D1553000

Wartime Notebooks

Wartime
Notebooks

France, 1940–1944

ANDRZEJ BOBKOWSKI

TRANSLATED FROM THE POLISH BY

GRAŻYNA DRABIK AND LAURA ENGELSTEIN

YALE UNIVERSITY PRESS ■ NEW HAVEN & LONDON

A MARGELLOS
WORLD REPUBLIC OF LETTERS BOOK

The Margellos World Republic of Letters is dedicated to making literary works from around the globe available in English through translation. It brings to the English-speaking world the work of leading poets, novelists, essayists, philosophers, and playwrights from Europe, Latin America, Africa, Asia, and the Middle East to stimulate international discourse and creative exchange.

English translation copyright © 2018 by Grażyna Drabik and Laura Engelstein. Originally published as *Szkice Piórkiem*. Copyright © Henryk Boukolowski and Wydawnictwo CiS, 2011.

Yale University Press books may be purchased in quantity for educational, business, or promotional use. For information, please e-mail sales.press@yale.edu (U.S. office) or sales@yaleup.co.uk (U.K. office).

Set in Electra and Nobel type.
Printed in the United States of America.

Library of Congress Control Number: 2018936160
ISBN 978-0-300-17671-1 (hardcover : alk. paper)

A catalogue record for this book is available from the British Library.

This paper meets the requirements of ANSI/NISO Z39.48-1992 (Permanence of Paper).

10 9 8 7 6 5 4 3 2 1

CONTENTS

Introduction, by Laura Engelstein   vii

1940   3
1941   175
1942   244
1943   379
1944   520

Afterword: Out of This Nettle, by Grażyna Drabik   592
Acknowledgments and Translators' Note   603
Notes   605
Index of Names   653
Illustrations follow pages 174, 378, and 560

INTRODUCTION

Laura Engelstein

Andrzej Bobkowski, an aspiring young Polish writer, found himself in Paris when the Germans invaded France in May 1940. For the next four years and three months, until August 1944, he kept a journal. He followed the progress of the war as reported in the press and in radio broadcasts, as reflected in rumors and the fears of people he met in his daily life; he read widely in both French and German and reflected on European history and culture. Safe on the home front, he ate, he drank, he smoked, he swam and bicycled. He thought of himself as a free spirit and developed a vivacious prose style on the handwritten page that expressed his desire to break with social and literary conventions. After the war, Bobkowski did not return to Poland, by then under Communist rule. His wartime notebooks were published in Paris in 1957 but, for reasons connected to the politics of postwar Europe, did not attain a Polish readership until Communism had ended. Once discovered in his homeland, Bobkowski was hailed as a bright new voice in Polish letters. A literary hero was born.

Opening the translation of Bobkowski's 1957 text, English-speaking readers will be fascinated to encounter a writer whose work remains fresh and surprising in its native context, even half a century after it was written. They will be fascinated by the unusual perspective his testimony provides, the outlook of an intellectual from the cultural margins of Europe who did not take Europe for granted. On the one hand, he was at the center of things. "Paris," as he later wrote, "was at the time an excellent observation post. The perfect armchair."[1] Bobkowski had come to Paris with his wife, Barbara, and the couple felt themselves very much alone, but they were not isolated. Bobkowski's observations reflect his wide social networks, both among the Polish emigration and among French acquaintances, neighbors, and colleagues. His omnivorous cultural appetite, embracing theater, music, the cinema, literature, philosophy, and politics, also offers a portrait of the historical moment. On the other hand, the occupant of that well-placed armchair was not a native Parisian but a visitor from Eastern Europe, a culturally amphibious outsider, able to observe his surroundings with a knowing but distanced eye. Readers will be intrigued as well by the complexity of Bobkowski's profile. Nothing is simple when it comes to this writer—neither his biography nor his persona, neither the saga of the note-books' publication nor the story of their reception in the Polish-speaking world.

So, who was Andrzej Bobkowski? This son of Poland was born on October 27, 1913, in Wiener Neustadt, Austria, where his father, an officer in the imperial Habsburg army, taught at the military academy. His early years, spent in Poland, coincided with those of World War I, the establishment of the Second Polish Republic in 1918, and the Polish-Soviet War of 1919–1921, in which his father served as chief of staff of an infantry division in the Polish army. The young man attended Gymnasium first in Toruń, then Cracow, where his mother was closely tied to theatrical and artistic circles and his father to the regime inaugurated by Józef Piłsudski in 1926.[2] From 1933 to 1936, he studied economics at the War-saw School of Economics and in December 1938, he married Barbara Birtus, known as Basia, whom he had met in Cracow.[3]

In March 1939, the couple left Poland for Paris, where Bobkowski was to take an internship arranged by the Polish Ministry of Commerce and Trade, with the goal of an eventual posting in Buenos Aires, Argentina.[4] But history was closing in. On September 1, 1939, Germany invaded Poland from the west; on September 17, 1939, the Soviet Union invaded Poland from the east; on September 27, 1939, Warsaw surrendered to the Germans. After a mere twenty years of inde-pendence, the Second Polish Republic ceased to exist. The French Third Re-public was soon to follow. On May 10, 1940, the Germans invaded France; on June 14, Paris surrendered. A week later Germany signed an armistice with the regime of Marshal Philippe Pétain and France was divided into the northern zone of occupation, including Paris, and the so-called *zone libre* in the south.

On September 7, 1939, Bobkowski had volunteered for the Polish army in France, but was rejected, and thus deprived, as he wrote sardonically, of the chance to die for the fatherland. Instead, he busied himself with a more mun-dane service. From February 1940 until August 1944 he worked for a special Polish Bureau created by the Paris office of the war industries section of the Polish Finance Ministry. The Polish Bureau was attached to the Atelier de Con-struction, a French munitions factory in the Parisian suburb of Châtillon, which employed Polish workers. An attempt to ship its personnel to England in June 1940 failed; instead, workers and staff were evacuated to the south of France in September 1940. Bobkowski accompanied the relocation but returned to his office in Paris, where, under the pretext of liquidating the Atelier's commer-cial affairs, he and his colleagues provided systematic support, financial, legal, and social, for Polish workers remaining in the occupied zone.[5] After the war, Bobkowski stayed in Paris, engaged in various occupations—editing a Polish-language journal, working for a bookstore, for the YMCA, and seeing a few short pieces into print.

Crucially, Bobkowski established an enduring connection with the most important center of Polish intellectual life outside Poland, the publishing house of Kultura, after 1947 established in Maison-Laffitte, near Paris. Its journal, *Kultura*, was modeled on Alexander Herzen's Russian Free Press of the 1850s, an outpost of free thinking beyond the reach of autocrats and official ideologues.[6] Its director, Jerzy Giedroyc, saw Kultura's mission as one of "widening the Polish arena for debate with the introduction of fresh ideas," even across the divide of Communist Poland.[7] Kultura published a broad range of authors, in Polish and in translation, including such writers of international stature as Czesław Miłosz, Leszek Kołakowski, and Witold Gombrowicz. Giedroyc would emerge as the publisher of Bobkowski's *Notebooks* and as the writer's lifeline to Europe, because in 1948 the Bobkowskis finally boarded ship, heading, not for their original destination, but for Guatemala, where they settled with barely a penny to their name and not a word of Spanish. There, Bobkowski ran a shop for model airplanes, a lifelong passion, from which he eked out a living, maintained an active correspondence with Kultura and with friends and family left behind, and continued his literary projects, including revisions of the *Notebooks* for publication. He died of brain cancer on June 26, 1961; Barbara Bobkowska remained in Guatemala until her own death in 1982.

When Bobkowski began filling his copybooks in May 1940, writing in a sure and steady hand on lined paper, he was twenty-six years old. His pathway to authorship and recognition was to be long and twisted. Immediately after the war, he published a few fragments from the notebooks in a Cracow-based literary journal and a piece in *Kultura*. In 1948, he offered the complete volume to the Communist-run publisher Czytelnik in Warsaw, but the manuscript was rejected. Finally, he gave the *Notebooks* to Kultura. "What a pain to deal with publication across an ocean," he complained to Giedroyc, while the text was in preparation.[8] He had hopes it might be a hit (a *szlagier*).[9] One thing for sure, it would be "monstrously fat—a damn brick."[10] Indeed, it appeared in two volumes. Preserving the journal's episodic form, Bobkowski called the published version *Szkice piórkiem (Francja 1940–1944)—Pen Sketches: France, 1940–1944*, or *Wartime Notebooks*, as we have titled them.[11]

The "brick" in two volumes was barely noticed at the time. Only in the 1980s did articles begin appearing in Polish journals recognizing Bobkowski's existence. An eminent literary scholar described the *Notebooks* as an "unknown masterpiece" of modern Polish prose, a fresh voice in Polish letters.[12] In 1985 a Polish-language publisher in London reprinted the Kultura edition, which was followed in 1987 and 1988 by underground versions inside Poland, as the Communist regime was losing its hold. A volume of his stories appeared in Paris in 1970 and in Warsaw in 1989, after the regime had fallen. The *Notebooks* themselves were published in their entirety for the first time in Poland only in 1995. The first translation—into French—had appeared in 1991, a German translation (of the first volume) followed in 2000.[13] After the long silence, Bobkowski now began to speak, and not only to people in Poland. A Ukrainian translator recalls how he first encountered the text in 2004 and swallowed it in one sitting. What Bobkowski had to say was "fresh and close to my heart," he remembered. What the Pole said about Poland "fit very well our national characteristics, our national weaknesses and stereotypes."[14] The Ukrainian translation appeared in 2007, the same year as the fiftieth-anniversary Polish reprint in Warsaw.[15] The celebration of Bobkowski and his *Notebooks* and the controversies they evoked had begun.

Beginning in Paris in May 1940, the narrative is organized in almost daily entries, with some long breaks. It describes the exodus to southern France in September of that year, followed by Bobkowski's return to Paris by bicycle, in the company of a Polish worker named Tadzio (Tadeusz Wylot), the resumption of life in Paris interrupted by several stays in the provinces, concluding with the months leading up to the Allied liberation in August 1944. The tone is notable for the absence of martial rhetoric, the failure to celebrate patriotic causes, military victories, or political crusades. Though fascinated by politics, political opinions, and political attitudes, Bobkowski insisted on the importance of everyday life, precisely under the relentless pressure of ideology. He insisted that the beauty of the French countryside, the pleasures of the table and of the open road, must retain their value even in the face of war and atrocity, if the human spirit were to survive. The *Notebooks* are indeed strongest in their vivid evocation of place, individual people, and the texture of everyday life.

They are nevertheless still very much a record of a war—albeit a war experienced from behind the lines, in a country that managed to escape its worst ravages. And toward the end, Paris too was subject to air raid alerts and Allied bombing; the French also suffered deprivation and hardship, as the war and occupation dragged on. Bobkowski records all that, yet, against the Polish tradition of somber patriotism, his energetic, playful, ironic manner is shocking. As it was meant to be. He understood the gravity of the historical events in which he was caught up, but he refused to be grave, though he was intensely serious.

Bobkowski saw a lot. Taking a circuitous route back to Paris, on a bicycle loaded with gear and provisions, he and Tadzio encountered local people, slept in barns and on the roadside, frequented local bistros, and even stopped briefly in a casino in Monte Carlo. Back in Paris after his unusual Tour de France, the writer spent part of each day in his office, a position that afforded him a salary and the essential ration cards. Otherwise, he scoured the shops and markets for food and fuel, rode his bicycle up and down the Paris streets, made deals on the black market, visited the town halls and police stations on official business, frequented the bookshops and bookstalls, attended the theater, went to the movies, sat on café terraces nursing a drink and eyeing the girls, or rather their wardrobes, avidly listened to the radio and devoured the newspapers, and finally in 1944 watched Allied airplanes flying overhead and took shelter, with his neighbors, from their bombs.

There was much also that he did not see or did not notice or did not care to record. A chronicler of decrees, speeches, and posted announcements, an eager reader of the German-sponsored collaborationist press as a source of information, he paid little attention to the situation of Jews in Paris or elsewhere. The published version notes the imposition of the yellow Stars of David in June 1942 and the great roundup at the Vélodrome d'hiver in July 1942, in which thousands of Jews from all over Paris were interned and then deported, and it is clear that he was aware of what was happening to them in the East.[16] But the fate of the Jews was not a subject of much interest.

Such omissions reflect the limits of his own direct experience and the focus of his attention on the circumstances of Polish immigrants and refugees in France and on the grim fate of Poland during the war and its grim prospects for the postwar, as the likelihood of Soviet domination in Eastern Europe increased. He comments briefly on the Warsaw Ghetto Uprising in spring 1943, but the Warsaw Uprising in August 1944 was of immensely greater importance, for obvious reasons. It was both heart-wrenching and infuriating, for its pointless heroism, for the Soviet treachery in allowing the slaughter of young Polish insurgents by German forces to proceed to its bloody end. The pathos of that futile act of resistance, as well as the massacre of Polish officers at Katyń in spring 1940, clearly even at the time the work of Soviet, not Nazi perpetrators, fueled Bobkowski's hostility to totalitarian regimes and deepened his anguished and ambivalent attachment to Poland.

The problem of politics—the decline of humanist Western civilization in the face of mass ideologies on right and left—was a central preoccupation, one he shared with many intellectuals of the day. From Oswald Spengler to the philosophical popularizer Hermann von Keyserling, it was fashionable to deplore the collapse of values and the emergence of an ominous modern age.[17] Bobkowski's cultural catastrophism was only confirmed by the picture of French accommodation to defeat and German occupation. Ensconced in an actual armchair in his hotel room, he took copious notes on his favorite authors, in particular Joseph de Maistre and Keyserling, but also Henri Bergson, Honoré de Balzac, and even some of the Russians. An opportunity to expound his views was provided by the bicycle journey back to Paris, together with Tadzio, whom he treats to seminars on European culture and civilization. The two engage in a running conversation, earthy and commonsensical on Tadzio's side, pedagogical and philosophical on Bobkowski's. The model for this relationship was Denis Diderot's *Jacques le fataliste*. The Bobkowski persona, rebel that he thinks himself to be, is the repository of cultural knowledge; Tadzio is the humorous sidekick, providing the saucy, off-color remark.

The ideas Bobkowski expresses may now seem commonplace, but they are interesting as a reflection of what was in the air at the time. They also reveal the dilemma facing an intellectual confronted by the great political challenge of the twentieth century—the dual threat of Soviet Communism and Nazism—a threat with particular resonance for the Poles. Bobkowski was very much a Pole, though one who wished to escape a narrow Polishness in favor of a broad European culture. He styled himself a "cosmopolitan Pole"—a "*Kosmopolak*." Yet this broader culture was under threat. Hence the flight from Poland to France and from France to the New World, not in its latest incarnation as the mass consumer society of the United States, but in the backwater of Guatemala, a refuge both from Europe in decline and North America in the ascendant. The young, aspiring writer was thus a man of contradictions: an iconoclastic cultural conservative, a professed "hooligan of freedom" and uncompromising individualist, skeptical of what the postwar future held in store, yet imbued—like it or not—with the prejudices of his time.

These conventional ideas included various stereotypes of national disparagement. The Germans were humorless, rigid, brutal, authoritarian. The Russians lacked any understanding of the concept of freedom, and Russia as a nation, whether imperial or Soviet, was always in the business of conquest and domination. Bobkowski loved equally to characterize the temper of France and French culture, which he loved, if only to find it wanting by its own standards. Such easy generalizations were coin of the realm in the 1930s. The widely read Hermann von Keyserling, whom Bobkowski greatly admired, made his reputation on philosophical travelogues replete with cultural clichés, including those respecting the Jews. This kind of casual anti-Semitism was endemic across the political and cultural spectrum at the time and hardly warranted comment. Despite his aspiration to free thinking, Bobkowski was selective in his rejection of clichés.

The participant-observer recorded his surroundings like a cultural seismograph and used his observations as the basis for philosophical reflection. Today's reader may find him more interesting as a writer than a thinker, however. The observations may appear fresher than the ideas, but the need to observe is in fact consonant with his intellectual posture. Hostile to ideologies of all stripes, he championed the importance of the individual person, of practical life (fixing a bicycle, pitching a tent, slaughtering a pig), of immersion in the material and sensual pleasures of existence. His lively, evocative prose, his echoes of conversations caught on the fly, his pen portraits of curious characters—all reflect a philosophical position, which he sometimes expounds at great length but more often allows simply to infuse his perceptions and choice of words. For his is a casual and vivid language, fluid and unpretentious, making the most of Polish plasticity, refusing a formal literary posture in favor of a literature of immediate sensation.

But, although Bobkowski's style and his playful disregard of sacred cows endeared him to the readers who discovered him in the optimistic context of post-Communist Poland, his ideas and prejudices have fared less well. After Barbara Bobkowska's death in 1982, the writer's papers, including the original notebooks, were deposited in the Polish Institute of Arts and Sciences of America (PIASA).[18] When, twenty-five years later, Łukasz Mikołajewski, while researching his dissertation, examined the original notebooks, he discovered certain discrepancies between the pages inscribed in Bobkowski's own hand and the 1957 edition.[19] Questions had earlier been raised, without access to the manuscript, about the text's "authenticity," concerning the extent to which Bobkowski had altered his notes for publication.[20] Mikołajewski's comparison revealed only a small portion of the text to have been altered, but the changes indicated shifts in the writer's attitude toward certain subjects, in particular, Communism, the United States, and, most controversially, the Jews and anti-Semitism. It is not unusual for diaries or journals to be edited for publication, but the question of Bobkowski's ethical stance was of urgent importance in post-Communist Poland. The figure of Bobkowski, as narrator of the published notebooks, seemed to have escaped the extremes of militant Communism, Polish hyperpatriotism, and unreflective anti-Semitism. It was disappointing to discover that the original notes had expressed, in unambiguously strong terms, a distaste for the Jews and displayed a marked indifference to their demise, despite professions to the contrary inserted in the published version.

The *Notebooks* thus became something of a minor cause célèbre in Polish intellectual circles.[21] The controversy spread through literary journals and internet sites, testifying to the degree to which the enlightened Polish public found the issue troubling. As translator, I too was disturbed by the revelations, but as a historian I was eager to explore a document with such a distinctive perspective on its dramatic context. I was also drawn to the mystery of what had caused Bobkowski to adjust his youthful notations in the mature rendering of his text. The question of Bobkowski's attitude toward the Jews had in fact surfaced soon after his death, but his occasionally disparaging remarks were explained by those who knew him as a feature of his quirky outspokenness, rather than a moral flaw.[22] Indeed, such remarks would not have distinguished Bobkowski from many other intellectuals, not to speak of ordinary citizens, in France as well as Poland. More interesting is the fact that he chose to remove the strongly worded passages from the final version of his text and to add others explicitly rejecting these earlier views. Anti-Semitism was incompatible with Kultura's basic principles, but there is no evidence that Giedroyc exercised any kind of editorial interference. Bobkowski left no explanation for his alterations. Perhaps he had not only changed his mind, but belatedly understood the consequences of his earlier opinions; perhaps in the aftermath of the mass murder of the European Jews, casual anti-Semitism seemed less casual. All we have is the text as in 1957 he wished it to appear. And this is the text we have used.

The English-speaking reader who, six decades later, approaches the reflections of a young Polish writer aspiring to free himself from the shackles of convention should be aware that the printed page is not the complete record of what he thought at the time. Yet the apparent imperfections of a man who engaged freely in moral judgments do not discredit him as a witness to the events around him or negate the value of his testimony as a reflection of prevalent views or make him a less interesting figure. He himself decried the Polish desire to celebrate national heroes. If he himself has fallen from the pedestal on which he briefly stood, then, as a fierce proponent of THE TRUTH, he would have been obliged to applaud the outcome.

The *Notebooks'* antiheroic message, the desire to break with the Polish litany of injured national pride, raises the question of Bobkowski's imagined readership. Who was he writing for? One of his models was Joseph Conrad, a Polish writer who transcended his Polishness by abandoning the Polish language.[23] Bobkowski had learned French and German as part of his education, and the notebooks even include an English word or phrase here and there, but he wrote in Polish. At the time of the *Notebooks'* publication and for many years thereafter, his reader could only have been found in emigration, yet Bobkowski was highly critical of the tenor of Polish émigré life. The reader he seems to have envisioned was in fact the reader of the future, a reader who did not yet exist. At one point in his reflections he entertains the idea that Tadzio's children might someday achieve a level of education, joined with a practical understanding of everyday life, that would establish the basis for a new kind of Polish citizen, as distant from the snobbish intelligentsia as from the culturally unschooled and therefore parochial laboring man. And it is perhaps this very reader of the future who finally emerged after 1989 and discovered Bobkowski, the reader for whom Kultura saw itself as paving the way with its cultivation of uncensored Polish writing. And the time has now come to provide English-speakers with access to this distinctive voice, at once Polish and culturally broad-minded.

Like all first-person accounts, the *Notebooks* must be read critically and in this case with an awareness that they were committed to print more than a decade after being composed. This translation presents the text as its author wished the public to find it. We have hoped to convey the spirit in which the notes were written, which also reflects the philosophical and cultural message their young author wanted to convey. He did not speak "for Poland," he insisted; he spoke for himself, as an individual person, but also for a certain set of values; yet, writing in Polish, unlike Joseph Conrad, he made a contribution to freeing the Polish literary language from the constraints of literary convention. In this respect, the *Notebooks* are a breath of fresh air, which should, in the cosmopolitan spirit in which they were conceived, translate into another language. They are a historical as well as literary document, which, as all historians know, cannot be read out of context. Yet the writing at its best—in its liveliness, immediacy, and joyful verve—transcends the moment of its creation.

Wartime Notebooks

1940

May 20, 1940

Silence and heat. Paris has been emptying out and becomes emptier by the day. Departure, however, takes place somewhat furtively. People leave on the sly, assuring their friends until the last moment that "we are not budging." But the sight of cars slipping through the streets, heavy baggage fastened to the roof, speeding off toward the south, becomes increasingly common. Better not to notice. Uncertainty and mystery have descended on the city. I was constantly struck, as I walked the streets, by how mysterious the most ordinary aspects of daily life now appeared. Cars were moving rather strangely, as though more silently and faster, and in the metro stations one waited not only for the train but for something more. Falsehood and evasion hung in the air.

Only this morning has the gloom that's been dogging everyone finally lifted. Weygand appointed commander in chief to replace Gamelin, Pétain in office.[1] Weygand immediately assumed command and left for the front. Naturally, rumors of treason got started: Gamelin has supposedly committed suicide, there's proof that . . . , and so on. Weygand is trusted, he's expected to set things right and patch things up. In the meantime, the French have lost the first phase of that battle in no uncertain terms.

The Germans are already in Arras and in Amiens, trying to surround the Belgian army.

May 21, 1940

In the Senate today Reynaud spoke the truth, or rather part of the truth.[2] It turns out that General Corap's army, defending the Ardennes line in the sector between Mézières and Sedan, was badly organized, composed of poorly armed divisions—last November I saw them marching through the city in their house slippers—and moreover the bridges over the Meuse have not been detonated.[3] In short, a scandal. The Germans, of course, directed their most powerful offensive in this direction, because they certainly knew about this before Monsieur

Reynaud had been informed. But for all that, tradition has been satisfied: everyone is heartened by this scandal. The French swear, curse, and finally come to the conclusion that "now we'll show them" and *Weygand va montrer.* Show them what exactly? The Miracle on the Vistula?[4]

The general gloom has been dispelled by the scandal, by the change in cabinet, and everyone seems to have awakened from a nightmare. Each Frenchman appeared to me this morning as the personification of the "Marseillaise." The slogan of the day is "hold firm"—this eternally French but by now moth-eaten—*tenir.*

May 22, 1940

Since May 10 unbroken good weather. Sunny and hot. Thousands of refugees from Belgium and the northern *départements* are flooding into France. They are being sent south. The French have taken back Arras. In Paris life goes on as usual. Antiaircraft artillery fire adds to our daily entertainment. The Germans have not yet begun to bomb Paris but they quite often fly over the city. That's when the cannonade begins, which is to say, showing off. Between bursts of fire you hear the buzz of the airplanes. We wake up and fall back to sleep again. I wonder when the Germans will finally make it to Paris.

May 23, 1940

The French are determined at all costs to create a unified front line. Unfortunately, the Germans have slipped through a gap and are threatening to take Boulogne. They've already taken Abbeville. The Belgian, English, and French armies are not yet completely surrounded, but according to the newspapers they have not managed to establish contact. They are forming a separate unit, the so-called Army of Flanders. The Germans attack in a different place every day, despite their losses, which, the papers report, are enormous.

May 24, 1940

Nothing new. The French have not managed to plug the breach between Arras and the Somme and the Germans are pushing through with motorized units, so fierce battles are raging near Boulogne and Calais. Total mayhem, *Eintopfgericht*—a big stew, from which the Germans are pulling the best morsels, which is to say, a new tactic that consists of confusing the enemy completely. The marvelous weather continues.

May 25, 1940

Saturday. Basia came to meet me at Porte d'Orléans. We went to the movies. The Paris police are organizing big raids, everyone—even the native French—must acquire personal identity papers. At the Préfecture there's no one to speak with—it's all a bit too late . . . The police are armed with rifles, but when I took a better look at these weapons today, I was tempted to ask whether the ammunition for such popguns didn't belong in the Musée des Invalides. The latest model in 1870, which probably served in the defense of Paris—now dragged out for use against the paratroopers.

May 26, 1940

The evening papers contained a brief notice that said a great deal. Fifteen generals have been relieved of their commands. The scandal is evolving on the principle that "a fish always rots from the head." Seven new generals appointed. The Army of Flanders is already practically cut off. It now forms a half-circle, one flank extending to the north of Dunkirk, the other to the north of Calais. In several places it touches the Lys and Escaut rivers. This army is supposedly being supplied from the air. The Germans are pushing them into the water.

May 28, 1940

It's getting better and better. Early this morning Belgian King Leopold surrendered, and along with him eighteen divisions. The news knocked everyone for a loop. It looks like clear and obvious treachery. He surrendered without alerting the French or the English, thus exposing their rear flanks. What's the result? It's a death sentence for the Army of Flanders.

May 29, 1940

In the afternoon I left the factory with Jean in his Ford. Yesterday Leopold surrendered, eighteen divisions gone to hell, everything is falling apart, and we are arranging *cartes d'identité de travailleur étranger*[5] for the Polish workers in the state munitions factory in Châtillon. The French bureaucrats are unyielding. The signature of the factory director is useless, the same for attestations—workers must be transported, group by group, from the factory, ten kilometers outside Paris, taking them from work for half a day, because "they are required to appear in person." A signature that has not been signed in the Préfecture is not valid—indeed, inconceivable.

Having accomplished exactly nothing, we dropped into Dupont's for a beer. The day is hot and stuffy. Dupont is red and silver inside. After the beer Jean flew into a rage. We got into the car and hit the gas. The poor Ford wheezed, policemen blew their whistles at every intersection of the boulevards, but we hurried on. Once outside Paris we took a lovely road, lined with trees. Covered all over in pale lilac flowers. I lit a cigarette and opened the window. Sank into my seat and half-closed my eyes. It was like plunging into a mound of flowers. The breeze and the scent came in through the window. I don't know what I was thinking about. Memories of distant springtimes, of silence, memories touched with the sadness one feels at the train station when someone very dear is about to leave. An internal hurricane that makes it difficult to breathe.

We turned into a dirt road, without slowing down. The Ford bounced and rattled. Yesterday it rained a bit and the road was full of puddles. Water sprayed off to the sides and onto the windshield. The road ran downhill, toward the forest. There was a small garden restaurant near the road. Jean stopped in front of it and said: "I once played here in the orchestra. I was the violinist, occasionally I also played banjo—and made a living that way." He became pensive. It seemed to me he was feeling the same thing I was. Perhaps he had come here to part with memories? We went for beer. The *patronne* greeted Jean like a son. I took my glass of beer and, sitting in the window, gazed out into the forest. They were recalling old times. A few disconnected words came my way—*fleurs, Suzanne, mignonne.*[6] The beer barely made it down my tightened throat.

An evening chill was already coming from the forest, the smell of wet vegetation and rotten leaves; a few rays of sun breaking through the high trees fractured against the pyramid of old champagne bottles stacked carefully near the garden fence. I poured the rest of my beer into a barrel of rainwater. Jean said good-bye to the *patronne* and we climbed back into the car in silence. Then we drove around the forest paths at full speed. Tossed, shaken, we suddenly burst out laughing—a silly, hysterical laugh.

May 30, 1940

What are the Italians doing? That's all that was missing.

May 31, 1940

The Army of Flanders is being evacuated by ship to England. A part has already been rescued. The Belgian defection now belongs to the past. It's said that the Dutch and Belgians, with the Germans' consent, have drawn the French and English from their fortified positions, thanks to which the Germans have succeeded in imposing the tactics most advantageous to themselves. In any case the Germans are operating as if on maneuvers, observing all the rules of the military art.

June 1, 1940

Saturday as usual. Basia came to join me at Porte d'Orléans. We walked to the Luxembourg Gardens. It was a lovely, warm evening. We sat on the wrought-iron chairs around the pool and read the newspapers. The gardens are deserted, and the pool without the children's sailboats is lifeless and sad. From the newspapers one thing is clear: the soldiers and officers are depleting their boundless reserves of heroism in patching up the mistakes of the short-sighted politicians and so-called statesmen. The precision of the German operations is terrifying. Like clockwork.

Disjointed conversation, thoughts formed but not expressed. Disaster. We were torn from our sad lethargy by the sound of a trumpet. Somewhere in the depths of the park a guard was playing a gay little melody. Rousing the public before closing time. It was now dusk and the foliage was turning black. Another guard cycled past us and cried: "*On ferme.*"[7]

"Come on, they're closing France," I said. We moved slowly toward the exit. On rue d'Assas we entered a small restaurant. Chilled white wine.

June 3, 1940

Before noon, at the Ministry of Labor on rue de Vaugirard. In front of the entrance there are a lawn and trees. Two policemen are walking about on the lawn, they bend over, pause, bend over again. I don't have the time, but I stop, intrigued. Finally I come closer and ask if they are searching for something.

"*Mais oui, Monsieur,* we're looking for four-leaf clovers. Do you want one?" At that, one of them, with a pleasant smile, hands me a beautiful specimen. I take it and insert it in my notebook. I, too, smile. On the day the Bastille fell, Louis XVI wrote in his diary: *Rien.*

I ate lunch in the factory. Afterward went to my room to work. Ever stricter police ordinances have increased the mountains of paperwork. A few minutes after one o'clock an air raid alarm in the city. There was no alarm at the factory, so I stayed at my desk. A few minutes later the antiaircraft artillery went wild. One continuous thunder. Suddenly, a penetrating whistle—barely a few seconds of silence—and a roar. Then—already closer—more of the same. Bombs.

People started rushing to the ground floor. The wait began for the next series. Still no alert at the factory. I sat calmly at my desk, pretending to keep my cool, though I was frightened as hell. That's supposedly what constitutes real courage. After half an hour of gunfire everything calmed down. A few minutes past two they signaled the end of the alarm. Around Porte de Versailles the houses were burning. A bit later I set off for the Ministry of Labor. On one of the streets in Châtillon the windowpanes in almost all the houses had blown out. People were gathering in small groups and talking. I asked if bombs had fallen somewhere nearby. Indeed, they answered. A moment later two guards arrested me on the excuse that I had been asking suspicious questions. They took me to the commissariat of police. After my papers were checked and my explanations heard, I was released. Near the commissariat a three-story building was completely demolished. Near Porte de Versailles a house was burning. War . . .

The evening papers report that the Germans have been bombing a bit everywhere and that there are already casualties in Paris.

June 4, 1940

They have dropped 1,084 bombs. There are nine hundred casualties, 250 killed—the rest wounded. For starters, that will do.

The French and English navies have performed a miracle of agility. They have evacuated the entire Army of Flanders from Dunkirk—about 330,000 soldiers. Under continuous German assault from all sides. Only the men were rescued. The entire weaponry of twenty divisions remained on the beach. This may be one of the most heroic defeats ever. They're starting to give us Poles some competition.

Otherwise nothing has changed. The weather is sunny, even sweltering. The canteen for refugees on rue Lamandé, where Basia works, will probably be winding up operations in the coming days. What will happen with me, I don't know.

June 5, 1940

Since May 10 the Germans have sustained the highest pitch. They hold it without taking a breath. It was only yesterday that they finished with the Army of Flanders. Today at four in the morning they launched an offensive along the entire line all the way from the sea as far as Soissons. It's still unclear whether they have advanced and where they are headed, but I wouldn't be surprised if tomorrow they were in Compiègne and in five days in Paris.

Infernal heat. Our attic apartment is an oven. After supper we went to the

café Le Cardinal on the boulevards to sit a while in less stuffy air. I drank rum
with soda water and ice. The boulevards were deserted and dark. I turned to
Basia and laughed: "Well—you predicted this."

In fact, I don't know how, but a year ago, even before the war began, she
already knew and always replied to my raptures over France that when the Germans attacked, the country would crumble at the touch. I didn't believe it. I was
raised on the myth of France. And now what? France is collapsing—and collapsing quietly it seems, snapping like basting thread, nearly without a sound.

June 6, 1940

A scorcher. In weather like this it's really a shame to have to think about all
that stuff. Fighting on the Somme and the Aisne. The Germans have thrown in
another two thousand tanks. The French are retreating to the shore.

June 7, 1940

The Germans keep advancing, mainly along the left wing. They're at the
Bresle River. It's like beating a dead horse. Nothing's been said yet at the factory
about evacuation, but it won't be long.

Paris is calm, no outward sign of nervousness. Only, from time to time a car
speeds down the street, filled with suitcases, bedding on the roof. People are
leaving, however they can. I can literally feel the pulse of the speedily unfolding events—so speedy as to seem unreal. I work as usual, drink cold beer in the
bistros, read the newspapers, and find it hard to believe the Germans are just
120 kilometers from Paris. I'm now only waiting to see what happens next and I
watch. It's all very interesting, that's for sure.

June 9, 1940

A Sunday. Like any other. People have begun to leave, but still in secret, on
their own initiative. Nothing is said about evacuation.

Dreadful heat. After dinner we went to the Parc de Bagatelle.[8] Sunshine,
thousands of roses in bloom. A rumbling reached us from somewhere very far
away. Maybe artillery, maybe a bombardment. I stood beside one of the shrubs
and listened to the remote noises. One blast sounded louder than the others
and at that very moment the petals of a white rose in full bloom fell silently to
the ground.

I had the feeling, standing next to that rose bush, in the deserted, exquisite garden, that I was bidding farewell once and for all to everything: to the France that was like a dream and like a dream vanishes; to my youth—perhaps to an entire epoch. The roses smelled strongly in the hot air and a distant woman's voice was comforting a crying child: "*Ne pleure donc pas, voyons . . .*"[9]

June 10, 1940

The cordon has ruptured, as Adolf Dymsza used to say.[10] Sudden evacuation. In the car with Jean. The Ministry of Internal Affairs abandoned Paris yesterday evening. It's like this everywhere. I got the order to send off all the Polish workers in groups. The first group left already at one o'clock this morning.

What goes on in the train stations defies description. Paris has suddenly woken up, suddenly acknowledged defeat—and has been rushing for the stations. Now the station was deserted. Here and there on the platforms people were sleeping, waiting for tomorrow's trains. I dropped into the Red Cross canteen, drank some beer, and smoked a cigarette. I went out slowly, in the darkness stepping over people asleep on the ground. They were sleeping even on the sidewalks in front of the station. I couldn't find a taxi anywhere. They had no doubt all already driven away. I walked home. I wandered slowly along the dark boulevard Raspail. A policeman checked my papers and let me continue. I walked slowly through the Louvre, deeply inhaling the fresh breeze coming from the Tuileries. The sky was completely dark. Near the Opéra I was startled by bursts of antiaircraft artillery. In that deserted and dark night their echo carried through the lifeless streets and accentuated even more the feeling of emptiness. It was like hollering into a bottomless well—prolonged, sad, ominous, and hopeless.

Above the hubbub of this entire day, above the burbling of the crowd, above the city—it is not so much dread that hovers, as complete and utter sadness. It's the end.

This evening the Italians declared war. It's almost three in the morning. I have to get up at five.

June 11, 1940

I got up at five and went to Gare Montparnasse. The metro was packed and hot as hell. Everyone was going to the station with all their belongings— suitcases, baskets, bedding, cages with canaries. The narrow subway cars seemed to be made of rubber: even when they were already full, people still kept getting on, still squeezed in their suitcases, and still found themselves a place. In front of the station, encircling the station, there was a ring of people, like a hundred-meter-thick layer cake. Suitcases, chests, mattresses, baby carriages, bicycles, cages with canaries—everything the poor possess and what they feel obliged to take with them. To transport all that would have needed trains from the land of giants.

By some miracle, I found some people from my group and by another miracle led them onto the platform through a side entrance. I had never in my life spoken so much French and so well. I escorted them through the police cordon, through the cordon of railwaymen, got hold of the stationmaster, and together we installed them in a car parked on a siding and unoccupied. Then I returned to the front of the station to snag the stragglers who had gotten lost in the infernal throng. On the platform an old woman had breathed her last—they put her on a baggage cart and covered her face with a handkerchief. A black fog hovered over Paris. After arriving at the Seine, west of Paris, the Germans have apparently released this artificial fog. Today it appeared over the city and is blanketing the sky. The Germans continue to advance and are surrounding Paris.

I popped out in front of the station and picked our people out of the crowd, grouping them at one of the side gates. We all had faces blackened from the fog—a kind of soot that was slowly descending. Around nine in the morning I gathered everyone and packed them into the railway car. They were in a good mood, toasted me with cognac. I drank almost half a bottle without the slightest effect. Maybe it's the fatigue. The train finally got going.

The newspapers had by now stopped appearing, there were no buses to Châtillon. I went off to the factory on foot. From Porte d'Orléans in the direction of Châtillon, which is to say, heading south, stretched an uninterrupted string of cars loaded with baggage and people. An astounding sight. In a single minute I counted twenty-six cars passing the spot where I was standing. The string had been growing without interruption since yesterday evening. The factory was agitated, even the French had already broken off work and were rapidly preparing to leave. In our Polish office a third group was being assembled for departure this evening. I said good-bye to my French colleagues and went home to pack.

The insufferable heat continues. I was so exhausted that I couldn't bear the thought of packing and of walking for the third time through that inferno in the station. Yesterday morning Basia closed down her canteen on rue Lamandé and began to pack. We went together to the restaurant for lunch. After lunch another stint of packing. Unclear what to bring along in such situations. We filled four suitcases, heavy as millstones. Mr. and Mrs. P. wanted to leave yesterday, but hadn't made it to the station. They decided to stay behind. Basia and I have been considering this possibility for two days. Around five o'clock I started carrying our suitcases downstairs. I was so weakened and worn out that I could barely manage, although normally I have no trouble with heavy weights. On the staircase we met Mrs. P., who said everyone had already abandoned them and now she would have to say good-bye to us, too. And finally she began to tell us that our departure made no sense, that anyway France had already lost, that it was already the end. We stood on the stairs with the four suitcases (our entire life, Basia's and mine, was practically one continual suitcase) and almost cried. I looked at the suitcases and was seized by fury. I'm not budging. Come what may, I've had it. I left them with the janitor (the concierge had once again disappeared) and that was that. I decided simply to go to the station, get the third group on board, do my duty to the end, then return home and get some sleep.

At the station the third group was already waiting. I quickly realized the trains were no longer leaving. Accompanied by the engineer who was supposed to escort the group, I went to the stationmaster. No hope of a train—maybe tomorrow morning, but even that's not for sure. What to do? From the commissariat of police I phone Châtillon. Director Chappel tells me to send the people back and have them wait until tomorrow.[11] An hour later a truck arrived and transported them to the factory. I returned home. By now I didn't care one way or the other. I decided just to drop by the factory tomorrow and see what was up. But first of all, get some sleep.

June 12, 1940

I woke in the morning, and after taking the metro to Porte d'Orléans, I walked to the factory. They were packing the last crates. The directors ordered the French and Polish workers to start walking in the direction of Nemours. One of the trucks, miraculously snatched from the French, carried the Poles' baggage and their wives and children—the worst kind of baggage in such circumstances.

There was nothing else left to do and I set out for home. Along the way I bought a newspaper, really a bulletin on one sheet of paper. The Germans have crossed the Seine, all draft-age men must leave Paris. I read it and rebelled. No, I'm not leaving. But after a moment I reconsidered. To remain in Paris really amounts to desertion. Perhaps not everything is yet lost. I have to part from Basia, because if I leave Paris to avoid being a deserter, it's in order somewhere and at some point still to fight. And then what good is it to have a wife along? When one joins the army, one doesn't take one's wife. I agonized, disgusted at myself for my cowardice: because they might call me a "deserter." So what? No—it's unacceptable, I have no choice but to leave.

My thoughts were gradually becoming clear and with revulsion, in pain, and with the urge to spit on all this "unacceptable" and "duties to the Fatherland," I made the toughest choice. I was now as calm as though I'd taken some vile medicine. I arrived home, climbed slowly to the seventh floor, opened the door, kissed Basia, and told her we had to part.

We looked each other in the eye and said nothing. It seems to me she has understood the necessity of this better than I. She was silent. Then she said: "We may never see each other again." Why did you say that? These words got lodged somewhere in my heart and have pained me since the moment we parted. No—we will see each other—I believe this deeply and you must believe it. We love each other too much for our life to vanish just like this. After all, we have taken almost nothing from life—so far it has given us only suitcases, heavy and jam-packed, and countless farewell kisses. The shadow of all this has haunted even our happy moments. But this will pass and we'll find each other again. I'm sure of it. "Believe me"—the only words I kept repeating for the entire hour. She helped me pack the most indispensable things into a blanket. I rolled up the blanket and used belts to make suspenders. The result resembled a backpack. We entered the metro. Before going down into the station, I kissed her. We both wept. "I'll be back," I mumbled, but then got a hold of myself. I stood on the platform and muttered under my breath something to make every Polish matron and staff officer swoon. I began immediately to think about the army, because what else is there to think about in such a situation? And at the mere thought I felt faint. I have always loved our army so much that at the call-up they instantly put me in the clink. I have known the military all too well. Beginning as a child.

When I arrived at the factory, the Poles had already set off on foot. I found my colleague Robert in the office. We both came to the conclusion that it didn't pay to go on foot. Quite a few trucks were still parked in the courtyard and we decided to attach ourselves to one of them. Meanwhile, we sat in the office and reflected on the events of the last two days. Our Polish superiors were applying here the skills they had learned in Poland. They abandoned everything and everyone and absconded on their own. We purchased some food and packed it in the bags used for the gas masks that had been distributed to us a few days before. The masks we left on the table. Then we deposited our baggage discreetly in one of the trucks and we too slipped under the tarpaulin, arranging ourselves among the piles of tires, two motorcycles and accumulators. We had to hide because the women who, for lack of space, had not been taken were still standing in front of the factory and if they had seen us would certainly have staged a revolt. While the truck was pulling out, we remained completely hidden, and only on the open road did we draw a breath of fresh air.

The road out of Paris was an unbelievable sight. An endless string of cars moving along in rows of twos and sometimes threes. All were loaded up with bed linen, bedding, suitcases, chests, boxes, and cages containing every sort of bird. All were rolling forward inch by inch, for if a dog escaped from a car, the car would stop to retrieve it, and everything would come to a halt. Whenever a vehicle broke down, and many of these jalopies broke down on the road, since driving constantly in first gear overheated the motors, everything would come to a halt. The roadsides were crammed with bicyclists and people walking. Everyone encumbered with bundles and suitcases. Anything with wheels became useful. An old woman was pushing a wheelbarrow loaded with stuff, somewhere else there was a tricycle with a box perched in front. In the box sat an old woman holding a large dog in her lap. A man was pedaling with difficulty. And so it went for kilometers, as far as the eye could see. I watched it all sitting in my truck and wondered why these poor folk and these old people were fleeing. Clearly no one here knew where they were headed. They were moving along with no goal, just to go, because others were going. Possessed, poisoned by the poison of flight. But at the same time, all this seemed to have nothing to do with me. All I feel right now is curiosity, intense, deep, collecting in my mouth like saliva. Observe, observe, absorb, remember. For the first time in my life, I am writing, taking notes. It's the only thing that absorbs me. Other than getting my fill of that magnificent freedom, that chaos, in which one has to fend for oneself.

The sky clouded over and a light summer rain began to fall. We slipped under the tarpaulin. From Paris to Nemours is about eighty-four kilometers. From five thirty in the afternoon to dusk, which means until nine thirty, we had traveled at most fifteen to twenty kilometers. I felt sleepy. I stretched out on the tires, huddled up, and fell asleep with indescribable pleasure. From the road came the continuous drone of motors, shouts, calling out of names, general clamor.

June 13, 1940

In fact I didn't sleep. I dozed. During the night it rained and several times I had to get up, remove the tarp, and pour off the water. It wasn't pulled taut and puddles formed in all the hollows. Luckily it didn't leak. Toward morning it turned cold. During the night we stopped for several hours, standing motionless outside a small town. At dawn we moved on at the speed of a funeral procession. We were diverted onto the side roads. The day was cloudless and hot. From the fields the smell of steaming wheat and flowers. Cars stretched in columns as far as the eye could see. Now we waited for the Germans to fly over and make mincemeat of all this. But they didn't show up. Along the way, some troops in broken columns, retreating in complete disorder. They were regrouping to continue their flight.

At noon we stopped and ate lunch, then onward. By evening we had entered Nemours. Eighty-four kilometers in twenty-six hours. Columns of retreating divisions were hurrying through Nemours—no one was stopping. The first group of Poles who had left yesterday morning on foot arrived at dusk. The factory vehicles did not stop in Nemours and continued on to the next point, Sully-sur-Loire. The only vehicle that could transport these exhausted people, with their lacerated feet, was the truck on which Robert and I had arrived. Moreover, we had to wait for those who had not yet shown up and were supposed to appear tomorrow morning. I expected that the French would force our group to keep going, all the more so as the French were panic-stricken and insisted that Nemours be cleared no later than this evening. I took our driver aside and told him to pretend there was something wrong with our truck and to go get some sleep. He didn't need to be told twice. He was off in a flash. I then told the director there was no need to hurry, that he and his staff could also safely get some sleep. Having convinced them, I began to look for a place to spend the night myself. On the river that ran through the center of the city was the barge-hostel of the Protestant mission. I sought out the pastor. He was affable and resembled Schubert. He told me there was no room on the barge, which was filled with women and their children and with mothers awaiting delivery or just after. He explained that he was Swiss. "What's the reason for all this, why?" he sighed, looking up at the sky. "To make things less boring," I answered. He looked at me aghast. I asked him for the latest political news. This evening Reynaud appealed directly to Roosevelt for help. The French government is now awaiting America's answer. Let them wait.

Night fell. The pastor found a barn and our people went there to sleep. I left to buy more provisions, especially bread, which is hard to find anywhere. I was dirty, my hair was covered in dust because I hadn't taken any sort of hat. I bought myself a beret. Robert and I decided I would sleep in the truck because it needed to be guarded. They might drive off stealthily in the night. I settled into the driver's seat. The river murmured and splashed in the darkness, from the distance came the throb of motors, as the divisions retreated. I stared into the dark windowpane and prayed, like every evening.

June 14, 1940

I awoke at six. Soon Robert appeared and we went down to the river. We stripped and slid into the water. The air was chilly, still saturated with the cold of dawn, and my teeth chattered. But the water, warmed by three weeks of heat, was summery and pleasant. Bliss. I even shaved. Then I began to search around for hot coffee. It was but a dream—the bistros were cleaned out, empty, bare.

All that was left was white wine. No shortage of that. The French management assembled and began to hurry us along. Luckily, the driver had disappeared somewhere. Meanwhile, every few minutes another small group of Polish workers arrived on foot from Paris. I packed them into "our" truck. Suddenly the French began to show up, with wives and children to boot. They had also come on foot. The situation became tense, because our people were ordered to release the truck for the use of the women and children. Our fellows began to protest and a scrap was brewing. The French were right. In the end our side gave in. Suddenly a large factory truck appeared. It had returned from Sully-sur-Loire to collect stragglers. A relief. We were loaded onto the truck. We drove out of Nemours at two in the afternoon.

We speeded up. The roads had by now somewhat cleared and things were more orderly. The troops directed traffic. Once again we drove amid a throng of army columns, mixed with civilian refugees. The army was not retreating—it too was fleeing. The soldiers wandered about without any discipline. A levée en masse. Only the chow wagons moved along in an orderly fashion, and at noon that whole team showed exemplary discipline with regard to tinned rations, bread, and soup. Toward evening we crossed the bridge over the Loire. The river was almost completely dry and I couldn't really believe that a creek like that could become a line of any sort of resistance. Sully was crammed with refugees. I had to hide my two loaves of bread because they devoured them with their eyes.

In Sully, the factory gathered together. The next morning the French workers were supposed to travel to Bourges and Moulins. No decision had yet been taken regarding us Poles. I went to the station to inquire about trains. A train might be leaving tomorrow for Bourges. This no longer interested me, because H., as group leader, had taken charge of the whole business. I made yet another list of our people—almost all had arrived, and then I went to have supper. Robert and I shared a bottle of cognac before supper and settled down in the attic of some house. In the evening the news went around that if America did not enter the war, the French would appeal for a cease-fire. That seemed to me very likely, although the French assured me that resistance would be organized at the Loire. I wanted to ask, with what? With the army I see around me? That's no longer an army.

June 15, 1940

This morning we slept late. When we arrived at the assembly point, we discovered that most of our people had already left by train for Bourges. The others climbed onto the truck. Robert and I had by now had enough of the crowds.

We took two bicycles off the truck and decided to go to Bourges by bike. The truck with our countrymen departed, while we slowly and solemnly sat down to breakfast. Done with the shrieking, the hurrying, the nervousness of the men, the jittery women, and the howling children. Around eleven we got going.

The road to Bourges was jammed at the beginning, but with a bicycle you can always slip between the cars. After riding half an hour in the chaos, we emerged on the open highway. An excellent road. Around two, with about forty kilometers behind us, we stopped for lunch. Then off again. The riding was splendid. Gentle inclines and long descents. Fifteen kilometers outside Bourges we were told to take a side road. We had to go five kilometers out of our way. We were by now very tired. Around six we entered the outskirts. Robert was so tired that riding quite slowly he toppled over and smashed his nose on the asphalt. His nose was scraped and he bled profusely. The blood poured into his throat and out through his nostrils. Some boys brought us water, and a couple of gentlemen started to offer advice. Hearing us speak Polish, they started speaking Polish themselves. Jewish refugees from Antwerp. We immediately discovered some mutual acquaintances, because the uncle of one of them had a fur warehouse in Cracow. "You know, he had furs on Vistula Street—you go from Market Square, it's on the right side" . . . Meanwhile, Robert had stopped bleeding and we soon rode into the city. We found all our people gathered at the station. The French manager ordered us to return the truck and said we would have to get to Quimperlé by train. There we would be shipped off to England. Yeah, sure—a cruiser will be waiting specially for us, and we'll be welcomed aboard with flowers. I went to the military commissioner. He was polite enough but told me bluntly that trains were no longer departing toward the west. We have to continue south and from there possibly head for Brittany. A veritable beeline!

It was getting dark by the time I bought a newspaper. The Germans are already in Paris. The paper didn't spell it out, but you could guess from the contents. Robert and I sat down at a table in a closed bistro, took out our supplies, and ate supper. Robert is a terrific companion: calm, conscientious, knows what he wants, and like me can't stand crowds. I took a great shine to him. We returned to the station, where it turned out that the bicycle I had taken did not belong to any of the Poles. A Frenchman had put it on the truck and hadn't reappeared. As a result, we acquired "our own bicycle." We now had to find a second bicycle, because a single day had been enough to convert me to this form of locomotion.

It was already night when we went to town to find a place to stay. The moon shone brightly in the cloudless sky. Not a room to be had. We spent the night dozing fitfully on the cement of the platform.

June 16, 1940

After our night on concrete, we were up by five. H., who until now had been responsible for the group, had still not showed up in Bourges. Around nine in the morning we began our assault on the freight train. The passenger cars were already full of women and children. Robert and I found two places still left near the door. We sat with our legs hanging outside. Baggage was crammed into the car every which way, making it very crowded. We wanted to introduce some order, but that was out of the question. The people from the Paris outskirts were unyielding. A paralyzed old man in a wheelchair started brandishing his cane at Robert. No one wanted to help anyone else. When I brought one woman a bottle of water, she tore it out of my hands and glared as if at the enemy. The train got going, we were off to Montluçon. Right outside Bourges we stopped. A German plane flew overhead but didn't do any shooting. Again we started up. The day was hot, the air in the car fetid. The old man grew impatient. Noticing that people were getting out at the stations and lying on the grass, he insisted he must get out and *prendre un peu d'air*.[12] Then he had a fit, swore, and pummeled everyone around him with his cane. His daughter began to cry and scream that he had lost his mind and was making a scene. She told the entire car what she had done for her father, while the old man kept swearing that the Boches were already here, that France was no longer France but simply shit—in short, completely on target and not at all insane. *"Vivent les fous,"*[13] I said to Robert.

The sky clouded over and it began to rain. We drank some awful, rancid white wine, because it was all we'd found in Bourges. My throat dried up, I got heartburn and could barely stand upright. Toward evening we reached Montluçon. We collected our stuff and headed for town, although most people claimed that the train would be continuing onward. I couldn't care less. In town we managed at last to eat a normal supper with soup and meat. Then we looked around for a place to spend the night. People were carrying piles of straw into one of the movie houses. We went inside—luxury. Soft seats, lots of room, and you can bring your own straw. Only I don't understand why they can't show a film. It would be great to lie on the straw and watch Marlene. We immediately returned to the train station for our things. There we discovered that some of our group had already departed, but those who had failed to get seats on that train were waiting for another one, which had not yet arrived. I looked at Robert, tapped my finger on my forehead, and we grabbed the bike and our baggage and went off to the movie house. We deposited our stuff in the care of a refugee dozing on a pile of straw and went into town.

The town was full of troops and refugees. They were sitting in the bistros,

drinking wine and coffee, and deliberating. The evening paper caused a stir because the French government, evacuated to Bordeaux, has changed. Reynaud
has resigned, Pétain has taken his place, Weygand has become vice-premier—
an almost entirely military government. Everyone's face reflects the fear that
this may by some chance mean that they intend to fight to the bitter end. Meanwhile the Germans have crossed the Loire at various points. It's already the end.

Out of curiosity, we went to the station. The second group had also now departed. But a minute later two workers showed up. Tadzio took me aside and
declared bluntly that he had missed the train on purpose because he couldn't
stand it any longer.[14] We took them to the movie house, and later they went out
again. I don't know what got into me, but noticing two well-dressed women, I
approached them and asked if they knew of somewhere we could spend the
night. One answered straight off that we could stay at her place. Robert nudged
me, but I decided to take a chance. We went with her. She led us through a corridor in a narrow street, then into a courtyard, and finally into a coach house.
Straw on the floor, an old carpet, she brought us a blanket, a bucket of water for
washing. Most important. We returned to the movie house, retrieved some of
our things—and off to get some sleep.

June 17, 1940

We got up at nine. *Madame* made us hot coffee and allowed us to breakfast
in the kitchen. A seamstress by trade. She runs a women's fashion shop, her husband has a radio shop and is currently at the front. Both shops are closed. Just
this morning he phoned her to say he was healthy and doing fine, that he was
retreating with the army near Montluçon. She said everything was terrible, that
any day now France would certainly appeal for an armistice, but what can you
do?—the main thing is for her husband to return. And for them to be together
again. She was probably right.

At the station we learned that trains were no longer leaving. It was noon.
A crowd of people had gathered in front of a bistro and the sound of a radio
came from inside. The "Marseillaise." We approached. I started to ask what it
was all about. I noticed the tearful faces of the women and the gloomy faces of
the men. Finally a young workman informed me indifferently: "France is asking Hitler for an armistice." The "Marseillaise" ended and the second part was
played again. Despite myself I mentally repeated the words *formez vos batail-
lons—marchons, marchons*, while at the same time I was aware of the absurdity
of these words given the situation. France is suing for peace. I wanted to cry
but only smiled ironically, whispering instead of *marchons—fuyons*.[15] I grabbed

Robert by the sleeve and said: "They've sued for peace—it's all over." Women walked past us in tears, cars crammed with ragged soldiers sped through the streets.

We calmed down. What to do? At that moment Tadzio came walking toward us, smiling and delighted to have found us at last. I've always liked Tadzio. A driver by trade, he was born in Warsaw, where he acquired a rich background in taxis and buses and a spicy tongue. Tadzio now stood still, watched the cars going by, spat, and finally pronounced drily: "We for sure have to push off, then we'll see." We started to consider how to go about it. Trains are no longer leaving, there's no sense going on foot. Tadzio slowly rolled a cigarette, or "spirochete," as he puts it, and at last declared it would be best to buy some bicycles.

I made up my mind in a flash. After searching around for a long time we found a shop. There were no more used bicycles, only new ones. Tadzio bought himself a semiracing model for 630 francs, I a terrific road bike for 715 francs. In the store I was overcome by a wild and impotent rage. Why was this splendid country, in which a new bicycle costs one-third the average worker's wage—why was this country going to hell? I still feel this is the absolute end. There is no return. Perhaps this very feeling, a feeling of limitless sadness, is the worst part of it all. Robert is now packing our things. I'm afraid these bicycles will be riding us, not us them.

June 18, 1940

We awoke this morning at seven. The sky was overcast and rain hung in the air. The Germans have already dispensed with France and don't need good weather. The Polish September and the French May–June were equally sunny and pleasant.[16] *Hitlerwetter.*[17] Poor, impoverished Poland held out just as long as great and wealthy France. We Poles, no less than foreigners, considered our own effort at self-defense a scandal. By contrast, the French effort at self-defense is simply a crime. We wanted to fight but didn't have the means. They had the means but didn't want to fight. I wonder if France will manage to get back on her feet after this blow. Such thoughts have been plaguing me since yesterday.

Making it out of Montluçon was no mean feat. For a few good kilometers we had to push the bicycles and weave our way through the compact mass of cars, artillery pieces, tractor trucks, and tanks. That's what they had, the French—hardware. Farther on, there was more room to maneuver. It began to rain. A group of soldiers stood next to a truck. They stopped us and offered us some rum. They had several barrels of it, with which they plied everyone on the road. Tadzio tossed down the half-glass they gave him, spat, and returned the glass with the addition of some choice adjectives aimed at frog-eaters. We're riding in the direction of Bordeaux. Toward evening a descent into the valley of the Creuse. Evening brought a chill. I leaned low over the handlebars and took the sharp turns, trusting to the bicycle. The ride was intoxicating. At a certain moment, I felt distinctly that nothing any longer concerned me. Now, as I write this, I feel that something has ruptured inside me. Perhaps it's a break with the past. At last. In the midst of all the commotion, I am free. Perhaps I've even broken with myself. Splendid. Raring to go. Regrets? For what, damn it? For my former life? It was a nightmare, an unremitting sense of suffocation. The nightmare of my Gymnasium years, the nightmare of the life I was cutting myself out for, never able to find myself. I talked with myself only through others. And through whom? Through what? Hell!

At the bottom of the valley a signpost indicated a village fifteen hundred meters ahead, with the caption: "Twelfth-century church and Roman bridge." Without a second thought I took the turn. A must-visit. The priest of this Romanesque jewel found us a house with straw mattresses. After a bite to eat I went out. Fog hung over the damp fields, crickets were chirping, and the moon shone. I walked out onto the bridge, full of emotion. I thought back to an album of Włodzimierz Terlikowski's genre scenes (how boring they were) and examined the round, narrow arches of gray stone.[18] Near the entrance were remains of boulders from the road on which the wagons had rolled and the Roman legions had marched with heavy step. *Gallia est omnis divisa . . .*[19] Why did the Gauls put up resistance back then, although their equipment and technique were so much worse than those of the Romans? From the distant road came the relentless roar of motors, while frogs croaked under the bridge. The stocky figure of Tadzio loomed out of the dusk. He lit a cigarette. "Mr. B., don't you worry. Tomorrow we'll be making tracks. It's a pleasure even to escape on such roads. That's civilization for you—makes everything easier. Not like in Poland. But the French are miserable f—— slackers, that's the truth." It's silent now. Robert and Tadzio are breathing loudly, the candle sputters.

June 19, 1940

The weather has improved. Sunny and warm since morning. For breakfast hot coffee with milk. At ten off to Guéret. The sun was already shining mercilessly, but the road is lined with plane trees and it's like riding in a bower. An hour and a half later we arrive at Guéret. On the road people with wheelbarrows, once again bewildered, with baby carriages, going in the opposite direction. It was impossible to learn anything from them. They were dazed. We keep going. We hit the outskirts. There we learn that an hour earlier there was a bombardment. The city is full of troops, the market crammed with cars, with artillery pieces. A couple of houses are burning, in the middle of the road there's a crater from the bombs and the skeletons of burned-out cars. Tadzio looked around and said matter-of-factly: "Time to push off, because these SOBs will be coming back. I know the Germans: they won't let up before evening; they knock off only at six." We stopped looking for something to drink. We push our way between hundreds of cars. We pick up the road to Saint-Sulpice. Blistering hot. Beyond Guéret we decided to eat lunch. We wanted to stop near a roadside bistro, right where we were, but Tadzio wouldn't allow it. "I want to eat in peace." He dragged us off the highway, into the fields. We were preparing to open the tins of pâté and sardines and were buttering our bread, when suddenly something starts to growl. Tadzio stood up, emerged from under the tree, and shouted: "They're coming, the m-f——ers . . . here . . . one, two, five, eight, ten." We left our food in the grass and bolted toward the trees into a shallow ditch along the meadow. A roar in Guéret, the Germans were dropping bombs. Then the racket of machine guns. Tadzio shouted: "They're strafing with their machine guns, I hope they get their comeuppance." Airplanes passed overhead. I flattened myself in the ditch like a scrap of paper, but I turned my head to look. A prolonged whistle, close, close by, and a rumble—rending the air. The racket of machine guns. They were chopping up the roadway. "Italian machines—Fiat B.R.20," I say to Tadzio. Tadzio swears. We return to our meal. Twenty minutes later more growling. They flew over Guéret and bombed it fiercely. Then they flew over us yet again, chopping up the road with their machine guns. I lay in the ditch, terrified. After this raid we quickly finished our meal and turned our backs on this ill-fated place. A bomb had landed practically on the very spot where we had wanted to sit. All the windowpanes in the bistro had blown out and some tiles had fallen, tree branches lay across the road, and on the doorstep of the bistro lay someone's bloody corpse. I thought to myself only: "At least it's not me." A dozen meters farther along, near a side path, were two bottles of wine. Someone had left them and fled. Tadzio picked them up. We now pay more attention to the sky than to the road. We were perhaps ten kilometers away and again, the devil take them. The same group of ten. A car is riding calmly alongside us. Enclosed in the limousine, the passengers hear nothing. We signal to them. They stop and rush like madmen into the field. Leaving a child in the car. I took the little fellow in my arms, carried him through the fence into a garden by the road, and crouched down in the ditch. The poor child trembled and tears ran down his cheeks. He could no longer even cry out loud—tears simply streamed from his eyes. I hugged him and comforted him, thinking how terribly afraid I was myself. Tadzio yelled from somewhere: "They're passing us by!" I gave the little fellow a kiss and carried him back to the car. The mother was so terrified that she had forgotten all about him. He hugged her now and cried soundlessly. *"La prochaine fois ne l'oubliez pas,"*[20] I said, discharging the anger I felt at myself for having been afraid. She no doubt thought I was very brave.

Tadzio looked at his watch and saw it was already after seven. "It's safe to ride, it's their time off. Now they'll land, get soused, stuff their snouts, and tomorrow start all over again. Where is the mighty power of the French? The Germans are getting away with it, just as they did in Poland." He's right. There are French troops all around, plenty of antiaircraft artillery and machine guns, and nothing, no one has answered back. Around nine I left the road in search of a place to spend the night. I found a farm. Everyone was at supper. The farmer willingly agreed to let us spend the night in his barn. He offered us soup and wine. After supper I burrowed into the hay. The chirping of crickets and the croaking of frogs. Already in my pajamas, I went out again and sat on the stones near the well. The dew was falling and my cigarette got damp. Late that night two workmen from Paris came to sleep in the barn. They had left a day after us. They said the radio had announced that anyone of draft age who had not left Paris by midnight on June 13 would be considered a deserter. When and by whom? Apparently, around six thousand bicycles were distributed from the luggage left at Gare du Nord, to give people a way of getting out.

June 20, 1940

We left late, because in the morning Robert performs such ablutions, scrubbings, and packing up of his things that we cannot leave before ten. The Germans apparently keep moving forward, but they are rather far behind us. Robert insists there's no need to hurry. At midday we rode through Saint-Sulpice. A small town situated in a valley, surrounded by mountains. The heat is tropical. The newspaper we bought there reports that negotiations for the armistice are under way, but until the moment when the act of clemency is signed the Germans will press on and fighting will still continue. What fighting? The Maginot Line is surrounded. The two Polish divisions that have finally joined the action are refusing everywhere to retreat and are fighting heroically. Part of one division was apparently wiped out while covering the French troops and refugees retreating toward Switzerland. The newspapers report that the Poles rushed at the tanks with bottle-bombs. That's at least a bit better than attacking with cavalry but still not great, if true. Really—we Poles are still unrivaled. The French government is in Bordeaux. At two we crawled into the woods and napped until six. Tadzio is singing fierce tangos and swearing because it's mountainous. It was already dusk when I found us a farm. I'm the guide, I set the tempo, and seek out places to stay. At the farm, we are received effusively. And they have four young girls. We eat supper from our own supplies at the host's table and I chat enough for everyone. The girls regard us with curiosity, and one knows a few words of Polish. Tadzio flirts with her and spouts nonsense. An aside to me: "Mr. B. — I'll stay here — she can twist me around her little finger. The girl's a doll, mouth-watering. Pretty as a picture." We are tired. We climbed up the ladder into the hay. We could hear the clank of chains below us and the cows chewing their cud. Silence. The smell of milk and dung. A firefly flickered in the darkness, an iridescent speck. A moonless night, but bright with stars. Marvelous.

June 21, 1940

Breakfast, washup, a shave. We're still heading toward Limoges. Without a map it's hard to find our way. Impossible to buy a map anywhere, all sold out. Around one in the afternoon we reach Limoges. No one is allowed to enter. I dismount and after hearing my long lecture they make an exception for me. I leave the bicycle and go on foot. In the center of town I'm caught in a downpour. I wait it out under an entryway and go to the train station. The station is also shut and only after a long explanation am I allowed in to see the military commissioner. I ask about our group from the factory. He knows nothing. I return. Our supplies are dwindling and so I go in search of food. Bread is hard to find. There's no jam, no tinned meat, the shops are empty. I wander around. At last, I get hold of some sausage and a few tins of pâté, some bananas and oranges. Also a map of France, published by "The Auto" during the Tour de France of 1936. One bookseller had a stack of them, which he was now selling for a franc apiece. They went like hot cakes. I also found a lonely volume of Byron's correspondence and bought it for fifty centimes. A bargain. We ate lunch on the road, then off to Angoulême, eighty-four kilometers. Tadzio is now riding next to me and recounts: "Mr. B. — all the hookers from the Gastronomia[21] and the Café Club used to know me on sight. When one of them got her hands on a drunken john, then presto into my cab, she'd do him, grab his dough, throw the guy out, slip me twenty złoty for my goodness of heart, and vamoose." At this moment two men walking along the road began waving at us and calling out. Two Polish émigrés. They had heard Tadzio's immaculate command of the Polish language and stopped us. "Where are you coming from?" "From the military camp in Brittany." They had been called up, but three days ago, during the night, they were told each man for himself. The officers had escaped by car to the ports and transport to England; some soldiers apparently also left, mostly those from Poland. I wonder where Basia's brother Jasiek is. So it's a good thing they didn't want to take me into that army. Overnight on a farm, this time sleeping on straw.

June 22, 1940

This morning it rained. We slept. Got going only around two in the afternoon. Intermittent rain. We got completely drenched. We threaded our way once again through the crowd of retreating troops. They were driving like madmen. At every step along the road overturned cars. Tadzio looked them over and cursed. Asphalt slippery and muddy. A centipede would break all its legs on this road. After thirty kilometers I gave in. I found a farm. A heap of straw under a roof, shielded only on two sides. Cats and dogs kept us company at supper, it drizzled, from the road came the relentless drone, growling, and choking of motors pitilessly abused. Sleepiness. Calm.

June 23, 1940

"Miserable vacation, the season is a flop," says Tadzio. Robert regales us with the wonders of sunshine in southern France, of the Mediterranean Sea. Meanwhile we slosh in the mud on the paved highways at the western edge of the Massif Central. We are approaching Angoulême. They don't let us in, detour, we lose our way on the side roads. It's already night when we find a tiny, miserable farm. They are just finishing supper and are courteous. The *patron* accompanies us to the hay. I notice a green salad in a large bowl on the table. The leaves are waiting for the oil and it's so appetizing that I can't restrain myself: "Is it possible to buy some lettuce?" The *patronne* immediately gets up and says she'll bring us two heads. She went out and soon brought an entire bowl of lettuce. We eat it in the blink of an eye, chomping on bread with pâté. They are marvelous, those nights on the hay, under the monotonous patter of the rain.

June 24, 1940

This morning more rain. The *patronne* brought us half a bucket of milk for breakfast. We drench ourselves in milk, I'm lying down and writing. It's pouring. Later I eat some chocolate, smoke, fall asleep, wake up, munch chocolate, and doze. Around four in the afternoon the *patron* climbs up the ladder to visit us, babbles something, and then remarks calmly: "The Germans are now twelve kilometers from here; they've taken Angoulême." At least we've learned that Angoulême is twelve kilometers away. We jumped on our bikes. Taking the side roads onto the highway to Périgueux. We determined now to head south. After an hour and a half's ride we're in Mareuil. Along the way we found ourselves once more among the troops. Obviously, it wasn't the troops from behind the lines that were retreating but the first line—the front army. Crowding and screaming, trucks, tractor-trucks, tanks, artillery pieces.

A total bottleneck and everything comes to a halt. We managed to squeeze through on our bicycles and get to the head of the column. We move, and then again, it's all blocked up. The officers run around and curse. Pushed to the side of the road, fifteen-centimeter artillery pieces slide into the ditches. Screams. In a feat of acrobatics, we make it to the head of the crush. Four trucks have stopped and the soldiers don't want to move, because they don't know what's happened to their food-supply vehicle. Only when an orderly drove up on a motorcycle and said that chow was a kilometer away did they get going. An hour later the same thing all over again. The fifteen-centimeter artillery guns tried to bypass the stopped column and they all ended up in a ditch. What was happening there is indescribable. An inferno. We push our way through and several kilometers later encounter a bucolic idyll. The head of the column is sitting at the edge of a grove, tables and chairs (which they had brought with them) set out, and supper is proceeding as calmly as you please. *A garden party.* With music. The phonograph is playing, ruby-colored bottles of wine sit on the tables, and a good time is being had by all. I can still hear the whinny of the horses being unharnessed, the clamor, the clanging. Tadzio took a look, spat, and asserted: "Lousy communications in this army of theirs."

How different a country appears in time of peace and in time of war. For a country, war is like ringing a coin against a counter; and although I hate war, it seems to me there's no better test. I recall what I used to think of France as she was in former days. Today I understand one thing: the traits that are charming in time of peace, which are valued highly—these French traits are disastrous at the present time. In peacetime, the French forgot about war, during the war they have not managed to forget about peace. The light was already fading when we entered a small town. Streets crammed with soldiers, people crowding in front of the houses. A man waved at the soldiers and shouted joyfully: "*C'est signé, c'est signé!*"[22] I approached him. Excited, as if by an especially auspicious event, he told me about the signing of the armistice with the Germans and Italians. Hostilities were to cease at one thirty-five in the morning. Meanwhile cars and troops kept filing through the streets. News of the armistice spread like wildfire.

A mood of joyful excitement had taken hold. The town inhabitants sat in their windows or stood in their doorways and waved and smiled at the soldiers. The soldiers drove by, singing songs, playing harmonicas. The armistice seemed to have straightened them up, made them cocky. I got the impression that they instantly felt absolved. Heroes who had done their duty to the end. The town was festive. In the bistros the lights were lit, the doors wide open, there was imbibing and songs. It was only the beams of light that were still catching the dark silhouettes of cars, artillery pieces, and soldiers marching out of step.

We left the town to look for someplace to spend the night. But troops were everywhere. A couple of drunken soldiers approached us. They started to ask who we were. It's a military zone and civilians are not allowed. I say we are Polish. And they then give us a lecture: This entire war is on account of Poland. Instead of coming to terms with Germany, Poland took the side of the capitalists and of England, and England dragged in France. Besides, everything is written here. One pulls out a crumpled flyer. I want to take it away from him, but he stubbornly tries to read it aloud, although it's now almost dark. He mumbles something about international trusts, about capitalists, concluding with a flourish: "*Fini—nous sommes trop intelligents pour nous casser la gueule . . .*"[23] Tadzio, furious, drags me away: "Why do you waste words on these ignoramuses. It's the same as in Poland. The Germans on the one side, Stalin on the other, and that's it. Except that the Communists had to come to us in person, because the population was too stupid for their scribbles, but the French are 'intelligent,' so this rag does the trick."

We continue on, now in complete darkness. Lights are not allowed and everything seethes in the total dark. Only the roadside bistros, filled to the brim with drunken soldiers, blaze with light, like open furnaces in a foundry. Like the Cossacks in Henryk Sienkiewicz's *With Fire and Sword*.[24] It was already after midnight when we burrowed into the hay. There were electric lights in the barn and we discovered some barrels of wine. Tadzio looked at his watch and said: "Mr. B.—in fifteen minutes bayonets sheathed, arms stashed, and festival of the sea." My head was splitting from inhaling all the exhaust on the road and from the throb of motors.

June 25, 1940

Lousy weather. From the *patronne*, I learned there's a large farm and a château about three kilometers from here. The owner is Polish, very wealthy, *un millionnaire*. Polish refugees apparently used to gather here and some are still there. We decided it was worth stopping by. Perhaps we'd manage to get something solid to eat and learn something. Twenty minutes later we entered an allée and soon found ourselves in front of a large and dilapidated château. Once it must have been a splendid estate. A garden, flower beds, a fountain. Tadzio says to me: "Now for the lord of the manor." We asked to see Mr. Budzyński. We were told he was working. We found him in the garden behind the house. The lord and master of three hundred hectares with a château turned out to be an ordinary peasant from central Poland. He wore a shirt, ragged pants held up by suspenders made of cord, and muddy shoes. He was carrying some boards and gathering branches. Later I learned that he had come to France as a miner, then started selling cold cuts, carrying his wares in a box. Then he bought a bicycle, then a horse and cart, then began to make his own cold cuts, finally bought a farm in the north, established a large cold cuts factory, next opened a big delicatessen, expanded his factory, made millions, bought this property here in the south, and now, forced to flee from the north, he had driven down to his estate in five automobiles, bringing with him three tons of dried sausage and cold cuts, tinned ham, and so on. He kissed good-bye to his assets in the north (worth five million francs) and cheerfully set to work here. He did manage, however, to transport several machines for the preparation of cold cuts, intends to start another factory here, has some livestock, that's just the beginning, the rest will come, "because in two months the French will get their appetites back"—as he himself told me. He takes care of everything himself, is capable of doing everything himself, and puts his hand to everything. He welcomed us graciously and with great dignity. Just a week ago, he told us, the entire consulate from Lille was staying with him, but at the news that the Germans were approaching, all the men took off and only the wives remained. He showed us the wing where they were living and said: "Let those countesses look after you. They do nothing all day but puff on cigarettes—Polish ladies . . ." I liked him immensely. He had put the entire wing, with kitchen and dining room, at the disposition of the countesses. They slept in the château. They received us kindly. Right away they offered us hot coffee, with a mass of bread, sausage, and jam. We discussed the latest events.

Pétain's radio address would lead one to believe that the French did not have the wherewithal to fight. Half a million fewer soldiers than in 1917, not to mention being less well armed than the Germans. Pétain put the blame on the English. They sent only ten divisions. Now the English have resolved to fight on their own. "*Depuis la victoire, l'esprit de jouissance l'a emporté sur l'esprit de sacrifice. On a revendiqué plus qu'on n'a servi. On a voulu épargner l'effort; on rencontre aujourd'hui le malheur.*"[25] Finally, a bit of the truth. But Pétain doesn't admit this was the reason for the defeat. No. "Too few children, too few weapons, too few allies—those are the reasons for our defeat." So as not to insult anyone. Otherwise everything is normal. Jean Prouvost has been named high commissioner of propaganda.[26] Propaganda for what?

After coffee, I set to work on the bicycle because something needed fixing. Then lunch was served. Excellent. I ate myself silly. After lunch the ladies went to lie down, and I used the laundry to do the wash for Robert and myself. I hung it in the château attic. Supper was also excellent, after which we sat for a long time and talked with the ladies. Vacation in a Polish manor house. I said I intended to stay longer and get some rest.

June 26, 1940

For breakfast a pitcher of coffee with milk. I stuffed myself. I spent the morning chatting with the squire. He's really terrific.

No one knows anything and therefore we decide to continue south. The French management of our factory told me back in Sully that they would most probably be going to Carcassonne. Apart from the money still owed us, I'm drawn to the south. Such an opportunity doesn't come twice. I resolved to keep going, wait it out, see what happens next, and then return to Paris. Meanwhile, off in the direction of Toulouse.

The ladies fuss over us like a flock of mothers; lunch was piled on high. In the afternoon I ironed our wash. A French division showed up and installed themselves in the château. They had gramophones, played music, enjoyed themselves. I wheedled an excellent road map from a noncom. Now we can plan our route. Talking with the soldiers led me to conclude that this entire war has been a stroll across France for the Germans. This division never saw battle. At the mere sight of a tank (through opera glasses)—they scrammed.

June 27, 1940

Finally the sun is back. We decided to have lunch here once more and then right after lunch keep going. We bought a lot of dried sausage from squire Budzyński and replenished our reserves. We ate another excellent lunch. On saying good-bye, I offered to pay the ladies for our keep, but they wouldn't take anything. I have to admit that for consular staff wives they were first-class. I was pleasantly surprised. Around three o'clock we set out. Two hours later— Périgueux. Full of soldiers and refugees. We paused for a while to eat five kilos of apricots and off again. Cahors-Montauban-Toulouse. "Let's bite the bullet!" said Tadzio and took the lead at racing speed. The road is marvelous, green hills on both sides, evening falls slowly, a chill. We tore along like madmen. The southern mood took hold of us. Overnight in a tiny farm. Excellent red wine.

June 28, 1940

Sun, blinding sun, down below winds the Garonne River. I inhale the odor of the warmed fields and squint my eyes, because the polished asphalt glistens like a mirror. The cities irritate me. I streak through quickly and exhale with relief when I leave. A wonderful animal sense of pleasure, when your entire attention focuses on speed, signposts, food, and the search for a place to sleep. I have the feeling that never before in my life have I so completely not given a damn — and perhaps that's why I feel so good.

It feels as if we've entered a different country, a different climate. Around noon the heat becomes unbearable. The road is made of white stone and I ride with my eyes practically shut. Tadzio keeps riding up alongside me and chattering. His tongue never stops wagging. "Mr. B.," says Tadzio, irritated, "you're always chewing the same bone. Germany and Germany. You see nothing but Germany. It's not only that . . . in France it's the same cabal as in Poland. Did you know that when a Polish worker works too well in the factory, one of the French workers will secretly tamper with the setting of his machine? I wasted time almost every day adjusting the automatic setting, because they knew me, they knew that I can deliver up to seven hundred fuses an hour, and when it was going well, even more. But they had an order from the party: no more than four hundred. And whenever one of them had the chance, he would work on the badly calibrated machines to produce as many defective pieces as possible. You know — defective pieces were produced by the case. How many times did I notice them at night passing around leaflets. One would stick one in his pocket and a bit later duck into the privy to read it."

"Why didn't you tell me about this before?" I ask Tadzio.

"What could you have done? Nothing. Until that clique is disbanded, our goose stays cooked."

Tadzio is right. Just like Poland, France was subjected to terrible pressure and had to give in. Hitler broke her physically, psychologically she was depleted by Communism. I feel like a certain chapter is closed. France was a dogma. Now I look at her and don't even have the strength to reject it.

At an intersection, unsure which road leads to Belvès, I enter one of the farms to ask for directions. A man is lying on a couch. I ask him in French. He looks at me a minute and asks in Polish: "Are you Polish?" It turned out the tenant of this farm was a Pole. He invited us in, a bit later the entire family entered. The man I encountered at first was the host's son-in-law. Drafted into the Polish army, he managed to escape from Brittany before it was taken by the Germans. He reported the same thing as the two Poles we met on the road. We sat down to lunch together. We ate our food, they ate theirs, but offered us sour milk with potatoes for dessert. I learned that around here there are many Poles who share the lease of farms. It is a rather arduous system, but, they said, one can survive. The French are deserting the land for the cities, it's easy to find a farm, because in some areas all the villages are abandoned and the land lies fallow. Tadzio to me: "Get a farm and I'll be your hired man." Around four we set off again. Mountains, difficult climbs. Suddenly Belvès, clinging to the slope of a steep hillside. Narrow streets plunging downhill at a breakneck angle. Curtains in the doorways of houses and shops, everything steeped in sunlight. We sped downhill, then up the opposite slope — the full view of Belvès, a mountain daubed with cottages and festooned in streets. A road along the hollow of a distant valley, a white viaduct against the vegetation. We hurry along. Again uphill. Tadzio furious: "Must have been a wh—— who had you baptized — another mountain!" At this very moment, that is, when the harlot was taking the mountain to be baptized, two women working in the field waved at us. We stopped. "Are you fellows Polish? We could tell right away." Tadzio whispered: "Hard not to" and immediately began hovering around the younger one and winking at me. The mother and daughter work tending beets. They manage a nearby farm and invite us to spend the night. The evening was mild, quiet, and warm — we felt lazy and decided to stay. The farm is clean, everything in order. The father turned out to be a bricklayer. Unable to find work at his trade, he took up farming. He is doing well. Cheerful, dignified, and smiling. "Ah, Polaks, Polaks!" — said with a hint of irony. Tadzio looked at him: "If you have anything that needs repair, better say so right away and don't mess with us Polaks." The old man indeed had a double-bladed plow in terrible condition that needed fixing. Tadzio and I took a look: without riveting, it can't be fixed. Tadzio looked at me: "Shall we rivet?" We brought over some charcoal, bicycle pumps in place of bellows, a hammer, pincers — an all-purpose forge. Tadzio knocked out the old rivets, I sliced an old iron bar into new ones. Three hours later the old man had a working plow. At this he became all warm and effusive. We ate dinner with them — they would not allow us to eat our own food. Our bellies burst from the soup and bread and it was great. Finally, this Mr. Krukowski says: "Why leave tomorrow — tomorrow is the feast of Peter and Paul. Stick around and you'll help me turn over the hay." "We'll stay, Mr. Squire."

June 29, 1940

After breakfast we went to the meadow to turn over the hay. The sun shone, the grass was still damp from the dew. Krukowski brought cold cider and home-grown tobacco. After each row of hay, we had a drink and rolled a cigarette. When the work was done, I went into the woods for wild strawberries. I gathered a full cup and ate them with condensed milk after lunch. (Chicken consommé and cooked chicken.) A nap in the grass, writing. The evening is white with stars and throbbing with crickets, the dew settles. We sat and talked and in the end we all agreed with Tadzio that "the French are slobs and muff-divers."

June 30, 1940

Tadzio woke me up: "Mr. B. — the day is shining like a czar's ruble; let's move on." We got going. The towns were full of troops. They are waiting for de-mobilization. The French have signed the armistice on very onerous terms. They are obliged to turn over all their military matériel to the Germans, accept the occupation of half the country and the entire Atlantic coast, and feed and sup-port an occupying army. The occupied territories will supposedly be run by the French administration. There's also talk of the "government" possibly returning to Paris. The further south you go, the easier it is to find bread and food. Tinned meat, by contrast, cannot be found anywhere. After five hundred kilometers of nothing, however, beer and lemonade have reappeared.

The white buildings of the roadside gas stations are toylike and glisten in the sun; palm trees appear here and there in the gardens. In the afternoon we enter Cahors. The Lot River flows along the bottom of a rocky ravine; we hurry along the highway on the right bank. The road is cut into the rock. I think of nothing and simply look. In Cahors we buy peaches, cheese, and white wine, sit on a bench, and eat. At dusk we leave town. The night is warm and starry. The area is full of rocky heights, arid, no farms anywhere. I forgot my tobacco on the bench in Cahors and have nothing to smoke. I'm ready to ride all night and go to sleep only at dawn, because there's no chance of finding a farm. We stop at a turn in the road because Robert has noticed something and goes off to investigate. A motorcycle patrol pulls up next to us and two noncoms ask politely whether they can be of any help. They have no cigarettes. A car also stops and they give us four cigarettes. It's now easier to contemplate night on the road. Robert re-turns and says there's a place to sleep. Something, he doesn't know what exactly. We come closer. An empty hut made of loosely fitted stones. The flat stones are placed so that the circular walls, narrowing toward the top, come together and form a roof. An igloo of stone slabs. I light the lamp and marvel at this miracle of shepherd's architecture. We cut some branches from the dwarfed oaks and the juniper bushes, making an elastic bed. I luxuriate in falling asleep.

July 1, 1940

It was only five when we were awakened by the cold. A penetrating chill forced its way in through the unprotected entry of the stone igloo and kept us from sleep. Fog still hung over the valleys and the sun had not yet risen over the hills. Teeth chattering, we gather our stuff and set off. Around nine we rolled into Caussade and ate breakfast. The town had been eaten bare, but we managed to buy cheese and tinned *crème de marron*.[27] Not far beyond Caussade four corpses almost ended up on the road. The road seemed to be empty and Robert, without a care in the world, crossed over from the right side to the left. At that very instant we heard the squeak of tires on asphalt; inches from Robert's hind wheel a car shot by, skidding on all four wheels as it braked. The car went flying over to the left side of the road, hit the edge of the highway, bounced on the drainage ditch, and stopped a half-meter from a stout plane tree. Silence. We froze. Tadzio whispered to Robert: "If he pops out and lands you one on the kisser, I'll just stand by and watch, because he's right. If you'd done that to me, mister, you'd be spitting teeth." A Frenchman with a cut on the forehead emerged shortly from the car. He was staunching the blood with his handkerchief. I don't know—either he didn't realize it was Robert who had caused the accident or he was convinced it was his own fault. He said nothing. Paced around and breathed heavily, ventilating his nerves. The two women still inside the car now also emerged, completely dazed. I tried to find something to say, we inspected the car together. It was undamaged. We went on our way. Tadzio: "Mr. B., what kind of country is this? How were they supposed to win the war? They can't even bust a guy on the snout."

An hour later we reached Montauban and beyond the town, on the banks of the Tarn, we lay down for an afternoon rest. I think about the emptiness of these parts. Along the road we have seen dozens of houses, formerly inhabited, and often entire farms, completely deserted, rotted, dilapidated. Three or four kilometers from the main road places can be found without a living soul. A desert.

At dinner we drink an excellent red wine for one and a half francs a liter. Wine is never lacking here.

July 2, 1940

This morning—washup and a shave, laundry. At nine in the morning it was already infernally hot. After ten we set off. For the last three days we have been encountering people returning north. Heading back where they had come from, they wave and signal that we are going in the wrong direction. Around noon we enter the outskirts of Toulouse. We ride alongside an endless string of Parisian buses—now inhabited by refugees. They dry their laundry on the railings, sit on the nearby grass, light fires, cook, and drink. We ride into town. In Toulouse there's still a Polish consulate, as we'd been assured along the way. We draw up in front of the building. The entryway and courtyard are full of our compatriots. Workmen, officers' wives, Polish soldiers. The consulate apparently pays some kind of subsidy and people are waiting around. The mood is grim. All are frightened, tell fantastic tales, dream of getting Spanish or Portuguese visas, just to get farther away. Others are returning to Poland, urgently, this very minute. The Germans are said to have a special agency in Lyon, which encourages and recruits Poles to return. One has already left straight for Warsaw, another is leaving today. Some character is running around swearing on a stack of Bibles that it's possible to get a Chinese visa. I have a weakness for such specimens and I accost him. "Really? . . . Chinese? Where?" "It's not so simple," he says and smiles mysteriously. I whisper: "As for me, I prefer Andorra . . . I'm in love with the female announcer for Radio Andorra . . . have you ever heard her voice?" He bats his eyelashes. I laugh.

I determine, first of all, to find out whether our factory is in Carcassonne. I go to the office of the Ministry of Armaments in the Préfecture, but by now they've all kissed good-bye to weapons and no one knows anything. We therefore go to the Polish House. People sleep in the garden at night and spend the time debating. Also, cheap meals are offered there. Completely by accident, I learn from a Frenchman that part of our factory is in Carcassonne. I therefore don't intend to spend another minute sitting around here. The atmosphere is pestilential. Tadzio was afraid we might want to leave him behind. "Even if you didn't take me along, I wouldn't hang around with these dunces for any price. People pass along what they've heard from someone dumber than they are to someone even dumber than that." I hug him and assure him that I'd never for a minute contemplate losing such a treasure. He's overjoyed. We buy some food for the road and get going. We were warned that no one is being allowed to leave Toulouse and gendarmes are patrolling the roads. I ride in front, on the alert. Soon enough, there are barriers blocking the way and black uniforms. I turn off, we take the side streets and a kilometer later return to the main road. There was no one. God forbid they should secure all the ways to get out of town. It's already six in the afternoon and ninety-two kilometers still to go to Carcassonne. I set a racing clip. In the first hour, we make twenty-three km, in the second twenty-two—it's now eight o'clock. We start looking for a place to sleep.

It's a lovely route—on each side gentle hills, meadows, here and there a cemetery glows white among the rows of dark cypresses. Peace, quiet, and harmony. Quite naturally I begin to think of Greece. Somewhere in the distance a clock tower chimes an entire melody. Tadzio whistles softly, then falls silent. He rides up alongside me and whispers: "How beautiful it is . . ." Night falls. The pale blue sky turns gray and the cypresses in the cemeteries grow even blacker. We find a farmhouse, next to it a pile of freshly cut grass under a lean-to. The night is hot. I lie on the grass, in front of me a hill, and on the hill, the roof of a little church sharply etched against the dark sky. The bells are tolling—a large one and a flock of small ones. Tolling. And the black cypresses, the meadows, the fields, the vineyards carry their sound, ever farther into the distance, ever more softly. I listen and I watch. Beauty can be as hard to bear as pain. Possible to tolerate only up to a certain point, to experience only to a certain depth. Beyond that, it makes you faint.

The sky had grown even darker and had turned violet. The stars glittered. We went over to a large tank near a spring to wash ourselves. We stripped, ladled out the water with our mess tins, and slowly dowsed ourselves. Is France the Greece of the period when it began to be called Achaea? Around us crickets were chirping, bats gliding through the air. An immense calm. For a long time I could not fall asleep. All that once was no longer exists. I had no regrets. I felt as though this night, here in the south, I had for the first time found my footing on this earth.

July 3, 1940

We got up this morning awakened by a concert of bells. Sunshine. We're moving on. The harvest has already begun. Twenty kilometers later we settled into a hollow along the road. The fields of wheat appeared white in the sun. A harvester, the latest model from the age of Marie Antoinette, a cross between a sewing machine and a hair clipper, crawled slowly along, pulled by cows.

Around one in the afternoon we entered Carcassonne. A small town, full of charm. Across the river the castle, a fortified bastion, like a stage set. Carcassonne is deserted, because it's noon and hot. In the Hôtel Vitrac we find seven of our colleagues from the Paris office. Part of our factory is in Carcassonne, even part of the management. You can get 500 francs, later 675, as an *indemnité de repliement*, or compensation for making yourself scarce, and today everyone is signing up for benefits: 23 francs a day, starting tomorrow. They're treating the Poles no differently than the French.

After lunch we settle into a big room with five beds. If we sleep two to a bed, it's very cheap. We set off for our "factory." It's been installed in the building of a deserted hat factory. They register us and tomorrow are supposed to pay us five hundred francs. We left the "factory" and headed to the river for a swim. While he undresses, Tadzio leans over and whispers straight in my ear: "Mr. Bee, as of tomorrow we enter the condition of rest. Holiday, time to knock off." This is no doubt possible only in France.

July 14, 1940

Carcassonne? No, an Olympic village. They have paid us everything, and now a daily allowance of twenty-three francs. The hotel costs three francs a day, lunch fourteen francs with wine and bread *à volonté*.[28] As in the old days. Red wine, served chilled in large carafes. When one of them has been drained, you take another from the next table. The war? All that the locals know about it they get from the stories of new arrivals. Sunshine, magnificent and lush; evenings and nights, as silky as the coat of a black cat. First thing in the morning, into the water, the lazy feeling of limbs relaxed by a swim. Feels absolutely great. I've caught up here with old-time France. And now I'll savor her slowly, in tiny sips, like a glass of good wine. Then? My God . . . "Tomorrow," "then," "in the future"—these are words from a bygone age. That age has disappeared, perished—and let history treat it kindly. If we didn't manage to get rid of these words, "the now" would lose all meaning, all its charm. I want to live only "now." From the very first day here, I felt most clearly that fate has allowed me to win an immense prize and I must cherish every minute. I'm hoarding them. The complete, round, fragrant minutes and hours.

First there was Dakar.[29] Not wanting the French fleet to fall under German control, the English bombarded, sank, or otherwise damaged half of the best units of the French navy. A regular naval battle unfolded between the French and the English. The English did the best they could. A pitiful sight. Most important, however, is the fact that the French nevertheless put up a fight. True, it was in Dakar and against the English, but they fought. Afterward they behaved like a gigolo who's gotten his face slapped—the newspapers all shed tears: I danced with you, but you, but you—boo-hoo, boo-hoo, you so-and-so. Now they've severed diplomatic relations with those disgusting English. All their hatred for the Germans, all the regret for their war of retreat, they've now unloaded onto the English. When I say I'm Polish, they nod sadly: "Another victim of the English." Today is July 14. The French government, now situated in Clermont-Ferrand, has proclaimed the date a day of national mourning; funeral masses in the churches. As in a fog, I recall this day a year ago. Crowds of people on the Champs-Élysées. How splendid the army looked . . . Why all this damned lying everywhere? Is it worth remembering? Surely not. I write this and involuntarily I smile. I'm seized by a wicked joy that everything has burst asunder, snapped, that still more seams will pop.

Today I was in the castle, in the cathedral. At the altar was a banner, a priest in a black vestment, Mass without bells. After the prayer the organ bellowed the "Marseillaise." My knees buckled, my throat caught. Tadzio had tears in his eyes. But the French left the church smiling. Before even getting outside many had already stuck a cigarette in their mouths, put on their hats, fumbled in their pockets for matches or a lighter. I clenched my fists. How much harder it is to live when one is—a barbarian. No, the future belongs, not to the stomach and the brain, but despite everything—to the heart.

The grand hotel in the castle courtyard is now occupied by airmen. Hearing us speak Polish, one of them approached and said he was Czech. Despite his broken Polish, it was easy enough to understand him. He began telling us about the French, speaking of them with pity. "They'll only begin to realize two months from now what has happened." Then they'll see. But can anything really bad happen to them?

July 28, 1940

Do you know the mood and the life in the southern towns of France? I think of you constantly, Basia, and I so regret that we're not together. We would have had so many subjects to discuss and so many occasions to experience things that elude other people, slip through their fingers, or seem monotonous and boring.

There was a war, it still continues, but the French seem already to have put it behind them, and the south was never affected at all. And the French haven't changed. I go out toward evening. The sun has set behind the houses and you feel it only in the narrow streets, where its warmth remains in the stones ashen from the heat of the day and radiates from the walls of the houses. The hours between sunset and nightfall are hours without colors: wherever you look, everything has the same ash-white tone, hazy as a faded watercolor.

The shutters, closed during the day, now open, and little tables, stools, chairs, and benches are brought out and placed in front of the entryways. They are occupied by old women dressed in black; sewing, crocheting, darning, and talking. They speak in the almost phonetic sing-song of southern French. As in Marcel Pagnol's *Fanny* and *Marius*.[30] At dusk they are all in front of their houses and sit there until late at night. The young girls are olive-skinned and have black hair; the fellows are also dark and usually short. In the evening they dash around on their bicycles.

I go to the castle . . . It's now entirely dark. I approach the rampart and circle the walls along the outside. Stars appear in the sky, like bubbles in soda water, the dusty cloud of the Milky Way stands out clearly. The castle, the entire town, encircled by inner walls, appear mysterious. Like illustrations to a fairy tale. Across the bridge, once a drawbridge, I enter the interior. I already know all the passages and entryways. I climb along the wall, then up the stone steps to the tower. I deeply inhale the fresh breeze wafting in from the Pyrenees. I lie down on the floor and stare at the sky. Then it seems like a real vault. At times I almost doze off.

I walk back slowly and in front of the hotel drop into my bistro for a shot of rum. At one table are several picturesquely dirty and picturesquely attired Spanish Gypsies. They are drinking beer and grunting. At another table the local inhabitants are playing belote[31]—they play with their hands, their feet, their heads, their entire bodies, and shout. Yelling heatedly. I drink rum and light a cigarette. The night is once again stifling and I won't sleep well. At eleven the bistro closes. The gray-haired *patronne* shuffles to the railing outside and keeps calling: "Toto, Toto, pussy, pussy . . ." But "Toto," a big, black tom, has vanished. Carried away by the stifling night. In the morning he'll turn up under the door of the icebox, sniffing the meat inside. The old lady will inform him: "*Méchant Toto, la viande n'est pas pour toi—oh non!*"[32] and, looking around to be sure the other old lady, her sister, doesn't notice, will cut off a piece of meat and hide "Toto," along with his spoils, behind the counter. Then she will yell in a shrill voice: "*Du café pour monsieur!*"[33] I'll be drinking coffee . . .

I ride through the narrow streets bathed in sunlight to the town hall. I want to go to the sea and it's important to investigate the administrative aspects of such an expedition. One is not permitted to leave one's place of residence without a *sauf-conduit*, and what's more, my papers are reaching their expiration date.

In the section for *étrangers* at the town hall I approach a policeman with bulging eyes. Like everyone else around here, at this time of day he speaks in a voice suggesting Swedish gymnastics in slow motion. First I have to extend the validity of my national identity papers, submitting the application at the Préfecture. At the Préfecture they send me to the town hall for the stamp of arrival and registration. Except that the Préfecture has prohibited the use of such stamps on the documents of refugees. If the Préfecture allows it, that's fine. So I return to the Préfecture. Yes—they can make a recommendation to the town hall, but I must bring an attestation from the factory. I go to the factory. I return with the attestation. Now they relieve me of all my papers and instruct me to come back again the day after tomorrow. The day after tomorrow I have already become someone else. All of me is in a lovely file and *mademoiselle* says conspiratorially: "*Votre cas a été examiné et Monsieur le Préfet signera cela à cinq heures.*"[34] I show up at five and learn that *mon cas* has just been sent by mail to the town hall. The town hall is five hundred meters from the Préfecture. The following day in the *après-midi* the town hall will stamp my papers with *arrivée* . . . I return to the Préfecture. *Demain après-midi*[35] I will obtain the extension of validity. By now everyone knows me. *Sauf-conduit?* The gendarme looks at me severely. For what purpose? I want to ride down to the sea, simply to the sea. A minute's reflection, and the gruff order: then kindly write "Family in Narbonne." I smile. He smiles, too, into his mustache. *Demain après-midi.*

Why aren't we together, Basia? We would laugh together, as we walked the narrow, sunlit streets, and we would walk as slowly and lazily as my papers went from the Préfecture to the town hall: five hundred meters in twenty-four hours. *Demain après-midi*, once again without you . . .

July 31, 1940

I bike to the river. I emerge on the far side of town and take a road through the vineyards to the "swimming hole." I lie in the sun. In fact the French never harbor any illusions; they do not have what can be called "a craving for the impossible." Only the desire to catch fish in the Seine may constitute a certain exception to this rule. Although even this doesn't belong entirely to the realm of the impossible. They possess a phenomenally advanced sense of life without ideals or illusions, something so difficult for the Poles to attain. Ann Bridge, in *Peking Picnic* (what a title!), jokingly catches this trait when she remarks that moonlit nights and love are equally natural to the French, but they never confuse one with the other.[36] A moonlit night—true—is a beautiful thing, and love indoors on a comfortable bed is just as beautiful, *mais il ne faut pas confondre ces deux choses.*[37] Not to be confused. For the French, conversations or debates amount to an endless pouring back and forth of glittering beads and sequins, and in general they never hope to achieve any particular result, they never want to convince anyone of anything. It's a matter of cutting everything into a great number of sample pieces (without lessening their value) and displaying the samples on the table before the customer, who admires their elegance and delicacy. The French manage to chat for hours about the business of everyday life, which for them is the only issue that really counts. Today one loves them, tomorrow one hates them, the day after they have seduced you yet again by some bauble or by the facility with which they approach whatever they consider a "PROBLEM." A splendid capacity to materialize the spirit, which is perhaps what their spirit is about. They disturb me, they do not permit me not to think, they do not permit me to take refuge in the commonplace that is at this moment poised at the tip of my tongue. One would like to despise them, but it's not entirely possible. Not allowed? Has France in fact been a religion?

During the month spent here, world events have taken their course. France has changed its constitution, dissolved parliament, and installed Pétain's authoritarian regime. The French have been deprived of the one thing to which they were most strongly attached: parliamentary bedlam. But that makes no difference—they will grow even more attached to it . . . And next they will begin to be deprived of something else essential to their existence: food. Rationing was introduced rigorously, the sale of fresh bread is prohibited. Everyone is anticipating a German attack on England. Thus day after day, the mornings and evenings of this strange life pass by.

Gruissan, August 3, 1940

I live in a red bungalow built on piles. I walk slowly along the beach. A warm wind blows from the meadow, the sea is completely calm. The azure blue of the sky merges with the azure blue of the water and everything is submerged in the pitiless light of the sun. I take off my dark eyeglasses and feel like a camera without a filter. In such clarity the eye loses the ability to distinguish clearly between colors; sky, sea, sand, distant mountains all become a flat, ashen mass. I walk a long way, leaving behind the colorful patch of bungalows on piles. I spread a blanket on the sandy dune and strip off my clothes. I bury the bottle of drinking water in the wet sand and stretch out. All around deserted. Hours of conversation with the sun slip by. A small crab crawls toward my bottle with a curious gait. I clear my throat and the crab immediately moves to escape. It runs sideways, backward, forward—always in a straight line. It doesn't manage to turn. One could use the expression: as direct as a crab. It slithers quickly into the water. Some kind of sand ladybug crawls along my hand. It reaches the end of my finger, twirls, opens its carapace, and flies off. The wind had shifted and was now blowing from the sea. The motionless sheet of blue water begins to quiver and glitter like pearls. A million luminous needles shoot forth. Arrows aimed directly at the sun. I enter the water slowly and walk far out, immersed to the waist. My blanket on the shore has already become very small when I finally begin to swim. My arms and legs work as steadily as a machine. Why did Byron claim that the most beautiful woman eating and drinking anything but lobster and champagne always looks vulgar? A snob, but he swam very well. I wonder in what style? In hexameter—I laugh to myself. The bottom is still visible, although it's now very deep. The beach is just a string of yellow sand, far, far away. I dive with open eyes, but the water insists on tossing me back to the surface. I turn back. I move in a slow, lazy crawl. I emerge onto the shore, pleasantly tired. It's quiet; only a short wave hits the shore with a splash. An inquisitive crab creeps once again toward my bottle . . .

I return to the bungalow on piles. The sun has already traveled to the other side of the sky and stings the eyes. My *patron*, owner of the bungalow colony, stands on the ramparts of the canal, holding a long, ten-pronged pole. He is wearing navy blue sailcloth trousers, a pale blue shirt, and a cotton sash of blue-gray gingham around his waist. Against the endless beach, in the blinding sunlight, he resembles an inkblot on a yellow tablecloth. Every so often he squats down, shades his eyes with his hand, wipes his sweat with the end of the sash, and inspects the bottom of the canal. Suddenly he bends over, and with a smooth and barely perceptible motion, he plunges the rod into the water and draws it up again. A large fish flutters on the sharp prongs. The mustachioed Monsieur Louis smiles in my direction and, removing the fish, says gaily: "After all, there has to be something for supper . . ."

Morning. Fog over the sea. From a dozen meters away, the bungalows are only a darker patch. It's sultry and I feel the sun, dissolved in this milk, burning pitilessly. It's the atmosphere of a sunny room in which thin tulle curtains have been drawn across the closed windows. I take the bike and ride to town for bread, wine, and water. There's no freshwater on the beach. I ride out on a long dike between the bays and frighten away thousands of small fish on both sides. They escape with a splash into deeper places, crowding one after the other, tracing zigzags and streaks on the smooth water. The fog has an ineffable smell— like a pinecone just fallen from the tree. The smell of pine forests sinks into it and reaches all the way here. A deep, condensed silence prevails.

I drop into the baker's. He's like a cat roused from sleep—drowsy, lithe, stretching himself. In a sleepy voice, he tells me: "Fog means a scorcher . . ." He hands me the bread and disappears into the depths of the darkened bakery. Next I stop by for postcards with views of the local beach. My witch invites me in and in the same drowsy tone as the baker, sighs to herself: "Fog means a scorcher . . ."

The first time I entered this shop, no one was there. Suddenly in the dim light the door behind the counter opened and a sight appeared that made me go weak at the knees. A woman-monster with broad mustaches and a bushy beard. I must have had a stupid expression on my face, like "just don't devour me," because she laughed with great tenderness and said affectionately: *"Vous désirez, mon pauvre?"*[38] Today she spread out a box of colored postcards, wiped the sweat from her brow with her apron, and turned them over with gusto, marveling at each one and explaining what they meant—"There on the left, which you can't see on the card, is that café: *Monsieur connaît ce café . . .*"[39] In the end, the most important thing on each card was the thing you couldn't see, but *"Monsieur connaît ça sûrement . . ."*[40] I stared at her mustaches and beard, dreaming of a postcard showing only her. I bought three cards for a franc. She sat down, exhausted, and in farewell reminded me: *"Vous savez,* fog means a scorcher . . ."

Tomorrow I'll stop in to see her again, because the shop has everything. The fog lifted suddenly and sunlight has flooded the town like a torrent of molten steel into the vat. Empty streets. Only here and there, shiny cats pad softly along in the shadow of the house walls. I bought a liter of white wine, a tin of beans with meat, and got water from the public fountain. Putting the bottle under the stream gushing from the column, I tease a big carp swimming in the pool. It greedily sticks out its snout, thinking I'll throw it something, but I only make *"marionettes"* with my fingers. I always tease it, because I don't like carp. This one resembles a sluggish banker, and the remnants of its golden scales shimmer on its belly like a watch fob on a waistcoat. I return, sweaty, to the bungalow, drink my coffee in *monsieur connaît ce café,* with a bite of bread and jam. Afterward I cover myself with olive oil from head to toe.

Shreds of fog drift in from the sea. A half hour later the sky is deep blue. The sun is delirious. I have the feeling I'm sizzling like a sunny-side up on the frying pan. On the shore, a wave laps at my feet and the water's loud licking at the shore deepens the surrounding silence. The wind ripples over the sand and everything looks as if it's covered by crumpled cellophane. Thinking stops from time to time, while Ravel's stubborn and tiresome *Bolero* keeps churning in my ears. Something about this unmelodious melody alone can convey the mood of these hours of stillness; it's the rhythm of inertia, hot, yet also icy and cruel, the rhythm of something cold on the inside, completely motionless, and burning hot only on the outside.

The sun eats all the colors out of me, blanches my insides and blackens only my skin. I am a chunk of meat. I enter the water and I'm a fish. The chill of the water affects me like a hand passing over the piano keys. I fill up on tones and half-tones, I take on color. It's the dream come true of Jack London and Somerset Maugham's southern seas. I dive in. The water is greenish. I turn over on my back and move slowly upward, like a silent *"lift."* On one of the floors I pass a pink jellyfish suspended in the emerald green. Then once again, sun.

In the afternoon the heat increased. I dragged the mattress from the bed and spread it on the veranda. I read. A book borrowed from some Belgians I met a few days ago. There are a number of them here, also refugees. My acquaintance, Dr. G., is the director of the Museum of African Art in Namur. With a very nice wife. Both young and appealing. They laugh when I make some comments about the French. They are serious when I talk to them about Poland, although I myself often barely believe what I'm saying. Every defeat has one great danger: in the search for mistakes it is easy to cross the line beyond which the search descends into ordinary baseness and self-denigration. We Poles belittle our stupid heroism, the Belgians belittle their own cowardice and their king. They say we were right. I think they were. Poland, Belgium, Holland, France are beginning to reflect. But as long as this reflection doesn't cross the line of self-respect, they will not truly be defeated.

Through the railing of the veranda I see a line of hills. A few little clouds hang motionless above them. Suddenly a gust of wind rocked the whole bungalow. Then a second and a third. A hurricane came tearing through, hot and violent. The distinct blows of the wind, reminding me at first of the successive opening and shutting of an oxygen tank, became a continuous whistle. A wall of hot wind pushed in from the northwest. I looked at the beach.

The band of sapphire water and golden sand was divided by a yellowish haze. I ran out to the shore. A few hundred meters beyond the bungalows I undressed and began to run. Close to the shore the sea was entirely calm. The sand blown in from the land was creating great dunes and bluffs over the water; the wind howled and lashed my legs with the sand. In the short intervals, you could hear a metallic sound, like the ringing of billions of grains of sand falling upon the water.

I ran along the water's edge, kicking up fountains over and over. I was seized by a wild joy, and though I felt the fatigue, having already run more than a kilometer, I kept running. The wind whistled in my ears, the copper sun sank in the west, and my giant shadow danced on the water. I noticed something black on the expanse of beach receding toward the horizon. I ran nearer. Half-buried in the sand the wreck of a tugboat protruded. Nothing around, the wind whistling, light the color of slightly burnt sugar, and the boat's tilted chimney pointing up toward the sky. Against the remnants of the steel cables the wind whistled more stridently still, roared in the chimney, and buried the steel corpse in the sand. There was something strange in the entire setting, a pallid and lifeless waste, mocked by the wind, which chuckled in every crack, shaking the pieces of metal and dancing about in funnels of sand.

I sat down on the bow and I was suddenly reminded of *Treasure Island*. I had the feeling someone was spying on me from the porthole half buried in sand. And Captain Flint, dying in Savannah, was crying out: "Rum, Darby,

McGraw . . ."[41] Then a piece of metal broke off completely, bounded away from the boat, and, wobbling, rolled with a clank into the sea. I ran away, looking around to see if it wasn't pursuing me. I skipped along the dunes, took handfuls of sand and threw it up in the air. The sand descended in a cloud, carried by the wind far out to sea.

In the evening the sky clouded over and the night turned black, absolute black. My bungalow buckled on its piles, shook and creaked, buffeted by the blasts of the demented gale. After supper I went out. I strode along sand that was hard as cement, beaten by winter storms across this great expanse. I followed the telephone poles, so as not to get lost in the emptiness. I lay on the wind, as on a soft couch. Despite the night and the wind, it was stifling. I took off my shirt and continued walking. The hot gale, flying in from the dark distance, is monotonous and exhausting. The telephone poles became a complete symphony orchestra. I keep stopping and listen. Reminiscent of Rossini's *William Tell Overture*. No, it's rather Scriabin's *Twelfth Étude*, which always made me think of just such a hot, sweeping wind.

Memories, comparisons, forgotten images meander, intermingle. I was once hiking alone in the Gorce Mountains,[42] during the hot southern wind . . . Regret is the stupidest feeling, sorrow makes you helpless. I most likely won't sleep all night. I will be observing myself and from time to time confirm that I've done a fine job of acting: this scene of insomnia, melancholy, and sorrow. It's amusing, when at the same time you feel that life is surging inside you and also laughing. Tomorrow at five in the morning I'm leaving this place, and I haven't yet finished my book. There's enough left to last until morning. It has begun to rain. I've lost track of time here—there was neither day nor night, hour nor season . . . I was my own time.

Carcassonne, August 10, 1940

Carcassonne. I burrowed myself in the corner of our bistro, ordered myself a glass of rum, dropped in four lumps of sugar, and I'm feeling good. Except that deep down I worry about Basia. I've received a letter from her in Paris. Now I think about her the way Staś thought about Nel when he left her inside the baobab tree and went looking for help.[43] I know that everything will be all right. It's now a warm evening; rain is falling lightly and the air is fresh. Rum (obviously) has the color of dark amber and smells good. Rum . . . I sink even deeper into the corner banquette and light my pipe. I feel a marvelous, calm aimlessness. Julian Tuwim once wrote that cows have an "otherworldly gaze."[44] My glances are exactly like that. People are hopeless in their urgent search for meaning. The company from the "common room" is hard to bear.[45] War? War! For

S. it ended there one day in September. He's constantly harping on it and says that "if only," then it might even have been possible to hold out for a while on two fronts. That's all that was lacking . . . War! This one has begun twice and has twice ended. Now there's a twenty-minute break and one should take advantage of it, as one took advantage of recess in school. We were tested twice and twice we failed. They'll test us again in the next class periods and we must prepare. Does it make sense? No—life, ordinary life, is what's most important. Some people, when riding on a train, stand at the window and look toward the back. Because if they look forward, the wind might blow something into their eyes. When they see something interesting, they stick their heads out for half an hour (despite the sign: *e pericoloso sporgersi*[46]) and miss what has appeared, passed by, and vanished. They get stuck at some long-gone milestone, and cheerio, as Tadzio says. I myself always loved to look forward. (*Madame, remettez, s'il vous plaît.*[47]) Why is it impossible to describe rum without the phrase "the color of dark amber"? The same with "the cold steel of a revolver"—as inescapable as "the deep-not-agitated inhalation of a cigarette." What a shame that Flaubert died before he could compose a dictionary of idiocies.[48] The crayfish is the female of the lobster and so on . . . Thoughts can be terrible. There's one that gives me no peace: in the Escorial, before the time of Philip II, there was a chandelier with 300 (in words: three hundred) candles. How did they light it? Before they lit the last of them, those lit first would certainly have already burned out. I know: they lit them continuously. Clear as a bell! Intellect?—life, not intellect. I return to the sea. A long break. Soon Tadzio will show up and we'll play chess. He'll checkmate me for sure. It has stopped raining, and the sound of girls laughing rises from the street. Toto stood on the doorstep and cocked his tail. He stands looking away from me and resembles the Eiffel Tower from the Trocadéro side. His two legs join in a fat stump and diminish toward the top. Tadzio entered and asked me why I was craning my neck. "I'm looking at the Eiffel Tower." The Spanish delight who lives three numbers down has now dropped in for a beer. She has rather dirty legs and a black velvet ribbon around her ankle. This makes the leg with the ribbon look cleaner. Tadzio sat down next to her and grabbed the leg with the ribbon. Now he's gotten up and brought over a chess set. But he's making a great racket, because he's caught a giant flea in it. The fleas here are really splendid. He crushed it against the table with the white bishop. Checkmate!

August 12, 1940

I have everything. I'm fully equipped and return to the sea. In a basket at the market I found a few books and I'm taking them with me. Caesar's *Com-

mentarii de bello Gallico, complete annotated Latin edition for three francs. *Manon Lescaut* for one and a half francs and André Maurois's *Climats* for five francs.[49] What bliss . . . One must take advantage of the remaining sparkles of this country of cheap food, drink, and books. Equilibrium is France's charm. For what good to me are cheap books if food is dear, or cheap food if books are dear? An old man came up to me and began to chat. Here, in the south, they don't recognize that I'm a foreigner and at worst take me for a Belgian. He went on about politics and finally said, winking playfully: "Everyone curses the English out loud, but each secretly hopes for their victory. It is now the last hope — what do you think? Will they win or lose?" I answered him Normandy-style: "The Germans are strong, but the English know what they're doing — *on va voir!*" He smiled knowingly: "*Je comprends.*"[50] I asked him where to find a *pissoir,* because I hadn't noticed any of those "wailing walls," as Tadzio calls them, in the vicinity. A tradeswoman heard me and with great effusiveness eagerly explained: "*Ici, à gauche, mon pauvre!*"[51] She sang the final "e" and pointed out the direction. Touching. Today I like them all very much.

When I think about you, Basia, and I think about you all the time, I feel like a carefree, unconcerned boy, who looks on the bright side of this situation and has a good time, lets loose — manages even to enjoy his longing for you, finding in it the meaning of his loneliness amid the sunshine. I'm ashamed — I'd like to apologize to you. I'd like to apologize to everyone who is suffering now. "You know, Nel" . . . Don't be angry, Nel . . .

August 13, 1940

A terrific wind blew at my back and I rode at a dizzying speed. My heart beat fast — hmm — from pure joy. The sun shone, empty fields of stubble. I entered Narbonne before seven. A summer evening mood pervaded the town. Men in navy blue sat in the bistros, drinking an evening aperitif. Indeed they drink something here all day long. It was quiet, calm, blissful. Old Narbonne was preparing for bed. I also entered the bistro. Rum? No — lemonade. A couple of locals winked at me knowingly from behind their glasses of yellow pastis over a mound of crushed ice and said: "*Tour de balade, hein?*" "*Ouyi, on se promène,*"[52] I answered and went back to my lemonade, in which a thick floe of ice was suspended. Once again I felt ashamed . . . A summer evening, lemonade, in half an hour I'll be at the sea, I'll buy some bread, eat a tin of sardines, some tomatoes, cheese, I'll drink water with a slice of lemon and nibble some chocolate; by the time the moon is out I'll be jumping into the water and then

I'll fall asleep, rocking along with the bungalow, dancing a wind polka on its six piles. By now I'd fallen into a swoon and had to revive myself with another glass of cold lemonade. Then I climbed on my bike and by dusk was at the fountain.

I bought some bread, filled my bottle with water (the old carp was now asleep), and followed the dike to the shore. Monsieur Louis welcomed me with a glass of Grenache, complained about all the vacancies (a bad season this year, for sure), gave me the key to the bungalow, and wished me good-night and good weather. The sun had already set, the bungalow swayed, I ate my sardines, tomatoes, and cheese. Indeed, a bad season this year; it's perhaps because they ended up losing the war . . . what? what? The w-a-r?

An enormous moon rose in the sky. Crystals of salt mixed with sand sparkled with a white light. I jumped into the canal and bathed in the living silver. I played with the water, entered the bungalow, and toweled off on the veranda; the hot wind dried me. I went to bed and started to read *Manon Lescaut*, trying to whistle the aria of the Chevalier des Grieux.[53] I was thinking of you, Basia, all the while; because you remember—once in the evening, at our place, we sat on the sofa and listened to *Manon* from start to finish. You recounted the plot. Outside the windows there was snow and frost, the tile stove gave off a pleasant warmth, a box of cigarettes lay on my desk. I munched on nuts and raisins and asked you for a cigarette. You brought me the entire box. Leaning your head on my shoulder, you said as usual: "Just don't blow the smoke in my face." In the desk drawer were still several of our wedding announcements. Now, I stopped reading and stared at the roof. Jolted by the wind, it was bouncing up and down like the cover of a teapot when the water boils. I thought that if it suddenly broke off and flew away, it would be just like ours. We lost the roof over our heads a long time ago . . .

August 14, 1940

The sun woke me up. It came in through the cracks between the boards and sliced my little room into a dozen parts. I got up, split some wood, and prepared coffee. Then I unpacked my treasures and made myself at home. I'm pleased with every trifle, every saucepan, jar, little knife. I lay them out carefully, and at the sight of the aluminum plate with a lemon, tomatoes, and eggs against the checkered napkin I went into raptures. I added the little knife; now it all came to life and acquired meaning. And when I added a small salt cellar with a green tip and a slice of bread, I pronounced the experiment almost complete. I had the urge to paint. In the style of Cézanne, of course.

Then I took a long walk, read, swam, and dozed. Caesar is horrible. Now I truly understand why old Bogucki never called the Romans anything but "those barbarians."[54] Moreover, this Caesar exaggerates unbelievably. Ideas straight out of Disney. That the Romans could suddenly pierce through several Helvetian shields one after the other and immobilize the left hands of several warriors with one stroke of a single spear. Obviously, the Helvetians threw down their shields and had to fight *nudo corpore*. I read this with hatred. His Latin is as repulsive to me as the German of Hitler's *Mein Kampf*. These books have something in common. Both of them relish conquest. They have the same hypocrisy, the same falseness and insolence. The Germanic king Ariovist meets with Caesar and says he was not the one who declared war on the Gauls but the Gauls who declared war on him. Caesar says the same thing. And between them they divide up the world, which seeks salvation from either the one or the other. By the way, Caesar's tactics are amazing: excellent intelligence, fifth columns everywhere, his position always supported, and terrific propaganda. The *vulgus militum* is always well informed *qua arrogantia in colloquio Ariovistus usus* and thirsts for battle.[55] Caesar already uses the word *arrogantia* in relation to the Germanic people. This makes it clear that this is not merely a Prussian trait but a national one. The Prussians brought it back from the banks of the Rhine. This *arrogantia* appeals to me enormously. I have learned entire sentences by heart.

Back home I made myself a splendid meal. The fish here cost practically nothing. I fry them on the grill. They smell good and brown slowly, greased with olive oil, like wood shiny with polish. Tomorrow I'll hunt for mussels. And "my dear witch" still has St. Bruno Flake English pipe tobacco in her store. I read until evening, stretched out on the mattress on the veranda. Consider this my confession of mortal sins . . .

August 15, 1940

I blew out the candle and stared at the large moon. The evening was hot and silent, except for the monotonous murmur rising from the sea. I closed the bungalow and went down to the canal. Silently the boats sailed off to their nocturnal fishing. I quickly pulled off my sweater, shorts, and espadrilles. A boat approached. I jumped into the water and grabbed onto the side. The fishermen began to joke and laugh. Submerged in the wake and gliding behind the boat, I retorted, as best I could. Laughter—one leaned over and held out a packet of cigarettes; he wanted to offer me one. I so love this laugh of theirs and their jokes. We emerged from the canal into the sea. They towed me very far out, then stopped, and began to lower the nets. *Bonne nuit!* I let go of the boat and turned back toward the shore. After a while I found myself alone at sea, far from the beach. The water was completely silver, a lighthouse shone from the direction of the Pyrenees. Silence. Such solitude at sea, at night, is so amazing, that I will probably never forget it. I removed my undershorts and wrapped them around my neck. It's best to swim naked, and I now had over an hour to get back to shore. I swam rhythmically and slowly. Literally thinking of nothing. Listening only to the rhythmic beating of my heart, as my body, propelled forward, glides ahead, still and soundless. I observed my lungs, teamed with my arms, and appreciated their work, as a mechanic appreciates the work of a motor being tested. I licked the salty water from my lips and felt the desire for something sweet. Then I began to fear I wouldn't make it to shore and immediately began to lose rhythm and tire myself needlessly. I quickly corrected the problem and kept swimming. I emerged on shore tired and frozen. I lay on the sand a while like a dead fish.

August 17, 1940

No—I'm incapable of understanding *Manon Lescaut*. It may be very subtle, but that doesn't alter the fact that, at bottom, des Grieux is a pimp and Manon a wh——. I can picture them perfectly today in the metro during rush hour, pressed together against the wall and kissing voraciously. At République she gives him a hundred francs, he gives her a kiss and gets off, while she continues to Bastille and goes and sleeps with someone else. He may be from a "good family," but if they catch her and discover she is "not registered," they'll stick her in La Roquette. Only nowadays, they wouldn't send her to America but would give her *une carte*.[56] Big difference. From this perspective the book is surely immortal.

Caesar is, by contrast, captivating. At first it was rough going, but after some twenty chapters I got used to his Latin, which reminded me of the multiplication table. Now I catch myself unconsciously beginning to formulate some thoughts in Latin. I could, for example, say to some German, that *Germani multum ab nostra consuetudine differunt: latrocinia nullam habent infamiam, quae extra fines cujusque civitatis fiunt* and so on, in other words, pillage committed beyond the borders of their country is not considered a bad thing and serves, as they say, as training for young men, reducing their laziness.[57] Caesar in addition affirms that the Germans' favorite form of government is dictatorship. He certainly learned it from them. He judges the Gauls soberly: they are easily excited and easily submit. Caesar treats the Gauls precisely as one wants to treat the French today: once upon a time the Gauls, more courageous than the Germans, declared war on the Romans and established colonies beyond the Rhine. (*Ac fuit antea tempus, quum Germanos Galli virtute superarent . . .*[58]) One would like now to repeat this *Ac fuit antea tempus* at every step. In today's situation the past tense already used by Caesar has something tragic about it, something that troubles me. The figure of Vercingetorix is noble and tragic. Will de Gaulle fare any better? Dr. G. rates him very positively. He insists he is the only one capable of salvaging the good name of France. He knows, however, very little about him—no more than a few hints. All my thinking about France, meanwhile, comes down to one thing: France was certainly a kind of dogma, and a dogma so great that it's almost impossible to free oneself from it completely. France cannot be considered as objectively as England, the United States, and others. France is an exception, a great exception.

August 18, 1940

I have made the acquaintance here on the beach of two older unmarried ladies. Their father was a ship's captain and they had lived with their mother in Marseille. When their father died, they returned to their cottage here and they live on their pension. They lent me *The History of Gruissan* and several cheap romances. Their books contain the dates and places where they were read: "November 28, 1924—Singapore," "January 1, 1926—The Equator," and the telling note "*quelle chaleur.*"[59] Every day, like clockwork, they arrive on the beach at five, bathe at seven, contort themselves in well-synchronized Swedish gymnastics, dress at the same speed down to the second, and at eight go back. When I see two white dresses on the long dike, I seem to see a watch hand approaching five or eight. They are rather prim, reticent, and kindly provincials. They were indignant at me for preferring Balzac to George Sand.[60] Horrors! The first time I encountered George Sand was when my mother read me Juliusz Słowacki's letters.[61] I was then fourteen and conceived an instant hatred for the old girl. I don't exactly know why. Słowacki writes that he met her on Lake Geneva, on the ferry, wearing pants, and made an ironic comment about her. And that was enough. Today I reacted violently and in defense of Balzac, and said excitedly that George Sand was quite simply *une loutre intellectuelle insupportable*, translating literally the Polish expression, "an intellectual otter."

The Mlles B., in a perfectly synchronized movement, froze, reddened, and both at once inquired in a tone of icy sweetness: "*Plaît-il?*" This *plaît-il* cut me to the quick and trying to make myself better understood, I dug myself in even deeper: "*Je voulais dire une grue intellectuelle.*"[62]

If I had suddenly dropped my pants, the effect would probably have been infinitely less dramatic. They only murmured, "*Mais Monsieur . . . ,*" exchanged glances, and coldly changed the topic of discussion. They clearly realized that in relation to such a savage one could not even take offense.

Last night I had a quarrel with Dr. G. about Maurois's *Climats.* He told me in the end that I'm too good a swimmer to be able to understand it. Based on my view that the kind of people in *Climats* should not be trusted with love. What did they do with it? People in general like to eat good food and maintain a proper diet, but they have a strange propensity to feed their souls with various substitutes and leftovers. No, no—this book has a hothouse temperature, stuffy and aimless. That's what usually happens when people begin to live too well. I must certainly be wrong. In *The History of Gruissan*, I read that this wind has always been here and the Romans already called it "Circius." Pliny the Younger wrote that "this is the most famous wind in the province of Narbonne and none of the others compare to it in violence and power."[63] It now continually blows out my candle.

August 20, 1940

This morning I got a postcard from Tadzio. He writes that he can no longer put up with that "holy intelligentsia" in Carcassonne and asks whether he might join me. "After all, Robinson Crusoe himself was not always alone but had his Man Friday. Can I volunteer as Man Friday?" He asks what he should bring and if he can come with the Señorita. The Señorita is the Spanish woman with the ribbon on her ankle. Tadzio clearly intends to abduct her. I wrote back immediately, that I would take him on as Friday, that he should bring jam, condensed milk, and sugar, but please not to bring the Señorita. I took the postcard to Narbonne, so it would get there sooner.

I struggled with the wind for an hour. I sauntered around Narbonne. Southern cities should only be explored between sunset and nightfall. The entire richness of the sun-drenched day settles toward evening, quiets down, stands still, and doesn't dissipate in the din and clamor of the unruly light. I wander through the narrow streets, so narrow that you almost have to squeeze your way through. Majestic cats moving sideways, always clinging to the walls, and in the doorways people sit and chatter. Here there's the smell of onion, there a whiff of garlic, aloft on a light cloud of olive oil, and below it all lurks the often inconspicuous but pungent gutter. You love fairy tales, Basia—here you would have the setting for all imaginable fairy tales taken together. These streets and houses, recesses and courtyards can be brought to life by all sorts of characters, of the most improbable kind. Who knows if they would not become real in this setting. In one dreadful street I discovered a Masonic lodge. The dirty door bore the marvelously gilded emblem of the lodge. Who here belongs to the Freemasons?

I returned at dusk, riding through the vineyards. The grapes are now ripening. I dismounted and tore off a heavy bunch of black fruit, covered with a superb bluish fuzz. I bit into them thirstily—I was hot and my lips were dry. The sky was now darkening and only above the mountains, on the side of the sun, was it still ash blue. The wind was blowing. I sat on a warm stone, gazed at the sky stroked by the hot wind, and the purple juice of the grapes torn from the vine trickled down my chin. Once again I was thinking of nothing—I was simply eating grapes. All I could feel was that life had reached its maximum intensity inside me. I sensed my youth in these few minutes with a feeling that should have caused my blood to gush from every pore and mix with the juice of the grapes. I seized upon life, for the moment, but firmly. A magnificent feeling.

During the night the wind abated.

August 23, 1940

Tadzio has gotten himself into trouble. I was chopping wood this morning in preparation for lunch, when suddenly the breathless Tadzio rushes up on his bicycle, pale, semiconscious, screaming: "The Señorita has killed herself. The Señorita has killed herself." It seems he has brought the Señorita with him to the seaside after all, and as they were descending from the pass in the mountains around Gruissan, the Señorita failed to brake and on the most difficult turn went flying onto the rocks. Tadzio pants: "Mr. B., it's centrifugal force— you understand? Now she's lying covered in blood." "When I touched her she was already getting cold," moans Tadzio. We rush to the site of the accident. The bicycle lies on its side in a puddle of blood, the Señorita has vanished. Someone must have taken her to the hospital in Narbonne. We rush to Narbonne. Along the way we meet the car belonging to the doctor from Gruissan. He tells us he has transported *la jeune fille* (if only he knew), condition not serious, someone is always crashing on that turn. We hurry to the hospital. The doctor sees that we are Polish (or rather hears) and, smiling, introduces himself with a quip: "I'm Trotsky, but not Leon." He took us to the Señorita. She lay semiconscious, half her face a bloody mask. Trotsky said she should "rest a bit" and after being bandaged could return to Carcassonne. Let her rest. Tadzio roamed the corridor nervously. We went out for rum. Over drinks, we switched to first names. He quickly brightened up and began to babble about Providence, saying "obviously it was in the cards." I told him there had been someone just like him before, known as Jacques the Fatalist.[64] Tadzio has picked up from me the phrase, "Perhaps we can talk a bit about that." This amuses him greatly and he laughs. He chortled and said: "Listen, perhaps we can talk a bit about that." "On the subject of Diderot?" I asked. "No, the subject of the Señorita. Too bad—she's a good worker . . ." "And you're the one who'll pay for the bandages—good for you!"

August 25, 1930

Tadzio rode off to escort the Señorita. He should be returning this evening. I've become attached to him. I'm from the intelligentsia, he's an ordinary, poorly educated guy. We're the same age. I'm once more impressed by the idiocy of the so-called turn toward the people, the "didactic approach" to "the simple man." A single precept from that intelligentsia catechism is enough to guarantee failure. There is perhaps no more ridiculous figure than a person from the intelligentsia "going to the people." It's enough to try deliberately to speak in a "simple language" for that language to become incomprehensible. There's no "system" here. Demagogy succeeds with the masses, but with individuals demagogy does not get far. Real contact, real interaction does not occur at rallies, with the help of slogans—only through thousands and millions of personal contacts in everyday life and the mingling of "simple" people and the intelligentsia. And the other way around. In short, the point in question is both very large and very small. Above all it involves abandoning the classification of "uneducated," "semieducated," and so on. Man is all there is. Recognition of this fact would have to come from both sides. Alas, this is the most difficult part. Most often, the intelligentsia does not consider the uneducated person a complete "human being," while the uneducated see many things in the intelligentsia, but little of "the human being." Mutual disdain, inbred, exacerbated on the one side by envy, on the other by fear of "the masses," does not help get over this little hump. Especially in Poland. Our intelligentsia resembled the Bank of Poland or health insurance. No—even worse, it was the Café Swann or Art and Fashion.[65] A snobbish café for the gifted, but also for utter imbeciles. No—I'm unable to write about this calmly. Not yet. I would certainly be unfair. But there's one thing I know and readily confess: when in the autumn of last year that "cream" sailed into Paris, I didn't feel sorry for them one bit. This deprived Poland of many worthy people, but it also rid the country, in one magnificent stroke, of the riffraff: those dames, gentlemen, and officers with the infantile mentality of "*Gebirgstrottel.*"[66] Nothing would have been able to change these people and it's unlikely anything will ever change them. They're fit only to be preserved in canning jars. No, I must stop. The experiment has only just begun and the results are not yet known. But the word "intelligentsia" makes my blood boil and I can't manage to be fair. I instantly run the risk of sentimentality in whitewashing "the people," of the same Socialist Youth–type fervor demonstrated by my schoolmate Halina regarding the class that, as her comrade at headquarters on Red Cross Street used to proclaim, will one day "suddenly strike the blow."[67] I remember how this "suddenly" got my goat.

What is the difference between me and Tadzio? The difference is in sensibility. Nowadays we share the same material conditions. For me, to stroke a cat basking in the sun, its pale green gaze behind thick eyelashes turning all colors of the rainbow at the edges—that is a true pleasure. For Tadzio this means nothing. Or perhaps simply not yet. His son, raised in relative comfort, well educated, might already outdo me in sensibility. Or maybe not. Such things are unpredictable, but I believe in probability theory. The likelihood increases in proportion to the increase in the number of Tadzios living in dignified conditions and of Tadzios who encounter, not the stratum of society that feels in each contact it must "lower" itself, but the stratum that simply behaves naturally. A problem of form. Through form and form alone, the French have managed to persuade the rest of the world that France is a democracy. However, there is much less social interaction in France than in Poland. The classes are hermetically sealed off, even more tightly than in Poland. Democracy is only superficial. Shaking hands, naturalness, *Monsieur, Merci,* and *Pardon.*

August 26, 1940

Tadzio has returned with alarming rumors: the French intend to intern the Poles in camps. He ended with his favorite phrase: "Festival of the sea and cheerio." This alarmed me. I had met a young Spaniard, employed in the local salt factory, who told me that the French in such cases can be brutal, pointlessly brutal. He had been held for a long time in the Argelès camp. The field was surrounded by barbed wire, the prisoners were driven like sheep into the pen. When the nights were cold, the gendarmes forbade them to light fires. They nevertheless dug holes in the ground and secretly lit fires, to warm themselves if only a little. Caught red-handed (literally) disobeying orders, they were put in narrow barbed-wire cages. Confined in these cages, exposed to rain, wind, and cold, they could neither lie down nor sit comfortably. The prisoners had to build their own barracks, while the youngest and strongest among them were taken to the villages and towns and displayed on the market square, where the peasants picked them for work detail. They stood still, while the French *paysans* felt their legs and arms, clucked or grimaced—depending on "the goods." An ordinary slave market, as in Caesar's time. The young Spaniard, a student from Barcelona, recounted all this with a calm bitterness and he didn't seem to be lying. He smiled ironically and told me, not without a hint of satisfaction, that "now the French will see what it's like when the Germans put them behind barbed wire."

After a long discussion, Tadzio and I decided to return to Paris as soon as the factory had paid us all the remaining "loose ends." The French have now begun to return in hordes. We'll go see "what's going on there," and if necessary, "We'll put your wife in a backpack and scoot back to that so-called free France," said Tadzio to end the discussion. After which he turned to rolling himself a well-formed "spirochete," or cigarette. He likes this scientific term.

He put three hundred francs into the Señorita's slipper and delivered her home to Carcassonne. Let her recover there. We'll stay at the seaside as long as we can. Robert will write to tell us if we should return. Tadzio has just picked up my copy of Caesar's *Commentarii* and painstakingly mouths the syllables. When he gets the hang of it, he tells me, "I'll sing you a Mass." Tadzio really does resemble a goldfinch.

August 27, 1940

Actually, a man should always be like a blank piece of paper, with enough space for everything. In reality, people very quickly become square-ruled or lined notebooks, or even just account books. They write themselves in only one way, because it looks "better."

It often seems to me that so-called common sense is the most hypocritical corner of the human soul. The site of the germs of the most pernicious type of hypocrisy. Very often.

Faith in something is actually nothing more than a cane supporting lame ideas. That's why separating from a person one likes or loves is often so painful and difficult, because it's a separation from oneself.

Why is the culture of a given nation always (usually) represented by the culture of the nation's collapse? It is not true that cultures collapse under the influence of external blows. They collapse first *on their own*. The external blow is only the thrust of the barbarian's *sica*.[68]

The culture and civilization of our day remind me of a madman who has torn to pieces a pile of old newspapers, on each of which he has written the words "a million dollars," stuffed them all into his wallet, and declared with great self-confidence: I am rich.

I sat on the sand, eating marinated olives and bread. I stuffed myself to the gills. The olives will drive me to bankruptcy. Tadzio circled around me and collected seashells "for Janeczka." Some are exquisite. He kept running up to me and showing me the nicest specimens. At one point a little boy came up to him and began peering curiously into his can. Tadzio proudly shows him all the shells, spills them onto the sand, says "jowlee," but the little fellow is not at all impressed. Finally, he waved disdainfully, looked at Tadzio as though he were a child, and declared drily: "*C'est pas bon pour manger.*"[69] After which he spun around laughing. Tadzio understood, turned white, then suddenly red, searched for a few French words, sputtered, and finally burst out in plain Polish: "O you snail-eater, you underage wine-guzzler, you French spawn of a pussy-kisser—'pa bong poor manjee'—you good-for-nothing appendix; if it can't be wolfed down, you don't give a damn, you knucklehead. If you don't know a good thing when you see it, you little tramp, scram, or I'll give you what for . . ." The terrified boy took off, I collapsed in laughter, and Tadzio, shaking all over, looked at me and concluded his "potpourri": "You tell me—can these scamps amount to a hill of beans, if even as kids they think only about stuffing their faces? You tell me . . ."

He kicked his can into the sea, sat down next to me, and gazed into the distance. I didn't know what to say. He muttered, as if to himself: "If I'd thought only of bacon and of crawling into a warm bed with my wife, I wouldn't be here today . . . Romanians, Gypsies, the Frenchies—it's all the same."

"Tadzio," I began. "You have to take into consideration, that . . ." I spoke perhaps for an hour, or maybe more. Charlemagne, the Maid of Orleans (he had read about her), Louis XIV, Descartes, the Revolution, Napoleon, the nineteenth century—the century about which one can talk for twenty centuries, so great and fruitful it was, the Great War . . .

Tadzio listened attentively, pouring sand from palm to palm. After a while his hand remained empty. I kept talking, staring at his game . . . Finally, Tadzio interrupted: "Fine, but you're always saying 'it was,' 'they were,' Napoleon, the Maid of Orleans. What's all that to me? I know what's what: She's a whore, my dear king, no Maiden!"

August 28, 1940

The days fly by as in a dream (for sure). In Narbonne, Tadzio and I bought ourselves a miniature chess set, and in the evening, after changing into white shorts, we go to the café by the canal and play, sipping white wine with ice. Today we had a very characteristic adventure. We were seated, as usual, playing and drinking quietly. The table across from us was occupied by a group of French officers. They had come by car to have supper. They kept knocking it back and became more and more rowdy. Suddenly one of them got up and swaggered over to me.

"Do you know me?" he asks.

"I don't have the honor . . . what are you talking about?"

"I am asking, do you know me? *Eh bien, répondez!*" and raises his voice. Shouts.

Tadzio bent over and asked under his breath: "Knock 'em out, Pops?"[70]

"No, not yet." Tadzio straightened up.

The officer shouted: "*Alors*, do you know me?"

In a completely even and quiet voice I answered: "I don't have the honor, what's the matter?"

"You smiled somewhat strangely at us. Are you German? Are you French? What nationality are you?"

(*Qu'ils sont chatouilleux, maintenant*,[71] I thought to myself.) Tadzio knocked over all the pieces and began slowly to arrange them in the box.

"If I laughed, it wasn't at you. It's all too sad . . . I am neither German nor French. I am *merely* Polish." I intoned this "merely" with an ironic smile.

The officer fell silent and, very embarrassed, said softly: "Excuse me, I didn't want . . . I thought you were German and I didn't want to permit . . ."

I interrupted him drily: "It's too late now! The next time . . ."

He echoed me: "Right, the next time we'll both together send them packing back to Berlin."

"*Avec plaisir! Monsieur.*" I bowed, without looking at him, and emptied the chess pieces out of the box. He walked away, exchanged whispers with his mates, and they went on drinking. Tadzio looked at me and I saw a look of regret. A frustrated noble fantasy shone in his blue eyes. Settle their hash, gentlemen!

"Tadzio, where'd you get the expression 'Knock 'em out, Pops?'" I asked.

"From *The Deluge*, Andrzejek. Those two Kiemlicz dopes always put that question to their old man whenever someone started to mess around, like that out-of-commission *Gefreiter*."[72]

Assignment for the half-hour before sleep: reflect on the influence of Sienkiewicz's *Trilogy* on Poland.[73]

"White opens!"

August 29, 1940

Tadzio often asks completely unexpected questions and demands concrete answers. Our conversations are like a fencing match, in which I am the accomplished fencer; I know all the moves, Tierce, Quarte, Octave, whereas my opponent has grabbed the foil in his hand, waves it about, and when he whacks me in the face, laughs scornfully and says: nice, elegant what you're doing, but you took a hit anyway, though it was not by the book. Sometimes he reminds me of the girl in a story by Światopełk Karpiński:[74] A father had a son who never took his nose out of a book. There came a time when the father realized he had to get him into action. He therefore sent a beautiful girl to his son's room. The young man was enchanted: Your face is as beautiful as an ellipse, your eyes are like its two focal points, and so on in that same vein, up to and including an equation for the ellipse. The girl came right to the point: That's all very well, but the ellipse will cost you extra.

Today we lay on the sand. Total silence. The sunshine was almost thick and flowed from the sky slowly and heavily, like apricot jam from the jar. Tadzio suddenly sat down, gathered his sun-bleached hair and blurted:

"Tell me the facts, what's happening on this earth?"

Now, this instant, immediately. To him the world is an internal combustion engine that worked fine up to now and has suddenly "conked out." He expects me to answer him off the bat, simple as that: the carburetor is clogged, needs to be cleared and everything will be fine. No—no, I can't pull it off, although I know that would be the simplest way; not to mince words, as they taught me on Basztowa Street in Cracow: Capitalism, of course, Tadzio! But capitalism is only one of the factors, the most noticeable, in "what's happening on this earth." It seems to me that in this kind of process, what's easiest to see is not at the heart of the matter. "What's most noticeable" is perhaps only an indicator of certain deeper processes, as a rule, out of sight.

I thought for a while and then began. These were long hours of "lacework" with the rapier. Tadzio listened attentively, but in the end he rose on his elbows, exasperated:

"Jędruś,[75] give me a break! No offense, but all this about Egypt, Greece, the Romans, the middling age, and that Ressenance, or what have you, is sure interesting, but you're going into a tailspin."

Those are Tadio's inspired, intuitive terms. I don't know if there's a better way to convey the essence of intellectual confusion than precisely the one he learned in the air force: go into a tailspin. Indeed, I fell into one. Have to recover my balance. I sat down. I admitted he was right, but asked whether he had basically understood what I was saying and whether it interested him.

"It's a fact, I'm not entirely dumb; but listen up, your royal highness, the point is that Hitler came, waved his d——, and suddenly everything falls apart, totally. This whole world, understand?"

Funny. In these conversations he usually thinks I don't understand him well enough, and I have the feeling he doesn't understand me. Yet we understand each other better than we think. Now I knelt, held my arm out over him, and began:

"Listen, everything I've been telling you at such length you'll have to relate carefully to what I'm saying now. It's quite simple. When a group of friends begins to play cards, as you well know, everyone puts something into the pot."

"Meaning, into the bank," Tadzio corrected me.

"Fine, into the bank. This whole world, about which we are talking, started playing the game almost at the same time. Three partners paid into the bank—each a considerable sum. The deposits were Greek, Roman, and Christian. But each of these deposits, while equal in value, was in a different currency. Consider: the Greeks deposited the concept of man and reason, ordinary human reason as the measure of everything. Reason and man were for them what the measuring stick is for you. Thanks to this they created theory. What theory is you understand (Ha!). The Romans deposited practical action, most important the law and how to observe it. And now for a change, imagine the world as a thermometer with a temperature scale. The Greeks and Romans deposited their stakes below zero. Frost everywhere. Everything was cold despite the best efforts of philosophers, who felt the chill but could not manage to escape it and could not manage to raise the temperature of the world because they lacked—despite everything—the concept of humanity. In their eyes, man was just a thinking lump of meat.

"And suddenly, at the point on the thermometer marked by a red line, Christ is born. The temperature immediately rises, because with his birth the true man is born. Christ and his disciples spread the word about the new man, about his earthly life and the life of his soul, about eternity. Only now, in this man, does warm blood truly circulate, sometimes even too warm. Only now does this man have a true sense of human dignity. In short, Christ discovers and raises the price of man on the human marketplace, which is held at point zero. Got it?"

Tadzio gazes at me with his blue eyes and nods: "Damn simple! Give me some tobacco and keep going."

I thus recap: "Greece deposits into the bank reason, the search for truth, the struggle against ignorance, prejudices, and fanaticism. She allows people to understand each other, she provokes discussion. Rome contributes the law, the science of laws and duties; while early Christian doctrine contributes the distinction between earthly life and eternal life, the concept of the dignity of the individual *person*, a value that is not merely utilitarian. Christianity delineates also the limits of the state's power over man. At point zero, beginning with the red line, the game starts. The three deposits remain on the table of the history of our world. The initial players die—others follow. Certainly, each one contributes something or loses some of the capital deposited by their predecessors. The deposits are often small, sometimes there are none at all, other times they are substantial. Some increase or decrease the Christian deposit, some the Greek, still others the Roman. This game is sometimes less honest, sometimes more, but one thing is certain: no one questions the great and perhaps priceless value—so, keep this in mind—the priceless value of the Greek, Roman, and Christian contributions. They are debated, their exchange rate varies, but there is no mention of withdrawing them from circulation, from the game. There are many problems on earth—that's the truth, but as long as no one loses faith in the three great contributions, the hope exists that with their help many problems can be solved. Many problems have already been solved, and when skillful attempts have been made to combine them, the value of the contributions has never failed. Better or worse mixtures have resulted, but—I repeat—until now the value of the foundational components—Greece, Rome, and Christ—has never been entirely doubted. Meanwhile, things on earth are getting worse. I'll explain all of this later, not to muddy the picture. (That's where capitalism will fit in.) And now here comes fascism, and in its wake Hitler. Claiming to be remedies."

Something is beginning to well up inside me. It hadn't occurred to me before. In recent days I've consciously turned myself into a radio that can only receive, and within only a very narrow range. And now there has begun . . . Now I'm no longer saying all this for Tadzio's benefit; I realize I'm now talking above all for myself. I'm adding it all up for my own sake, so the later accounting won't take too long.

"The characteristic feature of these remedies is what's called totalitarianism, which means in short the absolute and complete rejection of the value of these three great donations. For totalitarianism there is nothing intangible, and you as a person, depending on your abilities, are not above all Tadzio but only a shovel, a pickax, a screwdriver, a file, and so on. People like me are only pens, paintbrushes, gramophone records, or in general—and most often—hurdy-gurdies. One can do what one wants with them. Their fate, their lives depend on some central chart and the chart dictates whether people should fare better or worse. The mercury that with such great effort rose above zero plunges violently. The chill of the heathen world returns, a kind of heathen 'state-worship,' in which on one pretext or another the Einsteins, Manns, and Werfels are driven into exile, as Anaxagoras and Ovid were driven into exile, and others driven to suicide, like Socrates.[76] Monstrous and hopeless. What will result from this?"

I'm practically shouting. What do I care that Tadzio doesn't know who they were. I'm talking to myself. All this must not be forgotten. My thoughts are whirling. How hot this sand is. What can we do, what can we do? At the very least, not forget, even for a minute. I had the feeling that this time Tadzio was looking at me with real respect. Legs tucked under him, he said nothing, just spitting from time to time into the water.

August 30, 1940

We chose the itinerary for the return. Carcassonne–Nice, 570 km. Keeping to the shore. In Bandol I'll stop by Villa Pauline to visit the ghost of Katherine

Mansfield. I'd give a lot right now for her *Letters*. From Nice, we'll cross the Alps.

Meanwhile, we rest and eat from morning to evening. I must by now have eaten half a barrel of the olives kept in the corner at "my witch's place." Toward evening we get on our bikes, to keep our legs from getting stiff. Otherwise, Tadzio keeps asking me hundreds of questions, and I try to answer him. I tell him stories about the construction of the pyramids, about the temple at Karnak, about the Parthenon. He is interested above all in the technical details and keeps wondering at a number of things. Using the example of our water flask, I explain the system the Egyptians employed to erect the obelisks by pouring sand underneath. Taking two flasks, one held against the blanket and the other against the sky, I reveal the secrets of the Parthenon's architectonic harmony and the varied thickness of its columns. This provokes other questions: What was the angle of inclination of the columns in the first row? How many centimeters thicker were the columns against the sky? How sharply from the vertical was the Parthenon's longest side inclined? And what was the architect's name? And what year was it built? And so on, and so on . . .

In the end I always want to cry out, "My kingdom for the *Petit Larousse!*" because of course I don't remember such details. For dessert, I always have to tell him something about Napoleon. He can listen to this epic for hours. He's delighted at the thought that he'll see Toulon, that he'll follow the Route Napoléon from Nice.[77] All Poles are perhaps still born with this special feeling for Napoleon. I promise him that once back in Paris, we'll go see Malmaison.[78] And then, a sudden pang: For Heaven's sake, the GERMANS now ARE there. I keep on forgetting about them. What does the ghost of Napoleon, sitting now in that summer pavilion among the faded roses, think about France? The pavilion in which he created her glory.

What good does it do me to know these things? Today I regret not having a trade; if I were a machinist, a turner, or a welder, I would know I am something. But as is? People of my stripe are to some extent a relic—regardless of how this war ends. The world will burst one way or the other, and we will have to go along with it. A new order will have to be created and we will have to forget we were raised to maintain the old one. At best, I'll be thirty when I'll be able to begin a new life. It's interesting to wonder how I will begin it and starting with what. If I had . . . No. Thinking in the conditional tense annoys me more than anything. It can drive the sanest person into his grave. In moments like these, it's best to apply Scarlett's system: "I'll think about that later."[79]

In the afternoon I was summoned by the *patronne* of the café: "*Monsieur Bonbonski, une dépêche pour vous.*"[80] Ah, Robert has wired. I opened the telegram: We must return, the factory is being liquidated. Tadzio and I sat on the veranda and gazed sadly at the sky. Both of us, though we hadn't yet left, were already beginning to miss Gruissan. Longing in advance. And indeed the weather is now splendid. Sun and a breeze off the sea. Well, it can't be helped; it doesn't make sense to leave today, and tomorrow is Sunday and so in any case our factory will be closed. Tomorrow—farewell visits, packing up.

Today the last Belgians were leaving. Monsieur and Mme G. already left ten days ago, but I have their address. They are now in Montpellier, where he is director of the Belgian Red Cross. The Belgians have an excellent saying with regard to French hospitality, something along the lines of: "charming welcome, sour farewell." I can confirm that this time the saying has proved itself once again. I chatted with them a lot, and since I knew Belgium quite well from the days when "the young master traveled abroad," conversation was made easy. In general, they justify King Leopold's surrender. (Tadzio holds a vague grudge against him, referring to him always as "That Belgick Poldie.") The Belgians insist he had no other way out; he saw that the French army amounted to nothing and that the English had gone off to war as though it was a tiger hunt in Bengal. Perhaps was he simply not . . . a Romantic. But for us, who in such circumstances think in terms of "Ordon's Redoubt," this is hard to understand.[81] Although for me it's not so hard. I'm reminded of when my father, chief of staff of the Eleventh Infantry Division during the anti-Bolshevik war, was surrounded, along with the entire staff and a certain general (I don't recall his name), during the famous retreat.[82] He told me how they were sitting behind a hill and then the general began his briefing with the words: Gentlemen, we must now die, and so on. My father dared to observe at that point that "although the method proposed by the general is the simplest way to extricate ourselves from this situation, it would be worth first trying some more complicated means of survival." Clearly they managed in the end to make it out. I imagine that this general to the end of his days must have recalled not the fact that they made it out but his peroration, so full of pathos, in which "everyone was ready to die." Certainly not everyone. For example, it would have taken a lot for me to have been entirely "ready." And probably the same was true for each one. But with us Poles it's considered improper to talk about this directly, without this particular hypocrisy. In short, it seems that for us it's easier to die than to answer a letter or return the bit of change we have borrowed "until tomorrow."

In the evening, the farewell round of rum and the farewell game of chess in the café near the canal.

September 1, 1940

Toward evening, a farewell visit to the Mademoiselles P. I had to go in shorts, because I have no trousers with me. They live in a tiny little house, in one of those winding and charming lanes, full of cats, the smell of fish and tar, and vibrating with the monotonous sound of millions of mosquitoes. On the beach, near the sea, there are none; here, in an instant my legs were covered in welts.

The Mademoiselles P. greeted me with coffee and cookies. They are hilarious. They constantly exchange glances, as though tirelessly watching out for each other. When one of them starts a sentence, the other finishes it. Their mother, a sweet, gray-haired old lady in a black dress, doesn't move from her armchair. She has a black velvet ribbon round her neck and a little gold chain attached to a lorgnette, which from time to time she dangles from her hand and swings like a pendulum. Out of the blue, speaking of Poland, she said to me: "Near Białystok there are many Jews, *n'est-ce pas?*" This detail stuck in her mind from some article about Poland, which she read back in the nineteenth century. She then beat around the bush and finally I understood what she was getting at when she burst out: "*Eh bien, vous savez, je n'aime pas les Juifs.*"[83] The daughters exchanged sharp looks and cried out in unison: "*Maman, pourquoi tu parles toujours de tes Juifs? Monsieur n'est pas curieux de connaître tes opinions là-dessus.*"[84] I saw that they were terribly embarrassed. The old lady fell silent, pursed her lips, and from then on uttered barely a word. I had the feeling this anti-Semitism of hers was like tobacco, which her daughters were constantly forbidding her to sniff. It's curious, but with anti-Semitism this often happens. Some people need it, like cigarettes, black coffee, or alcohol. In Poland, especially among the older generation, it above all worked as a stimulant. Alas, among the young it often took the form of a narcotic.

The Mademoiselles P. asked me if I was returning to Poland. No, the French really still do not comprehend WHAT has happened. I didn't feel like enlightening them about "what in fact is going on in the world." Thus, the ladies were very surprised that I was voluntarily leaving "Free France" and heading back to the Germans. Cautiously, but forcefully, I explained that "Free France" is not at all free; second, that my wife is on the other side; and third, that I've no desire to end up in a concentration camp in "Free France." There, on the other side, the situation at least has the virtue of being clear. In any case, I can always come back. They deigned to agree with me.

An entire wall in the living room is hung with boxes, in which magnificent butterflies from the four corners of the world have been placed under glass. By the way, Brazilian butterflies look as if they were not of this world at all. Specimens I had never seen. The ladies quoted me the totally fantastic sum for which these butterflies could be sold. They appraised them one by one. Ah, the suspicious glances constantly darting back and forth between them, simply for fear that one might blurt out something the other didn't think, or might express it differently. As I observed them, I wanted urgently to make notes, to write, to discharge some of those phrases that suddenly come to mind and instantly vanish forever. In fact, all writing indeed has value only when it absolutely "can't be resisted."

While eating cookies, I had the distinct feeling that I was swallowing, not cookies, but the pages of a story I had written about them and that I probably will not write. I look at them and suffer greatly, because I have to keep up the conversation, while at the same time entire sentences, whole situations, form in my head. A mutual tyranny, absolutely identical on each side, both for the tyrant and for the tyrannized. Pressure and fear are tightly connected and occur simultaneously. My "witch" was telling me that one of them is in love with the doctor, *"mais c'est très compliqué."*[85] I can well imagine . . . They tell me about Rio de Janeiro (of course, their father took both of them) as though they were talking about the market in Narbonne. *"Oui, c'est une belle ville . . ."*[86] "That's when Papa bought this butterfly—no, no—that one!" "Yes, now I recall." Then we discussed scorpions, which abound here. They are gentle and their bite is not dangerous. But the same species on the other side of the Mediterranean is very poisonous. They were surprised when I told them that scorpions are beautiful. I regard them as works of art. Still later, we glanced through musical scores, among which there just had to be a book of Clementi sonatinas and an entire mass of waltzes in jackets featuring garlands, flourishes, and dancing couples— she in a corset, he with mustaches. But the piano no longer worked, "because in this climate it's hard to keep it tuned."

I left them toward evening, completely disoriented as to the time of day and the historical era. They themselves, their house, their old mother, the afternoon tea, the smell in the apartment—everything was complete, perfect. A Frenchness one can only call "praesens plusquamperfecti." The presentness of time beyond the perfective.

September 3, 1940

Today the factory gave us our severance papers and the rest of our wages. I got about 800 francs and altogether now have 1,600. Since July 3 they have paid me here 4,353 francs, which means 2,126 francs and 50 centimes a month for riding my bicycle, swimming in the sea, and so on. France is beginning to pay tribute for the lost war not only to the Germans but to its own people as well. This nonetheless reflects a certain old-fashioned good faith and a maternal relationship to the people. I keep having the impression that France, smiling sadly, is trying to reassure her children: "Pity, it didn't work out, well, at least have this." When they paid me the money, I wanted to plant a long kiss on the hand — of France. To kiss, as one kisses a lovely, beautiful, and occasionally insufferable older woman.

Afterward, running around all over town, which in Carcassonne seems like bustling about a room. I bought a light tent on sale for 150 francs and quite a lot of food. I changed for supper — the dining room is already empty, there are none of our former acquaintances. It feels like the end of vacation and the start of the new school year. Today, as usual, there was Mass, and beloved Father Cegiełka said: "Dear young people in the Lord Jesus Christ," knowing full well that we are not at all "in the Lord Jesus" and that most of us will be with Him only in old age.[87] In any case, those for sure, who now, during the Mass, were stuffing themselves with plums and as the altar bells rang muttering with a touch of gloom à la Przybyszewski: "He-he, full of worms, damn it!"[88] The only way fully to grasp a great and true idea is to kick it around a few times like a ball. Such an idea (its greatness) can be recognized, if only by the fact that it can be kicked around even when it's in operation. From this point of view, Hitlerism and many other "-isms," which do not permit such a game, will sooner or later wither away. Sitting at the table, peering into a glass of red wine, I wondered who, for example, will be teaching classical Greek at Saint Ann's. Could it be Jerzy Schnayder yet again?[89] Too bad — in that case trouble for me. Afterward Tadzio showed up, knocked back a whole "bucket" of wine, and reported that he had thoroughly inspected our machines. They are in excellent shape and there's no point moving them. We'll therefore set off tomorrow at dawn. The first stage is Carcassonne–Monte Carlo via Béziers, Montpellier, Arles, Marseille, and then all the marvels of the Riviera. How are we going to pack everything?

September 5, 1940

Yesterday morning Tadzio said he wouldn't leave without an adjustable wrench. We therefore went to town to find this wrench. As we began searching for the wrench, it occurred to us that we had no papers for the return to Paris. So we set about obtaining a *sauf-conduit*, without which one cannot cross the demarcation line. And so the day passed. We were supposed to leave today, all of us at the same time, though each in a different direction. For the moment, that's utterly impossible: the entire "common room" is drunk. I'm now sitting and thinking — about LOGIC in general. It exhausts me. Tadzio has been singing since morning, and soon, on an empty stomach, to get into shape, we went for rum. We got into such good shape that I now liken Carcassonne to a carousel with horses. We ride round and round and the music plays. Yesterday things went something like this:

Everyone dressed elegantly for supper and even donned the "intelligentsia" (Tadzio's term), which is to say neckties. After supper we began to drink. I proposed we drink only *mousseux*. The proposal was accepted all around—eighteen francs a bottle. No point drinking anything else. So it began. After six bottles, the Señorita (she was also invited) had already had enough and went to bed in our room. After this I kept bringing out fresh bottles. The *patronne* sat by the entrance, because the night was warm, and kept guard. She asked us not to make a racket. Of course, but I told her that *apud Polonos nunquam sine clamore et strepitu gaudia fiunt.*[90] She nodded her head and said: "Ça va, ça va." She gave me the key to the refrigerator and told me to fetch the bottles myself, because she didn't feel like getting up each time. Then S. recited some patriotic poem by Kazimierz Tetmajer and everyone shed some tears.[91] Next, Tadzio stood up and made a long speech, beginning with the words: "When that old buzzard Budrys told his three sons to hit the road, he said: 'A pox on you, push off and bring me back a load of stuff.' Now we too are hitting the road. We won't bring our mamas sh——, but, God willing, we'll get ourselves back in one piece . . ."[92] He spoke for a long time, and I fell under the table laughing. You hear this sort of thing but once in a lifetime. Then we sang "The First Brigade"[93] and again shed some tears (?), though I insisted there was nothing to cry about, because it's nothing but the melody of the "*Totenkopfhusarenmarsch*," and they are now the Gestapo.[94] "Right, Giestapo, Giestapo!" yelled Tadzio. In all arguments, Tadzio always takes my side. A quarrel began about "blasphemy" and J. only managed to calm it down by starting up the "Ballad of Miss Franciszka." Then I took the floor, but I don't remember a single word I said. We struck up the "Marseillaise" and "Dąbrowski's Mazurka," and again we all shed tears, and Tadzio gave a performance of some Polish tangos: "A ruffian was he, known on all the streets around . . ." He sang mournfully, and I was reminded of the novels by Kamil Norden.[95] When he got to "Better not betray me, bitch, or my fists will make of you short shrift," I sank to the floor in laughter. The bottles kept coming and coming. Then S. sang some Gypsy romances, naturally in Russian, and recited Pushkin. One poem stuck with me, which now won't leave me in peace: "*Moskva, spalennaia pozharom, Frantsuzu otdana,*" or something like that.[96] I requested *Eugene Onegin*, of which he knows entire stanzas by heart. He kept us in thrall. It's difficult and pointless to resist—the Russian language truly comes to life, sways, intoxicates, and enchants, when lubricated by alcohol. It's a language like pickled cucumbers: tastes best "under the influence." In the end I don't know what happened, but it was great. I remember only that a crazy game was being played in our room. The Señorita was unconscious and was sleeping, completely naked, on someone's bed. I knew that S. had been after her for several days and might now "rape" her. We had to hide her, since she had never shown any interest in S. and it might end in a fight. The room was dark, because Tadzio had turned off the lights in the corridor, so "they would not keep burning" (?). S. spotted the Señorita in the dark and was preparing for action. At that moment Tadzio and I stealthily transferred her to our bed. S. began searching for the Señorita—and so the game of blind man's buff began. As soon as he approached the bed on which she was lying, Tadzio and I would transport her to another one; all this in the darkness and accompanied by the curses of the crazed S. Seven beds, on each someone asleep, alone or by twos, and the Señorita being shifted from bed to bed. Finally, S. got so muddled that he started to make for—J. Tadzio squealed and pinched me, because J. got up and went at S. with his fists. He pushed him onto a bed and S., exhausted, dropped into sleep. Our foundling remained on someone's bed and everything calmed down.

I'm sorry to part with this hotel, with Carcassonne, with all of this. I'm sitting now on a bench in the square, the day is marvelous, warm and peaceful. One chapter of life and youth is over—splendid, rambunctious, and lighthearted. And this at the very moment when millions of people are suffering, when every night bombs are raining on London, and when there is war on earth. Here, on this bench, in this sun, I can't believe it. I recall how once we went to buy books on Szpitalna Street. All three generations of the Taffets were then, at that time, doing a good business. We approach Grandpa Taffet and ask: "Mr. Taffet, sir, do you have any logic?" The old fellow went through the shop, whispering: "Logic, logic?" and returned: "No—logic run out, maybe it come anoder time." No, dear Grandpa Taffet, there won't be any logic another time, either. Logic has "run out" of life, just as it has "run out" of your beloved shop on Szpitalna Street, where we would go to buy and—with even greater pleasure—to resell books for cigarette and vodka money, and muttering a satanic "he-he," to read Ernest Renan and Spengler's *Der Untergang des Abendlandes*,[97] to study Engels's *Manifesto*, so as to one-up the priest in ethics class, to the joy of the history professor. In consequence, graduation exams were flunked . . . Before then everything had been logical. Afterward, nothing was.

In Carcassonne I felt my youth with special intensity, illuminated by the sun, imbued with wine and grapes, bathed in the sapphire sea; I played with the gold of the sand, with the silver of the moonlit water, with the hot wind. My conscience will never reproach me for not having savored the years of my youth—and the absence of logic. A gust of hot wind brushed the dusty treetops, and the clatter of crushed ice in the bucket resounds from the nearby bistro. The silence of a southern town, at dinner time. The bead curtains, threaded on their long strings, are clattering, as though softly saying the rosary of peace. Once in a while, when the bottom-most bead breaks the knot, they all scatter onto the sidewalk, hopping gaily and mischievously, like children running out of school; they scamper and bump each other. They're free and happy about it. I have a few beads in my pocket as a souvenir. Can I myself be one of the beads that has broken away from the string? Tadzio has appeared. I'm writing, looking at him, and I report what I'm writing:

"Tadzio, I'm a bead. I managed to break away from the string on which I was once threaded. And I never again want . . ."

"You're drunk, Your Highness! I've ordered the old biddy to put two bottles of 'Vichy' on ice for us. We'll sober ourselves up. I upchucked three 'peacocks' (Tadzio's word for the multicolored after-effects of alcohol) and feel fine . . ."

Heat wave. I'd rather cover myself entirely with ice. Tadzio says: "What a white fever outside today." The fellow is making progress—words fail me. He's right—this heat is white. I rest my head on his shoulder and see only his lips and his enormous cigarette. The smoke drifts languidly from his mouth, fans out, and after a quiver or two, suddenly vanishes with the wind. Like everything else.

September 6, 1940

So we set out. Yesterday afternoon we packed almost everything. Today we rose at six and finished our preparations. Our friends left to catch a train leaving for Toulouse at a little past seven. Tadzio and I remained alone in the room, as on a battlefield. We were sorry to leave. We had grown fond of the hotel, the room, the people, of everything. And now simply to leave it all behind. Heavy-hearted, we carried our saddlebags down to the garage. Then began the comedy of packing. We spent two hours loading our things, until the bicycles had begun to resemble two-humped camels. On the rear baggage rack I had the full back-pack, on top of that a blanket wrapped in a slicker, on top of that a large haver-sack with the food, and to top it all off a mess kit clipped to the haversack, that is, to the "pantry." On the front rack I had a haversack holding all my underwear and a bottle of wine. All this baggage weighed over thirty kilos. Tadzio's bicycle carried a bit less than mine but was almost as heavy, since his backpack was crammed with canned food. When we tried to move the bicycles away from the wall, our hair stood on end. We could barely push them, how would we ride? We stopped by the old biddy's for a farewell coffee. The entire street, kindly "rue du Pont-Vieux," already knew we were parting ways. The proprietress of the grocery gave us a kilo of noodles without coupons and also some chocolate and bid us good-bye as though we were her own sons. Pouring our coffee today, the old biddy had tears in her eyes. After coffee, we went to say good-bye to the *patronne* of the hotel. I thanked her for everything and apologized for whatever might have seemed to her "out of order" and kissed her hand sincerely. She shook her head for a moment and burst into tears. Next she's pressing me to her ample bosom and kissing me on the cheeks. Then I kiss her, which reduces me almost to tears. Tadzio smiles uneasily and says: "Jędruś, as God is my witness, I'm going to howl." When it came his turn for a kiss, in fact he almost did. Madame Vitrac did not stop sniveling. I'd never thought it would be so hard for us to part. We wheeled the bicycles into the street. She stood in the doorway; behind the windows of the bistro the old biddy smiled through her tears; the Señorita leaned out the window in her dressing gown, waving, and coquettishly revealed her cleavage; and from the distance, in front of her shop the "*épicerie* lady" waved us good-bye.

It was ten o'clock. The sun emerged from behind the clouds, promising a beautiful day. We wheeled the bicycles around the bend, afraid to mount. In the end I was the first to risk it. Tadzio followed. Horrors! I panicked. My bicycle seemed to be collapsing, the frame twisting out of shape, something about to snap. Tadzio went white and barked: "It won't last twenty kilometers." We were both trembling with nervousness, so we focused all our attention on the handlebars and after a quarter-hour's ride through town, we rolled onto the highway like two heavy tanks. There the going was easier. Little by little we got into the swing of it. Ten miles farther along, my handlebars stopped vibrating, the bicycle stopped "collapsing." The same for Tadzio. We perked up and recovered our good humor. We're headed for Narbonne by the old familiar road. Marvelous weather, hot. In Lézignan we took a break. I bought bread, milk, and tomatoes, a piece of cheese. Around two we drove off the side of the road under a few pines; stretched out on the dry grass in the shade, we tucked into lunch. Pure joy. We chat and eat, later as we smoke we wonder how long it will take to reach Paris. Taking even the "shorter" routes, we face sixteen hundred kilometers. Perhaps by the end of the month? Will the machines hold up? We recall our first trip. Now we have all the conveniences: a tent, which means we needn't scour the farms for a place to sleep; and a hot meal in the evening. Unfortunately, there's nowhere to buy fuel for the spirit stove and we have to cook on a wood fire. Again, the marvelous feeling of the open road and freedom.

By four we are in Narbonne. Tadzio stayed with the bicycles while I went to a fishing shop to buy two bamboo rods for the tent, since we had no poles. An afternoon somnolence pervades the town, I walk the narrow streets, half asleep. It feels like a dream. I bought two bamboo rods, tied them to the frame, and on we go. Direction Béziers. Good-bye to Narbonne; it's the last part of what has been. By now we're really leaving "our" places behind. When will I see them again? The road to Béziers is excellent. The bicycles are moving more easily, and we take some inclines quite boldly. Descending the mountains, the tires sing on the asphalt, and the bicycle rolls like a greased ball. Twenty-seven kilometers to Béziers. We'll tackle them in little over an hour and reach the town. It lies on the crest of a hill. Evening is already falling. With an effort we make it up the winding street to the top. Surrounded by vineyards, the city is imbued with the charm peculiar to small towns in the south of France.

People are taking strolls, having drinks in the bistros, and obviously enjoying themselves. There was nothing to keep us here, so we didn't stop. A few kilometers outside of town we began the search for a place to spend the night. After a while we turned to the left, toward the sand dunes, under the umbrellas of a few pines. It was already dusk. Tadzio gathered wood for the fire while I pitched the tent. It is well made and comfortable. A hot night fell. We lit the fire and prepared the meal. After ninety kilometers, with only a meager afternoon snack, it was hard to wait for it to be ready. I used the time to make notes while Tadzio went to pluck grapes for dessert. We stuffed ourselves to the gills. Then a cigarette, lying on our backs, scanning the star-strewn sky, and a few moments of intense happiness. A kind of animal contentment with life. Today here, tomorrow somewhere else, sunny days and starry nights.

Montpellier, September 7, 1940

We slept the way one sleeps only at our age and in circumstances like these. A bit on the hard side after the splendid hotel beds in Carcassonne. We padlocked the bicycles and left them near the tent. Still new to France, Tadzio can't quite grasp that sleeping in tents is perfectly safe; that no knife-wielding "thugs" from the outskirts of villages or towns are spoiling for a fight, sniffing around for loot, and so on. You can sleep two hundred meters from a village and ten meters from the road and no one pays any attention. There are no belligerent drunkards, no curious BUSYBODIES (a special category), or other such Polish amusements. Tadzio shakes his head and says: "Culture and civilization." I shake my head too and tell him, above all it's wealth. Certainly, there's a large dose of culture and civilization in all of this, but on the subject of thievery and plunder, in whatever form, I'm a believer in radical materialism. A man who has something to eat and something to call his own, even if very little, is less in-

clined to thieving than a pauper. The Frenchman, at least until now, has always
had SOMETHING. He steals nonetheless, but on another, higher plane. He won't
pull a knife on the first person to come along but does the same thing by filling out his tax forms, fleecing his clients, cheating his closest of kin in all manner of financial transactions, and evading the law whenever the chance arises.
All this is serene, subtle, invisible. I'm not sure whether CULTURE isn't, among
other things, the mildest form of certain ethical and moral diseases, diseases innate to every person and nation from time immemorial, which depend only on
the economic climate to take their course. In some areas malaria is endemic, in
some a minor scourge, while others are spared altogether but suffer from different diseases, of an equally dangerous kind. I don't believe it when someone tells
me that in this or that place people don't steal. They don't steal the way we in
Poland may understand it, but they steal BY OTHER MEANS. Here in France they
don't steal as Tadzio pictures it, but that certainly doesn't mean that they don't
steal at all and that everything is "culture and civilization." Murderers, bandits,
plunderers, brawlers, thieves, pilferers, Figaro, spongers, Molière's *The Miser*,
Balzac's Gobsec and the Baron de Nucingen—it's only a matter of degree. Culture in this case functions as a staircase; as it mounts, each innate human trait
keeps changing its costume, depending on the size of its wallet. Tadzio understood this perfectly well but used fewer words. Leaning against the tentpole, he
declared: "In short, always the same sh——, just different shtick." Of course!
I hugged him. Then he, with a lordly gesture, says: "In that case, please note it
down." Oscar Wilde was right: life imitates art. Tadzio was speaking like Stefan
Jaracz in Antoni Słonimski's *The Family*.[98] I had to sit down. Tadzio has never
heard of that; he's only proud that I "note everything down," including about
him. At this I laughed till I cried, pulled out my notebook, and immediately
began to write. "Here, look, it's spelled with a 'sh,' like 'shindig,' 'shoes,' and
above all 'monkey-shines.' Monkey-shines, indeed."

At breakfast we each drank a "bucket" of coffee with condensed milk (heaven
in your chops) and downed an unbelievable amount of bread with jam. Afterward we dawdled rather long over the packing because we hadn't got the knack
of it yet. There was so much stuff, all of it essential. The sun was already beating
down when we rolled our tanks onto the highway. We were riding better now
and managed to climb nearly all the hills without dismounting. Unfortunately,
our bicycles did not have *derailleurs* (gears). In France, where only the north is
flat, they are virtually indispensable. Around midday we cross the Hérault River.
Before entering Montpellier, we resolve to take a dip. We therefore veered off to
the side, hid our bicycles among the grapevines, grabbed the soap, towels, and
shaving gear, and made for the riverbank. The vineyard reached down to the

water. First we plucked some grapes, enormous and sweet, and began eating. The white sun filters through the tree leaves, you lie on the grass, stuff an entire bunch into your mouth, nibble on it like an apple—the kind of experience about which I could write twenty pages. But I'm not sure such blissful moments can be conveyed—you have to live through them to understand. All of this is possible in these circumstances, precisely these and none other. For example, during holidays or vacations in normal times each pleasant moment of vacation is poisoned, if only subconsciously, by the thought of what is waiting upon the return: you have to pay this or that bill, Mr. X is a swine, though you must keep on good terms, because "he can pull strings," and so on. This entire burden of concerns under normal conditions, the burden of the future, has fallen away. There's a war; I'm struggling to return to Paris; I haven't the slightest idea what will happen tomorrow or a month from now, and I really don't care. The future may turn out this way or that, but in any case, not as I might have imagined. So I don't think about it at all—what's too distant to be seen doesn't count. This civilization may not be worth very much, but on most continents it has accomplished at least one great thing: the hardest way to die in our time is from hunger. If this too goes to the devil, then it's all over. But no such danger for the moment, so I'm eating grapes. The NOW is what really counts, and one mustn't be afraid to drain this NOW to the last drop, then toss it aside and figure out how to make the most of the next NOW. One thing alone gives me pause: it's neither the *Carpe diem* of Horace nor *Après nous le déluge*. For the first you need peace and quiet, the second comes from boredom or fatigue. I don't know.

I lie on my back, peer at the sun through the dark-green eyeglasses of the leaves, and eat my grapes. They're superb. Then we light up. In the afternoon heat the cigarette smoke lingers close to the ground and catches on every blade of grass. We shave with deliberation, slip into the water, wash each other's backs, and finally swim out to the middle of the river, leaving a trail of soap behind. There's hardly any current, the water is deep and warm. We're bathing in the buff, of course, though the bridge is only a hundred meters away. This is possible because there are no curious BUSYBODIES around here; one can melt into the general indifference. Unless you approach someone and ask a question. Then they answer with a smile, say something cheerful, ask how your trip is coming along, and continue on their way. Older people like to chitchat and then I chat back. Tadzio shakes his head and says: "They're all I-couldn't-care-lessers." We move on.

There's another good stretch of road before Montpellier. The highway is empty, from time to time we pass a huge two-wheeled cart. It's hot, and we are overcome by such indolence that we can barely pedal. No gasoline, so no automobiles; the road is a quiet boulevard. This is another exceptional circumstance, never to be repeated. We are engulfed by vineyards; to the left and to the right, as far as the eye can see, nothing but vineyards. Every so often we ride through a village and notice the seat of the wine producers' cooperative. It's always the largest and most magnificent edifice in the commune. None of the vineyard owners in fact works very hard. The grapes grow, tended for a pittance by Spanish, Italian, or Polish workers. The *patron* makes the rounds, stopping by to have a look, then heads to the bistro for a drink. There's a bit of a commotion at harvest time, then the cooperative purchases the harvest or the wine, the *patron* pockets the cash or the note, which he lives on till the next harvest. The sun shines, the birds chirp, the sky is azure, and the pastis is yellow. Life is simple, long set in its ways. The phylloxera pest likely caused more havoc around here than this entire war.

Around five in the afternoon we enter Montpellier. It's instantly clear that it's a nice town. We search for the address of the Belgian Red Cross, because I would like to drop in on Dr. G. Unfortunately, he has stepped out, but will return shortly. We rest the bicycles against the wall and look around. A few Belgian soldiers in ragged uniforms are wandering about. They are waiting to receive civilian clothing and places on the re-evacuation train. Tadzio says: "Andrzej, pal, we'll have to snag some loot from that dear little Red Cross. They should give us something—we, too, are long-suffering victims of the war." Just then Monsieur and Mme G. appeared. I approach and introduce myself. Delighted to see us, they began to inspect our bicycles and ask where we are headed. To Paris? Do you have food for the trip? Splendid—to Paris via Monte Carlo—*c'est formidable!* (To Otwock by way of Peking, said the servant girl in Słonimski's *The Homeless Doctor.*⁹⁹) Full of his usual energy, he told us to bring our bicycles into the hall, summoned his wife, and retired with us to one of the rooms and locked the door. He then opened another door leading to a second room, and the despoiling of the dear little Red Cross began. I protested, because we had no room on the bicycles, but Tadzio kept kicking me in the foot and whispering: "Quiet, before I strangle you." They filled our arms, while we flew back and forth, piling the stuff into a corner. Sardines, tinned pâté, sugar, powdered milk, cheese, chocolate, soap, a box of biscuits, T-shirts, underpants, socks, espadrilles. Dr. G. ran around, searching for what else to press upon us, finally telling us to pack up, because he had to be off in a moment. He regretted not being able to see us that evening but invited us to come for breakfast the next morning. We can leave the bicycles at the Red Cross, and there are many cheap hotels directly across the way. Monsieur G. left and the drama of how to pack everything began. I constructed some boxes out of cardboard and slowly everything somehow found a place. Then we changed from shorts to trousers and headed for town.

We took a room in a scenic by-the-hour hotel, where we deposited a few personal things—then off again to town. It was too early for dinner. A small green streetcar, like the Number One in Cracow, pulled up and we get on. Just to ride back and forth and gaze out the window. We stroll around, examine the displays. Terrific sport shops. Streets full of young girls and fellows. A warm evening descends, we are by now impossibly hungry. Tomorrow Montpellier will cease to exist, there'll be some other city. Time stops—time no longer matters. I'm all eyes, absorbing, taking it all in, not thinking, because it's impossible to think. Every detail is charming and each cigarette tastes better than usual. For supper there's soup, beans with meat (*cassoulet*), macaroni with tomato sauce, peaches. Then coffee in a dimly lit bistro, full of painted floozies. (I adore this word.) It's already dark, we saunter from corner to corner. Finally, we emerged on the street with the bordellos. From every door and window echo the sounds of laughter, singing, the piano or accordion, the thump of slippers falling to the floor, the clink of glasses, the clatter of dishes, the flushing of toilets. Shadows play on the backlit screens of the curtains in the open windows: here the light dims, there it blazes forth. The din suddenly fades, then the racket starts up again. I'm reminded of one of Oscar Wilde's best poems, which I read in a terrific German translation: "Hurenhaus." The poem is grating, *cassant*, with rhymes like "*Grotesken*," "*Arabesken*," dry, at the same time artificial and stifling. Silence again, abrupt and startling—somewhere the sharp, wheezing cough of someone gasping for air. Chest hiccups. The whole corner gives the impression of a stuffy cellar, full of hothouse flowers, smelling poisonously, with faded, snaky stems crawling the walls in a wormlike movement—an intriguing impression, with its own peculiar charm, also disgusting, clammy, and slimy. Quite compelling too. I think about absinthe, about the drawings of Constantin Güys, Goncourt's *La Fille Élisa*.[100] I have an irresistible urge to go inside, look around, see the colors, inject myself with the sharpness that permeates this atmosphere. But Tadzio pulls me away: "Jędruś, let's split." We're off. I sit at the little table and write. The window of our room opens onto a tiny courtyard and across the way another *Hurenhaus*. We laugh. The night is stuffy, sweaty. From one of the upper windows, the sound of someone singing. A warm, deep woman's alto sings a mournful Spanish song. Even Tadzio became engrossed in the sound and interrupted the story of his brother-in-law, who "filched an entire set of his tools, which he sold and then had the stuffing beaten out of him." We listen. The melody bounces from roof to roof and floats lazily, wanders through the stifling darkness of the courtyard, subsides, then suddenly erupts in words with a great quantity of "r." A different female voice, hoarse and worn (an old gramophone record), began hurling insults and the singing stopped. Tadzio swore and began to undress. Now he's already breathing loudly. In this heat, the light of the electric bulb seems to trickle down like sand. Suddenly I feel how tired I am.

In the Camargue, September 8, 1940

We woke before eight. There were some grapes on the windowsill and Tadzio slipped out of bed to get them for me. He stopped at the window and froze, like a pointer stalking a partridge. Then he signals for me to approach quietly. I drag myself out of bed, come closer, and—it's hard to describe. The shadowy courtyard, lit from above by the sun, from somewhere nearby the rasp of an electric saw cutting through boards. One floor below, across the court-yard, an open window reveals a dark, cavelike room; the furniture is too dark to make out, except for the bed, covered in something grayish, also dark. Against this background, a woman's thighs, enormous and splayed; closer still, bizarrely intertwined calves. The rest of the body is monstrously foreshortened, breasts sliding off to the sides and the cone of an upturned chin. The saw continues to screech, now and again reaching a piercing high "C" (must be the knots in the wood). The body glows in the darkness, arrests one's gaze, mesmerizes. I whisper softly: "Tadzio, it's Schiele" (I think that was his name).[101] Tadzio clearly doesn't understand. I remember, when a few years ago Franek showed me an album of drawings by that Austrian artist, I didn't "grasp" the piercing realism of those horrible bodies of prostitutes, brilliantly drawn in yet more horrible poses. I said he was "overdoing it" and that it was "improbable." In fact, it was inspired. I'm now seized with regret that I cannot draw. No—Schiele alone could really "pull it off." The disgusting mound, repulsive and compelling in its strangeness. And the foreshortening—monstrous. Tadzio is insufferable.

"I would do her, maybe, but only if they drugged me first. And now, arise, ye proletarian of love!" And he starts bombarding her with grapes. The cruelty of the mob now reveals itself in him. I shoved him away from the window. I don't know why, but my reflex stemmed from the same impulse that would have led me to defend a sacred image against sacrilege.

It was still too early to drop in on Monsieur and Mme G. We rushed off to town. The morning was sunny and fresh, but the heat was already quietly stealing up, ready to burst forth with the sun from behind the roofs. On the street next to the hotel a large market. We saunter among the stalls, looking for a wrench, but there was none. The women vendors were screaming, the sharp smell of cheeses mingling with the aroma of giant peaches. A multitude from all corners of France and Belgium has gathered in Montpellier. The streets are filled with huge two-wheeled farmers' carts from northern France, with complete living inventories attached to them: cows, oxen, mares with foals, a few sheep. The sides of each cart are festooned with cages of poultry: chickens, ducks, geese, turkeys—and inside a family reclining on piles of linen and clothing. They had traveled like this for hundreds of kilometers and soon will be going back. The migration of peoples. In the tumult of this old city, in the commotion and time-lessness of it all, I sensed something medieval. The wandering of Narcissus and Goldmund over the face of the earth, separated, searching . . .[102] Colorful and gloomy, like the stained glass of a stone rosette.

Around nine we set off for Monsieur and Mme G's. They were already ex-pecting us; the table was beautifully set, and on the table there was BUTTER. Since leaving Paris I have not seen butter. Mme G. brought in an enormous pot of steaming milk chocolate. (Make a note: the smell of hot chocolate in a sun-filled room at nine in the morning, open windows admitting the special chill that arrives only before the heat.) Sitting down to the meal, Tadzio and I gave a virtuoso performance, to the accompaniment of smiling: "*prenez, je vous en prie.*"[103] We chatted at length about our return and theirs, about how the situa-tion was shaping up, in short about everything. They were in a cheerful mood because two days ago they learned that their two children had been found and were alive. In early May they had sent them off to summer camp, but then everything had fallen apart; they were unable to reach them and fled with the wave of Belgian refugees. From May until now they hadn't known what had happened to the children. Perhaps the worst thing in this war is how people are scattered in all directions and cannot find each other. This began in Poland, then spread to all of Europe.

There was a knock on the door. A Belgian boy scout reported to Monsieur G. that several demobilized French soldiers were asking for assistance.

"French? *Tiens, tiens.*"

We peered out the window. There were six of them, ragged, dirty, practically barefoot. Monsieur G. pointed them out to me and said:

"You see, it's like this every day. They do have their own French Red Cross, but it throws them out and won't give them anything. It's pure bedlam, plus lots of bureaucracy. The job of the local French Red Cross is to assist the civilian population; it therefore neglects the soldiers completely. Why should we Bel-gians provide for the French?"

Mme G. started to insist they be given nothing. *Rien!* Why is it that women who get involved in charity work so often become particularly nasty and heartless? This perfectly sweet, soft woman of Flemish plumpness all of a sudden revealed a harshness and lack of pity. Most Belgians regard the French as a second-rate class of people. At the seaside, G. remarked repeatedly that the so-called grandeur of the French nation, the national genius, was a carefully buttressed edifice, constructed by past generations and constantly repainted in increasingly garish colors with ever shoddier paint. And now the French have even run out of paint.

Meanwhile, on the street, the Frenchmen were insisting on their demands. Tadzio observed them and just as disdainfully pronounced: "Give them a little something—why keep settling scores with these snail-eaters." Monsieur G. asked me what Tadzio had said and I had to translate. The term *escargophage* appealed to him and he therefore instructed that each be given a pair of cord-soled shoes, socks, shirts, and sweaters. They also wanted soap, but that they were not given. "*Pourquoi du savon? Ils se lavent si peu.*"[104] The soldiers went away. The entire scene left me thinking. How much on this earth depends simply on someone's good or ill *humor,* or on a *turn of phrase?* Each of us walks around with a hat full of lottery tickets, with one hand offering it to someone, with the other hand drawing the same sort of ticket from somebody else. When I do a good deed for someone, is it only because that person has drawn a good card from me, that he was lucky? Well, and what kind of feeling can exist between nations? Perhaps only a more or less friendly disdain. When the disdain reaches the same intensity on both sides, the nations begin to *tolerate* each other, maintaining the good manners instilled in them by a common culture and by their parents. The Germans, appearances to the contrary, must have been raised by different parents than those in other countries in the West and continually behave like louts. I hate them, not because of the war, but because they have betrayed their family and their parents. This war is no longer a skirmish at the common table over who has gotten more chocolate pudding but a battle between adults over the inheritance, the entire inheritance and estate. The war of 1870 was a dispute over pudding. In 1914–1918 the Germans initiated legal proceedings over the inheritance, lost in the first instance, and are now appealing. But for pity's sake, surely there is still justice. (I gaze at the star-strewn sky and pray for justice.) Stop!—remember Scarlett O'Hara's method—I'll think about that later.

It was already well after ten when we began preparing to leave. Mme G. pressed upon us yet another enormous bag of powdered milk (she was again soft and plump and offered me the milk as though from her own ample breast) and added cheese and soap. Thus supplied, we loaded the bicycles. The extra weight amounted to several pounds, and with such an overload each ounce is multiplied ten times. Around eleven we started saying our good-byes. Perhaps I'll see them again sometime.

Direction Arles. Sky overcast, weather warm. We leave Nîmes behind on the left and take a secondary road, thus avoiding gendarme patrols, to whom it is hard to explain that we are really heading for Paris. From time to time, there are a few drops of rain. We ride slowly. Leafy groves between the ponds, everywhere flat. Tadzio says: "Just like in Wawer."[105] In Saint-Gilles we drink beer with lemonade on the terrace of a large bistro. Tadzio bullies me: "Why aren't you writing, damn it? Later you'll be schreibeling till the wee hours and we'll run out of candles." A sleepy Sunday mood in a small town. Some of the pilots stationed here were wandering the streets, strolling with the young women, others stood in groups near the houses, and everyone was yearning for sun. A day without sunshine around here is like salad without oil and dinner without wine: hard to swallow. It was gloomy, and the ashen stone houses seemed made of dust. Completely colorless, hopelessly monotone. The roar of a motorcycle resounded like a hammer banging in an empty room. James Jeans writes that every twenty-four hours the sun emits thousands of kilograms of light.[106] Here in the south, a sunless day is truly not getting its "full weight." You clearly feel you are being shortchanged and you want to return this kind of day with indignation. I almost dozed off in my chair. After studying the map, we realized we must cover another good stretch beyond Arles to arrive in Marseille by tomorrow. We picked up speed and quickly flew through Arles. Still the same gray day, aimless and incomplete. No other way to describe it. I didn't even want to visit the Roman arena. Instead, I bought some eggs.

We turn south and enter the Camargue. The transition from the zone of vegetation to the boundless, russet, and stony plain is very abrupt. Toward evening the weather improves, except toward the north, where the black clouds have frozen in a motionless mass. The Camargue is indeed a desert: a well-asphalted road and nothing more. On either side, as far as the eye can see, the russet surface is scattered with stones. An occasional dwarf tree or thorny bush. This worries us, because you can't count on finding water anywhere. Five kilometers into the desert—nothing. Ten now behind us and still nothing. It's already late and darkness is slowly descending. Fifteen kilometers altogether and ahead—more desert. As usual in such cases, we are doubly thirsty. But I soon cry out to Tadzio: "Here it is!" "What?" he asks from behind. "An oasis!" Near the road emerges a black clump of bushes and trees and further along, almost on the horizon, the outline of a farm. We reach the oasis, which is in fact a giant electric well. Inside the building that covers the well an electric motor hums quietly, pumps draw the water and pour it into a stone trough, from which it flows into the channels that carry it further along. Near the well there is a strip of grass and bushes; beyond that a field of grapevines and a young grove. Vegetation grows only between the irrigation channels—after the last one it's a desert. A tuft of hair on a bald pate, carefully preserved—with "Silver Cream." At the sight of water, our thirst vanished. I quickly pitch the tent, Tadzio collects firewood. An excellent place to spend the night. We prepare the ritual bouillon with macaroni, scrambled eggs with tomatoes, biscuits in milk with grapes, wine. The moon has risen, blindingly bright. To the north, flashes of lightning bounce around amid the black mass of clouds. Dew begins to fall, so dense that we crawl into the tent to avoid being drenched. A marvelous night. Tadzio, as usual, falls asleep with a lit cigarette in his mouth. The silence is absolute, for even the well has stopped ticking. It has shut for the night. In the dying fire something occasionally hisses or crackles, a tongue of flame leaps up then disappears. "Our Father who art in Heaven."

La Bedoule, September 9, 1940

We rose after six. A pleasant, sunny day, not a wisp of cloud in the sky. We couldn't strike the tent right away; it was as drenched with dew as after a rain. Washing up and breakfast. The sun kept getting brighter; by eight the heat was already intense. We have at least another hour of desert ahead of us. We get going after ten. In a few kilometers the desert comes to life: on the left and right there are aircraft hangars, an enormous base, reflectors, runway lights, and so on. Somewhere in the distance a few people are walking around. Tadzio takes a look and says: "If I saw an airplane, it could only be one of those fata morganas." I laugh; before the war we were all shown fata morganas and made to think they were real. Especially in aviation. We discuss the fata morgana. It's supposed to occur here, but I don't know if that's true. It's a strange desert.

We reach the sea, passing the town of Fos, beautifully situated, with a lovely Romanesque church. From there we follow the seashore. At Martigues we hop across a narrow wooden bridge to the other side of the canal. On approaching the bridge, I almost toppled over. Luckily a gendarme was standing there and caught me at the last minute. I paled. Now he'll demand my papers. No such thing—he was sorry we had to ride with such heavy baggage. One fall and the bicycle would crumple. In that short exchange I'm sure I resembled Stan Laurel, who causes trouble then tries to undo it—waving his arms wildly, clearing his throat, smiling inanely. It's so hot we're sweating buckets, the sweat fills our eyes and they sting. On a rise above the lagoon we stop. We decide to eat something and we settle down in the meager shade of a few pines. Below us lies the sapphire lagoon, a few ships stuck in its waters. The sky is blue with a few small white clouds. The colors are bold: what's white is really white, what's sapphire, pure sapphire. There are no half-tones. The colors are banged out like the C-major scale with one finger and the pedal. The entire color scheme is quite primitive: you could paint this landscape in tempera, without mixing, straight out of the tube. I say this to Tadzio, who adds: "You're right, these colors are insolent." Tadzio is succinct and splendid. Wouldn't "insolent" also fit the African landscapes by Adam Styka?[107]

We didn't rest for long. Marseille was still far ahead, and we will need to buy something for supper along the way. In one town I managed to buy two beefsteaks and a loaf of bread, although here the sale of bread is permitted only until noon. But I was so eloquent that the butcher not only sold me bread after hours but let me buy meat without coupons. In the late afternoon we arrive at a mountain. The highway winds upward so sharply that we are forced to dismount. We trudge on and on; at every turn the mountain gets steeper. Then a mad descent to the bottom. A few kilometers farther on we hit the outskirts of Marseille. The strange wind makes me nervous. The day has been hot, the wind is now cool. I realize at once it must be the local mistral. Now, as evening approaches, the wind slowly awakes, sweeps the dust from the streets, and blows it into our eyes. I tell Tadzio we must make it through Marseille as fast as we can. The mistral here is so powerful that it often knocks pedestrians off their feet. (So I've been told.) If it hit us from one of the side streets, we would go down together with our bicycles. Alas, easier said than done. Already in the outskirts, the pavement becomes so rough that the cobblestones of Wilno seem as smooth as glass compared to these rocks. Our bicycles begin to bounce so hard that we have to slow to a crawl to stop them falling to pieces. Moreover, we keep our tires at low pressure because of the heat. On the asphalt this works very well, but here time after time we "hit the rims." It's tough, but we keep moving. An hour later we are still in the outskirts. It takes an hour and a half to reach the center of the city. The pavement is still the same, even worse. The streets are full of people; everyone is strolling in the road, since the sidewalks, crammed with café tables, are reserved for the chatterboxes. They cluster in groups, all speaking at once, yelling, and gesticulating. There are also the tram rails to be avoided. It's a real feat to ride through these streets. You have to ride around people; no one reacts to the bell. Tadzio takes it all in and says: "Jędruś, honest to God, it's Nalewki."[108] Now the mistral was pulling out all the stops. The sun turned copper red. Spirals of dust and trash whirl through the streets; we lower our heads and dive into them. Two hours later and the end of Marseille is not yet in sight. These horrendous cobblestones also refuse to end. We are so exhausted that my feet begin to twitch nonstop and my right calf keeps going numb. I'm seized with a wild rage: if I'd run into the mayor of Marseille, I'd have beaten the daylights out of him on account of this pavement. After three hours of this hellish ride, I know I'll carry a grudge against Marseille till the end of my life. Such a great city and its main streets so wretchedly paved. Three and a half hours, inch by inch. I see a hotel and wonder if we shouldn't stay the night. But that's risky in Marseille. Rumor has it that Poles are seized and deposited in the camp in nearby Carpiagne. Finally, we extracted ourselves from the capital of Marius and Fanny. It's been *horrible*. Everything hurts—kidneys, shoulders, arms. The mistral is blowing now for real. It's so cold that we put on our sweaters. The sun has set, but we keep going because there's no good place to spend the night. We pass Aubagne and bear right toward La Ciotat. It's eight when we enter a ravine. Another winding uphill road and we have to dismount. Darkness fell and the moon rose. Above, among the tall trees, the wind roars; on the road down in the ravine all is calm. The road is indeed excellent, but fatigue has numbed us completely. We push the bicycles ahead of us and chat a bit. Not a drop of water anywhere; we walk for an hour, for two—always uphill. Our arms grow numb, the road keeps climbing, the walls of the ravine are so steep there's no chance of pitching a tent. Not until ten thirty do we reach what looks like a very broad pass.

You could see a few houses, on the left a gentle slope and a few pines. But here the wind is blowing from every side. A savage hurricane—a moment of absolute, dead silence—then a sudden blast, cold and penetrating. We leave the bicycles on the road and after a long search find a patch of moss under one of the trees. We retrieve the bicycles, put on all the clothing we have, and light our cigarettes. We haven't smoked since two o'clock. We quickly pitch the tent, so we can crawl inside and warm up. Hard to manage against this wind. One careless motion and the tent will be torn to shreds. All the cords get tangled. We work during the moments of calm, but when the devil attacks we use our hands and legs to hold onto anything still hanging loose. Finally, our "hotel" is up. I bang the pegs in all the way and tighten the cords, but even so, the roof sags at every gust. At last we are warm. We don't cook supper—just cheese, sardines, tomatoes, and jam, washed down with wine. We are dead tired. From now on, even Pagnol's beloved plays will be colored by my memory of the cobblestones of Marseille. The mistral dies down, howls again, attacks.

Toulon, September 10, 1940

We slept soundly. If the mistral had ripped the tent off from over our heads, we would probably have kept on sleeping. We were warm and cozy. Even a dumb tent feels a bit "like home." Besides, everything I possess seems alive. You could call it "a feel for equipment." The mistral kept on wailing; no hope of lighting a fire in this hurricane. But I urgently wanted something hot to drink. Taking the thermos, the coffeepot, and the saucepan, I headed down toward the few houses we had seen yesterday. In the first, I notice an open door and enter. The room is clean, a fire is going in the kitchen, an old woman is standing at the stove. I greeted her and explained that we were sleeping in a tent a bit farther up and I would like to make myself some coffee. The old woman bestirred herself, at once filled a pan with water and set it on the fire. We begin to talk — I ask if she lives alone here.

"No, with my son. He went off today looking for work, but it's hard nowadays to find any."

Her accent tells me she isn't French. I also ask her about that.

"No, I'm Italian and my son too."

"And I'm Polish, *Madame*."

The old woman livened up: "My son had a Polish friend. He was such a nice fellow. He left for the army and we don't know what has happened to him. You Poles are unfortunate these days, we Italians, too. They've summoned my son twice already, to return to Italy and join the army. But he doesn't want to, *ah non*. And besides, it's so poor there. What's the point of this war?"

I had no answer. She asked where we were going and how we had still managed to find real coffee. A strong aroma arose from my coffeepot. I gave her a handful of coffee and told her to keep it just for herself. I poured the liquid into the thermos and began to say good-bye. She held my head in her hands and kissed me on the brow. Then, with tears in her eyes, with Italian devotion, she made the sign of the cross on my forehead. I slowly kissed her rough, work-worn hand. Poor old dear. What is left for her on this earth? Her son and coffee and the whisper of a prayer.

After breakfast, only a slice remained of our two-kilo loaf of bread. I told Tadzio about the Italian granny and he was also moved. "Look, Jędruś — one on one, people are decent, but together they're a gang of m-f——s." The wind was still raging, but the day was sunny and a bit warmer. We loaded our tanks and moved on. Soon we entered a proper village — wonderfully situated. Woods all around, small melon patches near the houses. I bought an enormous melon for two francs and tied it to the handlebars. Then downward — a marvelous serpentine descent through the forest. Suddenly — no, it defies description. Around the bend we hit a stretch of road carved into the solid cliff. A long balcony along the void — an abyss at least 150 meters deep — below, the sapphire surface of the sea, white with foam along the jagged shore. The wind smacks us in the face with such force that we lose speed without even braking. My gaze vanishes along the sapphire horizon of the sea, on the left the ashen wall of cliffs to which the road is clinging, to the right the abyss and another sea down below, this one of intense, almost black vegetation. Everything immersed in the wind-blown sunlight. The sun has a completely different color in the wind: cold as an enamel finish. We coast like that almost to the water's edge, to the very end of a craggy spit, and then take a left. Again we plunge into the forest twilight. The tires whimper softly on the asphalt and at each turn we tilt gently to the side. With all the sharp reverses, it's literally a dance on the speeding machine. At such velocity, the loaded bicycle "holds" splendidly. Tadzio has moreover flattened out our narrow racing handlebars and we rest across them comfortably, safely supported. After twenty minutes we shoot out of the forest, like two bullets from the barrel of a gun, onto a straight stretch of road. On the left a small bay, on the right an island with a small castle and cypresses. Arnold Böcklin in the sunshine.[109] The coloring of the water is fairy tale–like: sapphire, aquamarine patches, and clear blue streaks sprinkled with the white crests of the waves. A riot of tones, complete madness. It's already La Ciotat. The highway now runs along the seashore. We pass villas and for the first time I get "a whiff" of the Riviera. In this gale the large patches of water seem even more ragged; a damp chill and salt emerge from the sea. The mistral continues to roar and the entire, impossibly (impudently) colorful setting bursts, sways, and clamors. The mistral clears the deck, airing out the quiet corners that have grown stuffy in the heat.

Leaving the bicycles near the road, we take our food and run down to the water's edge, onto the large rocks. We eat slowly, savoring every little bite. We always pick a lovely spot in which to eat; today the spot is so marvelous that we fall into something of a daze. Each sardine, each piece of cheese acquires special meaning. The sun is shining, the wind lashes us in the face, and we are doused off and on by a rain of droplets as the water dashes against the rocks. At each beat of the waves a rainbow erupts, lingers a moment in the air, and vanishes. One can really go mad from such a wild assault of colors. A bazaar of hues. There are certain views I would classify as "intellectual." For example, an autumn sunset over the Seine. Bridges drowning in the mist, their lamps breaking into tiny points of light, giant trees frozen in stillness, sunlight filtering through very special clouds, each of which should be labeled "Made in Paris." Not everyone can find something in this view. Here, by contrast, any old "know-nothing" or "average Joe," in Tadzio's words, is knocked off his feet or at the very least lets his jaw drop. It can't be helped. As though faced with a magnificent cocotte, brightly and elegantly attired. Tadzio's impression: "It's truly a festival of the sea."

We consume our afternoon rations and move on. We still have about twenty kilometers to Bandol. The road is becoming mountainous. Once again we dismount and walk uphill. The road is so perfectly constructed that it's even more agreeable to walk than to ride. From time to time, the sea down below glistens through the thick forest. The air has heated up and smells of resin; the mistral has not penetrated here. It leaps along the treetops. At one of the turns we meet a funeral procession. Impossible! Do people down here die? The hearse moves slowly downhill, brakes pitilessly screeching, followed by mourners dressed in black. At their head, a priest in a white surplice shuffles along. In this cheerful, carefree setting, on this lovely day, in this sunshine, the scene looks completely unnatural. It doesn't fit. It's so clearly "unsuitable" that we watch with total in-difference. (Not quite—I wish I could paint it, like Bonnard.) Tadzio expertly observes: "If the brakes failed now, the venerable corpse would be entitled to rise from the dead out of fear." We begin to expand on this theme: "First of all, the hearse would run over the priest, clipping the boy with the cross, which might hit the priest in the head. The whole clan would initially pick up its pace, then begin to run, and in the end" (Tadzio concludes coldly) "the widow would then cling to the hearse and scream at the driver: 'Brake with the clutch, if you care one bit for the life of the defunct.'" Tadzio recounts this in a manner so vivid that I now see only "his" funeral, and not the real one.

Another descent. We hit Bandol. It's four in the afternoon. Bandol is a jewel in a charming setting. Set on a small bay, its broad seaside promenade edged on the landward side by a colorful screen of white houses, cottages, and villas. In the corner of the bay, at the foot of a hill dense with cottages nestled among the trees, lies a toy-sized harbor with the white masts of sailboats. Near the harbor, several fishermen move about and comb through their outspread nets. As slowly as spiders checking from time to time to be sure everything is in order. It always seems to me that the fishermen around here are playing at the job. They head a little way out to sea, fiddle around, snag a few fish, and return. Nothing like the tough lot of fishermen in the northern seas or on the Atlantic coast.

I leave my bicycle with Tadzio at the harbor and set off to visit Madame Allègre. In shorts and a T-shirt, I'm not exactly dressed for a visit, but it's the best I can do. Boulevard Pierre Plane is a bit farther up and I am soon ringing the bell at Villa Pauline. My heart is beating as though I expected Katherine Mansfield herself to let me in. A young boy opens the door. I tell him I'd like to see Mme Allègre. Smiling, he takes me to a small, clean little kitchen, where a woman is ironing the linen. Mme Allègre, a tiny, wrinkled old lady, is bustling about the sink. I introduce myself in a rather original fashion as the person who sent her photographs from Paris last year. I tell her about Hanka and Franek, whom she recalls very well; she received the photos. She begins to laugh comically. *Madame* and *Monsieur* did not speak French, but it was easy to communicate with *Monsieur*. "He is so amusing." She laughs so heartily that I cannot help myself and join in. I explain how we got to know each other and that I am now returning to Paris to join my wife. After a while we are all conversing gaily. Mme Allègre brings some of the figs that have been laid out to dry on a large wooden board in the garden and stuffs them into my pocket. We go out into the garden.

The tiny cottage next to "Pauline" is where Katherine Mansfield lived. A small stone table; a miniature terrace, no bigger than a bedside rug. On this table she wrote that down below, on the sea, a warship had dropped anchor, that the day was gray and cold. A few words—I remember and I don't remember. There was a war then, too. I remember the inscription on her grave in Avon: *But I tell you my Lord fool out of this nettle danger we pluck this flower safe.*[110] And I manage to do this, too. Safe and sound, I pluck the flowers, avoiding the thorns of danger. I sat down at the little table and looked around. Would I be able to describe the view as simply and naturally as she did? Good honest prose is like a dress from the house of Pacquin or Molyneux: a little nothing that says everything.[111] Something entirely elusive. They are activated grenades that the author gives the reader, crams into him, so they detonate inside. The longer they keep on exploding, the greater the writer. Such spectacular explosions around the reader can indeed be spectacular, can deafen him for a while, but in the end not much remains of them.

Afterward we chatted a bit. I was informed that what I'm wearing is now forbidden all along the coast. To walk around in shorts is not allowed; on a bicycle they are permitted, but in the city strictly forbidden. Twice I asked to have this repeated, since I couldn't believe it. So now the French are becoming moralistic—and in what a ridiculous way. A pitiful sight, reeking for miles of the Secession, of Philistinism. It's certainly not a German decree. All this reflects the absurdity of Pétain's authoritarian *régime*, which has begun its rule precisely in THIS way. It orders France to cover her legs (such lovely ones) and at the same time inveigles her into doing God knows what. Obviously everyone is laughing at the latest decree; even old Mme Allègre giggles and squeals.

I take my leave. They wish me a good journey and safe return. A final glance at the stone table and I go. Tadzio was sitting alone on a bench and looking around. I gave him some figs—he was delighted with them. We rode along the promenade for a bit, then stopped at a small café. Bandol is well protected from the wind and the mistral is not as penetrating here. At the table, in the sun, it was warm and sheltered. Beer with lemonade. Nearby sat an old dame, ugly as a Pekingese and outlandishly painted to the gills. Vermillion, burnt sienna, car-

mine, cobalt blue around the eyes—strawberries in her eye sockets (?). Tadzio
kept stealing glances in her direction and could not contain himself: "Jędruś,
what can these cinders, these old remains, this ruin still be expecting?" Meanwhile, the cinders scrutinized us with curiosity and, what's worse, smiled coquettishly in my direction. "Ooo—sickening!" screamed Tadzio aloud. This
made me wince. I instantly grasped what a young woman feels when an older
gentleman "undresses her with his eyes." Nearby sat a few gentlemen impeccably dressed in the nautical style. Fancy sandals, wool blazers, colorful sailcloth trousers; they were accompanied by two women with decidedly nice
legs, overdressed, and reeking of perfume. From time to time a breath of wind
carried the scent in our direction, mixed with salt and the odor of bodies in the
sun, tapping coquettishly like a fan against your face. A few women strolled
along the promenade. They are like roses blown by the wind, they bend and the
petals of their dresses flutter and flap. After they pass, the scent remains. Perhaps
that's how to do it—approach women against the wind . . .

This whole environment makes everyone feel they're someone, though until
now they may have been no one at all. Except for the natives, everyone moves
and dresses with a certain nonchalance, with a supple and lazy gait. It seems to
me that people here even walk as though they were classier than they are. As in
Poland, where everyone walked and moved as though they were classier than
they were, sticking their noses in the air, if only not to behave in a natural way.
But perhaps being natural is itself but a pose? (Oscar Wilde.) I peer through
my sunglasses at the glistening tabletop, at the women's shins glistening in the
sun, and I'm amused at my own thoughts. Once it was possible to dream; nowadays dreaming is so senseless that one practices dreaming simply not to lose
the knack. Like doing handstands. The problem of life, ordinary life, assumes
a meaning it never had before. I don't know how others feel, but I sense a clear
duality: there's myself and there's the life I share with Basia. When I think about
this, I behave like a physician at a patient's bedside: I examine, I listen for signs,
I observe. Great—he's still breathing. Good. At the moment, I'm riding through
the Côte d'Azur, but I don't feel the same excitement I felt, for example, every
Saturday, when boarding the Luxtorpeda,[112] wearing a new suit and kid gloves,
illustrated magazines in hand, and a packet of good cigarettes in my pocket.
(Lighting up without removing one's gloves.) Chronic discontent never permitted me truly to value what I possessed. Back then I didn't notice that women
are marvelous against the wind. Reflecting on this, I fiddle in my pocket with
the handful of beads I found on the sidewalk in Carcassonne. They will always
jangle loosely; I won't ever thread them on a string . . .

We had smoked two cigarettes each and it was time to get going. Everyone regarded us with admiration. The bicycles aroused particular respect. We mounted and set off, direction Toulon. Leaving Bandol, the road runs so close to the sea that we catch the spray of the waves smashing against the rocks. A rainbow hangs in the air. A rainbow shower, cool and pleasant. It's too late to get farther than Toulon today. The area is, however, so thickly settled that it's hard to find anywhere to pitch the tent. We reach the outskirts. Everywhere houses and dirt. We look around and find an empty wooded spot just outside town, near a ruined house. The mistral has gone wild and gets on our nerves. It's tedious, stupid, idiotic, unnecessary, dull. I'll give it what for. I dug in my heels and managed to boil the water. It took an hour and a half. Fried meat, and we fill our stomachs with stubborn resolve. Each spoonful reaching the mouth is like a crane in the harbor loading a ship. A few ships can indeed be seen down below. We fall off to sleep with one single desire: for the mistral to stop blowing. *But I tell you my Lord fool out of this nettle danger we pluck this flower safe.*

Le Lavandou, September 11, 1940

Today is the seventh day of our journey. We're moving along quite well and if not for the continual packing and above all this continual writing, we could be starting out even earlier. I often jot down certain things straight away, while we're still on the road. We stop for a few minutes and I write. Otherwise, I fear it might "get lost." It's enough to have a few disconnected words in the notebook. Afterward, it's like a roll of exposed film, the negative developed every morning and evening. Tadzio behaves like a patron of the arts. "You there, keep writing, I'll take care of the rest. About that right-hand brake, don't worry." He extracts the cable from its casing, smears it with Vaseline, adjusts, repairs, tightens it, collects the things and puts them in order. "Jędruś—have a look. Is it ok?" "OK." "Then it's schejn, sa va, nespa?" "*Oui, ça va très bien.*"

I was up today around eight. Tadzio was still sleeping. I left a note to say I was going shopping and would probably be back around ten. I didn't really know where to go, but an old woman in a completely empty shop said I could probably find something three kilometers away in La Seyne . . . "*Mais pas grand-chose, vous savez; maintenant . . . oh là là, c'est bien difficile . . .*"[113] I go to La Seyne. On the left there's an inlet where submarines are basking in the sun. I don't like submarines. They are somewhat amphibious. Their slender, gray bodies exude the chill of the depths, where they skittishly thread their way, nipping at your heels with the determination of cowards. A repulsive weapon. La Seyne is a suburb of Toulon. Crowds on the streets, especially in front of the shops. Sailors in the bistros with red pompoms on their caps. Lots of them everywhere; it's clear they don't know what to do with their time. Why is France marinating these ships? Ours would long ago have found another place. Here, the French must certainly have surrendered by correspondence, by letter or telegram. These sailors probably have no nerves, heart, or even reason. Things like this are beyond me. It's no longer even—Cartesian.

In one of the shops I found two cans of beans. I hunt for cheese, but no luck; and when I finally found the last Cantal in all of La Seyne, they gave me only half a pound. I search all over for jam, but there's none anywhere. By now it's hot, the mistral has died down. I stop for a beer. At the counter, a sailor and two civilians in heated dispute.

"*Mais, j'te dis,* the Battle of the Marne was the biggest. And most important."

"*Mais non!* Reims. That's where everything was decided."

"Reims? Because a hundred thousand Americans were sacrificed there?"

I don't know whether Americans were sacrificed there, whether the subject was the first or second Battle of the Marne. All I know is that submarines are floating in the bay. The discussion continues, a cascade of unrestrained words about laurels, long since dried out, which are good for seasoning. They keep trying to serve them as a hot main course, the so-called *plat de résistance*. Medicine recognizes a certain mild form of insanity in which the patient's initial two sentences make perfect sense, after which he talks and talks and talks—making no sense at all. It is called *la logorrhée*. The outpouring of words is like the oozing of pus in a certain venereal disease. *La logorrhée* is the French disease—and has been for many years. The beer seems to me to have the same musty smell as the words spoken at the counter.

This time I try a *charcuterie*, and ask if by chance they have any—preserves. They do, but only in large jars; the *patronne* warns me they are very expensive—twenty francs a jar. I ask her to show them to me. She brings out some splendid apricot jam, one of the top French brands, but doesn't want to sell me two jars. I whisper a stream of stories into her ear about the hardship of people returning to Paris on bicycles. She slips me the two jars, on the sly, so others won't notice. Terrific. I also get bread and eggs. I return with my hands full. The heat was now unbearable and I walk slowly. I no longer look at the bay but turn my head away. Something in me has burst, something bubbles up; words rise to my lips that I would never before have dared to say out loud. Everything I've married in life, I've married out of love. I have accepted no other marriages. Inconvenient, but what if you can't help it? I married France with a young man's ardor. And suddenly here, in Toulon, I see everything, fear the worst, I'm distrustful. I distrust the perfidious correspondence and the flirtation between the German General Staff and Clermont-Ferrand, between Clermont-Ferrand and Toulon. Here I see France naked, on her back in Toulon, like a slut. She waits and smiles in resignation, spreads her legs . . . She betrays me. Sweat pours down my cheeks, I whisper a few words. Ah—perhaps it's not true after all? I turn my head. The ships are lying there quietly, ash gray, slender. Further off, two cruisers. I hadn't noticed them before.

I return to the tent. Tadzio has lit a fire, I smell coffee. He is fussing round, tidying up. "Good morning, Tadzio, did you sleep well?" Silence. "You know, I found some excellent preserves. Liquid gold in a jar." Tadzio says nothing, behaves as though I weren't there. I come close, grab him, look him in the eye. "Are you angry with me about something?" He pushed me away and said: "Back off, I can't breathe." "What's the matter? Don't you feel well?" "How am I supposed to feel well? Come over here!" He drags me to the edge of the woods. We are on a hilltop and a broad view spreads before us. Tadzio has noticed the same thing I had and works up a lather: "Take a good look at that scrap metal." He points to the submarines and the ships. "See how the French have lined them up? What are they waiting for? To wrap them up and drop them obediently at the Germans' feet? This shows that Westerplatte[114] and Warsaw are fine, but only to pose for pictures. While the French are dining on tripe, or snipe, or a duck's windpipe . . . Why waste your breath." A great display of juicy adjectives and nouns follows.

We return to the tent. Tadzio swallows his coffee so loudly that you hear every gulp. From time to time he bends over, peers out through the leaves, then straightens up again. I'm filled with sadness and disappointment—he with defiance, the intransigence of a man of youthful race and class. I feel his rage affecting me, too. I want to spit and utter simple curses—no, not simple: colorful, prolonged, and elaborate. Afterward, Tadzio tightens the cords of the haversacks, as though he were strangling someone . . . He breaks one and we have to change our system of packing. This takes so long that it's already one o'clock before we're ready to leave. We won't get far today.

We ride through Toulon. A lovely city. New, attractively laid out. Smoothly paved, broad streets lined with trees and palms. Enormous white buildings dazzle the eye, spacious cafés—lots of fresh air and room to breathe. Built with panache in the pretty, modern French style.

After Toulon we take a right turn. There's a shorter road to Hyères, which we have to pass through, but we prefer the road along the coast. The day is hot, cloudless. We're refreshed by a gentle, humid salt breeze. Everywhere deserted and silent, there are no cars or people. The clean, filtered beauty of the shore.

We roll slowly through Hyères. Suddenly the quiet of the sun-filled afternoon is torn by the scream of car sirens. Two enormous gray Mercedes are speeding through the streets: filled with Germans, stiff as ramrods. They were gone in a flash, but I felt like I'd taken a punch to the ribs. The roar of the motors, the sharply upturned brims of their caps, the impeccably designed eagles: this was reality. Tadzio rode up to me and tilted back his head.

"Off to inspection in Toulon. The French will salute them, *mersi, pardon . . .*"

The Germans. I still keep forgetting about them. Around five, after a stretch of marvelous road, we arrive at the small resort town of Le Lavandou. It's only here that the chain of summer vacation towns begins, which at Saint-Raphaël becomes the true Côte d'Azur. This is already the antechamber. A fine sandy beach, forest and vegetation almost touching the shore. We decide to spend the night here. Dismounting, we trudge through the sand to a clump of large bushes. A sign says *"Camping interdit."*[115] I survey the scene. A young couple comes toward us and at the same time I notice a tent under one of the trees. It is no doubt theirs. I approach them and ask if the sign should be taken seriously.

"No, it's enforced only in normal times. Now you can camp up and down the coast, wherever you want. They've let us in, so you can pitch your tent here, too."

The fellow is courteous, the girl very pretty and shapely. Tadzio eyes her rather greedily and says:

"Good quality, first-class instrument, in working order. In that tent of theirs all the cords are slack and it looks like a rag."

The tent really does show a lot of "slack," but I explain to Tadzio that during the day one always loosens the cords. He laughs and suggests we keep some distance. "What you don't hear you don't see." The sun is slowly setting, Tadzio gathers firewood and inspects the bicycles. I'm to make supper. We're determined to stuff ourselves to the gills, since we've had nothing in our mouths since noon. In Toulon we were too upset to get anything down. We were inclined rather to do the reverse.

Night fell, a bright moon rose. It's perfectly clear, silent, with only the gentle lapping of the sea. We spread a blanket on the sand, Tadzio's small suitcase becomes a table, and we eat. I'm unlikely ever to forget that supper. A warm, bright night, silvery ashen sand, and a pewter sea. And an appetite. Incredible pleasure, sensual and healthy. This beauty arouses no memories, reminds you of nothing—neither music nor poetry. It is beauty to be taken straight, like our sunny-side ups with canned spinach, washed down with a glass of red wine. You don't feel obliged to excavate emotions, longings, or dreams. Here in one fell swoop you can unlearn that blue-eyed "Slavonic nostalgia" of the meadows and plains and wheat fields.

Here beauty just is, right on the plate, so tangible that I eat my eggs, my spinach, the moon, the sea, tomato salad and beans, and lick my lips. Perhaps it's that very tangibility that arouses neither desire nor the need to let your thoughts wander, to "air out the soul." Larks? Here in France one shoots them and eats them roasted. Nothing else occurs to me on the subject of larks. None of that "God's creature,"[116] no blah, blah, or whoo, whoo.

Biscuits with wine and sugar, some grapes. Afterward we settle down on the sand and light up, exhaling the smoke toward the moon. We've no desire to head for the tent. Stretched out, I write by moonlight. It's already one o'clock in the morning.

Saint-Raphaël, September 12, 1940

We awoke around nine. Still sleepy eyed, I stripped down (in the early hours it's already chilly) and stretched out in the sun, munching on some chocolate. Once I'd warmed up, I plunged into the water, swam two hundred meters out from shore, and followed the entire length of Le Lavandou. My eye skims the sapphire surface of the water, hurries toward the shore, and there, like a seaplane, zooms straight into the sky; a strip of yellow sand, the black-and-white keyboard of the sea-front houses and villas (the dark clefts between the houses are like the ebony keys), the striped curtains in the windows in every shade of yellow, orange, and red, the sprinkle of multicolored umbrellas on the terraces, then the dark green of the woods and the pale blue sky, like laundry bluing. I circle up there and touch down again. No, no — I would take a crack at anyone who said to me, well, you know, it's nice, but you can see it doesn't hold a candle to Koluszki . . .[117] There, you know, in Koluszki . . . and so on. I'm not the one who's the snob; that would be the guy from Koluszki. How Mickiewicz must have despised Paris and how out of sorts he must have felt there to have written *Pan Tadeusz*.[118]

I swam for over an hour; the water was warm, transparent, soft. Afterward, five cups of coffee and an entire loaf of bread with pâté and jam. We'd like to spend the whole day here and must force ourselves to leave. We've got another twelve hundred kilometers to Paris. We pedal slowly in the heat. Besides, the road follows such a marvelous path that one cannot hurry. We pass a series of little gems like Le Lavandou. They lie side by side, hidden among the seaside woods. Between them stand isolated villas, each with its own small beach at the foot of the slope and often a small private harbor for sailboats. We ride through Cavalière, La Canadel, Le Rayol, Cavalaire. In a roadside bistro high above the sea we drink cold beer with lemonade. We carry the bottles onto the terrace, sit down at one of the tables, feet up on the next chair, and bask in the sun. Below us the sea is framed in green, above us blue sky and sun. Tadzio's impression:

"The world is beautiful, it's only people who are m-f——s . . ." Thoughts of the war, of the mutual slaughter by highly elaborate means, here seem . . . no, altogether, they don't seem at all.

I'm obsessed by my thoughts. Trapshooting is going on in my head. First, the round German caps we saw yesterday go flying into the air and change into formless images of books and names: Luther, Hegel, Marx, Nietzsche, Hitler, Rosenberg—with Wagner's trumpets sounding in my ears: Ta, ta taaaaa . . . ta, ta, ta, ta, ta, teeee—Tra, tara, tara eeee . . . The third act of *Lohengrin*. I see the face of Miss Dora Vogel, my German teacher, who often stayed well past the hour (she charged by the hour), for her own pleasure, feeding me that culture with all the unhappy love, as Słonimski once put it, that a Jewish woman feels for the Germans. "Please also read this." For next time, fifty pages of *Nathan der Weise*, in the rose-colored "Universal" pocket edition.[119] Once she assigned me to write her description. I began with the sentence: *"Fräulein V. hat grosse Plusen, aber auch grosse Schuld-ers."*[120] In fact she had thin shoulders and was very petite. I loved her very much. I called her "Minna von Barnhelm."[121] She was determined to fatten me up, like a goose, which by the way I then was. "We are going to read Schnitzler, but the young man will please not say anything to his mother." The "young man" was sixteen.

What have I retained of all that? I don't remember, but I now sense most acutely a certain quality: the hysteria of German thought, the hysteria with which the Germans slowly poisoned us all. Another thing I remember: Luther wrote that he could not pray without cursing. Whenever he said, "Blessed is Thy Name," he had to throw in: "Cursed be the Papists and all those who blaspheme against Thee." Somewhere around here a stitch was dropped. How much hysteria is concealed in Marx and was later inherited by his followers. The entire theory of surplus value was spiced up by the sauce of hysteria. I remember once leaving the theater with Frydka after a silly, lighthearted French comedy. Suddenly, on Szpitalna Street, she says: "Now let's consider it from the point of view of class conflict." Hysteria! Blessed be Thy Name, O Proletariat—Cursed be the bourgeoisie, and so on. Who unleashed this hysteria? The Germans, German thought, hazy, unsatisfied, Gothic, like the Cologne cathedral, which I can't abide. The Germans created that dreadful, murky language, in which I never know what the word *"Kultur"* really means. Are they talking about an apartment with a bathroom, or Goethe, or finally perhaps *"Marsch, marsch."* The Germans taught us the hysterical use of adjectives, which one must treat as carefully as a loaded gun. They have theirs, we have ours. They have *"Volk,"* *"Blut,"* *"Boden,"* we have "Socialism," "Communism"—everyone gets carried away, German-style. A world of hysterics. Right now, this minute, immediately, I'd like to have the books to prove I'm right. Above all, a collection of Luther's works. Hegel is not needed, because anyway I wouldn't touch him. And others, many others. A book to spread open on the handlebars and read. Following the scent that has stayed with me after all these years, I arrive at what I now feel so clearly. From the *Chromatic Fantasy and Fugue* of J. S. Bach, we moved on to Wagner . . . This is trapshooting. Now it hits me: I stop, take out my notebook, and write: "Luther," "Marx," "Wagner." The hysteria of the adjective "hysterical" hits me now. It's all the fault of those caps and Toulon. In Toulon Tadzio and I became hysterics.

We now turn away from the sea and cut across a rectangular cape, on which Saint-Tropez is located. We pass many fig trees bordering the road. We eat figs. They are warm on the outside, cool on the inside, sweet. We have about ten kilometers to Saint-Maxime. The shore is rocky, the rocks are copper red. In places the road is cut into the solid stone, covered only by a thin layer of tar and gravel. Down below are dozens of small inlets, surrounded by rocks. In one place, about fifty meters beneath us, is a small beach; stairs cut into the rock lead directly down from the road. I could not restrain myself. We propped the bicycles against the balustrade and quickly ran down. Off with my shorts and shirt and straight for the water. I climbed a high boulder and took the plunge. The water is crystal clear—I dove in with open eyes. On the bottom are large stones and a forest of lacy seaweed. Crazy colors. Emptiness all around.

To Beauvallon it's a long, serpentine descent; some of the turns are U-shaped, with 180-degree bends, at most twenty meters wide. The switchbacks are surfaced like a race track, and the ride is a sheer thrill. *Dancing.* In the afternoon we cross Saint-Maxime. By now it's the real thing: the Riviera. Villas, minipalaces, a small harbor, yachts, a beach, palm trees. There's hardly a soul; it's deserted. Those who stick around look like permanent residents; *rentiers* and other paupers, in the French sense of the term. Most are older women, dressed with phenomenal pretentiousness and painted to the gills—plastered with every possible *produit de beauté*. Here you have the typical promenade and the typical grand hotels in classic Secession style. Various wrought-iron ivy, golden garlands, recalling the Au Printemps department store in Paris. These radiate the Secession so intensely that I was ready: *fin de siècle, Lady Windermere's Fan,* and in the end, despite myself, I began to recite under my breath Tadeusz Boy-Żeleński's "Esik in Ostend."[122] The area was in its heyday between 1890 and 1914 and much of that atmosphere has survived here. The postwar years were already but a clumsy imitation of the magnificent past. Something is lurking around here, something of the Old World diamond brooch in the bankrupt countess's dressing table drawer. The remains of a vanished fortune, a touch of sadness.

After Saint-Maxime we pick up the tempo. We want to get beyond Saint-

Raphaël today. The entire coast is like a palette. Approaching Saint-Raphaël we pass large airfields and seaplane bases. Every few hundred meters concrete blockhouses, like molehills, protrude from the ground beside the road; they are brand-new, as though just recently completed. Perhaps already after the armistice? The French are capable of anything. Who knows whether they weren't still building them even in July, for administrative reasons (for example, to enter the expenditures for the transport of cement or deliveries, etc.)?

Saint-Raphaël is lovely. More modern, with fewer Secession-style hotels. We stop in the center to buy fruit and find a bakery. We eat six pastries, then another two, and yet again two—the baker's wife stares, so we down the next two. To keep track I tear off grapes and arrange them on the cash register. There are still some pastries we haven't yet tried, so we snap up a couple more. The *patronne* laughs, the other people, too; that is, not people but the various housewives who have come in the evening to get their bread.

"*Mais vous avez un appétit terrible . . .*"[123]

"For sure, after 150 kilometers." I'm pulling her leg. They give us the once-over and with good reason. We are the color of chocolate and our hair is completely white.

"*Vous êtes Allemand?*"[124] Everyone suspects me of that these days.

"*Mais non; Polonais.*"

Now their laughter is warmer, and the baker's wife starts a political argument. The women certainly are better than the men at coping with what has happened to France. Only the women have the courage from time to time to say out loud, "Our men ran away and didn't want to fight," and when you utter the word "*Polonais,*" they immediately regard you as a hero. "You fought—*Varsovie ne voulait pas se rendre,* but you were weak. *Mais la France . . . c'est honteux!*"[125]

The baker's wife bellows from behind the counter like a captain on the bridge, encouraged by her clients' approving murmur. "*Nos hommes?* The loafers. *Ça mange, ça vient, ça dort.*"[126] Poor guy, that baker. But she is right when she says that before the war all they heard were "*balivernes.*" Slogans trumpeted everywhere: "France is a fortress of culture," the "cradle of great thought," the "*esprit français invincible,*" etc., etc. To prove the point, examples were cited: Descartes, Voltaire, *La Révolution,* Napoleon, or Louis XIV, usually ending with Foch or Lyautey.[127] And all that resulted from all this was—Pétain, or Peten, as Tadzio calls him. Everyone was convinced of France's greatness. To them it seemed Molière and Racine (I have a bone to pick with that one) died only yesterday, everything is *formidable* and everyone would go quietly to bed, swearing by what they have always sworn by. They have fed the world on their warmed-up greatness. Eating only warmed-up food is bad for the health.

Only the Germans had their number. *Nous vaincrons parce que nous sommes plus forts.*[128] The French believed it. The Germans considered this slogan just another *"Dubo-Dubon-Dubonnet,"* and when Hitler said, "They will collapse on their own," France mocked it, first last autumn and again this spring. In April, Hitler said he would reach Paris on June 15. The laughter reached a crescendo. And who knows if the German General Staff didn't deliberately slacken the pace on the march to Paris, so the Führer's exact words would come true.

How many illusions did we Poles create from afar! Freedom to criticize? Oh, how free the French are to criticize! Fine, but what? They criticize the politicians, they criticize the social services, they criticize everyone else, but never themselves. The French nation is great, it's splendid, inspired, but at the mercy of this or that, of this institution, of that person, and so on. You, the French nation, are beautiful and good and brave and hard-working, you have produced this one and that one (the personages cited in such cases mostly didn't give a fig about the nation and knew very well what to think of it, or else they would not have been important people), but you are being preyed upon. Isn't the nation ever responsible? In Toulon the sailors are not to blame, nor are the trainees or the junior officers, but only "the brass." They are traitors. They lost the war, because of treason. Where's the proof? Why don't these sailors, trainees, and junior officers sail out to sea? What are they waiting for? To be "gift-wrapped"? In Poland the big shots turned tail but the people fought. At home, in Warsaw, the people didn't wait for orders. Our antitorpedo craft, Wildcat and Lynx, would have left the harbor without orders. Because we are not a great nation. Lucky for us! The French are convinced that they think, therefore they are, but nowadays that's not enough. Nowadays you need to feel in order to be. I feel, therefore I am. If all I do is think, I can easily not feel it when they hit me in the face . . . The French do not feel, they no longer FEEL.

We ate another four pastries, eighteen altogether, paid up, and left.

We continue on our way through Saint-Raphaël. Villas and miniature palaces stretch into the distance. Hard to find a good place to sleep. At last I spy a small bay with a pebbly but flat shore. Also a lot of seaweed deposited by the waves and completely dry. There we pitch the tent. Inside we make a thick bed of the grass, a soft nest. A couple of meters from the sea. I set out in search of water. There was none anywhere. At last in the garden of a deserted villa I found a well. I squeezed through the gate and along with the water brought a cat. A glutton for petting, the cat immediately made himself at home in the tent. Once again we eat by moonlight. The cat very obligingly fell asleep beside me.

Nice, September 13, 1940

Good weather. The morning is already hot. I jumped straight from the tent into the water and headed far out into the sea. The water is tepid. This is probably the best morning exercise. Breathing in, breathing out—the movement of arms and legs. I can swim for hours without tiring. When I turned back toward the shore, I didn't recognize our rock. It looked like a green hill covered in poppies, strewn with red spots. Only as I got closer did I perceive it was a company of Negroes in red fezzes, out for their morning stroll along the sea. From far away you couldn't see their dark faces. They are sitting in groups, a dozen circle our tent. Tadzio gesticulates wildly, as if brushing away a swarm of bees. They point in my direction. I cover the final hundred meters in the crawl and hear the joyful chattering of the amused Negroes. As soon as I emerged from the water, they quieted down and whispered something. Tadzio is running around and collecting our scattered things. Addressing those nearest at hand, he delivers a long speech. Something like: "Compran pa franse, but—back up a hair, not so close; f—— off . . . you black bonehead from God knows where, or I'll do you some damage. If you don't want your mug smashed, scram, because this tent is not your lousy African straw hacienda. Come on, brother, hop to it and make tracks, no one's giving out candy around here . . . Jędruś, there'll be something missing. Tell them to move back." I dried my face and hands, took out a packet of cigarettes, and offered it to the ones standing nearest.

"Where are you from?"

"From Madagascar," answers one of the bolder ones, sounding childish.

"Do you like it here?"

"It's fine." Now they all want to talk at once. They explain they were brought here in the spring, were supposed to see combat, but never made it to the front. They are returning in a week to Madagascar.

"Aren't you pleased?"

"Very pleased." They laugh gaily, chattering among themselves. I tell them we're Polish. Again they laugh. One says:

"*Polonais bon soldat—Français pas bon, oh—pas bon . . . Français*"—his black fingers mimic a quick flight. The French were running away. It pains me to hear. O France, even these Negroes . . . I'm ashamed for you. Others right now are perhaps more ashamed on your behalf than you are yourself . . . It's curious, the kind of sympathy the Poles have aroused among the blacks. In Toulouse, where the retreating divisions assembled, the Negroes threw the French soldiers out of their quarters, and when one of them showed up they bombarded him with food cans, crusts of bread, anything at hand. The Poles they invited in, welcomed, and fed, and many Polish soldiers apparently stayed on. The Poles and the Negroes covered the backs of the fleeing French, covered the back of culture, of civilization. If a culture uses barbarians to cover its back, will this culture still be able to spread the light? Those too weak to come to its defense will not inspire others to respect it. What does French culture mean to these Negroes, to the Tadzios? Staś appears great to Kali from the moment he shoots the Bedouins. Kali loves Staś for his kindness, for his culture, whose superiority he understands, but he does not respect him.[129] Kali begins to respect him when Staś succeeds in defending that culture of his, those principles in particular that oblige him to treat EVEN Kali as a human being. The point is not, however, to treat EVEN this Negro as a human being, but IN GENERAL to treat all men as human beings. These Negroes certainly do not know this—and Tadzio doesn't, but perhaps they sense it? And for that reason they have no respect. At their level, the subtleties and fine points *de la raison pure* don't count for much.

A pompous white "gogo" of an officer, in white gloves, switch in hand, whistled for them to assemble and the Negroes marched off. The lucky ones! In three weeks they'll be in Madagascar. I would gladly go with them. I'm not quite twenty-seven, but even at this young age I've already had it with Europe, that cradle of culture . . . I regret I haven't already managed to leave. Life at first might be hard, but it would be life with a plan. Not a game of blind man's buff with fate, life lived like an eel, which slithers along from one day to the next. Instead of walking on firm ground, walking on jelly.

The cat greedily drinks powdered milk and carefully laps up the bits of undissolved powder while we drink our fill of coffee. After breakfast I carried the cat back to the empty villa, bid it a long good-bye, and then had to shoo it away because it ran after me. We move on. A technicolor travelogue unwinds before our eyes: the "Côte d'Azur." We reach Miramar. Once again, the great Secession hotels and some human "ruins" of both sexes. I think it was Henryk Sienkiewicz (*Letters from a Journey?*) who once wrote that in southern France you can grow old, but it's impossible to die.[130] That seems true of the people around here: they grow old, the women paint themselves mercilessly, but, as Tadzio says, "they'll never die." We ride through La Napoule and stop during the hottest hours in Cannes. The beach is nicer here than in other towns. Before entering the city center, which is quite "urban," we sit on the terrace of a small bistro under a canvas awning and drink lemonade. The heat makes you lazy, a light sea breeze puts you to sleep. I doze and keep dozing—the world be damned. An hour later we get going and soon reach Cannes. It has a small but attractive harbor, filled with motor yachts and sailboats. They glisten white in the sun like giant swans. Near the harbor a promenade, a large square shaded by trees, villas, hotels, cafés— farther in, the town center, as in every southern town—fragrant and a bit dirty.

We parked the bicycles under the trees, Tadzio rested on a bench while I went to buy something to eat. The shortage of groceries has one virtue: to find anything to buy you have to visit almost the entire town. I stroll around, keep my eyes open, search doggedly for eggs and a can of peas. There are none. By contrast, the displays in leather goods and jewelry shops are as rich and elegant as on boulevard des Italiens in Paris. After an hour of roaming around I had acquired everything and return slowly to Tadzio, carrying some of the items in a small pillowcase, the rest in my beret.

Tadzio is sitting on the bench, casually smoking a cigarette, surrounded by a group of curious onlookers. They inspect our bicycles, shake their heads, and ask him questions. He sits like a mummy. At the sight of me he jumped up.

"There you are, finally! Why are these cursed frog-eaters jammering at me? Quite an aristocracy around here—take a look at that oddball in white gaiters; he's just like the count in Helena Mniszkówna's tale."[131]

The older gentleman, elegantly dressed in gray trousers, a dark double-breasted blazer, and white spats, is very nice and pleasant to chat with. He asks me, for a change, if we are English, where we are headed, how we can ride on such overloaded bicycles, and so on. His afternoon stroll bores him, life is boring nowadays in Cannes, so he's happy to have a conversation.

Learning we're Polish, he commiserates, then utters the profound philosophical thought: "Well, well, *enfin*, you are used to suffering, but we? . . . What will come of this? . . ." I burst into hearty laughter. He has dispensed with us in few words and logically. "Oh, *mon cher Monsieur, n'ayez pas peur.* The French will certainly make it through less damaged than we are, although—*comme vous le dites*—we're used to it.[132] The issue of national resilience always causes us so much suffering. *Vous connaissez un peu notre histoire?*[133] For 150 years the powers have wanted to destroy Poland as a nation but they did not succeed— that's the reason for all this suffering! And you, the French? Money and comfort have corroded your hearts, reason has dulled your senses (this for Toulon, take this for Toulon); you won't suffer. When you say: '*Mon Dieu*, how you have suffered,' you are thinking of hunger, beatings, executions, prisons, but not about our greatest suffering. We may be broken, killed—but France will only deflate, like a rubber ball, and will either remain deflated, or bounce back."

The old man is visibly shocked. I said all this very calmly, with an almost melancholic air, shaping the sentences carefully. If you don't coat the bitter pill, they won't swallow. *C'est le ton qui fait la chanson.*[134] The old fellow swallowed, but did it move him? I take my leave politely; I expect my words are wasted because they won't reach his heart. That's our fault. We Poles were always teaching them to feel pity; and the lesson was learned. They say: *vous êtes malheureux*[135] as easily as they spit. I was wrong to write that my words won't reach his heart; they won't reach his reason. It's a thankless task these days to try to reach someone's heart. People no longer have hearts. Thus—if they turn out to show any feeling, it's like spitting—with the heart, out of habit. I don't want anyone's pity—I want understanding; then the heart often speaks of its own accord and beats gallantly.

We leave Cannes and soon arrive in Juan les Pins. The town became fashionable only in the 1920s, which is immediately obvious. Though deserted, it's raucous: jazz-and-rumba architecture, saxophone villas. Spotting a shop with tins of pâté, I enter and buy some. As usual, I start chatting and learn that the Polish Red Cross has opened a shelter here for the wives and children of Polish officers who have managed to leave for England, are interned in camps, or were killed. I shuddered and quickly ran out of the shop. We hurry off, not wanting to stumble across any of the graces from that slice of our intelligentsia. If two months from now the sea around here were to wash up bile and spleen, as well as poisonous foam, I know they would have emanated from that shelter. No doubt about it! I was reminded of the charity dinners on L. Street and the crowd that gathered there, especially "our ladies."

Late in the afternoon we ride through Antibes. It's really Juan les Pins, though called Antibes. Trombone villas. We want to arrive in Nice tidy, clean, and smartly turned out. We reach the mouth of the Var River and follow the right bank upstream. We want to pitch the tent here, so tomorrow we can bathe in freshwater, properly, with soap. In seawater soap "doesn't take." The Var valley is very wide, surrounded by the Maritime Alps, with a barrier of mountains on the horizon. In the valley, magnificent vegetable and fruit gardens cover both sides of the river. In general, the entire region, except for the beach resorts, is nothing but one garden after another. It's the source of most of the early spring produce in Paris farmers' markets. Houses and gardens everywhere, blocking access to the river. Eventually we find a path between the orchards, almost barred by fences bent under the weight of the grapevines, and we choose a place to spend the night. We gather dry reeds, from which we make a springy mattress, and over this bed we pitch the tent. As evening falls it's chilly near the water and Tadzio every so often cries: "Attention—air raid!" The mosquitoes attack us like dive bombers and the noisy slapping on our thighs, hands, and faces sounds like explosions. The air raid is infernal. We quickly light the fire and prepare supper. I throw some grass into the fire and the smoke disperses them. They no longer fly in formation. I kill one, take it in my hand, inspect it, and tell Tadzio it's a female. "How do you know?" "Take a look." Tadzio inspects it by the light of the lantern. I laugh. He doesn't want to believe that among mosquitoes only the female bites. "So what do the males use to prick you?" I don't know; at any rate, they don't drink blood. Tadzio addresses them in the feminine gender and pronounces a string of antifeminist opinions. "Just think how many people in Romania have been infected with malaria by these mosquitoes. All the worst diseases come from broads." We sealed ourselves hermetically into the tent, killed off all the mosquitoes, and fell asleep.

Nice, September 14, 1940

The bed of reeds was soft and we slept very well. We awake in the morning and I notice on the transparent roof of the tent what appear to be red bubbles, as transparent and unshiny as the roof itself. I take a closer look and understand. Our tent has no floor and is not entirely sealed, so the mosquitoes have crawled inside. While we slept so soundly, they fed with impunity and are now so drunk on blood they cannot fly. We delicately pick them off and kill them with pleasure. We couldn't let them stay, or they would have stained the entire roof when we folded the tent. We spend a good quarter of an hour squashing them, while Tadzio addresses each of the condemned with a long peroration.

Afterward, we slide into the water. The Var reminds me of the Dunajec. Bathing and breakfast. Followed by a great washing of linen, and thus we spent the morning. We set off. In three quarters of an hour we roll onto the promenade des Anglais, which follows a curve that vanishes somewhere in the distance. To the right the sea, to the left villas, hotels, gardens, and palm trees. It's a hot afternoon and the incandescent air shimmers above the asphalt. At one point I feel like I'm watching a newsreel. Tadzio cries: "Jędruś—a hotel." I see a modest, four-story house whose windows and balconies overlook the promenade and the sea. The Petit Idéal Hôtel is ideally situated. I ask the rate and can't believe my ears. The *patronne* shows me a large, carpeted room, with a bed the size of a landing strip, a couch, and a balcony overlooking the promenade and the sea—all for fifteen francs a day. I pay for two days in advance and run to get Tadzio. We untie our saddlebags, take the bicycles to the basement, and go upstairs. Tadzio is dazzled by the carpets, the built-in bidet, the washroom, the grand bed, the couch. He opens the faucet in the bidet, lets a stream of water shoot up like a fountain, lights a cigarette, and asks nonchalantly: "And you, sir, what business have you here?" We don't even put our things in the closet. We run out onto the balcony. Below us is the promenade des Anglais, a broad swath of sea, Nice off to the left. For fifteen francs a day. This seems to Tadzio suspiciously little and he fears it does not include the "service," who will later expect one hundred francs: "Perhaps it's a house of assignation and a working girl will show up any moment."

We remove our clothes from the backpacks and hang them in the closet, so they will "uncrease" for Monte Carlo tomorrow. Then we dress for the visit to H. I hope she has already received letters from our other colleagues. I put on navy trousers, a white sweater with a large seal of Carcassonne on the chest, and white shoes. Tadzio wears gray trousers with wide stripes and a slate-gray sweater. We look like Sherlock Holmes and Dr. Watson. Before leaving, we fill out the registration forms and ask where to get a cheap meal. We resolve to rest (?) and to stuff ourselves regularly.

We enter Nice at a brisk clip. Once again, villas, palaces and mini-palaces, hotels and guesthouses nestled in the green of gardens large and small, many palm trees—in short, everything that appears on postcards or in the movies and at the sight of which one would think, "I might go there some day," with the same feeling as, "I might win the lottery some day." Now I'm walking along the promenade, I've traveled the entire Côte d'Azur for little more than three hundred francs and I'm feeling pretty good, because I've got a small fortune in my pocket, about a thousand francs. I don't have a dinner jacket, I'm not staying in a grand hotel, I won't be trawling the night clubs and drinking champagne, but so what? France has thoroughly cured me of that idiotic Polish snobbism and those various highly overrated longings. I feel much better as a full-fledged, stylish vagabond than as some "neither fish nor fowl" left over from the olden days. And besides—the beads. Here they are—in my pocket. I don't like night clubs and indoor swimming pools. At this moment the problem of daily existence and of wrestling with the tentacles of fate is considerably more compelling. Perhaps the cause of this specifically Polish snobbism was the perpetual insatiability caused by the gap between our upbringing, our aspirations, and so on, on the one hand, and the costs and unavailability of a host of trifles, on the other. When you cannot afford the simplest things, even the smallest, the most ordinary, you dream of things that are out of the ordinary. It's a curious oddity of human nature, designed perhaps to distract oneself, to forget the absence of just SUCH trifles. I remember that when I didn't have enough money for a bicycle, I didn't think about bicycles at all: I dreamed right off about—a car. Not having a car, I at least behaved as THOUGH I had one. Though work was six miles away as the crow flies, I took the commuter train, the long way around, with a change of trains, gracefully, with dignity, while I dreamed about a car. Generally unable to afford second class, on the commuter train I traveled second class—at least there I *indulged myself.* If the *Literary News* was selling so well, it was because it took the place of books, which were beyond the means of readers aspiring to the level of the *News* and the subjects it treated, who not only could not afford those books but often did not have the miserable eighty groszy for the magazine itself.[136] It was like parading naked in a top hat, with a white bowtie pinned to the ancestral breast (even without the coat of arms), forever dreaming of completing the outfit. And this in fact was how the entire national economy appeared: Gdynia, COP, BGK,[137] magnificent buildings, expansion, STATISTICS, an always favorable balance of trade, paid for by the export of what was most needed, paid for by the export of armaments essential to our own defense; maintaining the high exchange rate of gold. Meanwhile, the average citizen was penniless, unless he borrowed, unless he bought on the installment plan and always took an advance. And if he did borrow, then he often spent the money, not on necessities, but on luxuries. This was particularly common among the intelligentsia. If you didn't have a roll of toilet paper, you bought a roll of film for your Leica, inevitably a Leica, and for the other you used a "borrowed" newspaper. For such a person, everything would take place as in a building without stairs, without apartments on the floors, just a basement and a top floor connected by an elevator. Moving by elevator between the basement and the top floor. Pressing the button with a finger in kid gloves, the kind "just right for the steering wheel." Not a Ford, God forbid, but straight to a Delage, Bugatti, Buick, or Minerva. As soon as more affordable German models and small Simcas came on the market, people became more sensible. The models from fiction turned into REAL-LIFE models. People also changed. They became instantly more natural and in this regard seemed overnight to be DIFFERENT Poles — tolerable, reasonable, capable of direct and informed conversation on the subject of cars and motors. Drinking a second-rate fruit wine as if it were a real wine is as offensive to a good cider as to good wine. And in fact much of what we in Poland used to do in the realm of culture was done "for show." There was talk in general of "the price gap"; but the "gap" between culture and reality was considerably wider and this was perhaps the cause of a certain cultural psychopathology. Literature, art, music were divorced from daily life, they became an escape, an artificially separate domain, effusiveness, Polish snobbism, entirely special and especially unappealing. People were introduced to the basic necessities, but a pack of unfiltered cigarettes costs 1/250th of the above average, not average, salary of an office clerk or factory worker. A gramophone, a camera, a bicycle, a bottle of wine, French sardines, cognac, good perfume, and a whole host of other trifles acquired supernatural, even magical properties. It cannot be normal to eat canned mackerel pretending they are sardines, to live mostly on the edge of your dreams and desires, not at the center. This resulted in that bizarre but sacred division of people into "intelligent" and "nonintelligent." The word "intelligent" in Poland had a quite specific meaning — and a stupid one. The designation "intelligent" usually arose in the course of "high-level" conversations, in which the common aspects of real life—such as a plain meal—were not suitable for such "intelligent" conversation, and the person included in this category was considered part of the crème de la crème. It is hard in fact to define exactly what it was, but I'm convinced that this dissociation has caused very serious psychological difficulties and that the sharp duality has turned us into a people whom foreigners have basically disliked. Let's have no illusions—we are not liked; we are disliked for this pretentious boorishness. If once in a life-time champagne has passed our lips, we behave as though we drink it every day at dinner. Whereas we were usually drinking ordinary beer—and that only on holidays, because a bottle cost ninety groszy.

Mulling this over as I stroll along the promenade des Anglais, I begin to see many things more clearly. I'm grateful to France, thanks to the availability of trifles, of ordinary objects, of little "knickknacks," for curing me of the fever that has imperceptibly consumed so many of us, distorted our character, and made us unappealing. Indeed, France was rich and that's the way it was before the war. Now a second, very interesting phase has begun. No doubt about it: the Germans will plunder France as fast as they can and will leave it impoverished. So I'm curious to see how long France can live off its capital. Unemployment will now set in, people will be taking as much as possible from under their mattresses and out of their socks. Only then will we be able to see for ourselves the extent of their wealth. Until now it was obvious, it could be felt everywhere (that's what gives people confidence), but it was hard to assess. I'll probably observe enough now to take its measure and I'm curious to see how the experiment turns out. The result will be the same as in Poland—the only difference will be how long it takes the rabbit to die. Overall we live in very curious times, which, if they weren't too curious, might be genuinely interesting.

We're out for a walk. I understand now why our hotel is so cheap: it's prac-tically at the beginning of the promenade des Anglais, far from the center. We finally reach boulevard Gambetta and plunge into the city. Nice is a big city in miniature. A little Paris. There are streetcars, the train station is probably no smaller than Gare Saint-Lazare, and it's hard to imagine you're only two hun-dred meters from the sea. Grand cafés, movie theaters, shops—in normal times there must have been a lot of traffic, as on the boulevards of Paris. We do some window-shopping. The bookstores are the only shops I avoid completely. Better not—books are too heavy. H. was very glad to see us. She tells us that some of the "common room" is in the Red Cross shelter near Grenoble. We might visit them. Her mother, a very beautiful woman, also joins us. She invites us to tea. We talk. A conversation straight out of *Fragments of Reports* from the exchange between the Castle and Klonowa Street.[138] People and events of the distant past are mentioned almost in the present tense, so powerful is the addiction to the past. I have repeatedly observed that many people stopped on the date of September 1, 1939, and got stuck in place. They manage to retreat, but not a single step forward. What once existed remains alive; people argue over things long in ruins, but reality to them is a nightmare. These are people whom reality has flattened, like a train. They were unable to jump on board, or didn't even try, but let themselves be run over. They are in fact corpses. But I can understand: the present reality is basically so horrifying, it's not surprising. Furthermore, they had already managed to acquire SOMETHING and have now lost everything; I had nothing, so it's easy for me to talk. And I'm young. In general things have to be very bad indeed for a young person to start reminiscing.

We finished our tea and leave with H. She claims we are paying much too much for our hotel. There are others with rooms for seven and a half francs a night. Her mother says good-bye affectionately—especially to me. While we were talking, she had forgotten about the war and for two hours immersed herself in gossip, chitchat, and tittle-tattle of the *ancien régime*. It's already dark when we reach the promenade des Anglais. The moon is shining, the sea glistens, the dark silhouettes of palm trees stand out sharply against the water. We had an excellent dinner with H. in a restaurant near our hotel and accompany her back home. We return alone. It's all completely deserted. We sat on a bench on the promenade and gazed at the moon. We listen to the sea. Then we sat a bit longer on our balcony, eating grapes and smoking. The moon had by now risen high in the sky and the sea was silver. The door to the balcony is open. We fall asleep on the soft bed. There is indeed no place on earth with beds as comfortable as in France.

Nice, September 15, 1940

We woke around nine. I leap straight from bed onto the balcony. It's a sunny day, a strong wind off the sea and high waves. Each surge breaking on the shore sends up a fountain of water and foam. We'll take a swim in the waves.

Breakfast in a restaurant. I had a good talk with the *patronne* on the subject of our meals. I told her we were tired, with a long road ahead of us, and we needed to eat well and plentifully, but cheaply. She will supplement the normal "menu" with a bowl of noodles with tomato sauce or with grated Gruyère cheese. Later we returned to the hotel and, after repairing the tent and washing our shorts, went for a swim. H. was already waiting for us on the beach, which around here is unimpressive. Tiny pebbles and not a grain of sand. France is urgently imposing moral reform: a recent decree prohibits lying on the beach with one's feet, instead of one's head, pointed toward the promenade des Anglais—feet must point to the sea. In addition, they've announced a campaign against alcoholism. The sale of "aperitifs" with over 15 percent alcohol will be banned. By contrast, wine as much as you like; cognac, rum, liqueurs—to your heart's content. Just to be able to say—and more important—write, that Pétain's government has embarked on the country's "reconstruction." And the French believe this, just as they believe that the unoccupied zone is actually Free France. Yet it would be difficult to imagine anything more damaging than the division of a country into two countries. The Germans have in this manner divided, not simply France, but also each individual Frenchman.

There's hardly anyone on the beach, for Nice is altogether deserted. The surf is high. I seize the moment between the crash of one crest and the next to push off. Like a see-saw: one minute I see the shore, the next only peaks of water. Afterward I lie in the sun and doze. My mind runs through everything my mother used to tell me about such places. Whatever once was is over and done with. With each passing year the world becomes more impoverished, although it could well instead keep getting richer. Not surprising—in the manufacture of any product the most expensive phase involves tests and trials. The whole world, perhaps under the influence of technology, long ago began experimenting with the management of life, much like what happens in an automobile factory before the release of a new model. Alas, more care is applied to the manufacture of automobiles than to the production of political regimes. Huxley (*Ends and Means*) is right: it's hard to grasp, in this technological age, when every ordinary engineer must be highly qualified, that public administration and politics are arenas open to anyone.[139] Any Tom, Dick, or Harry can simply show up and start messing around, like a back-alley midwife, one of those "angel-makers." And so, the production of adult angels increases from year to year. It's surprising that Huxley, writing so recently, has failed to notice how unfashionable he is with this whole topic and his campaign against the principle of "ends justify the means." Everyone else long ago came to terms with it. *Ends and Means* seems in places to be reviving the debate on how many angels can fit on the head of a pin. We have already gone considerably beyond that: "The ends justify the people who pursue them." The justified means were only a secondary concern. If today the means are so horrible, it's because they are employed by anyone with the mark of sanctity on his forehead, a mark acquired immediately upon spouting a few phrases about the need to "save the world." A moment's reflection is enough to realize that in this respect we live in a period of monstrous obscurantism. It seems altogether to escape Huxley's attention that the true causes of evil these days lie above all in people's inexplicably vast ability to ACCEPT whatever comes along. People have become as absorbent as blotting paper.

After our swim we went for lunch. Excellent. Then a short nap and we change. The day's high point was approaching: Monte Carlo. Tadzio cannot believe we are really going to Monte Carlo and is frantic. "Will they let us in? How much can you gamble? Can I go in THESE trousers?" and so on. He puts on his best shirt, with cufflinks, dampens his hair with cologne, preens and postures in front of the mirror. We don't wear our neckties for now, because in this heat we would suffocate. Even in blazers and socks we feel constrained. It's twenty-five kilometers from Nice to Monte Carlo. We fetch our bicycles and set out before five o'clock. Right off, we almost took a tumble. After nine days of riding on overloaded bicycles, we feel awkward. The road from Nice to Monte Carlo is splendid.

We climb a steep mountain; it's the other end of the bay. Below is the city, the port, to the right the sea, to the left the dark wall of the Maritime Alps. The sea is an amazing greenish azure, streaked with every shade of blue and green. The road winds up and down along the shore. On the right the sea, on the left steep slopes covered with villas and terraced gardens. Somewhere high up, a railroad slithers among the rocks, swallowed every few minutes by a tunnel. The turns are sharp and often we descend headlong toward the sea. The road disappears behind a rocky bend, then turns — and once again emerges over a bay, above the water and vegetation. One of the most picturesque roads I've ever seen. Everything is bathed in sunlight and the blue of the sky. We speed along. We enter Villefranche, which resembles a delightful toy, a doll's room. Although everything in these places is normal size (except the French), each object seems smaller. I'd like to play with the white sailboats in the harbor as if they were toy boats in the Luxembourg Gardens. We reach Monte Carlo. A policeman stands at the turnoff, in a gold-braided white uniform and an enormous plumed shako. He looks impressive. Stunned, Tadzio whispers reverentially: "Gorrrrrgeous cop." No, probably a soldier of the guard. We are sweaty and tired, choking and suffocating in our blazers, trousers, socks, and shoes. We had pedaled twenty-five kilometers in an hour and ten minutes. We roll down into Monte Carlo. The old town sits on a hill, off to the right; the road to the casino is on the left. I recognize it from afar. The building resembles a deluxe cigarette case. We enter a large park and leave our bicycles in the police station. A mustachioed policeman immediately offers to buy them, if we end up running out of money. Bicycles are now a highly prized vehicle. We laugh: *Sommes pas si bêtes.*[140] We knot our ties and sit down on a park bench. We are sweating buckets.

Tadzio sprawls out on the bench and says: "Can you believe it? *Monte Carlo.* For guys the LIKES of us . . ." We decide to set aside thirty francs for betting, fifteen each, dividing the gains evenly, no matter who wins.

"Fine, but do you know how to play?" Tadzio asks anxiously.

"No."

"Neither do I. I've played three-card monte, blackjack, and fool, but never roulette."

"We'll see once we're inside." I observe the entrance. People go in and out, sit on benches, step out into the large, elegant café next door. We both have the uneasy feeling that everyone is looking at us and smiling ironically. Finally we rise from the bench, circle around past a few shops with fantastic leather goods and jewelry, and approach the entrance. Oh so cool and nonchalant, with the air and gestures of seasoned players. But I fear we are more like Laurel and Hardy. We cross the threshold and are swallowed up by the semidarkness.

The doorman points us to a door on the left, where they dispense the admission tickets. A few gentlemen seated there ask to see our papers and record our data on a form, which they send to the manager. The manager after a while gives permission to let us in and we receive our personal admission tickets. We pay five francs each to "the cutpurse" (the purser—Tadzio is feeling the spirit).

We enter the hall. Again, semidarkness, large electric lamps above the tables, silence, literally all that's heard is the dry smack of the ball bouncing in the roulette wheel at the nearest table. Once, they certainly did not admit "guys" in casual trousers, but I now see quite a few others like us. Certain gentlemen have even removed their blazers and are sitting in shirtsleeves. It looks more like a poker game in the Wild West than roulette in the temple of casinos, the most famous of all casinos. We stand near one of the tables. The people sitting around it are holding little pads and tables of figures, busily noting the numbers as they appear. Some maniac is doggedly working a slide rule and whispers something to himself. From time to time a fellow entirely absorbed in the figures and in "his own system" bets on a number and—loses. Behind the circle of people with seats at the table stands another row of players, less formal. These casually throw their chips on the table, calling out a number after each of the croupier's sacramental *"faites vos jeux." Rien ne va plus* sounds like *item missa est* during a quiet Mass in an empty church. We stand and gape. Tadzio behaves as if he's in a cathedral. But he couldn't resist. He whispers in my ear: "Jędruś—now I get it—just like at home in Poland: shoot duckie in the belly, you play, you win, candies, goodies, chocolates, mackerels . . ." I snorted with laughter and several people threw me a hostile glance. Tadzio (the devil got into him) blathers: "That damn ball jumps as if fleas are biting it. Jędruś, I get it now. Go buy some of that 'stuff' (chips) and let's shoot the duckie."

"OK, but where do you buy them?"

At that very moment a man standing next to us prompted, in impeccable Polish and in a Mephistophelian whisper:

"Do you want chiiiips? Buy them from the croupier!"

Tadzio dragged me over to another table. We buy six five-franc chips and begin to play. Tadzio plays. He has never before revealed that he's so good at French numbers. With a sure movement he places one chip on two numbers and says loudly: "Trez-katorz." We lose. My turn, I bet on 13 alone. Nothing. Tadzio on 7, still nothing. I leave the fun to Tadzio. He bets again twice and loses. We have one chip left. Tadzio bets yet again on 13–14. The ball jumps, slides, and—we win. Tadzio flushed. This time he addresses the croupier at the top of his lungs: "Messie—isi—trez-katorz." The croupier doesn't hurry and Tadzio flies into a rage: "Why isn't that gardener raking in our direction?—Messie, isi, trez-katorz." The croupier threw him a mocking glance and calmly handed me a roll of chips—eighty-five francs. I put six of them into my side pocket as the return on invested capital and give two to Tadzio. He is now in a trance; his eyes sparkle as he shuffles and pushes his way through the people around the table. This must be how Disney's Donald Duck would have behaved in a casino. I finally realize who Tadzio reminds me of—obviously Donald. He loses once, then picks the 35–36 and wins. Another roll of chips finds its way into my hands. I give Tadzio four and, ignoring the game, observe the people. The place is full of older women in apocalyptic makeup, in garish, outmoded attire, hats dating from the cancan era. Necklaces, bracelets, lace, cloying perfume. Everyone stares at the ball, at the rakes, following with envious eyes every roll of chips handed to a winner. Large, gray five-hundred-franc notes travel from their handbags into the croupier's pocket, small towers of chips at times advance toward someone, at times retreat and don't return, or return in markedly larger amounts. Some people have feverish faces, one lady's hands are shaking, another steadily crushes her handkerchief in the palm of her hand and tries to make it into a ball. The man next to me doesn't even reach for his handkerchief but with a rapid motion wipes the perspiration from his forehead and neck—with his tie. The motion doesn't seem to belong to HIM; it's a reflex that escapes his consciousness. Everyone remains calm and only the small gestures betray what's happening inside them. They remind me of a steam boiler on its test run: likewise nothing is visible. The manometer needle has crossed the red line and I sense what's happening inside.

I don't understand how one can stoop so low that all one's inner peace, order, and harmony, everything, in fact—should depend on thirty-six numbers and a ball. Observing these people, I reflect that all of this—the players' nervous strain, the willpower needed to maintain the appearance of calm—is out of proportion even to a big win. Tadzio comes up to me; like the others, he, too, is now "ready." He hands me another roll of chips. He lost three times, then on the last chip he won at another table. I count up and see that "we've come out ahead" and that our entire stay in Nice has been financed by the casino. I take Tadzio aside and say, "enough." He's on another planet: "Jędruś, no—one more time—something tells me the 21 will come up . . ." I check my watch. Already past six o'clock.

"Enough, Tadzio. Our bicycles have no reflectors, in an hour it will begin to get dark and we'll be locked up for riding without lights."

Tadzio gives in, wilts, returns to life. "Good thing you stopped me—I was already getting carried away. If I'd kept going, I'd have lost all our 'stuff' and my own money too. Jędruś—it's terrible—you're entitled here to forget your wife, your kids, and hit bottom . . ." We stepped out onto the terrace. Then exchanged our chips for money. We leave. The sun is sinking over the horizon and it's already chillier. We have a beer and write postcards. Tadzio to Warsaw, me to Cracow. As though business as usual. Maybe they'll get there. (They did.)

We approach Nice when it's already dusk. The lamps are lit along the promenade, like a string of pearls. After supper we decide to set out again and look for a cheaper hotel. Perhaps we can stay here longer? We stroll around town and find a cute little hotel. We enter and the *patronne* greets us with a friendly smile. Rooms? Certainly, at ten francs, please. She takes us to the second floor, opens a door, and shows us a room. We go in and look around. The *patronne* slams the door and disappears. What's up? A moment later she knocks, towels in hand, and with the same friendly smile says: "When the gentlemen" (their classic *quand ces messieurs*) "have finished, please leave through the courtyard because *la grande porte sera fermée*."[141] And exits. I understand nothing, but Tadzio is already squealing with laughter: "Well, Jędruś, off with your clothes, for you must be mine—you won't find a better deal . . ."

I haven't laughed this hard for a long time. I lay down on the bed, calmed down, and once again went into convulsions. We left, and choking with laughter I explained to the *patronne* that we weren't interested in THAT. She looked at us with obvious suspicion—a couple of abnormals . . .

We sat for a long time on the balcony. Moonlit nights here are exquisite and it's a shame to go to bed. Now we really feel tired. And we were supposed to be resting here. We'll rest tomorrow. I empty my pockets before getting undressed and take out the six chips I had put aside. I had completely forgotten and failed to exchange them. Rest indeed! Tadzio is already rolling on the bed, squealing: "Clearly, it was meant to be. Tomorrow we'll go back to Monte Carlo and win for sure. It's a sign. I won't get a wink . . ." Tadzio is Disney's Donald and *Jacques le fataliste* rolled into one.

Nice, September 16, 1940

Breakfast at ten. Despite everything, we decided to push on tomorrow. We need to take advantage of the September weather. We're riding through the Alps. I didn't buy a topographical map because we don't want to be daunted from the start by the amount of climbing ahead of us. But I did buy fuel for the spirit stove. It may already be so cold that we might have to cook inside the tent, instead of playing hide and seek with the fire in the chill or rain. Unfortunately, they sold me only half a liter, though I used all the wiles *de mon charme slave irrésistible.*[142] The entire morning went on repairs and on washing our linens. At noon a swim across from our hotel. Once again the weather is sweltering. After lunch I took the things we had washed, which I wanted to iron, to the old Russian woman who lives in our hotel in a tiny cubby next to the laundry room and pays for it by washing and ironing the hotel linens. Discovering I was Polish, she began to lament our fate and compare their situation to ours. She said that for many years she had lived in Wilno and it turned out, naturally, that she knew almost everyone in my mother's family. She was particularly close to one of the cousins, a real pain. The old Russian woman didn't speak of Russia at all. For her, home was still the city of Wilno. We chatted like old acquaintances. As I ironed, I made the rounds of Wilno. The Redoubt had a theater on Pohulanka Street, dear Uncle Julek had an Essex automobile, and every three weeks a bailiff came to their apartment to seal it against the Redoubt's debts.[143] I fell in love for the first time with Hala, then with the pale Ala, who was always pestered after school by the hulk Towiański (I acquired a strong aversion to that name). In the end I smashed my pencil case into his mangy skull. He had some sort of bald spots on his head. This got me into trouble, after which at home my father took me on his knee and was very proud. "Remember that in such situations you must always defend the woman. But not with a pencil case. A man does it with his fists." Mother said: "Henryk, for heaven's sake, that's a fine way to raise him." I was eight at the time. On Easter we "rolled the eggs." How risky a game that was! I was reading *In Search of Castaways* and beginning not to understand fractions.[144] I still don't. In general I don't like fractions—of any kind.

Next, we set out for Monte Carlo. This time we stuffed our clothing into the saddlebags and changed only when we reached the town, on the road. With a dignified air, we crossed the threshold of the casino. I'd barely had a chance to observe the people and watch a bit of the game when Tadzio approached with a downcast look and said: "We can split now—the 'stuff' is gone." We didn't want to risk any more, because if the forgotten chips hadn't brought us luck, "the subject doesn't bear further discussion," as Tadzio says. We therefore entered the hall and began playing the automats, a game something like *rouge et noir* and *paire et impaire.* You insert one franc, press the handle, and wait. I began doing pretty well and one-franc pieces kept raining into my hands. Tadzio each time banged with his fist on the apparatus, "just in case," and behaved insufferably. At the sight of such *good fortune* we were approached by an old hag whose painted face weakened my knees and who struck up a friendly conversation with the obvious intention of wheedling a few francs out of us. This was so repulsive, sleazy, and humiliating (God, her smile) that Tadzio stroked his head in embarrassment and suddenly leapt toward her, spread his arms, and screamed: "Away, get lost, do you see the holy cross? Be gone, dammit. Jędruś—spit three times over your shoulder . . ." (Where did he get this "be gone"?) We both fled. "Jesus Christ—what rot, what a ruin," Tadzio whispered. This "ruin" no doubt hangs around the casino all day long, scrounges a few francs, then tries her luck at roulette. She lives by begging and roulette. Her attire incarnated the *fin de siècle.* I immediately thought of Józef Weyssenhoff's novel about the Riviera.[145] I don't remember the title. So far have we come from those times and those novels.

We sat in the park in front of the casino. It's splendid, full of exotic plants, an open-air orangery. The newspaper stands (I don't read them) sell an endless number of brochures titled "Surefire Method of Winning at Roulette" and other such publications about "the one surefire system." Indeed—human folly is unlimited and boundless, like the universe; which is to say, I can more easily imagine the limits of the universe than of folly. The human mind is incapable of embracing it. The philosopher's stone, Jerusalem Balsam,[146] and the system of roulette are all innocent examples in this domain. The problem is much worse when it comes to the one and only true ideologies and religions. That's obvious today. Last autumn, when I was in Mézières (almost at the "front" line), I saw posters all over the city with instructions on how to extinguish a fire. They began: "A certain retired fire captain used to say: in the first minute you can extinguish the fire with a glass of water, in the second minute with a bucket of water, in the third minute with a river of water, after which do whatever you can." We're doing whatever we can. This kind of fire is not so easily extinguished. The one and only true ideology ignited the fire. Ideology? Religion?—No. This division is as antiquated as "the ends justify the means." Ideology is today religion, religion—ideology, while I try in this regard to be like the first Christian. And I envy those who were actually the "first." Because I feel that despite everything it's hard for me to wring from myself THIS KIND of faith. They're the ones who "had it good"—oh, yes. The entire world was falling apart, everything was breaking up, but they kept going forward, eyes on the cross. The cross was for them a cane, an artificial limb—everything. And now? Who knows if we are not collapsing, just like Rome collapsed—once and for all. Only, what will come of it all? When you think about something, there's usually a point at which you can roughly establish the results of reflection; in this case absolutely nothing can be precisely established. One senses something (even too much), but it's like someone blind from birth who can recognize a shape with his cane but can't identify it. In fact, I'm afraid of these thoughts. Only now, perhaps under the influence of "that everything," do I suddenly recall books I read long ago, begin to understand their melody, while no longer remembering the tones, seem to discover the usefulness of things that once bored me, which I considered unnecessary but that my parents forced upon me. Music, languages (mother) — physical fitness, realism, and what the Germans call *Handfertigkeit,* that is, working with wood, metal, and other materials (father), education in general (father and mother together) — everything swirling around in my head, to the point that I cannot stop it. Writing this reminds me that my father prefaced my first lesson in shooting at a moving target by citing the important principle: "Allow for adjustment." As the bottle swung back and forth on a string, I allowed for adjustment and took aim. Several years later (I was by then a good shot) my father repeated the same principle during our first discussion. "Allow for adjustment." It was considerably harder than when firing a gun. I would like some day to learn how to do this properly. But how the devil is it possible on this earth to think while "allowing for adjustment"? Do what you can and call it quits. Besides, if the bottle was thinking while I was taking aim, it certainly did not "allow for adjustment." We're being shot at! I muttered this to myself, while scribbling shorthand in my notebook. Tadzio looked at me with obvious concern.

We set out for the old town of Monte Carlo. If museums of this kind existed, old Monte Carlo would belong in one of them. After leaving town, we change our clothes. The evening sea breeze is cool, the light is silky and gentle, peaceful. The entire coast, before going to sleep, wipes off its daytime makeup. Restful to the eye. After supper we sit for a long time on the moonlit promenade. Nevertheless, we are already eager to move on. With equal appetite we consume noodles and kilometers. Before turning in, grapes and cigarettes on the balcony. It's quiet enough to hear the sound of seeds hitting the asphalt.

Somewhere in the mountains, September 17, 1940

We rose early. A day as "shiny as a czar's ruble," in Tadzio's words. Packing, farewell visit to H., and an early dinner. The *patronne* has spoiled us: lunches and five-course suppers with wine at fourteen francs. Each time, it seemed I was eating not only supper but also the leftovers — of France. Over coffee, I kept on thinking it was too beautiful to last.

After Nice we turn north: the Route Napoléon. He took it after escaping from Elba. I tell Tadzio about his stay on the island, about the hundred days and Waterloo. The best description of that battle is perhaps the one in Stendhal's *La Chartreuse de Parme*.[147] Simple sentences, unobtrusive words, yet taken as a whole, so penetrating and vivid it's impossible "not to take part." As I read along, I fought in the battle and retreated. Napoleon's road runs continuously along the valley of the Var. After an hour of riding, the mountains close in on both sides and we are now entering the Maritime Alps. After so many months of a broad and boundless horizon, we feel caged. The mountains tumble down on our heads from every side, overwhelming; we feel cramped and uncomfortable. In fact we are continually ascending, but the incline is so gentle that it's hard to notice. You only feel it in the calves and thighs: the muscles bulge to the surface, breaking the skin. In places the road is cut into the slope, below is the river, on the opposite side a mountain wall. It's a long time since I've been in the mountains. Riding under a shady stone wall, seeping with water, I plunge with delight into the chill and smell of the damp rocks, mixed with the smell of invisible spruce. The valley is narrow in spots, then widens and undulates with the green slopes of pastures or cultivated fields. At points the gorge is no more than thirty meters wide, at others it broadens into a lush, verdant expanse. The road is superb and Tadzio, the expert, concludes: "That Napoleon knew which way to return."

We ride slowly. The mountains are completely different from the Tatra. The Tatra are really cramped, the peaks pressed together, like a pincushion tightly packed with pins. This is an enormous massif, broad and powerful. At its widest, the valley is an entire country. The transition from the sea to the mountains is so abrupt, the smell of the wind so different, it's sometimes hard for me to believe we are only twenty kilometers from the heat, sea, palm trees, and the beach.

In the afternoon we stop by the side of the road and take our afternoon tea. For dessert we have white grapes plucked in a vineyard higher up. They taste completely different from the grapes lower down; they are firm and small, refreshingly tart and covered in fuzz, as if their insides had been frozen. The sun warms gently and the surrounding mountains sink into the bluish, already autumnal mist. Deserted all around. We have encountered barely a single automobile on the road and only three people. We nap, then push on.

The sun is already striking the mountaintops when we arrive in Puget-Théniers. A small town straight out of *Peter Pan*. The houses here do not stand alone; they are all attached, often joined together, and what might be called a street ends abruptly at a great portal—you pass under the vault—on the other side the same "street" resumes its course. In any case, it's hard to call them streets. They are rather courtyards—rectangular, elongated, rhomboid, or tri-angular. The entire town is actually one single house and one single yard, and everything is "here." You cannot describe any house or shop as—"there." In be-tween them are great, broad-canopied trees, many arcades, and wide arched entryways.

In one of the small shops "here," I got my hands on some jam. In Nice you can't even dream of jam. The remains of former France can be bought now only in small towns far from the railway. No gas, no cars, hence no deliveries. The absence of automobiles disrupts the entire food supply. The larger cities are fam-ished and stripped to the bone; dozens of smaller cities experience no shortages at all, except that they, too, have stopped getting produce from the countryside. The missing links in the French railway system are now apparent. If, for ex-ample, in Germany, Belgium, and Austria the railway network is an actual net with square mesh, then in France it's an unfinished spiderweb. Paris is the spi-der's headquarters, from which the rails, like threads, extend to the larger cities, with practically no transverse lines crossing between them. The main lines are arranged like a star (Paris–Bordeaux, Paris–Strasbourg, Paris–Marseille, etc.), but between the sides of the star are hundreds of places accessible only by the excellent *routes nationales* of the first and second category, the *routes départe-mentales*, and finally the *routes communales*, which are often excellent, not at all third-rate. The network of roads is so dense that I was often tempted, looking at the map, to say it's really too much. You can get to every hole-in-the-wall from five different sides. And moreover on WHAT great roads!

Places the railroad doesn't reach still have jam, canned food, chocolate, con-densed milk—in a word, *la douce France*. But that, too, will soon disappear. Meanwhile, however, we resolve to indulge ourselves here in the mountains, where there have been no refugees and the trains don't saunter through very often. As Tadzio rides alongside me, I tell him about the exoticism of France. France is exotic. A strange country. As, for example: In Paris, as a rule, unreno-vated old buildings use kerosene lighting above the fifth floor, people cook on alcohol or wood stoves. Toilets and running water are in the corridors or on the landings. In French, "comfort" often means a toilet in the apartment (not on the landing), while an apartment with a bathroom is considered a luxury; rents for a room with bath and kitchen (the so-called studio) are about two or three times as expensive as in Poland. The pipes for central heating and the gas lines are as a rule attached on the surface—simply affixed to the wall, the elec-tric wires are also mounted on the surface, covered merely by wooden slats. The system for locking the windows has not changed since the time of Saint Louis and is still designed for the powerful hands of medieval knights. I'm the one who always opens all the windows, since Basia is not strong enough. Door handles are generally unknown. The French bed, made properly, cannot be aired without the kind of heavy labor that brings on a sweat. Rugs and blankets are shaken out from the windows directly above the neighbors' heads. That's because some ancient regulation forbids beating them altogether; carpets may only be dragged into the courtyard and cleaned with a broom. Papers, tin cans, rinds, ashes, and cigarette butts are thrown on the ground. The use of ashtrays is limited. Railroad cars are dirty and I've never seen any hooks in them for hanging coats. No coat in France, either for men or for women, whether custom tailored or off the rack, has a loop from which to hang it. In France, screws are not standardized. On our bicycles every screw is different and moreover Tadzio's are different from mine, because our bicycles are of different makes. For this reason the convex eight-caliber wrench we purchased fits barely a third of all the screws. Now I understand why a "French wrench" is called "French." It fits any type of screw, which given the millions of screws in France is necessary. Since it's hard in France to call this type of wrench "French," it's called "English." What applies to wrenches also applies to the spoiled "French lapdog," which here is called *un chien anglais*. Physicians neglect their patients and the practice of medicine here is considered an "occupation," no different from any other. When our concierge broke her arm on a Saturday, despite her medical connections, Dr. P. could not help her at all and she had to wait until Monday, because *le samedi et le dimanche on ne travaille pas*.[148] I have rarely in Poland seen cows as dirty as on French farms or such filth as in French villages. I was working in a large munitions factory (five thousand workers), which had barely heard of the scientific organization of labor. Perhaps because it was *une usine nationalisée*, which is to say, state-owned. No one gave a damn about anything. The system of bookkeeping meant errors were considered not only possible but inevitable. As a consequence, each payday there were around 3,000 (in words: three thousand) complaints. In correcting the errors, they made even more. The Poles immediately caught on to the possibilities and after each payday returned their *feuilles de paie*, with or without reason — "just in case." And as it turned out, rightly or wrongly, they were often paid extra. Bogdan, that amazing Varsovian, whom Tadzio jokingly called "a guttersnipe," told me repeatedly: "Mr. B., their payday is like the national lottery." Maybe it was better at Citroën or the Somua tank factory. I don't know. I just know what happened with us. Someone observing even this mess would likely say what was always said about France: "Sure, but in the end France holds together." What held things together were money and wealth; the French could afford the disorder. But that was peacetime. War struck and everything burst like a puffball. Money doesn't help in

such cases. Magnificent France collapsed faster (relatively) and more ignomin-
iously than beggarly Poland. Will they want to admit this? Will they want to take
the blame, instead of pinning it on circumstances, or on "treason," "because
America didn't help us," or on others besides themselves?

Recounting all this to Tadzio, I try at the same time to teach him to be RE-
FLECTIVE; if it's like this HERE in France, that doesn't mean everything was
necessarily better IN POLAND. I can't stand those "well, at home in Koluszki,"
or that "culture" which required that the colonel's wife refuse to occupy a
hotel room with a "built-in" bidet (these are usually the best rooms), asserting
hinnndignantly that "staying in a brothel is not what I intend to do." This French
"exotica" also has value. Question: What kind of "shortcomings" are in fact a
culture's saving grace? When I twist or untwist those disparate screws, I curse
like a sailor—it's true; but at the same time I reflect, I AM OBLIGED to reflect,
that these screws were made by human hands and not by machines. Besides,
the bicycles are superb, perhaps the best on earth. Even in these bicycles there
is a bit of France.

This area is not good for pitching the tent. The Var flows here through a
broad valley that is damp and chill. We pass a farm, not far from which I notice
a shed full of straw. We could sleep comfortably and without trouble. I bike to
the house, introduce myself to the owner, and ask if we can spend the night.
He is a bit reserved but agrees right away. His accent makes me think he isn't
French. As we keep talking, I ask about this. He tells me he's Spanish, and when
I in turn introduce myself as a Pole, his apparent formality disappears and he
immediately invites us in. There we meet the rest of the family. His mother, an
older woman, welcomes us ceremoniously, and when we kissed her hand, she
instantly rose and began behaving like a veritable *grande dame*.

"Please be so kind, gentlemen, as to take a seat, you must certainly be tired.
Some wine, perhaps? Sorry that I have to leave you, but we are making preserves
and the fire under the cauldrons needs tending."

I suggest we go together and we step outside. In the courtyard a fire burns
under two cauldrons, containing thick champagne bottles, wrapped in bladders
or corked and bound in wire. They're used to prepare tomatoes, peas, and green
beans for winter. At the cauldrons we meet both daughters—seventeen- and
fifteen-year-old Inez and Angelica. Both are pretty with large black eyes and
graceful figures. Tadzio immediately began to fling himself about and run at the
mouth, all the more so as both girls behaved with simple elegance. The whole
family had a dignity and good manners completely at odds with their bare feet
and worn clothing.

As we talked, it was difficult at times to believe I was speaking with poor, ragged farmers. The daughters were delightfully natural, unabashed, free, charming. The conversation touched on the school program and the French. And once again, as often before, I was struck by the way foreigners who have lived for a long time in France laugh at the French and even disdain them. The Frenchman is incompetent, doesn't know how to work. Akin to the disdain a healthy person feels for someone who is weak-willed and sickly. A large dose of forbearance derived from a sense of one's own strength and resourcefulness. The daughters regarded us with some admiration: Poles. They had read about the defense of Warsaw, about Westerplatte, about the conduct of the Poles on the French front. The Alcázar of Seville and Westerplatte created a spiritual kinship. Conversation, as though taking tea with Mr. and Mrs. X or Y.

Inez helped us prepare our supper, while Tadzio surpassed himself imitating a clumsy, clueless young man. He rolled his blue eyes and made the girls laugh. A table was set for the two of us—the family ate separately. Their son also turned up for supper, a handsome young Spaniard who worked nearby in the brick-yards. Before eating the whole family prayed. After supper we chatted still more. Around eleven Tadzio and I retired to the straw, after long and elegant apolo-gies on the father's part, that he could not offer us a more comfortable place to sleep. They were poor—he said this as though a bit ashamed. The land here is thankless and demands a lot of work. He's taking on what the French have left behind, what they found *trop difficile*.[149]

Tadzio turned and twisted on the straw and finally couldn't contain himself:

"Jędruś, what if I planted myself under the window of that Angelica. After all, Spanish women know how to appreciate Polish men, when they met Ta-deusz . . ."

"Where did you learn about 'Alpuhara'?"[150]

"We sang it in the army . . . But the younger one is a sugarplum. Oh, I'd love to caress her, give her a good kiss. What about another two days here . . ."

"Go to sleep, Almanzor of the Warsaw slums.[151] Good night."

In the mountains, September 18, 1940

We slept practically in the open air because the shed had no more than a roof. Like submarines, we dove into the straw and kept only our periscope noses above the surface. Warm. I woke at dawn. It was already getting light. The stars were pale, mist rose from the river and spread across the pastures. The air was like springwater. I swallowed a few huge gulps and went back to sleep.

After breakfast we set out again, the entire family bidding us farewell. They gave us milk and eggs for the road. They wouldn't take any money and would have been offended had I tried to insist. Inez and Angelica waved at us for a long time.

A few kilometers beyond the farm the road diverged: to the left the Route Napoléon in the direction of Digne, to the right the Route des Grandes Alpes to Barcelonnette. We bear to the right. The road began to climb more steeply. Sun and heat. These are still the Maritime Alps, but increasingly mighty. It's like swimming far out to sea: near the shore the waves are short, sharp, irregular — beyond they become longer and higher. It's the same now with the mountains. The Var River narrows here and is at times hard to discern amid the great boulders at the bottom of the valley. The narrow, well-paved road winds sharply and we are obliged to dismount from the bicycles. Walking slowly uphill, we talk. Tadzio prattles away, his mouth never closes. I sense we are approaching a high pass, below which is the minute village of La Salette, which looks like a settlement of doghouses. We begin the descent. Furious switchbacks, in places long tunnels. It's already a genuine high-mountain ride. Dazed by the sun, we enter the totally dark tunnels and are blinded. We orient only by the bright spot of the exit, visible at the end. The road is designed like a difficult racecourse. From the tunnel we emerge onto a slope, fly down a few steep switchbacks, and sweep again into a tunnel, as though making a goal. We hit speeds this way that bicycles don't usually manage — up to sixty km/hr. And so we sweep into the little town of Guillaumes. Lit by the afternoon sun, it lies, with its tightly clustered houses, at the bottom of a valley ringed by mountains. We prop our bicycles against a bench, sit down, and have a smoke. And, for the umpteenth time, as I observe the houses, the people walking calmly and slowly in the narrow streets, visiting the little shops, I say to myself: "Here's a place I'd like to live for a while." A film short begins to unwind, an animated feature of dreams: annual pension at adjustable rates, like the propeller of an airplane (in case of the devaluation of the franc), three rooms with kitchen, many books, a great many books, a few pieces of good sporting equipment, skiing in winter, and Nice within reach; here there's snow, there palm trees, lemons, and oranges, tiny *clémentines*, fragrant and juicy, the sea . . . How nice it would be to thumb my nose at life and fate . . . I'm off to buy something to eat. Everything's available, people here are STILL happy; time has broken down, like an old alarm clock, and doesn't work and doesn't ring. Alas, it will soon have to be taken to the watchmaker and switched to NOW-time. Then it will ring stridently . . . No — you can't "put one over" on life or fate, as Tadzio says. Do what you like, fate will at best let you give it a tickle from time to time. The gulf between the merciless blows and relentless schemes of fate and a person's exertions and marionette-like struggles is as wide as the gulf between the desire to possess a beautiful woman and learning to conjugate the verb *amare* as a way to succeed. Tadzio dozed off on the bench. I wake him and we get under way. I already know—the time has come for the world to examine its conscience and confess its sins. After which, it will—keep on sinning. If I were God, this time around I would not give the world absolution. God is definitely too good.

The road becomes increasingly difficult and we dismount more often and walk. Around five in the afternoon Tadzio punctures his rear tire. We decide not to ride any farther and strike the tent on a small roadside clearing. Tadzio busies himself repairing the inner tube, I cook. The days are getting shorter, and here the mountains shorten them even more. The sun disappears earlier behind the peaks, turning them red. We are probably by now in the proper Alps. The powerful massifs start off an orange-yellow, then pass through all the shades of brick and end up blood red. Nightfall in the mountains is marvelous, with its special silence, the silence of the inside of a violin, an "acoustic" silence. At the nearest farm I borrowed a bundle of straw, we sit by the fire and chew the fat. When you travel by train or automobile, live in hotels and pay money even to have conversations, you can observe a country, but you can't get to know it. You can get to know it only when you have to live there, earn your living, and count your pennies.

In the mountains, September 19, 1940

I was worried about the weather in the mountains, but it seems to be holding up. The day is sunny, intense, and fresh, like orangeade with ice. I have already forgotten the sea—I'm all mountains. The mountains alter one's movements, lengthen one's neck (one's eyes are always craning upward), and harden something inside. In the mountains I feel quite simply more manly. A recently mown clearing has had a crew cut and large drops of dew have settled on the stiff bristles of the grass. I crawled out of the tent and lying on my belly pressed my face to the earth. The grass moistened and prickled my lips and eyelids; it smelled of earth, of vegetation, and of nine o'clock in the morning in the mountains. I felt the chill on my chest from my drenched anorak and sat up. I munched on chocolate with sunshine and inhaled the smoke from my cigarette, mixed with the morning fog. A mountain hookah. The roof of the tent was steaming. I took back the straw, because there isn't much around here and the owner had asked me to return our mattress. Some animal had drunk up the milk we prepared last night. The coffee smells of smoke, the smoke smells of coffee. Off we go.

We didn't get far, because the road began to rise at an impossible angle. The signpost said, "Col de la Cayolle—17 km." We'll be climbing the whole time. The roadway twists continuously, like a startled snake. It is so steep that we must brace ourselves solidly with our legs to hold up the bicycles. After an hour of silent climbing we arrive at the first stage. At our feet we have the entire Var valley and from here more of the summits come into view. The vista opens out to ever wider expanses, expanses the likes of which I had not imagined. The valley beneath us is an entire country. Behind us is the narrow ribbon of the road, on which you can see large white milestones. We count those ahead of us—at least thirteen to go. It doesn't seem like much: hundred-meter stretches. I gaze at the full thirteen kilometers. Including breaks, we have four more hours of climbing ahead of us. Tadzio doesn't believe it and insists we can get to the top in two hours. I assure him he'll barely drag himself to the pass. We keep climbing. Tadzio began to chatter, but stopped very quickly. We are sweating buckets. The slope is southernly and the road so steep it's an effort for us to support the heavy bicycles. We walk like robots—slowly, rhythmically, firmly. After an hour and a half my temples are throbbing and I am near collapse. My calves twitch and my hands are numb from gripping the bicycle. We stop to rest.

We pull on our sweaters and stretch out on the grass. The pulse throbs in my temples, my legs, my hands, my stomach—everywhere. Even a light breeze up here is sharp—it lashes and freezes one's bare legs despite the sun. We eat chocolate with sugar and bread. We massage our thighs and calves. Then onward. We pass two posts, five still ahead. At times the road is so steep that, grasping the handlebars, we have to brace with our legs from behind the rear wheels. We lean almost flat over the asphalt. The final two kilometers are the worst. The pass looms above our heads but we cannot get there in one bound. By now we're climbing no longer on our feet but on our nerves. My temples are pounding so hard it makes me squint, my breathing had become shallower and I hear the strong and rapid beating of my heart. The bicycles keep slipping backward and when we stop to catch our breaths we have to apply the brakes. One more kilometer to go. We instinctively pick up the pace. We must resemble two fish, pulled from the water and climbing up the banks. We make the final kilometer in fourteen minutes and roll up to the pass. The bicycle has finally stopped slipping back. We head for the large granite post. It's the border between two *départements*: the end of the low pre-Alps. Low indeed! I read further and can't believe my eyes: "Col de Cayolle 2,326 m." And that's only the pass, not the summit. The summits pile up above us, in the distance loom the Italian Alps, their eternal snows glisten white. I had forgotten my exhaustion for a moment. But a cold wind is blowing. The sun is already dropping in the west and the gigantic rock walls and terraces emit a frigid draft. We leave our bicycles and pull on our sweaters and anoraks, hoods over our heads. We take shelter in a dug-out left behind by the French army.

It's warm in the dugout. I extract an entire five-hundred-gram bar of choco-late (the so-called big bar) and we each eat half. I don't know if I've ever enjoyed chocolate as much as at this moment. It's only in such situations that you can ex-perience the TRUE taste of things: extreme taste. Legs propped high against the wall, heads on the ground, we eat chocolate. Followed by *"Gipfelzigarette."*[152] We've conquered Cayolle and we're feeling good. What a pleasure to be young and able to exhaust oneself thoughtlessly, just for the fun of it, to exhaust one-self for no particular purpose, for the sheer joy of being alive. Sitting now in the dugout, I truly understand Sotion from Jan Parandowski's *The Olympic Discus* and I understand what the writer wanted to express through him.[153] We bulk up with chocolate and after an hour's rest crawl out of the dugout. The sun has already dropped behind the mountains and it is bitterly cold. Teeth chattering, we mount the bicycles. Hardly have we got going when I puncture my front wheel on a nail from an army boot. We curse. With fingers numb from the cold, we can't do anything properly. Icy blasts tear at our bare legs; gusts of wind, as hard as rocky cliffs sunken in shade, penetrate our bones. Twenty minutes later we start the downhill bicycle race. From Cayolle to Barcelonnette is thirty kilometers. The road is insane. We lie low over the handlebars, squeeze our fin-gers on the brakes, and start to drop downward, flying at over sixty km/hr. on the straightaways. The speedometer needle at that point reaches sixty and gets stuck. It can't keep up. Before every turn the brakes squeal, we hunch over, then the levers on the handlebars rattle as they are released, and the bicycle shoots ahead, as though it had a motor. On the thirty-meter straightaways we reach speeds of over fifty km. After ten kilometers of this kind of riding my hands are completely numb. Frozen to the brakes. I don't feel my legs at all; lashed by the icy wind, they hang beside the saddle like foreign objects. The only place I'm sweating is on my chest, under the sweater, from both effort and emotion. I'm getting drunk on the speed, the whir of wind in my ears, and the dance at the turns. Only once did I look ahead beyond the bicycle's front fork and for a brief moment was terrified: what would happen if the fork snapped? At this speed and with such a heavy load, it was vibrating from end to end, vibrating as fast as a struck tuning fork. Ah, no matter; another straight run. I release the brakes and jump immediately to forty, fifty, fifty-five, sixty—the needle again gets stuck and so does the breath in my lungs. A turn, a leap over a bridge to the far side of the river, the smell of wet logs piled beside the road, resinous and knotty, the dim mouth of a short tunnel. Inside the tunnel, the asphalt is moist and the tires clack as though it were spread with glue. A smell of mold and mushrooms. The bright opening at the far end expands rapidly as we approach, the gray ribbon of the road comes into view and plunges downward, into the forest, into the green of the spruce and the late afternoon red of the tree trunks. The sun still managed to break through a slit, from which it spurts out, like the beam of rays from the small aperture of the cinema projection booth. A screen of red vegetation, against which my bicycle speeds along. From time to time, for a split second, I see my shadow. When it vanishes, I feel as if I have overtaken it and it cannot catch up with me. A turn to the left, then to the right, once again onto the opposite side of the roaring stream, along the rocky wall. The road begins to drop more gently and presently we plunge directly into the marketplace in Barcelonnette. Barely able to stand on my feet, I check my watch: thirty-two km in forty-three minutes. Average speed forty-five km/hr. Our faces, hands, thighs, and calves are completely blue, despite our tan. Our fingers are so stiff that we can't draw the matches from the matchbox. This is perhaps the most beautiful day of our entire journey. But we are infernally tired. I feel it now, standing in the marketplace and smoking a cigarette. My hand trembles and my lips quiver, as though I were on the verge of tears. Six hours of climbing and thirty-two km of an infernal descent. Tadzio says: "I will remember this day even after death."

Barcelonnette is a small town and a bit exotic. Around here France has a tinge of Mexico. Many people from these parts had traveled to Mexico and returned with the money they earned to their hometown. Some still wear Mexican hats and have retained bits of the attire. It's hard even to say which. And they move differently than the French. About this Mexico I hear from an old grandpa who asked us for a light for his shaggy, clumsily rolled cigarette. The old man's hands are shaking and he cannot pack the tobacco evenly. He chats with us, smacking his lips loudly. He says that before the last war some people around here were still going to Mexico in search of gold. The grandpa smokes his cigarette with such pleasure that I'm tempted to chuck my own and take his stringy "roll-up." I visit a few shops—there's food in abundance: tinned meat, peas, lima beans and string beans, jams, milk, chocolate. In the blink of an eye I spend over a hundred francs and we are fixed for several days. The light is fading. I consult with Tadzio whether to keep going or pitch our tents right away outside town. No—enough for today. In a young woods a few kilometers beyond Barcelonnette, we collapse for the night. The valley here is broad, surrounded by mighty peaks. There's a splendid extravagance and disregard for the limits of space in this Alpine arrangement. Rachmaninov's *Prelude* played on the organ is the only comparison that occurs to me when I gaze at this land of giants. The Tatra are pocket edition mountains. We gorge ourselves and fall instantly asleep.

Beyond Gap, September 20, 1940

Yesterday the evening was chilly, so we piled on all the clothing we have and fixed supper inside the tent on the spirit stove. At five thirty in the morning we awoke as at reveille. Tadzio screamed: "Jędruś—I'm frozen to death." I couldn't utter a single word, because I had turned into an iron bar. A steel ingot. It felt as though what was left of me had curled into a ball and settled in the region of my diaphragm, shivering from the cold, as though my entire body—that other me—had become an inanimate object. But I moved; the way a little wooden manikin might have moved, the kind used by painters to capture the motions of the legs or arms, which are sold by the dozen on rue Bonaparte in Paris. I poured some wine into the pot, threw in some sugar and raisins, and lit the spirit stove. After a while it grew hot inside the tent and we blessed the alcohol. We drank the hot wine, burning our lips, and warmed up almost instantly. It was even too hot, since I hadn't switched off the stove. Then we crawled out of the tent. The view was so stunning that instead of moving to keep warm, we stood still as posts.

The sky was turning pink in the east and passed through every shade of brick, orange, and lemon, until it reached a violet sapphire, against which the stars still glittered. Everything in the valley was covered in frost, emitting faint little sparks, like millions of scattered diamonds. The mountain peaks, tinged with rose, were wrapped in a band of transparent fog. The sun was slowly rising, scattering ever new colors. The same tree, the same summit kept changing, discarding one costume and donning another. The spruce also changed their jewels, as the frost, melted by the sun, turned into large drops of water in every shade of the rainbow. The dark sapphire of the sky faded, as it turned ever more violet all the way to blue. The stars dimmed before our eyes and day dawned. A few final touches, casual brushstrokes of the sun, and the painting was complete. If the beauty of the entire coast from Saint-Raphaël to Monte Carlo was earthy, tangible, almost dense, then here it was diffuse and endless, inaccessible in its plenitude, like tones too high for the ear.

We stood like this for almost half an hour and felt cold all over again. But now the sun began to warm up. We sat down in front of the tent, thinking about breakfast. Oh, if only someone would bring me "breakfast in bed." I'm feeling lazy. And besides it's so hard to be patient and keep watching while the water refuses to boil—this very minute, already, on the spot. We're in luck with the weather; another sunny day. After breakfast another thirty-five-kilometer descent. The descent is much gentler than yesterday, but we reach the same speeds. The road drops down through a broad valley. Along the slopes, large comfortably sprawling villages and small towns intermixed—a relief map on a scale of 1:1. Over the next dozen kilometers one could glide a finger along the ribbon of the road, stop at some *bourgade*[154] — here turn right, continue straight — one can trace the route without taking the map from one's pocket. The entire vista reminds me of the little pictures painted on Tyrolean cuckoo clocks or of alpine lithographs from the end of the nineteenth century.

At noon we stop near the river, swim, and eat. The sun is hot, one's gaze gets lost among the summits. I'm overtaken by a typical mountain lassitude. One can lie for hours, gazing idly, munching on chocolate with raisins, smoking. One can cease being a person and become some kind of one-celled creature, an amoeba or plankton.

In the afternoon we reach Gap. The town is bigger than Barcelonnette. Food enough to eat your fill. There's an enormous Nestlé condensed milk factory and many sawmills. I buy several tins of sweetened milk. We eat it with the same purpose as Popeye the Sailor, who revives himself by eating his spinach. There's also fuel for the spirit stove; I purchase two liters right away, so we no longer have to cook on an open fire. It goes without saying that I also buy a huge batch of chocolate. We left the bicycles in care of the bistro *patronne* and went for a stroll. Splendid sporting shops with top-notch equipment: excellent ski boots and skis. I stopped in everywhere to chat with the merchants and "handle" the wares. They were happy to show me everything and shoot the breeze, though they knew I wouldn't buy anything. It pleased them that I had an eye for the goods. I came within a hair's breadth of buying a terrific goatskin wine flask from Spain. But it was too expensive and I regretfully left the shop. I almost swooned to see hard-frame backpacks at two hundred fifty francs. But I have to bring a few pennies back to Paris. In fact the prospect of the return worries me, ever more, the closer we get. I'll think about it later.

Directly after Gap we take the climb to the "Col Bayard" — seven km on foot. Evening is already falling as we climb. We walk very slowly. We plan to leave a stretch for tomorrow and we search for a place to spend the night. We choose a meadow near the road with a small stream. The sky has clouded over, the mountains have vanished in the mist; it's stuffy and hot. It will probably rain.

Beyond La Mure, September 21, 1940

Around ten o'clock the weather cleared and it became unbearably hot. We resume our climb toward the Bayard pass. Horseflies bite at our legs. The pass is 1,230 meters high. Almost the same as Turbacz.[155] Beyond the pass the descent begins, steep, but long, in straight stretches. The speedometer can't go beyond sixty and it doesn't keep up. I distinctly feel the resistance of the air. Suddenly I hear a thud and a crash; one of the bottles of spirit fuel has fallen. I did not slow down. Tadzio drew up beside me for a moment, cursed the bottle and "all these breakneck descents," and returned to his spot behind me. The repeated descents are wearing us out. In the next town I replenish the alcohol. Standing in front of one of the houses, we are approached by two gendarmes. I was sure they would want to inspect our papers. But they only stood and stared. Finally, one came closer and began to shoot the breeze: "My, you are really loaded down." I smiled. "And where are you headed?" "*À Paris*," I answer. "*Oh là là*—you've a long way to go. And do you have a *plaque de vélo?*"—That's a medallion showing you have paid your bicycle tax. "*Bien sûr*," I say, but make no move to produce it. "Well, fine—*bon voyage!*" And they went on their way. Tadzio stared for a long time at the two black silhouettes on the road and uttered a few complimentary remarks on the subject of all "French coppers."

The French policeman is not always clever; he is sometimes even stupid and narrow-minded, but often he is good-hearted and easygoing. Our Polish policeman was also not clever, but in addition was spiteful and drunk on power. A decidedly worse mixture. Rarely did the police treat anyone as a human being. In their view, the Polish citizen was above all a character "only allegedly without a record." This "only allegedly without a record" was a specifically Polish police term, unlikely to be encountered in the rest of the world. They still have no evidence against you, know little about you, but you are already "only allegedly without a record." Our policeman's first question on checking someone's documents was "What are you up to?" If the answer was "Nothing," this was considered mocking, disrespectful of authority—and was followed by arrest or, rather, "preventive detention," guaranteed. In France, during normal contact with the public (for example, examining papers), no policeman would ask such stupid questions. Papers in order, round seal of the Republic, and off you go. Since leaving Carcassonne, today was the first time we were approached by a gendarme and that for purposes of friendly conversation. The question about the *plaque* was only a mild reminder to us (and no doubt to himself) that he nevertheless was responsible for upholding order. Bad-mouth them all you want, but there's a sense of freedom here, what remains of the freedom that existed in Europe before the war, in my parents' time. And in fact the rules concerning foreigners began to tighten up only in the last ten years. I'd like to know in what other country, at the present time, in wartime, two foreigners could ramble so freely for hundreds of kilometers without any checks. *O douce France!* Life here is easier and simpler, a human being is first and foremost a human being. It's so easy and enjoyable here to "thumb one's nose" or "one's heels" at many things. There's something tragic about the fact that these freedoms, this prosperity, this superb *je m'en fiche*[156] were also the cause of their downfall. Who knows . . . No! I'll never believe it. I reject the possibility . . .

The road has become difficult. Up and down, up and down. We are having to dismount, push the bicycles for half an hour, then descend for a few minutes, then once again uphill. This is much more tiring than a single long ascent. We want to get past La Mure today and by tomorrow be in Uriages near Grenoble. There's a Polish Red Cross shelter there and a few acquaintances from the "common room" in Carcassonne. Perhaps we'll manage to recover for a couple of days after the Alps. The road was the same for the entire afternoon. Around thirty climbs and descents. And finally the nail in the coffin — the six-km ascent to La Mure. Nothing for it — we climb. By about eight in the evening we are in La Mure. The evening is chilly and we are so exhausted that we drag ourselves through the streets, one foot after the other. I would like to buy some meat for supper, so we stand the bicycles against a wall and look around. Two girls pass by speaking Polish. Tadzio immediately scampers over and says: "O beloved queens, lilac blossoms, dearest women of Poland, our compatriots, where around here can one buy some meat for two miserable citizens?"

The two "lilac blossoms," ruddy and plump (double lilacs), began to giggle and babble. And where are you from? And where are you going? And for how long? And our aunt has a bistro and a shop next to the bistro, and maybe she'll sell you something. Tadzio, without hesitation, seized the moment: "O pride of France, lead the way — we'll follow you even into bed (hee, hee, hee)," and so we landed in the aunt's bistro. Along the way Tadzio offered some private remarks of the sort: "Scullery maids, émigré pests, rockets (?), drudges," etc., etc., but aloud he worked his charms: "What are you laughing at, my lovely flower — you shouldn't, it doesn't become you . . . ," and to me in a whisper: "Get a look at those legs, Jędruś — nice enough, but only around the house or in the fields, yes?"

In the aunt's bistro there were a few Poles, emigrants. They invited us to their table and conversation was in order. Tadzio was not pleased, because like almost all the Poles who have arrived in France during the war, he basically can't abide the emigrants. I understand him, but I also try to teach him to understand this unique element. The old emigrant remained at heart a Pole and proved it in many ways, but physically, most often subconsciously, stopped being Polish. In this respect one can speak of a distinct nationality, an emigrant nationality. The Polish emigrant is a product of many features and conditions of both Polish and French life, a *cocktail* not always tasty, often hard to stomach, prepared by pitiless fate. Who was emigrating to France? In the main, unskilled and uneducated agricultural laborers. Such an emigrant usually followed a difficult path. Driven by poverty at home, he signed a contract while still in Poland selling himself to a French farmer or manufacturer for three years, then boarded the train with a placard around his neck, like a beast being led to the slaughter, and set off. Arriving in France, he worked for a farmer to earn his keep and four hundred to six hundred francs a month. All the while, he witnessed French freedoms and democracy, took his meals at the same table as his boss; by the end of the first year was dazzled, after two years, having met others like himself, had already "wised up," and after three years escaped from the farm to the city to work in a factory. In the factory he encountered the screwdriver and the file, and with typical Polish handiness and intelligence "grasped" what was expected of him and thus came to consider himself a "skilled metalworker." And he now told the world to go to hell. Torn from his own state organism and the civic discipline of his own country, at the same time he lived outside the bounds of French civic life. This is the source of that particular emigrant anarchism, innate in every Pole, but intensified by the French way of life. He earned good money, enough for sardines and champagne. "Here, you know, it's not like there in that Poland of YOURS, because here, you know, we have egalite and, you know, liberte; here, no one reproaches the worker, because the worker is super-respected—vuala, you know!" Deep down the emigrant retained the uneducated, unenlightened brain of a poor, landless village laborer, covered by a thin layer of lofty civilization and a standard of living based mainly on access to everything that, "you know, in that Poland of YOURS, only the intelligentsia got for itself—vuala!" Access to what in Poland was often a luxury even for the "intelligentsia" shaped his way of thinking. He was instantly the wisest of them all, a master, who knew it all and did it all, and it was all "because in that Poland of YOURS." A concentrated mixture of what in fact constitutes every Pole, a mixture of high-proof alcohol, champagne, and a thin veneer of good manners. There are exceptions, especially among the miners, that element dense and wise with the wisdom and danger of their work. Thus, even here, a distinction can be drawn: between emigrants in general and the miners.

Having forgotten his Polish, the emigrant butchers the French language, instead of "yes," he says "shi" or "vu-ee," and one has to admit that in most cases he has absorbed only the negative aspects of French freedom and French *laisser-aller*. His innate diligence and intelligence lead him to disrespect the Frenchman, who is not as tough or resilient. In the factory I worked with emigrants, with "our kind of people from Poland," and with Frenchmen. I noticed a lot. "Our kind of people from Poland" in general despised the emigrants, who returned the feeling. How many times in the cloakroom did I hear "one of ours" explicate condescendingly to an emigrant: "You, fellow, all this insurance, these paid vacations, in Poland we've had them from day one. Don't give me your France—you're ignorant, why bother even talking to you?" Tadzio typically isn't bashful: "What's the use of arguing with you, you wise-ass. Speak plain Polish:

what's with this 'shi'? You're not my 'she,' and I'm not your 'he'—I don't get it—kompran pa!"

Suffering occasionally ennobles, but usually only those who have not suffered before. Those who have suffered all along it ennobles very rarely. The emigrants suffered first in Poland, then here. When the crisis hit France most foreigners were fired from their jobs; our emigrant applied for unemployment. While unemployed, he did not pay rent and collected benefits, but since the monitoring of unemployment, like all French regulation, was highly erratic, he worked on the side (*bricolage*). He would repair a stove here, paint an apartment there, install a bathroom or central heating somewhere else (Poles are handy at everything), etc.—in short, his life in many respects was tolerable. His attitude toward the world was: "So, what are you going to do about it?" The government of Léon Blum[157] and the distinctly easier life in France, unemployment benefits, *bricolage*—these conditions ensured him a standard of living he considered his own achievement. Reading the French left-wing press, splendidly demagogic, completed his education. It's Poland's third sex, an element apparently hard to get along with, but of greater value on the inside, and moreover essentially gullible, which our politicians have taken advantage of, causing many to lose faith in the Polish state. This is the reason for the perpetual "because in that Poland of YOURS." Too often they were lied to.

The emigrants here in La Mure have a hard life. The work is awful. Almost all of them work in the local lead mines. The wages are miserable, but today's conditions don't allow them to throw off their shackles and seek a less onerous or at least healthier way of earning their bread. We talk about Poland; the eighteen days of the defense of poor Poland, compared to the fourteen days in which the Germans strolled across France, have filled all of them with pride. Almost none of them produced the eternal "because in that Poland of YOURS," instead I constantly hear "because in OUR Poland." But they curse our "intelligentsia" and they may be right. Our intelligentsia made them sick, like greasy food, when they observed the rancid cream of the crop that had fled Poland. Many of the "cream" saw the emigrants as their NEW SUBJECTS, a new folk in miniature, which they could govern on the spot. The emigrants' patience was sorely tested. They did not, however, foreswear Poland, although the temptation was great: the French eagerly enrolled them in their army despite the agreement with the Polish government in the Hôtel Régina.[158] The emigrants fought and fought well.

We had a beer and stopped by the aunt's shop. In addition to what we purchased she threw in, gratis, two tins of pâté and two bars of chocolate. I was natural, straightforward, and they were agreeable, neither "insolent" nor "arrogant." Occasionally they had trouble with logic, because they had swallowed more than they could digest, but when you tell them they are talking nonsense and demonstrate with a good (not far-fetched) example that they are full of hot air, they fall silent and listen. They like to be addressed in PLAIN language. It was already beginning to grow dark. We left the bistro, to a warm farewell from all concerned. They even offered us shelter for the night and of course began immediately to argue over where we would be most comfortable. I preferred, however, to keep going, because I sensed this would all end in a monstrous drinking spree. Tadzio and I had already sniffed the odor of rum in the bistro. The company around us made so much noise that two gendarmes asked to see our papers, but they then joined the others in showing their concern that we make it back to Paris. At dusk we left La Mure. The broad plateau here stretches as far as Vizille. Mist is falling on the meadows, cold and damp. Several kilometers farther along, already in the dark, we pitch our tent near the road, sheltered only by a few bushes. The night is clear and practically transparent. We fix supper in the tent, after which Tadzio falls instantly asleep. I write by candlelight. The crickets are clicking, and the rasp of a beetle ambling around the roof of the tent makes a perfect racket. I'm so tired I can't fall asleep.

Uriage, September 22, 1940

Already sunny first thing in the morning. We were aroused early, by hunger as usual. Tadzio's first words: "Jędruś—let's eat." I get out the chocolate and, still drowsy, we slowly munch. Followed by a cigarette and the day really begins. I go for water and milk. Tadzio strikes camp. I love my almost daily morning walks. Wrapped in sweaters and scarves (in the morning there can often be frost—it's autumn), I take the bottles and meander slowly down the road, then along the paths through the fields, stopping by the farms. As a rule the whole house is still asleep and only the *patron* bustles about the yard with an entourage of chickens, ducks, and turkeys. They track his every step, waiting for him to throw them something. I stand quietly behind the fence and watch. A lively discussion unfolds between them. The *patron* says: "*Allez, allez, attendez,*"[159] while the chickens loudly cluck in reply, the ducks, wheezing softly, nip at his pant legs, and the turkeys, with the look of corporate directors examining the morning post, describe casual arcs from afar and approach him around front. The way they walk, I'm sure they have their hands in their pockets and thick cigars in their beaks. In the silence, each sound is clear, framed by nothing. Fog hangs over the meadows, the grass glistens, and the mountain ranges stack up on all sides. The sight goes straight to my heart and casts a direct and quiet spell. As I look, I have the sense of hearing an older, wise, and beautiful woman who is talking to me in a deep, level voice, and her every word brims with experience and emotion. At other times, it strikes me as a splendid tale that creates a mood, dense and straightforward, like the stories of Ivan Bunin or Katherine Mansfield, in which nothing happens, and yet so much has occurred; in which the pages are written, not from left to right, but in depth, a bottomless depth.[160] At such moments I stand for a while against the fence or under a tree, taking it all in, mind wandering, exposing whatever it is in us most susceptible to sound, color, the rays of the sun, smells, or a breeze. I turn into an instrument and allow myself to be played. There's no exaltation in this—it's a shower for the soul, just like a shower for the body, and I experience the same pleasure in them both. Each shower leaves me with the same magnificently intense feeling of life. Under a cold shower I always drink the water that whips me in the face; here—against the fence, under a tree—I drink life. All of us possess an inner gearbox, but few know how to use it. I discovered mine only a few months ago. At first I disengaged the rear gear and for rather a long while was stuck in one place, but then I began to engage the other gears. Now I ride in fourth, if not even in the so-called *Schnellgang*, or overdrive, which the great Mercedes are supposed to have. But perhaps I'm mistaken? Perhaps we don't ourselves shift gears or release the clutch? Perhaps it's fate that does it. Often an entire life is spent in search of one's true self—and without success. It's a lottery that has few winners. Worst of all perhaps is to keep missing the chance to be oneself, always expecting to hit the jackpot, which for everyone consists precisely of finding oneself. Only from that moment can one become a true prize also for others. This is the only true prize—the rest are not true. My notebook page has become damp from the mist and the copying pencil writes so clearly. All this because of those turkeys. They reminded me of the morning mail, of company directors, and of myself bowing obsequiously at the door. I had imagined I would find my true self there. What a misconception . . . Tragic! . . . Brr . . .

I did not find any milk, but no matter: we have our own, in powder. It's excellent. Around ten we set off again. An hour later we reach the edge of an elevated plateau and at our feet lies Vizille, deep in the valley below. The road is like a spiral back staircase: straight down from the seventh floor. I almost took a fall. The asphalt was freshly strewn with gravel that hadn't yet sunk into the tar. I braked at the bend and my rear wheel went into a controlled skid. The pebbles sprayed like snow and Tadzio emitted a piercing scream. We enter Vizille. The center is quiet and dignified—a Sunday mood. We drink beer and eat cakes. It's hot and languid. Only nine km to Uriage. We'll have to bathe and shave en route, to be in good form when we arrive at the Polish shelter. There will be

nothing but "nobility" there, for sure, and *noblesse oblige*. After careful ablutions outside Vizille, we don our Sunday best: white shorts, navy blue shirts.
Uriage is a small summer resort, villas, guesthouses—the lungs of Grenoble,
ten kilometers away. Forests and mountains. The Polish shelter is lodged in one
of the grand hotels. We don't head there straightaway. First we sit in the park,
cooling off, because the heat is tropical. Three women pass by: the older one
in a long gauze dress, the two young ones just as elegant. Their hands are full
of gracefully draped flowers. "A garland of lilies in her hair, / A green stalk in
her hand. / Before her skips a little lamb, / A butterfly skims the air . . ." (from
memory).[161] They are speaking Polish, of course. We bow and inquire about the
Polish Red Cross hotel.

"Here, immediately on the left—you are no doubt new pensioners. Welcome, welcome."

"No, we're just passing through. We want to visit some colleagues."

"Very well. And where in fact are you headed?"

"We're going to Paris. Returning, because there . . ."

"What? To Paris? To the Germans? Traitorrrrssss! Zosia, Helenka, come. We
have nothing to say to these gentlemen."

And they turned on their heels, "tiggling their wails."

Tadzio turned purple and whispered something about old ——— and that
we would very well see who was a traitor. I clenched my fists. Tadzio: "You see
how nicely you were welcomed? How warmly, in the Polish style, on the Red
Cross dime . . ." I tried to calm him down as best I could, preparing him for other
surprises. I've had a taste of these people before. In Paris, the colonel's wife was
forging coupons for free meals, and when I once caught her red-handed it had
no effect. Three days later she did it again and there was a scandal, because this
time I didn't give her a pass. Mrs. X stole mandarins, Mrs. Y maintained that
once again she had wasted money in the metro, because all there was for dinner today was blood sausage. "You should warn me when we're going to have
blood sausage." "By phone or by pneumatique?" I asked ironically. She got the
point. At the same time, I was embarrassed in front of Tadzio. After all this is
my family.

At last we reached the hotel. Reminded me of a guesthouse in Zakopane.[162]
Besides our three colleagues from Carcassonne, there were also a few engineers.
A self-important, pompous crowd, decked out in stiff collars, spiffy clothing—in
a word, all very refined. Our two colleagues from Carcassonne, C. and S., barely
bothered to greet us and quickly made themselves scarce, because they were
supposed to play bridge with Mr. Director and Mr. Consul, who were already
waiting for them in the lounge. Only the amiable Stefan Hołuj was glad to see

us, helped us unload the bicycles, and promised to find us a room. Then he took us aside and began to unburden himself: "You have no idea what kind of gang this is. Here, where everyone is supposed to try to get along, where every-one is supposed to contribute something, instead they are constantly quarrel-ing. This entire intelligentsia, these directors, engineers, and so on, refuse, for example, to peel potatoes when it comes their turn and expect the workers or soldiers to do it. There's no one to serve at table, because our LADIES do not want their daughters doing THIS KIND of thing, because they are NOT housemaids, but GIRLS FROM GOOD HOMES, and as a result we are served at table by male VOLUNTEERS, while these 'girls from good homes' don't lift a finger. The upper crust goes on outings, plays volleyball and bridge until the wee hours. When I came to table once in my windbreaker, I was told I should wear a jacket to din-ner. But, you know, I lost all my things in the escape from Paris," Stefan con-tinued. "To be admitted to this shelter one needs connections, because it's not that easy to get a place. The decisions are made by various P.R.C. directors in Vichy, Lyon, and Toulouse. And all this is witnessed by the people who, above and beyond their normal duties, are told to peel potatoes because they are only commoners, not somebodies. But *à propos*—you'd better change clothes and stop parading around in shorts, because 'it's just not done' and may antagonize the shelter director."

This in short is the picture drawn for us by Stefan, a real engineer and also a human being. I replied that I had intended to rest here for two days, but in view of what he had said we would push on tomorrow. I was furious. No—people like this must disappear. They should be wiped out by some kind of insecticide or antibedbug spray. They've learned nothing; now living off the public dole, they continue to puff themselves up, noses in the air, are high-handed with people "of low station," and despise the "dirty work" in the kitchen. The ladies, the "girls from good homes," a cigarette between their teeth, all dolled up, playing volley-ball, flirting, taking strolls. How much more respect do I have for *ces demoiselles* from the not very good houses of Paris . . . A bridge-crazed, vacuous, insensitive, indecent horde. Peering down at them from Stefan's window, I suddenly had the urge to drop a few flowerpots on their heads. I sense that Stefan is as em-barrassed now as I was a while ago, when I was calming Tadzio. They sit around down there, play cards, and each one is likely to utter the perennial "What have we come to." That's it exactly: you've come to nothing and won't ever amount to a thing. Not with that attitude.

After much hemming and hawing they gave us a room—only because Stefan persisted. This involved much convincing and many questions about "who are they," and after determining that we were "this kind" (at least I was; and what if

I had been "that other kind"), the sponsor acting as director gave his consent. Stefan intended also to request supper, but I renounced that pleasure. Tadzio and I went to a restaurant. We returned in the evening. The lights were on in the hotel Basset, bridge was being played, the LADIES were strolling in the garden with the YOUNG PEOPLE, we were looked at askance. I had the urge to invite them to kiss my —— but only through a rose petal from the flower bed. And who knows whether there might not have been quite a few takers, if I had promised a hundred francs a peck. Because money is what they love and they'll do a lot to get it. Naturally, all on the hush-hush and oh so refined—so that no one knows about it.

September 23, 1940

We slept in a single, rather narrow bed and were uncomfortable. Tadzio swore and was ready in the middle of the night to go to the park and pitch the tent. In the morning we warmed some milk on the cooker and ate breakfast in Stefan's room. The day was sunny and hot. Right after breakfast we quickly began to pack our stuff, in order to clear out discreetly, on tiptoes. However, the word had got around among the blasé Mister Consuls and Mister Directors and others of that ilk that we were on our way back to Paris. So, while yesterday no one paid us the slightest attention or extended the slightest welcome (to us traitors), today every two minutes someone or other took me aside, introduced himself like a young man inviting a young miss to join him in a dance, was saccharine and officious, apologized "for presuming," in a word all sweetness and light: "Excuse me, would you be so kind. My wife and I left Paris with only a small traveling bag, but our two suitcases remained at the hotel. Here's the address and my authorization. Perhaps you'll be able to send them on to me here." Or: "You know, I left my pelisse and my wife's Persian lamb with the concierge of my building" (he slips me a piece of paper he had already prepared with the address). So I should have them sent. Another took me aside and after insisting emphatically that "you surely can't refuse me—oh, sorry, I forgot to introduce myself—I'm the consul from . . ." (Stuff it where the moon doesn't shine.) "It's just that I have a car here (*tiens, tiens*) and I'd like to sell it but I need proof of purchase. I bought it from a Monsieur M.—a Frenchman (but when?)—he lives on *rue* . . . he'll give you the document and you'll send it to me . . ." Business deals, shady deals, "you must handle this for me, I'm broke, and you've seen the conditions we live in here." I gazed indifferently at the mountains, I thought of the beneficent institution of the Tarpeian Rock[163] and answered drily that conditions here were altogether tolerable and I only hoped they didn't get worse.

All the while I wondered whether they had any idea at all of what it meant to be in difficult circumstances. In the end, Tadzio loaded both our bicycles himself, because they kept taking me aside in turn, pleading, naturally in secret from the others. One who began with the words "I knew your uncle very well" was struck dumb when I answered, "and, so what?" He lost the thread entirely. I know I was mean-spirited, but I refused all of them: transporting anything across the demarcation line was forbidden, and I myself had many compromising things (the notebook—how would I get that across?). I'm very sorry, but I must refuse. If one of them had approached me and said simply: "You know, after all it's not so terrible here, but I would like to do something nice for my wife—she was so fond of her foxes . . . If you could possibly, I would be very grateful, but if not, then never mind . . . ," I would have arranged it without hesitation. But they believed others were obligated to run risks on their behalf, because they ARE still somebodies and don't want to recognize that they once WERE but no longer ARE. You must do it for him, he counts on it, for besides the dollars he already has and the handouts from the P.R.C., it would increase his reserves. He could spend another three months smoking Chesterfields, having his linens washed, mooching and living off the Red Cross, while using private funds to keep up "appearances," playing the master and bridge, bringing suits in defense of honor, which he has not a whit of himself. If being natural is just a pose, as Wilde says, it's at least the most natural of poses. That pose is lacking in everything we do. People do not like us, they often simply cannot stand us, precisely because we do not have it.

They finally let go and I'm almost certain they will now show off to each other. "He refused you? To me, he promised to see to it . . ." And each will feel a step up in the ranks. The shelter reminded me of Saint Helena. Except that on Saint Helena there was only one Napoleon, plus two ladies and a dozen courtiers, all at each other's throats, while here every man is a Napoleon, nothing less. And just like Napoleon, each one constantly returns to his own Waterloo and imagines being victorious in the battle he irrevocably lost. Who knows whether they hadn't made me out to be a Gestapo agent. For if you don't give him a hand, and you don't "accommodate" him (that's one of the basest, most repulsive words), he'll just as soon dump a bucket of dirty water on your head. We leave the place with a feeling of great relief.

After half an hour's ride in the valley, we enter the outskirts of Grenoble. The regulations against selling food without coupons are becoming increasingly strict, and in this *département* (Isère) they are being applied as of yesterday with absolute ruthlessness. That's why I had to earn every morsel of food I purchased before we entered Grenoble by eloquence, jokes, and banter. I succeeded and even conjured up two bars of chocolate, which officially no longer exist at all. Grenoble is a nice city, surrounded by mountains. Pleasant boulevards along the Isère. I would love to return to being a student and study in Grenoble. We took a little ride around town, smoked a cigarette each on a bench near the river, and moved on. As we were leaving town a gendarme checked our papers. Irritated by our stay in Uriage, Tadzio addressed a long speech to the authorities while digging in his wallet. Naturally, in Polish. He began, no problem, OK. Then, in Polish: "I'll show you those *papie*. Watch out, so I don't show you something else, you bit player from a cheap detective novel. Instead of traveling in peace, a person is obliged for the sake of this horse's ass to spill the guts from his wallet and watch how this stick from the provinces is impressed to see folks traveling to Paris. Here, read, you lousy pain in the butt!"—and sticks all his papers under the guy's nose. I can hardly contain my laughter, all the more so since the gendarme replies to Tadzio's every third word with an offhand *oui* and takes the entire bouquet of Warsaw epithets for explanations. He bids us a pleasant *bon voyage*. Tadzio continues to grumble and overall can't get the episode of the shelter out of his system. He's in a bad mood. Doesn't say a word. Later, he rides up to me.

"If you one day became a minister, would you still call me by my first name and allow me to address you the same way?"

I admit, I was taken aback and for a moment was silent.

"First of all I will never become a minister."

"Why not? After all, you're well educated. You could be . . ."

"Leave off. Do you know what politics is about? A certain great French writer, Paul Valéry, said that in the first place politics depends on preventing people from getting involved in what concerns them, and then on forcing them to decide about things they don't understand. Leave me alone."

Tadzio laughs. The French *esprit* has the virtue of being understood by Tadzios all over the world. But he doesn't give up.

"But if you were a minister, would you call me by my first name and would I be able to call you by yours?"

"Yes, probably, yes." (I like to be frank with myself and I feel all the same that I'm not entirely certain. So I throw in that "probably," aware at this moment of how powerfully, despite everything, we are shaped by our social class.)

"But did you notice how the engineers from our factory looked at you when I called you by your first name?"

I had noticed nothing, but I understand that Tadzio was bound to notice.

"I didn't notice, but you surely know it doesn't bother me a bit."

"I was worried that you were upset, and in fact there in the shelter I wanted to call you Mr. Bobkowski. Except that by now I'm no longer used to it. Jędruś, tell me: Were you upset?"

"Not in the least; and I assure you, if you had, I'd have bopped you in the kisser just to remind you 'who's who.'"

Right after Grenoble we encounter the first signpost saying, "Paris—550 km." Getting close. We eat beside the post. We are exhausted and have no desire to keep on pedaling. The road is once again mountainous. A dozen kilometers before Les Abrets we pitch the tent in a thick little wood, making a mattress out of dry leaves. There's a farm nearby and toward evening I go there for water. The sky is overcast, but it's warm. Total silence. The creak of the farm gate is so loud that inadvertently I started. In the hut the kerosene lamp is already burning and in its light the heads of two little children bend over their homework. They scribble assiduously in their notebooks and squeak with their pens. Their mother greeted me with a calm *bon soir, monsieur,* as though I were an old acquaintance. Turning to the children—"Say good evening to the gentleman." The little boy and girl rose, gazed at me with great eyes straight from Mariette Lydis's portraits of children, said *bon soir, monsieur,* and sat back down.[164] Seeing that I was wearing shorts, the *patronne* brought me four eggs and milk, without any questions. She is young, pretty, and speaks in a calm, melancholy voice, as even as the ticking of a clock. Her husband is a prisoner of war, she's alone on the farm. She also gives me a full pail of water. I'll return the pail in the morning. It's already almost dark, the well creaks, the woman speaks softly and monotonously, she is pretty and sad, like the evening. I want to stop feeling, stop thinking, to be the silence, like everything all around.

Slowly I return to our little wood. Tadzio bustles about, singing under his breath. We prepare supper. From time to time a startled bird flutters in the trees, an insect crawling in the dry leaves makes a noise that can be heard for ten meters all around; the water in the pot begins to sing.

Bourg, September 24, 1940

The weather seems to be holding up. We have another hundred km to Bourg and could actually still make it today. We speed up to an average eighteen km/hr. and pedal like mad. Despite the sunshine and good weather, the region is already completely different. It's not hot, not as bright, the colors are different. We feel like we've crossed the French equator: the south has ended and that other France has begun—chilly and damp. The grapes are sour and the wine harvest has not yet begun. Floating over the fields, in the air, everywhere, there's already an autumnal sadness, which I did not feel in the south. The Alps, visible on the right, recede and vanish in the fog.

By tomorrow we may already be in Chalon and we are filled with emotion.[165] Will the Germans let us through or not? Tadzio predicts that all will go well: "What do they care about two guys like us. You'll sprechy a bit with them, we'll bow politely and say 'nach Parisch . . .' and they'll certainly let us pass." Around one in the afternoon the day became gray and overcast. We eat by the roadside, white grapes for dessert, sour as vinegar. In general, everything feels somewhat sour, chilly, and damp. The road is monotonous. After lunch full speed ahead. Along the way a well-dressed young fellow attaches himself to us and keeps close behind Tadzio's rear wheel. On the ascents, thanks to his gears, he passes us by, but on the level we overtake him and he resumes his spot on our tail. We decide to wear him out and pick up the pace. He rides up to me and says, "You're really making time, even with all that baggage." I start to talk with him and explain where we've come from. He was visiting his grandparents in the countryside and is returning now to Bourg. He tells me that two weeks ago he passed his baccalaureate exam and now wants to study for an advanced degree in forestry. An intelligent fellow from the French bourgeoisie. I question him on the subjects of the test, on Latin and Greek. "Did you have Tacitus, what about Livy?"

"So you passed your baccalaureate, too?" he asks, rather astonished.

I say, not only my baccalaureate but *études supérieures* as well. He became even more animated. We discuss his baccalaureate now with the shared knowledge of what's involved. He tells me the theme in history was very topical, probably dictated by the occupiers: "England's role in the ambitions of Napoleon." The point was to prove that Napoleon wanted to unite all of Europe, but England—awful, perfidious England—would not allow it. He confesses that they are all rather nervous, because they described England as the only country, thanks to its tenacious sangfroid and resolve, that managed to resist Napoleon and defeat him in the final match. I haven't been reading the newspapers or listening to the radio. At the moment it appears the Germans are bombing the English day after day, night after night, and the fellow tells me excitedly about their splendid determination. This really is war. We wonder if Napoleon actually wanted to create some kind of pan-Europe under the French scepter and when precisely the idea occurred to him. Certainly not at first, when things were just starting "to go his way," but only later, when the successive conquests and subjugation of other nations had to be draped in the trappings of a higher purpose—an ideal. Until now Hitler has said nothing about Europe; he speaks constantly about the eighty million Germans who need *Lebensraum*. When will he begin speaking about Europe and turn from a materialist into an idealist? Perhaps Napoleon really had such a plan? Maybe, but he started the war with Russia and that was his ruin. He made a stupendous blunder, which Hitler is unlikely to repeat. I remind him, however, that Napoleon in the beginning nevertheless met with Czar Alexander I on the Neman and everything was going well.[166] The trouble began only later. *Peut-être que maintenant ça va changer aussi; on sait jamais.*[167] We laugh. I ask him what he thinks of General de Gaulle. "He alone salvages our honor in the eyes of the world." And Pétain? I ask. "He's trying to save the nation." The French work double shifts. Having their cake and eating it, too. I won't pursue the subject with him. I don't get this type of reasoning. We fall back on Livy and Tacitus, Horace and Ovid, and finally on French literature. He is delighted to discover how much I have read. I inform him that every Pole with the least bit of education often knows French literature better than German, that almost all of Balzac exists in Polish translation. I explain the influence of French culture on Polish culture. He listens avidly. "It's curious, how little the French know about Poland." I don't mince words: France has spent too much time admiring her own greatness, she has not progressed, has failed to produce an enterprising youth that also has ideals, she has neglected economic and social issues, and has rested on her laurels. She has not managed, either in space or time, to occupy the position she aspired to. And she has collapsed. He saw the truth in what I said, but since he intends to study forestry and agriculture, he went on about that. He told me something interesting: it's now been estimated that France has lost roughly three hundred thousand horses in the war. "The soldiers neglected them," he says. "The horses were requisitioned whether they were needed or not, they were rounded up, and in the end the animals died, done in by hunger, the sun, and thirst. What will be used now to plough and thresh? There'll be famine."

As though to illustrate our conversation, we pass through a small village and are forced onto the shoulder, because the road is occupied — by threshing. They don't have threshing floors in the barns, so they use the asphalt road for threshing. They lay the sheaves across the road and pound with their flails. Rather inexpertly. The women stand alongside with brooms and scoops and after the sheaves have been threshed they sweep up the grain from the asphalt. The student says: "You see, this is how threshing is done everywhere now, and when a car comes along, it has to drive around, because the peasants don't budge. Admittedly, the Germans are supposed to provide two thousand tons of diesel to run the threshing machines and tractors, but what does that amount to? So, the coming year in France will be hard . . ." He asks me where we plan to spend the night. I tell him, under a tent. He offers in that case to take us to a park near the entrance to Bourg, which is designed specifically for camping. He'll put in a word and we'll be able to use it. During the summer season the park is used for camping by the *Éclaireurs* (a scouting organization) traveling through Bourg. The space is at the moment rented by the *Éclaireurs* of Bourg and has been prepared especially for them. I accept with pleasure.

Toward evening we arrive at the place. After introducing us to the caretaker of the park, who is also the owner of the adjoining farm, the young man bid us good-bye and promised to look in on us in the morning before we left. He was indeed pleasant, sturdy, imbued with the fellow feeling of a sportsman and a sense of disinterested camaraderie. The park is in fact a wide avenue lined with chestnut trees. At the end is a small shed for the WC, with a few washrooms and showers. Simple and functional. Farther on is a concrete trash bin, covered, of course. Aside from sleeping in tents, it's like a hotel. We pitched our tent under one of the trees. The caretaker brought us some straw and—an electric light-bulb attached to a long cord. He hung the bulb on the front tentpole and drew the cord behind a tree. Soon the bulb lit up. "Please turn it off for the night—*bonne nuit.*" We were speechless with astonishment. Finally, in a voice almost trembling with emotion, Tadzio whispered: "Jędruś—that's culture for you . . ."

"That's not culture, it's civilization," I answer. Tadzio falls silent and suddenly explodes:

"In that case what is culture and what is civilization? You're constantly going on about it but what's the difference? I don't understand."

I scratch my head.

"Listen, the electric bulb attached to the tent, this park with its trash bin, washrooms, and privy, that's civilization. Whereas, when we know how to use all this in the proper fashion, when we don't steal the lightbulb or tie up our bag-gage with the wire, when we don't do our business in the woods, when we don't dismantle the outhouse for firewood, and when the next morning we leave with-out quarreling with the caretaker and say good-bye without smacking him in the kisser, that will be CULTURE. Civilization and culture, it's like the password and the countersign in military training. They answer each other. One without the other is incomplete. As with nuts and bolts, both needed in order to make anything, affixing or attaching. It would also be culture in the next, higher de-gree, if right now, by the light of this bulb, I were to lecture you on the history of illumination in general, on the role of illumination in the culture of nations. Did you know that illumination was one of the most difficult problems for the high civilizations of the ancient world to solve? Something was always giving off smoke, and, for example, after the evening feasts the splendid Roman villas resembled chimneyless peasant huts. The walls were blackened by smoke and special slaves had to clean them every time. Tadzio, do you finally understand the difference between culture and civilization?"

"You'll see right away that I've got it."

The evening is foggy and damp. From time to time a drop of fog falls from the withered, autumnal leaves of the chestnut trees and plays an autumnal tom-

tom on the drum of our tent. It's cold and dreary. We dress warmly and go into town for mulled wine. Before leaving I stop by the caretaker to tell him we're going out for a while and ask him not to lock the gate. Tadzio bows and says in advance: "Merci Messie." Then winks in my direction: "That's culture, right?" "You got it." The roadside bistro is empty and ill-lit, there are bottles on the shelves and the counter, and behind it the fat *patron* is pouring something through a funnel. The interior of a medieval alchemist's workshop. Silence, the faint noise of glass clinking. The sound of the cat, sitting on a bench, scratching itself as fast as a small two-stroke engine. It starts up and dies down. We drink rum because he offered us wine with saccharine. There, behind the dark windows, there's nothing. A bistro from the other world, a tavern from beyond the grave. My damp cigarette burns inside its tube with a "covered" fire. We pay. The gate creaked, the *patron* leaned out the window. "*Qui va là?*" "*C'est nous.*" "*Ah, bien, bien. On aura de la pluie cette nuit.*"[168] We turn on the light. Tadzio opens a can of beans and a can of meat, takes the flashlight, and goes out. I hear him opening the cover of the trash bin and tossing the empty cans. He returns and crawls into the tent. "That's culture, right?" I laugh. "You see, I've got it." After supper we go wash up and lie down to sleep. At that moment the rain begins to drum on the roof of the tent. At first a few powerful knocks—boom, boom, boom—then an entire orchestra. Autumn is marching to the beat. It's the first rain since September 6. We had forgotten that such an atmospheric phenomenon exists.

"Tadzio, are you sleeping?"

"No, what's up?"

"Tadzio, do you remember how you were asking me back there, already in Gruissan, what in fact is happening on this earth?"

"I remember, what of it?"

"Tadzio, the world has issued a password but fewer and fewer people know the countersign. The world issued the password of civilization, but it doesn't teach people the countersign of culture. It has built and wants to keep building parks with electric lighting, but it teaches people nothing else besides; it doesn't teach them respect for anything. Do you understand me?"

"And how! Plus, they bop all those 'janitors' a good one in the kisser. Don't worry, I get it . . . If only it doesn't leak on us tonight . . ."

The rain is drumming, now harder, now softer, from time to time a large drop falls from the tree and knocks loudly. Autumn—we had also forgotten about that, down there in the south.

Stables in Chalon, September 25, 1940

All night long it poured. I woke several times, checked to see if there were any leaks, but finding everything dry and the tent holding up, I fell back to sleep. In the morning the rain did not let up. It lashed away, relentless and unremitting. We each ate a piece of chocolate, smoked a cigarette, and fell asleep again. How marvelous it is to fall asleep when the rain drums on the roof, it's warm under the covers, one's eyes fall shut, and one's thoughts wander aimlessly, disappear, return, flee. We awoke for the second time around ten. It's pouring relentlessly. We eat "breakfast in bed." How are we going to ride? Tadzio didn't pursue the matter, turned over, and dropped off. I extracted my notebook from the backpack and began writing. After eleven our student came for a visit, soaked and splattered. He asked whether we needed anything and invited us to supper in case we didn't intend to leave today. "My parents will be delighted to meet you." He promised to stop by in the afternoon. At midday we keep on drinking and eat from sheer boredom. It's raining, the wind has come up, and it's gotten even colder. Tadzio yawned, curled into a ball, and dozed off. I kept writing. Not a drop gets into the tent—we have time. Suddenly Tadzio roused himself, sat up, and declared categorically: "Let's pull the plug—time to roll." I put away my notebook and we begin to consider what to wear and how to manage our departure. We'd be soaked to the bone no matter what. Despite the cold, we decided on shorts and shirts, over that sweaters, then the waterproof windbreakers. We packed up everything in the tent, took our things and the bicycles over to the farm, folded up the tent, and finished the rest of the packing in the barn. It kept on pouring. Tadzio swore like a sailor. Around two we rolled out onto the road. Bourg resembled a dirty courtyard on a rainy day. Mud in the streets, gutters spouting in wide arcs, people scurrying along. Once out of town we set a fast pace, to warm ourselves up. The rain tapered off, our legs were spattered in mud up to the waist. We pedal like crazy—we still want to hit Chalon today and make it across the demarcation line. Will they let us past or not? The Germans! Tadzio says: "All year I've been avoiding them and now of my own free will I'm headed in their direction." We are both on edge. Our pace is so insane that it's only five when we enter Chalon, or rather the outskirts. Here the *zone libre* is separated from the *zone occupée* by the Saône River. German sentinels stand at the entrance to the bridge, which is blocked by a barrier. My heart is racing. We come rushing up and suddenly hit the brakes. I almost plow into a broad, gray-green chest topped by a heavy helmet. Legs in combat boots spread in the weighty pose of a Roman legionnaire. It's the first time I've laid eyes on them "since then." The soldier standing before me seems a mighty and powerful apparition. I take out my *sauf-conduit* and present it. He looks, looks again—waves and barks sharply, like the catch on a rifle: "*Nein!*" "*Non,*" he adds in French. "*Warum?*" I ask. Then quickly, I say inwardly, to myself, "oh, hell." "Why" is a word from that other world, from that other age, a word that has been proscribed. Here questions are no longer permitted; here only listening is permitted. The soldier is not prepared for such questions.

"*Haben Sie so einen Ausweis?*"[169] He shows me the pass that was issued to some Frenchman by the Kommandantur at Chalon. I try to explain that my pass is no less valid. The German words and sentences emerge ever more fluently from my constricted throat. "Minna von Barnhelm" would have been proud . . . But Tadzio now took the floor and wouldn't let me finish. He gestured dismissively and blurts out in Polish: "Why are you talking with such a souse (?). Go sprech a little with the stripes—there's a corporal over there, the one with the bayonet at his side."

The corporal took a look and gave a sharp bark:

"*Morgen, kommen Sie morgen früh. Heute ist's zu spät!*"[170]

We had reached the barrier, sweaty and drenched. Now our teeth are chattering with the cold. We turn back and pass alongside the French barrier. A gendarme is standing there and laughs at us.

"So they didn't let you through, just wait, today it's raining, so they're not letting anyone through. If tomorrow is sunny, they'll let you go. Sometimes they let people through, sometimes they don't—*on sait jamais de quoi ça dépend; de l'humeur des officiers sans doute . . .*[171] You can stay in the stables over there and wait until their mood changes. Some others in the same situation are already there."

He accompanies us to the stables, pushes open the door, and cries gaily: "*Messieurs, je vous présente de nouveaux locataires!*"[172]

The company in the stables play a welcoming fanfare with their penknives made of tins and sound off in unison: "*Salut, camarades.*" They approach us, introduce themselves, press our "mitts," like old pals. They point to a couple of vacant spots on the straw: "Hang your things on the hooks, or the rats will chew up everything during the night."

A few demobilized soldiers, a teenage boy with a squeaky voice, naive and cheerful. The gendarme lets them know who's been let through today, who hasn't, and why—"Oh, the two Poles were not allowed, because they don't like Poles." They all question us about what we've been told, and each one forms his own conclusions and opinions based on our case. One is waiting for additional papers, another has an aunt who has already applied for a permit which she is supposed to send him here, a third has nothing at all and tries five times a day to get across—until he finally succeeds. Everyone has something up his sleeve.

They seek advice from the gendarme, who instead of minding the barrier spends his time sitting in the stables, only jumping up once in a while: *"Il faut que je jette un coup d'oeil pour voir s'il n'y a pas de clients."*[173] In short, they are all in good humor: one is humming, three are kicking a ball around, others are playing belote with something that was once cards. Someone returned from town and affirms that sausage can be found in such and such a place and across the way there is also jam. Above it all, the squeaky voice of the young boy, an apprentice locksmith (*un apprenti*), who spouts endless silliness with a serious face, naively believes everything he hears, and would much rather be visiting his aunt in rue des Martyrs, eating "a nice plate of beans" (*un beau plat de haricots*). We instantly hit it off, because rue des Martyrs is my *quartier*, and a Parisian *quartier* is a city unto itself. Local patriotism above all else. Right away we discover shops we both frequent, we gossip about the familiar *épiciers*, we make fun of the tradeswoman selling sea urchins on rue Saint-Lazare, who screams at the top of her lungs: *"Allez-y, allez-y, très bon pour la toilette intime! — Tu la connais? — Ah, dis donc . . ."*[174] I see my balcony, high up among the chimneys, a flowerpot with a bunch of anemones and a bright dress. Seventh heaven. My throat tightens and it's hard to breathe. *Ah, dis donc . . . tu sais, Paris . . .*[175]

We change our clothes. We hang our things on hooks under the ceiling, turn over the straw, and start fixing supper. The downpour doesn't let up and the cold becomes more and more penetrating. We open a large can of pickled cabbage with sausages and heat it up. Hot wine. I shared the cabbage with the young boy, because the poor guy had no money and was eating dry bread for supper. He was touched, and everyone pronounced on how well we were equipped and observed that we clearly knew a thing or two about sports. "If you stay with us any longer, you'll see that it's fun around here."

The stables and the German barrier with its grim Fritzes in heavy helmets. Amid the jokes and songs of the people here, the other side seems like a gray prison wall. I lie on the straw wrapped in a blanket and sense two different worlds side by side. Almost at arm's length . . . And yet again, for the umpteenth time, I think about France. Say what you will, France has a certain special SOMETHING. It's the remains of something that once was—and that's perhaps what's so sad. What others sensed, what they unconsciously yearned for, the French managed to embody and display in a form that was clear and intelligible to EVERYONE, full of life. They didn't want any "supermen"—they wanted human beings and perhaps for that reason their influence went so deep and so profoundly transformed world culture. Later the momentum kept them going. The last war drained them. What did they give the world after that war? A lot less than they imagined. Decay?

Everyone goes on about it but no one understands why everywhere the Germans strike, they are victorious. There's talk of incompetence, treason, unpreparedness; all well and good, but everyone today forgets that their criticism depends on a faulty standard: everything is measured against Germany. And clearly no country can be as well prepared. As though hypnotized, everyone has turned the values upside down and used Germany's strength as the measure of their own weakness. In fact Germany is an anomaly that has stunned the normal world. The normal world has proved to be rotten, disorganized, and ineffectual, as ineffectual as a naked person attacked by an armed drunkard or madman. Neither Poland nor France nor England could have succeeded against Germany and would not have succeeded had they been a hundred times better organized. For in order to have measured up and withstood Germany's assault, not only Poland, but the other countries as well, would have been obliged to adopt a way of life just as abnormal and distorted as life in Germany, to have accepted the same unbending idea and subordinated everything else to it. And beginning much earlier. The last World War was a conflict between opponents; today it's two worlds that have collided, two religions. But the world of Germany cannot be considered normal, cannot be used as a standard. Today England will get the better of Germany only when she herself adopts the same methods and means, and perhaps also part of the same worldview. Napoleon . . . And I am almost certain that although the Germans will lose the war, many of the ideas derived from their view of the world, both economic and social, will penetrate throughout Europe, as did the Napoleonic ideas spread by HIS war. Today I see with perfect clarity that the world could not have beaten the Germans, for the simple reason that it was that other, old world of FREEDOM. The world of freedom, of the laws of freedom — often also harsh — could not have resisted a well-organized slave. I justify that old world here, on the straw, in these dirty stables, because I am listening to songs and jokes that could only have been produced by freedom of expression, of thought, and of opinion, by the lack of discipline and self-control, the lack of persistence. We are paying the price for all of that, the entire world is paying, because, though perhaps in appearance only, it was nevertheless governed by the idea of the human being of flesh and bones, not the idea of a creature sacrificing itself for the good of the so-called future generations and for greatness, for utopia. If that old world did not offer true freedom, it at least provided the illusion of it. The new world does not even provide illusions . . . I curl up under the blanket, because suddenly with terrifying clarity I see that the Germans are upending all ideas, all values. Until now we have believed in the power and superiority of the free man — the Germans have already taught us, have drummed into our heads, the idea that only the slave is capable of genuine effort, that he ALONE can in fact build and create. The Germans do us more damage from within than from without. The results can be monstrous. And at moments when my mind gets covered in goose bumps, I hum to myself the waltz from Gounod's *Faust*. In my mind I am also on the border, in my thoughts I also sense the demarcation line. Suddenly I again see Miss Dora's thin, shaven, ginger-colored eyebrows. The German words pour out, form sentences, fall with the rhythm of raindrops outside the wall. Memories, dreamy and blurred. Meaning? The helmets? There, in the Congo jungle, on the banks of some river, Leo Frobenius recalled a strange termite mound.[176] A high cone, topped by an exquisite dome, crisscrossed by corridors and arteries, in which tiny ants moved with a rhythmic sound. Quietly and calmly. Except that every four weeks the peace would suddenly shatter. The interior would emit rumbling sounds, as though from the muffled bursts of an explosion. Until one day the surface of the mound would crumble, the canals would be exposed, and thousands of yellowish corpses would scatter in the red earth of the ruins. The dome would explode. At night, in the light of the lamp, you would be able to see the young generation of the same species of termites, which had emerged from the bottom layers of the mound, as it murdered and destroyed everything on top. The following night the new generation would clean up the corpses and the debris, create their own order, and once again a period of quiet and calm would begin . . . Why did he begin the book, the title of which I no longer remember, with precisely this scene? *"Fräulein Dora, was meinte er?"* Fräulein Dora drew a cigarette from her handbag, listened to be certain no one was coming, and quickly offered me one. Then her gritty voice continued, breaking from time to time: *"Als höchste Ordungsform der Menschen wird heute von den Deutschen der Staat betrachtet. Nach der Hegelschen Philosophie war er der höchste Wert auf Erden und verpflichtete als solcher die Menschen, sich ihm bis zur Aufopferung des Lebens hinzugeben . . ."*

"Fräulein Dora, diese Wertung ist falsch. Das ist faaaaalsch, das ist ein Wahnsinn!! . . ."[177]

In the dark night the rain splashes, the wind sends the water streaming down the wall and bangs the door. I lie under the blanket, contracted like a caterpillar pierced by a pin, twisting and turning, unable to sleep. Except that something keeps dancing to the rhythm of the waltz from *Faust*.

September 26, 1940

We had to get up earlier because the clocks on the other side are set an hour ahead, to agree with German time. It's by that reckoning that the officers "officiate" on "the border." The rain has stopped, but the day is cold and dreary. We fix coffee, feed the young boy. Then pack up. Despite the cold we decide again to wear shorts, because it's easier to ride that way. Around nine we're ready and we make our way to the German barrier, forty meters away. Our pals stand together on the threshold and send us off with a *bon passage* for the occasion. They are as anxious as we are. Will they let us through, or will we be returning to them again? I'm tense and feel a kind of heartburn; also revulsion. I would like to have all this as quickly as possible behind me. We approach the barrier.

Three officers are standing there, in gray leather coats, with gloves on. The soldiers and a noncom process people passing through and only the suspicious cases are decided by the officers. We show the noncom our French identity papers and our *sauf-conduit*; he looks, collects the documents, and with a salute hands them to the officer. Two others also showed an interest and gather round us. The officer reads and says in broken French:

"*Vous êtes réfugiés?*"[178] He reads the information on my *carte d'identité* and suddenly smiles. "*Wo sind Sie geboren?*"[179] he asks suddenly in German. I am terribly nervous and automatically answer in German. I answer—also purely mechanically, not thinking at all, with the old joke:

"*In Wien bei Wiener-Neustadt!*" My expression is serious and I immediately clench my teeth. The officers burst out laughing, German-style, beery and ponderous. Ha, ha, ha . . .

"*In Wiener-Neustadt bei Wien*"—he corrects me—ha, ha, ha—"*Anton, er ist doch dein Landsmann . . .*"[180]

Anton has a narrow face and smiles sourly. The Austrian certainly interprets this as spiteful on the German's part. Some little joke, some dig. Friendly chatter. What makes me Polish? I explain in a nutshell. The German takes the wallet from my hand and begins to remove everything and inspect it. He comes upon the photo of my father in uniform, with the rank of colonel to boot. He shows it to the other one and is delighted. "*Was für ein netter Kerl . . .*"[181] My fists clench of their own accord and I swallow a lot of saliva. More talk. Where have we come from, how long have we been traveling. Now they laugh appreciatively, impressed with our itinerary. They ask what we have in our bundles, whether we don't have weapons or foreign currency. My notebook is at the bottom of the backpack. I make a move, as if wanting immediately to unpack everything. "*Nein, nein—na, fahren Sie weiter.*"[182] Thinking this was it, I hold out my hand for our papers. But he passes them along to the officer, who accompanies us to a guardhouse at the other end of the bridge. We say nothing and despite my anxiety I begin to recall the little poem by Heinrich Heine addressed to the customs officers. The worst is what I smuggle in my mind . . .[183]

"*Warten Sie ein Moment.*"[184] We wait. We prop the bicycles against the wall of the guardhouse. Soon a noncom admits us. What more do they want? We enter. Tadzio, as brazen as can be, slurring a bit, says: "Gut-Mugging" and bows.

Then nudges me and in a barely audible whisper: "Lord Jesus—Gestapo." Two uniformed men are sitting at a little table. They answer cordially, "*Gut' Morgen.*"[185] They are holding our documents in their hands and reading. Then they open a fat ledger—we notice a list of names. Typed—how else?—*Ordnung muss sein.*[186] They run their thick fingers over the pages. They whisper something to each other. They return our papers.

"*Na, da könnt Ihr weiter fahren. Warum kehren Sie nach Paris zurück?*"[187] I explain that my wife is there, that I've left her without means of support, and that it's now been four months since I've seen her. One of them smiles sadly:

"I haven't seen my wife now for thirteen months—*verstehen Sie*[188]—for thirteen months . . ."

I have a stupid expression on my face. An even greater surprise awaits me.

"If you want to take the train, go to the station in Chalon. At eleven the train leaves for Paris."

"Thank you very much; we'll continue by bicycle. It's only another three hundred kilometers—not much more to go . . ."

He smiled mischievously:

"*Sagt doch besser dass Ihr kein Geld habt um Euch die Eisenbahnkarte zu kaufen . . .*"[189] Here, take ten marks—and he draws the money from his wallet. If he had reached for the pistol lying on the table I would have been less astounded. An awkward situation, impossible.

"No, thank you, I cannot take it. We still have some money, but we WANT to continue by bicycle. We already have thirteen hundred kilometers under our belts and it would be unsporting now to go by train . . . ," I explain insistently.

"*Machen Sie doch keine G'schichten*"[190] (sometimes he uses the formal "*Sie*," sometimes the informal "*Ihr*"—usually when he's looking at Tadzio). "You can send me back the money when you get to Paris. I'm making you a loan."

"No, really, thanks a lot. You must understand us. It isn't sporting after thirteen hundred kilometers to clamber onto a train—*besonders dass wir weder krank noch müde sind . . .*"[191]

Laughing, he replaced the ten marks and they followed us out to the guardhouse. They patted the bicycles respectfully. I had impressed them. They observe us as we get going. We do so quickly and expertly. We enter Chalon. Tadzio looked back and proclaimed:

"There's a sweet one for you, that ugly mug. What were they up to?"

"Propaganda. Sand in our eyes. The point is that we're supposed to tell people in Paris how nice they are and how helpful. Any Frenchman would fall for it—but why play games with us? He knew very well that we're Polish. I don't get it."

We enter the street where the Kommandantur is located. We have to stop and wait, because at that moment the changing of the guard is beginning, solemn, an entire platoon. The soldiers emerge from the guardhouse, line up, a diminutive noncom steps to the side. There's a French expression for such types: "They're so small that when they fart they raise the dust from the ground." He issues an order, barks out a few sharp words, the soldiers are like automatons. Then a brief march in goose step. The hobnailed boots strike the paving stones, the tiny noncom leading the way. At every high step, the helmet quivers on his head, like a thimble balanced on a match. Hup, hup, hup — the hobnailed boots strike the paving stones of this small French town (as if someone were breaking my heart), the echo ringing against the walls of the old houses. — Halt! Silence. And once again, march. There's a poem by Rudyard Kipling — "Boots." I recall that every few lines the words "boots, boots, boots" are repeated rhythmically. I read it once, now I hear it for a second time, recited magnificently, in a language everyone understands, in the original, in the language of the most eloquent boots on earth and interpreted by true masters.[192] They can express themselves however they want: in truth they manage to speak their minds only with the stomping of boots, the pounding of hobnailed combat boots. Therein lies their soul, the true one, exposed. They are artists, the eighty million most talented composers of the music of boots.

I listened intently. Boots thud the same way in Oslo, in Copenhagen, in Warsaw, in Brussels, in Amsterdam. They resound everywhere. And where else will they be pounding? At the moment they are hammering the old stones of France. Is there a piece of my heart in every cobblestone? Now I truly feel how much I love France. I don't want to believe my eyes and the boots are crushing my heart. The changing of the guard ended and we continue on our way. The streets are full of soldiers. They walk around, window-shop, drink beer. They are neat and well dressed. The privates wear gloves. Well proportioned, athletic, and well fed. All Europe believed there was hunger in Germany; people laughed that they "are starting the war with ration cards." Now all the nations will be eating on coupons and the Germans will be stuffing themselves. The walls are plastered with large posters showing sinking ships and a drowning French sailor. The caption: "Remember Dakar." If only one could erase "Dakar" and insert "Toulon" . . . I grit my teeth.[193] We have entered a different country. That, after all, was the border. The weather suits the mood: the sky, the fields, the houses, and the uniforms — everything is *feldgrau*.[194] It is cold and relentlessly gray.

The day before yesterday we did a hundred km, yesterday eighty, and we're exhausted. The road is once again mountainous. The mood is so heavy that I dream of burrowing into the straw, of hiding somewhere in a barn, in order to withdraw into myself for a while. Every so often a German automobile or motorcycle flies past us, otherwise it's deserted and quiet. Here and there on the roadside are the remains of smashed automobiles, sometimes a French grave or a

German one with a helmet perched on the cross. The German graves are fenced in, well tended; people must be afraid to visit the French graves. The Germans do it for them. We see two soldiers who, after decorating their own gravestones, turn their attention to the French. *Anständige Buben—und so gut erzogen . . .*[195]

We're so thoroughly chilled that we stop in a village for a shot of rum. We drink a wineglass of rum each and drag ourselves onward. The cold gale lashes our bare legs. We decide to stop sleeping in the tent. A farmer's barn will be more comfortable and warmer. I wish I were already in Paris, but at the same time I am afraid of the return. To show up suddenly in this different Paris.

We had set our watches an hour ahead and we have a hard time getting used to it. It does violence to the sun, which until now had been our lord and master. At five in the afternoon we finally leave the road and head for a farm. The farmer is friendly and willing to let us bed down in the empty stables. Frozen to the bone and hungry, we settle onto the mounds of straw, wrapped in all our warm things. We hang the wet tent out to dry. The farmer came to the stables to shoot the breeze. I learned from him that a list has been ordered of the entire inventory of livestock and reserves of grain, potatoes, beans, peas, etc. He told me he had listed only half, because "I know very well what it's for." If they want to search, let them search . . . Père Grandet smiles craftily.[196] In the villages *ça ira*, but in the cities there will be hunger. Toward evening he left and promised to wake us in the morning. We eat supper and dive into the straw. Outside it is damp and cold. We had grown unused to the cold. Oh—the south . . . How good it was there. I understand how people who have discovered the south of France yearn for it the rest of their lives. I am already yearning.

September 27, 1940

The farmer woke us early in the morning and brought us half a pail of milk. Before breakfast we went to the well to wash properly, since the last time we washed was actually five days ago. The day promised to be sunny and a bit warmer, but in the morning everything was already suffused in the autumn fog. Pigeons cooed on the wet roof, while the lady of the house loudly berated the large cat, which had been up to some mischief during the night and was now performing a trapeze act on the wild grapevines over the door. We then talked about the farm. Feigning innocence, she asked whether I had any silver ten- or twenty-franc pieces, because she "collected" them. Numismatics is flourishing in the French village, as usual. I said I didn't have any. Certain laws of economics, if one can even speak about "laws" in economics (it is perhaps the science closest to meteorology: the weather will be nice, but it might rain), will always exist, despite all the "planned economies," the "closed circulation of money," and the intriguing studies of Pierson, Mises, and Barone.[197] In none of Enrico Barone's equations (ministry of production in a collectivist state) did I find the slightest trace of Père Grandet. Professor Lipiński was correct when he used to say in his splendid lectures that one must ALSO learn economics from Balzac.[198] I am curious to see whether France ends up with inflation. Every day of support for the occupying army costs the French 400 million francs, which is to say 12 billion a month, 144 billion a year. (That's what people were telling me along the way.) In order to manage that, the production of francs will have to expand. Père Grandet therefore "collects" silver. After which he'll go for dollars and gold; for louis d'or. Talking with the farmer I learned moreover that in a few days he expects to be allocated prisoners to work as laborers — French prisoners. The Germans have captured about two million Frenchmen (hard for me to believe). Some of these prisoners are kept in camps, in France. To spare themselves the bother of feeding them and quartering them for the winter, etc. — the Germans are assigning them to work for French farmers. The French prisoner will be working for a Frenchman, who will be personally responsible for him. My farmer scratched his head, grimaced, and declared he could not imagine it: "I, a Frenchman, was also in the army and the only reason I am not a prisoner is that I was good at escaping, and now I have to order around and treat like a hired hand this prisoner, who is also a Frenchman. I don't have the right to pay him, because he's a prisoner, and if he doesn't feel like doing any work for me, it will be hard to force him or complain about him, because he's a Frenchman. I'm obliged to feed him, because he's a prisoner assigned by the Kommandantur, and if he runs off home on me, I'm to answer for it." Indeed, it's a troublesome situation. It often seems to me that the French not only did not want to fight but didn't even want to run away. After breakfast we pack up and get going. It's a sunny day, but chilly.

We stopped in a village to buy some meat for the evening. I enter a little shop, get two nice cutlets and pay with a hundred-franc note. The *patronne* rummages in her cash register and offers me change in marks, which she extracts from the drawer with the aid of giant tweezers. In the blink of an eye I felt something rise up inside me and explode in wild laughter. She was getting hot under the collar:

"Am I supposed to hold THIS in my hand? This is money" — she waves some franc bills. "These calling cards of those *messieurs en gris-moisi*,[199] who have paid us a visit, these are not money at all!"

I stuck the three marks (sixty francs) in my pocket with the firm intention of getting rid of them at the first opportunity. It was France, my France, that spoke in those tweezers. They should give that shopkeeper the Legion of Honor someday—she should be the first to get it. I report this to Tadzio. He begins right off to sing: "For that's how it usually begins . . ."[200] Yes—it begins with this.

German divisions are quartered in all the villages. Automobiles and motorcycles roar along the roads. Powerful as they are, the troops seem to me somehow shoddy, like cheap toys. The feeling is absurd and impossible to justify. There's something cheap and tinny about this army. Tadzio notices the same thing, completely independent of me. Maybe it's simply the instinct for self-preservation—a kind of tweezers. Since there's no other way, then at least this. Now . . . Coupons for food are required everywhere, especially when it comes to bread and cheese I have to fight long and hard. Of course I always get them without coupons. In relation to the Germans, people hold their tongues, uneasy, disapproving. Yet one shopkeeper told me frankly that when it comes to armies, she prefers the Germans. "When our men retreated, they looted the shops and bistros, they beat up people who tried to stop them. The Germans could have taken everything; but though some people wanted to give them things for nothing, they refused and always paid. *Ils sont gentils, on ne peut rien dire . . .*"[201] I told her we would talk again, when the Germans began to withdraw . . . The area is becoming less and less interesting, more monotonous. We already think of our journey as something that's over. In one village there are German cavalry, in another tanks—lots of them everywhere. The men have already found themselves some girls and stroll with them in the streets. Tadzio, each time he sees one of these couples, goes on a rant as he passes by: "Ach, you sniveling slut, go ahead, keep going, and you'll end up . . . He'll give you what for up to here . . ."

If one could only think about the future in any way at all, to imagine what might happen even—but nothing, nothing, and nothing. To think about the past? No point. To think about tomorrow? How? With yesterday's categories? Nonsense. All that remains is the present moment. To simplify one's system of thinking even more and try to live—to endure and survive. But survive for what? Not clear.

The road is once again mountainous. We often walk, because our legs are tired. Even the toe clips no longer help. As we climb, we talk. We wonder what life in Paris will have to offer. We'll have to manage somehow. I have so often confronted the question "What next?" and so often failed to see anything ahead of me that I've finally gotten used to it; I don't get worked up and—I whistle. Suddenly we notice some motorcyclists in the road, guarding an automobile stopped farther along. The guards stop us. We stand still. The hood of the car is open and two soldiers are fixing something. Along the side of the road walks a fat individual in a bright overcoat, surrounded by several officers. I look and look again, remove my eyeglasses from the pocket of my backpack, put them on, and I can't believe my eyes. There, one hundred meters away, strolling past with his entourage, is Göring himself. Tadzio also looks, bends over: "Jędruś—I'll be damned—Gieryng!" Absolutely. No doubt about it. Tadzio claims the "Horch" has broken down and that this . . . (here there issues a stream of epithets, compared to which Pantagruel and Gargantua were babes in arms) is waiting for them to fix it. They try—the motor chortled. One of them runs and reports. Meanwhile the motorcyclists order us off the road into the ditch. We struggle, because the bicycles are heavy. Tadzio curses out loud. A pox on "Gieryng" . . . Soon the car passes us, still not going very fast. Yes, it's Göring. For a moment I see him five meters away. Dressed differently than the others. How is it that each of these great leaders must have his clown? Napoleon had Murat, but Murat came from the circus and it's hard to reproach him his ostrich feathers, leopard skin, and gold lamé.[202] It's amazing to observe how history is made before one's very eyes. How much of it will be manufactured in the next year or two or three? Because events are rushing along. The invention of the combustion engine and the increase in speed have resulted in the increasing speed of events. The history of the world brings to mind the short film in which the American comedian suddenly begins to hurry and after him the crowd. *Police*, with Charlie Chaplin.[203] It's been only a year. Tadzio keeps asking me how much longer it will be. I tell him that alas this is only the beginning—another two, three years, for sure. "And who will win?"—I declare it will be Stalin. He witnesses the growth of these two powers and is ready to be the third. Tadzio laughs and says I'm joking. A bit yes, a bit no. Besides I'm not the only one who thinks this way—that's what they're saying on the farms and in the shops. Clearly it's the fashion at the moment. It changes every month.

Toward evening we ride through Avallon. Troops everywhere, they sit in the bistros and sing their *Lieder*. By now there are also German women, probably officers' wives. They've already arrived. We pass by one such group getting into a car in high spirits. I now find German repulsive, although once I liked the language very much.

An old French town with a Romanesque church and *eine blonde Hure*,[204] laughing her head off, screaming at the top of her lungs under the advertisement for Pernod Fils. "*Rudi—da musst du mir aber eine Aufnahme machen!*"[205] I instantly recognize in myself all the impulses of a sexual murderer. What would I not have done to her . . . They make themselves at home. Tadzio is careless, letting fly at the top of his lungs: "Don't strut around here, damn it, buzz off to England to take your photos. There they'll snap you, in the snout and with a knife, you Swabian stumps (?) . . ."

I bought a pound of tomatoes and a pack of cigarettes and we hightailed it from Avallon. Anyway, we have to find a farm where we can spend the night, as the evening is again cold and damp. We still have two hundred km to Paris. We might make it tomorrow. The sun had already set when we inquire in a village if there's a farm where we can bed down. The fat *patron* of a roadside bistro gives us the address of old "Mère Marie," who "loves fellows like you and all the boy scouts always spend the night there."

"Mère Marie" turned out to be a cheerful old dame. Our *bonsoir* set her chirping and laughing. I regaled her with silliness and joked around, she was delighted. She ran about, wanted herself to bring the straw to the room she had set aside for us in the empty part of her house. She gave us a quilt and a pillow, warmed up some milk. She boasted to us that in June two generals had slept at her place, later a director of some large concern with the entire staff of secretaries and stenographers. She giggled impishly: "*Vous voyez,* they all slept together, *le directeur et les belles filles de Paris.*[206] Too bad you weren't there . . ." and smacked her lips. I hug her and clap her on the shoulder. The old girl seems to wish that everyone could sleep at her place. Altogether an echo of the bygone France of Anatole France and Alphonse Daudet.[207] We asked for a bucket of water. She would not allow us to fetch it for ourselves, but sent the shaggy, dirty Paulot off to the well. "This is MY prisoner, our prisoner, who was assigned to me as a laborer. He's from Paris—a big lazybones and doesn't want to do anything; all the ones from Paris are like this. Poor fellow, but I'll teach him how to work. Why should you fetch the water yourselves? All day long *il fume ses sales cigarettes et siffle ses chansons de Paris . . .*"[208] I gave this Paulot a few cigarettes. He confessed that Mère Marie goads him. In Paris he had been unemployed for the last ten years. I ask him what trade he practiced. It turns out he has a very particular craft: a pearl-driller. Those who make holes in pearls. The market in pearls had declined sharply, so he could not find work in his particular trade. And preferred to wait around for ten years, rather than learn some other one. They're like that. If their trade is "banging in nails," then for nothing in the world will they agree to pull them out, though they may spend their entire lives jobless. Because pulling out nails is not their métier. But Paulot already does quite a good job of cleaning the horses, carting out manure, and herding the cows. Tadzio also gives him some cigarettes and claps him on the shoulders: "Learn, my jailbird, learn. They'll make a man of you yet, you super-blockhead." We fix supper in "our" room and go to bed.

September 28, 1940

We got up in the morning and are happy to see that the sun is shining. It's not warm, but it will do. Mère Marie gives us three liters of milk and sits with us at breakfast. She starts chirping from the break of dawn, like the sparrows in the courtyard. A character from a novel, she is as complete and perfect an example of her type as a Bach fugue. We are off. Mère Marie kisses us on our foreheads, we kiss her hand, which sends her into a trance. She runs into the garden, plucks some asters, and hands us a little bouquet. "*C'est pour votre femme—ne les perdez pas . . .*"[209] Tadzio says good-bye to the shaggy Paulot: "*Salut*, you little shepherd of Bethlehem, *salut*." Paulot smiles cordially. The region is monotonous, but it's flat and we ride without much effort. Around noon the sky clouded over and it began to rain off and on. An autumnal drizzle, the French *bruine*, subtly and thoroughly drenching. It's cold and dreary. We pass an airstrip—still sitting there are two half burned-out French fighters (they look like Bristols).[210] It starts raining so hard that we have to change our clothes and repack our things. We enter a roadside farm and take shelter in the coach house. An old woman with a cane emerged in our direction, spiteful and grouchy. The exact opposite of Mère Marie. She very unwillingly agrees to let us shelter briefly under the coach house roof, muttering to herself and watching us the whole time. Tadzio says he would happily "smash this rotten casket in the beak," but he's afraid there would be too much dust. I imagine how she must tyrannize the rest of her family, which is only waiting for her death to claim the inheritance. Every few words, she knocks her cane on the ground, rolls her restless beady eyes, and throws suspicious glances. I'm sure she sees everything, even what happens behind her back. Condensed spitefulness and suspiciousness in a cramped, aged body. Tadzio changes his clothes and repacks, all the while keeping up a conversation with the old woman. "So, and what are you staring at, you old sourpuss—we won't nick anything from your lousy hacienda. Go on, you wickedy witch, knock with your cane, death will knock you with his scythe. What? You've never seen a blanket, madame, or what? It's ours, not yours—you old blubberer . . ." The old crone muttered something back at him again. Seeing that we were finishing and intended to move on, she followed behind us and began driving us away with her cane. That was finally too much for me and I snapped in "gentlemanly" slang: "F—— -*moi la paix, vieille crécelle, sommes pas des voleurs . . . Merde!*"[211] I sat down on the wagon shaft and took out my cigarettes. She calmed down and moved away. Tadzio in turn treated her to a long peroration in Polish and lit a cigarette. The rain let up a bit, the old woman fidgeted uneasily. We rolled out onto the road.

We enter Auxerre. The rain has picked up again and the black clouds are so thick that it's almost dark in town. There is no one on the streets—all completely deserted. I want to buy matches and bread. But matches are nowhere to be found. I run, drenched, from one bistro to another; there have been no matches for the last three weeks. I enter a bakery. The *patronne*, young and pretty, does not want to sell me bread without coupons. I explain, plead, tell her we're returning to Paris and we're hungry. Nothing helps. I see that she would like to sell me the bread, but she's afraid. She's shaking all over and close to tears: "*Chaque soir ILS me comptent les tickets*[212]—I can't sell you a single ounce without coupons . . ." The water is streaming down the bakery display windows, the gutters are rattling and overflowing. I stand still and no longer say a word. I'm quiet. Silence. Suddenly the woman broke into loud sobs, darted over to the shelves, pulled down a big loaf, and ran up to me. She wrapped one arm around me, pressed her head to my shoulder, and wept terribly, while her other hand thrust the loaf upon me. Sobbing, she practically shouted. The words burst out and tore through her tears: "*Prenez, mangez, . . . vous êtes jeune . . .*"[213] She began to shake her fist in the direction of the street . . . "*Tant pis . . . j'ai pas peur . . . ILS . . . ILS ont défendu de vendre . . .*"[214] Finally, she could no longer speak, wracked by her sobs, and only now and then blurted into my soaked windbreaker ILS, buffeted by impotent rage and protest. I stroked her head, slowly detached her, and sat her down on a stool. She sat bent over, with lowered head. I left, without a word. The splash of rain on the street, the semidarkness of the bakery, the single intelligible word, "THEY," wrung from her along with the sobs, it was all as intense as a tale by Guy de Maupassant.[215] I read one that was set in the time of the Franco-Prussian War. I don't recall the title, or even the plot, but I know that I experienced something like this and that it HAD TO BE that way then. Something heavy descended on my head and on my heart, an enormous, gray iron helmet. "THEIR" helmet. I'm standing with Tadzio under a little roof, surrounded by tassels of water. I put away the bread and all the while hear the weeping and sobbing in the gurgling emptiness of a rainy day. I keep feeling her face on my shoulder and I feel like crying, too . . . A repulsive boy barged into the playground of happy children, into the sandbox in which they were playing in the sun, demolished their sand castles, poured sand into their lunch baskets, and now pulls the hair of the little girls in white dresses and the little boys in white ruffs.

An old man is dragging himself down the street, bent over and wrapped in a hooded cape. He walks along tapping his cane on the sidewalk. Suddenly a motorcycle came roaring by, sent a giant puddle splashing into the air, and vanished. The water splattered onto the cape. The old man halted, stopped tapping his cane, straightened up, and shook his fist, muttering something under his breath, some kind of "Ahem . . . hm . . . hm . . ." And resumed his three-legged ramble.

I'm jittery, my thoughts, too, are merely "Ahem . . . hm . . . hm . . ." and I'm seized by that mute fear. Everything here strains the nerves, and it's more than simply the bleakness of an autumn downpour. We'll wait out the rain somewhere or other, anywhere but in this town. We draw on our hoods, I tie mine carefully and pull it down over my eyes, like horse blinders; we ride, plunging into the downpour. A few kilometers beyond the town we find an empty shed near the road—a small house for workers repairing the highway. We enter, light the stove, and heat up a liter of wine with sugar and raisins. That gets us back on our feet. The rain is slowly abating and the sky is clearing. Onward. The region is flat. In one of the villages I found another piece of sausage and a can of green peas. Toward evening we settle into a lonely straw-filled hut, in the middle of a field. I leave my bicycle and walk over to the village a few hundred meters away. Tadzio: "And where are you off to now?" "I'm going to find the owner of this hut and ask his permission for us to sleep here." "Got it, got it . . ." The *patron* willingly agrees: "Just be careful with your fire." The evening is freezing. As I busy myself with supper, I whistle. I don't know where it came from, but out of the blue I recalled one of Bizet's symphonies. I don't remember which. Tadzio listens. "Jędruś, that's great. What is it?" The stove hisses. "How far still to Paris?" "Tomorrow we'll see."

Paris, September 29, 1940

We continue to be confused by this German time. In the morning it's still gray, feels like it's only six, but it's already eight. In summer French clocks are set ahead one hour. When the Germans arrived, they set them ahead one more hour. By the time we had fixed breakfast and packed our things, it was noon. The day is already so cold, though a bit sunny, that we stow our shorts and put on trousers and sweaters. We hit the road and find the first milestone. "Paris 135 km." I looked at Tadzio. "Shall we cross the finish line?"

"If we really push, we can be there by evening. Let's finish!"

The road is flat and from the start we set a murderous pace. The speedometer needle hovers between twenty-five and twenty-eight km an hour. If not for the heavy load, this would almost be a race. It takes such an effort that thinking stops altogether. Thoughts turn into kilometers. My watch is affixed to the baggage in front and I keep my eyes glued to it the whole time. We roll. I'm returning, really returning. I haven't the slightest sense of foreignness, nor for the moment do I think about the fact that I'm in a foreign country. I'm returning *home*. Already, the long weeks of wandering in the sun have been erased from my memory. I'm thinking about *my* streets in Paris, as I once used to think about my streets in Cracow. The white milestones keep appearing up ahead, we're getting closer; yet again 100 m, 200 m, 300 m . . .

We fly through the town of Sens. Along the road, yellow and black signs and German milestones begin to appear. The distances they show to the next village are always one or two kilometers greater or less than those posted by the French. Because THEY always know better: not forty-five km but forty-six. *Das ist ja doch ein Unterschied.*[216] Have they remeasured? With them anything is possible. In any case, all the Michelin maps are useless. The names of the towns have not yet been changed. Apparently the French have managed in this respect to be exact, although it's unclear, for example, whether Melun might not have been called Mehlein in the time of Charlemagne . . . It's almost three o'clock. We hit Montereau. We've put almost sixty km behind us—we still have about seventy-eight to Notre-Dame. Half of Montereau is in ruins. It's Sunday and people are strolling in the streets. As soon as we leave town we resume our former speed. We leave Fontainebleau behind on the left and tear off toward Melun. Once again I plant my eyes on the speedometer and the watch, but I already sense the fatigue. My hands are numb and my shoulders ache. I can no longer maintain the speed. Four o'clock. Four hours without respite. Just before five we hit Melun and almost without slowing down return again to the highway. You can already feel Paris approaching. Many bicycles and tandems. He, she, and the tandem out for a Sunday spin. As in the old days. I steal up close to the rear wheel of one of those marriage bicycles (a tandem always reminds me of a French bed) and am drawn along in their wake. Instantly a bit easier. But after ten kilometers I can't keep it up. We're drained, from over five hours of "grinding" without a break, without rest, without a bite to eat. Another thirty km to go. I reckon we can rest a bit. We leave the road and hop off the bicycles. We cannot stand on our own feet. They have turned into rigid stilts. We sit in the ditch and begin to feel those hundred-plus kilometers covered in five and a half hours. Having to slow down when going through the towns lost us a lot of time. We eat sausage, cheese, and jam and drink milk. I add plenty of sugar to the mug of milk. After six we continue on our way, beginning a race against the night. There are many bicycles on the road—all loaded down, pulling trailers filled with sacks of potatoes. We now ride more slowly, our legs refuse to work, each kilometer lasts an age. The sun is setting, big and red. At all costs we must arrive before nightfall, because we have no lights. Yet again I summon my last strength. We're getting there. Roadside bistros with little gardens, gray automobiles parked out in front, and THEY are enjoying themselves. The sound of *Lieder.* Over the garden gates are large signs: "Bier." Well, well—*Biergartens* close to Paris.

Not far now, but riding in the road is no longer permitted and we must take the special bicycle path. But, naturally—Tadzio suddenly calls out: "Jędruś—my rear has blown." Just as we were about to enter the Parc Vincennes. We stop and consult briefly. There's a small nail in Tadzio's rear tire. "Let's leave it—I'll pump it up and next time it goes, I'll do it again . . ."

Twilight. I become more and more impatient, yearning for home. For the last two months Basia hasn't known what was happening to me . . . I rally yet again. We have to ride as fast as possible, because Tadzio's tube keeps deflating and each stop to pump costs us precious minutes. We cross the bridge over the Marne, we enter the woods, Paris. Near the Parc Zoologique we have to pump another time. It's not yet dark, but we already should be riding with lights. The zoo emits the pungent odor of the lion and tiger cages, some birds are screaming. I'm in a kind of dream. We hit Porte Dorée and mount avenue Daumesnil. I'm so moved, I want to cry. Because here already is "our" fountain, there is "our" hotel, where we once stayed. I greet every pebble, every tree. Oh—here a year ago on the first of September I tore the *Paris-Midi* from the paper boy's grasp and read that war had begun. I want to shake hands with the Génie de la Liberté, the Spirit of Freedom, atop the column on place de la Bastille, the endearing "*Bastoche.*" *Ça va?* No—this is not a foreign city, I am truly coming back home.

It's dark. The policemen are very tactful and try not to notice us. It's instantly obvious that these are French police, not Gestapo disguised in the uniforms of French "*flics,*" as we were warned in the south. Place de la République. The square is empty and we ride along calm as can be without lights. Paris is dark, plunged in the antiaircraft darkness. We stop for a while and have a smoke. We enter the boulevards. Pedaling slowly. At the corner of boulevard Sébastopol a policeman finally can't resist: "*Vos feux, Messieurs!*"[217]

I stopped, and showing him my lit cigarette, I say with a smile: "*Mais voilà mon feu . . .*"[218]

He gave a laugh.

"*Je vous demande votre éclairage.*" "*C'est mon seul éclairage,*"[219] I answer, waving my cigarette. He laughs and asks us to dismount. He assures me he's obliged essentially to give us a fine: "*C'est plus comme avant—les temps ont changé . . . ,*"[220] he adds sadly. I, too, uttered a sigh. *Ordnung muss sein.* If to top it off they start forcing people to cross the streets between the lines, I'll begin to speak of the end of the world. We proceed on foot. Not far now. The boulevards . . . The roadways along the riverbanks are full of cars, the boulevard cafés are full of soldiers. The Deutsche Wehrmacht is tasting the fruits of Paris. It's so dark that we practically grope our way along. Rue Richelieu, rue Laffitte. Soon I recognize the specters of the columns of Notre-Dame-de-Lorette. I whisper to Tadzio that we are now home. The streets are empty. My heart is pounding so hard that in the silence I hear every beat. My throat is tight. I open the gate, leave Tadzio and the bicycles in the courtyard, and run up the stairs. I ring the bell. Mr. P. opens the door. I push him aside and run to the kitchen. I had only uttered her name when I felt all over the warmth of her embrace, her body buried in my arms, the scent of her hair, the hollow of her eye under my lips, the taste of tears, salty and hot . . .

Paris, October 3, 1940

Paris is quiet. The only vehicles on the streets besides German cars are bicycles. The bicycle is the basic means of locomotion and Paris has turned into Copenhagen. There is not much traffic, Germans are everywhere. Food by the coupon, but one can make do. In the shops the Germans are buying out whatever they haven't already managed to buy out over the last three months. They pay for everything, perfectly legal, of course, with occupation marks, at the rate of one mark to twenty francs. And ship it all *in die Heimat*.[221] At every step one feels, almost palpably, that all of France has been bought out for scraps of paper printed over there, beyond the Rhine.

We have no kerosene and in the evenings we sit by candlelight. We cook on the spirit stove, but getting the fuel is increasingly difficult. Each trifle becomes a problem. Perhaps it's better like that? No time to think. I struggled through all the formalities and helped Tadzio do the same. We were at the Préfecture of police, but they are still not quite sure how to deal with foreigners. All they did was stamp the papers and set a date for us to return. We obtained the food ration cards at our district town halls without any trouble. All the offices are still in a state of disorder and everywhere officials give the impression they do not quite trust the freedom the Germans have temporarily allowed them. Our factory has been taken over by the Germans—entry is forbidden on pain of death. The former administration operates from the ballroom of the town hall. Starting tomorrow I go to work. Legal aid and social services for the Polish workers. Words can't describe how the French director, the engineer François Chappel, behaves toward the Poles. His every gesture, his every word and decision, reveals the greatness of French culture in its purest form, in direct descent from the noblest minds of France. A HUMANE regard for the PERSON. There are no Frenchmen, there are no Poles—there are HUMAN BEINGS, abandoned, helpless, in need of help. Nothing more. But this is EVERYTHING. In times like these, one SUCH man is all that is needed to restore one's faith in humanity. And in France.

October 27, 1940

I cannot stand to read in French. I cannot. Each word, each turn of phrase in this language stifles me. I cannot bear those smooth sentences and expressions, that dryness and the cult of words without feeling. I realize this is absurd, but I cannot. When I look at the books on my shelves, without exception good and well chosen, I cannot manage to take a single one in my hand. I feel like I've consumed too much of a heavy, overly sweet and extra creamy pistachio cake. Physical satiety and disgust at the words, sentences, subjects. Whereas I have consumed *Pan Tadeusz* with pure barbaric voracity and now sink my teeth into Sienkiewicz's *The Deluge*, as into a meaty leg of mutton. I lick my chops, smack my lips, wipe my greasy fingers on my trousers, and—dig in. It's amazing: every time I read *The Deluge*, it seems to me that THIS TIME Kmicic will succeed in abducting Bogusław, that THIS TIME Roch Kowalski will capture Karl Gustav, that now what didn't happen will happen and what happened then, now won't. One thing is certain. Kmicic is not a type worthy of emulation. The continuous bloodletting does not redeem the faults of character or the overall nonsense. The best way to redeem them is by wiping them out. To answer one's letters, to return the small change borrowed "until tomorrow," less "brash courage," and more solidity and naturalness.—But that's the rub: I probably read *The Deluge* precisely because that "brash courage" is missing around me. General Cambronne at Waterloo said *Merde!*—then, it seems, he added, "The old guard is dying, but does not surrender."[222] This time they said *Merde!* and added that "the old guard surrenders and does not die." And there's Pétain. Yet there was a third resolution: "The old guard is not dying and does NOT give up." People insist they have chosen this third resolution, but it's hard to believe.

November 2, 1940

Today is All Souls'. Like last year, we went to Père Lachaise cemetery. The day was sunny and warm, there were few people at the cemetery because most had come yesterday. First we went to Chopin's grave. There were many flowers on it, one bouquet tied in a broad, white-and-red ribbon. We placed our little bouquet, also tied in the Polish ribbon, and lit the candles left over from my birthday cake last year. Alongside this grave I don't think and I don't pray. I pray with the melodies that resound inside me one after the other. Those that recur most often are my beloved, but so rarely played, "Rondeau" and "Berceuse."

Near the grave stood an elderly Frenchwoman, who asked if we were Polish. Then she said it was nice of us to pay our respects, that she comes every year, and that she loves the Poles very much. "A brave and noble nation such as yours cannot perish and will not perish." Good lord! I can't stand to hear any more of this. As in, "Here, Pops, take this dime and go buy yourself something." Then the door shuts, one sits in an armchair and reads a book while eating chocolates. I responded, nevertheless, as though at a ceremony for Franco-Polish friendship, that the same could be said about France. For the first time in history, Poland and France are in a similar situation. Although for us it is a disaster, while for them merely a defeat. The difference is so great that it's hard to compare. When we suffer, they *bear* it; when we have nothing, they *still keep up appearances*; when we cannot *not* think, they *do not think and they get by.* They are like the rich man who, no matter how much he loses, will always find some kind of support; we are like the pauper who has staked everything on a single number, lost it all, and has to start from zero all over again.

This year, like last year, as I stood by Chopin's grave I thought of the similarity between his time and ours. Last year the Polish government was in Paris, along with the numerous and undistinguished emigration; just as in the introduction to *Pan Tadeusz*—just as in Chopin's time. This year many hopes were dashed, the emigration journeyed to England, while only a few remained in Paris, where, despite their small numbers, in the good Polish tradition they quarreled among themselves. Bridge should be recognized as the Polish national sport: bidding and games. That's all our countrymen manage to do correctly.

From Chopin's grave we proceeded to the grave of Oscar Wilde. My humble little bouquet was the only one that enlivened that large, indeed excessively large, tomb. Followed by a few moments of reflection at Balzac's grave. Down below lies his Paris. The sky is reddening in the west, closer by there's a sea of grayish-blue roofs in the fog. The roofs color the fog so strangely; they "bleed" into it. Along the silent cemetery paths, a crowd of graves and the fragrance of asters. The wreaths of metal or of beads resemble pretzels.

November 13, 1940

Everything is bearable on this earth, if only you have at least one person to love and are loved in return. Pearls of wisdom of the genre, "dumplings are a good thing." Fine, except that really good dumplings are hard to find.

November 15, 1940

Around eight I run downstairs, take the bicycle out of the cellar, and set out for Châtillon. I have almost an hour's ride ahead of me. Outside it's still rather dark. By way of rue Le Peletier, I reach the boulevards, which I cross, and enter rue Richelieu. It's darker there than in the other streets because it's narrow and tight. You have to be very careful. The Germans park their trucks there overnight and leave them without any lights. Today a boy riding ahead of me hit his head on the rear of a car, which he failed to notice right in front of him. He was knocked unconscious. There was no one around. I picked him up and carried him to the nearest bistro. I telephoned for the ambulance. Half his face was smashed to a pulp. We all swore loudly. The police regulations of course apply to everyone, but not to them. For riding your bicycle without a red light the fine is up to two hundred francs.

I pass the Comédie-Française and enter the Louvre. It's slowly turning light. Occasionally, near place du Carrousel a division of soldiers marches while singing. In the fresh morning air, the words of the German song carry a long way, bouncing off the wings of the Louvre and disappearing among the bare trees of the Tuileries. There's something so sad and improbable in this that I'd like to dismount from my bike, crawl on all fours, and howl like a dog. I cross the Seine, cut through boulevard Saint-Germain, and turn up boulevard Raspail. The wooden blocks in the roadway are being removed and pavement laid. People can often be seen pilfering the discarded blocks. For fuel. The policeman pretends not to notice while they feverishly stuff their sacks and vanish into the twilight. The streets are all empty and quiet, the fog is clammy, and everything around looks like it's covered in frog's skin—shiny and slippery. From Denfer-Rochereau I ride straight to Porte d'Orléans. I pass the German barrier that regulates the movement of their automobiles and carts. Alongside me, making an infernal racket, a platoon of brand-new French tanks (Renault) drives by, filled of course with Germans. They pass me. From each turret peers a soldier in a black uniform. They halt beside the road outside the city, climb out of the machines, and gather around a young officer. He barks out his instructions in a sharp tone. They are learning to drive on the French equipment . . . A short command, the motors begin to roar and the platoon starts off again, grating and clanking over the pavement.

I arrive at the factory, or rather the ballroom. I greet my French colleagues, who are sleepily preparing to rummage in their papers. *Ça va?—Ça va?* (With them it's always *ça va.*) I collect the documents I came for and return to town.

Making the rounds of the town halls, the Préfecture of police, the Ministry of Labor, the shelter. Every day something has to be arranged for someone, something resolved, something gotten hold of.

Everyone now listens to the broadcasts from London. Each day there's some bit of sensational news. Everyone is sure the Germans have already lost the war and that with a bit more patience, "our side will triumph." I have my own views on this war and don't get excited. What does it matter that the English have bombed something here or there. The game still has a long way to go and there are many unknowns. The Germans are humoring the French and at all costs want to win over French public opinion, to turn France into an ally and mold

Pétain's still rather resistant government like clay. This government has two tendencies: one, pro-German, favors cooperation; the other, pro-English, wants to establish Free France in the colonies and ally the colonies with the English. All sorts of rumors circulate about the government, but the truth is hard to discern. The newspapers are dictated. I don't read them.

I go home for lunch. The situation with food is still not too bad. On the street below our house the market closes down and the tradeswomen with their carts also go off for lunch. Some are still hawking what they haven't yet sold: *Allez-y, allez-y, tapez dedans, profitez . . . allez-y.*[223] After lunch I return to the factory or set out again on my rounds. By the end of the day I have often covered around eighty km in Paris alone. Toward evening, I return home. The sun sets over the Champs-Élysées, a mist falls. Our neighborhood, once quiet, is now very lively. All the bars, dance halls, and brothels, closed during the war, are opening one after the other. Signs everywhere warn *"Nur für Deutsche Wehrmacht."*[224] Long lines can often be seen in front of the brothels. A noncom keeps order. A *Schwester,*[225] filled with the fear of God, first escorts the lucky one for an injection. In front of the Alcazar, where a girlie show plays to great success, there is often an entire division lined up two by two. The noncom takes care of the entrance fee at the box office, comes back, yells, *"Rechts um,"*[226] and the whole company enters in pairs. After the show they will be bussed to place Pigalle, on command they'll disperse to the brothels and on command they'll return. If only Paris were Capua for them . . .[227]

One day follows the other and soon it won't be long until the New Year. Everyone says: "If we can just make it through the winter — in spring something will budge again." Winter will pass, spring will pass, everyone will say, "We are waiting for summer." Summer will pass, and the problem of getting through the winter will reappear. And so on for several more years. For I don't believe this war can end quickly.

November 20, 1940

The situation of Poles in Paris is clear. And in fact quite improbable. The Germans, or rather the Gestapo, have created a special *Polenreferat,* or Polish Department, headed by a certain Counselor Schwerbel. This German graduated from the Polish Gymnasium in Włocławek, it seems, speaks excellent Polish, and "looks after" all of us. The Poles are mainly concentrated in three shelters, which, after prolonged battles with the Catholic "Caritas," were taken over by the so-called Marquise, who is Polish by origin, French by marriage. She befriended this German Schwebel, and with his help got Father Cegiełka put in prison and the same for the directors of the institution attached to the Polish church in Paris, which had gotten in her way; the Gestapo compiled a detailed register of names and—all is in order. The Counselor acquired some gullible friends in the shelters, who give him letters to their families in Poland ("I'll send this for you"), he discusses Polish literature and culture, *et voilà* . . . In this idyll, obviously my turn may come and the turn of some of my colleagues. Or it may not. I do what I have to do.

All the French offices are still chaotic, and the worst is the police. I feel completely at a loss. Politics has become a part of life. The eternal questions: How will it end, what will Germany do, what will happen with the Balkans? I avoid these conversations. I know only one thing: today is November 20 and the Germans have not landed in England. That alone is certain. When I reflect on this war, I'm always reminded of the Napoleonic wars. It's my so-called *hobby*. Hitler has a poorly annotated textbook of the Napoleonic epic, on which he bases his orders and commands. Napoleon also wanted to invade England, he even massed his troops near the Channel, frightened the English, but it came to nothing in the end. The current war is a series of German campaigns in Europe and a continuous state of war with England, which never reaches a decisive engagement. Germany by now possesses almost all of Europe, but in fact does not possess it at all. And the most important problem in all of this is RUSSIA. Will the current war in this respect also end by resembling the wars of the great emperor? Recently one sees quite a few photos of Stalin. Will the craftily smiling *batiushka*[228] one day say: "And now come to me—I have a lot of room"? The Germans will invade Russia and dissolve in its territory like a sugar cube in a glass of tea. And then the English and Americans will finish them off in some Battle of Waterloo. I dream, I am Rzecki, a bit like every Pole.[229] This mad war will be long and what will emerge from it God only knows. Nevertheless, every day one has endured, every quiet day, is important, because it comes nearer to that unknown end.

November 25, 1940

Autumn this year is cold but clear. Sunny, enameled Parisian days. As evening falls I sit at the window, watching the sunset. The sea of roofs visible from our mansard grows more deeply dove-colored, then gray-blue and cold. At a distance, in the fog, is the Eiffel Tower with a swastika standard attached to its peak. She has lived to see even this, the fifty-one-year-old Parisian matron. And so they've dressed her up, too. I lit the little stove today and sat in the dark, staring at the mica aperture lit by the fire. I still cannot get over those burned notebooks, the Polish journals. Heroes! Mr. and Mrs. P. knew I had been writing. They ordered Basia to burn everything when the Germans entered Paris.

From fear. Good thing they didn't tell her also to burn our few Polish books. They made sure that she did it as they watched. She tore out some dozen pages from the notebooks. What remained of them was as much as I've retained of my past. I will not reconstruct anything and I don't even want to. Even what you write on the spur of the moment is already a bit of a lie, a deformed thought, a true sound warped in transmission. The melody is usually the same, but certainly written in a different key. What's worse—often a "major" key comes out as a "minor" key and the reverse. The best ear is no help. Perhaps what's good emerges only from a direct connection between the pen and that strange world of thought and feeling. How often does it seem that the connection is not direct but makes its way laboriously through various switchboards, in which the operators' silly voices can be heard. These operators' voices are easy to recognize in written works. What an effort it took Flaubert to eliminate them from his prose; how many have continued to jabber on in Balzac?

I ride around Paris all day long. From the expansive boulevards I enter the gloomy and always different (or the same ones, yet also always different) side streets, I observe, think and do not think, give a whistle now and then, at the intersections extend my arm to show the direction I'm turning, smile at the policeman. Sometimes I wait while a column of gray automobiles rolls by and then I continue. I direct a remark to Molière on his monument, to Gambetta[230] at the Louvre I always say: "It's high time the Germans dismantled you" (the Germans are apparently considering this good idea), I scoot by the Church of Saint-Germain or peek at the pictures, prints, and antique shops on rue Bonaparte. I dive into the old side streets and emerge in the antechamber of some ministry or board of industry. I know I'll manage to get everything arranged, but it will take three months. The men in the gunpowder division will also get paid. Meanwhile, one must write letters and hang around in antechambers. I hang around. Then once again I cross the Seine and enter rue du Faubourg-Saint-Honoré. Beautiful women, never before seen on the streets, now walk on foot or ride in horse-drawn carriages. Buggies, tilburies, carioles. Paris looks like it did a hundred years ago: a quiet side street, the clattering of horses' hooves and a small vehicle with a beautiful woman dressed also a bit à la Louis Philippe.[231] I think of George Sand, of Lady Dudley, of the Duchesse de Langeais, of Liszt...[232] The conquering army behaves impeccably. They are calm, dignified, well-mannered. I haven't seen a single drunkard. An army of subdued madmen, which executes everything under the direction of the commanding physician, also a madman. But they are impressive. Have you ever seen a man offer his seat to a woman in the metro? The German soldiers do it graciously. They domesticate the French with a thousand pretenses and prepare the ground for "collaboration," which is talked about ever more openly. And so we already have

EUROPE. It reminds me of the conversation with the student we met on our way back to Paris. The word "Europe" is for now dropped discreetly, like the first balls in a tennis match, when the opponents "feel out" each other's reactions. Cautiously, quietly, and discreetly in official language the great word "Europe" replaces "Germany." The German soldier no longer fights for the greatness of Germany, he will fight for the happiness of Europe and on behalf of Europe. A triumphant nationalism, wanting to keep a tight rein on the ever-growing number of conquered nations, must issue international and idealistic catchwords and slogans. Always the same comedy—the Napoleonic comedy, repeating itself down to the last detail. The formation of "independent" new nations. So far they have not yet created a king. For example, Göring would suit this role very well; that Hitlerian Prince Murat. The factory of history is working in three shifts and has introduced the latest equipment. The best is perhaps the machine for the production of lies. Its construction is truly worthy of admiration. These lies are like poorly faked banknotes. But so many have already gone into circulation that we all accept them and pay as though nothing was out of line. We know they are false, but we stick them into our wallets. The world? Humanity? Man? Please!! Fifteen hundred "lies"—this new currency, which has no underpinning, but is not threatened with devaluation.

November 28, 1940

Foggy autumn days. The sun shines evasively, with no sense of obligation. The leaves have fallen from the trees and winter is coming. Every day hides behind a screen of *gris-moisi*, mixed with an unknown number of other colors, and every morning it appears, passes by, and disappears. Like a taxicab meter.

I ran into Tadzio Piotrowski. He has been renting a room from a Frenchwoman. He fled Paris and recently returned to continue his studies. His landlady had burned all the Polish books in his room. *Par mesure de prudence!*[233] I understand: barbarity inspires fear, fear inspires barbarity. The Germans do not have to organize anything, nor impose anything by force; they THREATEN. The rest takes care of itself. Under the influence of fear everything crumbles in a split second. I suspect that if I were to feel fear, I myself would crumble before my very own eyes. And for that reason I DO NOT WANT to be afraid.

December 4, 1940

A few days ago Italy apparently declared war on Greece. "Rome" conquers the Hellenes. This time, however, the Greeks are beating the "Romans." The problem of the Balkans has not been resolved and awaits a solution. Meanwhile it's rumored that the French government in Vichy is sitting on its suitcases and awaiting the moment to flee to Africa, in order to pledge itself openly to the English side. The local newspapers are obviously attacking all the ministers in Pétain's government, calling them pro-English traitors. There's even talk of some arrests, but which and of whom no one knows. In any case, Pétain's government has not yet come to the point of open "collaboration." "Oh, I'd like to, but I'm afraid . . ." They're still a bit shy.

December 10, 1940

We live now like troglodytes. From morning to evening the most interesting subject is—food, fuel, light. The Germans have proven that the Roman principle *panem et circenses* can be applied *à rebours* and the result is the same. Either you provide bread so the people will not think, or you do not provide it and the people also stop thinking. Especially in France, where any process of thinking depends on the stomach. The head is not the warehouse of thoughts but a grocery store. The devil in you decides it's his sacred duty to search for opportunities to buy things without coupons. Paris has discovered a new snobbism. When someone says he's gotten a pound of butter without coupons, one is obliged to smile in disdain and let out casually: "I bought three kilos of sugar at twelve francs a pound." Most pitiable is the person who starts at the mention of butter as if scalded and asks in a loud voice: "Where?" In his limitless naïveté, he expects the other to tell him "where." But the other merely smiles and answers evasively. *"Il faut être malin."*[234] Egotism and envy wrapped in smiles have never had such a field day. Conversations in Paris these days always bring to mind conversations in the café at the House of Artists,[235] where everyone was ready to strangle each other. At present there are plenty of great talents—chocolaty, buttery, sugary, and milky—who refuse to recognize each other's talents.

December 14, 1940

Morning in the metro. Quiet, the cars are practically empty. At place de la Concorde an entire family got on, returning from a funeral. A dozen or so people dressed in black. At each stop in turn, when one of them got off, the smacking of lips resounded, so loudly that even the rattle of the wheels could not drown it out. *Allez, mon vieux, il faut descendre . . .*[236] and plunk, plunk, a salvo of kisses, a gallop of lips smacking, short, abrupt, then again prolonged, like the sound of a straw sucking the last drops of orangeade from an empty glass.

Finally only one couple remained. As they were getting off, I smacked my lips several times. They looked back over their shoulders. I smacked my lips in their direction yet again. I needed to complete the scene. Tomorrow the five-year-long haggle over the inheritance will begin and all the kissing will stop. One will say about the other: *Ah, ça alors . . . pensez-vous . . . quel salaud . . .*[237]

December 15, 1940

It's cold. Fog and drizzle. So fine and dense, that falling on my rainproof jacket it hisses. Unremitting hiss. I ducked into a bistro on rue Broca. I drink hot wine. Silence. A brewery cart laden with barrels moves down the street. Each of the horse's hooves strikes the cobblestones distinctly. I light up a cigarette and observe. The *patron* behind the counter is struggling with a piece of cork in the bottle, using the pick for crushing ice. Next he pours the remains of lemonade from several bottles into one and if I had ordered a *panaché* (beer with lemonade), he would have added some of that cocktail to my beer. I won't have one. One of the local prostitutes entered in very high-heeled shoes. Nice legs. She said: *"Quel temps"*[238] and downed a glass of cognac. She looked at me and smiled. *"Ça va?"* *"Oui, merci, ça va,"* *"Tu veux?"* and nodded in the direction of the hotel across the street. *"Non, ma cocotte, merci."*[239] They're making good money these days. They settle in marks. Before that the girls had pounds. And not only them. Some women workers at the factory are also "studying" German. One of them boasted to me yesterday that she was taking lessons: *"Ich lerne Deutsch."* "With the officers, or with the troops?" I asked indifferently. She laughed foolishly and left. All because a mark is worth twenty francs.

The girl left. The *patron* sits behind the counter and looks out the window. Me, too. I feel good. Something in the atmosphere of this sort of godforsaken bistro on a foggy day is comforting. One's nerves turn into angora wool that one can wind around one's finger.

December 16, 1940

Conversation with the cashier at the factory, a wise older woman.

"What's your opinion of the war?"

"It doesn't concern me. People are murdering each other for no reason at all. What do you think?"

"If I could count on getting there, I would go to England."

"*Mon Dieu!* What a thought. But you are much more useful here. Why, what's the point?"

"Surely you understand—there's something that compels one to ignore the demands of reason; a feeling, a desire to tell oneself the truth, faith . . ."

"I don't understand what you're talking about; after all you have a wife, you are earning your living—*il faut gagner sa petite vie et c'est tout.*"[240]

"You see, it's about honesty, about *the truth*, or simply a *sense of duty* . . ."

"???"

"Well, for example, do you have someone you love, do you have an ideal, even if it's just a person? Perhaps for me it also concerns an ideal."

"Yes, I have someone, someone I love."

"Would you be unfaithful?"

"I think, yes, I would. But not in my heart!"

"It amounts to the same thing. Would you feel the need, even the obligation, to tell him about it?"

Indignant: "ONE NEVER TALKS ABOUT THAT!!"

This conversation reminded me of a conversation I had with a postman I knew, still before the war. He showed me some pornographic photos of sexual encounters in a foursome: he with his friend's wife, the friend with his. He recounted all the details of what they did. I asked him:

"How is that? You allow this other man to do everything with your wife? To kiss her and . . ."

He interrupted me indignantly: "Everything, only no kissing. MY WIFE'S LIPS ARE MINE ALONE!"

So, go on, try to talk with these people!

December 17, 1940

It's cold. The subject everyone talks about: FOOD. The subject everyone thinks about: FOOD. Riding today past Notre-Dame I thought: "If only those sculptures were made of butter. And no one knew about it!" Later I tried to remember in which area of Tibet they indeed make large sculptures from butter. I'm certain that such sculptures are made there. And when the war ends, then in fulfillment of everyone's desires . . . first of all great ships will arrive carrying American canned goods . . . And then I thought about eternity and realized how strong our habits of thinking are. How much easier it is to imagine that eternity has no end, because that is what we've heard since childhood. By contrast, it's quite impossible to imagine that eternity also has no beginning. Such a thought is capable of turning the eyeballs around 180 degrees.

December 18, 1940

So typical. One evening at supper in one of the Polish restaurants. The saga of the lithographs and etchings that adorned the room and that depicted Polish military costumes from the time of the Napoleonic wars and the 1830 Uprising. When the Germans entered Paris, the French police came running and ordered the immediate removal of those "placards." (Good thing they didn't order them burned . . .) The *patronne* rebelled and did not remove them. Meanwhile the bar began to be frequented by German officers, often speaking Polish. A few of them even became *Stammgäste*.[241] The French police came rushing over for the second time and threatened to close the place down if she didn't remove those "placards." She removed the "placards," leaving pale rectangles on the walls — like footprints of the pictures. The Germans came and raised a fuss. Where are the pictures? What did the *patronne* do with them? She told them about the orders from the police. "We have nothing against the Polish army. It was always heroic. In Poland there was a real war, but not here . . ." This was said by a second lieutenant in the Wehrmacht.

Now all the pictures hang in their places and the Poles who come here are often delighted. Our credulousness has not changed from the time of the partitions. Wave a white and red flag our way, pay tribute to our heroes, allow us to sing "God Save Poland," "The Oath," "Dąbrowski's Mazurka," and "The First Brigade," and you can get away with a lot.[242] It's no surprise that so many Frenchmen daily take the bait of the Germans' apparent generosity, lured into collaboration with Germany in the new Europe, increasingly a subject of open discussion. Judging by what is said on the radio, the Germans botched the whole business in Poland with their stupidity. Fortunately. They hate us too much to be guided by psychology alone.

December 19, 1940

A very important issue in life nowadays is STANDING IN LINE. I stand in line and listen. I stand amid a crowd of women, a crowd of creatures like living caricatures from Daumier, etchings from the time of the Revolution in the Musée Carnavalet, the *tricoteuses*.[243] Creatures in filthy rags, splattered shoes caked in dirt, drooping stockings, with tangled hair. Each of them rates herself in terms of the number of lines she has stood in today, the amount of time she has waited. "Two hours, *pensez-vous*, we've come to this. Yesterday for dinner I had to . . ." Followed by a detailed inventory of her culinary labors. And once again, meat, sugar, butter, potatoes. A sudden shriek. Someone tries to sneak to the head of the line. Several enraged women rush up from the back and begin abusing this *resquilleuse*,[244] calling as witnesses those closest by. After a thousand repetitions in every tone of voice, *Ah non, ça alors* mixes with the general grumbling. The case becomes clear: the woman trying to jump the line is pregnant.

She purposefully displays her distended belly and snaps back at the women. She looks like a toy top that makes various noises and buzzes as it spins. Pregnant women have priority, they have a "certificate of priority" issued by the town halls and do not have to stand in line. The housewives return to their places, muttering: "No one wants to fight over a spot in line—*pensez-vous*—but fair is fair *quand même* . . ." They are particularly suspicious of pregnant women, because at the beginning, before the "pregnancy certificates" based on doctor's notes were introduced, many pregnant women showed up on line, successfully claiming *priorité*. They succeeded thanks to the French cult of pregnancy. When, however, it was discovered that under the dress or coat a small pillow was hidden and the majestic mother's belly turned out to be stuffed, the good times ended. Now the first impulse of these furious battleaxes, which they can hardly resist, is to pat down the stomach of the woman trying to beat the line. *On connaît bien ces femmes enceintes . . . ,*[245] they always add, moving back to their places, like bedbugs crawling under the slats of a bed.

The brief commotion subsided—the women resume their chatter. Meat, sugar, Olida pâté,[246] lard, beans. And once again, from the top: meat, sugar, Olida . . . Many of them bring their needlework and knit. I often had the urge to tie up their hands and pierce their tongues with one of those needles and leave it there. Like that battleax on the macabre April Fools' cards sold back home in Poland. These philosophical disquisitions on food can induce nausea. They talk about it so greedily, with such hatred, for example, for anyone who receives a package from the countryside, picking at each morsel, so that finally the entire world amounts to GRUB, DRINK, SLEEP, and S——. One of them is always slipping out of line and announcing to those in front of her, *je suis derrière vous* (a witness in the event of a squabble or accusation coming from those behind her), then peeking into the shop and returning with the news. With spiteful joy in her voice, she says: "There's not enough left for those at the end." She says this loud enough for those "at the end" to hear. And a rumbling arises at the end of the line, growing ever louder, because the woman adds with satisfaction: "*C'est pas la peine d'attendre,*[247] you should have come earlier." Instant shrieks: "Not everyone can come earlier . . . It's not always possible . . ." But the woman keeps arguing and begins to tell her tale: "*Mais MOI . . . ET MOI . . . SI JE . . .*" She alone is important, if they only followed HER example, everything would be different. Cries and insults. Then a policeman comes up, keeping order in the lines, and having checked the store reassures them: there's enough for everyone. In turn everyone begins to insult the woman; the entire line. And thus over and over again. Lines and lines, for everything and for nothing, lines for the sake of lines, from line to line. Meat, sugar, Olida, potatoes, lard, beans . . .

In this situation, one is a creature trying only to cram oneself with a certain quantity of carbohydrates and fat with protein, to evacuate after digestion and once again to obtain carbohydrates and fats. It's a question, not of living, but of having something to s—— from day to day. Life is limited to the functioning of the alimentary canal, regulated by the amount of money one has. Monstrous.

December 21, 1940

Interrogation. I stopped by yesterday evening at the Polish House. The workers tell me: "Schwerbel is upstairs, he's questioning people about the furs the Marquise obtained for the shelters and which she is now selling for 100 and 150 francs." I understand. I chat with them for a while, one of them needs help at the mayor's office, another wants to go south.

Suddenly one stops in and says: "Counselor Schwerbel asks you to come up." This surprised me. I had never lived in any of the shelters. They will already have informed him . . . I go. The man at the typewriter is still young, carefully dressed, smoking English Black Cats (they've lined their pockets on the English); he welcomes me with a smile and speaks excellent Polish.

"Good evening. Your name is familiar to me, either from literature or from history . . ."

I'm frightened, but I want to burst out laughing.

"Not yet from either. You're mistaken," I answer with a smile.

"Aaa . . . My mistake. What are you doing in France?"

"I arrived before the war, I worked for a French company and still work there . . ."

"You were never in the army?"

"No."

"Well, no need to conceal it. We have nothing against soldiers. It's a duty, like any other. So you were never in the army?"

"No, I wasn't. I was working. I was mobilized into industry."

"Well . . . You would probably want to return to Poland. The place of every good Pole is now in Poland. We must work, take up honest work . . ."

"No."

He is surprised, but continues to pull the wool over my eyes.

"I do what I can to facilitate everyone's return, but the action taken by Father

Cegiełka and certain activities on the part of Polish Communist elements have interfered with my work, delaying everything . . ."

"A shame."

"So, you see, how stupid people are. What's the point of these machinations? If a fellow wants to go to England, why not come out and tell me? I would give him a pass to the Island of Jersey, which Germany occupies and to which English Red Cross ships deliver food.[248] We've made this agreement with the English. Let him take a ship to England, to that hell. Please, go right ahead!"

I say nothing, but despite everything I want to laugh. He's laying it on thick. I begin to understand a bit of what they're up to. The Germans allow the Poles a certain freedom of movement, wanting to catch only the elements they consider harmful without worrying about the others, leaving them under the supervision of the Marquise in "her" shelters and placing the burden of financial and social assistance on the French. They have more important things on their minds than a few hundred Poles. The Counselor is complicating things on purpose, pretends to have his hands full so he doesn't himself get drafted. Anyone who gives him trouble, he locks up. Thanks to his "amiability" he has many devoted informants among the Poles, knows everything that's going on, and thus our position with the Germans remains tranquilly undefined. The conversation continues.

"What do you know about the sale of furs by the Marquise?"

"I actually know nothing."

"Ach, you are therefore testifying on her behalf?"

"I'm not testifying about anything."

He wrote all this down in German and read it to me out loud. I signed. The Counselor is the sole representative of the Germans and our "guardian angel." No other German authorities are interested in us—just HIM. And so it goes.

December 22, 1940

There's nothing more annoying than when people you can't stand give you so-called good advice and when their advice turns out in fact to be—good.

December 23, 1940

Sad. The Christmas feeling is absent. My thoughts escape to the few dear hearts for whom it's worth living and enduring all of this. It's cold and gray. Rain mixed with snow falls against the windowpanes from time to time and presses up against them. Along the Seine and around the Madeleine they are selling Christmas trees. I'd like to buy one, but they are very expensive. I sat near the stove and read my notebooks from the south. Trying to describe southern France is like wanting to paint the sun with ink. I would like to write about this endlessly, especially now. The wind shakes the door, slides through all the cracks, knocks raindrops against the windows, or suddenly drapes the roof in a sheet of snow that flies in from afar as though torn from the earth. Just a rag, dirty, torn from the trash can.

Loneliness. The acute pain of isolation. The absence of laughter, of company, of animation. It's more than loneliness; it's a complete emptiness that accentuates the foreignness around us. We're attached to nothing, tied to no one. We are alone, we two, and each of us clings to the other as if to a ship's mast in a storm. For an entire year we were able to ignore this feeling of isolation, perhaps even to be content with it; but now it hurts.

December 24, 1940, around midnight

It was an evening like any other. I lit the stove and it was warm. We washed ourselves in one of our pots and Basia went to bed. She was very tired. I pulled up the table and sat down dressed for the occasion. We put our family photographs on the table and we shared Christmas wafers in their company. We ate sardines, the traditional borsch with dumplings, some dates. And then I surprised her and pulled out a bottle of champagne. She smiled, kissed me: "How good of you to remember . . ." But though she likes champagne very much, she didn't want to drink. I turned aside so she wouldn't see that I had tears in my eyes. Because I was truly very sad. I didn't pop the bottle but drew the cork quietly. The wind was groaning outside the windows and insistently tried to break into the room. I drank almost the entire bottle myself, munching on the dates and smoking a pipe. The candle sputtered from time to time and the clock ticked loudly. "What time is it?" I stroked her head. "Sleep—this hour will pass and others will follow . . ."

Andrzej Bobkowski skiing in the Tatry mountains, Poland, 1930s.
(Family archive, Małgorzata Czerwińska-Miklaszewska, Cracow)

Andrzej Bobkowski with his parents, in Modlin, Poland, 1920s.
(Muzeum Literatury im. Adama Mickiewicza, Warsaw)

Andrzej Bobkowski in Brussels, early 1930s.
(Muzeum Literatury im. Adama Mickiewicza,
Warsaw)

Barbara (Basia) Birtus and Andrzej Bobkowski hiking, Poland,
late 1930s. (Instytut Badań Literackich, Polish Academy of
Sciences, Warsaw)

1941

January 3, 1941

We are on rue de Reuilly in OUR ROOM. It has been costly . . . I woke this morning and went to the Polish House to see Tadzio. It was still dark. I enter their room. Tadzio is sleeping. Igiełka, "The Needle," is already up and is tinkering with something. Boruc is lying in bed and dozing. Igiełka greeted me noisily: "Mr. B., old Tadzio here won't be much use to you, since he got back at two in the morning flat wasted."

I wake Tadzio. "Ahhh, Jędruś, ready to roll. Man, am I drunk. I'm dressed in a flash and off for the cart." He indeed got up and began to dillydally. The other two jeered, he snapped back. Tadzio is half-sober. I know him and I know that even when he's completely drunk, it's hard to tell. Meanwhile, Igiełka produced a quarter bottle of vodka from the corner, a tin of pâté and some bread, and declared we must drink to the New Year. We drank. We started to enjoy it. Tadzio said he already felt better, the mood became festive. Finally we passed the hat and dispatched Igiełka for a half-liter of vodka and some herring. He dashed over to Dombrowski's on rue Saint-Paul and returned with the lot. By now it was light, outside the window a thick snow began to fall. We all got sentimental and "chucked one down," as Tadzio says. Bang, bang, bang—a bite of bread with marinated herring and again bang. I was already good and tipsy. Tadzio and Igiełka were totally drunk. But we kept our cool. Igiełka offered to lend us a hand.

The three of us went downstairs on shaky legs, grabbed a hold of the cart, and took off. It was almost ten o'clock. A thick snow was falling, silent and peaceful. The banks of the Seine were deserted, a row of bowed trees, houses, the Left Bank—everything disappeared into the fog of snow and vanished before our eyes. The snow got under our collars, wet our faces, and settled in a thick layer on our shoulders and hats. It was so heavy that Tadzio, waving his arms, shouted: "Get a move on, make way for the esteemed porters," batted the snowflakes with his hands, and continued his monologue.

Near Arts-et-Métiers we felt thirsty and went for a beer, and after the beer a drop of cognac. We reached the boulevards and near Porte Saint-Martin stopped in for a kirsch. We were raring to go. By now I, too, was almost drunk. We spouted nonsense, passing some policemen Tadzio bowed and said: "Hail there, you . . . , in the cape"—in a word a drunken caravan, hanging onto the cart. Around midnight we arrived at rue Saint-Lazare. With a great racket and out of breath, we made it to the seventh floor.

It snowed and snowed, descending without letup over the whole city. We carried our things downstairs, piled them onto the cart, covered them with the tent, and set off. The blizzard was raging for real, we realized it would be heavy going. We began to move slowly, step by step, our feet sinking and losing their grip. From rue Saint-Lazare to rue de Reuilly it's about six kilometers. By the time we reached the boulevards we had sobered up completely. We trudged along, panting, one foot before the other. From Porte Saint-Denis the boulevard rises gradually as far as place de la République. But for the helping hand of a Frenchman who noticed our vain efforts and took pity on us, I doubt we would have budged from the spot. The snow did not stop falling and it covered the city in a thick sheepskin coat.

We fell silent and stubbornly advanced one pace at a time. Despite the frost sweat poured down our faces and we were soaked from head to toe. Finally, after a five-hour trek we arrived at the hotel. Tadzio was in a hurry to meet a date and left right away. Igiełka and I carried our stuff to the room. Then we took the empty cart back to the Polish House. This was a breeze, because rue Crillon is nearby. We returned the cart, I embraced Igiełka, thanking him for his help. Without him, the two of us could not have managed. Then I returned to rue Saint-Lazare.

I was so tired that I sank down in the hallway and began to cry for no reason at all. I rested a bit, and only then did Basia and I go downstairs with a few remaining items and take the metro to rue de Reuilly.

The hotel room, which was barely heated, seemed hot to us. Sixteen months of that pigeon coop under the roof had done us in completely.

January 6, 1941

We both feel like we're in a sanatorium for the treatment of nervous exhaustion. We're so comfortable here, so peaceful and at home, that we sometimes give no thought to anything at all. Everything delights us. The bed is delightful, the sink, the separate kitchen, the gas, the electric light, the wardrobes, the linoleum floor, and even the people are delightful: the *patronne*, cursing the German occupation and playing the radio full blast with communiqués from England,[1] the baker and the baker's wife, greeting us, as in the old days, with the smiles of fat, good-natured people, the shopkeeper and her daughter, an elfin little Frenchwoman, the contentious *marchand de vin*, a former pilot, who treats Basia with great sympathy and announces to his clients when she appears: "*Voyez-vous, madame est Polonaise. On les aura, n'est-ce pas, madame?!*"[2]

Everyone recognized us and upon our return accepted us into their *quartier*, among the great family of permanent residents of the Hôtel du Commerce. The *patronne* put in a word for Basia at "her" shops, which did not hesitate to add her to their ration lists. People here are completely different, a bit like the provinces. Not that awful, greedy, and shameless riffraff of the 9th arrondissement. The hotel residents have been here forever; not even our neighbors on the other side of the wall have changed. She is still fat, with an impressive abundance of curves—he is diminutive, good-looking, small-boned, and younger than she. And once again the sounds of their loud and complicated caresses reach our ears.

I return home in the evening and it seems to me that time has stopped, that things are still "as they were before." I gaze affectionately at the saint's figure standing before the entrance, at the artificial grotto overgrown with ivy and at the tree outside the window. It's strange—in a hotel I've found my home.

We have no desire to do anything, simply unpack, arrange our things. We go to bed, light the night lamp, and read. Lying down and reading. No more ice-cold stone floor, no more fussing with the spirit stove, no more tiptoeing around the room. One can wash one's hands in warm water and sleep in one's pajamas without a sweater and a scarf around one's head. As in a dream.

January 7, 1941

By now we know what's going on. Counselor Schwerbel came to spend Christmas Eve at the shelter on avenue Wagram and after the supper delivered a speech to the Poles. The speech was very positivist and ended with a stanza from a poem by Adam Asnyk, eloquent, programmatic:

One must advance with those who live,
And grasp what's new that life can give,
Not stubbornly adorn one's head
With the faded laurels of the dead.[3]

Verstanden? There's something piquant in this Gestapo man reciting Asnyk's positivist verses at a Polish Christmas Eve. After his speech, the Counselor withdrew to the room of Mme the Marquise and there they joined in singing—

Polish carols. The Counselor is musical and sings well. Our people listened to them from the hallway. Both E., an educated man, and B., a workman (E. jotted down the little poem and I got the stanza from him), insisted: "Mr. B., he must be Polish!" Because he recites verses by Asnyk and sings Polish carols. That's all it takes. I retorted that if he's Polish, then in that case I'm German. If the Counselor requests that a Mass be celebrated this year in memory of Piłsudski, Dmowski, and Daszyński, well great![4] Then Poland is already independent for sure.

January 10, 1941

Since the New Year there's been a steady frost and the weather is completely un-Parisian. It's fresh and the streets are covered in a thick layer of snow. They clear it very slowly and one could easily travel all over Paris by sleigh. The food situation keeps getting worse. The great turnip, the so-called rutabaga, has appeared everywhere. The newspapers offer a thousand and one ways to prepare this vegetable and they trumpet the virtues and benefits of eating the disgusting thing. Hence, an orgy of jokes on the subject of eating turnips. The papers are full of humorous cartoons. For example, a family sits around a bare table, the father with a book. "And now, instead of dinner, we will read about Pantagruel's feast." Apparently the German censor is surprised by this humor and considers it improper and harmful. *Schädlich!* How can one be witty and make jokes on this subject under the circumstances? I remember how the Englishman in André Maurois's terrific *Silences du colonel Bramble* says to the Frenchman: "Do you know why this war is so awful and tragic? Because the Germans have no sense of humor."[5] How true. A profound truth. No genuine culture lacks a subtle wit. I'm afraid of nations without wit, without lightness. There's a gulf between the Germans and the French that nothing can fill; not collaboration, or agreement, or the new place of the new France in the new Europe.

One hears more and more on this subject. Vichy has gotten rid of the Anglophiles and clearly begun to count on cooperation with Germany. It is influencing public opinion in this direction. While standing in line, I've already heard it said more than once that the Germans are *gentils*, that they're good organizers, that they're sending France their potatoes. What the devil has happened to the French *esprit de contradiction?* They direct their innate critical faculties at *notre gouvernement*, compared to which the Germans obviously look splendid. The Germans have left the entire administration in French hands, and this administration is clearly floundering, because it has suddenly become more "planned" than the German one; endless papers and forms, while stomachs are empty.

January 20, 1941

The Counselor is a good psychologist. He did not shut the lending library of Polish books in the Polish House. He simply requested the catalog, crossed out the titles that were *neblagonadezhnye* ("unreliable," as the Russians would say), demanded that they be delivered to him, and set about reading them. Among the discarded works was an anti-German book by Axel Munthe.[6] The Counselor read it through and a few days later brought it to one of the Poles in the Batignolles shelter. "You should read this, it's perhaps the best characterization of the Germans I've read." Axel Munthe seems to have livened them up considerably. (I haven't read it.) Can this be a warning? He's a real joker. The optimists insist he fears that the Germans cannot win the war and this is a way to guarantee his future. We are one big family, at the head of which stands the Counselor, the kind father, omniscient and omnipotent. Each of his catchphrases makes the rounds of Polish Paris with the speed of an arrow. To former soldiers, with no source of money, he gives a few francs for cigarettes from time to time. "And if the French police give you trouble because you don't have papers, then come see me. After a phone call from me, they won't lay a finger on you." What's more, he works up a sweat to enable everyone to return home to Poland. "Just watch it with your behavior — don't make my job any harder." And some of the children are polite. But not all of them . . .

January 31, 1941

America is like a cat approaching a basin of water. It wets a paw, shakes it, then stands and looks. Dips in another one and again quickly removes it and shakes it. Eventually it may decide to go in.

C. today expressed the opinions held by "enlightened" Frenchmen: "The Germans are still too gentle with us. They should tighten the screws enough to teach us a lesson. That's the only way to raise us from our collapse and moral disintegration."

I assured him not to worry. The Germans will certainly tighten the screws, because that's the one thing they manage to do well. But that will not save France from decline. When the Roman legions marched into Greece, I'm almost sure the Greeks behaved in similar fashion. With typical French objectivity, C. went on about the laziness and obtuseness of French youth, about the disappearance of crafts, and about the workers' shocking inefficiency. No discipline, no deference. He teaches in a vocational school attached to one of the factories. As an example, he reported that the results of the psychotechnical entrance exams for prospective students grow worse every year. This year, for example, many of the fourteen-, fifteen-, and even sixteen-year-old boys were unable to describe how they had spent the previous Sunday. Pen in hand they would sit for an hour without writing a single word. By the way, in many cases I do not know of any greater subjectivism than precisely this French objectivism. They manage to be splendidly partisan while maintaining the appearance of the most enthralling objectivity.

February 15, 1941

Today I was a witness at Antek's wedding. The other witness was the *patron* of his hotel, a fat and bewhiskered Frenchman: an appealing example of some-one who has remained a provincial "despite everything." He will never be a Parisian. I rode over on my bicycle and then we all four walked to the town hall. There we waited a while in the hallway. A sluggish custodian plastered with beribboned medals appeared and ushered us into the wedding chamber. It's a special room decorated with the usual paneling, a carpet on the floor, all very official. If you were brought there while deeply asleep and then awoke, you would certainly say, not "hello," but "*République française—Liberté, Égalité, Fraternité.*"

At the end of the room stood a large table covered in green cloth. In front of it two large armchairs for the newlyweds, on the sides along the wall two chairs for the witnesses. Also, a row of chairs for the audience and family guests. As at the movies. We sat there and waited for the other couples, because the mayor usually performs the ceremonies all in a row. A couple shortly appeared with a crowd of relatives. All already quite flushed with red wine. They smelled like a barrel which had just been drained of the last drops of *pinard.*[7] They began to chatter all at once and naturally about food and food ration cards. Then other couples arrived with their families and the room grew crowded. The custodian entered, closed the shutters, and lit the large, shining candlesticks and chandeliers. It's more elegant with artificial light. He went to the entrance and announced: "*Monsieur le Maire!*" Everyone stood, like children in school. The mayor entered in a black suit, with a tricolor sash. He took a seat at the table and then we in turn sat down. Two clerks took their places at the opposite ends of the table. They rummaged in their papers. Meanwhile, the assembled public began again to chatter. The jovial *patron* of Antek's hotel, his other witness, asked the mayor in a loud voice if one didn't need coupons to get married. The question aroused laughter all around. The mayor's answer, very witty, amused everyone even more.

"*Non, monsieur, d'ailleurs c'est déjà rationné: une femme pour toute la vie.*"[8]

Consumption is limited. A flood of jokes and double entendres on the theme of "one woman for life."

Meanwhile the custodian sat Antek and his future wife in the armchairs, us in the witness chairs. The room quieted down. I approached the table, showed my *état civil*, signed the marriage certificate. One of the clerks read out the young couple's personal information, tripping over Krucza Street and over the maiden name of Antek's mother. The mayor rose—and with him the whole room. He read out all the paragraphs, the husband and wife affirmed their intentions, followed by another few paragraphs, in which the husband was instructed to look after and provide for his wife, the wife to take care of the household, even something about food—short and practical—in the Napoleonic style. The mayor congratulated the young couple and shook the newlyweds' hands. We went out. At the door the custodian handed Antek the *livret de famille*—the family booklet, a booklet in which all the information about the couple and the date of marriage are inscribed. Additional rubrics: date of child's birth, date of child's death, date of wife's death, date of husband's death, date of divorce . . . based on the court's decision, etc. Everything is anticipated and there's a rubric for everything. It's certainly very convenient.

We left the town hall. The day was sunny and frosty. At the hotel the *patron* stood us a round of aperitifs, Antek stood us a second round, I a third. Then I returned home.

March 6, 1941

One of our workers, employed in Romania before the war, told me today how warmly he had welcomed Polish refugees in the fall of 1939: "I had a house. At times thirty people would come for the evening. Everyone felt completely at home. They all kept getting into fist fights . . ." Is it possible to convey any more bluntly or accurately IN POLISH how comfortable his guests felt and how much of a Polish outpost his house had become? He recounted all this proudly, in all seriousness.

May 1, 1941

May Day and Pétain's name day. Notices are posted everywhere, with his photograph and the absurd slogan: "I keep promises, even those made by others" (*Je tiens les promesses, même celles des autres*). Who are "these others"? That he will keep German promises, there's no doubt . . . Below it, a proclamation addressed to the French worker surpassing in its stupidity anything uttered on this theme before.—Things were bad, because of social inequality and the class struggle. Once social inequality has been eliminated, the class struggle will automatically cease and there will be Paradise on earth. All of this he—Pétain—will accomplish. No—it's not that simple, and besides it's high time to stop competing with the Lord God and his Paradise. Paradise is a very complicated machine and it cannot be replicated without obtaining concessions and detailed plans. Otherwise, it will end like all such undertakings usually end—in bankruptcy.

I don't know if there has ever been an age as permeated with lying as our own. Lying, backed by force, using the crudest methods and under intense pressure, is crammed into people's minds as the truth. They are ordered to believe, and that's all there is to it. And under this barrage of lying, the mind finally ceases to function on its own, it succumbs and gives way, like the support of a bridge under the crush of a swollen current or ice floes. People believe, without believing. This is the latest achievement of lying today. The surface layer of thought and the brain, which is intended for daily use, is not able to resist and succumbs not only to sophisticated forms of lying but even to those that are primitive and crude. Only the deeper layers of the brain and of thought function normally and from time to time react. It is then that one senses the extent to which humanity today is chained and shackled by lying. Powerlessness in the face of this lying further weakens resistance and even the most sensible people turn into a herd of sheep. I observe this in myself: I read something in the newspaper and it takes a moment before I notice that I've believed it. Entire nations have been trained to accept lying as the truth; they are forced to swallow—and swallowing keeps getting easier, as with sick children and castor oil. After the first spoonful, the rest go down more smoothly.

As is the custom, lilies of the valley are being sold everywhere today. But it's still cold and dreary. Yugoslavia and Greece now belong to the past. The Greek prisoners are being released and Hitler has given a speech in which he stressed how much he values the culture of that nation, if only as a result of his studies. I wonder how far Heinrich Schliemann's archaeological discoveries have turned the Germans' heads.[9] They have long considered themselves the Greeks of our day. They may be Spartans, but never Athenians. It's terrible when an entire nation suffers from such an obsession. I gaze at them every day and I'm repulsed, not by their appearance, but by a certain mud one senses in the soul of each one of them. This mud contains various things—but they are nevertheless covered in mud. That's the point. This mud clings to every thought about them, it clogs and sticks to everything. The mud of the first day of creation.

All the newspapers carry shots of German soldiers at the Acropolis, or (using the technical language of photography) "high-contrast pictures." Indeed!

May 6, 1941

I'm in the hotel room of the worker G., listening to him talk. "You know," he says, "in this hotel I met a very beautiful woman. Her room is three floors above me and she lives with an Algerian who leaves for work every day at six in the morning and returns in the evening. I also get up at six and as soon as he has left I go upstairs. We stay in bed until nine, she gets up, makes coffee, buttered toast, a good breakfast. What do you expect? I have no money for food and I must think of my wife. I have to bring myself back home to her in Poland, more or less in one piece and in good health. I have no job, but at least I have a decent breakfast every day." All this in a serious tone without the slightest trace of irony. He has found a method of survival.

May 17, 1941

Our first time in the theater since the outbreak of war. Sacha Guitry's *Vive l'Empereur*.[10] Perfect nonsense. The action is set in the time of Louis-Philippe. A loving couple is celebrating their thirtieth wedding anniversary and have invited all the wedding guests from thirty years before. The company arrives, a splendid sample of the French bourgeoisie. A couple from the provinces, quarreling continually by means of clever, lively, and pointed quips, allusions pregnant with meaning—everything smoothed over by the host with the constant cry of: *"Et le temps est quand même beau."*[11] Some old Napoleonic campaigner, a fervent Bonapartist and—what a great surprise—a long-lost friend of their youth. The man of the house has tracked him down and his appearance is intended as a surprise for the wife. After all, she had been so fond of him . . . The long-lost friend arrives, but the man of the house sees that his appearance causes his wife's good humor and liveliness to vanish. This seems to him suspicious. He asks her why. She is evasive but in the end admits that not long after their wedding she had caught Monsieur Robert in a tender scene with her sister. She had naturally been obliged to ask him to leave the house. As they were now joyously celebrating their thirty years of unclouded marriage, full of love to this day, everything had reminded her of that scene.

The husband, annoyed at the spoiled mood, takes Robert aside for a talk: "Robert, I know everything . . ." Robert: "That's great; you see, I myself wanted to tell you about it, but since you already know . . . In any case I admire you . . ." Obviously. The husband quickly grasps that his wife had betrayed him with Robert a few weeks after the wedding—thirty years ago. The ticklish situation is relieved by the entrance of the renowned Monsieur Daguerre, with his infernal photography machine. The company arranges itself in a group, which is simply a virtual photograph from that former time. A terrific trick, full of Guitry's particular zest. The theater rocks with laughter.

The next four acts are variations on the theme of the first and end in harmony. The poor husband hesitates over what to do. That was thirty years ago, but all the same, despite everything, he's jealous, his pride is wounded. What about a duel? That's what the old Bonapartist advises. "With sabers! Strike blindly!"[12] As a second, well versed in affairs of honor, he'll be useful in his old age. The husband's friend from the provinces calms the waters. Meanwhile, his wife is furious with him because he refuses to speak with her and demands no explanations. The monster—he doesn't even want to know how it happened. Finally, he yields to her pleas and agrees to hear her confession.

How many times? —Once. A single time? Maddening. Because if it had been ten, twenty times—well, one could understand.

Wife: "Well, you see, my betrayal was . . . patriotic."

Husband: "What?"

Wife: "Remember? We were having supper with Robert, the three of us, in that restaurant. And that evening came the news of the victory at Austerlitz. All Paris was going mad, but you were criticizing Napoleon. We quarreled and I left with Robert. I don't know—somehow we ended up in a hotel."

Husband: "In a hotel! . . . Well, and . . ."

Wife: "—And in the hotel . . . When you know . . . well, the victory, and you were criticizing the emperor. Even at a certain moment . . . so, at a certain . . ."

Husband: "At a certain . . . psychological . . . moment . . ."

Wife: "Yes, at a certain psychological moment I even cried: *Vive l'Empereur!*"

I wonder if Guitry hadn't built all this nonsense around this one idea, which is after all excellent. It's absolutely French and there's nothing improbable about it. I'm still laughing now.

Dialogue and more dialogue followed: sparkling, subtle. A WORD. A duel. The friend from the provinces says the wife would be able to stop the duel even at the last moment. The husband discreetly informs her of this. But she'll have nothing of it—she hasn't the slightest idea of intervening. On the contrary: she is delighted. He will be fighting on her account: AFTER THIRTY YEARS. How much he still loves her!

One can indeed go mad. There will be no duel. He will betray her—with the beautiful student who comes to him for singing lessons. This is how he will take revenge. A few scenes with the young Geneviève Guitry, Sacha's fourth wife. (They keep getting younger and younger.) The wife senses something and decides to assist him in this escapade. Then they'll be quits. And he'll no longer have the advantage of never having betrayed her. He goes to the *rendez-vous* arranged by his wife. They all await his return. He returns. NOTHING. His wife is furious. It's all thirty years too late. "If only it had been thirty years ago."

Sacha Guitry didn't even have much acting to do, his role was so simple. Nice costumes, wretched decorations, authentic props, likely from his private collections. It was getting dark when we left the theater. We walked from the Madeleine to the Opéra, discussing the play. The boulevard was deserted and quiet. Only the occasional rumbling of the metro underground or the hissing of an ash-gray German automobile. A pretty young woman kept stopping every few feet in front of the shopwindows and allowed the client trailing behind her to approach slowly. The Café de la Paix was empty. Two officers were downing the remains of their beer on the terrace. The shopwindows were dark. Despite the silence and the emptiness of an evening in one of the once liveliest places on earth, something in the mood drew me even closer to this city and charmed me. I have grown attached to these Parisian corners, I have lived with them in daily communion, both ordinary and amazing, in the course of my daily bicycle rides. I know every pebble, every bump in the road, which I avoid from memory at night. Yet, despite the old familiarity, everything is always new. Can these corners and stones have poisoned me, or what?

Could such a play be performed in Poland? I wonder how much it would lose in translation, whether in moving from the Théâtre de la Madeleine to some Polish theater it wouldn't along the way lose that intangible "something." These French plays are so French that when served in a different climate, at a different temperature, they lose their bouquet. And with plays, as with wine, it's precisely the bouquet that counts. In another climate either too much meaning is attached to such things or they are made too light of. What here is an hors d'oeuvre in Poland is often made into an entire meal or is not considered edible at all. And that's not surprising. It has to be that way.

Paris and French thought are like champagne, peaches, burgundy, sardines, cheese. Juicy, exciting, easy to digest, piquant, tasty, light. And practical. The French do not like supermen or superthought. This always makes them attractive—even when one has had enough of them in many other respects or has even disdained them as people. Can it be that their conduct in this war is only human, practical, and realistic? Practical, certainly. The best proof is that I am now walking along peacefully after the theater and that I'm able to think about such things. Are they without honor? At the moment. Perhaps in the end they will emerge with honor, and if not—even so, the world is ready to forgive them and forget. Is there anything that cannot be forgiven the beautiful woman one CANNOT live without? And Poland? The Cousine Bette of nations. The world will always "hold everything against us," as it would with a poor cousin. We live with constant, subconscious stage fright. And when we are obliged to say our "lines" and play our role, we overdo it. The audience does not like actors like that. In particular, the select, opening-night audience. But that's the way it goes in this world, this is the one that determines the play's reputation. France will coast on her good reputation, like students who study well in the early grades but pass the Gymnasium graduating exam—on their reputations alone. The French will wiggle out of it. Moreover: they will be heroes. And then it starts all over again: yesterday I couldn't stand them, today I like them, tomorrow I'll curse them . . . While in the domain of thought they will continue to be a laxative, a tonic, a stimulant for the appetite. For all the other nations.

May 24, 1941

Słowacki's *Letters* to his mother.[13] Until his mystical period he is dear to me and lucid. Then, that's it! I cannot, I just cannot stomach it, I retch. Very good comments on France. One senses an exceptional wit, refined and pungent. And then the curtain drops. The Polish tendency to fall into mysticism is rather terrifying. We often provide examples in which the line between physics and metaphysics is missing. In its place, stretch the "Wild Steppes," where the various Towiańskis roam with impunity and compete with the whirlwind in their nonsense.[14] But what else is left for an eternally impoverished nation, always being ravaged and oppressed, but at the same time having a very elevated conception of itself, garbed in traditional gentry robes and with the sense of freedom the gentry enjoyed. If we had been a wealthy nation, a nation in suit jackets and carrying wallets (not the inevitable "fat purse"), our history might have been the most glorious on earth. At the very least the most heroic. At the same time, the world's attitude toward us is at best benevolent and condescending. It treats us exactly the way "cultured" anti-Semites treat the Jews: "When it comes down to it, one shouldn't behave swinishly . . ." We often resemble the beggar who knocks at the door and, when offered soup and bread, suddenly straightens his shoulders and while stroking his whiskers and speaking French with an accent from the Vistula borderlands, shouts: "*Madame, je ne mange que la langouste au mayonnaise.*"[15] Our mania for unenlightened martyrdom, our eternal willingness to die, whether it's called for or not, our readiness for any sacrifice, has deeply convinced the French and English that we part with life more easily than the members of any other nation. Certainly—from the perspective of pure ethics and morality, of honor, we deserve considerably greater respect than others: but the world thinks in practical terms. The persistent conflict between our psychology and the psychology of foreigners rests on a continual misunderstanding, the opposition of theory and practice, the battle of cavalry against tanks. (I still can't believe cavalry was actually sent against the tanks.) We fence using the concepts of chivalrous honor, in which a stubborn inferiority complex combines with lordly gestures and—one has to admit—with boorish pretentiousness. We draw correct theoretical conclusions and oppose them to cold, commercial, strictly calculating reason, in which even baseness is permitted if it produces tangible benefits. This always reminds me of a certain friend with whom I used to play chess. On principle he never took pieces, or exchanged them, so as not to spoil the "aesthetics of the game." When I realized what he was doing, I began pitilessly to take advantage of every moment in which I sensed that for the sake of "the aesthetics of the game," he was committing blunders. I offered him my pieces to be taken, knowing he wouldn't take them. I more than once gained not only a piece but a POSITION. That was even more important. And I took everything he had. He would get angry, talk about "the aesthetics of the game," and—lose. He had to lose. We Poles are already known for this. For the sake of "the aesthetics of the game," we commit this and that blunder. And not only our pawns but also our important pieces are taken, although I don't know if we have ever managed to play with real pieces. One can count such games on the fingers of one hand. And clearly, pawns can be taken also *en passant* . . . Culture? Culture is often for us a kind of lipstick. Applied on entering a social gathering. After which, we act provocatively. A flurry of Balzac, Flaubert, Montaigne, Chamfort,[16] Marx, Tolstoy, Shakespeare, precise observance of the outer forms of *bon ton* (not always) and at the same time a horrifying lack of tact. The same lack of tact with which we so often reproach the Jews. We are very much like them and that is doubtless the source of our anti-Semitism.

The Czechs. Hácha has signed, the country was untouched.[17] During the period of lost independence they did not revolt, resolving not to submit *internally* and to seize the first opportunity to regain their external independence. And they made money. Now they will regain their independence, because they will also be heroes and will be esteemed more highly than we are and will be more widely known. I've heard that in Paris there are 240 Czech refugees. They do not wander from shelter to shelter, they do not display their heroic penury before strangers. Every well-established Czech family in Paris is said to have taken in a refugee and helps him out. They can afford to. What about us? The eternal attitude of the bankrupt aristocrat toward the Jew-tenant. Have a look, you Jew, at the portrait of my ancestors, look at the weapons on the walls, look at the scars inflicted in duels of honor, and—lend me, you boor, a few pennies.

And sometimes, smiling indulgently, the Jew will give him a few pennies and treat him with condescension, because scars, time-darkened portraits, and dried blood cannot be pawned. Old weapons? It depends what kind. And the master bears him a grudge . . . No. None of this "Together, arm-in-arm, Gentlemen."[18] One should sit quietly, remove one's jacket, loosen one's tie, and focus on the chessboard. And repeat to oneself, "I am Polish," without the song about the cavalryman and without the turbid metaphysics. We are far too valuable, too talented and clever, exposed to too many dangers, to permit ourselves to romp about on various "Wild Steppes."

Słowacki comments on George Sand appreciatively. I must have remembered it wrong.

May 31, 1941

There's a feverish mood in Paris, which is hard to understand. This evening we went to "our" cinema. Before the start of the weekly newsreel they now make a short announcement: "The management asks the audience to remain calm while the newsreel is running, because any sort of demonstration will result in the cinema being shut down and the culprits will be punished, starting with the owner." By order of the Préfecture of police. This is followed by the weekly news from the Association Cinématographique Européenne. We are now one great fighting Europe. The films show only English planes being shot down and only English ships being sunk. A French workman behind us said: "*En même temps* in the London cinemas only the Germans lose airplanes and only German ships are sunk. *Ils sont quittes.*"[19] No—the French are not a nation that can be classified in simple terms. In Africa it's tough going. There's nothing to show for it. Near Tobruk it's a war of position. In the cinema dead silence reigned.

June 1, 1941

I have two days off. Today and tomorrow. Today summer has suddenly arrived. Sun and practically a heat wave already. There was no spring this year. For the first time in many months I've taken up reading in French. I've gotten over my aversion. George Sand's *Indiana.*[20] Słowacki recommended her to me and I've decided to get to know Mme Sand a bit better.

A few weeks ago a large German bookstore opened on boulevard Saint-Michel. Tastefully designed, modern, the displays nicely presented, flawless books and bindings. The German graphics are simple, harmonious, subdued in color—outstanding. I took a look at the bookstore a few days ago. It was a sunny afternoon, the sky was pale blue, everything submerged in that sharp but never tiring Parisian light. Bistros bustling like beehives all around, small bookshops and large bookshops with book-filled tables on the sidewalk. Assorted books, stacks of Balzac at three francs each. Flaubert, Gautier, Dumas, Mme Sand. *The Lady of the Camellias* crowded by an album of Louvre masterpieces, *Cousine Bette* next to a booklet on Cézanne, *The Three Musketeers* along with *Mademoiselle de Maupin.* The letters of Mme de Sévigné and the letters of Mademoiselle de Lespinasse.[21] Octave Aubry with his Napoleons.[22] Book covers of every sort, mostly no covers at all. I gave the German bookstore and the exquisite editions a pass. I was annoyed by the Gothic type, marching rigidly and evenly, with mathematical precision, the immaculate and harmonious arrangement of lines and spaces, like a military march: dum, dum, dum, and fifes. The dreary visions of German Gothic in marvelously produced art albums. I went over to those messy tables and my spirits lifted. All those books, so casually piled in heaps, seemed to be laughing and joking on the subject of the bookstore across the street. And above them presided the smile of a print of Watteau's *L'Indifférent* — a pale blue, velvety smile of superiority.[23] Stirred by a light breeze, the print seemed to dance. Yes. Really. There was a spirit to this side — over there, for all the supreme perfection of the graphic art, hobnailed boots pounded to the beat of drums and pipes.

I gazed from afar at that bookstore, almost with pity and, saluting the sun, ate a buckwheat crêpe filled with jam. They're sold on the street without coupons. The German bookstore is one great misunderstanding. My fingers were a bit sticky from the remains of the jam and I rummaged casually among the books. I rummaged in the same smiling and free spirit offered to everyone here. And I purchased Mme Sand's *Indiana.*

June 5, 1941

One of the workmen living in the shelter on avenue Wagram, ill and driven to despair by Mme the Marquise's harassment (she orders them every three days to change rooms), jumped from the sixth floor. This suicide had a depressing effect on all of us. The unfortunate man's funeral was held today. Among others at the cemetery was the Counselor, who on behalf of the Gestapo placed a wreath of white and red flowers on the grave. He did not give a speech and recited none of Asnyk's verses. The Counselor has put me off Asnyk and the positivists for the rest of my life.

The English are apparently planning to attack Syria. All the concierges are talking about it. Therefore it must be true. Bu-bu-but will they ta-ta-take the pl-pl-plunge?

June 7, 1941

It looks like the English really do intend to invade Syria. The concierges have already invaded, but not yet them. Titans of the speedy decision. It's possible, however, that the French may yet fight.

June 9, 1941

The English have invaded Syria.[24] Amazing! The French have decided to fight! But without declaring war on England. They can tell the Germans: Look, we're on your side. Some day they'll tell the English: We did not want war—we were on your side. No—I can't believe that THIS is France. I don't want to believe it, because I know how quick we are to criticize others. But as for what goes on inside me . . . France nevertheless has good advocates. The issue is whether she HAS any at all, in fact; whether they are not too often the shades of the dead, speaking to us in the voice of the living. This is the mystery of France and France knows how to make use of it splendidly. The great pens and minds of France are not yet entirely dead, although they have long ago been buried.—Thank God! *Gott sei Dank!* If France should ever allow them truly to die, if she rejects them, it will be the end of her. And the end of us all.

June 12, 1941

Mme Sand's *Indiana* and *Valentine*. I have immersed myself with pleasure in the atmosphere of French Romanticism. A Romanticism of the manicured garden, of sexless moonlight. Words are endearments, sentences are epigrams, feelings are breezy, despite all attempts to give them the force of hurricanes. The grass, the little birds, the nicely tended ponds, espaliered trees and leaves, as in theater sets. Organdy. An overall impression of care and elegance. Everything maintained as it should be, well ordered and in tempo, like the sonatas of Karl Czerny played with a metronome.[25] Even crime or suicide are unable to move you. They simply mark the *forte* (God forbid *fortissimo*) needed for action, like punctuation in a text. Suicide or crime have the power of exclamation marks. Not even two exclamation marks, for no self-respecting person uses two exclamation marks. *Quelle vulgarité!* Perhaps only Balzac, that *enfant terrible* of French literature, of whom one often speaks with a smile, as of a naughty boy. But Sand is no match for him. I admire him for having managed to show that the regulated river of French literature can foam and stormily overflow its banks, that it's a real torrent, not a scheduled opening of the sluices. Reading Balzac, I feel like I've entered an enormous factory. The clatter of tangled sentences, here a wheel revolves, there something has broken down, and the oft-repeated *"dont"* screeches, like a badly greased ball bearing. (*"Un fauteuil* dont *les bras étaient terminés par des têtes de sphinx bronzées* dont *la peinture s'en allait..."—La Cousine Bette.*[26]) We Poles do not pay as much attention to style and good form as the French. That's why Balzac captivates us so much more.

Conrad's *The Shadow Line.*[27] I'm discovering him for the second time. What a splendid ability to convey ineffable things in simple words. By describing a particular, tangible thing, he manages to render a mood that no language or word can define. The smallest actions of his characters can convey an approaching storm. You think not about the actions but always about the storm.

It's finally summer. In the evening we walk to the Bois de Vincennes. The ponds and greenery are like a manicured landscape. Worse—like a cheap print. The cries of the peacocks reach us from the zoo, a pair of swans is swimming on the pond.

June 13, 1941

Afternoon on boulevard Saint-Michel and in the Luxembourg Gardens. Warm and sunny; everything seems to shimmer. A blinding sun. I ate a crêpe with jam and squinted my eyes. The clatter of wooden soles.[28] The books strewn on the bookstall tables are like heaps of confetti. One would like to take some handfuls and scatter them about. It's quiet in the Luxembourg Gardens. The crunch of pebbles under the feet of passersby and the cries of children near the boat basin. Basia makes friends with a young boy and listens to his expert comments on his sailboat; I assist in the launching of a large submarine, sticking my tongue out, just like the boys, as we wind up the machine. One of the sailboats has headed into the fountain and can't be retrieved from under the stream of water. My boy laughs. The submarine has taken off and vanished; the boys rush to the other side of the pond. I put on my eyeglasses and rush after them. It's very interesting. Afterward we sit on the bench, close our eyes, and feel good. The setting has a certain quality—as though the buoyancy of life, of thought were hovering... This can make up for a lot. And indeed it does.

June 14, 1941

The Champs-Élysées. Sunshine and hats, big and small, tiny turbans of flowers, a fog of veils. Painted legs, dresses with a hint of bustles, hairdos à la 1900. Strawberry tarts on the café terrace. Germans stomp by, prowling for "prey." There's a lot to choose from. Next to us are two Germans with their wives. Two giant Valkyries appear like "bolts from the blue" in this colorful and bright setting. They look like caryatids amid Tanagra figurines.[29] They reek of sour cabbage and beer and of a splendid kitchen with rows of faience canisters labeled: "*Reis*," "*Salz*," "*Pfeffer*." With adages embroidered on the dishcloths.

June 16, 1941

Today I ride through the Bois de Vincennes. It's where the Germans keep repair shops for their military vehicles. A great commotion reigned there today. They were packing up, winding up, driving off. People stood and stared. I learned from a Frenchman that people are being drafted off the street for the transport. Where to? Apparently, to Poland. That was enough for me. I was seized with excitement. I began to think about what this means and concluded there will be war with Russia. A Napoleon complex. I'm transfixed by the thought. But whenever I mention it, everyone smiles in disbelief. On the way to the factory, I rode a stretch with a French worker. I said the same to him. He didn't want to believe it. K. mulled this over with me and also smiled in disbelief.

June 17, 1941

I could go to Poland. I returned again to the Bois. They are literally pulling people off the streets. They don't care at all about qualifications. I'm completely certain about the direction of the war. But people are afraid to believe it. They say it would be too good to be true.

June 21, 1941

For the last four days the heat has been unbearable. Hot and stifling. Dreadful, humid heat. Suffocating. The asphalt in some places has become muddy. We walk around our room barefoot and in shorts. The nights are just as hot and the sheets are scorching. In addition, the mood is clearly tense. Once again everyone is waiting. People talk more and more openly about Russia. That would be a decisive turn in the war.

June 22, 1941

Sunday. In the morning I sat in my armchair and read. Basia went to the store. Suddenly she calls me from the courtyard. I stuck my head out the window. "They left this morning for the east." I thought I would jump out the window. I couldn't believe it. I was dazed. I ran to see the *patronne*. Her voice shaking with emotion, she reports the radio announcement: "*Monsieur,* now the Boches may get a good thrashing" (*Ils vont prendre une bonne pilule*). We argue heatedly about Russia's military capacity. The French believe in Russia. Above all in Russia's inexhaustible human potential. "They have enough people." But today it's too soon to tell. Three or four weeks from now things may be clearer. If they withstand the first attack and manage to prolong and drag out the fight, then who knows whether this won't be the beginning of the end. I wish this month were already over and one could know what to say. Because this is something entirely different. Until now a certain system has been battling a certain ideology, or rather philosophy, something considerably broader than a system. Now a fight has broken out between two systems, each built on its own philosophy and ruthlessly and uncompromisingly formed in terms of this philosophy. The enemies Germany has had until now have lacked this kind of philosophy and that's why they have taken a beating.

In Russia it will come down to a struggle of matériel and men. The Germans will immediately hit "high C" and try to finish off the whole thing in one breath. (Like Napoleon, I'm thinking now. Smolensk, Borodino . . .) But the Russians have freedom of movement, they can withdraw indefinitely—and will try to keep drawing things out, so that every succeeding German note will be lower and lower. I pore over the map. Europe compared to Russia is a cramped, one-room apartment.

Afternoon in the Bois de Vincennes. Terrible heat. In the woods there are crowds of people and crowds of papers. Each person seeks a patch of grass in the shade and spends Sunday in the bosom of nature. The disheveled and half-undressed men and women give off the stench of dirty, sweaty bodies. The Parisian commoner stinks, litters, and sweats. Everyone reads the newspapers and concentration shows on their tired faces. But maybe it's only the heat. Hitler's speech, or rather his appeal to the people, is in *Paris-Midi*. A pack of distortions and lies, twisted truth, and the perennial "we were threatened and were forced to act." We return home at dusk. Someone walks past us and I hear him say: "I suppose that now the real war has begun." On a bench, in the fading light, a couple is imitating Rodin's *The Kiss*; there are bouquets of flowers on the bicycles heading home. The dynamo hubs click. It's impossible to breathe in our room. I go out for a beer. The *patron* and *patronne* are sitting next to the radio, as though by the fireside, and wink at me. The beer is lousy, but iced. Everyone in the bistro is already an expert on Russia and of course they say many stupid things. The crux is that someone is doing their fighting for them. I'm reminded of the encounter with the Negroes at the seaside. And the amazing conviction that this someone "has the obligation" to fight for what they, the French, consider right. Thoughts are also sweaty. "What if Staś . . . if only Kali . . . Staś . . .

Kali . . ." The concierge, emerging from the toilet in the courtyard and flushing loudly, announced: "It's going to rain, because the toilet stinks." The butter melts instantly into the bread, flies dance around the lightbulb. War.

June 26, 1941

Today a major German communiqué summarizes the results of the week's battle. They have advanced somewhat and provide implausible numbers of destroyed Soviet airplanes and tanks. Over four thousand planes and two thousand tanks, so-and-so many cannons, machine guns, etc. No one wants to take this seriously, everyone's spirits are lifted, and something has awakened even among the French. The myth of Russia is at work. But it's not merely a myth. Something much deeper is involved, a sympathy based on class, a sympathy felt by the people in this country of unfinished revolutions for the country that finished the job in one fell swoop.

Naturally, England recognized Russia as an ally right away. America, to a certain extent also. In the streets a touch of hope is in the air. In the metro, tickets are more often being torn in the shape of a "V"—*Victoire*, or in the form of an "H"—de Gaulle's *Honneur*. Something is stirring, a tremor in what is otherwise complete quiescence and in Vichy's increasingly collaborationist measures. Syria is fighting "heroically" against the slowly advancing English invasion.

July 13, 1941

Infernal heat. The English have taken Syria, though the day before yesterday Paris was plastered all over with posters asking: "Why are we fighting in Syria?" Indeed: why? I throw up my hands at the stupidity of this propaganda and lying, elevated to the supreme institution in today's Europe.

Tomorrow is July 14, a work holiday; it has to be marked with restraint and decorum—no ceremonies or demonstrations.

This "Anti-Bolshevik Crusade" (the current official label) has now ended its third week and—nothing. The Germans have not even broken through the front. The Russians are retreating slowly, destroying everything in their wake and fighting as they go.

July 16, 1941

The weather has finally cooled down. The heat has drained us. We eat poorly, meat is scarce, and the slightest effort strains the body. Fruit is also scarce and very expensive. It's hard to make ends meet and we need to supplement my salary with some of our savings. Admittedly, on June 1 I got a raise of 1.15 francs an hour (wages have risen throughout France), but even that is not enough. Despite the regulated prices, efforts to keep them steady are having no effect. On July 14 there were scuffles, especially in the Quartier Latin. The display windows in the German bookstore were smashed, the police tore off the tricolor flowers people had pinned to their clothing and broke up trios of girls walking along in blue, white, and red dresses. Articles in today's newspapers warn: do not imagine you can do whatever you fancy. Whatever you still enjoy is only at our pleasure. Think about winter. Your behavior will determine what you'll have to eat, and so on. But in the metro tickets have increasingly been appearing in the shape of "V" and "H."

I wonder about the sudden surge of patriotism, precisely from the moment Russia became Germany's enemy.

July 20, 1941

The German propaganda stunt with this "V" tops everything. Today they plastered the town with enormous posters bearing a giant "V" and the caption "Victoria," and underneath: "Germany Victorious in the Fight for the New Europe." They have purloined de Gaulle's London "V" and are pleased with themselves. The Eiffel Tower flies a giant standard with a "V"; all the cars display a "V" surrounded by little laurel wreaths; the radio plays the "Victoria" march — complete tomfoolery and comic opera farce.

July 22, 1941

Germany's Russia campaign has now been going on for a month and the Soviets are holding out. One has to wonder now how much longer they will be able to keep it up. The Germans continue to push ahead. The French are waking up. Or rather, it seems to me, it's the French Communists who are waking them up. As long as the Soviets were allies of the Germans, silence reigned. Who knows whether the French defeat in 1940 isn't the result of France having lost the war from below, just as we lost our 1830 November Uprising. Obviously, on a different scale, several notches higher, because since then much has changed. But the principle remains the same.

London has announced that the "V" in the German version means *Verloren*,[30] while Moscow insists one need only look at Goebbels to conclude that man does not descend from the apes, but the apes from man. As you prefer. For my part, observing the entire human race—not just Goebbels—I'm inclined to the Moscow version of the theory of evolution.

July 27, 1941

There's some talk about a Polish-Soviet treaty. Anything's possible. The cobra and the rabbit also can sign treaties, but there can be only one final result: the cobra swallowing the rabbit. After drooling over it tenderly, to smooth its way down.

July 30, 1941

The Word became flesh and Russia is our ally. Władisław Sikorski's government in London has signed a treaty with Russia.[31] Russia annuls everything concerning the partition of Polish territories since 1939. Along the lines of: "I took your watch, he took the watch away from me, and therefore the watch is yours." Perhaps also . . . The most important thing is that a Polish army is being formed in Russia and the deportees and political prisoners will be released. How many are there? How many were deported? I understand nothing. I know only that the French tell me enthusiastically: "They're freeing your people, *c'est formidable.*" But when I ask them: "*Et de quoi étaient-ils coupables?*"—silence.[32] Nobody cares about this. The cobra is already drooling over the rabbit, is kind-hearted, friendly, and gives itself a good press. Russia stabbed Poland in the back, helped the Germans, signed off on the partition, deported hundreds of thousands of people whose only crime was to have been born Polish, and now is magnanimously releasing them, allowing them to organize, and displaying her "magnanimity" to the world. And the world believes them, and the world is convinced that *we Poles were the guilty ones and should now be grateful to the Soviets.*

August 3, 1941

Sunday. A nice, dimly sunny day. In the afternoon we took a walk through the narrow streets of the Île Saint-Louis, down to the Seine and up to Notre-Dame. The streets were deserted and sleepy. My thoughts dissipate in these surroundings, along with the smoke and the fog suspended over the bridges, roofs, and treetops. You can "wander about" so that the mind also "wanders." After following the twists and turns of the streets, we reached the Seine, opposite Notre-Dame. The used-book stands were open. I found an entire set of Gavarni caricatures and a bundle of newspaper clippings with reproductions of caricatures by Daumier.[33] The Daumier and Gavarni caricatures do not seem to be caricatures at all, but drawings of normal people and perfectly natural types. Whereas it's enough to enter one of these narrow streets a half hour later for normal and natural people to appear instantly as caricatures. These lines so brilliantly capture people that the drawings themselves do not offend, either by exaggeration or by excess—it's rather the living models, of which there are always many around, that are offensive.

After two hours pecking around in the bins of old books, we sat down in the bistro behind the garden next to Notre-Dame. The wretched beer and wretched cigarettes acquire an entirely special taste here. On this summer afternoon, framed in colors, sounds, and lazily gliding thoughts, they are excellent and full of meaning. I watch people walking by or catching fish. Everything is in harmony here, people have no problems or complexes, they're not building castles in Spain. Life is in them, they are life—*il ne faut pas chercher à comprendre.*[34] Take things as they come, swear and grumble out of habit, without foaming at the mouth, with a smile or a joke. And don't even hide your own egotism. A man is but a man and nothing more, and life is short. All this may not be so good, they will perhaps have to pay for it dearly later on—as we were taught. But in the end you'd have to be a fool to torment yourself on such an afternoon with thoughts that will be of no use to anyone. So I prefer to drink beer and smoke a cigarette. Why should I always be looking for wild strawberries among the treetops, while guiltily peering toward the ground? Climbing down is unacceptable, because at the bottom there are no winds or clouds, no Sturm und Drang . . .

August 5, 1941

For the past few days there's been a hint of revolution in the Paris air.

August 7, 1941

Radio London said today that Germany has presented England with an offer of peace. Unofficially. Armistice, withdrawal from Norway, Belgium, Denmark, and Holland—at a later date from France. Borders of the British Empire to be guaranteed. Alsace and Lorraine absorbed into the Reich—Vichy has already agreed. Occupation of European Russia for twenty-five years. Poland, Czechoslovakia, Yugoslavia, and Greece as semi-independent states. London has declined.

Big uproar. Furthermore, it appears that the Germans have begun to dig trenches near Smolensk. Devil take your Blitzkrieg.

Today's Paris-Berlin newspapers report that General Anders has been appointed head of the Polish army in Russia.[35] Noted without the least irony. With almost sincere respect. What's the purpose of this? The large map of operations in the east has been removed from the bookstore on rue de Rivoli!!! Perhaps it's become an embarrassment?

August 8, 1941

Yet again, all the newspapers report officially and in all seriousness that a Polish military mission has left London for Russia. It makes no sense to me. If I were Rzecki, I would entertain an entire parade of conjectures . . . K. and I sat at our table and spent the morning dissecting the communiqués. He's got a good head on his shoulders but even he couldn't think of anything. We reached the conclusion only that "something must be behind this."

The German notices are methodically being torn down. The Communists are putting their organization into gear. The giant posters with a "V" are being replaced by posters with the map of Europe on which arrows emerge from the countries involved in the war against Russia. The caption: "*Croisade contre le Bolchevisme.*" The letter "*l*" and "*visme*" are now scraped off, leaving "*Croisade contre le Boche.*"[36] Something is percolating under cover of the normal peace and quiet. Germans are rarely seen in Paris—it's emptied out. There are only a few spots where a soldier or two or the odd officer hangs around from time to time. Near the Opéra, on place de la Concorde, in Montmartre. But even on the boulevards they are rare—*feldgrau* has vanished.

August 9, 1941

The Germans have been halted everywhere. They've therefore started the Battle of Kiev against Marshal Budenny.[37]

August 10, 1941

A top-level conference is taking place in Vichy-État (who would have imagined the labels on Vichy-État mineral water would have turned out to be so apt?).[38] The Germans have apparently demanded that Pétain hand over Dakar and the fleet, that France enter the war against Russia, begin mobilization, and so on. They're no longer satisfied with the Anti-Bolshevik Legion now being assembled from "volunteers," with great fanfare under Vichy patronage.[39] At seven in the evening the radio said that the results of the talks would be broadcast at nine. At nine it announced that there was nothing to report. The newspapers are denying the rumors — allegedly, only domestic matters are involved. But the French are panic-stricken. Yet again mobilization threatens. Just when it had become clear that others were going to fight to win their independence for them.

August 12, 1941

"À *Vichy rien*" — that's the title of today's newspaper articles on the subject of the top-level conference. Anxiety is felt everywhere.

August 13, 1941

The conference ended with a rather uncertain speech by Pétain, in which he admitted outright that his policies have not produced the expected results but have met everywhere with incomprehension. He was therefore increasing the powers of Admiral Darlan and "*je doublerai l'activité de la police.*"[40] A disastrous impression.

I had a conversation today with B. on the subject of the war and he presented the French point of view. Simple and rational, logical, down-to-earth and easygoing.

"What do you want?" he says, "war is not interesting. I understand that in Roman times war had its benefits. A young man risked his life and if his country triumphed and he survived he would receive a number of hectares of land, a few dozen slaves, a couple of Greek concubines. There was something to fight for. But today? In 1919 I returned home, a victor, and then it was back to work as usual and taxes to be paid. *C'est pas du tout intéressant, la guerre.*"[41]

Said in jest, but the jest conveys something more general, the sigh of fatigue of an old nation.

August 14, 1941

Notices posted all over today on the dissolution of the Communist Party in France. Why only now?

August 16, 1941

This afternoon in the Musée Rodin. A thousand and one figures of lovers, not clear who with whom, who to whom, who where, which way, and by what means. A few exquisite heads, otherwise not very impressive. A nice mansion in a quiet and somewhat neglected garden. We sat by the fountain, farther off a few children were running around, like multicolored balls. The balls gathered in one spot near the pond. A drowned bird was floating on the water and the balls wanted to pull it out. Flies buzzed in the quiet air. A summer afternoon.

Modesty above all. While taking a pee you read the notice about a cure for syphilis attached inside the pissoir and out of sight, while you yourself are visible above the waist to everyone passing by.

August 18, 1941

Fresh notices. A million-franc reward for identifying the culprits responsible for constantly dismantling the railroad tracks. Only German trains are derailing—lately rather often. German notices are being pasted over by "butterflies" with the hammer and sickle. The Communists have declared war on the Germans on the territory of occupied France.

Today's communiqué from London is direct and to the point. In fact the German offensive in Russia has stalled, both sides are preparing to outlast the winter.

August 23, 1941

Yesterday a German officer was killed. Today, new notices: All prisoners of French nationality who have been arrested by the Germans or on German orders will be treated as hostages and in the event that such actions are repeated a number of them will be shot.

The fun is starting. One of my French colleagues was indignant: "It doesn't make sense—the price is too high."

Ministers Zaleski, Seyda, and Sosnkowski have been dismissed.[42] They probably objected to the Polish-Soviet treaty. Or perhaps they have foreseen the consequences?

August 27, 1941

Rumors of Göring's arrest. Too soon. Mindless gossip.

August 28, 1941

A short, narrow street near the Jardin des Plantes. Morning light filters through the fog. A golden half-light on the pavement, the curbs still lined with garbage bins in which the dogs are rummaging. Hugging the walls of the houses, a few giant rats slip by at a ponderous trot. A blind man with a white cane, pulling a heavily laden two-wheeled cart, wandered down the middle of the street. He groped with his cane and pulled the cart from point to point. It moved in a series of small jumps. A dirty purple rag hung from the cart.

August 30, 1941

Seven Frenchmen and one Dutchman have been shot. Three for spying, five for taking part in Communist demonstrations against the German army. Notices have been posted all over.

The police are organizing big raids and searches in the hotels. A dozen Poles have been arrested, but Schwerbel intervened right away with the police and they were released. The Gestapo looks out for us as if we were its own children and protects us from harm. But Father Cegiełka, Szymon Konarski, and Roman Rosinkiewicz remain in prison.[43] Fortunately, they are still in Paris. Since February 12, Schwerbel has kept them in Fresnes. He apparently insists that if it were only up to him, he would have released them long ago. But Father Cegiełka spoiled everything for him. Schwerbel is a curious man. He has taken various measures with respect to the Poles that are hard to interpret. He has behaved humanely, often with a marked sense of humor, which in a German seems incredible.

Paris is once again inundated with soldiers. They have obviously been brought in to calm the unsettled mood. Summer is ending, the days are growing shorter.

September 1, 1941

The second anniversary of the start of the war. I can't believe it. We've managed, so far we've managed to survive. Until now I've been lucky. I'm ashamed to say so, but despite everything we've faced, I've never in my life felt as happy as I have in these recent years, even the two years of the war. I've never felt so good in my life. I write this in full command of my faculties and I can't really explain it. But that's how I feel and there's nothing I can do about it. I may be the only such case at this moment. Life fascinates me, magnificent, succulent life, this wartime Paris, every single day.

September 3, 1941

September already. Summer has vanished in the blink of an eye. Today I'm dreamy, thoughts float through my head like cigarette smoke on a hot summer evening. Sometimes a mere trifle will put me in this mood. And today I encountered such a trifle.

I left the bistro after lunch this afternoon to go for a walk. I headed in the direction of the Châtillon church square. It's a quiet square, surrounded by low houses, with a small Gothic church. The sun was shining, the day was warm, the square was dozing and looked like the stage set for an opera. I sat down on a bench. Next to me I noticed a piece of paper secured by a stone. I moved the stone and read these few modest words: "Mark, come upstairs. Mama has gone into town. I'm waiting." I put the letter back under the stone and left the bench, my eyes half-shut. I felt like I was dreaming. The peace, the quiet, the sun, the little houses and the church and "Mark, come upstairs."

I wanted to cry from happiness, for both of them, I wanted to bless them, their embraces, their love. To cry from happiness because all this is still possible. Despite everything.

September 4, 1941

I pedal at breakneck speed from place de l'Étoile down the Champs-Élysées. I lean over the handlebars, whistle "Toreador," and carry in my backpack 5 (in words: five) kilos of bread obtained for me by our workmen from the shelter in Levallois. They have a baker, an amazing baker, who lets the Poles get bread without coupons. Because he likes Poles. So there exists such a madman. What does he like us for? I myself don't like us at all. And our good-hearted fellows buy some for me, too. From "Toreador" I proceed to a Schubert march, I observe the policeman's movements and turn into Rond-Point at a speed of sixty km an hour. At the sight of the obelisk on place de la Concorde, I whistle the march from *Aida*, I reach the banks of the Seine, hurry past the Tuileries and the Louvre. Now a small detour near Les Halles to inspect the garbage bins. I snake my way through the narrow streets. After today's market the bins are full. Lettuce leaves do not interest me. Besides, this hunt needs a system, it needs a compass. That compass is the dogs. A bin that dogs are circling may contain something interesting, something with bones or meat. There—I hit the brakes. "Beat it," I tell the mongrel politely and nudge him aside with my front wheel. The scoundrel snarls, it must be something special. I take a look and can't believe my eyes. An entire sheep's head. I take a paper from my sack, wrap the head, and stow it away. A bit "high" already, but all the same a lot to eat. I hurry once more along the Seine. Distracted by a poster for *Madame Capet* with Cécile Sorel[44] (she'll never die), I drive the tip of my shoe, armored with the bicycle "clip," full force into the fender of a German limousine. The fender dents horribly. Sabotage—luckily no one saw. I escape, satisfied. At least I've done something for the fatherland. I make it home and, whistling the *Salome* one-step, present the head.[45] War council with Basia. Does it smell? Mutton always smells. We arrange a dissection room. I cut through the skull with a metal-cutting saw—there are brains. Also the tongue and the cheek meat. I will stuff myself.

Then I sit in my armchair and read. I feel great. Often when I wind my way through the streets on my bicycle at a dizzying speed, when the sun is shining, I'm happier than ever before in my life. I've discovered the smile of thought. I don't know what else to call it. I want to clown around, to be silly for my own amusement; I'm bursting with simple joy and lightheartedness. Everything pleases me, everything around is like music. The moods of individual streets and the vistas, caught on the fly, revolve inside me like a parade of dancing couples, each in a different costume. I take great gulps of something I cannot define. Youth? I feel good because I'm young and strong; because I'm myself and I think more freely than ever before. And because I have Basia. What more do I need?

Basia is right. Once when I asked, full of pride and conceit: "And where would you find another such husband?" she answered tersely:

"In the loony bin, darling!"

Her humor is always sharp-tongued.

September 5, 1941

The mornings are chilly, but sunny. Everything is bathed in the sun-drenched fog and glistens delicately. Buildings, bridges, trees are not buildings, bridges, trees—they are their delicate evocations, as though softly saying: "Do you remember? . . ." I dive into the narrow streets near the Jardin des Plantes. Empty. Except for a cart full of wreaths of violet heather parked in front of a building. A few dim rays of sun flit over them and then the heather becomes almost red. Bins still full of garbage line the curbs. Front paws on the edges of the bins, dogs sniff and dig inside with their muzzles. Occasionally I hear the snap of bones being gnawed, tasty, brittle. I instantly feel hunger and envy the dogs. Further along a shutter rattled as it opened. Rats run along the walls with a slimy, repulsive gait. They are dun-colored, revolting, and at the same time enigmatic, mysterious.

September 8, 1941

The day before yesterday was Saturday. I left the office at noon and stopped by a bistro for a beer. Afterward I had to go to the other end of Paris, near La

Muette, to get butter and other rationed products off coupons. I stood, munching stale bread, and drank my beer. Some Frenchmen from our factory entered the bistro. The head of the financial department, the director's driver, two women from the office. They were drinking aperitifs before lunch. They invited me to join them. "What do you drink?" "Only cognac," I answer. The *patronne* puts a small glass in front of me. "*Non, madame,* in the same size glass they have and just as much." The men shuddered, the women turned green. The conversation began with the proverb or rather the expression, *soûl comme un Polonais.*[46] I explained to them that this phrase is supposed to have come from the lips of Napoleon and doesn't insult us at all. The Polish soldier was supposedly ready for action even after a good binge, whereas the French warrior was good for nothing. Discussion of Napoleon. I suggest they, too, have a cognac, and they agreed to try. The discussion of Napoleon proceeds. The head of finances attacks Napoleon. Why did Napoleon take on Russia? Because he had to. Why didn't he allow the guard to be deployed at Borodino? "Eight hundred miles from Paris one does not risk one's last reserves" — I cite Napoleon. Someone entered the bistro, the *patron* barely served him, but leaned on his elbow and listens. The baker's wife from across the street also entered and listens. We have an audience. The next round of cognac is on me and we broach the theme of "old French gallantry." The ladies attest that the renowned French gallantry is simply humbug. As an example of true gallantry they cite the way Polish men treat women. I bow and kiss both women on the hand. The cashier attests that our Polish workers are "much nicer" than her own colleagues. At this, the head of finances enters the fray with an analysis of the issue and asserts that Poles above all have *le charme slave* and that this is not the same as *la galanterie*. I offer the example of German soldiers. They give up their seats to women in the metro. They are better brought up — perhaps better trained — than you are. You have lost chivalry. A bit of conversation follows — something about music. The director's driver perks up. German music — Beethoven, Mozart, Schubert. I object — they were not Germans. The true spirit of Germany is Wagner. Can you stomach Wagner? I cannot — I order another round of cognac. Both men have had enough. Talk moves on to Poland. The head of finances asserts that in fact the French always confuse Poland and Russia and know us only by a few names: Mickiewicz, Maria Leszczyńska,[47] Sienkiewicz, Marie Curie . . .

"And Chopin?" I cry. Protests. Chopin was a Frenchman. Not on my life. We begin to quarrel. Suddenly the *patronne* emerges quietly from behind the counter. She is holding the great encyclopedia *Larousse* in her hand and says: "*Messieurs — silence!*" She reads from the Larousse: "*Frédéric Chopin, compositeur polonais d'origine française . . .*" This ends the dispute, the men pull in their horns. "Art is international," I console them. They nod. The head of finances checked his watch and swayed—three o'clock. He's completely drunk, the ladies laugh. We go our separate ways. I get on my bicycle and ride all the way to La Muette.

Today the wife of the head of finances was annoyed with me. She coldly offered me her hand. "I waited until three with lunch—there were *pommes frites*—in times like these *pommes frites*—and obviously they got stale. Pierre isn't a child, he could have phoned . . ." and a thousand reproaches leveled in my direction. And every third word "POMMES FRITES."

"Next time I'll call you," I snarled. She smiled sourly.

September 11, 1941

In Paris it's become the fashion to shoot German soldiers and officers. On September 6 and yesterday, September 10, a few were killed. Now the Germans are shooting hostages. This is how the Communists are saving the honor of the French, who after the war will say: "That was us."

September 14, 1941

Yesterday Roosevelt delivered a bellicose speech. He ordered his ships to shoot at anything German. And gave the Germans a crude dressing-down. What a boor! Mrs. P., an American by birth, told me once that a war against Germany is not popular in America and that Roosevelt will first provoke the Japanese and via Japan declare war on Germany. In America war against Japan will be a "sacred" war. Rather complicated, but in times like these the opinions even of crazy old crones must be considered. In the madhouse, after all, one must listen to the lunatics. If only everyone weren't totally mad.

September 16, 1941

Announcements posted of the execution of ten hostages. The mood is tense.

September 19, 1941

Another German officer shot dead. None of the hunters has been caught. Well-organized Communist work. In response, a criminal ordinance was issued today for all of Paris, according to which walking in the street after nine p.m.

on September 20, 21, and 22 is forbidden. Anyone caught after nine will be imprisoned as hostages. General Stülpnagel warns the population that if Germans continue to be killed he will be obliged to apply increasingly harsh methods.[48] At the same time, he apologizes to the inhabitants of Paris, insisting that true Frenchmen have nothing to do with these murders, that only the Communists are involved, but that the population nevertheless bears the responsibility. Failure to reveal the perpetrators shows that people are aiding and abetting the murders.

And this coddling is what they'll next be calling an occupation. Everyone is nevertheless depressed and even indignant at the Communists.

Kiev has been taken. Things are going all too well for the Germans in the south. The war in the east is starting to get a bit old. I'm now reading *The Doll* and I notice I've been imitating Rzecki for quite some time now.[49]

Afternoon on the Champs-Élysées with Lola. Marvelous weather, truly golden autumn days. We sat on a café terrace and observed the populace drinking beer. I smoked a cigarette, then dropped the butt on the ground. Soon a little girl approached, picked up the butt, and put it in a large can. A bit later a boy went by holding a metal box, his eyes glued to the pavement. Hosts of butt collectors now make the rounds of all the crowded and most elegant Paris cafés. Since limits were put on the sale of tobacco (120 grams per month per person), butts have become a valuable commodity. A pack of cigarettes on the black market costs forty francs.

The leaves on the trees are already yellowing, the sun is pale. The Champs-Élysées is full of people. Suddenly a large coach drawn by four horses emerged into the road. A groom, a bride, and their wedding guests, the party all singing, shouting, talking with passersby. They're amusing themselves riding back and forth between Rond-Point and the Arc de Triumphe. The company are all smiling, carefree. The wedding party moves away. Now the clatter of hooves is heard. A small red-painted two-wheeled cart flies by at an extended trot. The horse has a red harness and lacquered red hooves. The splendid woman seated beside a serious man has tinted blue hair. The movement, the colors, the smells. I half-close my eyes and feel good; completely and mindlessly good.

September 22, 1941

Again red-letter notices posted. Twelve hostages have been shot.

Real summer weather. Sunny, warm days enveloped in an autumnal fog. This evening we sat in the Bois de Vincennes. Total silence. The only sound was the continual rustle from the tall trees, as their leaves were struck by chestnuts falling to the ground with a loud plop. In the evening calm, the leaves fall gently and silently, like the petals of roses wilted by the heat. The chestnuts are making a racket.

In the evening Basia asks me how crayfish are eaten, what is there even to eat?

"The necks," I answer.

"That's not much."

"True. You need a lot of them. Do you want to buy some? Not worth it. Having traveled, I'm an expert on this . . ."

"I've also traveled."

I roll my eyes. I know she's never traveled.

"Yes. For example in — Poland!!!"

My sharp-tongued one.

September 27, 1941

Three volumes of *The Doll*. A great trilogy, greater than the trilogy by that Sienkiewicz.[50] It's hard to find a better book, a better revelation of all the unfortunate traits of the Polish character. Our society has not changed very much since those days. Traits of character that are "unfortunate," but not "negative," for our greatest misfortune may consist of those trivial faults, so hard precisely to define — in contrast to our great positive qualities — which spoil our virtues, virtues not encountered anywhere else, and so often deprive them of their value and worth. There's something irritating in the Polish character, certain irritating minor traits, most often manifested in thoughtless and tactless ways. You are not supposed to work in order to earn a living, and if you do, then you should make it seem as though you're "working for the good of the country." Poland is Poland, but I often think this poor Poland weighs so heavily on our brains that it leaves us stupefied. Then she serves to justify our stupidities. Instead of a fatherland, I all too often perceive her as a *Mädchen für alles*.[51] And the louder the talk of Poland, the more one should be on one's guard, because probably some "genius," with his craw full of Poland, is preparing some "stroke of genius."

Prus's description of Stanisław Wokulski in Paris may best convey everything the writer wanted to say and may be the best that can be written about that "something" that for the first time makes a Wokulski feel good.[52] At least as good as I am feeling. I often think every Pole harbors a deeply hidden guilt complex because Providence has not allowed him to die for the fatherland. Even I bear this sense of guilt. And that makes me rebellious. Because I always find death repugnant, even death for the fatherland.

This evening we went to the movies to see *Trois Valses* with Yvonne Printemps and Pierre Fresnay.[53] An old film, but charming. Some segments recall Dégas, the *plein-air* shots are Manet in black and white. We emerge from the theater to find it's now completely dark. People were emerging from the other cinemas, flashlights shining everywhere. As we walked home arm in arm, I hummed to Basia, "*Je t'aime quand même*," and I reached the conclusion that under no circumstances do I want to die. After all, no one wants to die, except that Poles consider it improper to say so out loud. No national myth has ever convinced me, and this, the most important of them, least of all.

September 28, 1941

A wonderful lunch—a true Sunday meal. Thanks to Lola, who yesterday brought us a big piece of chicken. I am constantly hungry these days. I often wake in the night, eat a piece of bread washed down with wine, and return to bed. Day after day fifty, sixty, seventy km by bicycle all over Paris and the suburbs and nothing decent to eat.

After lunch we went to the Bois de Vincennes. The day was as warm as in summer, though overcast, no sun. The grass has already turned brown and thinned out, at every breath of wind flocks of leaves went flying.

September 29, 1941

One of our workers, who's involved in the black market and lives in the shelter on avenue Wagram, celebrated his name day yesterday. Among the guests was the Marquise de Bonnières, the shelter director and a loyal client of the host, and our Gestapo, in the person of Counselor Schwerbel. The guests were having a splendid time, singing along gustily, and finally the Gestapo intoned the "March of the Sharpshooters" from the Insurrection of 1863: "Hail, Sharpshooters, together! The White Eagle flies overhead."[54] Almost surreal.

I heard this from the porter at Wagram, an eyewitness, and from K., who lives there but is eager to move out.

September 30, 1941

I'm sitting on a bench on boulevard Arago and chatting with an old mechanic. "Uncle" Galant, boozer and brawler, brought me a kilo of bread, in exchange for which I gave him a bit of tobacco and that's how life goes.

The afternoon sun is setting somewhere behind Denfert-Rochereau, the weather is warm and golden. We're discussing the war. "Uncle" was in the Caucasus and in Turkestan. We discuss the future. "You know," says old "Uncle," "after the war this whole Europe should pull together a bit. Instead of each country for itself. Otherwise this whole Europe will be complete bedlam all over again." Short and to the point. "After the war . . ." Whenever that is. Better to bask in the sun and stop thinking.

October 1, 1941

I've never seen this kind of weather. From morning to night the colors keep changing and all are delicate, gentle, strained through the gauze of the clouds. The woman who runs the grocery in Châtillon today sold me pâté without coupons. "What is it?" I ask. "How should I know? Maybe dog," she answered with the indifference of a southerner. She's from the Pyrenees. Woof, woof— grrrr.

October 4, 1941

That clown gave a speech. He said that for the last forty-eight hours a battle has been raging on the Russian front aimed at the total destruction and collapse of the Red Army. That the battle is continuing is one thing; that it will lead to the destruction of the Red Army is another.

This evening in the Bois de Vincennes. The pond, the trees, the lawns, the sky—all like an illustration from *Peter Pan*. The silence is broken by the plopping of chestnuts.

October 5, 1941

My afternoon rambles are never boring. The Louvre, the Tuileries, the Champs-Élysées. Then the Madeleine, the boulevards, the Opéra. The flower beds at the Louvre are exquisite, planted with fall flowers. Groups of people stop ostentatiously under the Arc de Triomphe du Carrousel and read the inscription aloud: "At Austerlitz the power of Germany was broken . . ."[55] Alas, this time the French are not the ones who will do it. But they will have their illusions. That's what counts for them.

It's a warm, gentle day. The Tuileries are crowded. Gounod's *Mireille* is playing in the open-air theater.[56] Around the low fence surrounding the theater, the nonpaying audience stands or sits silently. They catch the fragments of music and singing that reach even here—sometimes louder, sometimes fading out among the trees. The stage is a platform, divided in half by a partition of decorations. The actors can be seen entering the stage and exiting "into the wings." Mireille has finished her aria, left the stage, and, sitting at a little table, takes up her knitting. Now the tenor has appeared on stage, runs about on the few feet of boards in hot pursuit of Mireille. The chorus have tossed their cigarette stubs, straightened their costumes, struck an official pose behind the scenes, and slowly emerge. Mireille has set aside her knitting and also appears. A duet. Gounod's sentimental music floats gently in the air, a russet leaf drops onto the brim of my hat; a wrinkled, worse-for-wear blond kisses the hand of the fat fellow sitting at her side. "*Chéri . . .*" End of the act, sound of faint applause. The Paris of 1941 or my mother's Paris?

A German military orchestra is playing near the Grand-Palais. Some "potpourri" of operettas. A grandmother says to her little granddaughter: "You see, *mon petit chou*, here our army once played, *les soldats français . . .*"

Crowds on the Champs-Élysées. People are sitting on the café terraces. Pricy, dressed-up demimondaines tap the wooden platforms of their fanciful sandals. And ostrich feathers—the latest fashion.

Place de la Concorde has been dug up. They're removing the wooden blocks and laying cobblestones. The fountains are splashing. Bustle at Maxim's—it's the hour for *dîner*. The displays on rue Royale are increasingly depleted, women's leather handbags disappear and are replaced by showy bags and sacs of fabric or felt. Models from the latest races at the Hippodrome d'Auteuil—four hundred francs. The boulevards. In the most expensive shops prices have gone up, though not so very much. Except that there's less and less to sell.

October 6, 1941

Igiełka, "The Needle," was at our place for supper.[57] He's going to fashion me cycling pants out of a coat. He insists he'll manage to put it together. He's a tailor-artist, a tailor of the free spirit. He doesn't live in a shelter, but nests in a "cabin" at the Salvation Army, gets unemployment benefits at the town hall, and makes some extra by sewing. What he makes he squanders. "Sometimes I have nothing to eat, sometimes I eat supper at that Yitsek's place near the Hôtel de Ville for fifty francs, all without coupons." He has a lot of trouble buying thread, notions—and it gets harder all the time. He shares with me the mysteries of the black market, those fantastic hand-to-hand transactions. He tells me about a former Polish pilot who now deals in diamonds. Under the counter, from the back rooms of sleazy joints, where 120,000 francs move from briefcase to briefcase.

October 7, 1941

It's said that:
Józef Beck is in America giving speeches.[58]

Some people roll sixty-four cigarettes from a forty-gram pack of tobacco, using butts and the butts of butts. Another method consists in making five cigarettes out of ten butts, using three for each cigarette. First, one makes three cigarettes—leaving one butt aside. These three cigarettes produce three butts + the one = four butts. This makes one cigarette, which produces one butt. Thus, two butts remain. An additional butt is borrowed and the final cigarette is made, smoked, and the borrowed butt returned. Honor bright—no debts.

One thing is certain: Hitler has designated a certain number of people for execution and will be as good as his word.

In the unoccupied zone, Pétain is called *Saint Philippe qu'on roule.*[59]

In the fall and winter there is supposed to be a lot of meat, mostly mutton, because the Germans are slaughtering all the sheep to make sheepskin coats for the army in the east.

The best currency in the countryside is tobacco, old clothing, gasoline, and olive oil.

The war will start winding down three years from now.

C. told me today with a laugh that one of the largest surgical instrument companies, where he used to work and where he still has contacts, received an order from the Germans for ten thousand speculums destined for the residents of regulated brothels. Every *fille de joie* must have her personal speculum. And the Germans will do the inspecting. *Ordnung muss sein.* Typical.

October 10, 1941

P. asked me to help clear out the apartment of one of our former embassy attachés (Colonel Fyda) and supervise the operation.[60] It involved moving the furniture from the second floor for storage in the garage. I was offered a hundred francs for the job and naturally did not refuse. Ten hours of hard labor for two with an untrustworthy workman and an even less trustworthy domestic. Who would certainly steal the lot.

I returned after dark. There was a cold, penetrating rain. The leaves were dropping from the trees, torn away by sharp gusts of wind. I was dreadfully tired but with an odd pleasure dove into the rain, plunging into the dark avenues near Trocadéro and Alma-Marceau. It's autumn.

October 11, 1941

Situation critical on the Eastern Front. London is not hiding its fears at all and the English communiqués are very pessimistic.

October 16, 1941

An evening at the Odéon Theater for the stage adaptation of Balzac's *César Birotteau*.[61]

The play is well produced but less well performed. Popinot alone has succeeded in producing the authentic Popinot of Balzac. The play is moralistic through and through—moreover tendentiously moralistic. Recently a breath of "regeneration" has begun blowing across France, regeneration of character, morality, religion, worldview. It's a shame, though, that this series of truly wise statutes has been introduced by a government like this. The plan to "return to the land" (*retour à la terre*), bonuses for children, family supplements, social welfare—it's all under way, and if it doesn't uplift her, it at least allows France to survive and make it through this bout of the flu without grave complications. Pétain operates with money—he pays. He prints it and pays. In fact inflation began long ago, but resistance to inflation is incomparably greater in France than in other countries. Money is part of the French character, it's their tradition, their history, their morality, almost their life.

Strictly speaking, the entire morality of *César Birotteau*, the entire morality of the play, resides in the uncompromising attitude of this bankrupt man toward his own debts—it's money with a capital "M," which penetrates everywhere, sealed by life. And if one analyzes Balzac's work in its entirety, the morality and the character of figures who are supposed to say to the reader, "Look, this is how a strong, pure, and noble man should be," it's almost always about the hero's relationship to money. Balzac builds the entire morality of his *Comédie humaine* around the innumerable confrontations between his characters and money. He flings people at money and describes the sound. Money is for a given character what ringing a coin against a counter is for money.

The French character has not changed much and Balzac is still relevant. Long neglected, he is now returning slowly as the people's moral conscience. France is making an effort to renew herself. Except that it's not clear who's to be thanked for it: they themselves or the Germans. The *retour à la terre* is simply *Blut und Boden*. All this welfare and public assistance is nothing more than *Winterhilfswerk*.[62] The promotion of rebirth and crude nationalism is also a German invention.

October 17, 1941

C. told me a story today about someone he knows. Ten years ago the fellow had a small business and went bankrupt. He settled with his creditors on 50 percent. But he resolved nevertheless to pay the rest. He joined a small factory as foreman, worked hard for ten years, and repaid the other half of his debt. Three days ago he paid off his last remaining creditor, returned home, and shot himself in the head. César Birotteau in a revised edition.

October 18, 1941

Lunch with the couple who run my bistro should have worked out, but it didn't. They have rented a small apartment in the passage d'Enfer, a century-old little street. Quiet, empty—the provinces in the middle of the city. As soon as I enter, the concierge hands me a telegram. I must be in Châtillon at two this afternoon, signed "Chappel," the director himself. I sat down to table furious, everyone's mood had been ruined. I telephone at two to make sure. It turns out the Germans want to requisition all our factory cars. I'm to come immediately and compose some letters in German. For the last few days K. and I have done nothing but scribble letters in German. The Germans must really be hurting for means of transportation if they are tempted even by these old crates, converted moreover to run on wood gas.

By three I was in the office. The director greeted me with the words: "You probably never expected that in France your knowledge of German would come in handy." "True, and especially today . . ." He caught the allusion and smiled. In an hour I had finished writing that nonsense and by five had returned, greeted by an ovation from the already well-oiled company. Suzy, from the Châtillon bakery, was already in her cups and I extracted from her the promise of 350 daily grams of bread without coupons and without having to sleep with her. She was interested, but I care more about bread. *"Mais tu sais que j'te donnerai tout c'que tu voudras." "Donne-moi du pain et ça suffit." "Tu es quand même un peu vache,"* she said.[63] *Vache* or not, but I must have my bread. Sometimes I'm literally dying of hunger. But I haven't yet reached the point of giving myself for bread. Then I got drunk and in the metro it hit me so hard that I kept passing out. Fortunately the conductor kept an eye on me and put me out at Daumesnil. I groped my way home and was completely done in when I got there. Basia laughed.

October 20, 1941

Today I was sent to the Secrétariat d'État à la Production Industrielle, that is, the Ministry of Production, to compose some letters in German for them. The ministry has no one who can do it. When C. heard this, he said: *"Vous pouvez noter cela comme un signe de plus de la décadence française."*[64] Indeed, there's some truth in that. The worst is that K. and I must increasingly take the German phone calls from the Astoria Hotel, that is, *Zentralkraft*—general head-quarters.[65] I don't mind the correspondence so much, but I find the exchanges really unpleasant. I try to pull the wool over their eyes as far as I can, venturing into discussions of inaccurate translation. And these blockheads can often be distracted. The Germans are nevertheless blockheads. That's why they will lose this war, too.

October 21, 1941

The attack on Moscow has come to a halt. The French claim that Hitler is ruining his reputation. Napoleon, who set out two days later than the Germans, at this point was already installed in Moscow. On June 24 he crossed the Neman. Besides, everyone is convinced that winter this year will begin earlier than normal if only in order to resemble 1812.

Today Basia and I committed *Rassenschande* and went to the German film *Bel Ami* with Willi Forst. Adapted from Maupassant. Very good. It's a long time since I've seen such a good film. Doubtless because Willi Forst is Austrian.[66]

October 22, 1941

The Germans are an inspired nation, they predict everything, calculate everything, split hairs in four parts, except that something is always missing in these predictions. Most often it's some detail and because of this detail they fall apart, come to grief completely.

The day before yesterday, yet again unidentified perpetrators assassinated the *Feldkommandant* of Nantes.[67] In response General Stülpnagel ordered the execution of fifty hostages and if the perpetrators are not identified he will shoot another fifty at noon the day after tomorrow. And now the French have truly woken up. The entire plan of collaboration, the entire idea of collaboration devised and developed over the past year (not without considerable success), will fail.

October 23, 1941

The day before yesterday another German officer was shot—this time in Bordeaux. And once again they executed fifty hostages with the promise of another fifty if the perpetrators were not identified. Today everything is in turmoil. The consensus: this is not a criminal penalty, but an outright massacre.

C'est un massacre. A number of factories have apparently gone on strike. "And we're supposed to cooperate with them? Now finally they have shown who they really are"—this can be heard all around. If I were Hitler I would throw this Stülpnagel out on his ear. He has messed up badly. They should merely have announced right away that despite the assassinations in Nantes and Bordeaux no repressive measures would be taken, because these were not Frenchmen, one cannot imagine their being French—they are agents of Moscow and London, provocateurs—and we cannot punish the innocent. France would have allowed herself to be taken in, she would have swallowed the hook. Because at bottom the French want to swallow some hook or other, in order to cure themselves of the complex that has dogged them since June 1940. A battle for the soul of France has been going on for a year now, all of France yearns for absolution and seeks it wherever she can. And she was on the verge of accepting it from German hands via the Vichy-État. And now, here you are. The French themselves say so and pronounce with a disdainful smile: *"Ils ne sont pas fins . . ."*[68]

Success. In recent days, de Gaulle has won France to his side. Now indeed he can sleep in peace. With one kick of the boot the Germans have swept away the subtle cobweb they had spun. Stülpnagel should be awarded the Legion of Honor. The Germans are always the same. Now they will want to make amends because they are not stupid enough not to grasp the enormity of the psychological disaster.

October 25, 1941

Obviously! *La magnanimité du Führer . . .* The Führer himself has deferred the execution of the additional one hundred hostages. France should be grateful. No, France has at last understood, O you nation of unqualified corporals. Oof—I'm relieved.

October 29, 1941

Snow—at midday, snow mixed with rain.

October 31, 1941

Snow, cold. Our Salle des Fêtes is not yet heated and we sit at our tables working in only 7 degrees Celsius. The snow was so heavy that I was late to work, because biking was hard. A decree has been issued that officially prohibits listening to Radio London. The fine is one thousand to ten thousand francs and three months to three years in prison. Naturally, everyone will now listen with even greater zeal. *Ça fait du sport!*[69] They have again postponed the execution of the hundred hostages. Supposedly as a result of Churchill's intervention. He promised Hitler he would immediately shoot 250 German officers and non-commissioned officers in English captivity. If it's a rumor, then it's a good one, spread with typical English ingenuity.

November 1, 1941

We stay home and freeze. The cold is penetrating and of course there's no heat. I'm sitting in my armchair, my legs wrapped in a blanket, wearing five layers of wool, and reading Jacques Bainville's *Napoléon*.[70] The book illuminates the realities we face today, including the early onset of winter. After reading it, I understood. Germany must lose this war and Russia will win it.

November 2, 1941

The cold is terrible. In the afternoon we decided to leave the house in order to warm up. As we did last year, we went to Père Lachaise. To visit Chopin's grave. We bought some asters and Basia had two candles. There were few people around, because it was already late. Chopin's grave was covered, as usual, with lovely flowers. We lit a candle and then went on to the grave of Oscar Wilde. No one remembers him. This time, however, there were two lovely chrysanthemums. We deposited our flowers and lit a candle. Our candles were the only light in the whole cemetery because this custom is not observed here. Metal wreaths and garlands are hung on the graves, which then look like pretzel stalls. On the way out we returned to Chopin's grave. Our candle had vanished. Stolen. A practical nation.

We returned on foot. One of the ugliest parts of Paris, including the hideous fountain on place de la Nation. A giant bronze Marianne pissed on from all sides by pregnant crocodiles. It was only when I'd eaten some buckwheat crêpes with jam—two francs apiece—that my mood brightened.

November 3, 1941

Roosevelt delivered a speech. He said the first shots have been fired and we know who was the first to shoot. But this is not what counts; what counts is who will shoot last. The Germans have already sunk two American torpedo boats (today's newspapers report they sunk a third one yesterday). America has virtually been attacked already, because Washington possesses two documents of German origin. One is a map of South America divided into five parts under German rule. The second document is a plan to abolish all the world's religions (at least in the conquered territories) and replace them with the cult of national socialism: in place of the cross—the swastika, in place of God—the Führer.

The speech made an impression, despite the element of American *humbug*. It's probably intended mainly for domestic consumption.

November 4, 1941

"O memorable year . . ."[71] Oof—in Poland, fine, but in Paris . . . A thick snow has been falling since morning, the real thing, no ersatz. The roofs are white, the streets are covered in snow as in winter. And over there near Moscow, my friend? Can you believe it, old man—minus 27 Celsius, as the Englishers were reporting on the radio. The offensive is stuck in the snow. A month ago, that infernal Schweik sulked and lashed out, all in vain, promising a decisive outcome.[72] Not Kronstadt, or Leningrad, or Moscow . . . And what do you look like now? Like a camel's ———, Mr. Hitler. Snow is falling.

November 7, 1941

Dinner at the home of Mr. and Mrs. P. A true symphony. Soup. Followed by poached fish. Mushrooms in white sauce, fingerling potatoes sautéed in olive oil, accompanied by a 1926 Chablis. Brussels sprouts. Pears in cream. At table I conducted *eine wirkliche Vernichtungsschlacht.*[73] I laid waste. I stuffed myself to the limits of my shrunken stomach.

Yesterday Stalin gave a speech. He does not deny that the situation is serious, but says they will pull through. Hitler should not imagine he is Napoleon. The Russians are short on equipment and supplies, but England and America are sending more, and Russia doesn't lack for people.

November 9, 1941

Sunday. Afternoon stroll on the Champs-Élysées and avenue Foch. The Champs-Élysées is crammed. There's an enormous line in front of the Menier chocolate shop. Cups of hot chocolate are selling for five francs. And people stand for hours to be able to drink a cup of hot chocolate. In front of the movie theaters there are crowds and also lines. A mania for lines. On a side street off avenue Foch two carts are selling roasted chestnuts. We bought two bags of them. There haven't been any this year. The Germans take even the chestnuts. So that source of nourishment is also gone. All last fall we stuffed ourselves with chestnuts—now it's potatoes and turnips over and over again. My stomach is full but I'm still hungry. Prices are soaring. Sugar is not to be had even for fifty francs a kilo. I was promised sugar in exchange for cigarettes. Two packs for a kilo of sugar. Maybe that will work. I can afford it because I get tobacco from Lola and I save my cigarette ration. Four times a week I get half a kilo of bread from Suzy in Châtillon. From Brittany we sometimes receive a package with butter from one of my colleagues. In the fall I dried some beans myself, we have enough potatoes thanks to "my" workers—they bring me some whenever they can. Winter is breathing down our necks and we have to stock up on provisions. That's perhaps the most important problem in life today. What will we think about when a kilo of sugar is no longer a historic event?

On avenue Foch the leaves are falling from the trees. Mounted German officers are trotting along the sides of the road. As I walk I read the speech Hitler gave yesterday in Munich. But these are only excerpts translated into French. Tomorrow I must buy the *Pariser Zeitung.*[74]

November 10, 1941

Hitler's speech in the Munich Löwenbraukeller is cocky, threaded with vulgar irony, self-justification. Calls Churchill *"whiskeyselige"*—a souse. And you, I say, are *"schneetraurig"*—"snow-sad." From offense he has shifted to defense. He's no longer attacking the English, but just let the English try attacking him. *"Wenn es den Herren Engländern beliebt, sei es in Norwegen, sei es an unserer deutschen Küste, oder sei es in Holland, in Belgien oder in Frankreich, eine Offensive zu unternehmen, so können wir nur sagen: Tretet an, Ihr werdet schneller abtreten, als ihr gekommen seid!"*[75] What a moron! But he has to shout, shout loudest of all and dazzle the world. Victory in the east: *"Wenn ich zusammenfassend den bisherigen Erfolg dieses Feldzuges umreissen will, dann hat die Zahl der Gefangenen nunmehr rund 3,6 Millionen erreicht, d.h. 3.600.000 Gefangene, und ich verbitte mir, dass hier ein englischer Strohkopf kommt und sagt, das sei nicht bestätigt. Wenn eine deutsche militärische Stelle etwas bezählt hat, dann stimmt das! (tosender Beifall)."*[76] A pitiful argument. And this is what's causing the world to tremble, mobilizing the entire world, and killing millions of people. It's madness. And what next? *"Ich hoffe, dass wir in kurzer Zeit noch ein paar weitere Massnahmen treffen können, durch die wir ihnen Strang um Strang langsam aber sicher Luft abschneiden werden."*[77] He hopes he will be able to . . . *"Ich hoffe, können, langsam aber sicher"*[78]—these are words we have not heard before. But you must believe me, because I'm a genius, ME and MY INTELLECT. *"Da kann ich Herrn Roosevelt nur sagen: Ich habe auf gewisse Experten überhaupt keine Experten. Bei mir genügt immer mein Kopf ganz allein. Ich habe keinen Gehirntrust zu meiner Unterstützung notwendig. Wenn also wirklich eine Veränderung irgendwie stattfinden soll, dann entsteht das zunächst in meinem Gehirn, und nicht im Gehirn anderer, auch nicht in dem von Experten. Ich bin auch kein Gymnasiast"* (O God, and this is the speech of a statesman, a leader) *"der in einem Schulatlas Karten einzeichnet."*[79] Now, for a change, it's Roosevelt who's responsible for Poland taking a stand: *"Wenn nun der amerikanische Präsident Roosevelt, der einst schon verantwortlich für den Eintritt Polens in den Kampf war, was wir ihm heute genau belegen können . . ."*[80] Curious. He battles one enemy after another, but every speech is aimed almost exclusively at the English, whom he hasn't yet faced. What comes through is impotence, the furious impotence of a man who is bound and being buried alive inch by inch. Utter boorishness. Unbelievable.

Hope is growing. There's still a long wait ahead. Not weeks and not months, but now it's at least clear what we're waiting for.

The English have taken on the Italians in the Mediterranean. They have sunk an entire convoy—seven vessels.

November 11, 1941

Churchill's speech. Optimism prepared in the persuasive sauce of English reserve. The English air force is by now the equal of the German. That's what counts.

If not for yesterday's rain, Paris would be without electricity. Apparently the power plants of southern Germany were bombed and industry there is functioning on energy partly from Belgium and Holland, partly from northern France. In any case, the power plants supplying Paris now service the Germans. Paris is getting current from hydropower stations near the Swiss border. There has been no rain for an entire month and the reservoirs have run dry.

November 12, 1941

Sikorski is on an inspection tour in Egypt and Malta.

November 13, 1941

General Weygand was having tea with Pétain when he was apparently asked what he thought of the war in Russia and he answered: "For me the main thing is that they're beating the Boches." Present on this occasion was the collaborationist minister Georges Scapini.[81] Pétain had summoned him and demanded he give his word of honor not to repeat what he had heard. Clearly he did not keep his word, since everyone is telling the story. One of many rumors.

Since the Germans have relentlessly been jamming London on the short- and medium-wave bands, London now broadcasts on long wave—1,500 m. Since it is forbidden to listen to English radio, the same conversation can be heard ten times a day:

"*Avez-vous essayé d'écouter Londres sur 1,500?*"

"*Oui. Ça va épatemment bien . . .*"[82]

Now everyone listens. Even those who haven't listened for a long time, believing in the outright trash of Radio Paris. Collaboration has lost its popularity.

November 16, 1941

I've been totally absorbed in Chopin's *Letters*. All the biographies I know consider his music in terms of the pleasure it gives and savor it down to the very last note. But they say little about the process of work. Yet he went about his work methodically, working through everything, creating his style with the full awareness of an artist and artisan of composition. The *Letters* give the impression that he simply "worked like a dog," sitting for hours at the piano in Nohant. Without affectation. He knows exactly what he's capable of, works intensively with Bach, keeps on learning, is careful what he puts on the market, but when he finishes something, then it's "pay up." All his biographies are written in twilight colors, nocturnal, melancholic. Chopin suspended above life, floating in the mists of the preludes and études, and so on. Yet it seems to me he was one of the most normal members of that Parisian emigration. He was a clear thinker and an artist who had discovered his style and was sure that this style was also the style of the times, that his pieces "worked," and so he deepened this style and made a concerted effort to have it recognized, precisely where it was harder to find acceptance. The letters are simple, sometimes capricious, unpretentious, and discreet. A snob? Maybe. But I prefer his snobbism, accompanied by a sober view of things, to the case of Mickiewicz, for example, who is rather unappealing, despite everything, during his Paris period.

I bought myself some scores and after many years once again began tinkling on the piano. At the Châtillon factory I found an old instrument behind the stage, some "offstage" relic. And as I now go through Chopin's scores, he delights me all over again; I marvel at their simplicity and superb workmanship. If there is melancholy here, it is entirely deliberate, crafted. An inspired simplicity, clarity, music not for supermen, no metaphysics or grand ideas—simply music. With all the intransigence of the Polish heart and Polish sensibility. His intelligence is reflected in every one of his letters. The charming intelligence of a calm man and a powerful artist whose talent is at his service, and not—as often happens among the Slavs—a man at the service of talent. A good heart, an amiable skepticism and irony, much self-irony, as is the case with all natures who realize their own worth—a straightforward and practical mind, a touch of egotism. Compared to him, George Sand appears pretentious and coarse, turning out novels on the assembly line, promoting ideas and new trends with the anxiety of a sexually frustrated female, getting tangled eventually in typical French peccadillos. The letters convey the impression of him at the piano, observing all this and judging it for what it's worth. Finally, he has enough and breaks it off—breaks it off cold, logically and discreetly.

Afternoon at the movies to see *The Chess Player*, based on Dostoyevsky. With Pierre Blanchar.[83] A well-made film—immersion in the Dostoyevskian universe. It's interesting the degree to which the French identify with and re-create the mood and atmosphere of something seemingly so foreign to them. Perhaps for the same reason that the Russians are inclined to "technical" raptures and guilt complexes having little to do with genuine feelings. They are masters of coldness, cerebral crimes, and mathematically abstract spiritual complexes, inspired not by emotion but by thought. Dostoyevsky seems to me above all contrived. So contrived, that he doesn't move me at all.

In addition there's his phenomenal ability to evoke moral squalor. Zola shares many traits with Dostoyevsky. The French excel at the capacity for evoking moral squalor and its spiritual particularities.

The newsreels are reassuring. That satanic clown is visiting his troops in their winter quarters. Let them hunker down.

November 18, 1941

Tadzio arrived from Mińsk Mazowiecki[84] to spend his leave in Paris. He came over for supper. Brought a suitcase full of things from Cracow. The whole family contributed to its contents. Hanka brought it to Warsaw, then stopped by Tadzio's place—stories from a thousand and one nights.

At the sight of the shirts and long johns belonging to my father that my mother sent me, I wanted to cry. They themselves have nothing but are sending me this . . . Piasecki chocolates,[85] cigarettes . . . and Tadzio telling stories about Poland. On Monday he was still in Warsaw, Tuesday evening he's sitting with us. I'm not inclined to patriotic emotions, but I was torn up. An intense longing for the country, for my parents, for Hanka and Franek, for Maryna—for all of them. It was perhaps only at this moment that for the first time I experienced our loneliness, the foreignness of our surroundings, and the almost three years of an entirely different life, in which many feelings have grown dull under pressure of the unrelenting "don't give in." Tadzio and the things we had been sent gave off the air and odor of "ownership," of "one's own," of "ours." And Tadzio talked about the hope that sustains them there, about himself, about others, about everything.

November 19, 1941

What have they not sent us . . . We still can't get over it. Even money, which simply puts me to shame. We can't grasp what's been happening to us since yesterday. Cracow has come within arm's reach. At times it seems the war will end any day now, that we're about to return, that we'll first be getting visitors.

It has seemed to me that I have by now become so very attached to our surroundings and to our life here. But riding home today I saw everything as if on the first day of our arrival. Foreignness—at best a superficial and undemanding connection.

November 20, 1941

This evening we met Tadzio at the Rosinkiewiczes' place. Rosinkiewicz wants to return and spoke with Tadzio for three hours, pressing him for information about Poland. It was very interesting. Tadzio recounted what he knew, what he didn't know about he didn't mention. I know him, but for the first time I learned something more specific.

General Weygand has resigned, he's through with collaboration. Many rumors are circulating on that subject. Northern Africa is becoming very important. The English have launched an offensive in Libya in the grand style and insist they are making progress. The general opinion: Germany is beginning to lose the war and in fact has already lost it. Past perfect tense.

November 23, 1941

Tadzio runs around madly and buys up everything he can. We hardly see him. We met him finally this evening in the Polish restaurant on rue Saint-Paul. A portion of roast chicken for forty-five francs. The Germans have taken Rostov.

What are they doing with Africa? A meeting between Göring and Pétain is said to be in the works. The Germans want the fleet, Tunisia, and Morocco. On the other hand, it's rumored that at the decisive moment Africa will break away from the Metropole and declare itself to be Free France. Pétain will throw up his hands and tell the Germans: Go ahead, take it.

People keep saying that Pétain's policies are a delaying tactic, that he doesn't want genuine collaboration. Hard to believe, just as it's hard to believe that Africa would dare break away. If the French give the Germans the fleet and Africa, I don't know what France will do after the war. Why this servility, this lack of spirit and ambition? If Father Trublet once called Voltaire "the perfection of the average," I often want to say the same thing about the French nation as a whole and about the reasoning of each Frenchman.[86] Discussing the war with a Frenchman, even the most intelligent, can turn your stomach. They have no vision of the future. For some this is a class war and they regard it from the class perspective as a kind of European revolution, others talk of France as though it were still the France that ceased to exist in June of last year, still others fail even to grasp the meaning of those daily events, and in the end no one realizes they are weighed down by something that could be called the "Lord Jim complex."[87] It's always *la France éternelle* and the unfounded claim to greatness.

November 26, 1941

Basia is going all over town looking for presents for Cracow. There seem to be plenty of goods everywhere. But when you want to buy something, a gift for someone or something special, there's nothing to choose from. Everything vanishes in the blink of an eye, prices hit the roof. There are pretty women's stockings in the display windows, but the cards pinned to them say "sold" and there's not a single pair in the shop. A ruse, because the goods are hidden, to be sold later at higher prices. Tadzio and his pals operate only in the Polish section around rue Saint-Paul and naturally they buy what they want, because Poles can find anything. In any case, this is by now the center of the black market. They have each brought along twenty thousand francs and buy goods to sell in Warsaw. Their transactions involve five or ten dozen pairs of stockings, tea, fabrics, rum, cognac — everything at astronomical prices.

November 28, 1941

The Germans are beginning to requisition "Canadians" (water-resistant jackets lined with felt) and leather overcoats. In addition they're going after the monuments. The monuments to the Montgolfier brothers[88] and to Victor Hugo have already vanished. Of course the newspapers report that the monuments will be replaced by others composed of a different alloy, more durable than the present ones, and so on. Nonsense, providing the subject of mockery and jokes.

November 29, 1941

Each of the workmen who arrived here on leave from Mińsk Mazowiecki will be departing like a Venetian galley or Spanish caravel with valuable cargo. Tadzio got me fifteen pairs of stockings. I must begin thinking of how to make some extra money myself. But, for example, Piotruś F. is taking fifteen dozen pairs of stockings for a large exporter from rue Saint-Paul. Indeed, an outfitter in the grand style. Others take women's lingerie, sweaters, and so on. A single successful transport of such a consignment can increase one's capital six to ten times. As in the spice trade. Similar risks. This being the case, I, too, have taken a risk and Tadzio will depart from here as my caravel equipped with fifteen pairs of stockings. For himself he's carrying three kg of tea, fabrics, and other items. They're leaving tomorrow evening.

The Russians have recaptured Rostov—the Germans are retreating.

November 30, 1941

Deals, deals. I lent Tadzio five thousand francs and will deduct it from his salary here at DKW-Grün.[89] Later, one will have to buy dollars because it no longer pays to keep francs.

In the 18th arrondissement the brothel for German soldiers was blown up. Two people were killed, several wounded. As of today the entire 18th arrondissement is closed off after six in the evening. The order stands until further notice. Once again red-letter notices are plastered everywhere. Timoshenko is chasing the Germans beyond Rostov.[90] The English are stuttering in Libya, supposedly moving forward.

December 1, 1941

Tadzio left this evening. Around eight in the evening I was at his hotel but he wasn't there. His friend said only that he'd been seen somewhere, completely plastered. We sit around and wait. The rest of the group gathers slowly. Everyone was sure Piotruś would show up sloshed, but he arrived sober accompanied by enormous packages and a Jew with the extraordinary name of "Natsweter." Obviously everyone called him "Mr. Sweater." He is dispatching a large quantity of goods via Piotruś for export to Warsaw. He walks around the room, smacks his lips, puts on his hat and takes it off, scratches his head, finally with oriental resignation he concludes: "Either they'll take everything away from me or they'll take nothing at all." Suddenly, he demands in a loud voice: "A wet towel and an indelible pencil." Setting upon his packages, he moistens them with the wet towel, and writes in big letters: "DKW Grün—*Kriegswerkstätte.*" He turns back around, contented: "They will go as a factory shipment; the customs officers show absolute *désintéressement* at the sight of such packages." I assure him customs will confiscate them nevertheless. He gives me a menacing look: "What are you saying? It's clear you're not at all up-to-date . . ."

The others are still packing up the last trifles and the supplies of alcohol. Piotruś has an enormous flask of eau de cologne filled with pure spirits. He has made the rounds of Paris pharmacies buying up pure spirits. Tadzio enters strutting. In high spirits, drunk, cheerful—carefree. Fortunately Boguś had thought of him and packed his things carefully. Tadzio stretches out on the bed, looks at the Jew, and begins to squeal with laughter: "Mr. Sweater, I already see those German women wearing your stockings. Hey, where'd you pick up that crazy name? Bogdan, you guttersnipe, get a move on! . . ." The room is becoming more and more chaotic, because it's soon time to leave for the station. The hired porter has already arrived (the guys are done exhausting themselves) and is beginning to take down the suitcases. We leave.

The night is clear, moonlit. Tadzio chatters away, it's as if I'm going too. Basia is already at Gare de l'Est. Tadzio practically throws himself at her, takes her by the arm, not worried at all. He walks, chats, and gives instructions: "Boguś— bags onto the cart." He greets our Frenchmen, clapping them on the shoulders: "*Ça va,* bonzzur Robert, you French blockhead." Robert smiles and says: "*Ça va,* I understand with Polish." Finally we reach the platform. But the German guards at the entrance are checking papers meticulously. Tadzio snooped around a bit, found a side entrance, and we enter with the entire cart without being checked at all.

It's dark on the platform, the Germans are boarding the train, a cart goes by and a woman calls out in a horrid accent: "*Kuchen, Schokolade, Bonbons, Sekt . . .*"[91] A linen-haired Valkyrie buys a box of chocolates. While our lot, furious that seats were not reserved for them, holler and curse in Polish as though they were right at home. They pack themselves in wherever they can. We say good-bye, embrace Tadzio, I repeat all our instructions one more time, and we leave, again by the side passage. The station is now empty, the dead silence in the streets is lit by the moon. And somewhere underground the metro rumbles dully. War, Paris, Poles, Germans, Gare de l'Est, where Frenchwomen call out, "*Schokolade, Sekt.*" Sometimes I feel like I'm dreaming. If only I could by now wake up from this dream.

December 2, 1941

Today's newspapers are simply crammed with articles on the subject of yesterday's meeting between Göring and Pétain. Obviously, nobody knows what they talked about. Speculations abound: Africa? The fleet? Intensified propaganda from the "Anti-Bolshevik Legion" and the mobilization of industry.

Negotiations between America and Japan are proceeding in a tense atmosphere. America is trying its best to get Japan to declare war, but Japan doesn't want to. Fiercely cold outside and foggy. In front of the big flower shop on rue Lafayette an old woman wrapped in scarves and shawls is sitting on a folding chair behind a small easel. With a hand blue from the cold she is painting the strangely twisted orchids in the display window. People stop, look, and go on their way. Painting orchids in the freezing cold may be the height of perversion. But perhaps this is the way she has found to warm up? I stood next to her for a long time and suddenly I was seized by such longing for a country where orchids bloom that I wanted to cry. I literally felt the pain of longing.

December 3, 1941

Our *patronne* is extremely bellicose. She listens to Radio London; every few days we have long political discussions, ending always with the exclamation: *"Ils sont foutus!"*[92] One of her desk drawers is filled with maps. We study the Russian front, the cosmetic operations in Libya. The Far East. I advise her to buy a map of the Pacific. It looks like something will soon start up there as well.

Paris is in fact quiet, Germans are few, the harlots are losing their clients. "Now they get out of bed to get a little rest," as Mr. P. wittily put it (*Elles se lèvent pour se reposer un peu*). The criminal penalties imposed in the 18th arrondissement were rescinded today. The weather is as usual chilly and nasty.

I'm reading André Siegfried's *L'Amérique d'aujourd'hui.*[93] Terrific writing. With the lightly disdainful tone of a Frenchman in regard to these "barbarians" and the continent without cathedrals. Basically, it's a case of envy, which takes different forms—most frequently that of so-called cultural superiority. Yet in many cases, compared to America, cultured Europe comes off poorly. Culture? It depends what kind. In terms of political and economic culture, America beats Europe all the way. Everything we know about America beyond the store of "wise" and stereotypical judgments amounts to nothing.

December 4, 1941

Basia's name day. First thing in the morning someone brought her a plate of chocolates and cakes from Lola, and Chomętowski sent a lovely primrose. All this was delivered to our room by the hotel maid and the day began on a festive note.

Before going to the office I went to rue Saint-Honoré and bought her a pair of gloves, and on the way home bought three roses. Lola came by after supper for tea, and the three of us spent all evening together, discussing the war, as usual.

Yesterday, in the tenth district, another German officer was shot and starting today the entire *Bezirk*[94] will go to bed at six in the afternoon. Sikorski went to see Stalin, they concluded a treaty (a bad bargain, no doubt), and Polish divisions are forming in Russia. The Russian offensive is making progress and the Germans are retreating. They have stumbled in Libya; tension between America and Japan is increasing. An American-Japanese war would be the center of the third act of this tragedy, its high point. Afterward one would merely have to await the finale. God only knows what kind—the end of this war may be worse than the war itself . . .

December 7, 1941

Roosevelt has sent a personal letter to the emperor of Japan.

December 8, 1941

Yesterday the Japanese attacked all the American bases in Hawaii and have embarked on war. According to the communiqués, the entire attack was executed by fighters launched from Japanese aircraft carriers. The Americans were totally surprised, "caught with their pants down," as the saying goes. It's indeed hard to understand. After all, the giant Japanese squadron was no needle in a haystack, even in the Pacific. Where was the intelligence? Where was the deep reconnaissance around Hawaii? Were the Americans sitting around calmly, eating pineapples and dancing the *hula-hula*? All the ships in port and the planes on the ground fell to the Japanese and in a couple of hours were reduced to shreds. *Oklahoma* and *West Virginia* at the bottom of the sea, thousands of corpses, even from the first bulletins it's clear there must have been total mayhem. I don't understand why the Japanese didn't immediately land and take possession of this pearl of the Pacific. Now the war is complete, the circle is closed.

In Paris, further attacks on the Germans. The entire German hotel on rue de la Convention was blown to bits. As a result, as of today all movement after six in the afternoon is forbidden. The metro runs only until five. The order was received with good humor, all the more so as work stops at four. B. commented: "*La natalité française va augmenter.*"[95] It's said, however, that ensuing retaliatory measures may be even worse, that, for example, they will close the bakeries for several days or cancel a certain quantity of food coupons for December. The French consider this the very worst that can befall them. They simply can't imagine anything worse. But a feeling of solidarity and even satisfaction at these continuing attacks has emerged in the neighborhood. Standing in line today I heard some mothers discussing the assignments their children were getting at school. Questions, such as, "What do you think of Mers-el-Kébir?"[96] or "What do you think of the Third Republic?" Apparently in both cases the children wrote nothing, and one resolute girl answered the teacher: "How is it possible to think about the Third Republic if it no longer exists?"

Yesterday Dmitry Merezhkovsky died. There was only a tiny notice in the newspapers. His death has elicited no response. My mother practically fed me on his books, and his *Leonardo da Vinci* was the first biography I ever read.[97]

December 9, 1941

Sensation. Our German "minder," Counselor Schwerbel, seems to have vanished over the horizon. Various rumors are circulating on this subject, but nothing specific is known. It's also unclear who has replaced him. The Polish mood in Paris has darkened.

December 10, 1941

The German retreat continues. But it seems very orderly. On the Île de la Cité the first Christmas trees have appeared.

December 11, 1941

The Japanese have sunk one of the newest British warships, *The Prince of Wales*, and the armored cruiser *Repulse*. There is absolutely no doubt that the Americans were thoroughly surprised. Today, the American Mrs. P. rubbed her bony hands and told me: "Good for them—they were asleep, like the French—they were asleep on their electric refrigerators, on their peach jam and orange juice. And now they have to . . ."

This evening the Germans and the Italians declared war on America. Hitler delivered a speech in the Reichstag. Our *patronne,* understanding not a word, listened to the entire speech and offered me a short summary: "He shouted dreadfully." "It's all he has left," I answered. Well—the "i's" have finally been dotted after two years, three months, and eleven days. I remember that as early as September the English were talking a lot about the preparation of plans for the future, using 1943, for purposes of calculation, as a limit. They were reckoning well.

December 12, 1941

I rode around to twenty newspaper stands trying to buy the *Pariser Zeitung* with the text of Hitler's speech. But I couldn't find the rag anywhere because it had sold out in the blink of an eye. I had to make do with reports and excerpts from the French *Zeitungen.* This time it's truly hard to tell what to call this speech. Obscurantism in the mode of Towiański, either simply German or Hitler's own.[98] The Germans are the Christ of nations, the chosen people, whom the Creator has entrusted with the mission of defending Europe. And thus nothing can be done to save her. An elaborate explanation for why Germany attacked Poland, so elaborate that it's incomprehensible and suspect. The balance sheet of losses in the east is simply laughable, finally an attack on Roosevelt, who, like Wilson, is called a madman, and also a few words about Mrs. Roosevelt, which sound idiotic. In short, pure buzzing, the angry buzzing of a fly flailing around in a spiderweb. In contrast to these words, to this flailing about, in contrast to the military "exploits" of the Anglo-Saxons, the figure of Stalin stands out, menacing and majestic, imposing and terrifying. He hasn't budged from the Kremlin, keeps silent, has held back, and now, having signed a pact with winter, has started to advance. And still remains silent. He has been surprised by no one—he's the one who has surprised the world. A menacing and mysterious poetry emanates from the Kremlin, a great and inscrutable "X" in the equation that will emerge after the war.

A mild December this year, warm. It's only the humidity, which penetrates everything, that is nasty.

December 13, 1941

One could apply the title "Paris 1941" and begin the story like this: The male rose from his lair, prepared his morning nourishment, and, throwing a few worn-out skins over his shoulder, set off on the hunt. He nosed around all day long, encountered other males or females, hunted with cunning and cleverness, and what he had bagged—the beans, canned peas or butter, coffee, sugar—he shoved into the great sack on his back. And returned in the evening to his chilly cave, presented his loot to the female, and she let him come to her. And such was their life in the Stone Age, known as the twentieth century, when millions of other males butchered each other for the love of humanity, for the good of future generations, wanting to create the Bronze Age but heading straight for the Ice Age.

December 14, 1941

Sunday. We're at home. I'm reading. Basia is sketching. I'm reading Sienkiewicz's *Without Dogma* and my blood boils.[99] Leon Płoszowski should be spanked with nettles on his naked bottom, have his head dunked in ice water, and fed for five days on salted sardines with nothing to drink. Afterward he should be packed off to do some honest work. Although the devil knows whether, even in these circumstances, a character like this wouldn't create his own philosophy: of the waterish-sardiny-nettlish type. This is no fictitious character—there are plenty like him running around. Intellects of the most dubious sort. He must—damn it—think. Instead of living and thinking, he only thinks and considers himself somehow superior, because he has invented NOTHING. Such a cripple and intellectual freak knows from the start that he will invent nothing, but he persists in thinking. *Er denkt, er denkt, der Schlag hat ihn getroffen und er noch denkt.*[100] The simpler one's thinking in all matters concerning one's own "I," the more honest and open it is, based entirely on brief "yes's" or "no's." That's what it comes down to in the end when one truly wants to talk honestly with oneself, to live a more enlightened life. Alas, we harbor a constant and overwhelming desire at every opportunity to play a great role in our own eyes. We harbor an entire theater, no—rather a vaudeville show and we keep on mugging. The inner spectator, one's "I," takes all this in dead seriousness, goes into raptures, and watches, feeling moved and wringing a handkerchief. Without sensing the falseness, because one cloaks one's thought in words, one savors the form, not realizing the contents are rather vulgar.

Man has a tendency to transparent self-deception and a snobbish fear of seeming simple-minded in his own eyes, precisely in his own eyes. No one knows anyone else's thoughts, but people still most often take into account the opinions they imagine others to have when they do their own thinking. And therefore they lie to themselves, no less than they lie to others. Whether it's necessary or not. Basia once said: "Easy for you to talk about simplicity of thought, of its clarity, since you are happy." I answered: "You're mistaken, because imagine how easily I could be unhappy." I don't look for happiness, because I've arrived at the great realization that I have found it. It seems to me that I am shallow and superficial because I cannot manage to be a spinning jenny of thought. In any case I cannot manage to be Płoszowski.

December 15, 1941

Yet again bomb attacks on German restaurants in Paris and the outskirts. Today's *Bekanntmachung*[101] therefore informs us that a hundred Jews, Communists, and anarchists will be shot and that a tribute of a billion francs will be levied on the Jews of the *zone occupée*. The text of the notice implies that this nevertheless does not affect the French. Softening the blow. The French are indignant already. Even Radio Vichy has delicately said that it does not approve of such methods, because despite everything, all Frenchmen are in fact threatened by the death of these hundred people. This delicate demurral on the part of Vichy is from a certain perspective quite sensational, because IT'S THE FIRST TIME a statement of this kind has been heard from that quarter—and precisely IN RELATION TO THE JEWS. Many people I talked with today said: "Only now for the first time, when it concerns the Jews, is Vichy protesting. *Ne trouvez-vous pas cela un tout petit peu—étrange? . . .*"[102] One might entertain many conjectures on this subject, and very anti-Semitic ones at that. People who would never have had such thoughts before have now begun conjecturing in just this way, and from that point of view Vichy's "protest" has done more harm than good.

December 16, 1941

Riding the metro has now become a most refined form of torture—obviously during rush hour. In the last couple of months the trains have been shortened, instead of the complement of five cars there are now four or even three cars. The number of trains has also been reduced and the wait is now five to seven minutes during rush hour, ten to fifteen at other times. Half the lightbulbs in the stations as well as in the carriages have been unscrewed and the lighting everywhere is deathly pale. The escalators and elevators are shut. The passages once used only as entrances now also serve as exits. Between six and seven in the evening the metro becomes an inferno. Swollen streams of people throng the passageways, bump into each other, cram together, and rush to their trains. Today I took the metro at Porte d'Orléans. At Denfert-Rochereau the train was already full. The air instantly became heavier. At every stop a certain number of people burst out the doors like champagne corks, others pushed their way in and the doors again banged shut. Like closing an overstuffed cigarette case: you compress the contents for a minute, until click—it's shut. Everyone is sweating, stench and stuffiness. I change trains at Strasbourg–Saint-Denis. I was propelled from the train directly into the embrace of a poster politely inviting the French to volunteer for work in Germany. Entire walls in the metro are covered in posters: *L'ouvrier allemand vous invite, Allez travailler en Allemagne*, and so on.[103] In the passage—sudden screams. A long line of people extends all the way from the automatic door to the entry stairs. At the exit from the platform a metro official is checking to be sure people aren't entering through the exit. A woman with a child in her arms standing next to him wants to pass without waiting in line and board her train. But he won't let her through. At this, the people in line shout: "*Madame, passez!*" They roar and threaten. Enraged by waiting, they want this one woman at least to get through. The crowd would like to tear the metro official to pieces. A few men finally rush at him, the women shout: "Throw him onto the tracks." The woman passes through, the crowd screams with satisfaction. A hail of abuse rains down on the guardian of order. *Idiot, imbécile, ballot . . .*[104] The German soldiers are suffocating along with everyone else. Now they, too, have to ride the metro, often entire divisions travel this way, with their kits, backpacks, and bundles. I make it onto the platform for my line, push my way into a car. I'm flat against the back of a young woman, someone is pressed up against me—it's stuffy and stinks. The young woman pokes her dirty head under my nose, with a hurricane of intricately twisted and lacquered curls, the color of oxidized brass, reeking of brilliantine. She has heart-shaped earrings and despite the crush is reading a pocketbook romance. The title of the fascinating chapter is: *La chambre nuptiale*. She buries herself in her reading, every few seconds licking her painted lips. At each station, before the train stops, I'm kicked by the passengers "battling" their way out. It's a relief when I get off at Daumesnil.

December 18, 1941

They could no longer hide it. Today, for the first time. The Germans have admitted in their communiqué that they have been forced to retreat. In order to shorten the front and because of the winter, which requires the switch from mobile warfare to a war of position. In a word, as "Uncle" Galant put it, the Germans are moving ahead and the Bolsheviks on their tail. Meanwhile, the Japanese are doing as they please with the English and the Americans. Rumor has it, furthermore, that the Germans are concentrating their forces around Bordeaux and plan to attack Gibraltar together with Spain. Otherwise, the holiday mood is much more festive and positive than last year.

I have finished *The Połaniecki Family*.[105] Not entirely stupid. Many excellent remarks and observations.

December 20, 1941

Lola invited us today to the Théâtre Montparnasse to see *Marie Stuart* by a homegrown lady writer.[106] The play was a series of tableaux vivants against a backdrop of black curtains—either boiled potatoes or fried potatoes, which is to say, either London and what they are saying about Mary Stuart, or Scotland and what Mary Stuart is up to there. Attractive costumes, good lighting, but that's all. The French style of acting is artificial, affected, and pompous. Insufferable singing of the text. Each word starts with several letters, followed by notes, and all the actors, starting with those in the principal roles, thrum like a pack of grouse. Each one sings his role for himself, turning frequently toward the audience. Darnley slithers around the closed door of Mary's bedroom and batters her with an onslaught of words exuding desire: "Mary, your body is as essential to me as bread, meat, wine . . . ," and a whole series of other rationed products. The script is dangerous for today's public, for as someone in the audience observed under his breath, Darnley had not mentioned fats. There was tittering. After which Darnley called Mary a whore, belting out *"putain"* in every key. In a word, criminal.

The Christmas holidays promise to be excellent. From the twenty-fourth to the twenty-ninth and from the first to the fifth the Châtillon office will be closed, to save on light and heating. Time off, and with pay.

December 21, 1941

Seeking Basia's opinion, today I inform her, with a serious expression on my face: "When I get my money tomorrow from Grün I will look around for a way to invest it. Perhaps I'll buy . . ."

"Marks and yen!" Basia finishes dryly and categorically.

If the cold irony and hatred with which she said this could be transformed into energy, Germany and Japan would be smashed in five minutes. The gold dollar rises from day to day—it has already reached 525 francs. Only three weeks ago it was at 450. The gold ruble rises just as much. Yesterday I wanted to get some accurate information about prices, so I went to visit a Polish antiques dealer I know. He has his shop, or rather his corner full of spiderwebs, on rue des Francs-Bourgeois, between the Musée Carnavalet and place des Vosges. One of the nooks of Paris you don't simply enter but plunge into. Riding into such corners on my bike, I always feel I should bend over, raise my elbows, and move carefully as if into a tangle of bushes. Parisian lairs. Mr. Zygmuś, the antiques dealer, is by now an elderly gentleman. He in fact is never in his shop but floats around the city, always ruddy and a bit sloshed. When you drop in on rue Saint-Paul—Mr. Zygmuś will greet you, lisping slightly, with a broad, outmoded Polish "Gooooooddaaaay." When you walk along boulevard des Italiens—Mr. Zygmuś is there taking a stroll and elegantly tips his hat (elbow close to the chest), twirling a cane grasped by a mitt wrapped in an impeccably dirty cotton glove, formerly white. He has business everywhere, his pockets full of samples, such trifles as: a gold watch chain for 3,000 francs, a small lady's wristwatch with tiny diamonds for 8,000 fr. (junk, no sir, not worth it), and in general, "I don't sell anything these days, no sir, not worth it. Yes . . . well . . . when I need five, ten thousand I peddle something, but not worth it. When you're buying—they want a lot, when you're selling—they give nothing . . ." He waves his cane, tips his cap, again twirls the cane, and a half hour later you can find him on the Champs-Élysées.

The shop is tended by his "ssociate," as he calls her—an elderly Frenchwoman, who presides over the spiders and the spiderwebs. Mr. Zygmuś drops in, says a few words, and is off again somewhere, far away. When I came by the shop today, Mr. Zygmuś wasn't there. *Madame* interrupted her darning of the spiderwebs, received me courteously, listened to what I had in mind, then in the dusty voice proper to all antiques dealers, instructed me: "Take a right, then at the first corner a left, past one bistro on the right, then a second one, and beyond the second one an antiques shop next to a shop selling ladies' blouses. Go in there and ask for Monsieur Joseph."

I thanked her and I plunged into the narrow streets, until bubbles rose around me. I found the antiques shop and asked for Monsieur Joseph. But Monsieur Joseph was next door in the bistro. "Go over there and ask for Monsieur Joseph." The bistro was dark and mysterious. I winked at the *patron*, whispered "Monsieur Joseph." He pointed mysteriously at a little door in the wall, opened it, and bellowed until the glasses clinked on the counter: "Monsieur Joseph!" At that very moment Joseph jumped out like a jack-in-the box. A small, swarthy little Jew, somewhat dirty, somewhat elegant. "The price of gold rubles? Exactly half the gold dollar. Are they offering you some? For how much? Offer 260–265 to the ruble, maximum." He speaks French with an accent that immediately reminded me of Lopek Krukowski.[107] I thanked him and—he vanished. Near place de la Bastille I regained the surface, emerging after my sojourn in the depths of the city. There's one kind of life there, here another. There Mr. Zygmuś, Monsieur Joseph, and hundreds of others turn into deepwater fish, trading in gold, diamonds, everything. They pop up from time to time, splash about on the surface. In the quiet, narrow streets, hidden away, Balzac's Paris, with its array of characters, deals, and scandals, still rustles. The rustle of a basket full of snails. Time to read some Balzac again.

December 22, 1941

If only this keeps up, all for the better. Hitler has named himself commander in chief in place of von Brauchitsch and has sent him packing.[108] Officially it's said that von Brauchitsch had long been asking to retire because of heart problems and the Führer finally granted his request. What really happened we'll find out someday. At the moment the only known fact is that the Bolsheviks are flaying these invincible armies and keeping them moving. The French are rubbing their hands, and if this keeps up, in two weeks they'll be talking about Cossacks in Montmartre. Two opinions prevail: some people report miracles and attribute every rumor to Radio London (Of course! London says!), according to which the Germans have already lost and they're rushing headlong to the end. Others are skeptical: in the spring the Germans will show what they still can do.

It seems to me that the truth is somewhere in-between. Russia's current successes do not have the significance the optimists imagine, but I don't think that the Germans are capable of another monster offensive this spring. From what one hears from eyewitnesses working for the Germans, the Germans increasingly lack raw materials and means of communication. And what will happen when the mass production of American airplanes enters the picture? When the Americans begin to batter Germany day and night? The game will still continue, but happily the outcome is already by now clear.

December 23, 1941

I dressed a bit more respectably, got on my bicycle, and rode into town to order flowers for Mr. and Mrs. P. We had decided to send them something from the best florist in Paris. I went to La Chaume on rue Royale. One of the many elegant shops in Paris that still preserve the atmosphere of "Paris 1900." If the Secession is in principle a style that's hard to digest, the French have nevertheless managed occasionally to give it a lighter touch and here it even has its own special flavor. It isn't dead—it's still alive and breathing. The entrance to La Chaume is unremarkable, but an interior of marble, stucco, gold leaf, and garlands has all the subtlety of that most unnatural naturalism, the brothel style. The service is the same as in all shops of this category: older ladies modestly dressed in black, with a touch of the pious zealot from the provinces. Old maids from the best families now down at the heels, living portraits out of Balzac. Here, the flowers are arranged casually, mixed together, nothing ostentatious. Shops catering to upstarts, to the riffraff, may be showy; for this regular clientele, by contrast, for the true Parisian *noblesse* of rue du Bac, rue de Grenelle, the Île Saint-Louis, the Paris of the 16th arrondissement (many nouveaux riches can already be found there), ostentation is not permitted.

I entered with the refined modesty of a young man of good family and was approached by one of the impoverished female cousins who asked, as if intoning a Hail Mary: "*Vous désirez, Monsieur?*" "*Je voudrais une azalée.*"[109] She leads me inside and shows me an azalea bush. How much? 1,200 francs. I didn't even blink, although internally I flinched as though someone had heaved a weighty sack onto my back. "Ah, no—*vous savez*—I would prefer something more modest," I say slowly. "*Mais voilà, Monsieur—600 francs.*" A bit easier to take. I say nothing and look around. The impoverished cousin's respect has grown. My miserliness, my hesitation over the expense, positively reeks of the purest-blood aristocracy. Here you can boldly show you are a penny-pincher. This is the type they respect, as most certainly rich. I pick out a smaller bush, more modest, but pretty. 180 francs. I take it and ask that it be sent tomorrow morning before noon to 20, rue Saint-Lazare. The address seemed to her a bit strange. She pretended to have misheard, "20, rue Saint-Honoré?" she asked innocently. "*Non, non—*Saint-Lazare." It flashed clearly in her eyes: "Who's ever lived in such a neighborhood . . ." Mrs. P., when giving her address in shops like these, always adds: *Provisoirement, vous comprenez, les événements . . .*[110] I added nothing. The saleswoman leads me to the exit and when opening the door, says, in the tone of "now and at the hour of death": "*À votre service, monsieur.*"

Afternoon at the town hall of the 17th arrondissement in the unemployment department. I needed to obtain a certificate for one of the "lambs" showing the period he received benefits. I left the bicycle in the "garage." All government offices, town halls, and large cafés now have guarded bicycle racks. You pay one franc, leave the bicycle under a specially constructed overhang, get a numbered tag from the old fellow in charge, and you can go calmly on your way.

I enter the gloomy room. A low counter runs along the entire length, dividing the room in half. The walls behind the counter are covered in folders and papers all crammed into the shelves. From floor to ceiling. A few aged functionaries sit behind the counter, chatting away, someone creeps along the shelves like a shadow and searches for something he clearly doesn't want to find. On the right side, against the wall, stands a small, glassed-in booth with the sign "Information," and inside there's a bald old man with a beret perched on his skull. A nutshell on a brass knob. Up near the ceiling, a small window communicates with the room by means of a pulley for papers and documents. Below and above are two curtain rods, a few strings, and an old cigar box. The "case in question" is put into the box, the string is pulled, the box rises to the window. The head in the beret leans out, takes the "case," *le cas est examiné dans les archives,*[111] the response is put into the box, the box descends.

Silence and calm reign here, covered in dust. A few clients wait, conversing in a whisper. Nothing here is important, because everything is important—the deeds, dossiers, abstracts, documents are handled solicitously, with devotion, with relish. Haste, scientific methods for the organization of labor, the purposeful arrangement of furniture, efficient and speedy administration and paperwork—all are nonsense. Since thousands of papers have resided here for hundreds of years, the methods for handling them must also remain unchanged. We'll look the matter over, slowly; you'll get what you want, but meanwhile you can chat, tell stories, or say something amusing and clever. No need to worry about regulations, organization, that eternal "you should"—but rather adapt everything to . . . To what? To THAT. To this bedlam, to the power of stupid and unnecessary regulations, the power of procedures and needless requirements, and that's all there is to it. The law and the statutes are the law and the statutes, and the citizens have the innate capacity and compulsion to evade them. In this bedlam there's always the possibility of discussion, fair or not—one can perhaps *arranger* something somehow, one can talk it over, bargain *spirituellement* and smoothly, settle the business calmly and leave. It's the atmosphere of an old-time notary's office.

At the counter are two clients, good-natured old men. They speak softly. Now and then their laughter rustles quietly. The laughter of old men sounds like the rustle of old papers. I listen in.

"*Savez-vous,* that parish priest was put away a dozen years ago. For trading in seats in paradise. *Figurez-vous,* he was selling places in paradise to devout ladies. For a *fauteuil d'orchestre*[112] next to Saint Anthony he took three thousand francs, and for a seat next to that patron of the cuckolds, Saint Joseph, fifteen hundred francs. But they put him away before he managed to post a notice in the sacristy that all seats were taken."

They laugh heartily, rocking with laughter like two tops winding down toward the end of the spin. The clerk joins a conversation on the subject of superstitions and he now begins:

"*Vous savez* . . . I was on vacation in the *département* of the Tarn. A small village lost in the gorges, no roads to speak of. One day a woman runs up and begs me to take her husband to the local healer, because the doctor can no longer help. The husband is dying. He has a pain somewhere in the a——s, he's turning blue, please drive him over. I had my car at the time. I dragged the fellow out of bed, loaded him into the car, and off we go. Horrible road, the car bumps along, the fellow moans. We finally arrive somewhere up in the hills. We ask for the healer. They say he's out in the field. Another quarter hour of driving—the healer is mowing the hay. I called him, carried the man out. He's moaning and twisting with pain, can't stand up. The healer asks what he's got. Something in the a——s, I say. He pulled off the fellow's pants, looked up his butt, whispered something, waved his hands about, blew, puffed, murmured something else, spit, and says everything's now fine." — (By now I'm not the only one listening, the whole office is listening, and behind a stack of deeds representing the sick man's a——s, the storyteller apes the healer's every motion.) — "I can return him. I put him back into the car, he no longer even moaned. I'm thinking for sure he won't last till tomorrow. Again we drive. The road is unimaginable. We were tossed about, shaken . . . I finally made it, handed the fellow to his woman, and went off to go fishing. The next morning the wife comes to see me, a goose and a chicken under her arm, two dozen eggs, and she's laughing. '*Monsieur*,' she shouts, 'my husband is healthy again. You saved him, he's already working in the field.' I think to myself—she's out of her mind. I go with her, I take a look— and I swear on the heads of my children: the fellow is walking around the field. Still staggers a bit, but he's walking. Do you think it was the healer? He had hemorrhoids, was shaken up in the car, the ulcers burst, and he immediately felt better. But the whole village said it was thanks to the healer. What can you do about superstitions?"

Everyone laughs. The two old codgers settled their business, gathered up their papers, exclaimed appreciatively a couple of times: "*C'est pas mal, votre histoire*,"[113] and went out, bent over, telling each other yet another tale. In the courtyard they paused, rocked with laughter, and continued on their way.

Saint Joseph, le patron des cocus.[114] Seems right. Cynical, because it's cynical, but logical, I think, as I gaze at the cigar box rising and falling. I'm feeling lazy and in a good mood. It's supposed to be an office, but it's as snug here as in an antiques shop. They rummage in these papers just like they did a hundred years ago. One can rage and swear at France and the French, at their idea of organization, for the tenth, the twentieth, the fiftieth, and the hundredth time, and for the hundred and first time succumb completely to the charm of that "something," that special atmosphere. Everything here is deeply connected to life, to man, and to his peaceful and regulated daily life. Everything counts, each piece of paper, each building, each trifle passes from generation to generation, fits in and has its place in life, is connected, derives from something, and

LIVES. Like their streets, their monuments, buildings, and furniture. In other countries there is progress, life moves along and with the passing of the years topples antiquities and monuments, turning them into museums. When something has served its time, it is put to rest. It doesn't survive into the present, the connection is broken. The historical monuments are dead. Because everywhere else they are set aside for contemplation. Whereas in France they are contemplated while still in use. A historic monument may sometimes be damaged, for example, by being turned into a clinic for pregnant women or some other social service institution, but at the same time it's incorporated into the life surging around it, it's not allowed to die. The charm of Paris may amount above all to the continuing life of monuments, which in other places are consigned to glass cabinets.

The value of the franc keeps rising.

December 24, 1941

A contrast with last year's holiday. Somewhat brighter and more cheerful. As of this morning I was already free and did not have to go to the office. After breakfast I took the bicycle and went downtown to buy something for Basia. Once, some time ago, we were walking along boulevard des Capucines and she took a liking to a tiny elephant lapel pin in a display of costume jewelry. I went there today and bought it. I returned home for lunch.

Basia had bought a small Christmas tree. After lunch I straightened the room, we finished the preparations for Christmas Eve. In the evening our guests arrived—Lola and Ch. Two appetizers, borsch with dumplings, cauliflower with potatoes, noodles in tomato sauce, fruit salads, custard—Lola brought poppy-seed cake and dried fruit and nuts, Ch. brought wine. After the meal we lit the candles and set out the presents. We all missed our families and friends and no one pretended this would be the last Christmas Eve away from home. Now it's already late, the table is half cleared. Basia puts the remains of the meal "out to chill."

December 25, 1941

We're at home, I'm in my armchair reading Balzac. And we eat as much as we can. A feast for the belly.

December 26, 1941

Today is our third wedding anniversary. I've somehow gotten used to it.

This morning I had to go to the Préfecture on official business. Since my "lamb" had not yet arrived, I sat on a bench and waited. Next to me sat a couple of tramps, old folks. She was a bit bent over but still full of life, he was more apathetic and indifferent. Both were dressed in tattered old clothing, wrapped in an amazing number of scraps, rags, shawls, and scarfs. With dozens of pockets and pouches, which they both kept patting reflexively, automatically—as if wanting to assure themselves that everything was in its place. From time to time he or she would extract something in a cupped palm and, barely moving their hands from the pocket, inspect it and transfer it to another pocket or return it to its place. They took inventory slowly and carefully, layer by layer, without a word . . . Moving as though steadily scratching themselves in one spot after another. Then she leaned in his direction and started to straighten his scarf; then she removed his hat and with the fragment of a comb salvaged from the thirty-eighth pocket in the fourth layer she slowly combed the two tufts of hair on his temples. Finally, she took a piece of bread from the bag at her feet, broke it into smaller pieces, and put them in his mouth. He chewed with his toothless jaws, his chin dancing wildly around his upper lip, and gazed into the distance. He resembled a rabbit whose mouth is being stuffed with one leaf after another. Once in a while the old woman scratched him tenderly under the chin, while muttering with satisfaction, almost purring like a cat licking her kittens. He let himself be stroked, indifferent and seeming twice as motionless in contrast to the mad grinding of his jaws. A horrible but touching sight. I couldn't help thinking that these two might well be happier than many people on this earth.

December 27, 1941

I have read through Balzac's *Le Curé de village* and *Mémoires de deux jeunes mariées* in literally a single breath. It would be hard to find a better job of defining and capturing what it was that a hundred years ago began to erode the organism of France and a hundred years later brought the country to the third stage of syphilis—sociopolitical, ideological, moral, and, despite everything, intellectual. It's apparently a proven fact that in its early stage syphilis stimulates the organism, elicits certain of its hidden strengths, that in many cases it seems to have acted as the ferment of genius—but it ends inevitably in progressive paralysis. One might say the same thing about France and who knows if this is not precisely where the mystery of this "something" not to be found in other nations resides. A hundred years ago Balzac wrote: "The General Council of Public Works, consisting partly of men exhausted by long and sometimes honorable service, but who have nothing left beyond the power of negation, and who dismiss whatever they do not understand, is the damper used to destroy the projects of audacious minds. This Council seems to have been created in order to paralyze the limbs of this fine young generation, who ask only to work, who want to serve France. Monstrous things are happening in Paris: the future of a province depends on the signature of men at the center, who, by means of intrigues I do not have time to recount in detail, block the execution of the best plans; the best plans are in fact those that do the most to obstruct the greed of companies or speculators, that most unsettle or reverse abuses, and Abuse is always stronger in France than Improvement . . . One does not lay a single stone in France without ten Parisian paper-pushers having submitted stupid and useless reports."[115]

Balzac is splendid. French administration is a subject in its own right. I have encountered it from every side and I am no longer surprised by anything. Without encountering this monstrous administration, one cannot know France. It represents continuity since the time of Charlemagne—a continuity sustained and cultivated through all the revolutions, disturbances, and changes of regime (or rather changes of mood—France has never really undergone a radical change of regime). Layer upon layer—ending in a thick sediment: an enormous synthesis, created in a record short time, considering its size—the great Napoleonic administration. And this has endured until today practically without alteration. Rigid, ossified, forever demanding millions of printed pages, forms, statements, copies, certificates—all this PAPER. It makes one dizzy to talk about it and try to convey the enormity, the inertia and negative power of this monster. France was a model for all Europe—and she has choked. Balzac continues:

"A country . . . is weak when it is composed of individuals lacking any feeling of solidarity, to whom it makes no difference whether they obey seven men or only one, a Russian or a Corsican, provided each individual keeps his own plot of land; and this unfortunate egoist does not see that one day it will be taken from him. The only laws will be criminal or fiscal, the stock exchange or one's life. The most generous country on earth will no longer be governed by sentiment. It will have developed and treated incurable wounds. Above all, a universal jealousy: the upper classes will be mixed with the others, equality of desire will be taken for equality of power; true superiority, recognized and affirmed, will be inundated by the torrents of the bourgeoisie. One could pick out one man among a thousand, but nothing can be found among three million with ambitions such as these, clad in the same livery, that of MEDIOCRITY. This triumphant mass will not perceive that it will confront another terrible mass, the mass of peasant proprietors: twenty million living acres of earth, walking, talking, listening to nothing, wanting always more, barricading every way, with brute force at their command."[116]

December 31, 1941

I leave in the morning, return home at six, and thus the days go by, thus a year has passed, and if the new year is no worse, that will be good enough. I work at my desk, run about town, roam between various offices, and the French keep on pushing papers in the great Salle des Fêtes of the Châtillon town hall. And we along with them — day after day.

Meanwhile France attempts to lick her wounds after the lost war. Pétain's government keeps wavering, this way and that, here and there, up and back, sometimes collaboration, sometimes something snags, while cooperation between France and Germany is continually invoked as "the wish of both nations," and some gentleman from Vichy-État keeps repeating that "he hopes an understanding will be reached." In fact, there are really no "yes's" or "no's." The Vichy-État is, in short, entirely on the German leash, but Pétain himself has said nothing explicit about collaboration — he limits himself to evasive "hopes" and "desires" and meanwhile tries to build up the country, drawing inspiration in his legislative-social-administrative measures from the appropriate and not always stupid methods of German National Socialism. The clerical staff is being replaced, efficiency and order introduced into the administration, the battle against French-style bedlam is under way, regulations are being changed, the responsibilities of department heads expanded, in general the *République* has been dismantled and the *État français* erected in its place. One of the most backward countries in Europe when it comes to social legislation — before 1936 there were no paid vacations, no family supplements, before 1930 no social insurance — France, since losing the war, has taken a leap forward in the area of social policy. Pétain is manufacturing laws and — paying, paying, paying. I'm impatiently awaiting the financial report of the Banque de France to discover how many billions of francs the Banque de France has loaned to the government. There's still no inflation, but devaluation is evident.

Everyone is looking to the east. *Ex oriente lux*. After June 22, everything was put on the back burner and all attention turned to the east. Russia has been holding out and now is involved in a great counteroffensive — a successful one, at that. Today they took Kerch and Feodosia in Crimea. What will come of it is hard to predict. The Germans explain their failures by the need to switch from the offense to the defense and the difficulties that entails. Either Germany will go bust this year and the war will then enter its final phase or it won't go bust and the story will continue for another two years. If Russia beats Germany a new tragedy will begin—Bolshevism in Poland, Soviet occupation, and, who knows, perhaps Bolshevism in Europe. I know nothing, finally. It's said that victory for Russia is not in England's interest. Perhaps. Everything would be simple except for the eternal question mark: the Soviets. Tamerlane beats Attila—that's bad; Attila beats Tamerlane—that's also bad. In the end, the Poles always take a hiding. That's what happens when you live in a passageway. What were our respected ancestors thinking? Better not to say.

1942

January 1, 1942

Will the war end this year? Either the Russians beat the Germans before spring and that will be the end, or not—and therefore another two years.

January 2, 1942

We have been invited to the Chopins' for dinner the day after tomorrow. She has now recovered from the birth of their fifth child and they sent us a letter of invitation. Not to arrive empty-handed, I decided to buy their boys a book, something Polish in French.

After lunch I got on my bike and rode over to boulevard Saint-Michel to rummage in the bookstores. I was looking for *In Desert and Wilderness*, but I couldn't find it anywhere.[1] In general it's now impossible to find translations from the Polish in French bookstores, because the Germans have informed the booksellers that it's their responsibility to remove from sale any books that undermine the propaganda on collaboration, friendship, and so on. As a consequence, the booksellers, in a surge of eager servility, have removed everything having anything to do with Poland. I was already completely resigned to this and reflexively stopped in front of the big German bookstore to see what was new. I stood in front of the display of French books.—Imagine that: right in the middle was quite a nice edition of the book *Contes et légendes polonaises*, with illustrations by Jan Koźmiński.[2] I therefore went in and bought the Polish legends, including the story of Wanda, who rejected the German knight—in the German bookstore, because it's useless to look for help from our French friends.[3] *Ils sont plus Boches que Pétain*,[4] as the Gaullists say sarcastically.

I continued my rounds of the bookstores, asking each time for Sienkiewicz (indeed if not Sienkiewicz, I really don't know what else from our literature to give a foreigner) and taking the occasion to see what was on hand, but there was nothing anywhere. It was only in a small bookshop that a withered old man led me conspiratorially to the stockroom behind the shop and pulled out—

Sienkiewicz's *Teutonic Knights—Les Chevaliers teutoniques.*[5] I laughed, he winked and whispered: "*Vous savez, ça c'est très bon, c'est anti-Boche . . . oh là là, prenez ça.*"[6] I wanted to hug him, the de Gaulle of the bookshops, he had salvaged the honor of all the passionate booksellers. I chatted with him quietly, bought *The Teutonic Knights* and after a brief comment on the situation on the Eastern Front ("*c'est dur pour eux . . .*"[7]) I went out. The old man won my heart.

On the walls of a townhouse "*Socrate*"—a street caricaturist—has hung out his drawings. Some are very good. Formerly, in 1939 he had "exhibited" on boulevard des Batignolles and when we went for lunch on rue Lamandé we often stopped by to see him. That's how we came to know his wife, who was busy peddling his work. I hadn't seen them for many months; today I noticed them and stopped, happy to see this piece of old Paris surviving and still holding on. Madame Socrate recognized me and we instantly fell to chatting. She began to complain to me that her husband was too timid to sell anything. He didn't want to exhibit in normal shows because he lacked the courage and cunning to insinuate himself into the society of painters. Their intrigues, which are horrible in relation to people with talent, had forced them to earn their bread on the street. Socrate was wandering around at a distance. She pointed him out to me: "You can see, he's so timid he won't even come any closer." A tiny, dark-haired figure in a miserable short coat with a burnt-out pipe in his teeth. I said good-bye to her and at the end she made me a tempting proposal: "If you ever want your caricature drawn, he'll do it for you—not expensive—five hundred francs."

January 4, 1942

Dinner with Robert's family. A small house in Fontenay-sous-Bois, four sons and one daughter. He invited his friend with four daughters and one son. The small house was bursting but it was nice. The dinner was splendid, quite as before the war.

January 7, 1942

One of "my" workers was caught back in November with a suitcase containing four kilos of ham and two kilos of pork fat that he was bringing back to Paris. A summons—judicial hearing tomorrow in Senlis, where he has to show up. Naturally, he came looking for advice. I'll go with him tomorrow for the hearing because he doesn't know a word of French. I'll find him a legal interpreter and a court-appointed lawyer and I may succeed in getting the fellow out of this fix, which nowadays sounds like two months in prison. So-called progress, culture, civilization—in a word, the New Europe. When I occasionally flip through the dictionary, the sight of so many, many words evokes memories of my childhood. And the word "humanity" or *l'humanité* can send you into stitches, can cause you to laugh yourself to death.

January 8, 1942

I returned home and am still under the strong impression of the day in Senlis. It's as though I've been floating all day long in a small boat on a great, quiet pond, paddling nonchalantly and sending my thoughts skimming across the smooth surface of the water. The thoughts skipped along, my boat drifted along, and time passed by.

The entire day, all of its events were enveloped in *calm,* in the regular monotony and *self-contained* existence of a small French town.

I left the house early in the morning. Half asleep I descended into the metro, quite automatically changed trains at République, and got out, still drowsy, at Gare du Nord. The accused was waiting for me. We bought tickets and boarded a still-empty train. It was dark all around and the station sounds all reached the compartment one by one, like sparks. In such darkness sound is light and the least noise is as brutal and individual as a single ray.

Soon people began to board, find places, and take their seats. Across from us a couple sat down and began completing in the train the morning caresses they had started in bed. He inserted his hand under the lapel of her coat and lustily grabbed her breast, which did not prevent him from dropping off and bumping his nose on his own tie. She removed his hat, stroked his hair, and rubbed her cheek against his ear, kissing him every thirty seconds and whispering tender nothings. He murmured a vague "ehe—hm—aha," grabbed her breast more firmly, then fell back again into the lethargy of his nap.

The train got going and of course everyone pulled out their watches to check the time. I didn't do this, because at best I would get Gare du Nord time. No two clocks in France tell the same time, they each do as they please. I have my time, Gare de Reuilly, and don't deviate, otherwise I would have to spend the day resetting the hands. For the French, however, this is *une petite occupation,* an occasion to exchange a few words with a stranger, and most important—rant against one *autorité* or another. Thus even the sleeping lover released the warm breast for a moment, roused himself, looked at his watch, clicked his tongue (*ça va pas . . .*) and so as not to tire himself again, put his hand on her plump thigh. At that she crossed one leg over the other, thereby pressing his palm with the sweet weight of her other thigh. In this tender and intimate pose they began to doze. Me too. After riding for three-quarters of an hour we got off at Chantilly and changed to a local line to Senlis. By now it was already day. The train slowly started to move. Twenty minutes later we got off at the tiny station at Senlis. A small and quiet station house surrounded by large trees, the sky colored shiny ash gray like an artificial pearl, the cathedral spire outlined above the crowns of the bare trees among a swirl of black crows.

After the train departed with a grating and banging like pots and pans, we set off toward the town submerged in such silence that you could almost hear the fog descending and coating everything in a sticky membrane. From time to time only the shrill sound of the crows reached us from the direction of the spire, sharp at the beginning and echoing into the distance, vanishing, like a dot from which a line is drawn that grows ever thinner.

We enter the town along a street bordered by several houses that have been destroyed by bombs. People wander around the streets, stopping to chat a bit, and move on. We enter the town hall, I look for the concierge, and ask where to find the court.

The concierge takes me past the gate, shows me the street, and tells me the court is next to the cathedral. The town is modest in size and old, the streets are narrow and twisting, and, as in most cases in France, one encounters almost exclusively old men and old women. We take the winding street toward the cathedral. Peace and quiet everywhere and the general mood is interrupted by individual scenes, as distinct as scenes in a theatrical performance.

Scene one: Meeting of two old women and dialogue:

"*Bonjour Madame Duval, ça va?*"

"*Bonjour Madame Lepont, merci, ça va, et vous-même?*"

"*Oui, merci, ça va tout doucement. Ah! Quel vilain temps . . .*"

"*Oui. Il fait froid aujourd'hui . . . le brouillard . . .*"

"*Et votre monsieur le mari se porte mieux?*"

"*Oui, le pied est toujours enflé un peu, mais comment voulez-vous . . . Avec un temps pareil . . .*"[8]

Between nine and ten the entire town repeats the same lines, when meeting on the sidewalks, from window to window, in the shops. Along the street we encounter a large, two-wheeled cart, into which two old workmen empty the trash containers left in front of each house. One stands on the cart and stamps down the trash, the other hands the containers up to him and then returns the empty ones to their places. The sleepy horse moves and stops on his own before each building. At this moment on all the streets in all the cities and towns of France the same thing is being repeated, except in the bigger cities it's done by large, beetle-shaped vehicles.

Scene two: An old woman dressed in black appeared from around the corner, stopped near the cart, and said:

"*Bonjour, Monsieur Paul, ça va?*"

"—*Merci Madame,*" answered the trashman, "*et vous-même?*"

"*Oui, ça se tasse. Quel travail quand même avec ces boîtes . . .*? But if this continues people won't have anything to throw away . . ."

"*Mais oui,*" and here the same endless conversation about shortages of food and provisions. The trashman on the curb leaned on the wheel of the cart, the one on top sat down, and they all chatted away.

We reach the square in front of the cathedral. A lovely old Gothic cathedral—well-known and much visited. Like French Gothic in general, this cathedral, despite its solemnity, age, and mass, has a certain lightness, a vitality, that merges with the ensemble of the town—one object among many others, without fuss. It is not especially revered, no one insists that it is *weltberühmt*,[10] no one cuts it to pieces, to examine it stone by stone; one can chat with it as familiarly as one can chat with the trashman we encountered just now.

In France there are so many cathedrals, so many monuments, so much old furniture, and so many old houses, among which life carries on, that even the historical monuments are a most ordinary thing. They enter the program of daily life. Since they belong to everyone, it's easier to consider them "my favorite" and detect in them the charm that no one *orders* you to find; easier to enter into close contact with them. And no one burns with sacred indignation if I care to assert, for example, that Notre-Dame is medieval kitsch and that the gargoyles are nothing compared to Picasso's green horses.

The court is located in a Gothic building next to the cathedral. A sprawling edifice with thick walls, vaults, wide staircases, and long, narrow windows. It's like an enormous stone block out of which a house has been carved, the halls and rooms excavated with a great chisel.

Having extracted the necessary information from the concierge we went to see the court secretary. He sat among a great fortification of books, files, folders—surrounded on all sides by a thick wall of great folios arranged on shelves. Should you want, for example, to learn about the court cases involving your relatives in the year 1680 you could probably find many relevant documents here. The centuries live on here, dozing on the shelves to be awakened from time to time by events, which, however, have not destroyed them. Who would have destroyed anything about them? In the north, a bit, but otherwise practically no one and practically nothing. Mostly the centuries have inflicted the damage on themselves in the paroxysms of the great revolution, following ten centuries of equilibrium, after ten centuries of practically uninterrupted life, continuous as a thread wound around a spool. They laid waste *pour changer les idées,* they could afford such a whim.

What is our life? Short pieces of thread that cannot be tied together are wound around a piece of cardboard. Where should I look for the birth records of my grandfather? Where to find the traces of my great-grandmother? To what can I attach the thought receding back in time? To nothing—to the stories, almost legends of the country that rented itself a transit room in Europe and for ten centuries has attempted to live there with a sense of comfort and with the illusion that the room has a separate entrance, in the process exhausting all its energy in quarrels and battles with those passing through. How to contemplate decorating this room with lovely furniture, bibelots, display cabinets, when they are always dirtying the floor, breaking and chipping our objects? This is no life—this is the impermanence of a butterfly's existence and that's perhaps why our national character has so much in common with this insect. How could we possibly be ants? . . .

I showed the clerk the court summons, explained what it was about, and asked for the services of a court interpreter, because the accused does not speak French.

"*Mais parfaitement, Monsieur;* there are several cases today concerning other Polish people for whom an interpreter has been summoned, so I will merely note on this gentleman's file that he also needs an interpreter at his trial."

He pulled up the *dossier S.,* entered the note, and put it aside. Since he was so polite, I proceeded to inquire about the possibility of obtaining a court-appointed lawyer, since my accused was unemployed and although he didn't have any money, he wanted to exercise his right to legal representation. "But of course." He immediately took the summons and the certificate of unemployment and went to see the president of the court. (*Monsieur le Président.*) Soon he returned with the name of the lawyer assigned by the president. The lawyer is called Monsieur B. and lives at such and such a place. So off we go.

Again narrow streets and the windows of low houses. As we pass by, I glance inside: rooms submerged in dim light, crammed with old, inherited furniture, carpets, drapes, clocks on the mantelpieces—an atmosphere of permanence, inheritance, and prosperity. There's a feeling of stability, it's obvious these people are well established and live by stringing their even, round, and smooth days on the thread of life . . . Calm above all!

We open the iron gate, cross the garden, and knock on the lawyer's door. He opened it himself. Still young, plump, round, and pleasant, like a powder puff. The kind about whom one can say right off: they brought him into the world, fed him, gave him an education, gave him money, married him off, and settled him down. And this suits him. He is courteous, leads us into his office, we take a seat, and I tell him what it's about. I recount the entire history of our factory, the life of our former workers after the armistice. I paint in dark colors our fate in France, which the Germans do not want to let us leave, and where finding work is practically impossible (I exaggerate slightly) if one isn't French. My companion (the accused), for example, lives with three others in a hotel. The one who works for the Germans and earns good money helps the others, they have a common kitty, another one does the cooking, etc., etc. Every five words I say: "*mon cher Maître*," I form pretty sentences sprinkled with sophisticated expressions; I manage to interest him in us and in our case. As a result he declares that he doubts his defense will succeed to any significant degree in avoiding the unpleasant consequences of the offense, because as of November 15, 1941, sentences for offenses involving food can no longer be suspended. The prosecutor, moreover, is very severe and formalistic—but he will try to *faire tout ce qui est humainement possible,* especially since he sees that he is dealing with people *qui ne sont pas, enfin, quelqu'un.*[11] He's hooked! I smiled and tossed out a few sententious phrases about human hypocrisy:

"All the same I'm sure that these same judges, this same prosecutor, who will sentence this man and hundreds of others for carrying ham and pork fat in their suitcases, will themselves have eaten a good meal, half consisting of products bought on the black market . . ."

The lawyer chuckled: "Certainly not the prosecutor; I know him; he's a man who would be capable of starving to death were there such a statute. He absolutely will touch nothing that's illegal."

"Ahah, just like Cato the Elder—*caeterum censeo Carthaginam delendam esse*—but what was good for Carthage, does not necessarily apply to the black market," I say ironically.[12]

It seems there's nowhere one can sell one's own intelligence and higher education at a better price and for greater effect than in France. In this country, where the single general standard is the certificate of completion of elementary school and one or another vocational course (only eight thousand high school diplomas in France in 1938—thirty-six thousand in the same year in Poland), anything that rises above this average is considered exceptional, attracts attention, arouses something close to respect.

At my Latin citation, pronounced moreover with an impeccable French accent, the lawyer regarded me differently. And I kept on: "Nothing has changed, it's always the same hypocrisy, as shocking as I always find the death of Lucien de Rubempré . . ."[13]

I had charmed him. Although he was hurrying to lunch, he told me he had studied in Paris (and you, where?), that his father was the town notary, and that he was going to his parents' for lunch, that it was his own house—we chatted about this and that. He presented me with the crux of his strategy of defense:

"I will stress that your companion has found himself in France not of his own free will, that he has worked in defense of the same interests as all of us, that circumstances have destined him to spend time far from his homeland, that he does not know the language, has no one who might help him, that he has been obliged to seek provisions in this manner, having no acquaintances or 'trusted' suppliers in his neighborhood, etc., etc. In the end he is one of many victims of our government" (in France the government is always blamed for everything—the scapegoat on which to freely unload everything), "the government that sent him to work when he was needed, and now has left him practically without means of existence and without the possibility of returning to his family."

"Great." I thanked him warmly—and said good-bye until the hearing. My S. was reassured—I had handled everything for him like the best nanny. We went to find a restaurant. A woman gave us an address *où vous déjeunerez pas cher et convenablement.*[14]

A large, bright dining room—empty, because it wasn't yet noon. The atmosphere of a French *auberge*—snug, well-heeled, in good taste. Eating here is clearly treated as a ritual. In the center a large iron stove is crackling cheerfully, against the wall there's a piano. I sat down and began to stroke the keys. The *patronne* appeared from the kitchen and said in the voice of a good-natured auntie: "*Ne vous gênez pas, Monsieur, jouez, jouez . . .*"[15] At noon the guests began to arrive. It was obvious that these were people who came here every day, perhaps for years—feeling at home. Pensioners and retirees living out their days in the quiet provinces far from the Paris cauldron. The waitress hands each one a menu. Everyone reads attentively—*Mademoiselle* is summoned here and there for quick consultations. After it has been determined who will eat what, a moment of quiet falls. At almost every table someone takes out medication and swallows it before eating. An older gentleman, tidily and elegantly dressed, fussily extracts a single pill from a bottle, drops it into a glass, adds some water, mixes it—then observes for a long time under the light to see if it has completely dissolved. With the concentration of a priest drinking the wine at the altar, he swallows the contents. An older woman lavishly dressed and a bit *à la 1900* piously counts her drops of medicine, moving her lips silently, as though saying the rosary. Another oldster pours syrup into a spoon. His hand shakes and the neck of the bottle tapping the metal makes a soft noise.

I watch, listen, observe, on the verge of drifting off to sleep. The quiet, the calm, the relaxation—one has to move a leg or an arm in order to feel oneself. I awoke only when the waitress placed the wine, bread, and beet salad in front of us. We eat lunch—alas nothing like the good old days. Here, three years ago, for twenty francs I could have eaten so many good things—now it's salad, a small piece of meat, an orange, a quarter liter of wine, and a piece of bread for eighteen francs. Using valuable ration cards, moreover. Over coffee with cognac (an extra four fr.) I looked through a thick book containing a list of cities in the *département* of the Oise with information about them. I look for Senlis, and discover: two pharmacies, one old-age home (*maison de retraite*), a poorhouse, three lawyers, three doctors, two notaries, etc., etc. Finally, a list of the town's societies and associations. I wiped my glasses: this small townlet had thirty of them: the association of archers, crossbow shooters (not to be confused: a bow is one thing, a crossbow another), hunters, anglers, chess players, friends of belote, army veterans, a few charitable societies under the direction of ladies with the names "Madame de" and "Madame de la" (*noblesse oblige*); hard to remember them all. I admit, I was impressed. One can have doubts about the vitality of these societies and their purpose, but one is struck by their number and above all their apolitical character. No—it's just that some people enjoy archery, others the crossbow, still others playing belote, and they are all free. They form associations because they have the time, they do it for pleasure, and again, what fills me with envy: *They can afford to.* Enough to live in comfort . . . the dream of 98 percent of Poles, who inhabit their own country like nomads, searching for a bit bigger piece of bread, with no sense of stability, their heads full of ideas, ideals, schemes, God knows what, holding grudges against others, against the entire world; educated people, intellectuals without affiliation, snobs, artists with talent and without—all with eternally empty pockets, doomed moreover to suffer eternally for the fatherland. If one sometimes thinks this way, it is not from disdain for Poland—but simply from rage at our fate, at our bad luck, from envy, when one sees others often less deserving. They do nothing, sacrifice nothing, do not suffer, and fate smiles upon them. What can you do about it! . . . It's no surprise if as a result we are left with only one escape and consolation—national mysticism. The heart, the head, the emotions, oceans of unappreciated heroism—as against the sack of gold. An unequal struggle, in which we are always defeated, always convinced of our superiority. But one must console oneself in order not to take the Lord's name in vain.

   We leave the restaurant and slowly walk to the courthouse. The courtyard is already agitated; people are standing around and talking, entering the building in small groups. We mount the broad stairs to the courtroom. On the wall midway up the stairs hangs a large painting: Marie Antoinette on the tumbril headed for the guillotine. The painting is executed in the official style—an enlargement of a photograph. It nevertheless makes an impression—especially here, in the dim Gothic light so reminiscent of the Conciergerie.[16] The crowd pushing its way up the stairs is the same as the one in the painting; it exudes the same atmosphere of ignorance, envy, cruelty restrained by shameless cowardice—in a word all the attributes of the masses. It's as though invisible threads connected the painting and the scene it depicts with present reality. In France to this day something intangible has survived from that era. I stopped. Until someone tapped me on the shoulder: "*Dis donc, mon vieux, serre un peu à droite, on peut pas passer.*"[17] I thought to myself:—Yup, that's it, these are exactly the types who get familiar. He looked at me, laughed, and, nodding in the direction of the painting, tossed out: "*Pauvre fille.*"[18]

It's cold in the courtroom—the public is all the same: local farmers, basically FOLKS—ordinary French folk, always including a bit of each of the social strata, which taken together form a single stratum. A touch of the bourgeois, a touch of urban or suburban riffraff, a touch of the peasant, here and there something "better," all blended into a whole—everything mixed up and stirred around. A social hodgepodge.

The two old guys sitting next to me stink of wine and cheap tobacco. They have come to the courthouse to amuse themselves and to listen. They discuss expertly—with the full knowledge of the law innate in every Frenchman. The court has not yet appeared, so everyone is chatting, smoking—of course not removing their hats. The atmosphere of a rowdy family gathering. A man pushes his way through the crowd carrying a legless man on his back. A torso and arms—in the lapel of his jacket the discolored ribbons of his military decorations and the rosette of the Legion of Honor. His acquaintances greet him noisily and take their seats in front of me. My neighbors pat him on the shoulder.

"*Bonjour, mon vieux*, how did you get here?"

"In any case not on foot" (*à pied*), he answers with a wheezing laugh, pleased with his joke. The others laugh, too.

Suddenly the usher entered and announced: "*Le Tribunal!*" Immediately silence fell, cigarettes were extinguished, and hats removed. The president and two judges in robes and caps took their seats at the table, the prosecutor on one side, the clerk on the other; the lawyers on the benches next to the accused. The cases began to tumble out one after the other, quickly, an assembly line.

Two young women whose appearance only Balzac would be able to describe. Human swill—redheads, slovenly, horrid. Accused of stealing clothing from a villa requisitioned by the Germans. A rich criminal past, recited playfully and spitefully by the president. Something along the lines of: "Well, well—we've met before, *mes enfants*; in 1937 we had petty theft, then vagrancy, then sentenced again . . ." The girls laugh cynically.

"Well, what about this time? In this villa only the ground floor was requisitioned by the Germans, but *mademoiselle* took the clothing from a cabinet" (*placard*) "in the kitchen on the first floor?"

The girl was silent—her lawyer broke in:

"Correct, they slept with the Germans on the ground floor, but at night *elle est montée dans la cuisine pour, pour . . ."*[19]

The president: *"Oui, elle est montée au premier étage pour se remonter après les émotions de rez-de-chausée . . ."*—adding "*spirituellement*" (laughter).[20]

Lawyer (laughing): "*C'est ça*, she was a bit exhausted and wanted to drink some water, *vous comprenez . . ."*

The president: *"Et au lieu de prendre de l'eau fraîche, elle a pris un manteau, deux robes, des draps et quelques cuillers d'argent comme souvenir . . ."* (laughter).[21] The lawyer doesn't even bother with a defense; sentence: two years in jail. Case of the second woman; her lawyer is older, fat and bald, delivers a speech for the defense that is grandiloquent and elevated. There is mention of Saint Mary Magdalene, of the priestesses of Astarte. The president listens with interest; it obviously amuses and intrigues him. The lawyer indulges in further grandiloquence, in citations from Holy Scripture, doesn't hold back. Here grandiloquence is accepted, like any other way of making your case. Because in France it's not important WHAT is said but infinitely important HOW it's said. That's why you can say whatever you want here—if only form is respected. The admiration and recognition of form are so deep and ingrained that the content and even feelings at odds with the content capitulate before them. If you've got the gift of the gab, you're allowed to say anything.

The president, sufficiently amused, interrupted the lawyer: "As far as I know the story, Mary Magdalene was in fact a lady of easy virtue" (*une femme galante*) "but did not steal—you go too far, *mon cher maître.*" He waved his hand, read out the verdict: "A year and a half behind bars."

The cases tumble out, one after another, fast and furious. Petty theft, pilfering, crimes connected with the black market, barely a single case of battery. I'm struck by this, because in Poland the majority of such petty cases are brawls that end in court. I don't know which is better. A railroad warehouse guard appears before the court, the father of four children, no criminal record, eighteen years of impeccable service on the railroad. He was caught by gendarmes somewhere in the countryside when transporting a dozen leather straps in his suitcase. He was careless enough to admit in the interrogation that he took the straps from the warehouse he was supposed to be guarding. The lawyer delivers a powerful speech: The court knows it is not possible today to buy anything in the countryside without offering something in exchange. This man has four children and everyone knows that ration cards do not go far enough. Wanting to buy some food, he took a few small leather straps from the warehouse, went to the village, and with the help of this "premium" tried to obtain something from the farmers. Besides—here is the testimony of his superiors, who immediately undertook an inventory of the warehouse and affirm here, on this paper, that nothing is missing in the warehouse and the railroad is not bringing charges. This man is not a thief! Eighteen years of spotless service on the railroad, no criminal record, four children! . . .

Whispers among the judges. Sentence: a month in jail. Commotion spreads in the courtroom, discontent and indignation burst out suddenly like a flame. The crowd is agitated. What's this? The railroad confirms that nothing was stolen, and he's given a month in jail; which means he automatically loses his job, because he will be dismissed for having a criminal record. The president quiets the audience but from all corners cries are heard: "*Ah, non, quand même, c'est honteux—Hou! Hou!—merde—une bande de salauds . . .*"[22] There's something rousing in this loud, daring, and frank defense of the poor wronged fellow and the forthright criticism of the court. It made you want to jump on the bench and cry, "*Aux armes, citoyens*," set fire to the court, and hang the judges. At this moment I begin to understand the crowd full of hatred that accompanied *la charette* of Marie Antoinette. The president thumps the wooden ink blotter on the table and cries: "*Silence*," but the crowd is still restless. And I'm reminded of the monument to Camille Desmoulins in the Palais-Royal and the scream in my breast almost explodes, almost chokes me.[23]

The room finally quieted down. The legless man is called before the court. Now no one carries him. With the help of his arms he slides nimbly from the bench and with the motion of a spider with its limbs torn off rolls himself between the legs of people who jumped out of his way. The president even leaned over the table to get a look at him. I didn't hear what it was about. In any case, the human torso boldly and impudently parried the blows, cloaked in the war, the Legion of Honor, and his monstrous invalidism. These are arguments before which everyone in France bows their heads. Not surprising—sacrifice here is not a popular sport. He was given a suspended sentence. He rolls toward the exit whistling softly and there awaiting him is his bearer. As the bearer bends over, he grabs him by the neck, and, swinging himself like a monkey, lands on the man's shoulders.

The case of a Polish woman: erasing the expiration date on her identity card (*carte d'identité*) and inserting a different one. Three months in jail. The interpreter is a young émigré, dumb as a post polished in France. Peroxided hair, hat with a feather, fur coat, not a bad French accent (probably already born here), but only broken Polish: "How are you called, how many years you have, where was you born, and confess you scroobled something in your papers? No good, no good—dockument's a hoowly thing . . . for scratching—the clink . . ." A fine court interpreter, indeed. But the president smiles at her, says: *Madame, ayez la gentillesse* . . . And Kaśka feels important—she was swored to the coorte.

My client's case comes only toward the end. Barely had they read him the charges and barely had the interpreter bombarded him with something in Polish, barely had our Maître B. opened his mouth, than the president interrupted him: "*Maître*—you know that at this moment the minimum penalty for such infractions is a fine of twelve hundred francs" and he pronounces the verdict: "a twelve-hundred-franc fine." Great—we are pleased, better could not have been hoped for. Now it's up to me by means of various petitions, proofs of unemployment, to delay the deadline or annul the verdict altogether. I already know the French administration well enough to know how to arrange for an item to drift for months in a sea of papers and drown finally in the abyss of oblivion. Maybe by then something will have changed . . . We leave the court—it's already after five. The last train has left for Chantilly at ten after. We therefore decide to go by foot. From Senlis to Chantilly it's ten kilometers. We set out. The day is still gray, the clock stands still. Might as well be nine in the morning as one or six in the afternoon. On a day like this you lose all sense of time. We pass fields, houses, occasionally a denser concentration of houses, which is to say, a local village (*commune*). Everything is colorless and flat. The buildings, the forest, the hills are like cutouts of gray paper. Somewhere far ahead of us old women emerge from the forest carrying firewood on their backs. They walk slowly, bent over—like two-legged tortoises. Occasionally we step off the road to avoid a car, most often German.

After an hour and a half march we reach Chantilly. We pass the castle, set beside a pond in a large garden; a charming composition. The white forms of sculptures shine through the trees, here and there the black maws of artificial grottos loom, and the delicate bridges created for the frivolous sighs of the ladies of the Baroque spread their arches. A view whose precise and accurate description can be found in George Sand: "*. . . des paysages frais et calmes, des prairies d'un vert tendre, des ruisseaux mélancholiques, des massifs d'aulnes et de frênes, toute une nature suave et pastorale*" (from *Valentine*).[24]

"*Toute une nature suave et pastorale*," the phrase that embraces everything and best conveys the character of what the French call "nature," but which for the Poles is always a bit like a drawing room under the open sky. Descriptions of nature in French always sound to me like descriptions of stage sets. For that's what indeed they are, and especially in the Île-de-France.

We enter Chantilly, passing the famous racecourse. Chantilly lived off this once upon a time—now it lives off the Germans and capital. Some of the great hotels are shuttered, some have been requisitioned by the Kreiskommando[25] and other occupation institutions. The streets are pervaded by the melancholy of a January evening.

We rush to the station because a train had just pulled in. But the good-willed station agent assured us it was only for workers returning from construction of the airports. He winked: "The English will have somewhere to land."

So we went to the nearest bistro to get a bite, because after a light lunch and the quick march we were hungry. The bistro buzzes with movement and talk, it's time for aperitifs. We ordered bread and pâté and a glass of wine. I put my wine on the counter and, after a bite of bread, meandered from corner to corner looking at the lithographs on the walls. It was as though someone had suddenly poured cold water over my head. Pasted on the glass cabinet, at the far end of the counter, was a German saying. I approached and read: "*Sei was du willst, aber vor allem weiss was du sein willst*"—Albert Schlageter.[26] The devil take them. A revolver shot during a concert would be easier to bear than such a maxim by a hero of Hitlerism in a provincial French bistro. How foreign, dreary, rigid, repellant it is. There's something in that so-called *Deutsche Kultur* that won't go down. The rude insistence with which it's pushed on you. No—I want nothing from them—I want to be what it pleases me to be and not necessarily *planmässig*,[27] know what I want to be. I want to live, to enjoy living . . . like today.

We pay up and go to the station. Dusk is falling, a light frost is settling in. The train rolls up. I sit in the corner and doze off, waking at Gare du Nord. We walk to another bistro for a grog with saccharine. The *patronne* sits at the cashier with a cat on her lap and orders the garçons here and there, two *filles* withdrawn from circulation on the center streets are chatting, coughing hoarsely.

I put up my collar and go out. Under foot the metro rumbles.

January 9, 1942

This morning there was great excitement. The German sentries at the Paris checkpoints have disappeared. People explain this in various ways and are pleased that the Germans are slowly leaving Paris. Pétain's government, himself included, is expected to relocate from Vichy to Paris. Rumors. In any case ordinary Parisians are pleased and say, *Ils foutent le camp, nous serons libres.*[28] And everyone is in a good mood. It doesn't take much. But the less optimistic insist that these are petty savings against the great expenditures of springtime. Pétain's New Year's speech has not been published in the newspapers in the occupied zone, which arouses everyone's curiosity. "What did the Marshal say? Likely something unacceptable to the Germans"—and naturally a slew of conjectures are circulating on this subject.[29] Overall it looks like a good stage production. The supposed ban on publication of the speech on this side is calculated to enhance the old fogy's "patriotic" authority and it will be read here with almost the same fondness as leaflets from London.

Tadzio is back again. He travels between Warsaw and Paris like "a minister of superfluous trade," as he himself put it. This time, Janeczka, his wife, has sent us as a present a piece of pork fat and some sausage. In fact, ever since November we have been continuously supplied with the basic foodstuffs that are so difficult to purchase here—via Poland. A paradox. When I mentioned this to a Frenchman, his eyes grew round in disbelief: "How can it be easier to get food to eat in Poland than here?" he asked. "Because we're not collaborating," I answered.

January 13, 1942

Today a Frenchwoman of my acquaintance gave me Pétain's New Year's speech, "smuggled" in from the unoccupied zone. Vichy has certainly organized this "contraband" operation. The speech is a masterpiece of slithery language, saying so much while seeming to say nothing, or saying nothing while seeming to have said great and profound things. The speech contains a bit of this and that. Pétain spoke only about France—true, a France that is defeated, whose government is half-free, but a France that is still alive, still great and creative in the spiritual sense. "France cannot remain indifferent to current events. *Puissance européenne, la France connaît ses devoirs envers l'Europe. Puissance civilisatrice, elle a conservé dans le monde, malgré sa défaite, une position spirituelle privilégiée.*"[30] A broken record.

"France's unusual situation cannot escape Germany's attention—*elle lui*" (Germany) "*suggérera, nous l'espérons, une atténuation du status qu'elle nous a imposé après sa victoire. Le rapprochement sincère des deux nations, souhaité par les Gouvernements et par les peuples en découlera. Notre dignité s'en trouvera restaurée; notre économie soulagée.*"[31] Then, in order to be able if necessary to retreat and temper—let's be fair—the single collaborationist passage, he throws in a few more forceful words: "*Mais la conduite d'une politique française, inspirée des seuls intérêts français, exige le resserrement de l'unité française. Or, l'unité des esprits est en péril.*"[32] He complains of misunderstanding between the two zones—free and occupied—and regrets that France has succumbed to the unfortunate illusion of a false peace. He brands as deserters anyone, whether in the press or on radio, whether in London or in Paris, who does anything to damage this unity. The new constitution will soon be ready, but it can be dated only from Paris and can go into effect only the day after the territory has been liberated. He addresses himself to everyone, asking for work, trust, and unity. "*Dans l'exil partiel auquel je suis astreint, dans la demi-liberté qui m'est laissée, j'essaie de faire tout mon devoir.*"[33]

Everyone is rather moved, the general opinion holds that the old man is playing for time and hides behind a mask. But too many facts contradict this idea. As a result Vichy is a Sphinx—without secrets.

January 16, 1942

Today K. gave me a hundred dollars to sell, which he was unable to sell because they are from an old series, the so-called large ones. I decided to see whether Mr. Joseph would buy them and early in the evening descended into the tangle of streets around rue des Francs-Bourgeois. Cautiously, I entered the bistro and whispered to the *patronne*: "Monsieur Joseph . . ."

She examined me carefully for a bit and once my fantastical outfit of a Parisian *loustic*[34] had won her confidence, she leaned over and with her lips rather than her voice answered briefly and mournfully: "*Il est pincé.*"

I instantly understood and quickly went out. They'd put him away. *Il est pincé*, an excellent and picturesque "professional" expression in the *demi-argot* of the black market. Along the lines of an affectionate: "He was nipped; they nipped him"—like a blade of grass by a duck's beak.

I therefore dropped in on Mr. Zygmuś's antiques shop. It was already dark and I literally groped my way to the shop door. I entered quietly. Mr. Zygmuś was sitting at a table illuminated by a fantastic oil lamp, refitted in improvised fashion for electricity, and with an effort he put on his shoe. On the table was a large flask of hydrochloric acid. A small black kitten sat on the shelf over the table and played with the pendulum of an Empire-style clock, which looked as if it had stopped at the final hour of that bygone age and not run since. Mr. Zygmuś panted, the kitten nudged the pendulum with his paw, and it bumped with a soft sound against the gilt columns of the clock case.

"Good evening, Mr. Zygmuś! Are you trying to poison yourself with acid?"

"Ah, good evening, greetings . . . nothing better for corns than hydrochloric acid. Right now, myself—with this—here right now with acid—damn this shoe . . ." His tongue is thick, he draws out every "l" endlessly (the easiest letter to pronounce when you are plastered). I see that he's in his cups as usual, more even than usual.

"You're not exactly in good form today," I say.

"Look . . . I'm drunk as a sk——— . . . today they did me in . . . pfff . . . hey, you . . . ," and here he raises his finger, "me, I got me sloshed on September 17, 1901, and since then . . . y' know . . . damn this shoe . . . pfff . . ."

The kitten, taking advantage of the broad surface of Mr. Zygmuś's hunched back, jumped on the nape of his neck and began madly fooling around with the tassels of the scarf thrown over his shoulder.

"And shooo, blast it" — he feebly brushes him away. I took the cat and sat him on my knees inside my hat.

"Mr. Zygmuś . . . I would like to sell a rather large amount of dollars . . . could you do something . . . I'm offering them at 140, but they are 'large' ones . . ."

"Sheew me . . . damn . . . I'm drunk! Some magnate showed up, you see, a Polish magnate from the provinces, with a pig farm, then a drop of coognac, a sip of vino, liqueur — and clink, and there you've got it . . . and now I'm drinking Vichy!"

At the word "Vichy" he hiccupped loudly and it sounded like "Vi!" and then a long "shshshshshshy" emerging with the gas from the depths of his stomach, prolonged and hissing.

"Sheew me those doolllars." I pulled out two five-dollar bills. He spread them on the table, smoothed them with his fingers while balancing on the chair, and examined them carefully. His eyes seemed to swim in their sockets unattached to any nerves. The left eye was spinning around, turning somersaults and dancing; the right eye disappeared somewhere into the outer corner and got stuck motionless, lying in wait, as though wanting to jump out and attack the five-dollar bill.

"Why're you laughing? Good pictures . . . they'll get through. You got time, so wait a bit . . . a done deal." I gave him the whole packet.

"Mr. Zygmuś, maybe better tomorrow; today you're not altogether . . ."

"And how'd you know tomorrow'll bee any better . . . come on! damn, the magnate Pole with a pig farm from the provinces . . . a thousand francs — clink! and I'm plastered, but y' know . . . y' can trust me . . . pfff . . ."

He removed his hat, pulled out the inner band of leather, raised the lining, and began to stuff the hat with dollars, inserting them between the lining and the felt. During all this his eyes led such a wild dance that I involuntarily felt my head ache and I had to restrain myself from squinting in turn.

"Mr. Zygmuś . . . what are you up to with those eyes?"

"If you'd been plastered for forty years, no letup, everything would get unstuck in you, too. Orevuar."

He put on his hat, swept his white scarf around his neck, took his knob-handled cane, and left with an unsteady step. From the kitchen emerged his French "caretaker" and she began to entertain me with stories, since we'd already met before. We talked first about the war, then about food, and finally about Mr. Zygmuś. "The Poles from the Russian partition—*du côté de Varsovie*—are all like this," she says. "Whatever he earns, he gives away, he amuses himself, enjoys life . . . he's gone bankrupt perhaps twice already; could have made a great fortune, but try to get it into his head. I've put up with it now for thirty years . . ."

She offered me white wine and bread with cheese. She recalls the Great War, the Germans; the war caught her then on the Belgian-Luxembourg border. She speaks with surprising dignity, with the culture of a simple woman who has gone through a lot and seen a lot. It's a pleasure to talk with her about all the secrets of the antiquarian's trade. She tells me there's nothing in the store right now because they don't want to make any sales; they keep all the precious and valuable things at home—"for when the English and Americans return to Paris," she says with longing in her voice.

An hour and a half later Mr. Zygmuś returned. "I sold them at 135" (as I expected, he'd earned 500 francs). I was surprised, because no one had wanted to buy those "large" dollars, but he'd made out in an instant. He counted me out 13,500 francs. K. will be even more surprised, because he'd been offered at most 85. I said good-bye and descended once again into the dark well of the winding streets. I returned the favor K. had done me very well indeed.

January 17, 1942

Tadzio decided to leave sooner than planned and spend the rest of his vacation in Warsaw. He had run through all his money, bought a quantity of things—and after a week got bored with Paris. "Jędruś, if you only knew, this Paris is a morgue compared to Warsaw." First thing in the morning I went over to help him with packing. I then called the office to ask if I needed to appear, because I now didn't want to. But K. said that yesterday evening the youngest of our "sheep"—twenty-three-year-old Anatol—had been detained in the Préfecture and someone had to go get him out. The Préfecture is my specialty. Anatol was arrested because the date of birth on his *carte d'identité* had been altered.

I got on my bike and rode over to the Préfecture. I headed straight for the clerk in charge of extending the identity cards. A polite fatso—I've known him for ages, because for the past two years he's been helping me with "my" Poles. I ask him about Anatol. A silly business. While renewing the card, the fatso noticed that Anatol had altered his date of birth—substituting 1919 for 1918—

making himself a year younger. Unable to comprehend why Anatol had done it ("*il n'est pas une femme, et puis les femmes, quand elles font ça, elles ne se contentent pas d'une année . . .*"[35]), the fatso sent him home to get his passport, in order to check the birthdate in the passport, because Anatol dug in his heels and insisted he had altered nothing. Anatol returned to the Préfecture with his passport and there the fatso notes that in the passport the year 1918 was also scratched out and replaced by 1919. At this he was completely perplexed, but even so wanted to smooth things over and not make a case out of it. But the fool Anatol not only brazenly stuck to his guns but began outright to carry on. Then the fatso sent him under escort up to the fifth floor to the department of "removals" (*Éloignements*). This is the department that confiscates your papers, gives you a slip with a photo that is good for a month, but along the way you can end up behind bars if there are any irregularities—and, in a word, once you turn up there, all is lost: you are subject to constant supervision, obliged to keep coming back to get your papers stamped and the temporary slip extended, and other forms of police-administrative harassment.

I know one of the heads of this department, a Monsieur V., and after a long wait I managed to get hold of him. Asked about Anatol, he immediately remembered him. "*Ah, ce jeune garçon, il est de chez vous?*"[36] He's been under arrest since yesterday. V. cannot understand why he scrubbed out the date of birth from his identity card (and again: *il n'est pas une femme* . . . the same all over again. The French *esprit* is much overrated. In short, standardization) and he asks me what I think about all this. I also fail to understand, but I ask him to let the man go, insisting that all will somehow become clear. V. promised me he would release him this evening and even hinted that he would not make a case of it. They will correct his papers and hush the business up. I am reluctant to believe this, but I ride right over to Anatol's buddies to reassure them and try to find out something, because I was lost in speculation and unable to make sense of this business of tampering.

I find Staszek and he tells me what happened. He had advised Anatol to turn to me, but that fool replied, "I'm no child," and said he'd deal with it himself. "But why the devil did he change his date of birth and tamper with the documents?" Suddenly it occurred to me to ask if Anatol didn't by chance have a second ration card belonging to someone who had left for Poland. He had. The card of someone with a very similar name, born the same day and month as Anatol, but a year later. For the exchange of cards at the town hall they require proof of identity and Anatol altered both the *carte d'identité* and the ration card to make everything agree. My blood ran cold. For altering the *carte d'identité* he risks three months in jail; if the business with the ration cards comes to light, then it's a year in a concentration camp and they'll finish the fellow off.

Enough for today. I told Staszek that Anatol should come see me tomorrow. I returned home exhausted and drenched. Three hours of flying around on my bicycle up and down Paris, through streets covered in melting snow. I must get the fellow out of this one way or the other.

January 18, 1942

This morning Anatol came to see me at the hotel. V. kept his promise and he was released yesterday evening, told to appear at the Préfecture the next morning. Bad sign! Once they begin sniffing around, they'll sniff out something. Above all, I chewed out the snotnose for not having come to me straight off. Strange, how sometimes one suddenly feels the passage of time, that one is already different, that something deep inside has undergone a tectonic shift and the layers have taken a different form. With this twenty-three-year-old before me, I felt with surprise the weight of my twenty-nine years. Only yesterday I was twenty-three years old and so often it seems to me that I have not changed at all, that I am still well ensconced in the age of the "twenty somethings." Now I regarded Anatol as a "foolish child." At moments it even seemed to me that I myself, as a twenty-three-year-old pup, was sitting in that chair, minus the last five years of so-called experience, understanding of people, capacity for reflection and intuition — the entire baggage of Life. It's gone, flown by, the first half of my life reaching its end. Now I was sorry I had scolded him. If an older man bawls out his junior, it's probably simply to yell and get the yelling off his chest. I scolded him also out of helplessness, because the devil himself can't explain why he changed 918 to 919. Why? What for? And best not to mention the ration cards. The fellow has at last grasped what he was in for and is terrified.

I was most likely experiencing just what Vautrin experienced when Lucien de Rubempré was sent to prison.[37] What clever trick would get him out? As determined as old man Vautrin, I paced the room and pondered. I paced for about an hour and finally came up with a story, entirely plausible and innocent. I taught Anatol the entire tale until he had it by heart.

"In June 1940, I was working in a munitions factory in Brittany. The factory was due to be evacuated to England. We traveled to Brest. In Brest it turned out it was already too late, the last English ships had sailed. The Germans were now close by, Brest was being bombarded (so far the truth — the rest eyewash). In the general panic, amid rumors that the munitions factory workers would be treated as soldiers and imprisoned, I was seized by fear. Afraid that the lists with the names of the workers in the factory in Quimper had been left in the factory and would fall into the hands of the Germans, I decided to alter my civil status on my passport — surname, name, and date of birth. Wanting to see if this desperate idea could succeed, I began by scratching out the date of birth beginning first with the lower bulge of the figure eight in 1918. But seeing that the change was extremely noticeable, I left it alone. At the spot on the lower bulge of the eight where I had scratched, the paper was rough and the ink would certainly have 'bled,' and so—instead of rewriting the eight—I drew a thin line from the upper bulge down alongside the rough spot, turning the eight into a nine. The Germans enter Brest, the rumors turn out to have been totally false, normal life begins. Then, afraid, because the date of birth on my *carte d'identité* did not agree with my passport, which could cause many problems in dealing with the French administration and the French police, I recklessly and without a second thought repeated the correction in my *carte d'identité* so that the date of birth would be the same in both places."

Simple and clear, Cartesian, and just right for those blockheads on the fifth floor of the Préfecture. Anatol is delighted. I must admit, I am too. No lawyer could have lied—excuse me: *n'aurait pas corrigé la vérité*—any better.[38] Now everything depends on whether this explanation satisfies them, also on whether they pursue the case through administrative channels, because then things will get worse. I agree to meet him tomorrow at the Préfecture and this time I won't let him out of my sight.

January 19, 1942

A whole day down the tubes. I wanted to shoot V. and shoot down every policeman. On arriving at the Préfecture I go straight to see V. and explain everything. The story succeeds in convincing him, he shakes his head sympathetically over the foolishness of this *jeune garçon* but, but . . . But in order to resolve the case properly, Anatol will be sent in the company of one of the police inspectors (*inspecteur* means undercover agent) to the Polenreferat—the German section of the Gestapo that monitors all the Poles. Because it will be necessary to establish whether in changing his date of birth Anatol was not in fact trying to hide from the Germans. If the Polenreferat replies that Anatol is not wanted by them, then everything will be fine.

I was boiling inside. If they could have, the French would have licked those German behinds. What loyalty! What cooperation! But I didn't let any of this show and with a smile I say: "Ah, there at no. 72 avenue Foch, that's Captain Engelhaupt." V. looked at me with respect. He promised immediately to assign us an agent who would accompany Anatol to avenue Foch. We wait half an hour—nothing. An hour—nothing. Such moments make me feel a growing hatred for this whole beloved Europe and the urge to set out for some primitive country in which I will not have to keep *waiting and hanging around* administrative offices. Finally V. returns with all Anatol's papers, hands them to me, and says: "Right now I have no inspector at hand, why don't you go with him yourself. When you've settled the business, come back to me."

I was stunned. Above all fear. To barge in myself, for no good reason, except "to keep someone company," directly into the paws of the Gestapo, to run the risk of being questioned and perhaps finally never get out again? . . . Because with them you never know. I was terrified. I wanted to abandon Anatol, to ditch everything and have them leave me in peace. I didn't know how to convey to V. that I didn't want to go, because such a jerk might simply think I was in some kind of trouble with the Germans and might become suspicious. Anatol I couldn't abandon. At the very thought of visiting avenue Foch he began to tremble with fear, stammering that if I deserted him he didn't know what he would do. V. stood with the papers in his hand, I wrestled with my fear. In the end I took the papers and said I would go. Never in my life have I been so afraid. I did not let it show and Anatol picked up a bit of courage. We go to avenue Foch. A number of large houses, small palaces, and the apartments of wealthy people who have fled and not returned have been requisitioned by the Germans. At no. 72 avenue Foch there is *die Wache* at the entrance.[39] An SS-man is sitting there, whom I ask about Engelhaupt, the new director of the Polenreferat. He's not there—should be back about noon. The SS-man speaks no word of French; I speak with him in German. We wait. Noon passes, we kill time walking up and down the avenue. Finally the SS-man says we should come at three.

My fear had somewhat abated, we went to Saint-Paul for lunch, and after lunch back to the Préfecture. I had hoped V. might relinquish his project. But he ordered me to go and without fail get access to Engelhaupt. O God . . . The same SS-man is sitting at the entrance and tells me that Engelhaupt is not there, but his deputy, Lieutenant Redel, is. I explain what it's about; the SS-man telephones Redel. Redel answers that this doesn't concern him and we should—go to the Préfecture of police. I tell the SS-man for the second time that it was precisely the Préfecture that sent us here—it's about such and such and such and such—I tell him the whole story. He rings up Redel once again—who yet again doesn't want to see us, this time sending us to the devil. I'm delighted. Our spirits restored, we return to the Préfecture. I tell V. that Redel doesn't want to talk with us—that he should call him on the phone. But V., after practically a half hour searching for the phone number, which in the end he never found, instructed us to come the next day. "I will send an inspector with you, and he'll be obliged to receive him." I wanted to embrace and squeeze him slowly enough to hear the crack of each broken rib one at a time. Small, lean, easy to strangle. I'm totally beat.

At nine in the morning I meet Anatol at the Préfecture. After a short wait

V. gives us an agent and this time there are three of us off to avenue Foch. The agent is a typical French *fonctionnaire de police*. Intellectual retardation approaching the ideal. We arrive. At the entrance there is now a different SS-man. I explain to him what it's about, the agent shows his papers and smiles ingratiatingly at the German. He looks exactly like a black man from Central Africa gibbering in French with the corresponding gibbering gestures. I'm scared stiff (practically pissing in my pants), but at the sight of this agent I want to burst out laughing. If he grovels like this before a noncom, how will he behave toward an officer?

The SS-man phones, Redel sends us for a change to the Quai d'Orsay, Gestapo headquarters. I prefer avenue Foch. *Mon agent* is a complete dunce, but fortunately he is stubborn. The SS-man makes another call and Redel has clearly had enough, because he gives in. The SS-man hands the agent and Anatol passes to fill out. I want to do the same, but the SS-man waves his hand: "*Sie brauchen nicht . . . !*"[40] I feel—honored. We take the elevator to the fifth floor, enter an apartment made at present into an office, knock on the room labeled "Polenreferat." We are greeted by a young lieutenant who seems rather likable, but of course very *stramm und wichtig.*[41] He does not speak French. I therefore get to the point and explain what it's about. Redel smiles. After my account he went to a drawer containing file cards, searched for Anatol's name, and read what he found.

"Tell this person" (nods toward the agent) "that Anatol T. is known to us—we are not looking for him. In any case it's good that the Préfecture checks with us *und ich danke der Präfektur dafür . . .*"[42]

I repeated the first half to the agent, omitting the appreciation for the Préfecture's conduct. The police would begin right away dispatching every Pole to the Germans. The agent bowed—*oui, oui, parce que . . . vous comprenez*[43]—and begins babbling obsequiously, that it's only to clarify, that they don't know . . .

Redel listens with a smile, waves his hand: *Schon gut*[44]—turns to me and indicating the worried-looking Anatol:

"*Warum arbeitet er nicht?*"[45]

"*Der arme Junge ist Lungenkrank,*"[46] I blurt out. Skinny and frail, Anatol is now terrified and completely lost. Redel looked on and nodded.

"*Und was sind Sie? Wieso kommen Sie mit ihm?*"[47]

"*Ich arbeite in Paris. Er ist mein Kamerad. Er ist jung, er ist dumm*"—I look at Anatol—"*man muss ihm helfen. Er spricht nicht Deutsch . . .*"[48]

"*Na ja . . . also.*"[49] He says good-bye. He offers me and Anatol his hand, ignores the agent completely, though the latter keeps kowtowing and starts up once again with his: *Merci monsieur, parce que . . . vous comprenez . . .*

"*Alors . . . sortons, sortons,*" and I drag him out of the room by the sleeve. He backs out, bowing the whole time and still blabbering from the doorway: "*On sait jamais . . . vous savez . . .*" I wanted to push him down the elevator shaft. What a pig! He would not bow to his own president this way, because *la dignité du citoyen . . .* ,[50] etc., but before this German lieutenant he kowtows Oriental-style. Many Frenchmen, particularly the police, behave toward the Germans like savages toward the white sahib.

Once out the door I breathed a sigh of relief. I regretted having shaken hands with the Gestapo man, but there'd been no questions, none of the many questions I had feared . . . On avenue Foch, covered in thick snow, fresh and white, I felt so elated and joyful that I had to restrain myself from rolling around in it. We return to the Préfecture, but since it's already eleven thirty, no one wants to begin to work on Anatol's case. *Venez à deux heures!*[51] We go to Saint-Paul for lunch and at two return. We sit at the desk of another idiot and he begins to write up a report. A bad sign. I dictate my intricately concocted story, so he can enter it into the record. Around five we finish and prepare to leave. The official lets me out but stops Anatol from leaving. He will be held under arrest until the judicial hearing. I rush out, look for V. (he's gone), nothing helps, these are the rules. Anatol is done for.

I get on my bike and ride over to his mates to tell them to bring him some cigarettes and some warm things. I return home at eight in the evening splattered up to the waist, drenched, and tired. On top of it all my bicycle is on its last legs.

January 21, 1942

The Bolsheviks have retaken Mozhaysk. In minus forty-five Celsius. Big news. I have the flu and I've had it up to here.

January 23, 1942

I have a slight flu and am staying home. *Vieux papiers, vieilles maisons*— two fat volumes of stories about various figures from the time of the Revolution and Empire.[52] They bring to life old-time Paris, buildings still standing today, in which so much transpired. They are written by an amateur collector, one of the many fortunate Frenchmen, able to forget that we live in the twentieth century, enjoying private incomes, their own apartments, and calm, comfortable daily lives, who can afford to indulge their passions with calm, tasteful, and attentive devotion. With the delight of a connoisseur, the leisurely pedantry of a worm gnawing its way through the archives of the town halls, the Préfecture of police, the notarial offices, the parish administrations—through the unknown and previously unexplored virgin forests of papers and files amassed over the centuries by this country's inexorable bureaucracy, a country that in the act of doing something, writing a document, is already in love with its past, lives off the future of its own past, if one can put it this way.

The French bureaucracy writes the biography of each citizen and each piece of real estate—it notes each successive life stage on dozens of forms, in dozens of reports, and files them in the archives. And when one has the time, when one's life doesn't hang by a thread, as under the blade of the guillotine—one can search here and resurrect personalities and facts, even those of little importance, completely unknown, but more interesting and more expressive of the period than anything else. Two volumes of hors d'oeuvres and historical petits fours. Desmoulins lived here and not there, where the plaque is mounted. His apartment was furnished in such and such a way, as indicated in the report drawn up when the place was sealed. And you can envision the apartment, get to know the petty cares of daily life, while outside the windows Paris was contorted in the convulsions of revolution. And the strange chair on wheels, propelled by two cranks at the ends of the backrest, and all in wood? It's Georges Couthon's *chaise roulante*.[53] Still in the Musée Carnavalet. The book contains the complete history of that chair, on which the paralyzed Couthon hurried down the steep, narrow streets from the Panthéon to the Hôtel de Ville, where he was condemned to death—the end of the Terror. The cold-blooded Saint-Just, accomplice of Couthon and Robespierre in their unique triumvirate, Robespierre's sister, the first marriage plans of poor lieutenant Bonaparte, the capture of General Pichegru, and other events often hard to believe, as for instance the escape of a certain English naval captain from the Temple.[54] I'll take notes and when the time comes for Basia and me to wander about, we'll take our strolls on quiet and sunny afternoons rummaging among the houses, narrow streets, and old nooks. I don't know if I'll ever again or in any other place experience a time like the one I'm living through here and now. Living so well, calmly, evenly, without internal twists and turns, with that splendid satiety and that indescribable something that fills every one of the most ordinary days. Often it makes me rebel. Under the influence of those antiquities, of the past that seeps from every stone, something within me goes to sleep, something with all its force rejects the present, this whole era. I fall asleep on antiquities and on quotations. Indeed, France has been doing this for a long time.

Anatol is behind bars and today he slipped me a note saying the trial will be held on Tuesday the twenty-seventh. He'll need a lawyer.

January 24, 1942

I'm reading, lying down. I fall asleep, then wake up again and read some more, and occasionally I have the feeling the stories I'm reading are happening now. The episode of the "language professor" Rotondi Rotondo is splendid. A suspicious character—Italian by origin, wandering about at loose ends. The Revolution catches him in Paris. November 13, 1790, the mob goes off to sack the Hôtel de Castries on rue de Varenne. Rotondo turns up there as well and to make himself seem more imposing climbs on a mound of stones and "supervises" the workers of the Revolution. The crowd is cheerful and laughs as it "cleans out" the entire building, tossing the furniture out the window and burning the paintings. It was agreed ahead of time that revolutionary citizens would not steal. Rotondo from his mound eggs them on, shouting from time to time in French with an accent that arouses general laughter. It's a kind of French mixed with English and Italian, a verbal "bouillabaisse."

At this moment, Lafayette and his entourage come riding through rue de Varenne, barely able to guide their horses through the crowd busy enjoying its work of destruction. Seeing Rotondo on his mound of stones shouting with the verve and dignity of a tribune of the people, Lafayette rides up to him and asks what was going on. Rotondo replies with something in his fantastical dialect. Lafayette—intrigued—asks him: "Ah, ça . . . et de quel pays êtes-vous donc? Anglais ou Italien?" "Professor" Rotondo, very concerned, mumbled: "Moitié l'un, moitié l'autre."[55] Struggling, however, with his pronunciation, the poor man pronounced moitié as motié, which produced a wild ovation from the crowd. The rabble began to yell, to applaud: "Did you all hear that reply? Long live Rotondo!" Rotondo's reply flew from mouth to mouth, he's embraced, Lafayette's entourage is mocked. Why? Lafayette's family name was Motier, and in the surge of revolutionary democracy he was called by that name, just as Capet stood for the king.[56]

No one knows who—probably Desmoulins—got hold of Rotondo's reply and began to circulate it in newspapers and brochures. "Motié l'un, Motié l'autre"—a nasty bon mot, full of irony and hidden meaning, that unmasked Lafayette, the "man of two faces, the Marquis of democracy, the revolutionary courtier." A general outburst of laughter, the joy, the "payback" for eighteen months of admiration and popularity. Now Rotondo became famous. Except that he did not know, he was the only one who did not know, did not understand the reason why. He had answered Lafayette without a hint of spite, afraid even of getting into some kind of trouble, not at all grasping the double meaning of his reply. He senses that he has said something "famous," he relished the ovations, but at the same time realizes that he is the one and only one to whom no one has explained the meaning of his own words and the only one not allowed to ask what they mean, because that would entirely destroy his fame, which was increasing daily. In the course of three days Rotondo, understanding nothing, becomes the star of Paris and Lafayette's rival. The scene at the Hôtel de Castries is presented in two-bit theaters, a hundred thousand *citoyens* admire this Italian patriot who left his own country to fight in France for the sacred cause of the people's freedom, a hundred thousand other *citoyens*, taking the side of Lafayette and joining with the entire Garde nationale, become enraged at this *étranger*, this tramp and renegade. While he himself *understands nothing* . . .

It's cold in our room, but engulfed in coats, blankets, and throws I wander about Paris together with Rotondo. Eyes half-closed, I encounter an entire crowd of other figures, alive to this day in Paris, although they have never existed but were imagined by Balzac, Flaubert, and others. I doze off, I awake.

January 26, 1942

Tomorrow is Anatol's hearing. Today I got down to business, which means that first thing in the morning I launched an attack on the Palais de Justice. Easier said than done. I went inside and immediately lost my way in the labyrinth of corridors radiating out from the famous Salle des pas perdus.[57] The hearings begin at noon—the lawyers in black gowns were already prowling around—some with white fur trimming on their wide sleeves. Stopping to greet their colleagues, they accompanied their clients, whispering, gesticulating, conferring. I was up to my ears in Balzac. The lawyers, the murmur of conversations permeating the vastness of the courtroom, the gallery of types walking back and forth preoccupied with the same thought: "To get out of, wriggle out of, wrangle a way out of, talk one's way out of"—an atmosphere imbued with slyness, cunning, dialectics, *esprit*, intelligence, and the game—the great game that has been played for ages and that is created by man himself: the law and getting around it by legal means. The atmosphere is laden with thousands of cases and shades of dishonesty, cases entangled, impenetrable, and complicated, as complicated as the human soul. I stand for a moment and suddenly it occurs to me, as I look at this courtroom and at the same time realize what is happening outside, out there in the world, that the Law, the essence of the law, is perhaps in fact the capacity for humane, legal, and lawful evasion of the law by defending oneself against its blind force, against the dead letter of the law. My hatred for the Germans, today, as Russia rises on the horizon like a bloody glow, is even greater, even more intense, because it's only against the Russian glow that one perceives the fearful enormity of the betrayal perpetrated by the Germans with

respect to our entire culture, the culture to which they have themselves contributed so much and which today they trample so monstrously that Asiatic Russia,
foreign, always hostile and alien to anyone imbued with the West, this Russia
seems—civilized. I have hated Russia since childhood, spontaneously, like my
father, who found Russia so unbearable that even in Warsaw he already caught
the scent of—Russia.[58] As for the Germans, I came to hate them as one hates an
unfaithful mistress, someone dear who has been disloyal, betrayed one's trust.

I search out the office of the Lawyers' Association located at the end of a hall
that one enters through a gloomy corridor. A smiling, gray-haired old man, lost
in one of the thousand gloomy, domed rooms, gives me complete instructions.

"You must find out when, at what time and before which court your friend's
trial will be held. Then come to me at eleven forty-five and you'll be assigned
a lawyer."

"And where can one get this information?"

"*Aux renseignements généraux.*"[59]

I go to the indicated office, or rather I lose my way. Following an unlighted
exit I end up directly behind the Conciergerie, through a square gate reaching the famous "meadow"—beyond it the windows of the corridor next to the
toilettes. I know this place better than the tourist guides. I turn back and end
up at the entrance to the detention area, in front of which stands a gendarme.
He shows me where to go. Through the great courtyard next to the Sainte-
Chapelle I enter the other court building. Only when you have to find something do you realize the enormity of this labyrinth of justice. Eventually I find
the right door—of course I have to wait—but at last I present a piece of paper
with Anatol's name. They search, they search—they find nothing. "You should
go to the clerk of the *petit parquet.*" Again I lose my way and after a long walk
arrive at the proper place, passing through a broken-down door, a room full of
scaffolding, and stairs in the process of being repaired. Naturally I end up waiting, because the clerk has stepped out somewhere. When he returns from this
"somewhere" he searches for a long time in a monstrous book of fabulous proportions—about a meter square and twenty centimeters thick. The book of bad
and good deeds from the Last Judgment. He moves his finger, ending in a typically dirty fingernail, murmurs, smacks his lips, repeats Anatol's name each time
a different way—finally his finger stops and a brief answer emerges:

"The trial was held on Friday."

"And what was the verdict?" I ask.

"That I cannot tell you, are you perhaps a family relation?"

"No."

"*Alors je ne peux pas.*"[60]

"But I know the trial was supposed to take place tomorrow . . ."

"There's nothing more I can tell you. Maybe they can tell you something in such and such a place."

I go to the indicated address. After almost three hours of wandering I begin to find my way pretty well. I began at eleven, now it's almost two. I get there and again end up waiting, this time in a line. I wait over half an hour. Finally my turn came up and an old codger, stuck between the pages of his books, like a pressed flower from the spring picnic called youth, mumbles an answer with his toothless lips:

"If you're not a family relation—I cannot tell you anything."

"I am more than a family relation, I am a friend. The accused has not a single relative in all of France, he is on his own."

"On his own! *Il est seul*"—and the pressed violet bats his reddened eyelids at me.

"Where can I get some information? Please help me!"

"Perhaps in such and such a place, but it's not guaranteed," he answers.

I cross the courtyard once more; from the bustling halls I plunge into completely silent nooks and back again into the crowd thickly sown with lawyers. Occasionally a willowy woman lawyer, with the appearance of a lesbian, flashes by, thumping loudly with her wooden soles, and trailing the scent of strong perfume. The young male lawyers, dressed elegantly *à l'anglaise*, pass by dignified and pensive, seat themselves at the little tables, rummage in their briefcases, and "concentrate." They read a bit, then stare for a long time with a remote gaze at the twenty-third pane in the stained-glass window. And doubtless they dream about great cases, about their careers, with their briefcases full of trifles.

The Palais de Justice is a world apart. Somewhere else there's another world, many other worlds, entire worlds. The metro rumbles in its long tunnels and the world of the metro pulsates. In the narrow streets around Carnavalet the world of the Mr. Zygmuśes rustles mysteriously—hats stuffed with dollars, walking sticks with screw-on heads concealing gold rubles, diamonds, and "such nonsense." Les Halles, place Clichy with the meadows of bleached heads *de ces demoiselles*—all that's out there, this is in here . . .

I make it to the indicated office. Located in a garret. Gloomy, low-ceilinged, and cramped. From the little cast-iron stove in the middle runs a long, cast-iron pipe suspended on wires from the ceiling that winds between the shelves and vanishes into the wall. Shelves along the walls, dividing the whole room like screens, are full of papers everywhere, of folders, and deeds bound with string, tape, or rubber bands made of old automobile inner tubes. In the midst of all this are tables, at which several young men in gray smocks service the shelves. The cashier sits in a cramped cage made of brass mesh in a corner of the room, distributing payments to the witnesses. Every so often he sticks his little mummylike head in a little beret through the small window. This is what an office in the Palais de Justice looks like. A hundred years ago it looked the same. I try to get some information, but no one knows anything. All the same, I stand there and look around. After a while an old fellow appeared from behind the shelves, stood next to the stove, and began warming his hands delectably. He seemed to be roasting them on a spit, so that he could enjoy munching on them later. I like such old men and trust them. I went up to him with a pleasant smile and started a simple conversation: "You know—I have a certain problem—it's now been four hours . . ." I choose my words, I am *young, embarrassed, and shy*. He was touched. These are three things old age cannot resist.

"I'm not supposed to, but wait a bit . . ."

I gave him the name of the "youngster" on a piece of paper and the old man toddled off. After a good quarter of an hour, he returned, we went into a corner, he pulled out a piece of paper: "The hearing was held on Friday, but due to the absence of an interpreter was deferred until tomorrow, twelve o'clock, room 17, but shshshsh . . ." He puts his finger to his lips. "This is just for you—don't tell anyone who you heard it from . . ." Touched, I said good-bye, thanking him sincerely and at the same time *respectfully*. We are both pleased with ourselves.

At last, after more than four hours. Tomorrow is the next installment. I feel as though I've taken a long journey—now pleasantly tired and full of new impressions.

January 27, 1942

Early this morning I met with the "youngster's" mates. All four came—one even missed work to make it to the hearing. I left them in the bistro across from the Palais, and went with only one (S.—my client from Senlis. He already knows his way around a bit . . .) to the office of the Lawyers' Association. It was still too early, we had to wait a while. A few minutes before twelve a young lawyer entered, exquisitely dressed. A white silk scarf spilled with a splash from the low collar of his navy blue and heavily brushed overcoat. The small knot of his tie is tucked into his high shirt collar *English fashion*, on his head is a black "homburg" à la Eden.[61] He holds a briefcase, white knitted wool gloves. In the swing rhythm of a slow foxtrot he approached the old man's desk and asked casually:

"Is there something there for me?"

The old man pointed to us and to a tearful woman in a corner of the hall. The young counselor looked us over, said *"bon,"* and disappeared for a moment. He has returned now in a black robe with white fur trim. A dreamboat. A tall brunet, with sharp, masculine features—as in a Florence Barclay novel.[62] Practically a Robert Taylor.[63] He lit a cigarette with a flourish and, turning to us, said: "*Je vous écoute . . .*"[64]

In a few words I laid out the "youngster's" case. He took some brief notes with a sweeping hand. Then came the woman's case—rather troublesome. She had been working and at the same time drawing unemployment and they caught her at it. But how was she to survive with three children when earning nine hundred francs a month, her husband a prisoner. She begins to cry—following her in turn, the children clinging to her skirt start wailing like organ pipes. I feel sorry for her, I would like to blow up this Palais de l'injustice, but I'm beginning to feel nervous, because it's now five after twelve. The Maître calmed the woman down, took a last drag on the cigarette that he'd smoked down almost to his front teeth, tossed the five-millimeter butt, and, without picking it up from the floor, accompanied us out into the corridor. There, after a few steps, he leaned over to me and said a few words—delicate and how human—about the reimbursement of expenses, *frais de transport*, etc. Without a word I pulled out a hundred-franc bill and handed it over discreetly, explaining that alas that was all I could manage. Ah, yes—he certainly took it! Despite all his English phlegm he couldn't hide his joy. He became instantly more effusive, now we had his full attention. The poor woman, whimpering and moaning, trailed along far behind us, receding into the background.

We entered the hearing courtroom. The "youngster" was now sitting on a separate bench together with the other defendants, who had been brought from the "Santé" for the hearing. He greeted us with a joyful smile. I winked and signaled him to pay attention.

Soon the court entered and the cases followed one after another. After a few charges (breaking and entering), compared to which the "youngster" appeared an innocent angel, the judge read off the "youngster's" name. "Nationality Polish? Is there an interpreter? No?" Postponed until Friday. I clenched my fists. They'd once before postponed the hearing for lack of an interpreter, now for the second time—and they will no doubt do it again several more times, while he's still behind bars in the "Santé." But before I managed to grasp the implications, our lawyer rose from the bench and turned to the presiding judge: "Will the Court permit the role of interpreter to be filled by the defendant's employer" (*patron*), "now present in the hall? He's Polish but speaks excellent French" and—without waiting for the court's assent calls me from the audience. The "youngster's" mates propel me like a torpedo, crying under their breaths: "Mr. B.—go for it, do your thing, stick it to 'em, go get 'em . . ." I want to laugh, but I approach with the serious expression of an "employer." They ask my name and surname. "Please raise your right hand." The president mutters the formula of the oath and says loudly: "Please repeat: *Je le jure.*" With my arm raised in a fascist-style greeting, I repeat "*je le jure*" and in the course of several seconds I have become a sworn interpreter. I was now charmed by the simplicity of the solution. No court interpreter, so they take me from the courtroom, administer an oath, and the hearing is not postponed. If there's a lot of formality and red tape in this French administration, it nevertheless dazzles you from time to time with the unexpected and nimble, simply humane evasion of the letter of the law. Perhaps it's simply the instinct of self-preservation against the letter of the law? If all the acts and regulations in France were applied by the book and put into effect, this country would long ago have turned into one great concentration camp.

The judge reads the record—the pure fable concocted by me—and smiles benevolently. After my intercession, he turns to the "youngster": "Did you scribble in your identity card?"—The "youngster" nods and confesses. At which the president next addresses me as the *patron*.

"Were you satisfied up to now with this fellow's work?"

I recite an entire hymn in praise of "this fellow," choking on the adjectives: *Un travailleur excellent, toujours parfait, minutieux et soigneux*, etc.[65] I'm enjoying my role. The sentence: Eight days arrest with credit for time already served. The lawyer immediately came up to me and added smartly: "They'll release him this evening." We all leave the hall. I thank the lawyer—he is very dignified and pleased with himself: "If you gentlemen" (he now takes us for some kind of gang) "ever need anything again, please always count on me." The poor guy has no business cards and writes his address and phone number on a piece of paper. Naturally, he lives in the Quartier Latin and I even know in which hotel. We leave the court and all go together for a celebratory meal at Jan's wife's place in Saint-Paul.

January 30, 1942

For three days now our room has been unbearably cold. Basia is worn out. On top of it, they've limited our gas supply and it's even impossible to make a hot water bottle. When I get home, we eat and go to bed. I've stopped riding the bicycle because the tires are no longer fit for use. If I manage to find new ones, then I'll fix up the whole bike. After ten thousand kilometers it'll do for another ten thousand.

The Russians seem to be advancing slowly and in one spot are 225 kilometers from the Polish border. There are some who rejoice in this. Besides they have given the Polish government a three-hundred-million-ruble loan, for which at some point . . . But no, this is defeatism on my part and I shouldn't be thinking like this. Which doesn't stop me from thinking . . . Overall everyone's mood has improved (though improving our intelligence is too much to expect) and once again almost everyone believes the war will end this year. I don't think so.

January 31, 1942

Hitler gave a speech yesterday. I bought today's *Pariser Zeitung* so I could have it *in extenso*. In fact, he said the same thing as always except that he no longer promised anything. Quite the contrary—he boiled everything down to "*Ich weiss nicht. Ich kann an diesem 30. Januar nur eines versichern: Wie dieses Jahr ausgehen wird, weiss ich nicht. Ob damit der Krieg sein Ende nimmt, weiss ich nicht.*"[66] Very interesting—this "I don't know" nevertheless has such magical power that everyone who reads it, says: "Ah—but I do know . . ." The ending is also in a "minor" key: "*Herrgott, gib uns die Kraft, dass wir uns die Freiheit erhalten, unserem deutschen Volk, unseren Kindern und Kindeskindern, und nicht nur unserem deutschen Volk, sondern auch den anderen Völkern Europas. Denn es ist ein Krieg für ganz Europa und damit wirklich für die ganze Menschheit.*"[67] It would be better in this regard if he thought less about other people and stopped worrying about humanity. Humanity is never as unfortunate as when someone begins to worry about it. Nothing good has ever yet come of it. What a boon if one day so-called Great Men were no longer born and no longer waged wars "for the sake of and on behalf of all Humanity."

A lot more interesting is the financial report of the Banque de France for 1941. Loans made to the government by the Banque de France (money simply printed and handed over to the government) amounted in 1940 to 80 billion francs and grew to 150 billion in 1941, meaning that over two years the Banque de France gave the government an injection on the order of 230 billion—in printed paper. The circulation of banknotes offers an even more interesting picture: 1939 — 151.4 billion; 1940 — 218.4 billion; 1941 — 266 billion. They are printing paper while the country is economically dead. Actually, France is already experiencing full and quite severe inflation. Prices have risen, but the most surprising phenomenon is that prices have not risen in proportion to the increase in the amount of money and generally remain in most cases within reasonable limits. Despite the inflation in the full sense of the term, it is still not felt. No comparison with Poland, where the price level is skyrocketing. Why? Why also on this point has the fall in the value of money and its purchasing power so far had a relatively moderate course? The mystery is rooted simply in French psychology. Since the Revolution there has been no inflation in France. There has been devaluation, but inflation is to date unknown. The franc *still amounts to* something and although it buys increasingly less and less, the average Frenchman *is not afraid* to put it away and considers the sum of five thousand francs to be *une petite réserve* or even *une petite fortune*.[68] The franc is plummeting, losing value daily, but the devaluation has not yet undermined confidence. People trust this money and cannot accept the possibility that the same thing might shortly happen to the franc as happened to the German mark after the last war. Moreover — they trust the franc to the extent that they do not take into account that after this war all the European currencies, including the franc, will fall sharply, being tied to the mark. And therefore France keeps traditionally saving as it always has — and stuffs its old stockings and mattresses — with paper money. Good luck! The present moment is a transitional moment and at the same time the mildest in terms of inflation. *Physical* inflation already exists, but *psychologically* it has not yet arrived. There are many thousand-franc notes in circulation, in people's pockets, in the purses they clutch to their breasts, and at the same time everyone considers each note of great value, treasuring it, and still believing that *un billet c'est quand même quelque chose* (*un billet* in colloquial speech means a thousand-franc note).[69] The Frenchman keeps saving — and he saves in nothing else, but precisely in banknotes. He loves to put away banknotes (also a kind of national trait), and as a result still today and for some time to come he will be withdrawing money from circulation, cushioning the effects of the printing of bills, which is to say of monetary inflation. Inflation is like a certain shameful disease. It can be divided into three stages (Ernst Wagemann: *Wo kommt das viele Geld her?*[70]):

The first stage of inflation consists of the creation (that is, printing) of money, which serves to conceal the deficit in the state budget. This kind of inflation affects only a certain part of the national revenue and, as in the case of the first symptoms of a certain disease, is not dangerous in itself so long as other symptoms of inflation do not appear.

The monetary disease becomes more dangerous when it is joined by a secondary form of inflation, as when the pathogen infects the blood: the inflation of credit. This consists of the creation of money with the help of the credit mechanism, which sets off speculation in securities, gold, currency, and goods.

The third form, and the most threatening, simply the third stage of inflation, consists of the increasingly rapid circulation of money, of inflation "via the cash register," which means inflation that appears when people *immediately* exchange their money, their cash, for purchases. In a word, the instant exchange of money for goods—for anything at all, if only not to hold on to money. These three stages will run a much milder course in a normal economy, which is to say where there are enough goods on the market. By contrast, with today's current deficits and the scarcity of products of every kind, each of these stages will run a considerably more intense course. Prices are doubling—on the one hand as a result of the glut of money, on the other hand of the shortage of everything. In France, on the one hand, people are still saving, thus depleting the money supply; on the other hand, the market in goods is not yet completely exhausted. Hence the mildness and delayed reaction. What stage of inflation is France in now? Let's see.

France traversed the first stage very quickly and already in 1939–1940. Despite all of its wealth, the sums which had to be amassed for the purpose of the war already exceeded not only the potential revenue from taxation but even the capacity for absorption of the capital market. Which is why the Banque de France had no other recourse but to print money and "lend" it to the state. It paid the government in advance. From 1939 until August 31, 1940, the expenses of the French government increased to 260 billion francs—of which 180 billion was for military expenses (though they didn't seem to have spent even a million on the war). And yet France's annual national revenue in this period amounted to barely around 120 billion, which is to say that if every Frenchman's entire annual earnings were sequestered, about 120 billion would be obtained. Taxes yielded 67 billion. It was impossible to sequester annual earnings (besides, they would not have sufficed)—therefore the printing presses went into action—not to speak of other means of increasing revenue (treasury bills, etc.). In short, in less than a year of this celebrated French war, the fiscal economy of France came to look just like Germany's in 1916–1917, in which the same methods of war financing were used. It's yet another aspect of the overall picture of France. In addition to the overall bedlam, incompetence, and ignorance reigning everywhere. In the course of the single year of the French *drôle de guerre*,[71] prices shot up by 25 percent, and the franc was devalued in relation to the pound by 20 to 25 percent. Then came the armistice—and fiscal policy did not change. The government was paying for everything and is still paying. At first there were all kinds of indemnities. Then the unemployment benefits. After the armistice everyone went on unemployment. Next came the bonuses for children and family supplements, then bonuses for "returning to the farm," indemnity for damage from bombing—in the end millions in benefits under the Secours National.[72] France entered the second stage of inflation—the inflation of government credit. Pétain pays for everything plus 300 million francs a day for wartime indemnities, which the Germans of course keep pumping into the

French market. One should have no illusions about the Germans' fiscal economy and one should not idealize it. They insist that their methods of financing are entirely different in this war than those used in the last. Agreed—but
after all they didn't invent anything new and the only difference consists in the
fact that instead of printing their own marks, this time they're printing francs,
złotys, crowns, guilders, and so-called occupation marks. The entire burden of
inflation and the suffering it causes fall on the defeated nations. France, with
its riches, is the mainstay of this system. This year the circulation of banknotes
will certainly reach 300 billion. And I have the impression, they're not yet at
the brink. Why? In the first place the French still respect the thousand-franc
note and are not afraid to save in francs, thus withdrawing the excess of money
from circulation, and in the second place the level of this saving remains high.
The French save in *banknotes*. And in what proportions? In 1934, of 80 billion
francs in banknotes then in circulation, 24 billion were permanently hoarded.
They were stuffed into socks and mattresses, according to the principles of Père
Grandet (Richard Lewinsohn—*Histoire de la Crise*, p. 209[73]). One can then
grant that one-quarter of banknotes in circulation continue to be withdrawn
as a result of hoarding. This year therefore about 75 to 80 billion francs will be
stuck in straw mattresses. Who knows, perhaps even more, considering the level
reached by agricultural earnings as a result of the black market. And the French
peasant is precisely the one who saves the most. People in the cities, in addition
to wages, earn profits from all kinds of legal and illegal trade. One can make a
profit from anything. As a result everyone has something. If you add that France
was the country with the most equitable distribution of national income, it's
easy to understand why it is surviving this period relatively well. And there's
movement—money is flowing. But this is temporary. Because at some point
the third stage will certainly be reached, unless America immediately props up
the franc with the dollar. If this does not occur, there will be a catastrophe such
as France has not seen since the time of the assignats of the Revolution. Eighty
billion hoarded banknotes will be dumped suddenly on the market in the search
preferably for gold and currency, or whatever else, if only to escape from money.
This will mean the ruin of every small fortune, which in France means general
ruin, the ruin of rentiers and small proprietors. France will really lose the war
only after the war—and this in every respect.

February 1, 1942

Snow and frost. In our room it's really unbearable. The cold and the shortage of fats cause nasty drying and cracking of the skin. Especially on the hands.

February 3, 1942

American airplanes have been dropping leaflets. Smart pieces of work. The French swallow them eagerly. On the first page is a drawing of the Statue of Liberty, and under it the caption: "You gave us our independence, we will restore your liberty." It would be hard to think up anything better, knowing the French even a bit. Today everyone was hawkish. Paris is swarming with Papkins.[74]—*Ah, alors, les Américains, vous verrez.*[75] Alas. It has always seemed to us Poles that the French haven't changed since the Battle of Eylau, when they let themselves be slaughtered and did not retreat, that they are the sons of Cambronne.[76] And we should get this legend out of our heads. These French no longer exist. Today they want to eat and think about nothing else but beefsteak, and it's up to others to fight in their place and leave them in peace. Besides, France is all that matters on earth.

February 4, 1942

Thaw.

February 5, 1942

Freezing. You can get dizzy—but that's all you can get, nothing else. No vegetables at all—not even rutabaga. Not a single potato or carrot. Nothing. If we hadn't gotten a sack of potatoes and some supplies in December, we would have nothing to eat. People have become touchy and the proverbial French humor and informality have vanished. I now take the metro and the bus and not a day goes by without some kind of fracas. In the metro people quarrel, in the buses everyone yells at the conductor—unheard of things.

I squeeze into the metro this morning, next to me sits a *citoyen*—he then gets up and appears to be looking for someone in the back of the car. An old woman with a basket standing next to him therefore takes his seat. But the *citoyen* shoves her aside and says: *"C'est pour ma femme."* At which another *citoyen*, squeezed against the door, turns on him indignantly: *"Depuis quand les places sont-elles réservées dans le métro?"*[77] He's right. I rise and give my seat to the old woman. The two men are by now arguing. As I approach the door and the citizen who is right, I whisper to him: *"Laissez-le, c'est un goujat."* My citizen, delighted that I have suggested the term that had escaped him, yells at the other one: *"Goujat . . . regardez-moi ce goujat!"*[78] The other one jumps up, screams, they trade abuses . . . It's like this everywhere you go.

February 6, 1942

Mr. and Mrs. P. were at a gathering where they met the sister of Pétain's ambassador in Washington, just back from the United States. She said life for members of the French embassy in Washington had become completely intolerable. Everyone boycotts them, no one greets them, official conversations with the ambassador are conducted standing up, they are never invited to anyone's home—in short they are given on every occasion to understand what people think of them. Comforting news.

February 7, 1942

We heard Adolphe Borchard[79] in concert at Salle Pleyel. He played Chopin, Liszt, and Debussy. Big crowd. An elegant devotee of music sat down next to us and began to chat with another devotee sitting in front of her. I always wonder how much is "blather" and how much is truth in talk about art. Probably more "blather." In the course of five minutes our neighbor strolled through all the concert halls of Paris and discussed all the pianists who have recently performed. I'm always amazed at the extraordinary fund of commonplaces that can be uttered in a tone of expertise. The French language lends itself to this especially well. The adjectives *merveilleux, sublime, formidable* (vulgar), *inoui, épatant, saissant, émouvant* (academic) are designed to be uttered in the voice and tone of Phaedra or Iphigenia[80] so as to come off as *très intellectuel,* usually without knowing what it's really about. The French language is like a costume for both everyday and special occasions. The costume for special occasions has enormous richness, with which the beginner is easily beguiled. Essentially it's most often form without content. The woman next to us, emphasizing her sonorous words by moving her umbrella, waving her gloves, and nervously crossing and uncrossing her legs, was—speaking the language for special occasions *très vexante,* in everyday language *très emmerdante.*[81] The lights dimmed, Borchard entered. And so he proceeded to execute Chopin polonaises. In truth it could be said that *il les exécutait,* but in the sense that a death sentence is executed. Halfway through the first one I'd already had enough. I looked meaningfully at Basia, she at me, and we understood each other without a word. I preferred to observe our neighbor, who was closely following the music.

She rested her forehead in one hand, grabbed the armrest with the other, and remained motionless. Only her tiny slipper rose and fell, beating the rhythm as precisely as a metronome. Just before the chords were struck, both hands rose to the top of the backrest, hung in the air, and then together with the chords her little white fists dropped down onto her round thighs. The slipper worked tirelessly nonstop. Meanwhile Borchard was working in the "free style," meaning he was practicing the "crawl" above the piano and finally concluded the whole production in the start position. At the last stroke he drew his arms back. I waited for him to jump into the piano. Applause and sharp whistles filled the hall. At the beginning of the second half of the concert Borchard's entrance was greeted with whistles and shouts. He was unable to begin. At a certain point, taking advantage of a moment of silence, he shouted from the stage: "*Les goujats à la porte.*"[82] This time the applause of his fans was mixed with a perfect roar. Borchard is considered a collaborator and the concert turned into a political demonstration and a face-off among the audience. He played an entire piece by Debussy to the accompaniment of an alarm clock, set off in someone's pocket. Later on more screams, hooting, and whistles mixed with applause. We left before the end.

February 8, 1942

Sunday. We stay home in the freezing cold. I finished Władysław Reymont's *The Peasants.*[83] Made no impression on me. I'm reading Diderot's *Jacques the Fatalist* and enjoying it despite the cold. In fact, that Jacques even warms me up. I'm struck by the modernity of what seems to be nonsense. And it may be one of the most amazing books I know.

February 9, 1942

Bitter cold, minus twelve degrees Celsius. People comfort themselves with the latest joke supposedly straight from Berlin. The optimist says: "One thing for sure, we're going to lose the war." To which the pessimist replies: "Yes, but when? . . . *um Gotteswillen.*"[84] Otherwise, there's still nothing to eat. The French farmers are keeping all the vegetables in the ground. Now, when the ground has frozen completely, it's impossible to pull them out. Leeks, carrots, beets are stuck in the ground, poking out their frozen tops in the fields, and can't be dug up. Deliveries to Paris have stopped. Instead, they're handing out miserly rations of beans and peas, enough for a single meal. We're living on potatoes.

February 11, 1942

Now that I'm riding the metro, I read a lot. I'm intrigued by the Goncourts' rather blunt description of Voltaire's *Candide* as simply "La Fontaine in prose, Rabelais without balls"[85] — I've reread it and I agree with the Goncourts.

There's no better way to describe *Candide* from the literary point of view. But only literary. Otherwise it's a sad book—it could all be written today and would be just as vivid, topical, and hopeless. Maybe even more hopeless today than in its own time. For reading such a satire in the eighteenth century, one could entertain the illusion that mankind would nevertheless emerge from this barbarism, that the era of enlightenment was approaching, that something was happening—there was light on the horizon. Man believed in his own power, philosophized about everything, God included—he felt he was moving ahead—he was creating, getting drunk on his own power, looking with a joyous smile on the bright dawn of the nineteenth century. "Liberty," "Fraternity," "Equality," "Law," "Constitution," "Parliament," "Democracy"—concepts that were vital, practical. Man *believed* and was able to believe. And today? Today *Candide* is simply a childish satire, because the object of satire, at which Voltaire so bitingly directs his wit and pen, is all in fact very innocent. Everything Candide endured, which at the time exceeded the normal conditions of life and existence, is today the lot of every man, it is simply the normal life of contemporary man. Poor Candide is impressed into a division of the Prussian guard and assists at the burning of one village—suppose even ten villages. He sees how the soldiers slit the throats of women and children. A dozen—let's say even several dozen—corpses are strewn on the ground. Later on he's in Spain and observes the abuses of the Inquisition. He travels to South America, where he falls—oh, horrors—into the hands of the Jesuits, and so on. A perfect idyll—and yet he gets so incensed, flinging poisoned darts of irony, considering the world a terrible madness. It seems to me that if he had lived today he would lose his sense of humor. How innocent were the despotism and oppression exercised by the monarchs and "tyrants" of his time compared to today's slavery. What a fuss over one ridiculous Bastille, the likes of which the world is teeming with today. A single Auschwitz beats the Bastille a hundred times over. And all this is happening in the name of culture and the regeneration of the world. Do we have any idea at all of the meaning of LIBERTY and LAW? My generation already has a very weak understanding of them. My father's generation can still remember something, but me?... *Niente.* If I had never known France, the prewar France, I would have died in the conviction that I had been living in freedom. You can say what you want about France—I myself will lambaste her more than once—but France was the only country in prewar Europe that may not have offered true liberty but at least provided the illusion of liberty to a very great extent. And all of us, accustomed by now to thinking in the categories of slaves, the categories of—hmm—barbarians, hold this against the French, considering its one result to be—*their defeat.* And from our barbaric, youthful, and dynamic point of view we are right. The defeat of France—from too much liberty. Perhaps, liberty is poorly understood and reminiscent of our "Golden Liberty" from before the Polish partitions.[86] The France of 1939 from the moral and ideological perspective is the Poland of the Saxon dynasty.[87] "Eat, drink, and eat some more." Well? I've tasted liberty and I know—and cannot forget it. Today I understand things I could not grasp when I first got here. A few weeks after I stepped off the train at Gare du Nord I was freer here as a foreigner than (O horrors!) as a Pole in independent Poland. I did not fear the uncertain future, I did not lose myself in gloomy thoughts about what would happen next, because I was free. I could change apartments, I could move to another city, I could do whatever I felt like—and even the commissioner of police himself was not interested. Voltaire was a writer—and spent time in prison for writing. Today he would have perished without trial in one of hundreds of Bastilles. Each of his ideas and words are blasphemy. Humanitarianism, the law, freedom, culture (oof) are really synonyms for decay, destruction, lack of willpower and vitality, and the absence of "Strength through Joy."[88] Not thoughts but schemes. Not feelings but instincts. Not men but a herd of sheep with Panurge leading the way.[89]

February 15, 1942

Thus the war will not end this year. Yesterday the English allowed three enormous German vessels to sail out of Brest and they paraded safe and sound through La Manche and entered one of the German harbors without any bother. And now they're laughing at the English. They're right—I myself would laugh, if I still had it in me.

This evening Churchill himself, the *whiskyseliger* and *besoffener* Churchill, informed the world in a brief speech on the radio that Singapore has fallen. Success all around. The *Scharnhorst*, the *Gniesenau*, and the *Prinz Eugen* are sailing all over La Manche.[90] The Japanese are conquering "unconquerable" Singapore, and you miserable citizen of the New Europe, you must go on believing. A joke is going around Paris on this subject. What is the difference between the English and the Good Lord? None. Both the English and the Good Lord are invisible, but one must believe in them.

February 18, 1942

Below zero for three days now. Better not to write about the temperature in our room. I spend the whole day in a well-heated office, but Basia endures torments.

Everyone is now talking about the American plan. It involves letting the Japanese take whatever they want and focusing all efforts on Germany, to put it out of action by the end of the year. To "feint" in the East and the Pacific—but everything against Germany. Nice plan . . . and good propaganda.

The Russian winter offensive is not producing the expected results. As if any results could be expected. I expect from this war only the unexpected. But people console themselves as best they can. Otherwise, there's a smallpox epidemic running around Paris and everyone has to get inoculated. Smallpox in the New Europe. And in Paris, that's really something! I feel like I'm in the Middle Ages, I plan to meet Quasimodo in a bistro, with Narcissus and Goldmouth.[91] I would like to catch smallpox and someday, someday, as an old man tell my grandsons: "It was the year 1942 in Paris and notices were plastered on the walls of all the town halls, on all the facades of buildings about the free vaccination of the population . . ." I would not complete my sentence, struck down from my armchair by a raging plague.

February 19, 1942

We got together today with B. and his girlfriend. We arranged to meet them at La Coupole on boulevard Montparnasse. We arrived a bit early and ordered toast with jam and tea. People were beginning to gather at La Coupole—that typical Montparnasse crowd: elegant hussies, sarcastic "lady savants," a bit unwashed and a bit tarted up, young men with long hair, dressed with studied elegance or artistically disheveled, shuffling nonchalantly and scanning the room not in order to see anyone but to be seen themselves. Here and there buried in the corner of a banquette a couple whispers to each other. A young man took a seat next to us, handsome and masculine, with an intelligent face—a pleasant contrast with this entourage of "peacocks." He was waiting for someone . . . Soon she arrived, very attractive and svelte, beautifully dressed, in age between a young girl and a woman. Self-confident in her movements, a touch of coldness in her eyes, floating on her lips the "remote" smile of Leonardo da Vinci's Lucrezia Crivelli. The man came to life and although he remained almost motionless in his seat, one felt he was all atremble and aquiver. He bent his head and looked her in the eye with well-masked flirtatiousness, making himself into the kind of guy he wanted to seem to her to be. I savored the moment along with him. What a pleasure—the chance suddenly to be different, the chance to draw oneself through this woman's eyes in vigorous, assured strokes, occasionally to "soften" the edges—like a perfect sketch. She took out a pack of cigarettes, offered him one, lit up herself, and, gazing into the distance, listened.

Maybe she sensed the game . . . maybe it amused her . . . Men are so ridiculously similar in such situations. When this occasionally happens to me, I want to howl in self-pity. The search for another woman is perhaps above all the desire to find oneself in another form, the desire if only for an illusion and for an escape from one's own by now monotonous self. It's not the woman who bores me, but I myself am bored with my own image as reflected in this one woman.

Madame A. arrived — B. was late. We chattered about everything and nothing. Mme A. is a calm person, full of distinction and rather reticent. B. came rushing in and made a stir. He hasn't worked for us since last summer but in five minutes managed to tell me all the rumors — even those I knew nothing about, although I'm on the spot. Who's with whom, since when, why no longer, that C. was kissing Mme B. (husband a prisoner of war) in the Odéon metro station with such ardor that even students cried out: "*Censure, censure.*" A provincial small town, not the capital of the world and a great city. I once caught Tyrone Power with Annabella in the same act — on the tower of Notre-Dame.[92] They at least might have imagined they were well hidden.

B. called the waiter and ordered *quatre coupes de champagne*. We decided to go for supper together. On boulevard Montparnasse it was already completely dark. We walked from restaurant to restaurant reading, by the light of a match, the menus posted near the entries. Down to the nubbin. Nothing to be found anywhere. Only in a small eatery, which B. assured us offered things not on the menu, did we find a supper fit to eat. Moules and crayfish, soup, good sausage served hot, vegetables, pears, cheese — almost like old times in a working-class restaurant. We talked about the French lack of sincerity. B. with complete frankness declared that as a Frenchman he knows what he's talking about: the French are terrible hypocrites. That modest supper cost over three hundred francs. Prices are becoming quite impossible. To finish, we went for ice cream at the Dome, where the approach of closing time was in the air: a cat walked around the empty room, sniffing out something to pee on, while in the corner sat a lone beauty looking for someone to bestow herself upon.

February 20, 1942

Yesterday the trial of those responsible for the French defeat opened in Riom.[93] On the defendants' bench were Daladier, Blum, and Gamelin. From the word go, from the very start, it was an operetta, because the defense as well as the accused began outright to accuse — Pétain and the Vichy government. The newspapers write about it cagily, but between the lines one senses that sharp words were said. Comedy. The general reaction in Paris is negative — something like shame and embarrassment.

February 22, 1942

This morning Oleś K. came by and brought us a package from Cracow. These packages are our salvation, especially when it comes to fats.

In the afternoon we went over to Robert's place to look after the children because he and his wife had to go out. In Fontenay it's as quiet as the country-side. Basia fed Filip from a bottle, which looked rather peculiar, I played with the boys. A great bunch. The couple returned around nine and we stayed for supper. A lovely family.

February 23, 1942

Black ice like I've never in my life seen before. Paris appears to be coated entirely in ice. At freezing temperatures there's a light drizzle, precise and per-sistent. The buses have stopped running and I went by foot from Porte d'Or-léans. Near the bridge, in the middle of the road, blocking the way, was the first bus that had departed in the morning and skidded as it started uphill. People wrap rags or string around their shoes and walk like paralytics. But I went crazy with delight. I would run a few paces and then slide a good stretch. Each tree, each branch is coated in ice. We quit work an hour earlier, so the employees could get home at the usual time. Because of the ice. Returning home on foot, I executed a terrific, long descent on the soles of my feet from one end of the bridge way past the other. I was dreaming of ice skates and could have skated all the way home.

I'm again reading Balzac by the pound. *Splendeurs et misères, La Peau de chagrin.* I travel in the metro with a sack full of Balzacs.

March 2, 1942

It has finally warmed up. On the last day of February winter seems to have ended. We breathed a sigh of relief. Most important, we can once again use almost unlimited gas. When the hotel owner informed us of this joyous news, the whole world meant nothing to me compared to these humble words: *Le gaz à volonté.*[94] You can even gas yourself to death without fear of being saved. I went to the kitchen and turned on both burners full throttle—let them burn, since it's *à volonté.*

March 3, 1942, eleven twenty p.m.

Not bad at all. The windowpanes are rattling. We had just returned from Lola's. We were sitting there at her place and suddenly around ten we hear some booms. A moment of silence and again the whole chromatic scale. I'm a bit of an expert on this. The Jews and the Freemasons have arrived.[95] Meanwhile the rumble and roar became almost continuous. We climbed to the top floor "to take a look." The western part of Paris was all lit up. Bright lights illuminated the sky and hung there for a long time, like stars. So-called bombing with flares. Weak rumbles from the antiaircraft defense—the Germans were caught un-awares. And the English kept on pounding relentlessly. I don't know what the target was, but it's the first time things have gotten this hot. It seemed that over there everything was shaking.

At one point a flare burst right over us and it became as bright as day. As for me, now my heart began pounding. Saliva filled my mouth, especially when I heard the discreet, gentlemanly buzz of a Blenheim,[96] heading for us at a lei-surely pace. The imagination goes into overdrive at such moments. I was already seeing the same kind of enormous pill, breaking away from the fuselage, as in June 1940. But the plane passed over, looked around, and—left. You could see it quite clearly. Basia almost fell out the window from sheer joy and wanted to scream. We left Lola's place to the sound of these echoes from the Thames and began walking back home. People were standing in the streets, in doorways and in bistros, remarking how strange it was that no alarm was given. No sirens sounded. From the distance could be heard the honking of the fire engines and the peals of the ambulances rushing west somewhere, toward that inferno. Ex-plosions are still being heard. The English have been bombing for two hours without pause.

March 4, 1942

There's probably no other place on earth where it can be said with such cer-tainty that "everyone's talking" as in Paris. Here in fact "everyone's talking"—and how!—and moreover exclusively about one thing only. There is no other subject. As of early this morning everyone has been talking about yesterday's bombing. In the streets, on the metro platforms, in the buses there's nothing else to be heard. Everyone now knows "something," "someone" was there and saw it, everyone is contradicting everyone else—and arguing. The newspapers have only a short notice about "the bestial attack by the English on the inhabi-tants and residential housing of one of the Parisian suburbs." Since the neigh-borhood has no churches or hospitals, everything focused on the poor museum of Sèvres porcelain. Let them . . . no harm will be done if some of those huge and horrible vases shatter. In any case everyone knows the issue was something altogether different. There was no alarm, people did not manage to take shelter, there are victims. Too bad. The main feeling is one of satisfaction and despite some whispers about two thousand killed, people applaud this move. Here and there some are heard to express indignation, but these are exceptions. Besides, this first decisive incursion of the English has awakened springtime hopes. Paris is bubbling—everyone is talking.

People say the English were using atomic bombs. *Ils ont jeté des bombes atomiques.* I left work today with P., an engineer and pilot. We discussed these rumors. He insists it's not possible, that probably these were high-powered explosive bombs, that some new type of explosive material may have been used. But nothing is impossible. Louis de Broglie, in *L'Avenir de la physique*, describes how when the uranium nucleus is bombarded with neutrons, the nucleus breaks apart, and its splitting into lighter nuclei is accompanied by the emission of neutrons, which in principle can in turn cause the splitting of other, neighboring uranium atoms.[97] It seems reasonable to expect that an explosion at a given point in the mass of uranium would continue further and cause an enormous liberation of energy. "Calculations have been made in relation to the dispersal of the disintegration" (*la propagation de la désintégration*) "of the uranium mass and have demonstrated that its realization is not 'a priori' impossible"—says de Broglie. I don't understand much of this, but I imagine this as a great munitions depot. The explosion of one missile can cause the explosion of those next to it, in short, a hell of an explosion. Estimating the difficulties of such a little experiment, de Broglie writes: "It is obviously desirable to perform experiments that promote progress in nuclear physics" (*la physique nucléaire*), "but it is equally desirable that people survive to benefit from the results." Fascinating. They should give it a try. Blow the entire world to hell and then at least there would be peace, once and for all. Everything is possible. The development of technology is so incredibly fast, acceleration is so insane, that nothing can be excluded. The war magnifies all this even more. To the point that concierges now talk about "atom bombs."

March 5, 1942

Yesterday the dish was prepared and today we got the latest news in the right kind of sauce. Tomorrow will be the funeral for the victims, which is being turned into a great and tasteless comedy. The day of the funeral will be a national day of mourning—they're putting a symbolic catafalque on place de la

Concorde, it will be a day off from work *pour donner la possibilité à tous de manifester leur solidarité et exprimer leur dédain*, etc., etc.[98]

Today I finally got hold of new tires for the bicycle. One hundred twenty francs and two packs of cigarettes. Time to fix the wreck, because it's barely holding up. I've had it with the metro where you can drop dead of rage. That's the main thing.

The newspapers are splendid: *"La France meurtrie," "La barbarie anglo-saxonne," "Le peuple français et l'ouvrier français en deuil,"*[99] but not a word about what happened to Renault and that the English reduced these large factories to smithereens. No, they were supposedly targeting the *quartiers d'habitation*,[100] the museum of Sèvres porcelain. People don't let themselves be fooled. Above all, there was no alarm. Besides, before the bombing an English siren-airplane flew over the factory and nearby houses, the Germans did not allow people into the shelters, and so those in the know add conspiratorially: "When the English had already flown off, two German airplanes arrived and dropped bombs on people's houses — on purpose, *vous comprenez?*" Tough — it's war and there must be victims. What are the English supposed to do? Calmly watch as the Germans manufacture tanks and airplanes at Renault? People are very distressed by the victims, whose number grows from day to day as more are found. But what can be done? Sometimes a simple argument can be just right. Today in the bistro I heard someone begin to say that the English shouldn't have, that they would do better to fly over Germany, and *et qu'ils nous foutent la paix.*[101] To which a woman in the room retorted: "It's all our fault. If there were no Germans here the English would not have bombed us." In their flyers and on the radio the English have announced that there's more to come.

March 7, 1942

This evening I brought Oleś a package for Tadzio to take back to Poland. This time Oleś was staying in a hotel near place de la Bastille, in the red-light district. When I arrived, Oleś was not yet there. I therefore sat down in the *patron*'s "office" and waited. The fat *patronne*, proportioned like a poppy head, sat behind the desk and counted money. The *patron* lay on a couch and stroked a large, black tomcat. Meanwhile there was constant movement on the stairs and in the corridor. Couple after couple passed by and two maids in white aprons ran all over the hotel. Just like ushers in the cinema, who show each person to his seat, here the maids accompanied each couple to their love nest. One after another they dashed into the office, grabbed a room key from the board and rushed breathlessly after a pair of lovers. Figures kept flitting past the glass door

of the office and every time the door opened I caught the waft of a strong perfume. Most often Chanel No. 5, much in fashion this year among the fallen
angels, the Lorettes and harlots. (I am very fond of the term "harlot.") A young
fellow from the fire brigade in a dark blue uniform climbed the stairs, after him
a slender and modestly dressed girl. It's instantly obvious that it's about "making
love." The girl is even somewhat abashed, avoids the maid's eyes, and clings to
the wall. The fellow is blushing but puts on a good face. Can this be their first
time? That means he with her, and she with him—because what happened before? That doesn't count. *Maintenant c'est du vrai amour*[102] . . . And now the
next couple: he's thin, impeccably dressed in a long jacket reaching halfway
down his thighs, an operator. She—condensed love. Like tinned milk. A tiny
hat on the peroxided tangle of her curls, a black *tailleur* with an enormous white
camellia in the lapel. Slippers with very high heels and legs, ah, such "come-
hither" legs. Legs in constant motion as though saying: "gzz" and "wrr"—"take
me, take me" . . . The sway of her hips—a poem, the promise of a boat rocking
on the calm waves on a hot afternoon . . .

The maid rushes in and calls: "A bottle of champagne and two glasses for
number 32." The *patronne* rises lazily from her chair and feels under her belt
for the key. Digs it out and hands it to the maid. The maid returns with a bottle
of Mercier on a platter and restores the key. The clock ticks, the board with the
keys gets emptier. Fewer and fewer shiny brass keys glisten in the dull light of
the bulb. The maid pops in yet again. "They don't want champagne. Half bottle
of bubbly. *Merde* . . ." The *patronne* pulls out the key like an automaton and
mutters under her breath: "*Ça fait alors 90 francs tout compris avec la chambre.*"[103] Damn—it's cheap. Silence again. Suddenly a dark-haired guy already in
his shirtsleeves approaches the office. His suspenders hang down behind him,
he's keeping his pants up with his hands. "Once again I've got a room next to the
toilet; they flush it all night long and I can't get any sleep." The *patronne* looks at
him from under her spectacles and in the same indifferent voice summons the
maid: "*Lucie, changez la chambre, donnez le 43.*"[104]

The hotel is filling up and despite the silence you feel it pulsating and shud-
dering, like a great factory. *On y fait l'amour.*[105] Oleś arrived and I went to his
room. We chatted a bit and around eleven I left. The factory was already in
action. From behind every door sounds emerged and dissolved in the silence of
the carpeted hallways. Here the sound of slapping, there rapid breathing and
broken-off words, syllables tossed out in moments of ecstasy. Somewhere whispers and nervous laughter. A prolonged "Noooo" resounding like the yelping
of a she-wolf (don't fight it, silly girl . . .). On every floor, behind every door the
same. And down below sat the fat *patronne* counting banknotes. The *patron*,

dozing on the sofa, stroked the cat in his sleep. "G'night" and I dove into the darkness of place de la Bastille.

March 12, 1942

In the district bombed by the English on March 3 victims are still being pulled from the ruins.

Hitler gave another speech. Always the same old thing. They ought to make a recording and play it once a month. The result would be the same. This time he criticized the trial in Riom. He's not pleased that instead of seeking out and denouncing the "perpetrators" of the war, the French criticize themselves and keep searching for the causes of their defeat. He wanted Riom to show the world, and above all the Germans, that he was not the one who instigated the war, but rather such gentlemen as Daladier, Blum, and Co. Meanwhile in Riom not a single accusation has been leveled concerning the declaration of war, instead the entire debate has aimed at identifying the causes of the defeat. The Führer is beside himself. Because France insists she had no air force, that ammunition and tanks *were in the rear* and did not reach the front, that the soldiers were undisciplined, that they were short of this and that—otherwise, who knows whether the Germans would have entered Paris . . . The generals are attacking Gamelin, who remains stubbornly silent. The accusations directed at Daladier are undercut by his counterarguments, from which it emerges that Daladier wanted to do a lot, but all his intentions and organizational-administrative plans were continually being frustrated by the apathy, red tape, and deadwood of the executive organs. And Blum lets it rip and with the flair of a socialist rabbi drowns everyone in a flood of splendid phrase-making. A splendid operetta, in which the accused emerge as heroes—especially by contrast with the present French government. A cartoon has already appeared in one of the newspapers: Blum in the prosecutor's robes cries: "Will the accused Pétain rise." With the caption: "*Si on les laisse faire à Riom.*"[106] The whole trial has tanked and today all of Paris says with a laugh: "This is no accusation—it's a rehabilitation of Daladier, Blum, Gamelin, and others." And so the Führer is sulking and thrashing about and will likely soon order the trial to be discontinued. But the prank has already succeeded and now everyone takes it all merely as a malicious joke.

March 17, 1942

Once again Paris is full of Germans. Now it will get hot for the English. As of today we've been here three years and we're starting the fourth. I wonder how much we've changed, how far we've come from the worldview of our family and friends in Poland and how different they will one day find us. Because that we will be different, that our point of view will often clash, perhaps even rather harshly, with their point of view—is more than certain. In general what will happen? A question I often ask myself. I already foresee how much effort it will cost me to readapt to our Polish mentality. Today I know how much we Poles are worth, because I constantly make comparisons and this is the problem that always interests me the most, but at the same time I know, I see, and I shudder at the thought of these subtle and vile faults—unfortunate and pointless, which do us such harm. We are somewhat strange: some bizarre mixture of heroism, nobility, perseverance, and yet also thuggishness. Plus getting on our high horse at the slightest occasion. Well—circumstances have endowed us with hysterical patriotism, but since human nature is stronger and obeys its own laws, when it's time to face up, patriotic hypocrisy results. It's something I cannot bear. Our eternal plague—lack of money. Innate intelligence and mental acuity (quite dazzling compared to other nations), but on the other hand an eternal shortage of money and a gulf between desire and the possibility of satisfying it that turn every Pole into a kind of "hustler." An exalted sense of honor, innate in the worst of cads to a degree not encountered in Europe (except for Spain), requires that every "hustle" have an excuse. And here's where the fatherland comes in handy. The poor fatherland covers for everything, and whoever forgets it is a scoundrel. You earn money—for the fatherland, you go bankrupt—for the fatherland. If you're accused of something, if you're called a crook—don't forget to shout that you're a patriot. You'll be forgiven. Complete confusion of idea and substance. If a guy visited a brothel in Paris, it was for Poland; if an officer's wife hung around the barracks and competed with the French wh——s, it was also for Poland. Enough already—time to end this once and for all. Earning money should not be considered a crime. One must make demands, but one must also give. Overtime should be paid, not treated as a gift to the fatherland. But all these thoughts are for later. Perhaps I'm mistaken? Perhaps I'm wrong and I'm just another Mr. Podfilipski.[107] Better to read *The Doll*. It's still relevant.

March 18, 1942

Either this is mockery, or undue subservience toward the Germans, or complete shamelessness. The trial in Riom. General Besson testifies and says:
"*Les gens me demandaient pourquoi ils se battaient. Eh bien, j'avais du mal à leur répondre*" (*Le Matin*, March 18, 1942, p. 4).[108]
But who knows if it didn't really happen this way. The soldiers asked the

general what they were fighting for and the poor general didn't know what to tell them. And so they kept talking—this was France 1940. Perhaps they were right? Someday, when there are no longer any wars (some people believe this), who knows whether the inhabitants of the pacified globe will not consider the French of 1940 as precursors of the "New World." The French escape saved the English; instead of attacking England the Germans got drawn into France. I will write a doctoral dissertation on the subject of "The meaning and role of Parisian brothels in the decisions of the Reichswehr General Staff," and so on. I don't understand why people discuss and argue. Everything depends on one's point of view and everyone can be right. Once the Jews believed they were the chosen people, today the biggest brains pray to the proletariat as the chosen class (why such certainty?), only because a hundred years ago a bearded gentleman developed a theory of the messianic proletariat and called it "scientific." The absolute of God has been discarded and the urgent search is on for an ersatz absolute, with a fanaticism inconceivable to the most fervent participant in the Crusades. Terrible are the times in which humanity throws itself into the quest for an absolute. Józef Hoene-Wroński would today do a first-class business.[109] Why can't one live without the absolute? Until now I've managed quite well without it. And when I have to, I'll return to God. The great advantage is that God cannot be scientific or proven, which is to say, you can calmly believe. Or not. But that already depends on one's mood and state of mind. I begin to suspect that at the bottom of this war lurks a grotesque quest for the absolute and it is laughing up its sleeve. As I do now myself, in this dim bistro after three glasses of rum. Beginning with Gregory of Tours and ending with André Gide I don't give a damn about all that and beginning with the Virgin Mary and ending with Zofia Nałkowska I also don't give a damn—I'm out of here.[110] I've had enough of this cradle of culture and concentration camps called Europe, I've had enough of the quest for the absolute—I want to live, simply to live. What is the absolute compared to a girl's breast and her kiss? Rubbish. I want to talk directly with myself, not THROUGH the absolute, I want to learn to live free, FREE, without the desire to believe in anything at all, I want to be good, not because the priest or Friedrich Engels demands it, but because you should love every man, since you are yourself this creature called man.

March 20, 1942

Mr. and Mrs. P. had a few social obligations and repaid them by issuing invitations. They organized an afternoon tea party. Two days beforehand Basia went to help them arrange the apartment, or rather something that barely passed for an apartment on an ordinary day had to become an apartment fit for afternoon tea. The chests, trunks, and suitcases that normally stood in the living room ended up in the master bedroom, and in their place all movable items (*le mobilier*), representing value and money and show were dragged in from all corners of the building. Thus carpets, tapestries, crystal, paintings, and engravings, plus a few pieces of furniture—everything antique, old, precious. The china was taken from the chests in the cellar and examined, the choice falling in the end on an old English service, in which a single cup is worth five hundred francs. The drawing room was decorated from the point of view of "admire and calculate—and eat your heart out." An armchair in the Directoire style bumped against a chair in the Empire style, in reproach for a coup d'état. In the corner a sofa Louis XVI *ancien régime* strutted its stuff, and a taboret Louis-Philippe expanded broadly and comfortably, evoking those pleasant times. An old, apparently very costly painting, representing the rear end of a horse with all the details (a gelding) and the head of that same horse protruding from behind it—hung next to another painting, on which the body of an enormous sow emerges from the gloom of oil paint darkened by the greatness of the past. Underneath, a hideously shaped (at least in the ninth month) Sèvres vase stands on a small, run-down table. Elsewhere, a priceless wall hanging and on it several etchings water stained at the edge. (Without such water stains they don't count.) Chairs along the walls, each different and each from somewhere or other—expensive antiques, their innards gnawed by worms. Altogether, an antiques shop—hundreds of thousands of francs gathered in one place without taste or judgment, for the sole purpose of testifying to the affluence of the hosts. Because generally the point is not that one has something, but how much one would have if it were sold. Everything is first of all about money, and only then about the object itself. Not "how" and "what," but "how much." The object's artistic value is appreciated, but the compass pointing the way to that appreciation is almost always the price. It's the rare Frenchman who manages to regard "nonmonetarily" what he possesses and what others have. Cousin Pons is an exception.[111] Furniture, artworks, clothing—everything expresses above all a certain amount of money. This is the aspect of possession that evokes the strongest emotions. Artistic responses, enthusiasms, passion come only later. Completely and impeccably arranged, the drawing room was presented to the guests like a promissory note. Take a look and do the sums—so much and so much on the market.

When I showed up direct from work, the guests were already sitting in the drawing room and the buzz of conversation was heard through the closed door. Mme X., one of the impoverished "girlfriends" who from time to time, like

Basia, come "to help out," was hired for the day—and played the role of house-maid. I felt rather awkward because I've grown entirely unused to such social gatherings. After three years of life as a "trapper in the great city," the old days came back to me as if through a fog and I faced the task with the feeling of someone who has not played the piano for several years and now pulls up to the keyboard and begins to recall a waltz he used to know by heart. In the draw-ing room everyone was sitting in a circle (*cercle*) engaged in conversation. I sat down next to Mr. F., a seventy-four-year-old "dandy"—the owner of a large sport and hunting shop on rue L . . . and shareholder in a munitions factory in Bel-gium. At present he is ruining himself on a shopgirl, who is his mistress. Next sat the wife of an important Paris lawyer (he handles Mr. and Mrs. P.'s estate and hence this afternoon tea) and the wife of an important industrialist from Alsace who nowadays works with the Germans. He was supposed to come, but was of course detained at some conference. Mrs. P. was disconsolate, because she thought through him I might wangle myself a better position somewhere in his business. I told her that *not even she* could now make me into a bureau-crat. I prefer to be a bricklayer or tramp. For three years now I've been breath-ing freely, living, living for all it's worth. I have finally become "something" and here they are, insisting I become "someone." Both ladies were dressed in black, very modest, but elegantly and expensively—as expensive as only modest ele-gance can be, where the string of delicate pearls is real, the brooch hidden in the folds of a dress from Paquin's is entirely of diamonds, and the price of the one or two rings on carefully manicured fingers can only be imagined. Pumps from Pinet's, a little model hat from rue de la Paix.[112] Compared to this Mrs. P. looked a bit like an Indian chief, because she had adorned herself, with all the "willfulness" of her American character, with the entire contents of her strong-box. She looked like a desiccated Christmas tree, stripped of its needles, but still adorned with trinkets. I struck up a conversation with Mr. F., asking about his shop and so on. Wishing to reciprocate and learning that I was *Polonais*, he told me the history of all the orders for hunting weapons he once used to receive— from the czar and the Russian grand dukes. All this in a tone of self-satisfied courtesy: "You talk to me about me, so I'll talk to you about you." Gently, but making it very clear, I explained to him that *la Pologne* is not *la Russie* and that it's much farther from Warsaw to Tsarskoye Selo than from Paris to Versailles.[113] The poor old man lost the thread and both of us began to listen in to the story being told by the lawyer's wife, who stocks up on now hard-to-find products at charity sales, where a dozen eggs or a kilo of butter are auctioned off and thus officially reach black market prices. The auction is nothing more than a legal sale at illegal prices, the whole thing sanctioned by charity. The woman's lawyer husband, knowing German, serves as defense attorney in all trials held before the German military court. He defends people who are bound to be sentenced to death—which does not prevent him, any less than his wife, from holding the Germans in high regard and admiring them in every way. Among the wealthy and middling French bourgeois classes such admiration and respect—practically universal—arise not only from the fact that this social stratum was the easiest to convince of the "red danger" and of Germany's mission to defend the New Europe, but also from a certain kind of intellectual astonishment. Living until now, in typical French fashion, navel-gazing (and even lower down . . .), with that intellectual narrowness of views (often quite sophisticated) but restricted by the tradition of greatness, perfection, and admiration exclusively for what is French—with a slight, rather snobbish pull if at all in the direction of England—*they suddenly discover Germany*. Pétain's government assures them of continuity and the conviction that France still endures, the occupation doubled their chances of earning money, German coquetry seems to work and wins them to their side. Money allows them to avoid experiencing the same food shortages affecting the poorer classes. So far the most painful aspect of the occupation does not touch them. At the same time, *Deutsche Kultur* is presented to them from the perspective of literature in ever-new translations from the German, performances by the Berlin Opera, lectures by famous German professors, etc., etc. All this, previously unknown, is presented skillfully and tastefully, logically, as logical as only perfidy and lying can be—and it falls on fertile ground. The Germans are viewed from an "intellectual" perspective, the new ideas and socioeconomic concepts of National Socialism are like fresh air and captivate people. Snobbishly people talk about their own faults and inadequacies, comparing everything to what is done "there." Having an inferiority complex is fashionable to the point of sh—— one's own nest. It reminds one greatly of the reactions of the inhabitants of Milan after the invasion of Napoleon's army. They were not so much tired of Austrian rule as bored with it. France had gotten bored—she finds entertainment in the occupation. In Paris fashion is everything—the current fashion is for Germany. They'll get over it, they will . . . We discuss Pétain—naturally with appreciation. He alone upholds France, he is her symbol, although under his wife's piercing glance Mr. P. adds a timid bit about "the old fool." The talk moves smoothly—Mr. P. displays his talent for this kind of typically French *causerie*. He is charming. French drawing room banter often sounds like stage dialogue.

Dressed as the housemaid, Mme X. announces tea. As we sat down at table the comedy began. Everyone raised a thousand objections and a hundred thousand protests as they took each petit four, each little sandwich. *Oh, non, merci, c'est vraiment trop, enfin, j'accepte pour vous faire plaisir*, and so on, with great fuss.[114] Each morsel was offered by the hosts and forcefully pressed upon the guest, the guest would defend himself with equal force, while everyone knew perfectly well that the former would prevail and the latter give in. All of this is called *politesse* and *savoir vivre*. It was the first time I had encountered this so clearly and I had the feeling I was not in so-called good society, but had rather found myself among the ragtag, invited to the lord's table and doing everything to maintain the *bon ton* known to them from cheap fiction about the aristocracy or from a manual of proper conduct in society. That afternoon tea was torture and I was relieved when it finally ended. All along I wanted to smash a teacup (at five hundred francs) or take five sandwiches onto my plate at once. Again I confirmed that I cannot stand so-called good or elegant society. "These are entities without value constantly searching for zero—the zero that would increase their value ten times"—as the wonderful Gavarni puts it.[115] Hypocrisy in social life is the thing I find most tiresome, and I am horrified by the atmosphere of hypocrisy that predominates in "society," that is, in gatherings in which people mostly have nothing in common except envy and the desire to extract some benefit at the moment of encounter. I don't know if there's anything I can stand even less than "contacts"—paying visits for the sake of "contacts," accepting invitations for the sake of "contacts" or because "there's someone one must get to know," and so on. And yet life demands it—otherwise it's hard to get anything done. What can I do? Which is why every day of the life I'm leading here now, this amazing life untroubled by "careers," snobs, nonsense, and social titles, is as dear to my heart as the most precious treasure.

When we finally finished eating, or rather nibbling, Mrs. P. brought in a huge, carefully packaged box and extracted another box, wrapped in meters and meters of paper, from inside it, which she began to unwrap, like a mummy removed from its tomb. Finally the gathering laid eyes on a chest the size of a large travel case, covered in embossed leather, with gilt recesses. Mrs. P. opened the lid—the chest was full of chocolates from Foucher. Fifteen kilos of chocolate. Enough to last this war—and the next. Everyone uttered "ahhhhs" of appreciation and since the whole thing was too heavy to be passed around, the guests formed a line, each took a chocolate, stepped back and although insisting they would not take another, impatiently awaited their next turn. The rest of the afternoon tea proceeded around the chocolates—standing up. Mme M. recalled that the last time she had been to Mr. and Mrs. P.'s for dinner was in 1937 and asserted, with a bookkeeper's precision, that *au fond je vous dois un dîner*, while old Mr. F., saying proudly that he was born in 1868 and wanting to be *spirituel*, added: "*À un an j'ai manqué . . .*" and winked with senile frivolity.[116] This was supposed to mean that a year later it would have been sixty-nine and then his birthdate would not have lacked a certain—hmm, spice . . . The ladies pretended—how surprising!—not to understand. A few compliments for the host, a few standard and ritual turns of phrase about "the lovely tea"—and the guests went their various ways. We then threw ourselves unabashedly on the abundant remains, of course not forgetting instantly to clear the table of all the precious and delicate 150-year-old English teacups and replace them with the battered "everyday" china. I asked Mr. P. if such complicated rituals were a requirement of good breeding. He said, yes, one must refuse everything, one must even say one doesn't especially like this or that and *que ça ne me dit pas grand-chose*.[117] By nature a gourmand, like 99 percent of all Frenchmen, he finally admitted this was all dreadful, and when I told him how we did things in Poland, he listened with delight. "*Alors, j'irai en Pologne.*"[118]

How very French is the letter from Mme de Mortsauf to the young Félix de Vandenesse in Balzac's *Le Lys dans la vallée:* "Politeness, dear child, consists in appearing to forget oneself for the sake of others . . . Be neither confident, nor banal, nor zealous—three pitfalls . . . Too much confidence diminishes respect, banality earns contempt, zeal makes us easy to exploit . . . If you attach yourself to certain men more closely than to others, always be reserved, as though one day you will have them as competitors, opponents, or enemies; those are the chances of life. Maintain therefore an attitude that is neither cold nor warm, know how to find the middle ground on which a man can remain without compromising anything . . . As for zeal, that first and sublime error of youth, which finds real pleasure in exercising its powers and thus ends by becoming its own fool before becoming the fool of others. Keep your zeal for the feelings you share, keep it for women and for God. Bring neither to the marketplace of the world nor to political speculation the treasures for which you will receive baubles in exchange."[119]

Terrific. I feel as if I'm pressing my face into a great bouquet of aromatic white flowers. The brilliance of ideas does not consist in speaking about things great or small in a dry, detached, speculative way and, wanting to fathom man and life, escaping from such things into abstraction, because then words mean nothing, are but empty signs. Genuine thought succeeds in grasping and expressing what everyone feels subconsciously and is unaware of, while at the same time being conscious of what we know without knowing. And only such thought—always human—is truly authentic, persuasive, leaving an impression on the soul and changing the world. When it comes to this kind of thinking, at the same time important and authentically human, the French are unique. France produced no Hegel, Marx, or Engels, she produced no *Übermensch* and did not compose minuets of ideas over the abyss of nothingness or pirouettes of Slavic mysticism. Russia and Germany have convinced every thinking man that the more one wants to be "humanlike" or "superhuman" and the more one wants to refashion the world, being, and man with the help of the "one and only true" ideology, the more everything becomes inhuman, the more the man of flesh and blood is forgotten. The current war is a result of this forgetting, a result all the more grotesque since its purpose was the desire to find this very man. But he will not be found, as long as the word "man" is replaced by epithets fashioned by some Stakhanovites, *Schaffenden Menschen*, corporatists, and other fanatics of "-isms."[120] And therefore let's wait patiently for Descartes, who, after thirty well-armed but fruitless years searching for man amid the chaos of moribund medieval thought, succeeded in providing the world with ideas of flesh and blood. For a time he satisfied the longing for thought, that most dangerous of all longing, for which millions have perished from time to time. Oh, how much better it would have been if humanity had reserved its passions for women and God.

March 22, 1942

Today I finished repairing the bicycle. For two weeks, day after day until midnight. The *patron* has an entire workshop in his basement with a set of tools. None of the parts I bought were suitable, because in general parts are scarce and you have to take what you can find. I had to rethread the nuts and rings, the pedals, and even a new cog. I sprayed the varnish myself and the bicycle emerged as good as new. Basia complained, because for two weeks the room was piled high with screws, balls, threads, and so on. Then I took a trial run to the Bois de Vincennes. One of those marvelous Sundays of early spring. The trees are covered with buds. Silence, sun, and warmth. In the afternoon we went strolling along the Seine—to drink sunshine with wine on the terrace of a bistro, squinting our eyes, dozing in the brightness and warmth. Both of us had the expression of cats emerging from the cellar into a warm afternoon. We took long, drowsy pauses in front of the used-book stands. A book or packet of reproductions would rouse us from time to time, then we would fall back asleep. After the hard winter, the sun stunned and dazzled us. The Seine, Notre-Dame, the booksellers, the people, the trees—everything was painted not in watercolor but in water in which a bit of color had been dissolved. The white and gray arches of the church resembled the skeleton of a monster, excavated from the earth. I'm looking for the memoirs of General Comte de Marbot, but can't find them.[121] Returning home on the metro, we overhear a conversation between two conductors. They're talking across the track—one on one side, the second on the other. We hear the word "Chateaubriand" cropping up continuously in their dispute. I nudge Basia and we come closer, intrigued. Must be a literary discussion—what can people like these be saying about François-René de Chateaubriand?[122] Indeed, how deeply culture, reading, and curiosity have penetrated. We listen . . . keep listening . . . and both of us burst out laughing. Because the subject of this lively discussion was—steak à la Chateaubriand. Chateaubriand flies from mouth to mouth in the shape of a thick and bloody beefsteak. And we were thinking, that . . . Józef Wittlin, along the same lines, enthusiastically describes a conversation between two policemen about Mauriac, and in that case the subject was no doubt only about a good bottle of Montbasillac wine, and not François Mauriac.[123] And thus are forged the legends about French intelligence. While in reality at this moment Chateaubriand the writer is just as remote to them as a beefsteak. *Beefsteak*—speaking of France, one must not forget this factor, this *most important* issue in the lives of Frenchmen from the lowest to the highest. Patriotism, liberty, the fatherland? No—*beefsteak*. Thick, bloody, juicy, and tender—à la Chateaubriand. The French are waiting for the Americans. Are they waiting for liberty, freedom, independence? No. Above all for *corned beef* in tins and fruit preserves . . . Do I exaggerate? No. Théophile Gautier in his wonderful *Tableaux de siège* (the siege of Paris in 1870) writes excitedly: *"On a beaucoup vanté le courage, le dévouement, l'abnégation, le patriotisme de Paris . . . Un seul mot suffit:—Paris se passe de beurre."*[124]

Courage, devotion, resignation, patriotism attain apocalyptic proportions and even butter capitulates before them. They don't have butter, but they still fight. On your knees, O ye nations. But perhaps that's right? Perhaps one shouldn't die as recklessly as us Poles—not only without butter, but without water and bread? We were always so ready to sacrifice ourselves (in the name of foreign interests) that, for example, the French are convinced it's easier for us to die than for them. *Vous avez l'habitude.*[125] It's not at all certain that it's hard to die for one's country. Sometimes it's a lot harder to live for one's country. For example, to live for it, even without butter . . .

The metro rumbles and stops at the stations. The breezy dresses of the women entering the car bring with them snatches of sunlight. Up above, it's already spring. SPRING . . . oof . . .

March 24, 1942

The fronts are quiet, nothing new anywhere. The weather is splendid. The English and Americans deserve to be called "Allies." They are the allies of Russia in the same sense that Austria was Germany's ally in the First World War. They are helping Russia win the war and the logical result is that after the war they will have as much say as—any mere assistant. This war is at bottom a war between Russia and Germany, all others are extras in this bloody performance and no more than that. K. and I were considering all this today and we came to the conclusion that there's no reason to harbor any illusions. In a dozen years Kaiser Willy's *die gelbe Gefahr* will have come to pass.[126] K. is right. He said to me today: "Hitler's greatest crime is the betrayal of the white race and the incitement of fratricidal war among us." And he added: "So, dear Andrzej— better to bid farewell to Europe beforehand. Because, you see—under Franz Joseph..."[127] And we began to laugh the bitter laugh of people who understand and perceive reality.

March 25, 1942

The English have returned and are destroying factories on the outskirts of Paris. New posters keep appearing on the walls, inviting people to go work in Germany. The most recent poster shows a sad, unemployed worker, looking through the window of his miserable shack into the distance, where on the horizon you see a splendid factory, sunshine, and brightness. The caption: "If you want to earn more money, go work in Germany." Most of these posters have been improved by local artists who draw airplanes and the bombs they drop onto the factory on the horizon. With this addition a caption such as, "if you want to earn more . . . ," acquires an extra and enticing meaning. Other posters with the caption, "Go work in Germany—your family will be happy," get an added note: "and you'll be a cuckold" (*Allez travailler en Allemagne—votre famille sera heureuse—et toi cocu*).

March 26, 1942

Today we went to "our" cinema. The French film *Mam'zelle Bonaparte*, set during the Second Empire.[128] If all branches of production in France are in trouble, film is flourishing. German films flood the market and squeeze in everywhere, but the French don't give in and keep up with them in terms of quantity—and outdo the Germans in terms of quality. Nearly all French films produced after the armistice are good, or if not entirely good, then at least watchable. They are refreshing, full of the French *je ne sais quoi*, finesse and attitude, delicacy and subtlety joined with truth about humanity.

Pagnol's latest film, *La Fille du puisatier*, with Raimu is wonderful.[129] Full of humor, entirely specific, and incomprehensible without knowing France even a bit, full of goodwill and the sunshine of Provence—of life there in the south, which has a very special color and tone. Another film, this from the French Alps, *L'Assassinat du père Noël*, is a fairy tale perched always on the border between fantasy and reality, spun out against the background of life in a small village, blanketed and buried in the snows of the Haute-Savoie.[130] *Le Joueur d'échecs*, after Dostoyevsky, with Pierre Blanchar, is full of that demonic mood, light, and terrific images that make your flesh creep.[131] A "grand piano" film, *Nuit de décembre*, also with Pierre Blanchar, though not a complete success, is certainly good.[132] The recent film about the life of Berlioz is said to be musically much better. A return to the years 1820–1850, the reversion of a public exhausted and stupefied by the New Europe to the tastes of a bygone Europe, one of the most beautiful Europes of all. There is *La Dame aux camélias* with Edwige Feuillère in the Théâtre Hébertot, for which the seats sell out three weeks in advance, also the film *La Duchesse de Langeais*, after Balzac, in which she stars, and today's *Mam'zelle Bonaparte*, also with Edwige Feuillère.[133] A version of the *Lady of the Camellias* and the public pushes down the doors. German films have to be shown and are not "a draw." Only the films of Willy Forst have any success—*Bel Ami* played endlessly—but then Willy Forst is a master craftsman, practically French, since he's Austrian. The kinship of cultures closest to each other affects the French viewer automatically.

Today we settled into our seats in the cinema and after watching the newsreels from the front lines, during which the audience always have terrible colds and cough a lot, and at the sight of "the big shots" cough even harder and get so hoarse that everyone has to clear their throats, we dove into the era of Napoleon III. The film is good and interesting—but—at the most interesting moment the lights went on and—alarm. The English have flown over. Everyone began to exit, dawdling, arguing with the ushers and making jokes *à propos*. But when it turned out the tickets could be saved and tomorrow the same tickets be used for the rest of the film, the crowd dispersed peacefully. On the streets illuminated by the clear, silvery light of the moon, silence and peace. A night perfect for love and for an air raid. And tomorrow we'll go for the rest of the film. No one can tell me life isn't grand.

March 27, 1942

The Riom Trial has been turned completely on its head. The outcome was entirely different than intended. Too bad—they were not trained in Moscow. The occupying scumbags are frantic. Today people are already asking outright *si c'est un procès de la France ou un procès français.*[134] The trial leads to only one conclusion: Daladier and Gamelin were heroes and honorable men. Although they knew France was not prepared, they declared war in order to keep their word and honor their treaties of alliance. Now people are already saying that the trial will be called off. It doesn't matter, because one way or the other it's all lies. Some of the witness testimonies are nevertheless interesting. A certain colonel, in typical French fashion, characterized the French army of 1940 as *un troupeau et non des troupes.*[135] A levée en masse without weapons in their hands and with weapons in the rear that never made it to the front lines. A bit of truth has been spoken there nonetheless and it will be a shame when this operetta comes to an end.

March 29, 1942

On the night of March 27 to 28 the English attacked Saint-Nazaire in a perfect example of the art of troop landing. À la Zeebrugge in the last war. They even came ashore, fought for a few hours, entered the city, destroyed the submarine installations in the port, hoisted their flag on the town hall, and returned to England.[136] Sensational. A thousand rumors make the rounds on this subject. One thing is for sure, namely that the population of Saint-Nazaire helped the English and that severe retaliatory measures have been taken against all of Saint-Nazaire. But the newspapers say that Saint-Nazaire has proven that the French shores *sont inexpugnables.*[137] Quite right.

April 4, 1942

Two heavy bombardments in a row on the second and third. You can hear the terrible explosion of bombs somewhere outside Paris, the antiaircraft artillery is going crazy, the English are flying over Paris and buzz like furious wasps, and bomb fragments bang on the roofs. This time they pulverized the Matford[138] plant in Poissy on the far outskirts of Paris.

April 5, 1942

Easter. We're staying home and gorging on holiday treats. Mrs. P. has gone to Brittany and we're left in peace. Today we're off to Lola's—tomorrow there's a small party at our place, which means the reverse: Lola and Janka come here. This is now our fourth Easter in Paris. I'm sitting in my armchair and for the fourth time in my life trying to make it to the end of Tolstoy's *War and Peace.*

(four in the morning, the night of April 5 to 6)

Alarm. The English have arrived. For the last half hour there's been one continuous rumble. Deep booms, arriving from farther away, bass tones dull as thunder—that's a series of bombs. Short and quick, staccato, that's flak. In moments of silence you hear the buzz of airplanes sometimes flying over our heads. In the hotel no one sleeps, but neither is anyone eager to go to the cellar or the metro. The only sound is the continual slamming of the toilet door. Such a shooting spree helps marvelously with the digestion. During the holidays this is even advisable. Every time the shots come closer, our neighbor on the other side of the wall cries "aye." She conducts an energetic antilove defense, speaking at the tempo of a twenty-millimeter field gun. Because Maurice takes advantage of the English raids and immediately starts to descend on his Jane. Except at mealtimes, he executes his raids relentlessly and at every opportunity. She calls out incessantly, *"ça me fait mal"*—and gives in.[139]

Almost five o'clock and silence has descended. It's a moonlit night, clear enough to read by. The English are returning and work steadily. Again, one continuous rumble. Paris is surrounded by flak—the Germans wised up after the raid on Renault. As the English fly over, the field guns can be heard somewhere in the distance and then one boom after another. As in a duck hunt. Basia opened a window and said: "The Jews and the Freemasons have flown away— we can sleep."

April 6, 1942

They've bombarded Gnome et Rhône in Gennevilliers and the Goodrich plant in Colombes.[140] Everyone now says the English and Americans will land in France this year. If they don't land, in any case they've created a pretty good distraction.

April 9, 1942

Today I'm speeding on my bike down rue Saint-Honoré and about to cross rue de la Paix when I practically run down a phenomenally elegant lady. I brake so suddenly that I almost fall over. I take a look. Jacqueline Delubac in all her magnificence.[141] Fabulous legs in super high-heeled pumps, ash-gray suit with a long jacket (ash gray as well as long—the last word in fashion), on her head a high, elaborately pinned-up pale green silk turban—the whole thing a work of art. But in the empty and rundown rue de la Paix that beautiful and well-dressed woman looked rather sad. As sad as a gold tooth in an empty jaw.

April 10, 1942

Enough! Tolstoy's wife must have had an iron constitution. Seven times she copied over what I cannot read through even once. *War and Peace* is certainly a terrific piece of work, but enough! I cannot stomach anything Russian. I'm ashamed to admit, but there's such a fundamental anti-Russianness inside me, if you can call it that, that I cannot get this book down my gullet. It repels me. My only consolation is that Joseph Conrad, when asked if he had read *War and Peace*, would apparently mumble something unintelligible, suggesting, that yes, but only "in translation," although he knew Russian well. So, as for me, neither the original, nor in translation. It's alien to me, completely alien, repulsively alien, almost an obsession.

Somewhere in *War and Peace* Tolstoy considers the causes of the war and comes to the conclusion—perhaps very "eastern," but who knows if it's not closest to the truth—that the war had to break out, that war is like a ripe apple, which at a certain moment falls to the ground. The botanist will say it had to fall because it was ripe. That the fall occurred as a result of the stem drying out. The physicist will say that the fall was caused on the one hand by gravity, on the other hand by the branch shaking in the wind. Someone else will say a greedy boy knocked it down with a stone. And they all will be right. But in the end the apple would fall because it had to fall—independent of external reasons, of which there might be thousands, of which each certainly contributed to the fall but was not the exclusive instigator of the fall. Because the fall was the result of everything—the result of ripening and the unavoidable consequence of this fundamentally intangible process.

Reflecting on this war, it seems to me that nevertheless its main cause was the greedy and foolish, mentally underdeveloped boy-Hitler, who knocked the apple down with a stone. Yes, ripening, intangible processes, and so on—but a personal decision, the decision of a single man played the fundamental role. Perhaps even more so than in the case of Napoleon. Will this war thus lead not only to an economy of distribution and consumption but also to an economy in the service of MAN? To the creation of a system of the whole, and not merely one sector, or a fragment? Because it's in such things above all that "ripening" is concealed in today's world, things that are exposed to the stones of insufferable greedy boys (world fixers), who hypnotize the half-baked intelligentsia of the Bouvards and Pécuchets, people who get their wisdom from brochures.[142] If the victorious Anglo-Saxon world turns in on itself once again in egotistical, short-sighted gestures, if in defending its own world and its "feeling for life" (according to Frobenius, culture is the feeling for life), it does so not in order to create something new and great, more human and brighter than its opponent—

culturally Russia is the opponent of the Anglo-Saxon "feeling for life"—and if this Anglo-Saxon world once again gets bogged down in half-measures, then in fifteen years there will be another slaughter that's even worse.[143] Then the apple will truly ripen and war "will have to" come.

April 11, 1942

Laval is in Vichy and is negotiating with Pétain. It looks like the Germans want to impose him on the government, so he can help extract even more from France. At the same time, other sell-outs like Doriot, Déat, and others travel around giving lectures and writing in the newspapers that the final hour has tolled: France must either choose collaboration or forfeit her last chance at salvation.[144] Huge to-do. The public considers Laval a traitor and waits to see what will come of these negotiations in Vichy. Again it's said the Germans will demand mobilization, the fleet, and so on. Radio Paris is filled with ideas of collaboration. Such a fuss has never before been made on this subject. The Germans must really be depending on France.

A sunny, spring Sunday. We went to the Luxembourg Gardens and sat in the armchairs—and simply sat. I have recently been attaching great importance to such things as "simply to sit," "simply to walk," "simply to eat," and "simply to s——." It's not clear that in the future world man will be able to allow himself any kind of "simply." Freedom . . . I feel almost physically how its territory is diminishing day by day, how the *peau de chagrin* is shrinking. Actually, *de chagrin*. Today this is the greatest anxiety for all seekers after the absolute, absolute happiness, absolute equality. Next to us sat a well-dressed older couple—from the "upper" crust—and she was reading aloud to him. *L'Histoire de l'armée allemande*, by Jacques Benoist-Méchin.[145] One of the recently fashionable books among Paris intellectuals. Anyway, it's really terrific and I read it in one fell swoop. From across the way we heard the splash of the fountain, at our side the monotonous voice of the elderly lady reading the book with a superb accent—French must "age" in a family like wine in the cellar—from time to time a sparrow, living without coupons and without lines, whirring under our noses, the crunch of the gravel under the feet of passersby . . . I closed my eyes halfway and savored the repose, calm, and tranquillity all around us. Stretching myself in my armchair I felt so completely relaxed that I seemed to be reaching boulevard Saint-Michel with my head and rue de Fleurus, on the other side of the park, with my feet.

And I was thinking. I was thinking that since reserves, national parks, are created for animals, because we are concerned to prevent, if only on a limited terrain, the disappearance of bison, bear, and reindeer, it would be high time to think about creating some reserves for free people, reserves of freedom. Because the man who wants truly to be free, who truly loves that most beautiful of all creations—freedom, is now becoming as rare as the bison or reindeer. He is hunted at all seasons and with the help of ever more refined weapons, or put in the modern reserves and national parks known as concentration camps. He is being exterminated at every step of the way—*in the name of freedom.* This is perhaps the best joke of all. It often seems to me that things began to go bad for freedom from the moment it began to be fabricated all over the place, when anyone at all, in thousands of fly-by-night distilleries, began to bootleg this splendid drink in any which way and as much as possible. And the result was "booze," an awful moonshine, used to make the millions drunk, while persuading them it's the real thing. Ask the twentieth-century man you encounter on the street how he imagines freedom. He begins with the words: "First you must eliminate and exterminate, imprison and neutralize . . ." Every program for freedom begins today with the slammer and the gallows, places of confinement and the hunting of a certain category of human mammals. That's fine—it's logical. What's more, understandable and appropriate. And then there will be freedom. What kind, damn it? Freedom for whom? For the slaves of "freedom," for the galley slaves. Only on Sunday will it be permitted to sh—— "simply," and not for a political party, for the happiness of future generations that are "already free," for the fatherland, for one's mother, and for mother-f—— freedom.

After a time we continued on, through the entire park, and stopped into one of the cafés on place de l'Observatoire for so-called ice cream. Then a long stroll down boulevard Montparnasse, rue de Rennes as far as Saint-Germain-des-Prés. Sunny, warm, concierges sit and do their knitting in doorways still emitting a winter chill. At their feet cats weave around like soft yarn, and here and there birds in cages suspended from the window handles rock back and forth. Observing them makes me think that in order to feel free people need the sight of something confined. In contrast to the bird in the cage these people feel free. In contrast to the millions of people perishing today in German and Soviet camps, I feel free. "By contrast" a person can be persuaded that sh—— is caviar. The acceptance of life by millions of people is today accomplished "by contrast." "By contrast" one can do anything with a person and—it's being done. Contrast—is the most up-to-date weapon of all modern ideologies, the perfect tool. Deprive of liberty one man in ten, decimate the group—and the remaining nine will feel free and bless life. With conviction. Will let themselves be torn apart or imprisoned.

Polish communiqués from London. One shouldn't mouth off in this situation (contrast—by contrast) but the blood boils. They've learned nothing. The radio announcer reporting naval battles never knows the difference and does not distinguish a battleship from a cruiser and an antitorpedo boat from a torpedo boat. The news bulletins teach you absolutely nothing, because they are produced by some incompetent bureaucratic slacker whom reality does not touch. Specific information about Polish forces (I would call them Polish weaknesses—the army, the military—these are Polish weaknesses)—not to mention the overall situation—can often be gleaned from English or even French communiqués but not from ours. Because ours provide fragments of plays, sermons, and other such nonsense and tall tales instead of brief and intelligent overviews. Obviously they will offer Poland to us on a platter, nicely garnished, because that's how someone over there fancies it. Patriotic weeping, sniveling, sobs, groans and moans. In Poland people are really suffering (not pretending as in France and places where the only ones who suffer are those who want to), but the radio provides weepy religious sermons and neutered information, that for example Alfred Falter represented Poland at the economic conference in Washington, which debated the organization of the postwar world.[146] A nice adviser for postwar organization. Tears. In Poland even this cheap item is now out of stock. But we love to cry cheaply.

April 14, 1942

Tension in Vichy has reached a peak. This morning when I came to the office, everyone was whispering among themselves that Pétain had absconded to Africa with a part of the government, that Laval had remained and all of France would surrender completely to the Germans. *Nous serons comme la Pologne . . .*[147] I couldn't believe it. How come? Is it possible that Pétain has finally decided to abandon the politics of *leur petit bonheur*—he who signed the armistice for the sake of that *petit bonheur*, instead of escaping to Africa right away and creating Free France there? The French were terrified. What will happen? Indeed—they want freedom, they do not want the Germans, but God forbid they sacrifice any of their *petit bonheur*. Let others do everything instead of them, they have already done enough for humanity. They want to work only on the day shift. I went around drunk with joy. Such trouble for the Germans as a result of this flight of Pétain's . . . Alas—in the evening it turned out that Laval came to an agreement with the old fogy, has entered the government *et tout s'est arrangé très bien.*[148] That's most important. The French have already adapted, each of them has managed somehow or other to settle in, make his own bed, arrange *sa petite vie*, including Saturday and Sunday—and all within a hair's breadth of everything going to the devil. But thank the Lord—*heureusement, parce que, pensez-vous . . . on souffre déjà assez et encore . . . rendez-vous compte seulement de ce que ça serait . . .*[149] It makes me want to puke.

April 16, 1942

This afternoon I join Mr. P. at Gare Montparnasse and we await the arrival of his wife. She's returning from Brittany laden with provisions and we are supposed to ease her passage through the inspection and the "octroi," dividing the suitcases among ourselves.[150] It's the first time since the flight from Paris that I've been here and walking along the platform I recall the hell of June 1940. Amazing what went on here . . . Now the sun is shining, it's quiet, and Gare Montparnasse resembles a station "somewhere in the beastly boondocks."[151] All of France, all of Europe, is today "the beastly boondocks." From the Volga to the Pyrenees everyone is being beastly. Mr. P. tries to *soutenir la conversation,*[152] which isn't working, and utters endless words and dozens of ideas, purely for the sake of making talk. Porters dressed in blue uniforms trail along the platform, lazily pushing their carts and smoking pipes, shooting thin threads of saliva between the rails. The train is obviously delayed, like all trains these days. Finally it pulls in and the clamor begins. In one of the windows we spot Mrs. P., a beret perched on her head, summoning us with her bony arms. With typical Anglo-Saxon disdain for other nations she had brushed aside a bunch of "those Frenchmen" and began to pass along the suitcases, arguing with her competitors in a dialect little resembling English and even less French. She leaned toward me and, in a whisper no doubt audible as far as Montmartre, said conspiratorially: *"Fet attenshn, say plen duf . . . ,"* which in the language of Rotondo-Rotondi was supposed to mean "Attention, it's full of eggs." With the motion of an old guards grenadier, she emerged from the carriage and after noisy greetings we made for the exit. Everyone was loaded down and accompanied by extras carrying the suitcases. We pass through the slapdash inspection and go directly to the "octroi" office. There's already a long line. Each one declares a modest dozen eggs and a pound of butter (the amount allowed), while having five or six pounds of it, pork fat, meat—an entire grocery store. Mrs. P. had transported seven hundred eggs and a quantity of other items. I struggle under the weight of two suitcases. Two years of fasting have left their mark and I'm now no longer in condition to juggle heavy cases as I used to do. I'm ashamed to admit it and make a superhuman effort somehow to haul them to the metro. In any case by the time I got home I no longer felt my arms. But supper is splendid. An omelet with more than enough eggs. Mrs. P. talks about Brittany, about that most patriotic, that is to say, pro-English corner of France. Soon true patriotism will consist in being pro-Russian, pro-American, or pro-English. To maintain even a part of one's own nationality, it will be necessary to accept another one, entirely and uncritically. The population of Brittany lives in expectation. Thanks to Mrs. P.'s American accent, the farmers gave her everything she desired. Every night one hears the sounds of bombing, the glow reddens the sky. The Bretons are playing hide and seek with the Germans and hide everything they can. The traditions of the Chouans have survived there, the survival of an attitude more dignified than in the rest of France.[153] "*On était trop heureux,*" as people now say who have truly grasped what has happened.[154] Because in general France is like Gare Montparnasse before the arrival of a train — waiting for the train that brings provisions — but also freedom.

April 18, 1942

Laval has formed a new government consisting exclusively of his own supporters or leading collaborators. *Eine kleine aber nette Gesellschaft.*[155] Pétain remains *chef d'État,* Darlan is commander of the armed forces of land, sea, and air. Well, and all of them together are undertaking the regeneration of France following the rules of art of National Socialism. Large posters in the style *das III Reich* promote reproduction (in the absence of entertainment and other forms of birth control this might succeed); young people march through the streets singing; "*l'Empire Français*" is written everywhere instead of "*la France*" — in a word, the more colonies they lose, the more there's talk of *l'Empire.* Meanwhile, the "Empire" has surrendered Indochina to the Japanese; the English are in Syria; Tahiti and other islands, including Martinique, are under American protection; and very shortly the English will take Madagascar. And what will remain of the "Empire"? But the operetta could not be doing better.

April 21, 1942

The English have created a distraction behind the lines, which was successful. Today London said the Germans have transferred part of their forces in the east to France and entrusted the command of these forces to Marshal von Rundstedt.[156] And indeed — for a few days now Paris has again been full of Germans. Again they set up house in the best hotels, and parking spots with signs "*Nur für deutsche Wagen*"[157] have once more filled up after several months being empty. Occasionally, with a great boom and crash a platoon of Renault 7 tanks moves through the city and rumors fly that Paris is being fortified. But these are just rumors. By contrast, the concierges are all saying that the English will certainly attack Madagascar and so there must be something to it. I never disregard the information of concierges because they always know best. The great military and offensive preparations of the so-called democracies are supposedly secret, but everyone typically knows about them two months in advance. With the concierges it's three months.

April 27, 1942

Hitler gave a speech. A bit different than usual. London commented pointedly: "We were waiting to see who Hitler would launch his spring offensive against—England, or Russia—meanwhile he has launched it against his own people." The speech was very firm. It leaves the impression that after two and a half years of war something in Germany has begun to break down, that some kind of fatigue and apathy has set in, that in certain cases even people in high positions have begun to resist the iron discipline. And the Führer reacted by demanding absolute authority from the Reichstag. Perhaps now he can send even Marshal Keitel and all his other marshals to the place from which no one returns.[158] He's the master of everyone's life and death, as was incisively and unequivocally affirmed by Hermann Göring in his closing speech to the Reichstag. As befits the twentieth century. *Tout va pour le mieux dans ce meilleur des mondes.*[159]

April 28, 1942

Hitler's speech has made an enormous impression. London carries on about it in every possible way, in all languages, and in every communiqué. In a word, victory's around the corner. The same in Paris: everyone says that something's amiss, that something in Germany is crumbling, and that not long from now ... Very short-sighted. I say nothing to anyone about this, because I would obviously be taken for a bad Pole, but everybody keeps making one mistake, always the same one: they underestimate German power, certainly by now quite weakened, but still very great. They do not consider the possibility that the war may end with the use of an entirely different weaponry than the one it began with, they do not take into consideration technology and inventions. What are the Germans cooking up? The combustion engine is basically as much of a relic as the piston steam engine, which has already been replaced everywhere today by the steam turbine that vastly increases the number of RPMs. A few years before the war Opel had already conducted experiments with rocket-propelled airplanes; the Germans have always been leaders in technology. England's potential has been overestimated; it's in fact nothing compared to America, which is only now beginning to complete prototypes and put manufacture on full throttle. On the Anglo-Saxon side nothing but preliminaries that are still incomplete. And then there's—Russia. If not for Russia, I really don't know who would be fighting the Germans and tearing away at them. And for that we'll have to pay through the nose. As yet nothing's been heard of the great German offensive that everyone is anxiously awaiting. Will the Germans pull it off, or will they have to spend another winter over there? But there's hope in the air that the war will end this year for sure. There are even some who are celebrating already, in advance.

April 30, 1942

The *Mémoires du Général Comte de Marbot* are terrific.[160] Despite everything, how much gentlemanliness in the mutual slaughter. Wellington's operation in Portugal consisted of boarding ship and turning tail each time the French went on the offensive, disembarking and marching into battle each time the French decided to retreat. In all of this only the Portuguese were actually fighting and letting themselves be slaughtered—for the sake of the English. The English operation in Portugal depended essentially on making sure Marshal Masséna's corps always had a few English officers on the side, who would ride up very close, pull a notebook out of their pockets, and at a distance of a few feet calculate and record the condition of the corps.[161] And it was never possible to catch them because they were mounted on full-blooded racehorses, which the ordinary French cavalry horses could not overtake. The entire operation of the English in Egypt until now has consisted of such Wellington-style movements back and forth at the head of almost exclusively foreign divisions.

May 3, 1942

A few days ago I managed to buy a women's bicycle on sale. This morning we went to the Bois de Vincennes for the first lesson. A sunny spring day, with pleasant gusts of wind. After fifteen minutes of being supported, Basia began to ride on her own, after an hour she had learned to mount and dismount. We sat in the sun. I then rode home, picked up some bread, cheese, and wine, and returned to the park. We ate nestled together, because the wind had gotten chilly, and then we rode together along the avenues and paths. And we were very happy.

May 4, 1942

Now I'm shopping for bicycle parts, because I want to fix up Basia's crate. I can't find anything anywhere and have to look all over to find something at all.

Today I went to a bicycle supply shop near Porte de Versailles. In the shop were two German soldiers—one of them an older guy, the other perhaps nineteen or twenty years old. They were trying to buy an electric flashlight. It was hard going, because they couldn't communicate with the Frenchman, and when the merchant began to explain that he couldn't sell them a lightbulb because he had none, they understood not a word, kept demanding a bulb, and refused to leave the shop. Although I never do this, today I was in a hurry and decided to put a stop to the endless misunderstanding. I explained in German what was going on, that the bulbs for their type of flashlight were simply unavailable, but if they took a French-produced flashlight they would get the full set and spare parts. They were very pleased, immediately bought the most expensive flashlight—the Frenchman warmed up to me on the spot—and they began to chat. How did I come to speak such good German, I didn't seem to be French. No—I'm Polish, from Cracow, but born in Wiener-Neustadt. They were both startled. The older one, delighted, grabbed my arm and cried: "*Dann sind Sie mein Landsmann. Ich bin ja auch aus Wiener-Neustadt und der Junge ist aus Baden.*"[162] Compatriots—I swear! They engaged me in conversation about Vienna, how did I end up in France, was I in the army. I say, no. "*Na, na—sollen Sie glücklich sein . . .*"[163] The conversation becomes ever more intimate, they ask if the Poles in France are being persecuted. I say, not so far, but he should know what's happening in Poland. "*Ja—das ist ganz einfach schamlos,* but do you think in Austria it's any better?"[164] Everyone has to work, even the infirm are forced to work, his mother has to work although she can hardly walk, though he's in the army. *Schauen Sie sich das an . . .*[165] He lifts his cap and shows me his gray hair. He is fifty-four. He begins to curse the war, Hitler, everything. "*Und denken Sie wie viel das kostet, diese verrückte Spielerei . . . und wozu, warum . . . weil der sogenannte Führer von Anfang an ein Idiot wurde . . .*"[166] I give them a wink and, not wanting to get deeper into the discussion, quickly say good-bye. They almost embrace me, are genuinely moved. Me too.

After supper an excursion on our bicycles. A nice ride along the avenues fragrant with young growth, drowsing in the silent end of a day in the German era.

It's already May and the Germans have not yet launched their offensive. The great and decisive offensive.

May 5, 1942

This morning the mood is tense—a quadrille of rumors and commentary. The English have attacked Madagascar, landed in Diego Suarez. So, the concierges were right. An official communiqué has already appeared in the evening papers about the "cowardly English attack on the French possessions and the heroic defense by the garrison at Diego Suarez." At least that. I was afraid the French would hand it over to the Japanese.

May 10, 1942

This morning we rode down to the Marne. A warm, sunny day—as busy along the Marne as on the promenade in Cannes. All the places to rent boats, kayaks, sailboats, and canoes were open, the riverside bistros and *guinguettes*[167] bustled, and the patter of conversation mingled with the music of the gramophone; on the terraces and in the street lots of women and girls in shorts, men in white trousers, and a crowd of cyclists heading in both directions. Laughter, songs, commotion. As in the good old days. We rode quite far along the banks of the Marne, sat ourselves down across from some hills and a compact mass of greenery as dark as the landscapes of Courbet, and again we felt happy.

Returning, we wandered through the small villages on the outskirts of Paris, as provincial as though they were hundreds of kilometers from the city. For some reason, you relax here better than at any time anywhere else. In France, even in Paris, there's no sense of anxiety. Sunday is Sunday, everyone tries to make the most of it as best they can, without concern for others. Live and let live and you'll be left in peace.

This evening Churchill gave a speech. As usual, optimistic, except that he warned the Germans not to use gas. There's been a lot of talk lately about gases and you could get the impression that the Germans might be intending to use them. In addition he said that England's situation in 1940 was quite critical but that obviously since then much had changed, that there would be this and that—broad-ranging preliminaries, in which America plays the main role, while allowing the Japanese to take whatever they please. But you have to have faith.

May 11, 1942

Sentenced in January in Senlis to pay a fine, my S. once already applied to have it annulled. Now again an inquiry and an *enquête* have arrived at his commissariat of police. The commissariat sent him a summons, I went with him, and the case once more set sail on the calm ocean of the French bureaucracy. It will sail for two, three months and return—and then I will launch it again into open water.

After the visit to the commissariat we strolled in the vicinity of place Clichy and ended up in a bistro on the square. The early evening hour, bustle, tables crowded with girls waiting for clients. One of them, older and heavily made-up, sat down next to us. I don't know if there's anything more repulsive, and at the same time worthy of pity, than a prostitute at the end of her career. Her face, her entire appearance, is worn, crumpled, and exhausted. All the more terrible for being concealed beneath thick lipstick, gaudy clothes, and grim smiles. It's obvious with what effort and desperation she clings to what once was, clings to her past, trying to turn it into the present. In the blink of an eye the thought entered my head: "This is France." Then I felt ashamed and tried to see in her only what she once had been. She signaled to the garçon and he took an empty glass from another table and placed it in front of her. She will be able to sit for an hour or two, until someone winks at her or sits down next to her, pays the waiter for the aperitif she has not drunk, the waiter will pocket the entire sum, and the client orders another round. Then the two of them will go to one of the countless little hotels near rue Biot, Lemercier, or Nollet. Perhaps no one will fancy her today . . . so just in case, she smiles my way, narrows her shiny eyes, and flutters her barbed-wire false eyelashes. She wears no stockings, and her bare, withered, and unpainted legs have the color of boiled fish. Warm spring rain began to drum on the canvas awning over the terrace and it grew dark. The red neon signs lit up. And we sipped our saccharine Grenache.

May 12, 1942

The Germans have launched the offensive at Kerch. Of course, they are advancing.

May 14, 1942

The Germans are proclaiming victory and the seizure of Kerch, Timoshenko is beginning the attack at Kharkov.[168] This evening we were returning from town by metro and in an overcrowded car someone sprayed sneezing powder. Everyone began to sneeze uncontrollably and to laugh at the sight of three German soldiers hopping about in paroxysms of sneezing. Someone at the back of the car yelled: "Put on your gas masks—a gas attack has begun." The three got out at the next station. The whole car shook with laughter, rocked by universal, good-humoredly wicked laughter.

May 20, 1942

It's a massacre at Kharkov, but neither side has advanced. The Germans claim this is the greatest battle in the history of the world and of the current war and they will win it. Moscow says she will not lose. While the English are watching and commenting on the radio.

I sometimes feel I'm too happy and will have to pay for it. Then I recite to myself softly *Der Ring des Polikrates*.[169] But I don't finish because it's too dreary. I prefer to whisper in French: *"Qu'est-ce que tu veux—c'est la vie. Quand ça va bien, il faut en profiter et c'est tout."*[170]

The weather's turned bad and we're staying home. I'm reading Bainville's *Histoire de deux peuples*.[171]

May 26, 1942

Darré, Reichsminister for food, has submitted his resignation.[172] The Führer put him on indefinite leave.

May 30, 1942

A noisy night. The English were finishing up at Colombes and Gennevilliers outside Paris.

May 31, 1942

Sensational. A thousand English airplanes have bombarded Cologne and the Ruhr. The Germans complain that even the cathedral was damaged, but the news might cause one to rejoice and regret only that the entire cathedral did not crumble into dust. This is the best demonstration of the degree to which *Großdeutschland* has managed to turn us into cultured people. When I watch the artistic short subjects in the cinema, showing the beauty of Regensburg or some other German city slumbering in Gothic calm (there are many such shorts lately), my single most vivid reaction is the thought of how nice it would be if it were all reduced to ashes, while Cossacks, drunk on *echt kölnisches Wasser 4711*,[173] danced on the ruins. And it's only the thought that this might easily happen, but on our own ruins, that cools my ardor a bit.

The Russians have said that another two or three victories like Kharkov and the war will be over. And in Paris it's springtime. And although everything is increasingly harder to come by, there have never been as many so elegantly and fashionably dressed women and as many new bicycles, which are also in fashion. There are lines in front of the cinemas, the cafés are full, prices keep rising, but everyone is living and somehow has money. Clearly, this year the war will end. Perhaps . . .

June 1, 1942

Le Matin of May 21, 1942, in a short article called *"Les visées soviétiques en Europe,"* writes: *". . . les Soviets désiraient occuper Trondheim, Bergen et Norvich avec leur hinterland."*[174] The French language has lately been enriching itself at an amazing rate. *"Hinterland"* has now joined the words *"le Führer," "la Wehrmacht," "la Luftwaffe," "un Ausweis," "la Kommandantur," "le Militärbefehlshaber."*[175]

In addition, it was announced today that as of June 8, the Jews throughout occupied France must wear a yellow star on their left breast.[176] They will receive the stars in their local police commissariats in exchange for two points on their fabric ration cards. These two points on their fabric ration cards have driven me almost insane. The French smile sympathetically. When you are in need of the French and want to encourage their cooperation, you really must have a screw loose to issue such a decree in order to show off before the nation that despite everything did produce the Declaration of the Rights of Man and to this day is imbued with it. Tragic, repugnant, and hopeless.

June 2, 1942

A letter from Hanka—a real one, uncensored. Too real. I read it over and over and am ashamed that I could have filled five notebooks just with nonsense. Here two idyllic years, there two years of something you can't call a life. One such letter is enough. I translated it into French and show it to trusted Frenchmen with a brief commentary.

June 5, 1942

A big to-do about Libya, where the Germans have launched another offensive, and about the murder of Heydrich in Czechoslovakia.[177] The great Battle of Kharkov has ended in a draw. Laval rules in Vichy and has strangled the trial in Riom.

June 7, 1942

All the same, under Franz Josef those were the good old times.

June 8, 1942

The latest sensation: Radio London is ordering the population to evacuate the French coast as far south as the Pyrenees. They're making a big deal over their plans to hit the shore. The French are pleased, no one talks about anything except the Anglo-American landing, a second front, and dancing on July 14 with the "Tommies" to the sounds of "Tipperary." All this is nevertheless a well-staged comedy, designed to tickle the Germans in the back. They will indeed be landing, though the Germans will already be gone. But there's no harm in playing around a bit and having some fun.

June 9, 1942

The English landing is nevertheless causing the French some trouble. What then will happen with their vacations? Half of Paris is preparing to spend the summer in Brittany, because it has the most butter, eggs, and milk, and now the English are becoming quite threatening. One of the women in the office was until yesterday a fervent patriot, which means pro-English, a person "of faith," as it's now said of those who listen to Radio London and who "are observant," which means they own short-wave radios. Today she almost had apoplexy. A fine kettle of fish! In ten days she's leaving for Brittany, *justement sur la côte,*[178] and now it looks like it won't be possible. And everything she was saying yesterday about the Germans, pursing her lips, today she says about the English. *"Ces Anglais — qu'ils nous foutent la paix — au moins pendant la période des vacances."*[179] Another sensation: German refugees in Paris. Apparently, after the bombardment of Cologne a large number of German refugees arrived in Paris.

Starting today, the Jews are wearing yellow stars with the word "JEW" in black characters, formed to look like Hebrew letters. I try not to notice them because I'm ashamed. How few people realize what savages we, WHITE PEOPLE, have become. I'm ashamed for the entire race, the marvelous race that built the modern world, created technology, conquered nature, mastered so many diseases — for what? In order, in 1942, to compel their brothers, perhaps their most valuable element, their leaven, to wear a humiliating badge, like medieval lepers. If I were a colored man, I would lose all respect for the whites. There may come a time when the highest price will have to be paid for the amusements of madmen. The price of our existence. Our technology and our savagery will be used to destroy us.

June 11, 1942

The Germans are repeating the attack on Kharkov and have begun to besiege Sevastopol. The battle for oil in the Caucasus has started. I'm curious to see how long the Russians will be able to hold Sevastopol. In Libya things keep getting worse, Rommel is pressing the English.[180] Continuously back and forth along the shore. Time goes so fast that it makes your head spin. When will this war end! The question, being asked by millions of people, is in the hands of fate, of evil powers.

How horribly numb we all are now. Only, on occasion, when one considers it calmly does one's hair stand on end. Yet never in the history of the world have the basic principles of the law been so trampled, never has there been such destruction of everything with any connection to justice and humanitarianism, to man and his spirit. What has the world come to? An accumulation of creatures, who are progressively losing whatever could be called the inner life and spiritual culture. Life has become superficial, ever faster and more greedily striving for something it is not even aware of, as it numbs itself with speed and amusements, stuffing itself to the gills with all the spoils of civilization, taxing the capacity of nerves and brain. Political and economic systems have turned the whole world into one huge prison, in which the bodies and souls of billions of people are chained by the "new," "one and only true" sociopolitical ideologies. What, then, are all these contemporary systems, contemporary ideas and assumptions, the current views of man's life and his task? They are simply one great and universal negation of man. Everything of value that might develop in this most unsuccessful of God's productions and flower over the course of the generations—all of this is destroyed in him systematically and precisely—scientifically. What have we come to? That today we take for granted and generally accept what would have tugged at the heartstrings of Stone Age man. But our hearts beat normally, because we have become numb, indifferent, and behave like animals during the hunt: from chase to chase, we crawl and hide, trying not to attract anyone's attention.

This is a century in which the basest instincts have been released, deliberately and by use of the most refined methods. The eighteenth century gave us the Declaration of the Rights of Man, in order for the twentieth century to outdo itself inventing the "one and only true" ideologies, which allow the sheep of various Panurges to forget the true sense and meaning of the terms "rights" and "man." The modern state has become a Moloch devouring millions of people, a monster demanding endless victims and slaves, in which man as an individual representing a certain idea and spirit is obliterated, crushed, destroyed. What we today recognize as the law, as statutes and codes, even worse—what we've come to consider the factor that governs human relations, is plain lawlessness. Today we take it for granted that our letters are opened and read, delivered or not delivered, that our homes can be entered without a warrant, that we can be packed off to a camp or killed without due process. The statutes and codes of the new world are lawlessness compressed into articles, crammed into the numbed minds of the two-footed herd, which have already *gotten used to* this and react only when it affects one of them directly. It makes you want to scream, spit, howl—that the principle of "the ends justify the means," which is taken for granted and considered normal, is ALWAYS A CRIME—a crime that will bury us some day.

Codes of lawlessness are crammed into the defenseless citizen's head with the aid of revolvers, machine guns, armored cars, and surveillance of his private life. And propaganda, presiding over all of this, exploits everyone and everything in order to give the appearance of truth to lies that become ever dirtier and cruder. On the battlefield people are dying, all over the world Man is dying, becoming an animal, purged of everything, and ever more preoccupied with how to fill his stomach and how to live a day longer than other specimens of this herd, prodded with the whip and poked in the back by the barrel of a loaded pistol. All this will leave a mark, the degradation will last for years. For it takes years to transform the animal that is man into a man. To turn a man into even more of an animal takes only a moment. When the war is over will we have to return to some version of the regimes that debase mankind? Bolshevism has brutalized and murdered, fascism has done the same thing with the help of more "Latin" methods, Nazism has already debased half the world. That leaves Anglo-Saxon liberalism, as weak as every liberalism, but in the end the only one. Will it still be possible to create something new in the generation that has been battered and debased, that is lost in space and time, often no longer now distinguishing the law from lawlessness and God from the devil? I don't know. Pessimism? Lack of faith in man? Misanthropy? No. It's only a moment of reflection, a moment of thinking on the part of every man trying to remain a man in an age in which thoughtlessness and "the one and only true ideologies" are put on a pedestal, and humanity worships before it with the help of prayers taken from prayer books full of the litanies of lawlessness, insanity, stupidity, brutalization, and blood.

June 20, 1942

Today I went to take care of a certain case at the Ministry of Labor. We managed, that is, to place a few dozen workers in the so-called *chantier de chô-*

mage,[181] where for digging around in gardens they get a passable midday meal, sixteen hundred francs a month, and are not jobless. K. got wind of this and developed the plan, I was supposed to carry it out by obtaining permission to hire them from the Ministry of Labor. I therefore set out for the Ministry of Labor and went straight to Mr. Pagès, one of the biggest fish involved in *la main-d'oeuvre étrangère*.[182] I had already been to see him several times and he was always very pleasant, never refusing to see me, and often cooperating in cases concerning Polish workers. When I arrived today and presented my card, I was immediately received. He gave me the permit then and there, without fussing over details, though the papers of some of the candidates were not entirely in order. Turning to leave I thanked him warmly. He looked at me and suddenly said: *"Et surtout n'envoyez pas vos ouvriers polonais travailler en Allemagne."*[183] Startled and muttering *"Monsieur, Monsieur,"* I again approached his desk. He rose and seeing my emotion embraced me and patted me on the arm: *"Allez, allez—vous faites du beau boulot, mon vieux."*[184] ("Well, well, my friend—you're doing a great job"—a touch of "argot.") The argot, the trust in me, his understanding—it all undid me. I clasped his hand firmly, saying something about my joy in finding there were still some people like him in top positions, that not everyone . . . He stroked my head and said, also with emotion: *"Mais nous sommes nombreux comme ça—du courage—on les aura."*[185]

There are still people, and in top positions, in this case crucial ones, who have not let themselves be bought. This short conversation has affected me all day. Here was the France I love speaking.

June 22, 1942

The English have ceded Tobruk.[186] Paris went wild, while German propaganda exploits the English defeat to perfection.

Laval yesterday gave a big-time propaganda speech, in which he strongly urged the French to volunteer for work in Germany. The speech was so despicable it was simply hard to believe. This page in the history of France will be truly a black one. The entire Vichy regime, its entire politics, it's all one big disgrace. And if it weren't for people like Pagès, who the day before yesterday allowed me to see something else, one could well give up on this nation.

The Germans are besieging Sevastopol and will likely take it, after which they will launch a great offensive, most likely in the Caucasus. After Tobruk the English landing sounds like a fairy tale for well-mannered children.

June 25, 1942

Meanwhile in Paris summer is beginning. The city is bathing in sunshine and warmth, life—adapting itself more or less to present conditions—flourishes with typical French nonchalance, laughs at everything. Politics is politics, Sevastopol is Sevastopol, but what does all this amount to when there's fruit, lots of fruit. All Paris is on bicycles. The bicycle is the latest word in fashion. The declining prewar bicycle industry (growth of automobilism) has been resurrected. All those who once had cars are now buying bicycles at dizzying prices, because a new bicycle becomes harder and harder to get. Bicycles are purchased with money, butter, eggs, and tobacco. But all the same there are more and more new bicycles. Any self-respecting elegant woman must have a bicycle. The same goes for clothing. Never has Paris been as elegantly and fashionably dressed as this year. All the women have new suits with long jackets, and since leather is hard to come by they all have large leather bags with shoulder straps. In addition they have fanciful sandals with wooden soles and their legs are artistically painted, some even with straight seams drawn in. The reigning perfumes are Chanel No. 5 and Guerlain. Not much work in the office, the free lending library in the town hall of the 12th arrondissement is well supplied and suffices for my spiritual nourishment. Boring.

June 26, 1942

Quite amazing how the Germans are playing with the French. They don't hold back in any of the countries they have conquered, but they flatter the French and fawn all over them. They make compromises, squeeze their throats but with gloves on, practice extortion but offer something in exchange. Four days ago Laval gave a speech urging people to sign up for jobs in Germany. By October 15 the Germans want to have 150,000 specialists. And Laval promised them they would. He promised that by October 15, 150,000 people would be leaving for Germany *voluntarily*. He began with the speech. Today came the German response. The *Militärbefehlshaber*[187] issued an edict, saying that potential civil or commercial suits brought against anyone who signs up to work in Germany will be suspended.

I can draw credit for a million francs and not repay it, I can write a bad check, I can—I can do a lot of things and after signing the contract to go work in Germany, cheerio!—I don't have to worry about anything anymore. What a come-on. This is indeed the "new morality" in the "New Europe" and in general *l'ordre nouveau*. À propos *l'ordre nouveau* not a bad joke is making the rounds. Two *clochards*, like those who live near the Pont de Grenelle and survive by digging in the garbage, are standing near two garbage cans (the French *poubelles*) and shooting the breeze as they search in the rubbish for valuable loot. One asks the other: "Hey, listen, what exactly is this *ordre nouveau?*" They think it over but can't come up with anything. Suddenly a magnificent limousine pulls up, stops, and out steps a German officer. One of the *clochards* approaches him and asks politely, what is *l'ordre nouveau*; surely he will be able to explain it. The officer smiles with satisfaction and says: "It's like this. When Germany wins the war, there will be the New Europe and the New Order. Now I'm the only one who rides in such a car, but then everyone will ride in cars like these. Got it?" The *clochard* nods, thanks him, and returns to his friend. "Well, did he explain it?" "Yeah, here's the deal. When Germany wins the war, there will be the New Europe and *l'ordre nouveau*. Now only the two of us are digging in the *poubelles*, but then twenty people will line up here and everyone will be digging. Provided there's any garbage." Interesting how far Nazism often converges with Communism. The same jokes could even be told under them both. This one sounds a little like Zoshchenko.[188]

June 28, 1942

Sunday. A beautiful, sunny day. I love Saturdays and Sundays. Our *patronne* by now knows in advance that if anyone phones she should answer that *Monsieur et madame sont sortis*[189] — and we have blessed peace. This morning I opened the shutters and sunlight instantly spurted into the room. The sounds of the radio reach us from afar, always with the same Sunday program. Ever since our arrival, we awake each Sunday to the sounds of Liszt's *Second Rhapsody*, Chopin's *Tristesse*, and Ravel's *Bolero*. These three melodies are part of early Sunday mornings. And though we laugh at this — every Sunday — it has its own charm. The repetition of certain things in life — all the more so in our present life — offers the illusion of stability. In general, many of these simple things, what's often called "French backwardness," give precisely the sense of "peace despite everything." The workman in the Paris metro who walks slowly along the station platform, sprinkling it through the perforated bottom of an old tin of conserves, into which he pours water from a jug; the train conductor who calls out to Basia hurrying down the stairs: "*Dépêchez-vous, mademoiselle*,"[190] and delays the departure of the train; the institution of the lady-concierges, always curious and talkative (Napoleon's Gestapo); and the obligatory "baker-cat," "butcher-cat," and so on, often found lying in the shopwindow among the goods for sale — all this oddly grows on you, transforms life into a pleasant series of these "despite everythings" — despite Germany, despite the New Europe, despite Laval, despite the Führer. I observe, with growing trepidation, that I have by now so deeply adapted to this environment, grown so accustomed to this life and to the French approach to living, that it's hard for me right now to think about going back. Perhaps it's an attachment to these past few years, which have helped me so much to come into my own. Finally, it's perhaps also an attachment to the country in which I've grown up. Admittedly, I grew up in Poland, but there I had rather the feeling of foundering. Something in me snapped irreparably, leaving me indifferent to many things.

A lovely, warm day, already summery. I made breakfast. On Sundays we always drink tea and there's still always butter for the bread. Then we spread out the map of the area around Paris and chose a route for today's bicycle ride. Boissy-Saint-Léger. Shorts and we're off. On the bicycle, a backpack with a blanket and books; in the side bags, bread, butter, a piece of sausage. Wartime Camembert (*zéro pour-cent de matière grasse*[191]), plums, and a bottle of wine. If not for the *zéro pour-cent de matière grasse* in the Camembert, it would be almost the same as before the war. The situation with food is considerably better this year and there's lots of fruit. I imagine that if I phoned Cracow right now and recounted all this, the family would think I had gone mad. In occupied France, in the third year of the war, it's still possible to stuff a sack with decent food, hook it to the bicycle, and ride out of town quite freely, off to the fields or the forest, encountering along the way not a single German policeman, almost no Germans. Occasionally a gray car may pass by and that's it. There's still freedom—by now reduced, but entirely possible. Today you have to register when you change your address or your place of residence, you have to put up with many regulations unknown before the war. But essentially it's freedom—and almost daily you still hear someone in some bistro giving Pétain a hard time or referring to Laval as *ce sale Auvergnat*[192] and uttering threats at the Germans. Out loud. It's still possible not only to think but also to speak your mind. This freedom is so ingrained here in France, so deeply rooted in blood and soul, in the entire past—that probably even the Germans have a *Minderwertigkeitskomplex*[193] in relation to the French and avoid getting too tough for fear of causing trouble. They are still affected by the history of France, the myth of greatness, everything Poles and Germans have been taught *über Frankreich.*[194] The Germans believe the Poles and Yugoslavs are easier to crush and destroy than France. I don't think so. France is old and weak and these second-string beaten-down nations are more likely to react. Well, the same goes for nations as for people. It's always a bit handier and easier to beat up an insignificant and down-at-the-heel person than someone just as down-at-the-heel but aristocratic. France was the aristocrat, recognized and worshiped by other nations, especially by the half-baked intelligentsia—like the Germans—climbing the cultural ladder. They still admire France, if only in their hearts, and although *die deutsche Kultur ist selbstverständlich die grösste*,[195] nevertheless in regard to the French they feel awkward, clumsy, embarrassed. Like a heavyweight boxer in the presence of a great lady. The Germans handle the French with kid gloves, as though seized by impotence. They flirt—as though fearing an explosion of that popular energy, which for good or for ill, has exploded so many times in the course of history. Today's France, however, is not the France of 1789, 1830, or 1848. Today a single German in the Palais-Royal or the Hôtel de Ville would be enough to keep everything in line. And at the same time, how comfortable France is. Like an old, hand-me-down slipper. Or armchair.

I write this lying under the shady trees in one of the forests around Boissy-Saint-Léger. It's hot. Basia is sketching. I had no matches and went to the road-side auberge to ask for a light. An old house, a large courtyard with stables, a plaque on the door with a no longer legible name and the date 1828. Stage-coaches must have stopped here. I entered an enormous dining room. At one end a large and blackened hearth, at the other a clock, tall as an obelisk, evenly ticking. How many hours has this clock struck . . .

June 29, 1942

The communiqué after Churchill's visit to Roosevelt offers a "long-range" view. People are annoyed. I explain as best I can, but it seems defeatist, when I say that the "simplest" airplane requires eighteen to twenty months before going into production. And this war is above all about airpower and tanks.

July 1, 1942

London very energetically denies the existence of a *gentlemen's agreement* between England and Germany not to bomb each other's capital cities. Finland is demobilizing the older cohort—for the harvests. And all this is what's called war.

July 2, 1942

Sevastopol has fallen—a great offensive has begun. Except it's two months too late. The battle for the Caucasus and the Volga. At considerable cost.

Churchill explained the reasons they were defeated in Libya: (1) tactical blunders, (2) tanks unsuited to desert warfare, (3) better German equipment. That's it—no more than that. The Germans have spent years in Egypt and adapted their tanks to desert warfare. Those pesky grains of sand were no longer seeping in, engines functioned despite the heat. The English had nowhere to test their tanks. Because the English have a sense of humor, they call these miserable English tanks Churchills, which Churchill himself acknowledged with a smile in his speech to Parliament. The war drags on. I'd hoped the end would come in 1943—now I'm beginning to have my doubts. Vichy under Laval is collaborating hot and heavy. France is assuming a serious responsibility. People curse, whine, feel that something is wrong, but they don't realize the kind of situation all of France will face after the war as a result of this government and its policies. Meanwhile, however, Paris is not concerned with politics. Besides, food coupons keep the population in line better than any police. Having enough fruit this year is more important than anything else. In any case, everyone is getting ready for vacation. Especially to Brittany. There you can eat without coupons, *Vive la France!* No question of obtaining the tiniest room in the smallest and most remote town. Train tickets in the direction of Nantes and Rennes must be reserved two weeks in advance. There are so many bicycles that the railroad does not guarantee the bicycle will arrive at the same time as the passenger. It has to be sent three or four days in advance; in Gare Montparnasse they had to build special bicycle sheds. In short, we're back in business, an almost prewar atmosphere. We're forgetting about the war.

July 26, 1942

I've had no time to write. Tadzio arrived on the third, left on the ninth. Then Bogdan arrived on the fifteenth and left on the twenty-second. They travel between Paris and Warsaw as often as possible. I've made a profit from these trips. I'm beginning to save for the departure from Europe. A hopeless backwater.

It's a lovely day, a summer day. This afternoon we went to the Galerie Charpentier to see the exhibit "A Hundred Years of French Landscape." Nicely hung, but a weak collection. A few good Courbets, dense with somber greenery; a few misty Corots; a few sunny and flowery Renoirs; a pair of lemony Van Goghs; two or three of the worst Gauguins; and otherwise a whole crowd of contemporary dabblers, seeking but not finding, yet hoping against all odds to find something. Indeed, that's the meaning of art—the eternal hope of finding something.

After the exhibition we dropped into Café Rebattet for afternoon tea. One of the elegant and venerable cafés of Paris, frequented almost exclusively by the wealthy old bourgeoisie, nobility, and aristocracy in search of bygone times. Elderly *comtesses*, unstylish and prudish; elderly gentlemen dressed with exaggerated elegance; and the young generation of *fils à papa*[196] and daughters, nonchalantly flaunting the most expensive wardrobes and jewelry. The waitresses look like poor aunts or nieces, and the chocolate or ice cream you ordered takes half an hour to arrive. Everyone comes here to satisfy their cravings. Next to us two pious biddies had an entire mountain of petits fours in front of them, which they crammed down with the help of ice cream. They then ordered tea and a jar of preserves for each of them, discreetly extracting their own sugar and their own rusks from their bags. And they ate. Savoring, slobbering, relishing every bite, feasting, soaking it all up. The greed on their faces thickened, like a layer of greasepaint. They slurped, smacked their tongues, licked their lips, played with each morsel like a cat with a mouse, turning it in their fingers; and chattered away.

I cut a path through the elegant public rather rudely because they were all jostling each other like fishwives standing in line. Reaching the glass counter with my plate, I loaded up with twenty little cakes and returned with my loot. Two franks a pop. We then ordered ice cream and set about demolishing it. Next, I paid the bill, the likes of which I have never in my life paid for afternoon tea, and with the expression of a loutish upstart took my leave of the place. On the way back we surveyed the display windows, excitedly discussing a classic wartime subject, that is to say, the aesthetics of perfume packages and the difference between Lanvin and Lelong, Schiaparelli and Guerlain, not Chanel — that's for servant girls and hookers. Chanel — *fi donc*, that will not do . . . Basia dreams, besides, of a gray sheepskin coat. We should also take a vacation.

July 27, 1942

Stasiek has arrived. He's leaving in ten days. Then Karol will come. Even better. Certain laws of economics are functioning and are inviolable no matter what the economic system, planned, centrally directed, etc. The "law of communicating vessels" is strict and when it malfunctions becomes interesting. I trade in "hard" and "soft" dollars and in moments of self-loathing, I justify myself the way Poles always justify themselves: "At the moment it hurts the occupiers and is thus patriotic. Long live Poland! How much for hard?"

August 1, 1942

Summer. Pleasant, warm weather. Vacations have begun. Every other shop is closing and announcing they will reopen on August 15, 20, or 31. Government offices are beginning to switch from on duty to on call and the most common answer is: *Après les vacances.*[197] One person has already left, another is supposed to return, and those who stay put also do nothing, because they're waiting for "the other one" to return, so that they themselves can leave. Everyone is hot—*quelle chaleur*[198]—in the metro you can drop dead of the heat and stuffiness, but almost everyone is going somewhere, although the average rate for room and board in a godforsaken hole-in-the-wall in Brittany or Anjou (the more godforsaken the better) amounts to a hundred francs a day. It's practically a psychosis, the desire to make up for the two years of uncertainty and wavering. People have by now adapted to circumstances, settled down within the limits of the possible, which in France are still rather broad, thanks to the relative freedom she still enjoys.

We went out this evening. The streets were peaceful and quiet. In front of Maxim's on rue Royale there was a row of carriages, Tilburies, coaches, and other vehicles from bygone days. Paris 1900. We went to the cinema to see the new French film, *Le Lit à colonnes.*[199] The prison director in a small town has a composer-murderer in his prison. He provides him with the conditions needed for work, takes his compositions, and publishes them under his own name. From a dull, two-bit provincial bureaucrat he becomes a somebody, shows off, marries his daughter to a count. His crowning triumph is the production of "his" opera in the Paris Opéra. Then things get complicated—he meets his death finally at the hand of the prisoner, who has discovered the whole thing. The action takes place in the 1890s. With the image in mind of Parisian streets today, the coaches and Tilburies in front of Maxim's, the film seems almost contemporary. Well played, but that's not all. The film is literally a painting, or rather a gallery of French Impressionist paintings. Quite extraordinary. As we watched we frequently exchanged a few words under our breaths, unable to contain our admiration. Costumes, interiors, light and shadow, landscapes—everything was full of color. You felt the colors, the sun, the play of shadows, the splashes of light, the base coat, the background . . . With only black and white, they brought out all the colors. We left the cinema full of excitement.

August 4, 1942

The roundup of foreign Jews on the territory of Paris has been accomplished. From July 14 to 15 a Saint Bartholomew's Night, or rather a Saint Adolf's Night, was organized, later on those who remained were rounded up as well—at present on the territory of the entire occupied zone all foreign Jews have been interned in camps.[200] This has made an enormous impression on the French. The separation of children over three years old from their mothers has aroused particularly vitriolic comments. I can only note it down, I have no strength to comment. Only an internal scream and the feeling of everything ripping apart. At the same time, a rumor, most probably from Jewish quarters, claims the Poles are next in line and everyone believes it. It's pandemonium in Paris. The more fearful have left for the countryside, others have not slept at home for several nights, everyone is convinced that any day now they will come for us as well.

More from a sense of obligation than from desire, I've become a fatalist in these things and at such moments I always think of Keyserling's *"il faut subir son époque pour agir sur elle."* [201] I tried my best to get some information, but none of the better-informed Frenchmen had heard anything on the subject. It's probably a Jewish rumor, quite understandable, started out of despair. Are they supposed to love us? Back in 1940 I was standing in line speaking Polish with an acquaintance. A Jewish woman at our side regarded us with hatred and said: "It's true, isn't it, that things are good here in OUR France? But Poland, sir, will not exist anymore." I did not reply, although usually I'm a loudmouth. Perhaps she was right? But even France didn't help her.

August 11, 1942

We're going on vacation. Robert and his wife have invited us to their aunt's house in Chambellay, in the very center of Anjou, where every year the entire family gathers for vacation. It's the family house, what remains of the fortune once possessed by Robert's clan, stemming from the so-called *bourgeoisie terrienne* (landed bourgeoisie). We're leaving on September 4 for ten days and returning along with them to Paris.

I'm reading a book about the United States and reaching the conclusion that I actually knew nothing about America. Naturally, except for the load of rubbish that every self-respecting European is supposed to know and which he must not renounce, because what then would remain of Europe. Why am I reading all this? I want simply to see things in their true light and not have any illusions. And I have none. Our immediate future, and what will soon follow, is dark in any event. Today they're knifing us in our bellies and we're suffering. Later on, they will poison us gradually and with a smile. Today we complain that we are slaves, we feel it every minute of our lives. And we have reason to complain. Later, exhausted and beaten, we will also be slaves, with the difference that we will have the pretense of freedom.

Meanwhile, having galloped from Tobruk as far as Egypt, the English have stopped at El-Alamein. That is, it's unclear who stopped: the retreating English or Rommel Africanus on their tail. [202] Probably the latter. He raced to El-

Alamein, extended his communication lines, on both land and sea—and ran out of breath. And Mussolini was not able to make a big speech under the Pyramids. Too bad! In any case, the front has stalled at El-Alamein and the Germans did not reach Cairo. Logically, one should expect the English after a time to push Rommel back. In Africa every offensive is *aller et retour*.[203] The German move toward the Caucasus, from one side, and toward the Volga, with Stalingrad the main focus, from the other, promises to be of much greater importance. Capturing the Caucasus and severing a communication artery like the Volga will be a death sentence for Russia, if anything at all is capable of doing her in. But let's not be optimistic. You have to admit that with each passing month Russia becomes an ever-greater surprise. I'm beginning to doubt whether Hitler and his general staff recognized her power. Marshal von Brauchitsch is the only one who understood—and he washed his hands of the business.[204] But at the present moment General von Bock is in fashion and Marshal Rommel Africanus, fresh-baked in the African oven.[205] Rommel is ready to become a national hero and, who knows, perhaps the heir. A star, greater than Gary Cooper. Rommel is all over the newspapers and illustrated magazines. Handsome and with a certain "something" nevertheless in his expression. And in Paris the Vélodrome d'hiver is offering a "real bullfight." *Gran corrida de toros.* The people of Paris are therefore already anxious to know whether the bullfighter will have enough meat coupons to entitle him to stab the bull to death. Sometimes I really think I'm dreaming.

August 16, 1942

I'm tired and nothing interests me. I haven't taken a vacation since October 1940. I simply need a few days in a row without having to take care of other people. I can hardly wait to leave.

Interesting exhibit at the Musée Cognacq-Jay.[206] Original photographs from the Second Empire. Naturally, it's full of Napoleon and Eugénie, Napoleon and Génie together and separately, with their children and without them, the children by themselves, and so on. But also, many photos of famous and celebrated figures from the theater and literature. Terrific daguerreotypes of Balzac and Théophile Gautier and many photos from one of the amateur exhibitions at Gautier's home in Neuilly described with such charm by the Goncourt brothers in their *Journal*. Plus all the dancers and singers in the Paris Opéra, photos of painters and their models, photos of the saucy showgirls from the boulevard theaters and dance halls whom our great-grandfathers and grandfathers lost their heads over. The flirtatious *déshabillé*, corsets, black stockings, bosoms overflowing the whalebones like waves breaching the harbor breakwater, and other charms of the day. The old goat Alexandre Dumas with a young, charming, and truly delectable tart. Crinolines. A whole series of portraits, more beautiful than any modern photographer can manage to produce. Portrait photography of that time was surely superior to what is done today. The ever more perfect materials, the "improvement" of lenses, plates, film, and paper have eliminated the transitions between light and shadow, which "flow" so perfectly in the photography of the nineteenth century. Today everything is sharply defined—like our whole era. What a lovely model Corot had.[207] What a splendid head on that Michelet.[208] A shame that he scribbled so much nonsense. Renan, the two Goncourts, Flaubert, Gautier, George Sand. I'm full of memories; each face has special value now. You can escape into them and hide out in one of Balzac's novels, you can take refuge in the bronze resonance of Flaubert's prose and not hear the idle squawking, the deceitful abuse of good sense that can lead to madness. This is already a sullying of lies, a desecration of lies.

August 19, 1942

At midday a fever, eagerness, expectation, a thousand commentaries flying from mouth to mouth. At dawn the English landed in Dieppe and to the south and north of Dieppe. Since morning they've already been fighting inside the city itself. They landed with artillery and tanks. German garrisons are all on the alert. Radio London appeals to the people of France to keep calm and not get involved in the operations. It all seems like a fairy tale. The tension lasted all day, although everyone realizes that this is not an "actual" landing, but only a kind of dress rehearsal. With stage sets. The unloading of tanks and artillery on the shore arouses general admiration. Radio Paris is silent, likewise the newspaper midday editions, and only London offers any information. The evening communiqué reports that the English expeditionary corps has withdrawn in an orderly fashion and shipped out, taking some prisoners with them. What counts is that the English disembarked, spent an entire day in France, and left again. They've demonstrated that they can land, while not a single German—with the exception of Rudolf Hess—has set foot on the English shore since the start of the war.[209] And yet the Germans could have managed, in July and August 1940, to accomplish almost with impunity what they are no longer now capable of doing. History will one day show how this happened. Instead of penetrating deep into France, why weren't the German forces taken from Belgium and Holland and directed at England? Hitler was seduced by the myth of "unconquerable" Paris, which during the four years of the Great War the Germans were unable to reach. The myth of France saved England. It was powerful enough.

August 21, 1942

Now begins the hurdy-gurdy of victory. We repulsed the English attack, we foiled the creation of the second front that Moscow is continually demanding, we have disheartened Churchill, we laugh and mock, and make such a big deal out of Dieppe as though we'd conquered at least all of England. And that's how it will be for quite some time now. All this proves that we wet our pants from fear, that we lost our heads, and that by shouting at the top of our lungs and repeating the same thing over and over we try to obscure the real meaning of this fact and prevent people from thinking about it the way they should be thinking about it. This amounts to the conscious dissemination of ignorance. By comparison, the Middle Ages seem like a Renaissance. To turn the masses into a herd of sheep, to destroy their common sense, both collective and individual (if the collective is capable of common sense at all), to wear them down by lying, to *anesthetize, annihilate* their thinking and their reflexes of internal resistance. But I'm repeating myself. Like propaganda.

Today Robert and I bought our train tickets and in two weeks we leave. Will the Germans take Stalingrad or not? That is the question.

August 24, 1942

Vichy has sent the Führer a telegram thanking him for the successful defense of France. Whereupon the Führer assigned (from Vichy's treasury) ten million francs for the city of Dieppe as a reward for the population's exemplary and disciplined conduct during the English attack. Touching. The newspapers are naturally full of photographs, descriptions, accounts, and reports about the Germans' magnificent defense. But since it was impossible to conceal the bravery of the Canadians, who in many cases went into battle with pistols and knives, the reports mock their "cowboy methods of fighting" and "Wild West brawling."

August 26, 1942

Still nothing but Dieppe. This time in reward for the exemplary attitude of the city population, the Führer has freed all prisoners who come from Dieppe. After a short leave they will be sent to work in Germany. And this stupid corporal thinks this is the way to buy off the French. Who exactly? The French lack the sense of the *Volksgemeinschaft*[210] and this theatrical gesture moves no one. If, instead of releasing the prisoners, he had increased the rations for Dieppe fourfold, he could be considered a genius and a great psychologist. Then all of France would stop in its tracks and buzz with excitement. Then, until the end of the year, everyone would keep talking enviously, on and on. *Ah, ça alors, ceux-là, par example, voyez-moi ça, ces Dieppois, ils ont de la chance, etc.*[211] Collaboration with France was at their fingertips. All they needed was to allow the French to eat their fill. Propaganda, the crusade, the cultural mission, Arno Breker,[212] the new order—all of this misses the mark when it comes to France. Culture makes no headway with them because they have too high an opinion of the culture of their own. In 1940, when three-quarters of France was psychologically favorable to Germany, when their positive feelings were widespread and strong, when the Germans were impressing them, these sympathies should have been fortified with bread, butter, eggs, meat, and wine. France would today be ready to take on all Germany's enemies. But as it is? A remark by one of my French colleagues, expressed at table in our factory canteen, can serve as an answer. It contains everything:

"No point the Germans pestering us with their greatness and genius, their fabulous organization and culture, if they have never managed to organize some decent, ordinary chow, fit for human consumption" (*casse-croûte*).

This short sentence captures France. No use trying to impress the French with the sacrifice of *die deutschen Grenadiere*,[213] Breker, Wagner, the Führer. Chow down—and then maybe we can talk. Ideals? Not many when the stomach's full, even fewer when it's empty.

August 29, 1942

According to the newspapers England has already ceased to exist. The victory at Dieppe is the best proof of that. You can really go out of your mind. The assumption is that everyone is mentally ill and can utter whatever nonsense comes into their heads.

August 31, 1942

This morning I sent off our two bicycles. To send the bicycles, you have to wait in line. I arrived at Gare Montparnasse rather early and after completing all the paperwork I still had time before heading for the office.

I feel like a schoolboy before the holidays—I'm restless with excitement. On leaving the station I dropped into a bistro for a beer. There is probably nothing more agreeable than on a humid Parisian summer morning to snuggle into a corner in some bistro and sip cold beer. Light up a cigarette and simply—exist. Nothing more. Live and pray. Increasingly, I pray over a pint of beer or a glass of rum, because these are the moments when I truly feel I'm still alive. And I give thanks. Today, too, I performed this kind of morning prayers, looking up toward the sky, then down along boulevard Montparnasse, which was growing ever brighter in the sunshine, and then I started to pick up a conversation between workers drinking their morning *coup de blanc*.[214] The conversation concerned the subject of the Russian front. Will the Germans take Stalingrad, or won't they? The universal question. Personally, I believe in the prophecy that says: "By a great river, they will be cut down and return with broken wings."[215] I've twice already bet some big money that they won't take it. The Soviets will defend the name itself if nothing else. It's beginning to look more and more like the "decisive battle." In America, bets are apparently running in the thousands of dollars. A funny species, this so-called humankind. The future of Europe, lousy one way or the other, is being decided on the Volga.

September 5, 1942

At last, we're in the countryside. Yesterday I went home early and packed at top speed. It will be about forty kilometers by bicycle from the station to Chambellay, so the baggage had to be organized for the ride. I packed the backpack and two tote bags. Basia packed a small valise and a handbag. The weather is marvelous, a hot Paris evening. We met Robert at Gare Montparnasse. We had reserved places in second class, but we still had to show up an hour before departure, because it's a total zoo in the stations. To get onto the platform you have to wait in line, then you have to accomplish the feat of pushing your way through the crowded train corridor to reach your compartment and your seats. We finally sat down, pleased with our success. Right before departure the cars filled up completely, meaning that all the seats as well as the corridors and toilets were occupied. At ten the train pulled out. The curtains were drawn and the compartment lights were on. Notices on all the walls said: "*Achtung mit den Gesprächen. Der Feind hört zu.*"[216] We were supposed to arrive in Sablé at one in the morning, stay overnight, and then continue on our bicycles to Chambellay.[217] I was as excited by this journey as though it were the first time in my life I'd traveled by train. Two years of staying put, two years somehow lost in the past, hard to take the measure of. One's relationship to the past these days is indeed reduced to the overall satisfaction that a certain amount of time has gone by, that one has managed to live through it, that time still goes on. That we manage to keep afloat, like corks.

It became horribly stuffy in the compartment, because the French have an innate fear of fresh air. A slight *courant d'air* equals death. Robert and I discussed the question of the deportation of workers to Germany. The Germans have given Laval until October 15 to comply and by then 150,000 specialists must have left. But no one goes voluntarily. What will come of it? I took some pears from the backpack and as we smoked we switched to subjects related to the war. Like the overwhelming majority of the French, Robert knows nothing about the Germans. I try to enlighten him, but it's hard going, because I have to struggle against the kind of *spell* the Germans have cast over very many of his countrymen. Not knowing the Germans, having been defeated by them, the French are aware of how weak and broken they are. They see the Germans as powerful and impressive, introducing many reforms in France which the strongest French government would not dare enact, and displaying an extraordinary vitality. As a nation of external forms, the French admire German form, do not penetrate beneath it, and are under its *spell*. With the same feeling with which the great-grandson of a veteran of the Persian wars probably regarded the Roman legionnaire. Culturally he still despised him, somewhere deep inside he still called him by the crude epithet "barbarian," but his body, as well as the vital, everyday layer of his mind, had already submitted to the charm of the power and vitality emanating from the Roman military machine. France drowns in prejudices, in brilliant formulations, in generalizations, which are so often misleading. In the course of a conversation, someone or other will suddenly say: "At this latitude . . . ," or "This fact is stunning," or—what is worse—throws into the conversation some great question, such as, "And what has humanity come to?" and "Here is our progress for you." How many times have I allowed myself to be taken in and treated this as an invitation to discussion. I would begin and—my words would fall into the void, I would come up against views narrower and more impoverished than I could ever have imagined. France is a country with a half-baked intelligentsia, which is to say, an intelligentsia that has been diluted and widely spread among the masses. Mass culture is a French invention, it's the French nineteenth century, but this culture was arrested in its development, it fossilized along with the rest of French culture and its development. France has lost her vision, she has lost contact with reality and—will pay for it. The social class that sets the country's tone and is the dominant class is the half-baked intelligentsia and the quarter-baked intelligentsia. The country of appearances and of ossified formulas. The mentality of the French, based on principles enunciated by the Revolution of 1789 and on a handful of facts drilled into their heads by a school system that has not evolved since Napoleon's time, does not change at all. France to this day cultivates the principle of self-enclosed thinking and feeds off platitudes *"made in France."* She is incapable of understanding any thought that's not French, cannot *grasp* anything except in the French way. She is satisfied exclusively with the activities of a few dozen

French geniuses, high-caliber mediocre geniuses who have entered into history, and considers them a threshold no one else has yet or will ever manage to cross. Appearances will always weigh in favor of the French, but *the essence* of things will betray them. France is a genius of *form*, but almost exclusively of form. No nation on earth has managed in the domain of thought and its formulations to create as perfect forms as the French (I grasped Hegel in French; in German, for all my knowledge of the language, I could not make him out). In the realm of language and expression no one has beaten them in terms of form. Hence their renown, but hence also the misconceptions about them. We extend to everything their genius for form. Not surprising. Sight is the most animal of human senses and man lets himself most easily be guided by sight. We are always inclined to identify the culture of Greece first of all with what remained of it in terms of form. Yet Greek form has lasted much longer than the spirit that gave it birth. Temples were built and statues carved at a time when the people were no longer capable of repeating the Battle of Salamis, because the spirit had decayed and frozen in form.[218] The people no longer lived, but still continued to act, like a mechanism set in motion. France is the modern Greece. What Greece was for the ancient world, France was for the modern world and her role is ending. France has ceased to live, France now merely acts. This activity may still give something to the world, but it will be rather like the striking of the hour—even sonorous and beautiful—but merely the striking of the hour by a clock running on the momentum bestowed upon it at the moment of its creation, a force that has enchanted us and that we continue to think still exists. France will for a long time probably remain the Greece of the new world that is arising today before our eyes. But the French and the nation will be for us young people what the Greeks and Greece of the Hellenistic period were for the Romans. They will be admired, they will be marveled at, but not—respected, just as the Roman could not respect the merchant of Alexandria or the Athenian living off his past.

France has now entered the phase in which she exploits her past, selling it off, and if she creates anything at all, in most cases it's a skillfully renovated antique, even more skillfully promoted on the market. She excels at this and reaches a level of perfection encountered nowhere else, but that very perfection is the best demonstration that something has been exhausted and has somehow to be replaced. It's a dying fire that occasionally emits a burst of showy sparks—which is the rule for dying fires.

In his predictions about the war, Robert cannot believe the Germans are further from victory at this point than in summer 1940. Their triumphal march toward Stalingrad through the Don basin and the Kalmyk steppes and their attack on the Caucasus are impressive. I explain to him that you have to look carefully at the map to realize that though this operation appears to be a great idea, in fact things look decidedly risky. They themselves are creating a second front. One mustn't forget that the occupation of the Don basin does not undercut Russian production to the extent the Germans would have us believe. Besides, the Anglo-Saxons are fattening them like geese and delude themselves that Russia will thank them for it. Russia will thank them in her own way, in her usual, Russian style . . . Hitler asserts that his victories are *einmalig in der Geschichte.*[219] I remind Robert of similar victories: the year 1806, the war with Prussia. Napoleon did not spare his caustic comments on Queen Louise of Prussia, like Hitler's comments on Mrs. Roosevelt, which do not surprise me. Napoleon did not like Louise; Hitler directs his sharp corporal's quips at Mrs. Roosevelt. But then, Napoleon's *Blitzkrieg* is better than the Germans'. On October 10, 1806, General Maison beats the Prussians at Schleiz.[220] On October 14 Jena-Auserstädt, October 16 Erfurt surrenders, October 17 Battle of Halle, October 18 capture of Leipzig, October 19 Admiral Murat enters Halberstadt,[221] October 20 General Lannes and General Davout cross the Elbe,[222] October 24 Napoleon in Potsdam, October 25 capture of Spandau, October 26 entry into Berlin, October 29 Murat's ten-thousand-strong cavalry corps beats the sixteen-thousand-strong Royal Guards corps under Prince Hohenlohe and takes prisoner Prince Augustus of Prussia, Prince von Mecklenburg-Schwerin, the emperor's son-in-law, and General Tauentzien, stopping at Prenzlau.[223] Finally, on October 29, General Lasalle, leading twelve hundred cavalrymen, takes Stettin, defended by five thousand men and 150 cannon.[224] Even General Wieniawa never did as much at Adria.[225] In the course of nineteen days, without the use of motorized divisions, Prussia is conquered as far as Pomerania. It remains only for Davout to get control of the lower Oder, General Mortier is beating the Elector of Hesse-Kassel,[226] Lübeck and Magdeburg are captured — the entire Prussian campaign is completed in twenty-eight days. So what is it about Hitler's campaign that's *einmalig in der Geschichte?* He wins his battles one after the other, except that . . . alas, when it comes to the encounter with Russia, the *Blitzkrieg* falls flat. The Prussian city of Eylau is a literal bloodbath. It's Kharkov. Then there's Friedland — these are the current victories, and at last the retreat from Moscow. That's bound to happen now. But I'm not sure one should be so pleased about it.

Train compartments all go through the same stages at night. At first everyone is dressed and sitting upright. Then someone removes an article of clothing or unfastens something, next begins to nod and comes to rest in a more or less bizarre position, possible only in a train. Finally, a deadly stillness and silence descend. I turned off the light. In the bluish half-light of the night lamp, the

whole compartment looked like a battlefield, like a Goya caricature. The neck-
tie on the man next to the window was undone in a revolutionary fashion, his
shirt, as though on the barricades, was open at the chest, his head tilted to the
side, his body bent as though smitten by a sword. Another man, right next to
me, had dozed off with legs spread wide, his head on his chest, leaning over as
though suspended above the passage between the two seats. By contrast, the
woman across from him had bent her head back, resting it against the upholstery, and arched herself forward like a bow, pressing one foot against the edge
of the seat between the outspread legs of her vis-à-vis. It looked like that kick
in the soft spot, known in French as the *coup de Vénus.*[227] Basia sat with her
legs tucked under her in her favorite treble clef position, while I kept turning
around, because my legs are always too long in such situations.

Around one o'clock Robert awoke and we prepared to get off. It looked like
we would have to exit through the window, but we managed to push our way
to the door. Our things had to be handed to us through the window, because
there was no hope of getting past with the bags. The train stopped and we got
out at Sablé.

Dark all around, you can't see three paces ahead of you. After making our
way to the baggage check, where a sleepy railroad clerk issued us a group pass,
we went into town. Robert knew the way, the nocturnal wind and chill revived
us. Suddenly, "*Halt.*" Out of the darkness emerged a solitary German gendarme
(in Poland they do not make their rounds solo) and demanded our passes. He
tries to light his lighter and asks: "*Vom Bahnhof?*" "*Ja, ja, vom Bahnhof, nach
Hause,*" I answer.[228] He returns our document unread and we continue on our
way. Robert has a distant cousin here, at whose place we are supposed to spend
the night. Lucky for us—otherwise we'd be sitting like the others in the station
waiting room. French towns are all booked up—filled with summer visitors.
We stand in front of a house and ring the bell. Madame Vigné herself opens
the door. She had been expecting us. We enter the dining room—the table is
set. Madame Vigné welcomes us very courteously, with the courtesy typical of
a well-bred older Frenchwoman. The good old bourgeoisie. Ladies from this
French milieu have retained to this day something of the Bourbon Restoration.
Despite their courtesy, freedom, subtle humor, they always wear crinolines and
their hearts beat only as hard as the world permits. Robert introduced us as
his Polish friends, for which we earned what is called in French *quelques mots
aimables.*[229] We sat down at table, Mme Vigné served hot coffee with milk.
It's been two years since I've laid my eyes on milk. Bread, butter, and fabulous
rillettes in small stoneware pots. A large slice of Brie slowly made the rounds
on a large plate. I felt faint. The conversation naturally began with the sub-

ject of shortages of everything in Paris and the abundance of food in the provinces. "Until just recently we almost did without coupons," says Mme Vigné. "Now even we are getting a taste of the inventions *de ces messieurs*" (the Germans), "though we still cannot complain." I say nothing and eat, although it's two in the morning. Mme Vigné mentions her lodger, a young German officer. She speaks of him with a smile, with an ineffably ironic air, with a pursing of the lips that makes each expression whistle and hiss, acquiring an incredibly elegant malice. The officer has found himself a *petite amie*, a Russian woman from Crimea moreover. "Seeing as he can't conquer over there," she says with a thin smile, "he conquers Russia in Sablé." I stopped eating. This is a concert, a French concert. When the beautiful Russian began to pay him nocturnal visits, removing her shoes in front of the house—"wooden soles are not well-suited to love trysts" (O France, long may you live! for God's sake, long live France! I was thinking, as I looked at Mme Vigné with my maw full of bread with *rillettes*)— and climbed the stairs in her stockings, Mme Vigné lodged a complaint with the Kommandant and the visits stopped. Meanwhile, I'm thinking about the occupation in Poland, about what I'm told by the guys who come through, what Hanka writes . . . Basia has a special talent for polite chit-chat and I left her the full burden of conversation. I ATE. It was after three when we went to our room. A small, clean room, a large bed, and an enormous down comforter. I couldn't fall asleep until dawn, probably from overeating.

In the morning I went to the station to fetch the bicycles. Miraculously they had arrived at Sablé unharmed. I returned with them to the house and after unpacking everything, we went to breakfast at Mme Vigné's. The day was once again splendid, sunny and warm. Silvery, September weather. After last night's gluttony, I am like a tiger that has tasted human flesh—I'm relentlessly hungry. For breakfast there was hot coffee with MILK, again butter, again *rillettes* and golden mirabelle preserves. I ate, as though in a dream. Life is a splendid invention—on condition that you can live well. After two years of living in a cave I suddenly found myself in the aura of a sunny morning, with the aroma of coffee and fruit preserves. The war is forgotten and I have a sense of complete freedom. I seemed to have grown several years younger, my inner tension relaxed, but despite my quite animalistic delight in everything around me, I was in fact all shaken up. The greatest nervous shock for millions of people will be the end of the war. When, after breakfast, I ran out to the garden, which sloped gently down to the riverbank, when I again observed the leaves glistening with morning dew and the boat tied to a post, against which the water lapped and smacked, I had to convince myself that this was real, that once I had had a different life and that in future, if I make it, there will be yet again another life.

With a farewell from the household, we mounted our bicycles and followed the lovely road along the Sarthe. We drove through the little town in which the Germans are quartered. They are all SS, the "Adolf Hitler" and "Großdeutsch-land" divisions of the Führer's guards, which in July paraded down the Champs-Élysées. The soldiers wander around in bathing trunks to the indignation of the inhabitants. They're on holiday here, coddled and protected. Machine guns are set on the rooftops, cars and tanks kept in the barns and coach houses. It's the same in every town and the entire *département* of the Sarthe is now filled with SS-men.

The road is difficult, by noon it's very hot. Finally, around one we encounter Lina on the road with her four boys. She has come out to meet us. Basia is very tired, barely pedaling, but somehow continues to move ahead. Chambellay is now visible. The houses look like blocks, above them rises a church tower. Along the sides and in the middle of the fields, clumps of trees surround the châteaux of the local gentry. This *département*—Maine-et-Loire—is still very patriarchal and feudal and in general royalist. As we enter the town we pass a wedding. The wedding party walk in pairs, already well-oiled and singing. The women and men are dressed mostly in black, and a fat woman, reeling and supported with difficulty by a small, thin man, shouts and sings, drowning out the entire company. Colorless and lifeless. Black clothing, the bride in a fashionable dress and a hat against the background of the white stone houses in the sunshine, bursts of tuneless songs, rather monotonous—everything moribund. Sienkiewicz, in one of his letters from France, wrote that in Poland "the popular imagination and poetry nourish our literature; here it's the reverse—literature nourishes the culture of the folk." You see it everywhere. The French village is moribund and drab. It evokes Balzac's *Eugénie Grandet* or, even more, *Le Médecin de campagne*.[230] No other French writer has succeeded so well in capturing the feeling of the village, in its inertness, dullness, and monotony, in the materialism and callousness with which it works the land, all in evidence here.

We ride up to the house. A large, well-proportioned, two-story building from the Second Empire. A garden slopes down almost to the river. We introduce ourselves, we are welcomed by the lady of the house, Robert's aunt, Madame Bazin. A small, elderly lady, with an energetic face, gray hair, dignified comportment. Some years ago her right side was paralyzed. Today, thanks to her efforts and energy, she is walking again, limping slightly and skillfully managing with her feeble right arm. Her language is refined, her sentences have a whiff of bygone times, strewn with expressions no longer used in daily speech. Robert's parents and his mother-in-law are also in the house. From the first moment, however, one feels the hand of Madame Bazin throughout. She offered us her own room and we are delighted. I sit in the armchair, looking out a window framed by yellow cretonne curtains, and softly recite André Maurois:

Dans votre salon Directoire
(Bleu lavande et jaune citron)
De vieux fauteuils voisineront
Dans un style contradictoire
Avec un divan sans histoire
(Bleu lavande et jaune citron).[231]

From below we hear the bell calling us to table. We enter during the prayer, which is being sung by the children. During lunch we talk about our journey, about Paris, about the Germans. Madame Bazin refers to them with a magnificent, refined malice and disdain that can only be conveyed in French. I listen as raptly as I did last night when Madame Vigné was talking about them. Everything is conveyed by a few expressions and by her tone, a specific vocal intonation that sometimes can escape the untrained ear. It's as though every step of the hobnailed boots on the well-groomed staircase, on each slat of the parquet floor, echoed as a sharp twinge in her heart. "There, at the bottom of the garden, they put their cannon . . . and they clipped branches of the apple tree to conceal their cars . . ."

After lunch, tired and lazy, we pass to the drawing room for coffee. The drawing room is a work of art. Conversation about the family. Robert even presents some old documents and is obviously proud of these promenades through the seventeenth century. The history of his family's rise and fall. Madame Bazin listens attentively, adding a few well-considered words from time to time, a few corrections. I experience an atmosphere I had so far known only from French novels. I say to myself: this is Flaubert. A family gathering in the drawing room of Madame Moreau, when Frédéric had returned home from Paris (*L'Éducation sentimentale*).[232]

After coffee we went to our room and slept until supper.

September 6, 1942

Sunday. In the morning we were brought café au lait, bread, and butter in our room. We had a jar of honey and sugar, which all together made a good breakfast. I opened the window—sunshine. We ate in our pajamas. After breakfast we dressed and went downstairs. Half the family had already been at morning Mass, we are going with Robert and little Elisabeth to the one at eleven. Near the entrance to the foyer, several prayer books for guests were laid out on a small table. We each took one and left. The local parish priest, *né* the Marquis de Chateauvieux, is also a Spanish grandee, a rare species. Our marquis-priest has a rather easy job here, because the whole *département* is traditionally Catholic, conservative, and known for its royalist sentiments. On the way to the church Robert told us, not without a certain pride, that the proprietors of the neighboring château support, at their own expense, the local elementary school, in which the history teacher is under orders not to teach the children anything about the French Revolution. Right in the middle of this democratic France. I asked him to repeat this because it was hard to believe. French democracy— yet another myth, a legend we were taught. Democracy here is a paper-thin external layer, a light, well-tailored coating, concealing a cramped and resentful caste system. The French clergy here remains an estate in the prerevolutionary sense, an estate fighting with the support of the Catholic faction in society, which is divided into a dozen self-enclosed conservative factions. The aristocracy, the hereditary bourgeoisie, the wealthy landed bourgeoisie—poor, poorer, and impoverished. Discrete layers, with minimal interpenetration—all under the cover of the semicultured masses, all of whom at every turn say *merci, pardon, excusez-moi, permettez que* . . . and who constitute the people, *le peuple*, with whom the caste of professional politicians (a special caste) does what it wants. Democracy is the form, inside which the feudal caste system persists. The relationship between the highest and the lowest social classes is democratic in form, but in practice points of contact are still lacking. So, if the language of politics in Europe as a whole has made progress, in France it remains at the level of 1789. The French worker or labor leader still speaks in the style of revolutionary pamphlets. I often get the impression that the great revolution in fact resolved nothing here, but stalled in the middle of the road, unsettling the equilibrium in which everything is counterbalanced, neutralized, pacified by means of constant chatter and half-measures. Of the slogan *"liberté, fraternité, égalité"*—only *liberté* was partially realized and the slogan in fact penetrated more deeply in countries such as America, above all, and after it England, that did not inscribe it on their state emblems. I don't know whether even Poland has not been a more democratic country *in practice* (not in form) than France. I remember a debate about Poland, which I had in 1939 with our émigrés in one of the most pro-Communist Polish milieus in Boulogne-Billancourt. To all arguments concerning the rights and privileges won by French workers in 1936 with the support of Blum's regime, I answered: "In Poland this has existed since the return of independence." The many reproaches they leveled against Poland made me realize that it's a matter of form that troubles them, the question of the "Polish lords," while France impresses them because an engineer shakes their hand and allows them to stand him a drink at the bar. They did not know that this "engineer" was most likely not an engineer at all but a trained and politicized sansculotte; they did not know that an actual engineer is more inaccessible to a worker here than in Poland, that the social gulf between them is many times greater. Even if he offers his hand, even if they exchange a few pleasant words, inside he despises that worker, that *canaille*,[233] more than our Polish aristocrat would; he exploits him like a colored man, and his true attitude is a hundredfold more "lordly" than the aristocrat's attitude back home. The revolution did not solve France's social problems and who knows if it didn't make them worse. Those who survived the revolution retreated behind a wall even thicker and more impenetrable than before. A new elite was created, which in the course of time took on the features of the hereditary aristocracy. The Napoleonic gentry enclosed itself in its own circle, and since it was drawn from the lower classes, and thus inexperienced, it often became more aristocratic than the old aristocracy. The bourgeoisie, having concentrated all the money in its hands, behaved similarly. And at the bottom, the people continue to agitate, envious and demanding, like any people prevented from moving gradually up the social scale. France is socially ossified. The revolutions have resulted above all in the destruction of the elite, the sapping of its vitality, its closing in on itself, and in the amazing tangle of all kinds of contempt. As after every revolution, thus also in France, what comes to the surface is boorishness, a coarsening that keeps spreading, though imperceptible at first glance, because it hides under the French *familiarité,* which nevertheless conceals thick skins and a degree of tactlessness rarely encountered anywhere else. They lack gentlemanliness, because they don't understand it. Where a superficial *politesse* counts as everything, it's incomprehensible that one can be a gentleman in the absence of form. I return to form, because without an understanding of form, one can't understand France. In France you can play the nastiest trick on the person you love most, you can commit the most despicable deed, while observing correct form. The French in general do not understand the difference, they do not grasp the fact that form does not get to the essence of things, either bad or good. Because here the essence of everything is form. The German occupation can serve as the best example. In France, the Germans behave the way they do in Poland, but here it's tempered, slower, and with the legal pretense of Vichy. And there's no way to explain to the French that it comes down to the same thing. Even worse: the French are incapable of understanding the great difference in the behavior of the two countries, they do not understand that Vichy is a stain on their history, a stain on their past. "If they are doing the same thing to you as to us, what's the difference, since the final effect is the same. We should both cede to their demands—why didn't you create some kind of government—it would have been easier for you . . ." They say this, not understanding our reasoning, convinced that their government assures their protection and that it's better that way. Perhaps . . .

We entered the church and sat down in the pews. The priest emerged surrounded by six altar boys with candles. He looked over his shoulder, grumbled at someone for some fault, and began to say the prayers. A latecomer banged the door. The priest turned and snarled loudly: *"Il est vraiment temps de venir."*[234] He read from the Gospels in the tone used to give soldiers their daily orders and began the sermon. He spoke plainly and immediately got down to the most important point—denunciations. The Germans are now inspecting the horses in all the villages and good horses are immediately requisitioned. Horses are the best machines on the Russian front. Around here the peasants have resorted to the trick of borrowing their neighbors' unfit horses to show to the inspector, instead of their own good ones. Everything was working very well, until right away someone naturally reported to the Kommandantur and the ruse, so extremely clever for the French, collapsed. The priest fumed: "This is not the first time . . . this depravity . . . envy . . . iniquity." He spoke to them of the most sacred of feelings, about envy. Envy here has assumed apocalyptic proportions. At this moment all over France envy and iniquity have joined hands and dominate the country. It's enough for a neighbor to notice that someone is being successful, that his business is doing well, for him to sit down and write a denunciation to the Germans. Hundreds of prisoners fleeing German captivity had been denounced, tens of thousands of people have had more or less serious experiences as a result of denunciations. The unsigned letter is to a degree the symbol of today's France. It betrays envy, the fruit of the incomplete revolution, the fruit of all revolutions. We Poles behave these days in a dignified manner, but just introduce the "dictatorship of the proletariat" in Poland, and the biggest patriots will start sending anonymous letters to some kind of Polish secret police, spreading depravity and iniquity the likes of which we would never have imagined before. With the help of Vichy and Pétain's *Révolution nationale*, the French have taken the occupation for the Revolution, the Kommandantur for the Committees of Public Safety, each Militärbefehlshaber for Fouquier-Tinville.[235] Thus, one of the booksellers along the Seine, seeing me, out of curiosity, pick up a *Guide to Writing Anonymous Letters* (indeed, it exists), told me: "Guides like this" (*les manuels*) "are currently in the greatest demand."

September 8, 1942

The weather continues to be marvelous, the days pass quickly. We go for walks, we stuff ourselves with blackberries, which grow abundantly along the roads, in the evenings we swim in the river. This afternoon Robert and I did ninety-two kilometers on our bicycles and for supper there was roast goose. After almost a hundred kilometers . . .

September 9, 1942

The sun is shining, the children are playing on the lawn in front of the house, and little Michel, in a large straw hat, has climbed onto a cow and is breaking it in. Basia is playing croquet with Jean-Claude. Robert comes up to me, carrying a newspaper, and says: "There's an interesting article. The German high command reminds us that they *never* predicted the capture of Stalingrad." I smile. Unfortunately they won't take it. I am firmly convinced of that.

After supper, the table cleared, everyone will play games. With typical Polish intensity, I will build an enormous pyramid of cards, which little Elisabeth will enjoy knocking down.

September 10, 1942

Yesterday afternoon we visited La Bourgonnière. This is a large farm, resembling a manorial estate (*la gentilhommière*), that long ago belonged to Robert's family. A large, old, two-story house with a small tower, once surrounded by a moat, its remains now reduced to manure. Altogether depressing. You can see how nice it once was. Having been purchased by some boor with money and now rented out to a tenant farmer, it's falling apart, rotting in dirt and slovenliness. The filth of the French village is horrible. Everything is exacted from the land, the buildings, and the machinery and nothing is given in return. This is a voracious, wasteful exploitation, using methods moreover that date from the Middle Ages. The local peasant often has a car and agricultural machinery, but everything drowns in such neglect and slovenliness that it all seems very primitive. I have never seen such filthy livestock, even back home in Poland. France is the image of the most backward capitalism, a reserve of that nineteenth-century capitalism I had until now learned about only in the history of economic theory.

We circled around the house, I peered into the interior. Filth and primitive conditions, life in a cave, with electricity. Robert walked around, looked the place over, and explained that once it had been like this or like that, something had stood here, something hung there . . . and so on. He behaved much more like a tourist than I did. I was reminded of Balzac's astute remark in *Modeste Mignon*: ". . . but to pass the time of day they had their horses saddled and ventured into the country that was as unknown to them as China. Because what is most foreign in France, to the French, is France."[236]

Balzac is practically a contemporary writer, because with the exception of insignificant social rearrangements, the CONTENT of France, which he grasped better than any other French writer, has remained the same to this day.

As evening fell, we went to another farm, this one belonging to Mme Bazin. A winding road through small fields, marked off by crooked trees. Lina bought a goose, we lay down next to a haystack on a pile of chaff. The stars slowly peppered the sky.

September 11, 1942

Yesterday Madame Bazin had some shopping to do in the nearby town of Château-Gontier, sixteen kilometers from Chambellay. Besides, she had to visit one of her cousins, who lives there in an old-age home. An ailing, elderly spinster pushed to the edge of the family plate, like a bone from the soup. She nevertheless salvaged something from the family pogrom and plunder, and having a small private income, she settled in the old-age home.

In the morning, Madame Bazin's farmer arrived in a small, two-wheeled cabriolet. She and Lina, with the little Jean-Claude, sat inside, covering their heads in straw hats and a palanquin of parasols, like our grandmothers used to have. The allée, shaded by chestnut trees, strewn with patches of sunlight, resembled a canvas by Manet and a fragment of Proust. Robert, Basia, the two boys, and I rode our bicycles. The weather is marvelous. Day after sunny day, almost a heat wave. Except for the chill mist in the morning and evening, a reminder of autumn. A pretty road, hilly, like all of them around here. Going uphill we hop from our bikes and walk, going down we're full speed ahead. We ride into town along a long allée of sycamores that overshadow the road. It's noon and hot. We follow the narrow streets to the upper part of the town and sit ourselves down in a cool bistro. We have cold meat, tomatoes, bread, cheese, and apples. We ask for wine, but there is none. How odd: in the very middle of Anjou—no wine. Obviously, it's the Germans. Robert is disconsolate—he can't offer me a taste of the *specialité du pays*, young white wine from Anjou. Instead, we drink soda water with grenadine, which tastes synthetic. In the dim bistro it's cool and pleasant and we're reluctant to leave. The heat is unbearable. We sit in the park and have no desire to move, but Robert is pitilessly conducting his tour of France and drags us through various spots, pointing out their beauty with the enthusiasm of a young man. We both love him for his entirely un-French enthusiasm, intelligence, and open-mindedness.

The houses here are built on the slopes, one next to the other. The roof of the house below becomes the garden of the house above. The gardens contain the withered remains of vegetables, nasturtiums tired from the heat, and dried-out asters. Well, it's already autumn. Down below, at the river, the grass has already turned brown and only in the small gardens are the flowers still blooming. Someone in a blue apron and large hat walks around watering them. In the silence of the hot day you can hear the whisper of water pouring from the spout in thin streams and bouncing against the leaves. I dream of watering flowers in my old age. How peaceful it is here. Both people and nature have the gentleness and calm of a genial Polish pensioner from Galicia. Basia and Lina remain in the park, I go with Robert and the children to examine the church. A few imposing black carriages are standing in the broad square. Everything is drenched in sun. The sight of the carriages reminds me of *Madame Bovary*. I see her walking quickly and fearfully toward one of them and I seem to perceive the silhouette of a man in a dark frock coat behind the window.

Then we go to meet Madame Bazin. The old-age home resembles a barracks. A large, three-story house with wings, a large, paved internal courtyard separated from the street by an iron fence with gilded spikes. The two women are standing at the entrance and talking. Madame Bazin's cousin is a small, older woman, who smiles amiably and conveys a piteous sense of abandonment, like a lost dog. Madame Bazin talks to her with the self-assurance of a person of means, masked by a courteous pretense of equality that only underscores her smooth condescension. "*Chère amie*" flies from mouth to mouth. Madame Bazin ate lunch in her apartment, because though the *cousine* lives in the old-age home, she has two rooms, furnished with the remains of her own furniture, and a young girl as a maid. In this milieu in France, this counts as extreme poverty. In Balzac the height of poverty consists of three rooms and a kitchen, a maid, and wine by the liter, not *bouché*—in corked bottles. Since then, there's been progress, indeed, in the downhill direction.

After a warm good-bye, the ladies climbed into the cabriolet, while we went to a bistro to look for wine, because Robert absolutely wants to show us the native *fillette* (the local name for specially shaped bottles of wine). After much haggling with the *patron*, we drank a *fillette* of white Anjou. Chilled and delicious. We overtake the cabriolet. Climbing, the cabriolet takes the lead, descending we pass it. The sky is ash blue, the fields are becoming silvery. A delightful day.

September 13, 1942

I spent the entire morning on the bicycles with Robert. It's easier to arrive than to depart. Tomorrow we are leaving and the trip had to be arranged. We went to Châteauneuf to enquire about the trains and "hire" a car. Robert took the occasion to settle some inheritance business with one of his aunts. This concerned a collection of silver belonging to a late cousin, who willed almost all of it to charity upon his death. A terrible man. The aunt lives in her own house, now entirely taken over by Germans. They left her only one room. An energetic, bony, elderly woman, of a tough disposition, categorical and dry. When speaking with us in the courtyard, she discusses her tenants at the top of her lungs, referring to them as *ces punaises qui ont apparues celle année*,[237] for which there's no antibedbug remedy. A large brooch pinned to her breast is shaped like the tricolor flag. A sun-filled silence. I stepped aside, leaving them both to *causer de leurs affaires*,[238] while I sat under the shade of a wall, observing and listening. I sat for an hour or longer, because Robert and his aunt had gone to inspect the silver that had been kept in a convent by the sisters. The silence was suddenly rent by the sound of the Germans singing as they went to bathe. The soldier on guard made an occasional clicking sound with his heels, but it was all encompassed in the calm of the sunny square with a monument in the center and blades of green grass growing between the paving stones. Robert returned and recounted the story of the inheritance and the silver, after which we went to the station. We arranged for a car. The train leaves before seven in the morning.

In the afternoon Basia and I ran out to pluck some blackberries for preserves. A storm was coming up. We picked them quickly, before the rain could start, because wet berries would not have survived the trip. As we were returning it already started to rain. The first rain for many weeks. We were thoroughly drenched, but we felt like laughing. In a way, we had let ourselves get drenched on purpose. Back at the house this drenching met with silent reproach. If they could understand that someone might want, from time to time, to get completely drenched, they might understand many other things they do not understand.

Yesterday afternoon we went for a ride on our own. A back road took us through some rough terrain overgrown on all sides by blackberries. We lay down on the grass and looked up at the sky through the leaves of the trees. Occasionally a swallow flashed by, occasionally a crow flew over on heavy wings. I don't know why, but it always seems to me that no crow on earth can ever be thin. Lonely ants were running around with silly expressions on their faces. A lonely ant, so "individual," always has a silly expression on its face. It can't help it. And nervous movements. If things continue the way they are headed, the average man will not know how to be alone. And when he is alone, he will have a silly expression on his face. Then we plucked the blackberries and ate them. We kept discovering ever more patches and bonanzas and we returned to the house with blackened lips and teeth. Again we were regarded with silent reproach. Because blackberries are not considered real fruit.

Our last evening. It's cool and fragrant after the storm. The last odors of greenery, like the perfume of a girl who has gone away. And the same sadness. The last hot rays of the sun. I said to Basia: "Tomorrow we're going back home" and both of us burst out laughing. To Paris—going home. A strange feeling. I feel that whatever else happens in my life, Paris will be home.

September 15, 1942

We left yesterday. We left Chambellay early in the morning. It was still dark. In Châteauneuf we boarded the train that took us to Le Mans. It was a lovely day and we both stood at the window the whole time. An autumnal haze and melancholy now hung over the fields. The train crawled slowly, the locomotive behaved as though it had angina pectoris, the small stations were dozing even during the stops.

At Le Mans the spell was broken. A big railway hub, everything electric-powered. A network of rails on the ground, a network of wires overhead, twisted into a great tangle. A brain made of wires. The hum of conversation, crowds of people pushing their way in all directions, platforms buried in baggage. We boarded our train by a miracle (I began to believe in miracles), losing the others in the crush. Basia and I planted ourselves in the corridor next to a window and stood there until Paris. The express train was doing over a hundred kilometers an hour, while I was thinking the whole time that one day at this same speed I would say "adieu" to Europe and transport myself to a sanctuary where you don't have to start pummeling your way through crowds first thing in the morning.

At Gare Montparnasse we said good-bye to Robert and his wife and the rest of the family. The metro was crowded and rank, stifling hot. Our room was messy and sweltering.

Today I returned to work and was immediately caught up in the feverish mood of expectation. Laval's promise of 150,000 volunteers to go work in Germany has not been kept because practically no one has gone. Vichy therefore has passed a national labor decree. All Frenchmen between the ages of eighteen and fifty must be employed. Registration at the town halls, factories must provide personnel lists, etc.—in a word, forced consignment to Germany under the patronage of Laval and Pétain. The French are upset, they gripe, but are afraid of everything. Moreover, the entire consignment occurs under the sign of the "changing of the guard." For every three specialists sent to Germany, the Germans will release one prisoner. It's called *la relève* and the act of leaving for Germany becomes—an act of patriotism. *Pour la France.* Even so, no one is rushing to comply, despite the great propaganda campaign. After this one day of discussions, rumors, *on-dit*, I returned home exhausted, as though I'd never gone on vacation at all. I have therefore stopped thinking.

September 17, 1942

I have therefore extracted Flaubert's *L'Éducation sentimentale* from one of our many suitcases and am reading it. I read it exactly three years ago, when I knew little about France. Now I'm smacking my lips. Each sentence becomes more significant, I see absolutely everything. Flaubert might have had cirrhosis of the liver, was perhaps a "workaholic," but he's great.

September 25, 1942

Yet another correction to the decree on "national labor." Everyone's in a panic. But I don't give a damn. Because I'm reading. Because Madame Arnoux did not show up at the rendezvous and Frédéric instead brought Rosanette to the room he had prepared for her. "Toward one in the morning, she was awakened by distant sounds; she saw that he was sobbing, his head buried in the pillow.

"'What's the matter, my beloved?'

"'Too much happiness,' said Frédéric. 'I have desired you for too long.'"

This is probably one of the most moving chapter endings in world literature. I searched through the snatches of notes I took three years ago. Under September 30, 1939, I wrote: "Evening: the sky has clouded over, the moon looks like a candle shielded by the palm of a hand. You don't see it, but the light breaks through along the sides. I went out onto the balcony with a cigarette. A warm night, silent. Below, the street is empty except for a car starting its engine. It growls a bit and chokes. Up above, the black outline of the chimney and the whole sky, across the street from time to time someone coughs. The sputtering car and the man coughing in the garret have something in common. The car pulled away, the coughing stopped, and silence returned. It's beginning to rain. Frédéric became Madame Dambreuse's lover."

The decree on national labor . . .

September 29, 1942

Basia had a prophetic dream last night. She always dreams. At night she sleeps—and dreams, in the daytime, she doesn't sleep, but dreams anyway. She gazes at sparrows hopping about on a tree and—dreams. The moon's daughter, as Kali said about Nel. Today she dreamed that a giant bust of Washington appeared in the sky. People gathered in the streets, gazing at the apparition. And suddenly Washington began to speak. He said the war will end in thirty-six weeks. That is, in June 1943 it'll be over. Nine more months. She dreams of Washington, but I can't even manage to dream of a slice of *corned beef*. It seems to me, however, that Washington was pulling Basia's leg with a bit of ordinary American *humbug*. I try to convince her that it was probably Mark Twain disguised as Washington. And he is making silly jokes.

October 2, 1942

Yesterday in the Berlin Sportpalast that satanic clown gave yet another speech. The same as ever: *"Taten gegen Reden"* (I'd call it rather, *Reden wegen Taten*), *"Dilettantische Gegner, Erreichte Ziele."*[239] Exactly. In a communiqué of September 26 the Germans announced triumphantly that in Stalingrad they had conquered—a bakery. Unbelievable. They only forgot to mention, it was a bakery with fresh bread. No big deal. Let's continue. Thus: *"Gigantischer Aufbau, der europäische Kreuzzug"* (*Kreuzrätsel*, no?), *"erkämpfte Volksgemeinschaft und so weiter."*[240] His speech-making style is horrendous. Demosthenes for louts. It's always the quintessence of vulgarity, lame jokes, and infinitely stupid self-assurance. It's truly a corporal's language. Although I don't know whether this isn't in their national character and even Goethe, having become a dictator, would not also have made speeches like a corporal. Because they don't understand any other language. Can the world be any different, when one of its most powerful leaders makes speeches SUCH AS THESE? Not to speak of the content. But the manner, the style. Listening to it, I feel like Petronius listening to Nero.[241] And those hopeless prophecies: *"Wenn wir zum Beispiel in den nächsten paar Monaten zum Don vorstossen, den Don abwärts endlich die Wolga erreichen, Stalingrad anrennen und es auch nehmen werden—worauf sie sich verlassen können (brausender, minutenlanger Beifall)—so ist das in ihren Augen"* (in the eyes of the English) *"garnichts . . ."*[242] Does this buffoon want to show off in front of the English? Clearly he cares about their opinion. In any case, Stalingrad gives him no rest, because he goes on: *"Jetzt ist es insbesondere die Inbesitznahme von Stalingrad selbst, die abgeschlossen werden wird, wodurch dieser Riegel vertieft und verstärkt wird. Und sie können der Überzeugung sein dass uns kein Mensch von dieser Stelle mehr wegbringen wird. (Tosender Beifall.)"*[243] We won't be moved! But I'm not convinced. I'm no staff officer, haven't finished military school, was never a corporal, but I have a good map, and for a long time I've considered the entire Southern Front to be an over-inflated balloon. It's not the Germans who are pushing the Bolsheviks back, it's the Bolsheviks who are drawing the Germans in and driving them into difficult positions. The whole German front, strategically speaking, is untenable in the event of a smartly conceived counteroffensive. I'm ready to draw arrows from the points from which the Russian counterattack should be launched and I'm ready to prove this thesis *jusqu'à la preuve du contraire*.[244] But people are so easily swayed by all this that it's no use wasting words.

Nevertheless the English are giving our Führer no rest. What a moron. Why does he talk about them? If not for Hitler's speeches, one could forget about them. But this way he supplies the English with a ready argument for talks with Stalin. They can say: "But Hitler mentions us all the time, although you, comrade, insist we are sh—— and worthless." If not for the Russians and Hitler's stupid babble, I swear I don't know what the English would use for their radio propaganda and what they would talk about. But Hitler keeps repeating himself. In English you could call it *personal talk*, so person-to-person: "*Herr Churchill, Angst haben Sie mir noch nie eingejagt. Aber dass wir nachgrübeln müssen, da haben Sie recht, denn wenn ich einen Gegner von Format hätte, dann könnte ich mir ungefär ausrechnen, wo er eingreift. Wenn man aber militärische Kindsköpfe vor sich hat, da kann man natürlich nicht wissen, wo sie angreifen—es kann ja auch das verrückteste Unternehmen sein. Und das ist das einzig Unangenehme, dass man bei diesen Geisteskranken*" (Roosevelt) "*oder ständig Betrunkenen nie weiss, was sie anstellen werden.*"[245]

Better and better. Hitler believes that a *Gegner von Format*—an enemy of stature—ought to give him advance notice of where he will strike or behave in a manner that would allow him to calculate the target exactly. An original concept of strategy—indeed completely new. Compared to this strategy I prefer the alcoholic strategy of Churchill. Besides, Roosevelt is a paralyzed nutcase, Churchill is a drunken loony, London says Hitler is mad, and so on. If things are this bad now, what will happen at the end of the war? Compared to all this, Stalin, who is never mentioned, seems like the caretaker of the madhouse.

October 4, 1942

Yesterday evening we went to the Champs-Élysées. The weather is nice, mild and autumnal. The setting sun made the falling leaves seem even redder than they were. Sacha Guitry's new film, *Le Destin fabuleux de Désirée Clary*,[246] has opened in one of the cinemas. I bought tickets for the evening show. But we were hungry and there wasn't enough time to go home. We went for supper to the Marignan. One of the most elegant restaurants on the Champs-Élysées. How comfortable to take a seat on the padded benches, shielded from the world by a table pushed toward us by the solicitous garçon, and pore over the menu. While our thoughts are running over *tomates à la provençale, huitres, foie grillé aux pommes*, and so on, the garçon arranges the plates and glasses, positions the knives and forks, as though they were precious jewels, and lays out the napkins with the motion of a croupier dealing the cards. He then discreetly inquires *quel vin Messieurs Dames ont choisi.*[247] "*Un bordeaux blanc,*" I answer, preoccupied with the choice of dishes. We start with a salad, after that Basia takes the grilled liver, for me the pig trotters *en vinaigrette*, followed by the tomatoes *à la provençale*, ice cream, black coffee — more black than coffee. I light a cigarette. Next to us a young German is eating dinner in the company of a classy *fille*. A large plate of oysters and the neck of a bottle of champagne, poking out of the silver cooler. The girl eats carefully, so as not to destroy the lipstick on her artfully painted lips, babbles, fawns all over him — behaves with the kind of self-assurance that instantly shows that she is not sure of herself at all. The young Hans with faded eyes tries to affect the attitude and gestures of a gentleman, which Germans rarely succeed in doing. Their parvenu culture always rises to the surface.

The garçon discreetly slips me the check under a napkin. I pay with a single large bill and get change. Money is not supposed to bring happiness. Quite possibly. But when you are happy, money certainly brings happiness. I was very happy.

We entered the movie theater. I settled into the comfortable seat and lit a cigarette. In the Sacha Guitry style, the film is not so much about Désirée Clary as about Sacha Guitry. The story of the life of Marshal Bernadotte's wife set against the background of the empire.[248] Sacha Guitry is as accurate in his historical accounts as the French in spelling the maiden name of their queen Maria Leszczyńska.[249] He went to town on the subject of Napoleon's love for Bernadotte's wife, the love that flowered in Toulon and that, according to Sacha Guitry, lasted to the end of his days. But that's not the point. The point is whether Bernadotte was a traitor, and a subtle sophistry threads its way through the film with less subtle allusions to Pétain's current situation. *Hier liegt der Hund begraben.*[250] Was he a traitor or was he not? Not, says Guitry. That's the point. General Moreau never became a king, thus he is unanimously considered a traitor.[251] Amen to that! — death to the losers. And Sacha Guitry will not be among them, that's the main thing . . . Sacha Guitry will never lose. He's not that kind.

Yesterday Göring gave a speech. Because the English have recently begun to bombard Germany FOR REAL, the head of the Luftwaffe had to speak up and raise his compatriots' spirits. He, who in 1939 was promising that not a single bomb would ever fall on Germany, said today that people subject to bombardment will receive—extra meat rations. All Paris is now rolling in laughter, people haven't laughed like this for a long time. Everyone everywhere is saying: "*Vous savez*—Göring has invented a new antiaircraft weapon—extra meat rations." And so, progress is being made.

October 11, 1942

Yesterday we spent the whole afternoon wandering around the Left Bank. It was warm and drowsy. I looked in every possible bookshop for *L'Avenir de l'esprit* by Lecomte du Noüy and finally found it.[252] Basia rearranged all the window displays in the antiques shops. On rue Bonaparte she showed me an interesting one. A small shop, specializing in the sale of costume jewelry from the Second Empire. Brooches, pins, crosses, earrings, flowers—all made from microscopic pieces of polished steel, resembling diamonds. Some items were pretty and inexpensive. Ten, fifteen, twenty francs apiece. Basia bought herself a couple of things. The nicest was a small cross on a wide chain, all made of superfine braided black wire. And so we strolled endlessly through the spots we know by heart and never tire of. At one point I said to Basia that if I ever published my journal, I'd call it *War and Peacefulness*.

October 14, 1942

Monsieur Pagès from the Ministry of Labor called to tell me that the prior of the Dominican monastery in Étiolles[253] had been to see him asking to be allocated some farmhands. That was about ten days ago. With the aim of inspecting the conditions there and discovering whether I couldn't use the situation to harbor some of our Poles, I set out this morning on my bicycle for Étiolles. It's about thirty-seven kilometers beyond Paris in the direction of Melun. An autumn day, a pleasant, ash-gray morning. It was a few minutes after seven when I left, taking along some bread and cheese and a piece of chocolate. Silently I flew along the asphalt pathways of the Bois de Vincennes. The trees had the color of oxidized copper—a reddish green, and the fallen leaves rustled under my wheels. In the all-embracing calm, spun like a spiderweb, the rustle of the leaves crushed under my wheels suggested a whisper and magnified the silence. True silence requires some noise and can only be experienced truly through the delicate contrast. A room is never entirely silent unless in some corner a clock is ticking or a sleepy cat purring.

I rode down to the Marne and out onto the road. A chilly sun began to shine through the ash-gray clouds and light up the roofs. The multicolored advertisements for pasta and *biscotte* factories, which abound here, splattered against the background, like paint drops trickling onto blotting paper. The bicycle flits silently over the asphalt and the wind pounds in my ears. I place myself under the colors, sounds, and images as under a stream of water. A shower of impressions. And fun. Pedaling mechanically, I say to myself: "Now pay attention to the colors." After a bit: "Now catch the details, the minutiae, the nothings." The imperceptible "nothings" that together make "everything." These "nothings" are the details that, taken separately, mean nothing. But the more there are of them, the stronger the mood, the stronger the "Something" floating through the air and creating an atmosphere. When I'm inside Notre-Dame I cannot feel the mood, because these "nothings" are lacking there and as a result it's just a dignified but boring desert. Interesting only for stonemasons. But when I approach from outside, from the side of the garden, when the doves floating across the sky form moving patterns, when a ripe chestnut slaps the ground, when an old man feeds tame sparrows from his palm and near the fence a toddler discreetly pees—then I get a feel for everything, I even comprehend the Middle Ages, toward which I have a Gothic aversion. I always find the Gothic alien, I see it but I don't have the feeling for it that other people have. Now, moreover, it is for me the incarnation of something else. I have told myself I can do very well in life without that Gothic of theirs. Including Dürer and Cranach! If the German Middle Ages were to take a bit of a hit from some four-ton bombs, I wouldn't care at all. The kilometers fly by. The day has become completely sunny. I stop and roll a cigarette. Nearly four years of this strange life here have made me into a perfect vagabond. I'm happiest wandering around, with or without a purpose. And when I don't have something particular to do, I can sit and take ten minutes to roll a cigarette. I have a smoke. A *feldgrau* motorcycle passes by— probably gendarmes. No—ordinary Morituri. I regard them always from the grammatical standpoint, in the Participium Futuri Passivi of *morior*—doomed to die. I open the map of *Paris et ses environs* and check the route. Then I continue. Small houses with gardens, a minipalace surrounded by trees. In Étoilles I inquire about the monastery. I'm soon driving through the gate and entering a large park. To the right there's a large building under construction, to the left a smaller old one. I enter the smaller one. A corridor and a hall. The benches and tables are piled with books—a Catholic publishing house. Two friars in black-and-white habits are carrying large trays with brass mugs. I ask for the prior. They go off to find him. I sit on one of the benches. Monks in monasteries all move as silently as though on pneumatic roller skates. My friar rolled off and melted into the shadows of the hall. He returned shortly and invited me into a separate room. A small vaulted chamber, freshly whitewashed. In the corner a large fireplace with a hood in the form of a half-cone. In the middle a heavy table, on which several beautifully bound volumes are lying, large Normandy arm-chairs against the walls. The ensemble is simple, even severe, but tasteful. I leaf through a magnificent history of Assyrian culture, translated from the English. The prior enters. I had expected someone older with a potbelly, I see a young, thirty-something man, slender, with an energetic and strikingly intelligent face. The suggestion of a smile flits across his eyes and his lips, something cutting but also appealing. At the sight of this face, one can't help starting to hear all the sharp maxims of Chamfort, La Rouchefoucauld, and others. I introduce my-self. For the sake of politeness, I describe how I found the place and looking out the window pay a few compliments to the enormous building, a mountain of cement and stone, heaving itself up into the sky. The prior looks at me with his cutting smile and says: "Indeed, it's big, but as you yourself know, it's hard to call it beautiful. *C'est grand mais ce n'est pas beau.*"[254] I burst out laughing. "*Vous ne me permettez pas d'être aimable.*"[255] We both laugh and our glances reflect the instant and pleasant meeting of humor and intelligence. I come straight to the point and ask about the possibility of placing several workers in the monas-tery. Alas, now it's not possible. It's autumn and in addition he had to hire sev-eral liberated prisoners. I want to take my leave, but the prior offers me coffee with milk and bread and cheese. I decline the bread, because I have my own, but I'd gladly drink some coffee. They bring me an entire pot. The prior leans on the fireplace and we chat. He tells me that Mr. Pagès has described me as something of an ambassador for Poles. That's an overstatement, I explain, but our office attached to a French factory and, in particular, Dr. K. and myself at the moment constitute something of a diplomatic outpost. I tell him about our work. He asks about my studies, about the level of university education in Poland. One of those conversations evolves that you remember for a long time. I learn that the monastery is a center of learning, that students of theology and students from Catholic universities come here to take courses and that in nor-mal times the place swarms with a multilingual crowd. The monastery publishes a range of work, has its own press, and so on. For several years he was professor of canon law at the Vatican university, where he encountered many Catholic clergy from all over the world. He was mobilized during the war, was a lieuten-ant in one of the rare motorized divisions in the French army, and after Dun-kirk was taken prisoner. About a year ago he was released. "We were firing with your ammunition, and your mine-throwers were terrific," says the prior, when the conversation touches on Châtillon and the factory where I work. The defeat of France? Rot, decadence. In this war the French were Communists, socialists, pacifists, anarchists — everything except Frenchmen. Our present regime? A sad operetta, backing the wrong horse. Better not speak of it. We're aging at lightning speed. His impression of the Vatican? The best face of Catholicism is the American clergy. Yes — that's true renovated Catholicism, moving with the spirit of the times. Materialism is a thing of the past, we know, but we still can't tear ourselves away. We don't want to admit we made the wrong calculations and recognize the negative results, because the entire calculation began with blind faith in a positive result. Measured words are spoken and wise glances peer from behind the gold-rimmed eyeglasses. Delicate observations, permeated by a critique of the "old" Catholicism, emit an elusive freshness. He has known several outstanding Polish priests, whose names he does not remember. "These were not men of this world. One of them spoke six languages and held a doctor's degree in three faculties, *mais vous savez, il nageait dans l'absolu . . ."*[256] The Spanish priests are horrible. *"Ce sont des fanatiques tout à fait du temps de la Sainte Inquisition."*[257] I had long ago drunk all the coffee and finished my cigarette. I don't want to leave. But finally I stand up and say good-bye. The prior gives me the addresses of a few farms where I might eventually place some of our men. I thank him, but apologizing in advance for my honesty, I say I'd rather see them in a concentration camp than working as farmhands for a French peasant. The prior smiles: "I see that you've gotten to know France very well." *"Oui*—quite well, Father, quite well . . . ," I answer and leave.

October 18, 1942

Today an infernal racket. Yesterday the English dared bombard the Schneider-Creusot plants in Creusot. Of course there were victims, but just a few. All the same, a great cry was raised — in the newspapers, naturally. However, people have learned to see this as a military necessity. Schneider was working exclusively for the Germans. There's apparently been a lot of damage to the factory. That's what really counts. The French should thank the Lord that the English bother to destroy things for them, especially when it comes to industrial plants. They should pray for them to destroy as much as possible. At least after the war they will be able to rebuild everything, installing the latest equipment, instead of working in those junkyards in which the newest machines date back to the Dreyfus Affair. And this will allow them to compete successfully with those horrible English, who, under pressure of the war, are now updating their industry. Not to speak of Germany, which will rebuild with the help of American loans, just like they did after the last war.

For a while we have been hearing more and more about the American "flying fortresses." They are not new machines. The prototype was already finished a few years before the war, now they are going into serial production. A four-engine monster, carrying around eight tons of bombs. The English are currently bombarding Germany with two-ton bombs, but one hears also of four-ton bombs. The Germans call these bombs *Bezirksbomben,* because one alone destroys an entire district. That's progress! Heartwarming. We feel a childlike joy hearing of such marvels. This is the savagery to which THEY have reduced us. We are paying them back with their own "culture."

October 20, 1942

Laval gave a truly piteous speech beseeching the workers to go work in Germany. The workers don't want to. In the end they'll be taken from the factories by force. Many plants have already drawn up lists of those obliged to leave. Transport is being organized, but barely half of those designated show up at the stations. Fear and anxiety. But even so, how much more delicately it's done here. There are no "roundups," deportations, raids.

October 27, 1942

My birthday. It would be nice if time could really slow down just a bit. I have not yet entirely recovered from the shock of failing my Gymnasium exams (in Polish, moreover—likely the origin of my passion for writing), but ten years have already passed since then. As a birthday present I received a cigarette holder from Basia, and from the English a great offensive in Egypt aimed at defeating Rommel Africanus.

November 1, 1942

For the first time since arriving in Paris we did not visit Père Lachaise. We stayed home all day. I'm reading the ten-volume *Memoirs of the Duchess d'Abrantès,* the wife of General Junot.[258] It's said that Balzac helped her write them. A caustic dame, so caustic that poison spouts from some of her pages. What stories! . . . She was a fervent patriot. Didn't mince her words with the French. Their villainy is as disturbing to her as to me. When the Russian and Prussian armies entered Paris, the French behaved just as they did in 1940. Sucking up to the conqueror, turning away not only from Napoleon (which could be justified) but away from honor, pride, and a sense of their own dignity—this was as horrifying then as two years ago. The dame's memory is a good one and often embarrassing, because it's based on documents. She managed to quote the exact list of jewels and ex-votos stolen by General Lannes from the churches of Saragossa. It's a sorry tale, this siege of Saragossa. One general after another, one marshal after another, fighting tooth and nail at every building, to no avail, while there in Paris, one leaf after another withers on the invincible emperor's laurel wreath. I read this and see before my eyes the same thing today. Over there, on the Volga, the generals and marshals of the invincible Führer, fighting fang and claw at every building in Stalingrad. Day after day the leaves on the *Eichenlaub*[259] wither and fall. New appointments and medals don't help, just as the entailments and titles awarded by the emperor failed to help then.

November 2, 1942

We did not take Stalingrad. And — what's worse — we intend to get a spanking at El-Alamein. Montgomery continues to press, as he has since October 27, and we're beginning to run out of breath. We're already writing about the "overwhelming superiority of the enemy" and are preparing public opinion for "a victorious retreat."

November 6, 1942

Veni, vidi, vici. Sir Montgomery can say the same. Rommel Africanus took a licking at the Battle of El-Alamein and is retreating at breakneck speed, pursued by a swarm of English airplanes, relentlessly pelting him with bombs. The German air force is running into trouble, the real beginning of the end. Thus Rommel is throwing the Italians to the wolves, and they gladly let themselves be taken prisoner en masse. The *patronne* sitting at the radio became quite deranged and goes on raving: "*Dites donc, ils ont dit que . . . ils ont expliqué . . . enfin je ne sais pas répéter . . .*"[260] and hops around the radio. People are radiant. It's about time the English did something, because one might have thought the war involved only Germany and Russia.

November 7, 1942

This evening we went to the Odéon Theater to see Paul Raynal's new play, *Napoléon unique*.[261] The three acts, with only five characters, that is, Napoleon (as the title indicates), Joséphine, Madame Mère, Fouché, and Talleyrand, are an unsuccessful attempt to compress the great drama of Napoleon's divorce from Joséphine into the confines of a few endless dialogues.[262]

The business of his divorce from Joséphine is nothing new in 1809. It's been the subject of conversation for a long time and Joséphine has been progressively distanced from the court. Exposed to the insults of people who not long ago prostrated themselves at her feet but now turn away, no longer seeing any use in worshiping the fallen goddess. Joséphine withdraws slowly from the life of the court and, having formed her own minor court of several loyal, but no less calculating women friends, moves back and forth, with her innate restlessness, between Malmaison and Paris. She ages and puts on weight. Left on her own, sensing that something unpleasant is happening behind her back, Joséphine cries and laughs, alternating between the high tides of pessimism and the low tides of optimism, as Monsieur Prudhomme might have said.[263] She seeks oblivion among the tailors and milliners, hanging out with this vulgar horde, who always have something to sell. Visits by all kinds of *marchandes de frivolités*,[264] sessions with fortune-tellers and astrologists. The bills pile up relentlessly on Napoleon's desk. While he, indeed *"Napoléon unique,"* knits his brow and—waits.

War with Austria delayed the divorce, the unfolding campaign sped it up. Essling, Aspern, Wagram—these are no longer swift victories but hard-won branches of the laurels added with great effort to the crown of glory. (I should be holding forth at patriotic morning assemblies.) France has bled profusely for these successes and no longer rejoices as she once did. In the villages, the draft provokes riots, often repressed by force. For the legend to endure, France needs peace. It's a turning point in Napoleon's life. Dreams of the dynasty, long concealed and impossible to realize for obvious reasons, are reviving. (Rzecki would be proud of me. This introduction captivates even me.) Napoleon feels that he must settle down, must break with political skulduggery and with his stormy past. He wants to enjoy the fruits of his victories in peace. His marriage with Marie-Louise of Austria will allow him to join the world of legitimate rulers, to open the doors to the chambers of monarchs, and turn the adventurer into the equal of those divinely anointed heads. Divorce—put off from day to day, from month to month—becomes irrevocable, *conditio sine quo vadis*, as Edmund Krzymuski liked to say.[265] But Napoleon senses and foresees the consequences of this step. Divorce from Joséphine is divorce from Bonaparte, from the glorious past and the legend that drove the people wild. Joséphine is his youth, the years of the young general's blinding flashes of genius. Napoleon feels regret, is fearful and ashamed in front of France, while still deep inside harboring feelings of attachment that revive memories: the wedding, Egypt, the return, the small palace on rue Chantereine, the coup d'état, First Consul. Then Malmaison. Work . . . The small pavilion near the gate, the table covered with papers, the hot summer days and quiet evenings. The silhouette of a woman in a white dress flitting among the trees, stopping at the rosebushes . . . He so loved the sight of women dressed in white among the greenery. No—it's impossible. Reports keep coming, piling up on his desk. The English are threatening to land, the reports from the coast are inaccurate. Illegible scribbles fill the margins of the documents. Divorce? Yes—a necessity. He cannot work calmly. He scurries across the room, looking out the window. Autumn, the leaves are turning yellow in the Tuileries . . .

That's my version. What about Raynal? Raynal has failed completely to make the most of the subject. He based the entire plot on a minor incident, discovered by an alleged spy posing as an astrologer who wormed his way into Joséphine's company. The spy was no doubt Fouché's invention, as a way to expedite Napoleon's decision, providing a pretext for the divorce. The first act is a monologue by Napoleon directed at Fouché, after which Talleyrand pokes his nose in for no obvious reason. Perhaps to be able at the end of the act to express an opinion of Napoleon that he never actually held. Napoleon speaks, reproaches him with everything, insults him, loses his temper. This is one of those attacks of volubility, a burst of interminable sentences, to which the emperor was prone from time to time. They would last two, often three hours, without any restraint in the choice of expressions and epithets. *Merde, assiette de merde,* and other select bits enriched his stormy outpourings. In the first act Raynal offered an example of one of these great tirades. Fortunately, though true enough to the general tone of the monologue, he was not pedantic when it came to its length. Even so, the imprecations flung at Fouché and Talleyrand lasted almost forty-five minutes and thoroughly exhausted Henri Rollan (Napoleon) and the audience.

Second act in the apartment of Madame Mère. Joséphine, foreseeing her impending doom, looks for help from Mama Letizia.[266] But Mama's initial sympathy for the cause of the daughter-in-law she never particularly loved vanishes when Napoleon tells her about the spy. The mother lion, always protective of her beloved son, awakes within her. All this would be fine, except for the excessive realism in the portrayal of Mama Letizia. We know she never learned to speak French properly and had no qualms butchering the language. So Madame Lily Mounet did the same thing and for the entire second act spoke Italian French-style and French Italian-style. She tried so assiduously to conceal her ignorance of Italian that her French became entirely incomprehensible, except for moments when she forgot about Italian and pronounced a few French phrases according to the proper rules.

Third act in the library at Malmaison. Nighttime. Napoleon is working. Joséphine enters and, in the absence of witnesses, a rather vulgar scene ensues be-

tween the married couple. Each heaps reproaches on the other, in language as
free as the costume Joséphine is wearing—a nightgown with *sex appeal*. The
dialogue vividly evokes an exchange between two housewives fighting over their
places in line. As a proper Frenchman, the author could not go beyond the limits
of an ordinary *engueulade*,[267] in which the man runs at the mouth just like the
woman and just as much. Seeing that all this chatter is getting her nowhere,
Joséphine takes another tack, luring Napoleon—into bed. This piece of furniture had been standing to stage left, practically a symbol of France. Joséphine
alters her voice, meows and minces, like a purebred Parisian she-cat, fawns and
writhes, but then again, her senses alive, her muscles tensed, she pants like the
panther in the well-known Polish tango. Napoleon also hisses, grunts, and runs
around—but, no. Wounded in her woman's pride, on the principle that nothing so touches a woman to the quick as not being touched when she wants to
be, Joséphine gives up and—walks out. This would have been fine, if after all
this, Napoleon had not banged on—the open door, which he had not wanted to
open, and had not dropped to his knees beside the empty bed, writhing in pain,
exciting himself with morbid memories of a warm bosom, firm thighs, and other
splendors. He is indeed *unique*, Monsieur Raynal's *Napoléon unique*.

November 8, 1942

Strange things are beginning to happen. This morning I pass our *patron's*
"office" and I see his wife waving to me through the glass while dancing wildly
around the radio like a Sioux Indian. I enter and am inundated with a flood of
quite incredible news. The Americans have landed in North and East Africa.
Algiers, Morocco, Casablanca, Dakar. They're landing everywhere. In some
places, the French make a semblance of fighting, but judging by the tone of the
communiqués, the landings are happening in places prepared in advance for
this kind of dirty trick. Hitler's plans for Eurafrica are kaput! Admiral Darlan
has apparently flown to Algiers in order to organize the defense, Pétain issued
an order to the army, and General Giraud, having escaped from captivity, is
also in Algiers, they say.[268] In a word, a fine mess, as we used to say in my family.

Very impressive. The French are beaming. The French fleet in Toulon has
apparently been ordered to put to sea. This evening, supper at Mr. and Mrs. P.'s
place. I turn on the radio and listen to Hitler's speech. Some strange notes
have crept into this speech. The Führer is responding to accusations. Whose?
Not clear. He denies that the Volga offensive was a mistake. Rolls out the figures to prove it and says: *"Ich weiss wirklich nicht, ob das alles nur Fehlern
waren . . ."*[269] Who's making these accusations? You could feel the fury in his

voice. He thrashed around, beside himself. I haven't heard him for a long time and I have to admit that the sound of these words, spit out in a fit of rage, sent shivers down my back. As though I were listening to Lucifer himself. Tens of millions of people at the mercy of a cursed madman. It's obvious he did not count on the occupation of Africa and was not prepared for it. If Roosevelt says Africa must be defended against Germany and Italy, he barked, *"so braucht man über diese verlogene Phrase dieses alten Gangsters kein Wort zu verlieren."*[270] A blockhead, a complete blockhead and for that reason so dangerous. I dialed Radio London. A calm voice announced an address by Mrs. Roosevelt to the women of England. Then came the blah-blah-blah of the president's wife . . . Pearls for the girls! Funny old dame, but her prattle warmed my heart. God, what a different world . . .

November 10, 1942

Armistice in Algiers. In any case, Darlan has surrendered to American "captivity." Our admiral, our great collaborator, who only a week ago was on inspection in Africa and gave a belligerent speech to the troops (*Nous défendrons l'Afrique contre qui que ce soit*[271])—has turned traitor. Pétain's successor has gone over to the other side. It's not yet official, but it's the obvious consequence of everything that's going on. The French are rehabilitating themselves. Characteristically, by deception. Somewhat stinky Wallenrodism.[272] But good that they can at least afford it.

What was left for the Germans to do? They have entered the *zone libre*, occupying the rest of France. They are "conquering" what was conquered long ago. It's almost pitiful. Hitler sent Pétain a letter and has entered unoccupied France. Someone is mocking the Germans shamelessly. Pétain himself must have had a hand in it, too. A nasty little trick. And then the Italians are taking Corsica, the Riviera, and Savoie. Finally, they too have "conquered" something. Unfortunately the Americans don't have the stamina to occupy both Tunis and Bizerte, where the Germans are landing, in order to defend the French possessions. Panic and pandemonium! The newspapers have not yet received their guidelines from the Berlin *Propagandastaffel*[273] and merely repeat the bulletins without commentary. It's as if the war were starting all over again. "It's not so far from Africa to Paris," people are saying. "Another few months." Even I have the impression that it won't be long, although I'm convinced this game will last at least another year.

November 12, 1942

I have reread *Madame Bovary*. This is the first time I've gotten the true taste of this novel. Homais, the pharmacist, is the classic type whose authenticity can only be truly judged when one has to deal with such specimens every day. And what's worse, France keeps "homaisizing" itself more and more all the time. The effect of reading this novel is elusive. A certain hardness. Basia, who has been reading about some conversations between Wilde and a certain Frenchman, mentioned today: "You know, Oscar Wilde said that *Madame Bovary* is a book without pity." Interesting and very much to the point. In general there is almost no pity in French literature. There's no equivalent of Dickens. Wilde's remark has made me think.

November 13, 1942

Darlan has turned traitor and that's the end of it. Vichy is doing everything to undo the damage and appease the Germans and talks as though it had nothing in common with this Wallenrod. In his concern for the *petit bonheur* of his citizens, Pétain talks like a German, acts like a German, and still besmirches French history with actions for which, despite everything, he should someday be hung from an old oak tree without regard to his age. He licks the Germans' boots and plays politics. He's like Joseph Conrad's Heyst, while de Gaulle is Conrad's Lena, and all together it will be called *Victory*.[274] If the French go for this, it means they are really done for.

November 15, 1942

A visit to Eleonore D. in Arcueil. A product of the emigration in the best sense of the word. Her Polish father married a German woman. Her entire childhood spent in Germany, then France. Always at the service of Poland. An unmarried middle-aged woman, slender, with a pretty, fresh face, in a long, wide skirt and a vest, a shawl thrown over her shoulders. All in black. Like a woman straight out of a Grottger drawing.[275] She has a tiny house in Arcueil, near Paris, and has taken French citizenship, but would that all Poles were as good citizens as she. She knows us Poles, indeed knows our faults very well. But also our virtues. And she knows the French. She tells us that when she worked in the international commission for clearing war debts, she once received an invoice for a medal the French had awarded to a Pole for his actions on the front — the French front and in defense of France. Indeed, the height of fastidiousness . . . In the manner of Monsieur Homais.

November 17, 1942

A terrific show. Like people standing in line, mouthing off, grumbling. De Gaulle in London can't cope with Darlan in Algiers. London hurls crude insults at Darlan in French, while the Germans laugh up their sleeves. No surprise, because it really is a funny vaudeville.

November 21, 1942

This afternoon in the Galeries Charpentier to see the retrospective of Kees van Dongen.[276] He's one of those painters it's hard to say anything about. Some canvasses are good, some horrid. Everything he does has a certain edge, but it's all somehow "artificial," *pour épater les bourgeois.* The pursuit of a new style so characteristic of the 1920s and 1930s, but it's a fake pursuit. The pictures are contemporary, but at the same time musty. Looking at them, I couldn't help hearing the *shimmy,* the *one-step,* the *blues,* and the *Charleston.* Such dances were fashionable and often played not so long ago, but at the same time terribly long ago. Nothing ties me to that era, I even feel a certain hatred for everything from before the war. Perhaps one of the most abysmal periods of all. Recently I fell upon Aldous Huxley's *Point Counter Point.*[277] Unreadable. After a few pages I put it aside. Back then it caused a big stir.

Paris is truly beautiful only now that the cars are gone and carts and bicycles fill the streets. It's peaceful. The neon lights are dark, and sounds of the waltz emerge from the dimly lit cafés. In the midst of all this, troubles like the forced departure of workers for Germany and other "pleasures" seem to be happening on another planet. The theaters are packed, there are long lines in front of the movie houses, women and men dress more elegantly than ever before. No one pays any taxes, the black market is by now well organized, and if you have money you can buy anything. The height of elegance consists in watching American films in private showings at a high price. After watching Clark Gable or other stars, one has in addition the pleasant sensation of risk (the showings are of course secret) and the feeling of taking part in the Resistance.

After the exhibit we went to Rebattet for tea and petits fours. I go there to make a study of gourmandise. It was already growing dark as we walked around the Madeleine and along the boulevard to Opéra. A splendid November. Dry and warm. If only the winter is mild, because the *patron* of our hotel will have hardly any coal this time around.

November 22, 1942

In the afternoon we went to hôpital Cochin[278] to visit one of "my" patients. An interesting case. A driver from the Poznan region. As he was fleeing Poland, he was wounded during a bombardment. A piece of wall fell on his leg. In Romania the wound began to heal. Afraid to go to a hospital, he kept dressing it himself. He arrived in France with his leg incompletely healed and worked in the factory. Odd things happened with the wound. The leg stiffened, the torn tendons and bits of shattered bone began breaking through the skin. He kept cutting them or gouging them out with a knife and applying bandages. And so on for two years until it healed. But the stiffness remained, and the leg, a bit elongated, was now deforming his spine. He decided to have an operation to shorten and straighten the leg. Now he is recuperating from the operation.

It's no picnic in French hospitals these days. Hunger. The sick are fed mostly by their families, who bring what they can. The nurses, besides their normal duties, are also cooks. They prepare meals for the sick or warm up their food on the gas cookers. People even bring raw potatoes. Those with no family, starve. We brought our man potatoes and left him a few bread ration cards, because his biggest complaint was lack of bread. I'll buy some counterfeit coupons. After leaving the hospital we strolled around Parc Montsouris. It was a sunny, warm day. We walked among the streams and rivulets, artificial grottoes and cliffs. The French are good at making gardens and parks.

November 24, 1942

Charlie can't get along with Darlan, which is to say, de Gaulle is picking fights. But if de Gaulle won't have anything to do with this gang of turncoats (wherever the wind blows, as the Russians say), it's not surprising. France once again gives quite a revealing performance. In 1940 she enthusiastically welcomes the armistice and forms a government under Pétain, whose slogan is cooperation with Germany. But a year later, when the Germans start up with Russia and they don't succeed, when America enters the war, and when the power of the Anglo-Saxon bloc begins to be noticeable, if only in the superiority of its air force, *diese kleine aber nette Gesellschaft aus Vichy*,[279] still under the leadership of Pétain, realizes it has bet on the wrong horse. It realizes that the Deutschmark is falling and the dollar rising. Therefore the group enters into secret talks with America and prepares an attack on Africa. General Giraud escapes from German prison and arrives in Vichy, where he gives Pétain his word of honor that he will not engage in politics. Darlan takes a tour of Africa, where he pledges loyalty to the old fogy from Vichy. On November 8 Giraud is in Algiers as the head and leader of the dissidents, Darlan seems to have been taken prisoner. He doesn't even have the courage clearly and openly to announce he's gone over to the American side. And how does Giraud look now, with his word of honor? Maybe he was compelled to give it, because otherwise he would not have been able to act. But "the ends justify the means" is good for scoundrels and Jesuits, not for generals, and does not justify a general breaking his word of honor. My father never broke his, even during the May events, as a result of which he was dismissed from the army prematurely.[280]

One must rejoice in this turn of affairs, because it has great significance for the further course of the war, but one can't help feeling disdain for these trickster generals and admirals, for the whole cabal based on such vulgar iniquity. Have the French now lost even their elegance, their style? Even the Germans, in their iniquities, have more style.

November 25, 1942

It looks like the Russians have guessed my strategic schemes and launched attacks from the points I've had marked on the map for a long time.

November 27, 1942

It's looking really bad. According to a stubborn rumor making the rounds, twenty-two German divisions have been surrounded. The Russians have launched a winter offensive on the Southern Front.

November 28, 1942

Better and better. The Germans wanted to enter Toulon and take over the French fleet. The entire fleet was therefore scuttled. Another scandal on a grand scale. The one subject of conversation since this morning. The French are both pleased (the stupid ones) and saddened (the intelligent). Almost eighty-eight naval vessels, the most advanced on earth, went to the bottom and into the scrap heap. This is where the politics of "running with the hare and hunting with the hounds" has led them. The suicidal gesture of sinking the fleet is attractive—it shows they're not yet rotten to the core. It's satisfying to know that so much hardware has slipped right through the Germans' fingers, but otherwise the feat inspires only pity for the boundless stupidity and short-sightedness of Vichy politics. My blood was boiling today when I vainly tried to explain to my French office mates that if the Republic put France in a coffin, it's Vichy that's carefully banging in the nails. They couldn't get it. You have a grudge against

the English—I practically screamed—you're afraid *ces Anglais* will take everything from you after the war, but you don't understand that scuttling the fleet is
just another step toward submitting to the mercy and mercilessness of England,
America, Russia, and even San Salvador and other Hondurases.

Because the French see only their *petit bonheur*, the damned food coupons,
for which you can still get anything. But one shouldn't ask for too much. It
could have been worse, they might have obediently and *gehorsamst*[281] handed
over the fleet (to spite the English, for example) and then adieu to ending the
war for a long time to come. Of course, the Germans must have a sour taste in
their mouths.

This evening in the Théâtre de l'Étoile. A *music hall* program. Acrobatics,
dances, songs. Lys Gauty was terrific in several songs.[282]

December 2, 1942

Mussolini delivered a speech. It's nevertheless a bit different from Hitler's
barking, full of loutishness, lies, and suicidal swagger. Mussolini's speech was
solemn and you could almost say—honest. It seemed almost as though he were
delicately reproaching Hitler. How else to understand it? "This new blow by the
English and the Americans," said the Duce, "did not surprise the Axis, considering that we possessed enough information about the cooperation between
the French and American armies. When the landing occurred, I immediately
informed Berlin that the only possible way to react was the immediate occupation of all of France, including Corsica." Who bungled it? The Duce says it was
the Führer. He lays the responsibility entirely on Hitler and unambiguously
reproaches him for allowing the French to make a fool of him. The Duce had
notified Berlin of what had to be done. Did Berlin hesitate? Berlin did not know
whether Pétain and his entire government would not flee to Africa as soon as
the Germans crossed the demarcation line. For crossing the demarcation line
annulled the armistice. Conclusion: Berlin did hesitate, because even Berlin
did not count on Pétain and his consorts taking their lack of dignity so very far—
Berlin could not imagine that Vichy would still calmly accept even this and not
react. It's positively comical, when the archvillain hesitates, unable to imagine
someone might be yet an even greater villain. It's the only logical explanation
for Berlin's hesitations. What will the Germans think of the French now? Despite three years of occupation they still harbored illusions.

Another of the Duce's allusions to Germany is truly a faux pas. He said outright that Italy was the only state that openly acknowledges its losses, publishing
the lists of dead and wounded.

The details of the self-scuttling of the fleet in Toulon are moving. The Germans stand on the shore and watch as eighty vessels slowly sink, to the accompaniment of ammunition exploding. A malicious trick. But it's a senile malice. And all of this after so touching a letter (already the second) from Hitler to Pétain. The atmosphere is charged. The Russians are advancing, farewell Stalingrad! Rommel has stopped at El Agheila, Montgomery is regrouping. If the Russians conduct their offensive according to my plans, then in March the Germans will be at the Dnieper. The next line is already Klaipeda-Kolomyia. After which, *"finis Poloniae,"* as Kościuszko did not say.[283] I got into terrible trouble today and will likely be considered a traitor. I said out loud: "I would like Poland to be occupied by the Americans." Patriotic howl. No occupation—but independence, sovereignty, churchness, the strings from our underpants, latifundia and loose ladies, breeding and divorcing, family planning and breast feeding. They convinced me—not to go back.

December 4, 1942

Basia's name day. I could write an entire poem about my wife. It would be rather original, because in fact there seem to be few poems about *one's own* wife. I bought half a dozen roses in the large new flower shop on rue Lafayette. Never in my life have I spent such money for roses for *my own* wife. For supper this evening we had oysters and good white wine.

December 5, 1942

This evening in the Théâtre des Ambassadeurs to see Henry Becque's *Clotilde du Mesnil (La Parisienne)* and Georges Feydeau's *Mais n'te promène donc pas toute nue!* with Alice Cocéa.[284] It's really amazing how many variations French dramatists have managed to discover on the theme of the so-called ménage à trois. It takes a lot of ingenuity to form so many triangulated configurations out of an ordinary triangle. *Clotilde du Mesnil* was first performed in 1885 and immediately recognized as a classic. Soon it moved to the Comédie-Française. The great Réjane, playing Clotilde in the Théâtre de Vaudeville, confirmed its glory with her talent.[285] But it was André Antoine in his theater who provided the play's greatest success.[286] Throughout the evening I wondered vainly what was "classic" about it and why this play had entered the permanent repertory of French theater. Clotilde du Mesnil is the wife of an older man who wants to get a high position in the administration. Their house is often visited by a friend of the husband's who, thanks to this friendship, is also a friend of the wife's, to put it in a friendly way. Clotilde is a cunning female, like all silly women. To enable the husband to obtain the desired position, which at the same time will allow her to stabilize her relationship with her lover (in the sense of "certainty," "trust," and "calm," in a word, the National Bank of love), Clotilde casually goes to bed with a well-connected young man. The husband gets his position, the lover resumes his role, everyone is satisfied.

This in the course of three acts. If at least it were piquant . . . But it falls flat. The entire plot, if you can call it that, is entirely mechanical. It feels constructed, obviously not without precision, but without any nerve. Clotilde is the perfect type of the Parisian *bourgeoise*. She executes her plan coldly, maintaining every appearance of a good wife—and what's more important—a loyal mistress. Because what comes to the fore in this play is the betrayal, not of her husband, but of her lover. The lover is depicted from the first act as a completely accepted part of the du Mesnil household. The conflict is the betrayal of the lover. All of it is pure calculation, cold and precise, not only without a drop of feeling but not even of sensuality. No one here loves or particularly desires anyone else, everything is a well-arranged transaction for everyone under the leadership of the cunning Clotilde. The husband obtains the desired position. The lover—momentarily desperate that he has lost not only her regard but also the Tuesdays and Fridays to which he has become so accustomed that he can imagine no other life—resumes his role and, after a brief storm, finds himself again in possession of his Tuesdays and Fridays. And Clotilde, thanks to her husband's position, will rise a step higher in the social hierarchy, acquiring a wider field on which to display the diplomacy of a widely respected (that's key) woman of the world. And thus endlessly, until menopause, when all of a sudden she will become a pious biddy. Maybe it really is a classic? Because Clotilde is classic, her cunning is classic, her hypocrisy is classic, the particular intelligence of a French female is classic. Besides that, the husband is classic, the lover, for whom Tuesday and Friday with Clotilde in the coach and in the hotel—is also classic, finally the entire plot is classic, not to mention the truly classic language.

The second play is a boulevard one-act by Feydeau set a few years later than *Clotilde*. It's already 1900. A deputy's wife walks around her apartment in a nightgown, high heels, and a hat. Why? Because it's July, Paris is broiling, and she's hot. This results in a series of quid pro quos ending in the visit of a reporter, who instead of interviewing and reporting on the deputy, writes the report, gazing with interest at the backside of the mistress of the house. And what does her neighbor Mr. Clemenceau have to say about this?

This has more character. A boulevard farce, at which our grandfathers got excited, spying out the charms under the nightgown. And the fun was in also catching a glimpse of her leg. No substance at all. That's from the literary point of view. Altogether different when it comes to the staging.

The Théâtre des Ambassadeurs, under the direction of Alice Cocéa, is currently the most refined theater in Paris. Cocéa is a wonderful actress. The staging and her performance have done so much to rescue the vacuousness of the two plays that one leaves the theater somewhat dazzled. The sets and costumes were designed by André Dignimont, who is very *en vogue* and has real talent.[287] With a Frenchman's feeling for that period, he displayed on stage all the opulence of a fin-de-siècle drawing room, in the best and worst style. Splendid original Art Deco furniture, knickknacks, fabrics, flowers, palms. Against this lavish backdrop, Alice Cocéa wears a splendid dress and a hat of the period, draped in jewels of the time from the private collections of Maison Boucheron.[288] The set is quite extravagant, Cocéa's acting is flawless, classic. The same goes for the one-act, with its equally splendid decorations, in the midst of which she managed to elicit all the features of a silly goose, wandering around the house in her nightgown, which she excuses with deceitful naïveté, *qu'il fait trente-cinq degrés de latitude à l'ombre* (thirty-five degrees of latitude in the shade).

The theater is packed. People have turned away from modernism. As though sensing her end, France looks back avidly at the time when she still counted for something. Both bits of nonsense have had a great success. Memoirs of all kinds, as soon as they appear in the bookstores, instantly sell out. If things continue like this, the fashion for corsets, crinolines, updated prudishness and modesty, and romantic love will take over after the war. The public in theaters and other places of entertainment teems these days with nouveaux riches, or profiteers, as they were called after the last war. People are racking up fortunes on the black market and display their wealth wherever they can. Young men with long hair and in long jackets, the so-called *zazous*, ladies in great hats or fantastic turbans. Everything new, shiny, dazzling. *Paris de la Belle Époque.*

December 6, 1942

Sunny and warm. The winter is promising to be mild. Could this be the last one? I'm waiting impatiently for 1943 because I keep thinking that this madness will already end next year. Some say, no—and they are probably right. We ate lunch early and rode our bikes to the Bois de Boulogne for the afternoon. There were lots of people in the park, lots of bicycles, and lots of children. The sun was a lot warmer than is usual for December, and a vague suggestion of summer hung in the air. We rode along the pond, then past the Parc de Bagatelle and entered avenue de Neuilly, where Basia instantly ran into—a policeman. He deftly grabbed the bicycle by the handlebars, like a bull by the horns, held it up, and prevented Basia from falling over. After we exchanged smiles and jokes—better to run over a policeman than a pedestrian, because you don't have to call the police . . . I'm already on the site of the accident, the policeman laughed—we went on our way. I imagine one of our Polish "cops" in such a situation. How pleasant to live in a country in which policemen make jokes, and the suburbs are not full of "thugs" and "brigands." We had a drink of hot wine in a bistro near the Étoile. The Arc de Triomphe turned red in the rays of the setting sun and threw a long shadow over the Champs-Élysées, sprinkled with the many-colored patches of the *vélos-taxis*,[289] painted in every hue. From the Étoile we rode down to the Trocadéro. The Eiffel Tower looked like a colorful lace curtain spread out against the ash-blue sky. The Trocadéro is deteriorating. Neglected since the start of the war, it is turning black. The gilding on the impressive sculptures is wearing off, the dried-out pool basins on the lower level enhance the sense of abandonment. The ensemble resembles a luxurious but run-down bathroom.

From the Trocadéro down to place Alma. The statue of Mickiewicz. From Alma along the Seine. I love this area. On the left, the Art Deco glass mountain of the Grand Palais, on the right the Pont Alexandre III. Enormous golden horses, and farther along a splendid view of the Invalides. We hit place de la Concorde. In the December dusk, it looks like the nave of an enormous church. The altar of the obelisk, two walls of the dark and gigantic Ministry of the Navy, in the distance the columns of the Madeleine, stiff and cold, like a bank of organ pipes. Silently, we glide like cats along the wall and fence of the Tuileries, which smell of dry leaves. The Louvre. Then a short stretch in the shadow of the wall and there's another Art Deco mountain of glass. The Samaritaine department store. A bit farther along, the sharp crests of the Conciergerie stand out black against the granite sky. The dusk softens its reliefs. Silence and a sense of dread. Châtelet and place de l'Hôtel de Ville. On the Seine, the Île Saint-Louis floats like a huge raft. On the left, the tangle of narrow streets of the Saint-Paul district, which form black openings in the monotonous wall of shabby stone houses. The entrances to the twisty burrows, to one of the underworlds of Paris, where the hotels are dirty, the men don't walk but prowl, and the young women resemble rotten fruit.

All the exits of Gare de Lyon are discharging the black lava of the crowd, which divides into separate streams, as in the crevices of a volcano, and pours slowly into the openings of the metro or onto the streets. When we pull up to the house, it is already dark. At the entrance we look in on the *patron* and his wife. Madame Bessières is resolutely darning the hotel linens, mending and patching them. There are no more in reserve, and new sheets and towels are not to be found. None are being allocated.

December 8, 1942

Persistent rumors about a Russo-German agreement hovering in the air. I try to convince myself it's absurd, merely Russia blackmailing the English and Americans, but it doesn't leave me in peace. It spoils my mood, spoils my day.

December 11, 1942

Nothing concrete. The Russian offensive is developing slowly, but decisively. There are no details because neither side says anything. Montgomery continues to regroup at El Agheila. And in France the forced departure for work in Germany continues, under the slogan, "For every three specialists a prisoner of war will be freed." Laval and Pétain are working *pour la France* like two of the greatest specialists. These two should be exchanged for at least two entire divisions. *Ceterum censeo Lavalum et Petenum* on the gallows *post bellum* danglendi *essent.*[290]

December 12, 1942

This evening we went to the Théâtre de Châtelet to see Shakespeare's *Richard the Third*, with Charles Dullin in the main role.[291] No. In a naturalistic production, this Richard III comes off as an amateur at a provincial horse fair. Dullin, apparently excellent in Molière's *The Miser*, reminded me too much of that role as Richard the Third. The number of corpses is entirely up to current standards. Hard to count them without a special calculator. For every corpse, I took a match out of the box and put it in my pocket, but I could still not keep up with the count, especially in the last act. Strewn on the battlefield were so many extras, over which others kept jumping with such zeal, brandishing their swords, that I should have emptied the whole box in one fell swoop and perhaps even bought another one, which at the moment is not so easy to do. Thus, the king's dramatic cry, "My kingdom for a horse," had no echo. It was impossible to believe this offer, while twisting in laughter at the sight of the extras jumping about on the set like monkeys at the Vincennes zoo. They finally offed the king and we were able to leave, which we did with no little pleasure. Going to the theater is a pleasure, but leaving is often an even greater one.

December 13, 1942

It doesn't feel at all like mid-December. Dry, sunny, and warm, as in autumn. We spent the whole afternoon on our bikes.

December 16, 1942

Rommel has lost another battle and is retreating from El Agheila. The English are advancing. Again a general optimism prevails. But it's not all that simple. It's much easier to conduct a war than to stop it. Especially the kind of war in which the allies are always keeping an eye on each other. Germany will lose it for sure, but it's hard to imagine England, America, and Russia winning it *simultaneously*. Someone must be eliminated from the winners' circle, because in war, as in poker, only one party can *really* win. The victory of more than one is the beginning of a new war. And that's precisely what threatens us today. Allowing Russia to remain in her current position and to dominate Poland, the Baltic States, and the Balkans would give her a deciding voice after the war and plant the germ of a new conflict in ten, fifteen, or twenty years. This war must be won *exclusively* by the Anglo-Saxons. Otherwise the war would have been senseless and the English and Americans would be faced at its conclusion with exactly what they faced at the start. The English and Americans must stretch out the game of *waiting and seeing*. They must aim for the greatest possible exhaustion of Germany and Russia in order to strike the final blow and present Russia with a series of faits accomplis, which she would not be able to reverse, being far too exhausted. At the moment the Russians have launched something of a monster-offensive. People are glad, but they don't understand that the point is not for the Russians to defeat the Germans *completely*, but to defeat them only *by half*.

December 17, 1942

A misty, rainy day. The air, saturated with moisture, seems like a liquid in which you swim like a fish in an aquarium. In the early evening, riding through the Left Bank, I dropped into a bistro for a glass of rum. It was at the intersection of rue l'Arbalète and rue Lhomond and when I entered, I remembered that somewhere near here was the boardinghouse run by Madame Vauquer.[292] The neighborhood has remained special to this day. One of those Parisian lairs that only Balzac managed to describe well enough for you to sense it from a distance. Here is where Father Goriot lived. I looked through the windowpane. Dusk was falling fast and seemed delighted to be creeping out of the dark streets in which it dozes through the day. A gray, winter hour. A few regulars stood at the counter having a lively political discussion. At the corner, right next to the wall, stood a young and very pretty girl. A neighborhood *fille*, probably living not far away and warming herself up between *tournées* in front of her hotel. Well built, classy, with splendid legs. I began to look her over rather covetously while sipping my rum. The regulars were talking about what today's *citoyen* could do against the violence of the occupation. Revolution? With bare hands against the armored cars, against the portable cement blockhouses that monitor each street corner? *Non, c'est impossible, c'est fou.*[293] A man is a patriot, wants to fight, but there's no way to do so. He has to sit quietly and watch. The girl slowly drained her coffee, listening with a strange smile. Suddenly she burst out in a hoarse laugh, from the depths of her ravaged lungs. That laugh, from the dark corner, sounded so uncanny that everyone fell silent and looked in her direction. Head propped on her arm, she stood leaning sideways. With her elbow on the counter, she slid back and forth, swinging her whole body, rocking her hips. And kept laughing. Then she started to speak—loudly and almost tenderly, as though speaking to children: "What can you do? Everyone can do something. I have syphilis and I offer it to the Germans. Each of them leaves Paris with a souvenir. *Je ne fais que ceux qui partent.*[294] Yesterday I did my sixteenth." And a long outburst of wheezing laughter. She tossed a franc on the counter and left, laughing. You could still hear her laugh out in the dark street. It truly made my blood run cold.

December 19, 1942

Important Russian communiqué. Voronezh has been retaken, they're advancing everywhere. It looks like they'll take back Stalingrad. It's a massive attack across the entire Southern Front with every chance of success. The English are bombing Italy. Almost every night they fly over Paris and we are awakened by antiaircraft fire. In Italy, about a million people have apparently been evacuated and the roads are clogged with refugees. I feel sorry for the Italians.

December 24, 1942

Christmas Eve. We're alone at our small table, engrossed in faraway thoughts. "On Sławkowska Street they haven't yet started, on Grodzka Street no doubt they already have . . ."[295] We laugh to ourselves. We light the candles on our tiny tree and turn off the lights. The tree stands on the mantelpiece in front of the mirror and the whole room is flooded by the soft light of several small flames reflected on the glass surface. Under my breath, I hum carols whose words escape me. Basia laughs. I gaze at the ceiling and think. I'm thinking that I'm feeling good.

December 25, 1942

The Russians have launched a new offensive in the Caucasus. I spread the map on the floor, get down next to it, and "make war." At the top, attack along the Voronezh line, at the bottom, flanking operations in the Caucasus. Above, Kharkov; below, Rostov—operations meet at Dnepropetrovsk, then envelopment, siege, destruction.

December 26, 1942

We're staying home and reading. We went for afternoon tea with Robert's family, where we met the Fontenay-sous-Bois parish priest. A charming man. He was imprisoned in the Poznan region, where he encountered many Poles. He could not say enough in praise of the population and his Polish prison mates in the camp. I told him that clearly he'd spent too little time there, and besides, in such situations we are proverbial charmers, especially with foreigners. Basia got angry at me, because when it comes to Poland she is Oleńka[296] and "why do you say such things to the French, when already . . ." I've never let myself be duped by this national business and I never will. I very likely detest nationalism even more than Communism, and if I were very rich I would endow a department of cosmopolitanism and critical judgment at one of our universities. The Poles are no better or worse than anyone else. The difference is in the tone, not the melody. We have created no style except the noble style of the Polish gentry, and our whole future is before us. Above all, we should learn to be free and not just mouth off about it. And learn a lot of other things besides. The raw material is first-rate.

December 31, 1942

Another year is ending. I'm in my armchair, a bottle of champagne is chilling outside the window to welcome the New Year at midnight. Still another two hours. Like Rzecki, I want to tote it all up, to talk politics. Another year behind us. "How time flies"—as Prus's Counselor Węgrowicz would have said.[297] In general terms, this entire war can be characterized briefly: in 1940 Hitler said "we have won," in 1941 "we will win," in 1942 "we must win," and in 1943 he will probably say "we cannot lose," and—he will lose. If the war does not end this coming year, then at any rate it will begin the process of *really* ending. The enormous and much-touted German offensive has in fact produced no tangible results. In any case, it did not achieve the most important goal: to reach the oil of the Caucasus and sever communications on the Volga. The enormous effort came to naught and expired finally at Stalingrad. Admittedly the Germans have taken the Donbas, but it's done them little good, and in any case Russian production is taking place east of the Urals. Besides, the Anglo-American support is enormous. It's not clear what would be happening without it. Lacking long-range airpower, the Germans are unable to attack the Russian rear. At this moment a massive Russian counteroffensive has begun, which if well executed can deprive the Germans of the fruits of this year's victories and render their effort of 1942 completely futile. The Russians have every chance of recovering whatever they lost this year. That would be a great success. Incomplete, but that's exactly the point. From the perspective of Polish interests, it's crucial for the decisive moment not to occur in the east. There, the Russians and Germans will have had to wear each other down, both exhausted by their gigantic battles. Complete victory then should be achieved by America and England coming from the west and from the Balkans. It's hard anyway to say anything about this, because if the problem of this war is rather easy to resolve in strategic terms, from the political point of view it still has many dark sides. The darkest of all is the side concerning Poland. What they will do with us, God only knows. I can't get as easily excited as others do. But it's not yet time to worry about this kind of thing. While at the moment in the east two colossi are again wrestling and exhausting each other, England and America grow more powerful with each passing day. The course of the African campaign is the best proof of that. The fact of the American landing in Africa is of great significance. A base is already being created there for the attack on Europe. The final liquidation of Germany is now only a question of time. The growth of Anglo-American airpower is becoming ever more apparent. And the war will be won by airpower. A few months from now, in this regard the wonders will begin, when mass production goes into effect in the United States. Beyond the numerical superiority, there will also be an advantage in quality. The English, but especially the Americans, are now building their entire air forces from scratch, introducing the latest models, while the Germans are still relying on models from 1939, simply tinkering with the details. By now the famous Messerschmitt is over four years old and although it remains the fastest warplane, it is not easily maneuvered at high speeds, while the Stuka is practically a museum piece. Fine—but it's all gone on too long already, people say. What else can they say, since they're suffering, suffering terribly. Next year should be interesting to contemplate—obviously, for those with the luxury of contemplation.

Biuro Werbunkowe Ochotników
Armii Polskiej we Francji
42 rue Jean GouJon 42

Paryż, dn. 7. 9. 1939
Paris, le

Lista № C / III / 186
Liste

Zaświadczenie tymczasowe - Certificat provisoire

P. *Bobkowski* *Andrzej*
M. (nazwisko - nom) (imię - prénom)

Rocznik: *1913* miejsce urodzenia: *Wiener Neustadt*
né le: lieu de naissance:

w dniu dzisiejszym zgłosił się ochotniczo do Armii Polskiej we Francji na czas trwania wojny.

s'est inscrit comme volontaire dans l'Armée Polonaise en France pour la durée de la guerre.

Pieczęć Komendy Polskiego Biura Werbunkowego
Sceau du Bureau Polonais des Engagements Volontaires

Komendant Biura Werbunkowego
Chef du Bureau

(above) Temporary certificate of military registration, France, September 7, 1939. (Fondation Jan Michalski, Montricher, Switzerland)

(left) Andrzej Bobkowski writing in his notebook, early 1940s. (Muzeum Literatury im. Adama Mickiewicza, Warsaw)

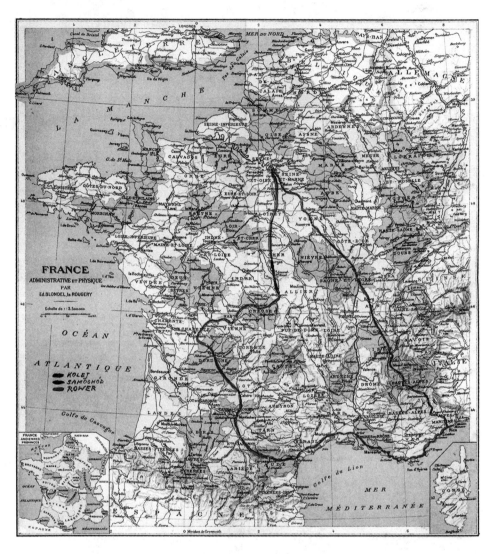

Map of France ("Cahier III," 1940). (Polish Institute of Arts and Sciences of America [PIASA], New York)

ne. W pokoju, choć prawie nie opalanym, wydało nam się
gorąco. 16 miesięcy tego gołębnika dało nam radę.
To, co z początku było zabawne, stało się nieznośne – z
pp. P. na czele. Teraz zaczął się nowy etap. Dokąd po-
wędrujemy stąd? Co jeszcze przeżyjemy tutaj?
Kupiłem dziś rano gazetę i na pierwszej stronie –
– nasza fotografja z wózkiem. Reporter, robiąc zdję-
cie niebywałego w Paryżu śniegu, chwycił nas. I mam
ilustrację.

Les cantonniers, sur les boulevards, enlèvent ce qu'ils peuvent
de la neige durcie.
Reportage photographique **Le Matin**.

Tadzio jest oburzony tą fotografją. Uważa to za kompro-
mitację. – Irenka – ja z wózkiem w Paryżu – żeby to moja
Janeczka widziała.... strach pomyśleć. A potem dodaję:
"Człowiek w tym Paryżu ruszyć się nie może, żeby go nie fotogra-
fowali – na prefekturze ciągle fotografje, w gazetach fotografje
– tępicielu!"

Manuscript of the entry for January 3, 1941 (in "Cahier V").
(Polish Institute of Arts and Sciences of America [PIASA], New York)

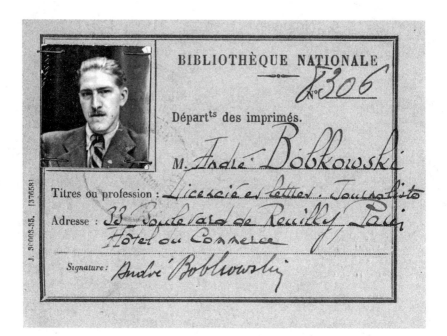

(above) Reader's card, Bibliothèque Nationale, Paris. (Fondation Jan Michalski, Montricher, Switzerland)

(right) Andrzej and Basia Bobkowski on vacation, July 1943. (Instytut Badań Literackich, Polish Academy of Sciences, Warsaw)

(left) Photograph presented to Jerzy Giedroyc, Paris, during the war. (Instytut Literacki–Kultura, Le Mesnil-le-Roi, France)

(below) The nine "cahiers" of the wartime notebooks. (Polish Institute of Arts and Sciences of America [PIASA], New York)

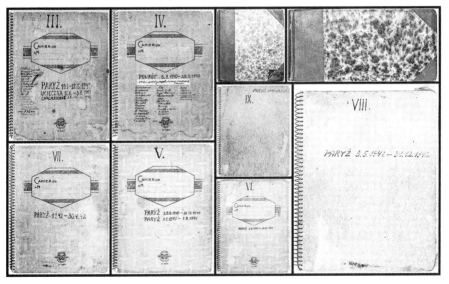

1943

January 2, 1943

Supper at J.'s this evening. For many years she has lived with a French family, or rather with the elderly mother, head of the family. Both daughters came for supper. One is sophisticated, a journalist who works for fashion magazines; the other is a dentist, modest and unbecoming. This is the kind of conversation in which I've had to make an effort to restrain myself from uttering sarcastic nonsense and impertinences. Like parrots, the French pick up "intelligent" questions, ask them, and then don't even try to provide answers. Now the "red danger" is in fashion, but in fact no one knows anything about Russia. As though André Gide had never gone to Russia and never returned, as though nothing has been known for a hundred years. Yet Condillac and Rousseau, Michelet and the Marquis de Custine wrote splendidly about Russia, and more recently there's Jacques Bainville's excellent study *La Russie et la barrière de l'Est.*[1] A web of inanity is spun by otherwise informed people who allow themselves to be fooled by appearances. A few days ago I heard: "Russia is becoming democratic." Quite possibly, if Stalin has so ordered. As Alfred Rambaud has written in his history of Russia, Peter the Great, using the cudgel and the whip, induced his subjects to feel like free people and Europeans. Communism is one issue in all of this, and Russia another—the most important.[2] Already in 1937 Bainville wrote: "Under Bolshevism, obeying the law that more than one western revolution has demonstrated, another Russia has emerged. And this is the eternal Russia, moving in search of space and air, as Russia has always done. The Bolsheviks having abandoned us" (the French) "in the heat of battle, we should not wish too hard for Russia to recover her strength and reappear in the world as a political power . . . Those who continued to yearn for the rebirth of Russia were reckless. She is reviving and, despite her anarchy and poverty, this is already troubling for Europe . . . Soviet or not, Russia is Russia." In this study, Bainville is almost prophetic. And today I'm not at all happy when people, with a mischievous wink, say to me: "You know, a lot is changing . . . epaulettes have returned to the army, the officers have orderlies . . ." (*pogony* and *denshchiki*, as the Russians call them) ". . . slowly other changes will come."[3] As though this were a change for the better. I don't fear Communism, because ideologies, even one as obtuse as Marxism, are not eternal. I fear Russia, precisely those epaulettes and orderlies, and everything Bainville writes about. I especially fear that when it comes to Russia, people always fail in their judgments, particularly since Lenin came to power. "It would thus be unwise," writes Bainville (p. 68), "to trust the signs of moderation and common sense (*sagesse*) the Bolshevik government seems to display. Abdül-Hamid and the Empress of China were also very good at the art of promising reforms when they needed to be in the good graces of Europe."[4] Stalin is nothing but a Russian Abdül-Hamid and for the sake of Hurricanes, Spitfires, and American trucks he will promise God knows what. Communism is not a problem, except insofar as it is tied to Russia, that eternal Russia, where the cudgel is used to teach people "to be free."

This evening I put a red dot on Velikiye Luki.[5] Russia is advancing. Asia used to begin already at Warsaw. That's how it was for Michelet, for whom the world of laws reached only to the Vistula and the Danube.

January 10, 1943

Winter this year has been very mild. I was riding my bike slowly and thinking. The bicycle taxis, the so-called *vélos-taxis*, got me going. It's 1943 and in Paris, in the center of Europe, men are pulling other men around. Other reflections followed . . . Progress. I gazed around the street. A row of houses, the streets—they're even attractive—but it's sickening to think that tens of square kilometers, hundreds and thousands of them, are covered by these houses. A great city, a monster city, that's also progress. An absurd progress. How many hours does every city dweller waste each day going to and from work? Underground the metro rumbles, crowded with people who push and shove, riding for what seems like forever in the stench and stuffiness. The same in the stations, the same in the suburban trains. They return to homes in which, except for the furniture, most often indeed except for a few personal things, nothing belongs to them. They get up early and rush to work, work to which usually nothing ties them, to which they contribute no part of themselves. All under the ashen veil of *anonymity*. You don't know who it is you're working for, you've never met those you depend on for your livelihood, you fulfill their orders automatically, you're a termite, you're nothing. Hoping progress would lead to freedom, we found chains heavier than even a feudal lord might have imposed. We hurry blindly forward, with a foolish faith in progress, with a childish delight in the latest achievements of technology and the newest *inventions*. Somewhere deep inside, thought, true and peaceful thought, lingers silently, like a little spring hidden in the woods, but increasingly drowned out by the thunder and deluge of clever ideas. How many people today live by thinking? They live on the candy of prepackaged answers to *everything*, scattered among the stupefied throng.

Paris is so beautiful these days because it's Paris without cars. It probably won't be long before lines of cars will again appear in the streets, tree leaves will start yellowing as early as June, singed by the exhaust, and people will be talking more and walking more quickly, drunk . . . What have we gained from so much suffering? The development of the machine, which has enslaved each one of us and separated us from everything. It has killed the soul while promising to liberate the body, promised everything, delivered almost nothing. Progress has done nothing but suffuse our blood with a single immense and authentic feeling—FEAR. The race toward unknown death. Deception and lying, deception in both time and space.

January 12, 1943

Nikolay Berdyaev's *The New Middle Ages.*[6] An émigré Russian philosopher. He founded a journal in Paris and became the center of a kind of school. I don't like Slavic philosophy. We feel everything too intensely and manage too seldom to express what we feel in a clear and intelligible fashion. We write with our feelings, not with our minds. Slavic philosophy hence contains so much confusion, disorder, and obfuscation. The analysis is usually tortuous, full of unexpected syntheses, in which extreme realism mingles so thoroughly with extreme mysticism as to result in such creations as Adam Mickiewicz's *Books of the Polish Pilgrimage,* Juliusz Słowacki's *King-Spirit,* Dostoyevsky, Tolstoy, nihilisms, and Leninisms.[7] In fact I'm repulsed by Slavic philosophy. Above all it has caused a lot of harm to Slavic art. But what can be done about it? If a Slavic person has any talent, in nine out of ten cases he will take up philosophy. When I read the second part of Słowacki's letters to his mother, I want to say: "Julek, my friend, for your sake and mine, drop this and get down to some honest writing." In *War and Peace* I would like to tear out a good number of pages and plead: "Dear Count, in this spot please, a bit of description, something along the lines of Napoleon at Smolensk or an account of the Battle of Borodino." Alas. Neither Count Leo, nor Juliusz, nor Cyprian Norwid, nor the Great Adam, nor the other Great Slavs have managed to guard against this great disease.[8] It's almost a rule that among the Slavs, poets and writers become philosophers, damaging both literature and philosophy, while in the West the opposite often happens—with the opposite result. Here, philosophers often become poets or writers, enriching literature and making philosophy more accessible. A line of great writers in France and in England are philosopher-writers and in many cases poets of thought—thought that is clear, simple, humane, and wonderfully expressed.

I picked up Berdyaev with reluctance. The Slavs—apart from their confusion—have other, quite unappealing habits: a tendency to create "systems," which in the blink of an eye turn into "religions." And that's the limit—I can't bear it. Each philosophical system immediately encases itself in a temple of mysticism and formulates DOGMAS. An Eastern atavism. All great religions have come from the East, because only in the East does man truly know how to believe and one of the Slavic people's most characteristic features is the eternal desire for a boundless faith in something. We, for example, are decidedly unhinged on the subject of Poland. This poor Poland, like a terrific painting coated with endless layers of color, as a result of constant "restoration." Colors of a peculiar chemical composition, where the Virgin Mary mingles with hunter's stew and borsch with dumplings, with Mickiewicz and the game of bridge (the Polish national pastime), with Catholicism and Towiański, with the bulwark of Christianity and Byzantine anarchism (an entirely specific Polish feature, expressed in the shorthand—I adore you, you mother f——), and with the absolute obligation to die for the fatherland, not only when it's necessary, but above all when it's not. In that case, try not to die. Necessary death doesn't count because it's suspect. The person might have had a personal interest in dying. True heroism is to die an unnecessary death and naturally with style. And we die unnecessarily and magnificently.

Why always look for answers in a dogmatic-mystical synthesis, even if it were to concern Poland? When one begins to think like a man and in the interest of man, one must decide whether to write a treatise or cook a stew. The Slavs usually concoct their stew with condiments that are often truly spicy, like the powers of Satan or impotent goodness. God, werewolves, night and hell, all knock about and roll around among truly marvelous observations and flights of thought. Having dressed everything in the colorful robes of liturgical explanation, investigations, and other excitable Slavs, they create a religion whose adherents either waste their talents on it and become deadly boring characters or ignite a real hell, like the adherents of Communism. All of Marxism in its Communist edition is nothing other than socialism in a Tatar-Slavic sauce, which even a retarded child knows and understands.

The New Middle Ages is precisely such a mixture of splendid ideas and superb observations, served up in the sauce of God and Satan, the Night, and nonresistance to evil. Many of its elements display a tendency to unexplained "inexorability." The entire responsibility lies with God and the unclean powers, mixing God and Satan to such an extent that I never know what the Slavs believe in more—God or Satan, the remission of sins or eternal damnation.

January 14, 1943

Everyone knows that the Russians have taken Velikiye Luki, but the Germans are writing incredible stories and refuse to acknowledge anything. It is impossible to obtain a single map of Russia in all of Paris. Everyone is listening to the radio and studying the map. First-class propaganda for Communism. Everyone is now a walking war bulletin. England and America have ceased to exist. They've disappeared. Radio shops are doing a boom business, because any halfway reasonable set costs between four and five thousand francs. Excellent weather. It's warm, so the fuel shortage is not a problem.

January 15, 1943

German ingenuity knows no bounds. In Africa the French are fighting on the side of the English, but because they have been "forcibly" drafted by the English, French soldiers captured by the Germans will not be treated as prisoners but immediately released and sent home. Important articles on this subject are in all the Paris newspapers. The Führer's magnanimous gesture. But it now has no effect. Magnanimous gestures do not work when you're getting shafted . . . They should have thought of that earlier.

I run downstairs to my *patron* and his wife, summoned by three blinks of the light in our room. Something important. It's the agreed signal. Indeed, Monsieur and Mme Bessières are bending over the table, their noses in the map. The names of cities and towns seized from the Germans emerge from the radio. Advances everywhere. The entire German army is surrounded at Stalingrad. Over two hundred thousand men, of whom only a few will survive to the end of the war. Berlin was bombarded twice in a row. American war production is beginning to reach the front. Four-engine Liberators will now be harassing the Germans more and more often. In Africa things are progressing, *langsam aber sicher.*[9]

January 19, 1943

The blockade of Leningrad has been lifted.[10] Everyone's in a fever. Stalingrad will be a scandal, or rather is one already. Propaganda in the German newspapers has changed tack. It relies on pessimism. Goebbels himself doesn't know what to write in his *Das Reich*, of which I have become a fervent reader. Even people with no sense of humor are beginning to manufacture jokes out of the Wehrmacht bulletins and the "tactics of bluster."

January 20, 1943

General Montgomery is sixty kilometers from Tripoli. He beats Rommel in each round and advances. As if with the wave of a magic wand, the Germans are being beaten everywhere and are retreating. Impressed by this, even pessimists like myself hint from time to time that the end of the war is not impossible this year.

January 23, 1943

Tripoli has fallen, Rommel is retreating "artistically," but he's retreating. The Russians are taking something every day. The newspapers no longer hide the facts. German propaganda has suddenly torn the veil and is beginning to show the naked truth. It's beginning to drum up fear. To terrify everyone with Red Power and describe the fate that awaits us in the event of its victory. We all know this (not all, very few in fact), but we have nevertheless begun to hate this "European" culture and European hypocrisy so intensely that we sometimes don't care at all. Let me perish along with it, but let me witness its end before I die. Every evening I now run downstairs to the *patron* for the communiqué.

January 27, 1943

An important communiqué about the meeting between Roosevelt and Churchill at a major conference in Casablanca. A series of decisions taken with regard to the joint conduct of the war. This makes very good propaganda. The president of the United States is attending a conference outside his own country. Something almost unheard of in American history. And so on. I can't get too excited because there's one important and ominous point. Stalin, though urgently invited, did not appear. Why? Because he doesn't give a damn about them and wants to win the war on his own. Why, why? I'm again turning into a Rzecki.

January 29, 1943

Hannibal ante portas, periculum in mora—that's the tone of the German newspapers and propaganda at the moment.[11] And therefore they're initiating total war. The total mobilization of the population in Germany. Men between sixteen and sixty-five years of age, of whom those between seventeen and forty-five to be sent to the front. Women from age eighteen to forty-five. That's in Germany. What about the rest of Europe? The mood is once again growing darker. Tomorrow that clown is supposed to give a speech on the occasion of the tenth anniversary of the seizure of power. What will he say?

January 30, 1943

Hitler didn't speak. He preferred to write a proclamation and let Göring read it. Except that *der dicke Hermann* was unable to read it at the time designated for the ceremony, because the English flew over to bomb Berlin and in the most tactless manner delayed the panegyric for two hours. What a horrible nation, those English. All Paris is rocking with laughter. The Russians are speeding toward Rostov.

January 31, 1943

A splendid Sunday. The boulevards shine in the dull winter sun. Everything looks as if it's coated in glass. We are too warmly dressed. Basia throws her fur coat over her arm, I unbutton my coat, and off we go. Slowly toward the Madeleine. All over Paris there's a sense of barely muffled joy. The anemic January sun already considers itself springlike. People stroll lazily, stopping to inspect the shop windows. There's not much in them, because regulations prohibit the display of *marchandise de luxe*. It's unseemly to tease the heroic defenders of Europe with luxuries exhibited in exquisite shops, while over there "Europe" is bleeding and retreating under the pressure of the barbarian hordes. The displays are practically empty. By contrast, the street is a display of insouciance. The Parisian crowd dresses more elegantly than ever before. Women and young girls are sporting cheap rabbit-fur coats in all possible colors and styles. Rabbit is in fashion and even the truly elegant, who have much classier wraps, wear rabbit, styled by the great fashion houses. With the Parisian's innate taste and artistry. The wooden soles of sandals and little fur-lined boots clatter along. Large over-the-shoulder handbags and long umbrellas add a touch of nonchalance. Hats grow ever larger, in the form of romantic cloches. Elaborate turbans and imaginative berets have become true works of art.

Even men have become more elegant. The French are civilizing themselves and the young set the tone. Inside the glassed-in café terraces on boulevard des Capucines and rue Royale people float along lazily, like fish in an aquarium. Fashion and women rule the roost. In one of the kiosks near the Madeleine I buy *Das Reich*. What has Herr Goebbels written? It's good to catch the lies red-handed. After all, what Goebbels writes has not only hands and feet, but often even a head, and would certainly have one if it weren't Goebbels who was writing. The Germans are a stupid nation, without an ounce of sensibility. And that's what produces blind faith in systems. They are the Bolsheviks' closest kin. Can one even mention systems, when the subject is man? I think not. Because man is an eternal atom, which when smashed releases ever greater powers. It sometimes seems to me that the entire direction of contemporary thought is simply absurd. There can be no talk of systems in relation to man — or worse — of FAITH in systems. Man is eternally on fire. He must be extinguished like a fire, which is to say, *however it can be done.* Perhaps even in extinguishing fires, many systems may be involved, but they are not of much use in the end, because nothing ever catches fire according to a system. Man, that permanent surprise, cannot be captured by a system. If someone were to ask me today what political regime, ideology, or system I believe in, I would have trouble. I don't believe in any regime, I'm fed up with all ideologies, and I despise all systems applied to man. I would rather be inclined to answer that I believe in any regime, ideology, or system that is *truly* concerned with man. "Let man LIVE" — that's the only system and ideology. Let man live, not ORDER him to live; allow him to choose his goal in life, and not impose one on him. And end the glorification of death.

We enter Rebattet's pastry shop. I order tea and buy a mountain of petits fours. I read an article by Goebbels about the mobilization of the population and total war. As an example to his Germans, he offers — Russia. He speaks of the women of Leningrad. Russia. The immense effort of man-the-termite. Everyone is filled today with boundless, uncritical admiration. Because there, in the Urals and beyond the Urals, in monstrous factories, plants, and labor camps thousands of slave-termites forge weapons for the termite-warriors, to defeat a different termite and turn the whole world into a giant termite mound. What does man amount to there? I admire nothing. I prefer to admire the petits fours and those lovely young women, not defending any Leningrad, for whom the only Leningrad is a bed. And that's how it should be.

February 1, 1943

Indeed, Stalingrad is over. But they don't admit it. They continue to write about the heroic battles in hopeless conditions. Not for a minute do I doubt the conditions are hopeless. No one feels either pity or admiration. Everyone's hatred is focused on Stalingrad. People speak with satisfaction and the deepest pleasure about the death of thousands of people and no one stops to think that these are also people. Not even me . . . All of occupied Europe sits in the arena and observes the horrible spectacle in complete cold blood. And they do not grasp the evil twist of fate, the infernal paradox that they are at the same time watching their own funeral. It's the death of those who have betrayed Europe and are digging her grave. K. is right. The Germans' greatest crime is the betrayal of Europe.

February 4, 1943

Well, they've admitted it. With fanfare and with all the gloom of Vikings and the mendacity of Teutonic knights.

Stalingrad has saved Germany from defeat. By concentrating Bolshevik power on itself, Stalingrad allowed the Germans to organize their defense behind the lines and spared them certain defeat. Very likely, but for how long? In the meantime we had fun. Madame Junot, describing the mood in Paris after Napoleon's Moscow campaign, quotes some sharp anecdotes and puns, which spread throughout France at the time. Plastered on all the walls, often right under Napoleon's windows: *"Qu'est-ce que tu as fait avec ton armée?"*[12] Napoleon answers: *"Je l'ai, je l'ai"* (spoken aloud this sounds like *"gelé,"* which can mean either "I have her" or "frozen stiff"). I've the urge to plaster something similar under the windows of the Führer's Hauptquartier. The Russians have taken Kupiansk, in Ukraine.

February 6, 1943

On the way to the public bathhouse on rue de Charenton today, I bought a copy of Balzac's *Colonel Chabert.* I read it in one fell swoop. It's a long novella, not a novel. Who is Chabert, this Napoleonic colonel, taken for dead in the Battle of Eylau, who digs himself out from under a mass grave and after years of wandering across Europe, arrives in France?[13] The specter of a great and bloody epic. The ruin of a man, at war with a life that's no longer for him. For those around him it's a bloody hiccup, for him it's a dream ending in madness.

How many such Chaberts will this war produce? War itself is terrible, but its results are more horrible still. For how long after this war will every society be filled with such human ruins? The ruins of former soldiers, the ruins of former prisoners, the ruins of those deported, of broken families, of deadened feelings and youth thrown off track? And, despite everything, the aureole of a legend envelops it all—the aureole of an *epic.* Each new war is born of the legend of the war that went before. Each war is but the continuation of the *very first war.* Who knows whether the murder of Abel was not cloaked in a legend, which then seduced the next Cain. Myth, the legend of sacrifice, the epic of death, tempts each new generation. In a few years Stalingrad will have become the burning bush whose image will lead a new round of young men to march forward toward their own execution. A vicious circle.

February 8, 1943

Germany has finished four days of national mourning over the defeat at Stalingrad. All for the ambition of a single man. I can't get *Colonel Chabert* off my mind. How long did the legend of Napoleon persist in France? How much blood has flowed in the name of that legend long after he himself was no longer alive? All over Europe. A legend of blood, a legend of disaster, misery, and death wrapped in the smoke of incense. A corpse, an ordinary corpse, obscured by the fumes of glory, that drags on, generation after generation, like a ball and chain. What is all this compared to the millions of human lives and the millions of hearts in tears? How long will the legend of Hitler survive in Germany? What will yet take place in the name of this legend? Hated today throughout Europe, he will appear to later generations in the aureole of a legend. The stories of those at Sevastopol, Kharkov, or Leningrad will ignite the imaginations of the young and lure them by the promise of a great adventure. The story of those who have returned will travel from the hot sands of the desert to the eternal glaciers of the north. They will never understand what happened and will die in their sleep. Man loves suffering, and when it's over adorns it with flowers. War ends not because one side beats the other but because the legend of one of the opponents fades faster than the other's. The image of the myth, that composite image made from feelings, memories, ambitions, erstwhile glory — gives way to the image of cold reality. But getting drunk on legends is alas one of the most stubborn addictions. The hangover is short and the desire to get drunk again returns quickly. How long will the German hangover last?

February 16, 1943

Kharkov has been taken, and two days ago Rostov and Voroshilovgrad. Let's not forget the English, who have once again triggered the psychosis of the landing. All of Paris is convinced that in March the Americans and the English will be in France. What for? It'll get them nowhere. Meanwhile, there's the game with Tunis. Rommel is retreating toward Tunis, where General von Arnim has installed himself with significant help from the French and faces the Americans approaching from the other direction.[14] In the end, Tunis will become a minor Stalingrad. All that needs to be explained is whether von Arnim — like General Paulus at Stalingrad — will also be named marshal *in articulo mortis*.[15] Otherwise, one must believe that Russia is no longer Bolshevik Russia but a lamb, with whom one can engage in discussion. Abdül-Hamid and the Empress of China . . . Until the time that . . .

February 18, 1943

Mass deportation of French workers to Germany. Obviously with Vichy's backing. France today presents an image of destitution and despair. Villainy flourishes, informing has expanded with elemental force, the absence of basic information about history, politics, and the life of other nations leaves the entire nation at the mercy of written and spoken lies. Propaganda does what it can to destroy sober thinking and Vichy, with *la France éternelle* always on its lips, sullies the history of this country as no government, beginning with Julius Caesar, ever has before. There's a limit to how far one can take subservience to the victor, if only the limits of one's own dignity. But Vichy, the French press, and that entire clique observe no limits. There are literary people, *French* writers, who follow German orders with such fervor and such total disregard for their own dignity, who write and speak in a manner that simply defies description. It's the *absolute fervor* of absolute self-abasement. Some Frenchmen understand this, but not very many. In general, such behavior is taken in stride. It's enough for someone to be *anti-Boche* and the rest doesn't matter. What does it matter if the majority of people are basically anti-German (now) and anticollaborationist when the nation produces such aces as Laval and Pétain. Every government is to some extent an expression of the nation. Today's France cannot be identified with what is said and written officially, but the two cannot be separated *completely.* There are still hundreds of these "lapdogs" of the occupation, ready to fulfill German commands with greater tenacity and zeal than the Germans themselves. Newspapers produced by the French outdo themselves in fulfilling the demands of propaganda. They lie shamelessly, they distort the facts, ten times more than the German press. Compared to this *Das Reich* seems like an honest rag. Yet the French are not under compulsion, no one forces them to write more than is demanded by the *Propagandastaffel in Frankreich.*[16] But they write, bark, and kowtow.

February 21, 1943

This evening, *Marriage of Figaro* at the Odéon Theater. A wasted evening. It was anything but theater. A fair booth. The sets, the costumes, the acting— less than zero. The only interesting thing: instead of the clever and sly Figaro, this Figaro was an ingratiating boor. And what's more, it was very clear that this was not a performance but expressed his own *nature*. Figaro was natural, to the marrow of his bones, in all the scenes with the count. He personified the revolutionary rabble that allows those of higher station to take such delight in feelings of liberty, equality, and fraternity. Above them by birth? No—by culture. This was the Figaro of the Republic, not Figaro of the Rococo. One felt the bonds of close friendship between Figaro and the audience and between the audience and Figaro. One felt that everything Figaro said was still relevant for this crowd. Each of Figaro's *boutades*,[17] sharp and malicious, was deliberately made coarse and vulgar, on purpose. This was the rebellious republican boor, a product of the half-baked revolution—to everyone's satisfaction. The continuing relevance in France of the Revolution and its dust-covered slogans is sometimes puzzling. I sometimes wonder whether instead of moving them forward, the Revolution did not merely set them back, but much worse—simply stopped them in their tracks. One often gets the distinct impression that after shaking things up on July 14, 1789, they have never stopped doing so, stuck in the same place and on the same level.

Russia is celebrating the twenty-fifth anniversary of the Red Army. People are confused nowadays on the subject of Russia, thanks to English and American propaganda. England and America are stuffing the Russians like force-fed geese and giving them a good press to boot. This is modern barbarity and nothing can be done about it. Although I would never contest Russia's progress in material terms, at the same time I consider its spiritual progress to be negligible—if there is any at all.

K. reads newspapers and magazines, I read books. Every morning, we meet at our table on the stage of the *salle des fêtes* of the Châtillon-sous-Bagneux town hall and review the current situation. Today K. said: "My dear Andrzej, if there were any sensible people in London, instead of preparing to return, they would immediately start building a strong and cohesive emigration." Occasionally we're joined by P., an engineer and philosopher. He speaks softly and deliberately. "So, do you think the English and Americans will allow Russia to reach the center of Europe?" He smiles. "They will. Let's have no illusions. They'll wait until Stalin dies and then—they'll see."

February 22, 1943

And so, the king of England has offered the sword of honor to the city of Stalingrad. Another terrific film, *Pontcarral, colonel d'Empire*.[18] It's been playing since the fall, but at first it was impossible to get a ticket. And whenever I can, I avoid standing in any kind of line. A line is one of the most perfidious methods of repressing independent thinking. As soon as I begin standing in line I feel *la bête humaine rampante*[19] within me, I turn into an amoeba, into some sort of plankton, indifferent to everything, inclined to tolerate anything, whose spirit has been collectivized and turns into a sort of kolkhoz: I lose my sense of self, and finally, after a long wait, when I get some little scrap, the world seems beautiful and nothing seems really all that bad. With an optimist like that you can do anything you want. This is also a method, and quite a clever one. Like a judicial interrogation, a line "softens" people up.

February 25, 1943

On the occasion of the twenty-third anniversary of the founding of the National Socialist Party, Hitler has issued a proclamation to the Germans and to Europe. But again he did not announce it himself. It was read by Hermann Esser.[20] As to why such works of literature are being read by others, speculation naturally runs rampant. From serious illness to death itself. The whole proclamation was yet again nothing more than the furious buzzing of a fly trapped in a spiderweb. "We will not hesitate even for a second to force the nations responsible for this war (?) to make an effort to help us in this decisive battle . . . In full accord with our allies, we are taking steps to mobilize Europe, materially and morally." Of course—into the train and off you go. Only now do we see what a resilient beast man is. This is what distinguishes him above all from the other animals. Everything that's happening today seemed absolutely unbearable to us even ten years ago. Aerial warfare, for example. We thought the one with the strongest air force would win right away, because people cannot endure bombardment. Yet, today it takes but half an hour for a city to be destroyed, thousands of people perish—and the comedy goes on. For the past half year London has been shaken by bombs, now south Germany is being smashed to pieces, and there's no end in sight. The Führer issues a proclamation, the English have finally gotten down to serious business, the Russians have demonstrated totally unsuspected capacities. Now, the war is really starting.

February 26, 1943

This is for posterity—to show how far basic depravity can be taken, even when compulsion is not involved. An article by Robert de Beauplan in today's *Le Matin* (no. 21420) can serve as an eloquent and multifaceted illustration of what I mean by absolute depravity. Robert de Beauplan is not the only one.[21] He writes what many people are saying and writing, following the lead of the entire Vichy clique. What Beauplan writes and what others write and say on the radio *is not dictated* by the *Propagandastaffel*, because even the Germans would not dare feed the editors items *such as these*. They themselves would consider them too coarse, even though their own sensibilities are rather limited. No—let's have no illusions. This is typically French depravity. The title of this screed is *France, pays d'Europe*. And it goes like this:

"Only the seriousness of the tasks detaining the Führer at his headquarters has again prevented him from appearing in Munich among his oldest comrades in arms to join them in celebrating the twenty-third anniversary of the founding of the National Socialist Party. The proclamation read in his name by Secretary of State Esser is nevertheless of capital importance.

"The German armed forces, which thanks to a string of victories have penetrated to the heart of Russia, have been subjected for the past three months to the most ferocious attacks of modern times. That their leader still declares his confidence in the final outcome is not surprising on the part of a man who, thanks to his energy and unshakable will, has up to now surmounted every challenge. The Führer owes this confidence as well to the certainty of having behind him a great, unified nation, which he has galvanized by his faith and which will avoid no sacrifice to achieve the goal he has put before it.

"But Germany does not fight for herself alone. She defends all of Europe against the menace of the Bolshevik invasion. That is also why Germany does not intend to fight alone.

"Some of the Führer's words are pregnant with meaning: 'We will not hesitate even for a second to force the nations responsible for this war to make an effort to help us in this decisive battle . . . In full accord with our allies, we are taking steps to mobilize Europe, materially and morally.' Who can help but acknowledge that this language is addressed above all to France? We bear much of the responsibility for the war and for our defeat, which has put us at Germany's mercy, gives her the power today to demand from us the support she needs. She is not taking advantage of her power. She is exercising a legitimate right, recognized by the government of Marshal Pétain and President Laval, whose policy is designed voluntarily to put the maximum of our available resources and manpower at Germany's disposal. Whoever tries to obstruct this policy fails in his duty to France. Besides which, resistance is useless, as the Führer has made perfectly clear." (This unbelievable sentence is unbelievable in its depraved sincerity, which is quite disarming.)

"But it is not the victor's harsh law to which we must submit. One must view these things from a higher perspective" (from the gallows). "If Europe goes under, France—a country belonging to Europe—will perish along with it. And if thanks to Germany Europe is saved, we will benefit only insofar as we have collaborated in the work of salvation. This is the dilemma we face. Let us not therefore say that Germany is keeping us in servitude, but rather that she offers us the unexpected chance to repair the disastrous consequences of our errors and be able, in the reconstruction of the New Europe, to assert our rights."

Can there be anything more base in its servility and depraved toadying? What swine!

March 1, 1943

The Russians have gone too fast. The Germans have turned to the counterattack and have already recaptured some positions over there. Everyone's faces fell and noses were out of joint. The Germans remain strong. Clearly—but that no longer alters the situation.

Berdyaev writes, among other things: "In the *Utopia* of Thomas More it is not easy freely to change one's place of residence. In the *Utopia* of Étienne Cabet there is only one newspaper, the government newspaper, and the free press is categorically forbidden. Utopias were not well known—or had been forgotten—and the failure to bring them about caused all too much regret. It turns out, however, that they are easier to achieve than it used to seem. And today we face an urgent question of a different kind: *How to avoid the full realization of utopia?*"

We have not avoided it. But we don't understand. "How did we come to this?" almost all of us ask nowadays. This question contains almost our entire era, and these six words harbor the enormous tragedy of our times. This question has begun to envelop everything, penetrate everywhere, assuming the shape of a great question mark in every glance of millions of people. Those who don't manage to think, *feel* that something strange, incomprehensible, and terrible has happened. The feeling is that of a prisoner who has been promised freedom, but is transferred to ever lower and darker cells—bitter disappointment, astonishment, fear, and finally dull resignation.

The mind seeks an answer and beats helplessly against the limits of sterile reasoning. War? No. War cannot be a cause, because war is always only a result, merely a symptom of a prolonged, hidden sickness. The result of what? Capitalism, crises, shifts in the social structure? Fine, but . . . But the farther one goes, the more complicated everything gets, the bigger the vacuum becomes. Somewhere even farther along the power of reason ends, faced with reality intellect breaks down. Man *does not understand* and gives up.

Yet everything must have some meaning, must be connected to something.

Giving up, "nonthinking," can only work for a short time. The next prick of reality arouses the same thought yet again. There's something humiliating in "nonthinking" and giving up. Today, in this age in which man has begun to be ashamed of being man, the abandonment of thought, the retreat to "I don't understand," humiliates us even more, brings us closer to the animal each one of us has long ago started to become. We didn't sense it—today we see it. For if even today millions of people have not yet become animals, it can happen to them very soon. We are in a period of accelerated "dehumanization." How the devil did we come to this?

In first tackling that question of our age, we each feel helpless. We observe that our entire intelligence is not enough to break through the wall of questions provoked by the first one. Our entire education, the entire way of thinking instilled in us, are worth less than nothing in contact with the life that has fallen to our lot. We feel that our reason is in fetters that cannot be unbound, that in reflecting on this subject we behave like a drowning fly, swimming around the sides of a smooth glass and sliding back repeatedly into the water. Unable to find an answer in our disorderly thoughts, we cease for a while to think at all but merely observe the feelings that arise in us when everything proves a disappointment and when we find ourselves once again helpless before the facts. Feeling is the basis of every thought. Feeling is the raw material, thought the work-in-progress, words the final product. Very imperfect, it's true. But one without the other cannot exist.

Beginning with our feelings and proceeding through our thoughts and words, depending more on each of the three elements (at certain moments), monitoring and categorizing, we extract from ourselves further observations. Analyzing our feelings, we observe that the most expressive of them, the one that encompasses all the others without exception, is our infernal *disappointment*—a feeling so great it leaves us completely numb. It's as though someone had been stroking our heads for a long time, while making tender promises, and—had suddenly struck us. After the first blow, others followed. As soon as we raised our heads, more, increasingly powerful blows rained down upon us. Everything we were taught, everything arranged in our minds and carefully classified, howls with pain.

Hard objects react to blows much more violently than soft objects. If today the content of our skulls explodes, it's because what was installed inside them was very rigid. This inelastic material is our entire system of thought. Our entire misapprehension of reality stems from the existence of a hard and inviolable "taboo," which blocks our access to new observations. We see it, and we *feel* the inability of thought to bend.

True understanding always depends on making concessions, on relinquishing, if only partially, what was considered the truth until then—with the goal of discovering a new truth. *To understand* means to *humble oneself.* We will understand the pain of these blows, we will understand that if today *we do not understand* it is only because—willingly or against our will—we do not want to concede and relinquish certain truths, those we grew up with and on which we were fed. The torpor and immense puzzlement which beset us in the face of reality today are directly proportional to the force of the resistance with which we cling to our deeply inculcated "taboos" or simply to dogmas. Because our century, which has taught us that skeptical thinking about everything is the embodiment of *liberation,* has bound our minds in new fetters of dogma or so-called irrefutable truths. The conflict of thought in confrontation with current reality unfolds in a way that demonstrates with near certainty that this is indeed the case.

The man who relies on dogmas of any kind reacts in the same way to new ideas or to phenomena that disturb his previous system of thought or religious faith: he adopts them but cannot accept them. It's the irrational negation of the existence of anything that imposes itself—the desire to turn away from reality, the fear when confronted with the collapse into ruins of what had until now been considered indestructible. Nothing has perhaps done more harm in this world than this cowardly (often also self-interested) desire to turn away from reality. Men or ideologies come to a halt, in the instinctive fear of a vacuum, and being unsure of what they will find around the next corner stubbornly prefer to mark time. To defer the catastrophe. The closer a given dogma was to the heart (never to the mind—dogmas do not withstand the force of the mind), the more deeply venerated, the harder it is to come to terms with a new truth, the longer the marking of time. This marking of time takes the greatest toll.

Human reason behaves like a bankrupt person who hides his bankruptcy and flaunts what remains of his fortune in the effort to convince himself that he'll manage to conceal his situation not only from others but also from himself. It's the desperate defense of positions that have already been lost. Faced with reality we mark time. We feel the bankruptcy of former beliefs, but we do not want to admit it. The desperate defense, the intensity of the struggle, and the misunderstandings that arise from it are typical features of the conflict between thought and dogma. For dogma is not thought—it is above all feeling, just as every feeling is to a certain extent dogma.

In every struggle with dogma or during the period of its collapse, whether we like it or not, a general confusion ensues, which obstructs the understanding of newly emerging things, since the battle is not between ideas but between thought and feeling. The stormiest periods in the life of the community as well as in individual lives are always those in which previously absolute belief-feelings are collapsing. The defense of feelings brooks no compromise and does not recognize common sense. Hence the feeble resistance of conservatives, who usually defend, not ideas, but feelings. All of us today are conservatives, and the defense, the blind defense of dogmas, clouds our minds. We are all adherents of the dogmas of *progress* in the most fallacious meaning of the term, of faith in man and his inevitable development. We are fanatic about the dogma of matter and numbers. We cannot resolve to refute them, fearing to break with our most precious beliefs. We defend our illusions and cannot comprehend reality. We do not manage to make the facts fit any of our plans, because each idea stumbles against the beliefs in which we were raised but which are *no longer sufficient.* Our reason twists and turns, defending already lost positions and marking time. We cannot believe it, we're afraid to admit bankruptcy, the bankruptcy of all ideologies.

Yet this bankruptcy has already become clear and only accepting it will allow us at least partially to understand what has so far escaped our understanding. Let's come to terms with the collapse of dogmas, and this will allow us to create our own dogmas—new ones. How hard it is to accept the fact that true wisdom and true faith are not faith in the perfection of what once seemed perfect, but *the ability to lose one's faith* at the right moment. It is also the readiness to start again from zero. We have to start again from zero and correct our false calculations. How wrong indeed, we see today.

I am trying to gather together the scraps of ideas that will not leave me in peace. Everything in me rebels, because it seems to me that we have taken the wrong road and that if we do not change direction the future will be dark. François de Curel once jokingly said: "Nature has no laws. People have invented them for their own convenience."[22] This witticism is in fact no joke. Today we are all bent under the weight of the "laws of nature" and of ideologies invented by those for whom man, the ordinary man, has become inconvenient. Man with a capital M is the greatest obstacle to all systems and ideologies. We are bent under the burden of "laws," "systems," and "ideologies," by now entirely false. We are hurrying, like the locomotive driver, with eyes only for the manometer and the speedometer. And only the pressure increases, only the speed. Nothing else.

March 4, 1943

The day before yesterday they again bombed Berlin. A conflict has arisen between Sikorski and the Soviets.[23] Concerning Lwów. The Poles do not want to give away something that at the moment is not ours, while the Bolsheviks do not want to relinquish something that never was theirs. Eternal discussions about the stolen watch. Obviously the Germans are making the most of it. Today there was already a long article in the *Pariser Zeitung* under the headline "*Polnischer Schuldfall.*"[24] A bit more of this and the Germans will begin shedding tears over us. They're making Poland into a nation tortured by the Bolsheviks. And that will be right. But it won't be right, since it's the Germans who say it. Now we're quarreling over Lwów and—we have good reason. Except that when the English get tired of quarreling with their loyal Polish ally, they'll zip our lips and tell Sikorski—in English—to *shut up!*

March 7, 1943

They are sixty kilometers from Viazma. For ten days now, every night, Germany is being bombarded. *Deutschland erwache. Und Deutschland erwacht. Jede Nacht.*[25]

In his splendid *Considérations sur la France*, Joseph de Maistre offers a few statistics, which say a great deal and, despite their date, are amazingly still relevant.[26] In chapter 7 of the *Considérations*, he says the following:

"Between July 1, 1789, and October 1791, the National Assembly enacted 2,557 laws.

"The Legislative Assembly, in eleven and a half months, enacted 1,712.

"The National Convention, during the 57 months between the first day of the Republic and the 4th of Brumaire in Year IV of the Revolution (October 26, 1795), enacted 11,210.

"For a total of 15,479."

"I doubt," continues de Maistre, "that the three royal houses of France could have produced such a mighty collection. This infinitely large number of laws arouses two quite different reactions, one after the other. The first is admiration, or at least astonishment. One is surprised, like Mr. Edmund Burke, that this nation, whose frivolity is proverbial, should have produced such tenacious workers. The edifice of these laws is a work of immense proportions, of stunning appearance. But astonishment quickly becomes pity, when one considers the worthlessness of these laws; and one sees nothing more than children exhausting themselves to build a great house of cards. Why so many laws? Because there are no legislators. What have these would-be legislators achieved in six years? NOTHING, because DESTRUCTION is not CREATION."[27]

All of that can be repeated today in relation to today's France and in the future (if all goes well) probably to all of Europe. After the armistice, after

Pétain took power and following him Laval, France entered the murky waters of "internal renewal" under the banner of "National Revolution" (*Révolution nationale*—they can't do without revolution). Beaten, stomped on, fallen from the heights of her self-image (often very exaggerated), she decided to beat her breast and—find the culprits. Instead of searching for guilt in herself, she brought the "perpetrators of the defeat" before the court in Riom. These were the *circenses* for the people, in the absence of *panem*. To debase and smear a few more or less eminent people in the national limelight, that is, to elevate the throng, satisfy its instincts for "revenge," while concealing the truth, which in these cases is what's most important.

The entire operetta in Riom was supposed to give the public something to chew on, deflect attention, in a word, a French edition of the Moscow trials. Nevertheless it turned out otherwise. The accused accused the accusers. The atmosphere grew more tense with each passing day, the winds of scandal spread, France—with the taste she typically displays in such situations—sniffed the odors from the judicial kitchen and had quite a bit of fun. The strict censorship somewhat spoiled the fun, but whatever got through was spicy—so spicy that the trial was called off. The Pétain regime's propaganda campaign failed. Interestingly, over the past hundred years no "one and only" political ideology, from the extreme right to the extreme left, has thought of anything better than these ridiculous trials. Hence, in order to save its remaining authority, severely strained by the comedy in Riom, the Vichy government initiated the canonization of Pétain during his lifetime. A senile little Stalin *à la française*. Everything now happened with the *maréchal*'s name on everyone's lips, in their mouths, and in every other part of the body. This is accompanied by the promotion of an "inferiority complex," slowly and maliciously injected by so-called intellectuals. Look at the Germans—they are brilliant, they have invented everything, they have composed the best music, they are disciplined, they are true citizens, Hitler is a genius, we are less than nothing. Muddy the waters, set France to quarreling with herself, break her up and split her apart. All in the name of the regeneration of the nation. Bubbling with French fans of totalitarianism, Vichy began to revitalize France—with decrees and laws, secret police, and concentration camps. This is how the great burlesque began, perhaps the greatest in the history of totalitarianism, the burlesque of totalitarian France under the dictatorship of Pétain, and now of Laval. It has all the features of a black-comedy skit in a third-rate music hall.

France is determined to "revitalize herself," taking the Germans as her example, in particular their orrrrganization. Reconstruction, orrrrganization, rrrrregeneration have become the slogans of the day. Seeing all the causes of

France's decline in the sudden surge of objectivism, the greatest French patriots suddenly noticed *nothing but evil*. The opinion of well-paid collaborationist intellectuals (intellectuals in such cases are always the greatest scoundrels and whores), proclaimed in newspapers, weeklies, monthlies, and on the radio, full of the colorful "inferiority complex," joined with the judgment of people of goodwill, critics of good faith, and those who are the most anti-German, all in unison disparaging their country and going so far as to deny even its best-known and most incontrovertible values. France is rotten and in decay—she has to be regenerated. As a nation that pays attention, at all times and places, only to *form*, not content, France has discovered in herself only errors of form. Instead of seeking the causes of her decline in her essence, instead of looking *inward*, she sees only the dead letter. In her self-psychoanalysis, she stopped only at the *results*, not at the ultimate, most obvious causes.

Recognizing and understanding *form* alone, she decided to regenerate herself through *form*, for the umpteenth time in her history using *form* to deceive and delude herself. The entire Revolution was in fact form without content and therefore produced no essential results. Seeing the cause of every evil in the failure to execute the laws, France decided to cure herself—*with new laws*. New laws and decrees were supposed to correct the evils of the past and prevent new ones. The result: doubling and tripling the number of unimplemented laws. The "new" France (*la France Nouvelle*) inundated the country with laws and decrees that no one wanted to apply. As the French are not inclined by nature and from birth to do this, they are being compelled by means of police, militias, national shock troops and concentration camps, prisons and fines. The France of today is confined to the camps and prisons of the occupier, pays fines, and serves time in her own camps and prisons, put there by her own government, her own police and administration, fulfilling the slogan—the regeneration of France. Tortured by the Germans, she torments herself a hundred times more—for her own "good." (Many say that life in the occupied zone is considerably freer than in the so-called free zone. This is no longer the case.) As though a delirium has overtaken even otherwise completely sound minds and many that are incorruptible. Something for Voltaire—though I'm sure he would be serving time in Vichy today.

The new organization has led to complete chaos. Interesting as a sign of complete helplessness. This nation, which has created so many laws and fed the whole world on them, which has enormous patience when it comes to regulating all aspects of life with the aid of separate declarations, questionnaires, documents, and official forms—this nation is completely helpless when it comes to the application of theories to life. The more I analyze France, the more often

I observe that the most characteristic feature of this nation is the constant discrepancy between theory and practice. The constant struggle, the constant clashing of theory and practice, is both the tragedy and the greatness of this nation. The innate ineptitude and helplessness of the French when it comes to the application of ideas is to a certain extent an instinct of self-preservation. Every Frenchman is at bottom a born legislator, theoretician, and ideologue. Every Frenchman is more or less inclined to resolve all life's issues with the help of laws and decrees. If all the laws and decrees, produced in such great abundance since the first attack of revolutionary fever, had been applied literally, France would have already completely disappeared or have become a nation of automatons and robots.

This constant clashing of theory and practice is perhaps the most essential cause of all the unexpected, often dazzling thoughts, ideas, and movements, that incessant ferment that gives so much to the world. France is in constant internal struggle, in constant movement, in constant negation, in incessant "feint," to use the language of fencing. Her tragedy is this constant internal struggle, the constant ferment, which is exhausting for her but which endows her at the same time with much of what the world recognizes her for and itself yearns for. France is the ideological boot camp of the entire world. When one gets to know France, one sees to what extent she has made all her revolutions instead of others and for their sake. While exhausting herself in internal contortions and herself withering away, she irrigated the entire world. She nourished the globe with ideas, tested good and evil on herself, experimented with her doors wide open. Others took from her only what proved to be good, which they applied and perfected. France is a country of the most brilliant reforms, a country of a million reforms, at the same time a country in which the fewest of these reforms have been enacted. France limits herself to issuing laws and applying the laws, if at all, in a *formal sense*. Everything that concerns the material side of the law is executed with blind precision, everything concerning the content of the law remains a dead letter. This is also why so much lawlessness in France occurs under the cover of the law.

But nevertheless, despite the endless examples, a Frenchman remains fanatically attached to the law, to art for art's sake when it comes either to the law or to ideas, attending to every word and every letter. This "political" credulity is in fact rather unexpected. It is the sole reason that nowhere but in France have so many governments and statesmen been able with such impunity to lie and to make the great promises they so often fail to fulfill. At each change of government, each time a dignitary speaks, the Frenchman eagerly grasps the pathos and the promises of reform, often appearing to mock them, but deep inside he

BELIEVES. At every minor change of cabinet minister, the widespread revolutionary fervor abates. Because the Frenchman believes—he believes that the external change, the *form*, changes everything. That's what's happened now, too. Having discovered her mistakes, but in form alone, France decided to regenerate herself by means of form and the reform of form. German power impressed her, Prussian organization dazzled her, the animal, herdlike obedience of a nation that not only issues laws but, what's worse, applies them most precisely—all went to her head. And then the dance began, the macabre burlesque began.

In *Les Employés*, Balzac says that in France there are about forty thousand bureaucrats. In other words, in 1840 the entire French administration consisted of forty thousand men, of whom Balzac says, that for the sixty million francs they are paid *"la France obtient la plus fureteuse, la plus méticuleuse, la plus écrivassière, paperassière, inventorière, contrôleuse, vérifiante, soigneuse, enfin la plus femme de ménage des Administrations connues."*[28] Fine, but in 1914 France already had eight hundred thousand bureaucrats, in 1924 a million two hundred fifty thousand, and today over two million, whereas the population has not grown significantly since Balzac's time, and it's possible it may even be the same, as a result of the missing three million prisoners of war and a million deportees. What's going on today beggars the imagination. I'd like to repeat the words of Guglielmo Ferrero: "Fascism promised to exterminate the bureaucracy but has finished by increasing its size, *because all revolutions have resulted in the multiplication of the number of bureaucrats."*[29] (If only for this reason one should avoid revolutions. A good idea.) France swims and drowns in a sea of acts, laws, and paperwork, orders and notices, regulations, edicts and decrees, executed with the help of over two million bureaucrats, who apply them only with the strictest, external formality, tormenting with paperwork, declarations, forms, questionnaires, and bulletins the thirty-eight million people who for good reason try their best not to observe them.

France is regenerating herself and to regenerate herself "truly," she promotes respect for the law by distributing to left and right all possible penalties. By now, no bureaucrat or citizen takes any of this seriously. Vichy emits a flood of edicts of "regeneration," a continuous stream, regulating EVERYTHING by decree. Dazzled, in her weakened state, by German totalitarianism, which she takes as a model, France has become with respect to the issuance of decrees more totalitarian than her model—*Großdeutschland*. To study totalitarianism in all its excesses, in particular in its crippling mania for the regulation of everything by decrees and laws—one should study today's France. I'm beginning to doubt whether after this experiment France will in future manage to be a nation of freedom and liberty.

In *Le Député d'Arcis*, Balzac put it very well: "In France, such a clever land, it would seem that to simplify is to destroy."[30] Not wanting to simplify, France is today destroying herself—with laws. Everyone, the entire country, is victimized by this. The more laws, the more ways there are to violate them, the more idiotic the laws, the greater the NECESSITY to break them. In today's France it is already necessary to break the law, thus demonstrating the absurdity of totalitarianism, which is to say, state control over every aspect of life. If we're still alive today it's only because we've managed up to now to get away with breaking the current laws and decrees. The situation becomes entirely absurd, paradoxical, surrealist when the legislative organ itself has to break the laws promulgated by itself to allow life to continue. Planning is a useful means of monitoring the overall economy. When it goes too far, it becomes nonsensical. For example, there has recently been a shortage of skins in the leather industry. The skins provided by the legal slaughter of horses did not suffice. At the same time, harsh penalties are being levied on the undeclared slaughter of horses, cows, or calves. However, to avoid a shortage of skins, a decree is issued accepting all kinds of skins and exempting providers from the need to explain how the skins came into their possession. Thus, on the one hand, illegal slaughter is punished, while on the other hand, because leather is what's at stake, the skins are accepted despite their illegal origins and—no penalties ensue. The French administration goes even farther, however: in a certain village near Paris, a peasant was penalized for having concealed the skins he had obtained from illegal slaughter. Right out of Zoshchenko or Averchenko![31] This is one of hundreds of examples. What's most interesting, however, is that after all this the tanning business immediately recovered. It seems that if France still eats meat, it's only because of illegal butchery. If I have enough bread, it's because I buy counterfeit bread coupons, which my baker accepts with a smile, praising the "excellent imitation," and if Europe is still somehow breathing, it's only because according to the law, each of its inhabitants should long ago have been thrown in prison. Totalitarianism always leads in the end to some monstrous abstraction, to a madhouse in which no one dares to question the theory, even when practice demonstrates something entirely different. "Why so many laws? Because there are no legislators." Not only in France—all over the world.

In a speech to Polish pilots returning from the bombing of Essen, Sikorski said, among other things: "Let those who are so critical remember that at the moment of victory England and the United States will also have something to say." At this I couldn't help cursing at the radio, something like "That's sh——, Mr. General, I respectfully submit, that's sh——." Curious. Of course, one can only hope the general is right and that this "something" to say is as important as possible. This means, however, that people in London are criticizing and some people fear that England and America would have nothing to say. They are right to be afraid.

March 8, 1943

A perfect duo, separated by a hundred fifty years. Paul Valéry wrote in "Rhumbs": "I do not value and cannot value any writers but those capable of expressing what would be hard for me to express, if the question of expressing it were offered or demanded of me. It's the only case where I can measure value in absolute units, that is, in MY OWN."[32]

I used those very units to measure what was said about France by de Maistre in the eighteenth century and what is said about France by Keyserling today. Both voices reach to the heart of things, complementing each other, creating two sides of the same coin. De Maistre writes:

"Among the peoples who have played a role in modern history, none perhaps more deserves to catch the philosopher's eye than the French people. None has been endowed with a more singular destiny and qualities more clearly apt to achieve it. France, such as she existed before the Revolution (no one knows what fate awaits her in the future), was destined to exercise the same supremacy over all parts of Europe that Europe exercises over the other countries of the world.

"I doubt that nature has done as much for any other people. France is placed at the center of Europe and she can just as easily ally herself with all the surrounding powers as disrupt their coalition. Situated between the two seas, she attracts the commerce of all nations, and her navies can reach and strike everywhere with unequaled facility and speed. No other nation is as well protected by nature and by art. The Atlantic, the Mediterranean, the Alps, the Pyrenees, and the Rhine! What boundaries! And behind these ramparts, you see a triple ring of imposing citadels erected and repaired by the genius of Vauban, whose disconsolate ghost bemoans having worked for the National Convention.[33]

"You may search the world for a state whose various parts are as closely connected and form as impressive a whole. France has both mass and volume; no political body in Europe is more populous, more *compact*, more difficult to rupture, and whose impact is more tremendous. Her population is immense, her products infinitely numerous and not lacking in diversity. Her riches depend on neither fashion nor opinion; her wines, her oils, her woods, her salts, her hemps, etc., make her independent of other peoples, who are nevertheless obliged to pay her tribute. And as if her natural riches were not enough, she has also received the scepter of fashion, so that her reign extends over dreams as well as needs and her empire is complete.

"Superb rivers traverse this vast realm and connect to each other by a host of navigable waterways that flow in all directions and whose endless networks seem to have been arranged by the hand of an engineer. Catherine de Medici did not exaggerate greatly when she said that France alone has as many navigable rivers as all the rest of Europe.

"This people would be a threat to the others if it could be a conqueror; but that is not its mission. Invincible at home, when it takes its forces abroad one is astonished to see its armies, victims of their own victories and of the vices of the national character, dissolving and disappearing like a puff of steam.

"The Frenchman is not suited to maintaining his conquests: his character alone snatches it from his hands. On this subject Mirabeau's *L'Ami des hommes* light-heartedly remarks that 'the warriors who succeed in expelling the French from a conquered country can take their place in the temple of memory alongside the geese of the Capitol.'[34]

"But if the French cannot dominate foreign nations by force of arms, they have at all times exercised another, much more honorable kind of dominion over them, that of opinion. From the moment when this people was united into the body of a nation, it has attracted the attention of the world, and astonished it by a brilliance of character that has always been envied. Charlemagne was the Sesostris of the Middle Ages; his paladins made such an impression on the imagination of peoples that they became the subjects of a kind of particular mythology; and the Rolands and the Amadis were for our fathers what Theseus and Hercules were for the ancient Greeks.[35]

"In order to exercise the kind of supremacy she possesses, France received a dominant language, whose hidden character remains a mystery, despite everything that has been said on this subject. Those who deny the superiority of the French language accept an effect without a cause. I do not in fact see any way to refute the experience. Even before this language was made illustrious by masterpieces in every genre, Europe sensed its superiority, loved it, and was honored to speak it. Today its reign, which has become so fateful, is all but too indisputable. It has been said a thousand times that the French language is hard and resistant, and this is true. But if one takes this as an objection, one is greatly mistaken. Like steel, the most obdurate of metals, but which more than any other achieves the most beautiful sheen when art manages to subdue it, the French language, when handled and mastered by true artists, acquires in their hands the most durable and the most brilliant forms. What is called precisely the art of the word is eminently the talent of the French, and it is by the art of the word that one reigns over men. Someone has said that a thought never belongs to the world until a writer of genius has seized upon it and clad it in the right expression. Well said; and here precisely is the source of French influence; the good writers of that nation express things better than those of any other nation, and they circulate their thoughts throughout all of Europe in less time than it takes a writer of another country to make his own thoughts known in his own province. It is this talent, this distinctive quality, this extraordinary gift that has made the French the dispensers of fame. Self-regard, more adept and stronger than national pride, had revealed this truth to the famous men from all over the world who all aspired, more or less openly, to obtain the approval of the French, unable to conceal from themselves that they were condemned to a local reputation until the moment when Paris should consent to praise them. I do not know if it has been noted that English literature owes all its fame to the French, and that it was perfectly unknown to the rest of Europe before France became enamored of its rival's literary productions. Its throne being situated between the North and the South, the French language lends itself without too much difficulty to the voices of other peoples and becomes for them a universal and indispensable interpreter for the commerce of ideas.

"With this *intermediate* language, the French have received from nature another analogous advantage: a universally suitable taste. One will undoubtedly find in foreign writers traits of equal, even superior beauty to the best that France has produced; but an impression is made, not by certain traits, but by the whole. French writers could easily produce traits of this kind; if they are less common among the French, it's because they submit to enthusiasm only with a timid boldness that agrees to be transported, but never carried away. This is the great secret of taste: for that which does not attain the sublime can still be beautiful, but that which surpasses the sublime is certainly foolish. The art of saying what needs to be said and when it needs to be said belongs only to the French; method and order are their distinctive qualities; and these men, who are so thoughtless, so impetuous, so eager to succeed, are wisest with pen in hand. You will find nothing in them that is hard or exaggerated, nothing unclear or out of place. Always elegant and eloquent when necessary, the most notable feature will not redeem a platitude in their eyes, and the value of thoughts cannot atone for a lack of style. *He writes badly:* here is the unforgivable fault, the mortal reproach for a philosopher, as for a poet or a novelist. One sometimes blames this sensibility of the French, but that is another mistake: this sensibility had to penetrate the character of the nation made to reign over opinion by its writings.

"In all the genres of eloquence, the French have no rivals. The eloquence of the bar, which among them has produced masterpieces of the first rank, does not exist elsewhere. Italy and Spain, so religious, and the masters of two such sonorous languages, have never been able to produce a sermon that Europe would have wanted to read. Hume, to whom one cannot object, says somewhere that he is ashamed to admit that a French lawyer arguing for the restitution of a horse is more eloquent than the orators of Great Britain promoting the most serious interests of the nation in the houses of Parliament. The invaluable talent of which I speak is so particularly the prerogative of the French that it has never abandoned them, not even on the occasions when it abandons all other men. The most dreary sciences have no thorns that the French do not know how to prune: physics, natural history, astronomy, metaphysics, erudition, politics are all explained, all embellished, and made accessible to common good sense; and it's possible that nothing is well known in Europe until the French have explained it. Eloquence applied to the most serious subjects and the art of explaining everything clearly are the two great talents of this nation. The mass of men, continually excluded from the sanctuary of the sciences by the difficult style and the detestable taste of the scientific works produced by other nations, do not resist the seduction of the French style and method. No sooner has foreign genius produced something of interest than French art seizes on the discovery, tortures it in a thousand ways, forces it into forms that astonish it and make it proud, and transmits it to the wide world on the wings of the universal language. Such books seek the germs of talent, dispersed across the globe, warm them, fertilize them, and bring them to maturity. They teach few things to true scholars, but what is indeed more valuable, they make them come alive.

"The experience of all times leaves no doubt about the empire that France has always exercised over opinion. But today this influence is so striking, and Europe pays for it so dearly, that it is no longer possible to dispute the point. Is it not an incredible phenomenon that essentially mediocre men, if taken one by one, and of whom the most capable has thousands of superiors in the world, that such men, without education and without experience, removed from all the world's great affairs by their social status, when united suddenly and strengthened by contact, like the strips of an artificial magnet that draw all their strength from their union, should have succeeded in five years in giving the most frightening shock to all the peoples of Europe?

"It will be said, perhaps, that these men owe their success only to the nature of the dogmas that they preach and that are, unfortunately for us, all too seductive for the human heart. But were there no revolts or toppled thrones in the world before the revolution in France? The one that cost the unfortunate Charles I his head hatched the same systems, the same exaggerations, and the same furies. The democratic pamphlets that appeared at that time could perhaps not have held their own in Westminster Hall, but the *Roundheads* and the *Levelers* of the day did not have the influence of the Jacobins; and other peoples, peaceful spectators of the tragedy being played in London, could not imbibe the poison of fanaticism that shattered England. Today, Europe is agitated because these same systems are being preached by the French, and when one preaches in French, Europe listens and understands."[36]

Thus wrote de Maistre in his *Fragments sur la France*. An encomium to France, to great and magnificent France. A hundred fifty years have passed. What is France like now? Keyserling, in the preface to *De la souffrance à la plénitude*, devotes an entire passage to France and writes, among other things:[37]

"And now, to conclude this Introduction, let's consider the special problem of France. The Frenchman, more than any other European today, has preserved deep in his unconscious the Christian mentality, dominated by the basic dualism between God and Nature, or in their two constitutive terms, Spirit-Flesh, with the accent on Spirit. The Middle Ages, whose vitality no problems could sap, were able on this basis to construct a rich and vital synthesis, established as a kind of equilibrium. The Renaissance *seemed* to rehabilitate Nature, and in fact the discovery of Nature, neglected until then, dates to this moment. But in reality Spirit did nothing but discover in Nature a new and fascinating *object*, so that in the end, it was Spirit alone that benefited from this direction, the rapid and seductive results of which flattered it with the illusion of being all-powerful. In France, Rabelais's *Pantagruel*, which devised a program of upbringing and even instruction for the new individual, is the first book to suggest the new and dangerous course taken by spiritualization. For, however vigorous and healthy the ideal human type whose exemplary image is presented by Rabelais, *Pantagruel*'s defining trait is nevertheless not an intense spiritual life but, much more narrowly, the appetite for *knowledge*, for an immense knowledge, whose quantity is more important than its value. Thus, in reality the Renaissance in Western Europe accentuated the traditional dualism of Spirit-Flesh and especially accentuated its latent imbalance. Insofar as spiritual values were represented — proportional to the weakening of vitality evident since then — by less vigorous individuals, the imbalance in favor of Spirit became more and more obvious. This is due above all to the fact that reason, or even intellect, alone came to represent for consciousness the totality of Spirit.

"This rationalization and this intellectualization were particularly evident in France. In the first place, the breach in the Catholic tradition was much less serious than in countries in which Protestantism was strong. Second, this rationalization seemed to signal a culmination: the full flourishing of the culture of the era of Louis XIV, a culture which it would seem, however, emerged from layers deeper than the intellect and borne by the most secret of instincts. As expressed in official formulations and policies (Descartes, Bossuet, Boileau[38]), this culture, the flower of a very particular land, the aroma of a special emotional terrain, the expression of only a very small part of the country and the nation, since then—and progressively more and more, aspired to the universal . . . It is true that resistance was not lacking. Molière, for example, is the extreme expression of bourgeois resistance, which opposed the new culture. Its existence demonstrates well enough that this culture was only a sublimated expression, representing only an extreme *point* of the nation, though also containing—despite official claims—profound values that are quintessentially spiritual. Whatever the case, this culture carried the day and the destiny of Louis XIV traces symbolically the course of the culture on which he put his stamp—notice the distance between the young king in his prime (1660–1670), cheerful, brilliant, sensual, and ardent (though perhaps less basic than Henri IV), enthusiastically 'earthy,' and the old husband of Mme de Maintenon.

"This general direction of French thought and culture suited only approximately the type of Frenchman formed by a long, largely uninterrupted history. As I tried to show in the chapter on France in my *Spectrum of Europe*, the Frenchman is someone whose basic and principal aptitudes are not rational and intellectual, but emotional, sensual, and thus moral, because what is called *le moral* has absolutely nothing to do with intelligence and reason. All the deepest roots of the French soul are irrational; thus the Frenchman is DEEP DOWN, despite his reputation, not the most rational, but the most irrational of Europeans. If, intelligent and refined as he is, he were not governed essentially by irrational forces, how would he understand so little of what was going on around him, how would he, more than any other European, cling to his prejudices, how would he play a part in an ideological and verbal politics preserved like a fossil from a past age, in a stock of stylized gestures which, for a German, make even Mr. Blum resemble at times Robespierre, at times Richelieu? No less can one say that French rationalism and intellectualism are entirely superficial. Nevertheless, this rationalism is ALSO an expression of the fundamental irrationalism of the French type. For three reasons. First, because of the French passion for ideas. The fact that this passion attaches itself to ideas in no way renders it intellectual in itself; it remains a purely emotional phenomenon, and moreover, where passion is involved, ideas are quickly reduced to little more than words." (In French it's also "passion," here in the sense of stamp collecting, for example.) "Next, as a result of historical developments, it turns out that the worldwide success of French ideas since Descartes and the eighteenth-century philosophers seems to have become one of the causes of French glory and certainly was a cause of France's *prestige*. Patriotism therefore impels the French to venerate them.

Finally, let's not forget that in France, more than anywhere else, quarrels over ideas are quarrels between people and coteries. It's enough to read the studies by André Siegfried, Albert Thibaudet, or Daniel Halévy to discover to what extent, alas unconsciously, and in the course of electoral mishaps, general issues are at base personal ones.[39]

"It is fascinating to note the degree to which the scientific and positivist official France of 1880 to 1890 and more generally the secular University exerted themselves to maintain a 'quantity' of sacramentalized mummified ideas. The Sorbonne deserves today to be considered its standard-bearer. But the Sorbonne in fact preserves only the official doctrine. It claims above all to 'safeguard the Spirit and defend it against the troubling forces of Instinct.' This by extension has become a slogan of current thought, a motto, a trademark recognizable in all public discourse, if only as an expression of the most egotistical politics.

"At the point to which we have now arrived, the special reflections I have permitted myself on the subject of France enter into the general theme this introduction attempts to establish and define. France is considerably less Americanized, much less mechanized, in short, much less 'termiticized' or 'insectified'" (from insect) "than the Germanic nations. But because she lives to this day still largely on premises established by the eighteenth century, premises vitally out of date . . . she has become incapable, without solving the problem of continuity, of progressing in the direction of the worthiest possible human synthesis. The problem of Flesh-Spirit or Earth-Spirit, as it is still posed by official France, is no longer a question for the vanguard of humanity today. Nevertheless not only official France, but almost all the representatives of intellectual and literary France continue to pose it. If the world of the Americans and their European rivals suffocates in a straitjacket of mechanical objectifications, the world of the French runs the risk of suffocating in a straitjacket of fixed prejudices of an intellectual kind. To take a single example: an incredible number of French intellectuals still today take the side of Soviet Russia, allegedly the champion of democracy, of the republican spirit, or even of freedom and world peace, which must be supported in the name of progress in the battle against counterrevolution." (This written in 1937—what is happening today, in 1943, under the influence of the Russian victories at the front and Anglo-American propaganda, is beyond belief.) "Well, anyone with the slightest open mind could have, indeed should have noticed as early as 1918, or at least by now, what is already an established historical fact: the current Russian regime represents absolutely nothing that points in the direction of a better future in the human sense. Sovietism initially marked a return to the spiritual condition typical of Russia in the fifteenth century, barely modernized by the addition of a nineteenth-century ideology, and subsequently has evolved into a regime of the most bloody Asiatic despotism, more oppressive, more antiliberal than even that of Tamerlane. Nevertheless, many good French thinkers persist in ignoring the facts before their very eyes and continue to believe in the possibilities for development in the direction of their ideal, although no actual evidence suggests it will occur. And if André Gide, upon his return from the Soviet Union, confessed his disillusionment, he stubbornly refuses to see that the development he deplores reflects the core principle of Sovietism. I realize that it is not simply a question of an outmoded rationalism, set in certain rigid prejudices, that has produced this very incapacity to see and understand anything that clashes with these prejudices, which are produced by an excessively mechanized critique." (Germany.) "I know very well that it also involves a sincere leftist idealism, a blind faith rooted in Tertullian's *credo quia absurdum*, and also an authentic revolutionary passion, a psychological inheritance that is therefore conservative, which cannot envision a future, no matter how remote, except in the watchwords inherited from the Revolution. But its origins do not prevent the results of the emotional irrationalism of the French from converging remarkably with the results of the intellectual and moral mechanization of the Americans. I admit that in discussing such things with intelligent Frenchmen I often have the impression of speaking with human termites—prodigiously intelligent creatures, possessing a tradition deeply rooted in antiquity, not only venerable, but incomparable, creatures who are refined but who, since the age of coal, have lost the sense of light. It's well known that termites live completely shielded from sunlight and that the least ray of light strikes them dead.

"For these reasons, the problem of France, despite all the superficial differences, is basically identical to that of more mechanized peoples. It is simply posed in different terms. Replace the term 'mechanization' by that of 'rationalism' or 'intellectualism' and the equation connecting the past to the future is exactly the same. In a certain sense, the problem of France is even more serious than the problem of more mechanized peoples. That is because a straitjacket of ideas that are clear, but petrified, threatens to suffocate the soul even more than a straitjacket of external mechanization. In the end, it blocks the power of sight. France is in clear danger of becoming blind. Besides, every misdirection distorts the individual, degrades and stunts him. The rich emotional treasure of the race is in danger of being entombed. And it is her superior emotionality and not her intelligence that has constituted the grandeur of the French race up to now."

Excellent. For someone acquainted with France, for whom the problem of France presents itself at every turn, who has been observing France from morning to night for four years, as I have tried to do, these two fragments provide a splendid picture and complement everything I have written on the subject.

The analysis of the two fragments, supported by my own observations, shaded and colored wherever de Maistre and Keyserling resort to intellectual short-hand, can convey the full picture and exhaust the theme—for a few months. The life of every nation, of every person, is an unknown film and you can't tell how it's going to come out. But it can be stopped for a moment, it can be moved forward to decide what it's worth and what vistas open up before it. The film of France is fascinating and provocative.

The first four paragraphs of de Maistre's fragment sound like a fanfare. It's the fanfare with which all Europe was raised—France included. A loud and power-ful fanfare that has continued to daze the world for centuries and that dazed the French so forcefully that they continue to hear it in its original strength, whereas for us there remains only—an echo. And herein lies the danger. For an echo is an illusion, easily mistaken for a live voice. And then thinking proceeds in the wrong direction and runs the risk of getting lost, or—what's worse—returning to its point of departure, that is, getting nowhere at all. It also runs the risk of taking the echo for a fanfare.

De Maistre is cautious, however, in tooting his horn and his small paren-thetical remark to the effect that no one knew the fate awaiting France in the wake of the Revolution is in this case an expression of caution entirely out of keeping with *la France éternelle*. For if the Frenchman observes moderation in everything, on the subject of France in general—not in the details—he is over-come by a blindness verging on the mystical. The same mysticism that led Joan of Arc to equate France with God. Which is why, very likely, every Frenchman contains on these subjects something of the obstinacy of the Maid of Orléans and why Friedrich Sieburg, in his book *Dieu est-il français?* is right to begin his series of observations with Joan of Arc.[40]

De Maistre, like all Frenchmen, moreover, commits an error right at the beginning, ignoring a certain basic thing. Describing all the trump cards with which France entered the game of History, he considers them nothing less than a mission. Adhering to French messianism means that he treats France like an emissary of God. Or of Nature. He does not see that France simply had good luck, while we Poles, for example, had bad luck. In short, the reasoning of every Frenchman rests on the conviction that France is what she is because fate itself endowed her with everything and thus destined her to play the role of the shep-herd of mankind. This, and nothing else, is to a great degree the origin of what every foreigner is inclined to call "parochialism." French "parochialism," the inability to see beyond certain, *always French*, limits, emerges consciously or unconsciously from the unshakable belief in her "mission," a belief perpetually sustained by every French writer, thinker, or politician everywhere.

The certainty of having a mission, of a monopoly on messianism, leads not only to parochialism but to a casual indifference to everything that lacks the element essential to Frenchness. Anyone who comes into close contact with the French must notice that he is considered a cultured person only so long as he kowtows before everything French. From the moment he dares demur, he is obviously still listened to, but with the smile (if only internal) of superiority with which one listens to—a barbarian. The belief in France's mission, which de Maistre develops so colorfully in his fragment and for which he offers various proofs, and which is rooted in the soul of even the least educated Frenchman, leads France to reduce her judgment of others to two disarmingly simple conclusions: if you acknowledge my mission without reserve you will become a somebody, but if you harbor reservations you are—a barbarian.

The best proof of how certain France is of her truth, to what degree she believes in her mission, is perhaps her magnanimity with regard to her ideas. France does not want to impose her thoughts, does not attempt to instill them in anyone at all costs. She does you the honor of giving them away. Whoever accepts them is expected always to feel unworthy of the gift, to lower his eyes and whisper reverently: "O, France—I am unworthy of your entering my heart, but only say the word . . ." Whereas when someone does not want to accept them and raises questions, France is insulted and turns away in silence. For France recognizes only two categories of people: total converts or barbarians. In this sense she is strikingly similar to ancient Greece.

One can offer countless examples of this. If it was relatively easy before the war to obtain French citizenship, it was not only because of the fall in the birthrate and the desire to repair the deficit by absorbing fresh blood from outside. It involved something one might call "the joy of conversion." And one can also say without much exaggeration that in France a single "converted" Polish Jew, shouting at every opportunity *Vive la France*, arouses in those around him greater recognition and esteem than a whole pack of Englishmen and Americans spending millions of francs but stubbornly skeptical with regard to *la France éternelle*. You just have to talk with the local Polish immigrants to learn how much humiliation, harassment, and abuse have been experienced by those who have not wanted to naturalize their children. France absorbs and accepts anyone who accepts her. She gets cross with the others, feels insulted, and treats them as barbarians.

There's nothing in this of the truculent brutality of the Germans, provoking conflict, no compulsion, no *Drang*. The Frenchman is like a snail. Wounded in the most sensitive tip of his missionary horn, he retracts it, shrinks back into his shell *d'une indifférence aimable*. But at the first sound of *Vive la France*, shouted by anyone at all, he is ready to jump not only out of his shell but out of his own skin. This may be the only circumstance in which a Frenchman's materialism temporarily abandons him.

One simply cannot understand France without understanding this messianic complex—perhaps her only obsession, but it's deeply ingrained—without understanding that the authenticity and exceptional character of this messianism constitutes such an absolute truth that France is not at all aggressive about it. (A totally self-confident person is not aggressive—he either listens or doesn't hear.) The true tragedy will begin when France becomes the only one to still believe in her mission. And that's already begun.

The rest of de Maistre's entire fanfare is in fact a series of variations on a single theme, with messianic leitmotivs in all the spiritual domains. Everything de Maistre goes on to say was once a vital sound, was once the truth—but that is no longer the case today. This is the source of the ever-widening intellectual gulf that has separated us from France. Because France continues to insist that this sound is still alive, while for us it has become, ever more distinctly, an echo. And because we have become so accustomed to France playing not only the loudest but the best, and because the memory of the prayer to Mother Mary, which once comforted us, is still in our veins, we would like to be able to keep repeating it. Alas, we cannot and we're sorry for it—and we sulk.

De Maistre speaks of language and its superiority. Quite right. But here, too, he forgets to mention that—as in everything—so on this point as well France was lucky and if she was a leader in so many domains and for so many centuries, in Europe and even the world, it's because she was THE FIRST. Like Greece in her time. This cannot be forgotten, although unfortunately it almost always is. As Europe emerged from the so-called darkness of the Middle Ages, France was the first and best integrated, most homogeneous national organism, with the best-preserved spiritual ties with Rome and she thus entered modern history with an enormous *handicap*. France had long ago left the starting block in the race of culture and civilization, when others were just gathering at the starting line. France was already writing when others had not yet learned to speak. France had begun to think when others were still mindlessly repeating their prayers. When others were still learning to think, France was already able to express everything the others couldn't express. This is all true, but not as a result of supernatural forces, but because France was the first and for a long time ran out in front. Today others are catching up, even passing her by, but she doesn't notice and doesn't want to—no doubt to the secret despair of many people.

All the virtues of the French language and the benefits they confer, all the advantages enjoyed by French writers that de Maistre enumerates, are genuine and justified, but only within limits. They are genuine and justified in relation to the mind and spirit of the eighteenth century, on which people of today still largely rely (to this day there is no shortage of people who swear by that old light-weight Voltaire), but which are increasingly inadequate. The French language is ideal when it comes to the materialization of spirit. All its glory and the glory of French writers is based above all on rendering tangible what to others seems intangible. De Maistre said that "a thought never belongs to the world until a writer of genius has seized upon it and clad it in the right expression." This is the best definition of the materialization of spirit that the French were able to culti-vate so much better than anyone else. The clarity and tangibility of ideas, though always only an ideal and must always remain so, nevertheless entails a great dan-ger—the danger of simplifying and limiting everything by the accuracy of de-scription. De Maistre mentions this and even takes pride in it, insisting that in every word written by the French "the value of thoughts cannot atone for a lack of style." This remark contains everything and is tightly connected to a series of other signs apparently remote and with no direct relation to concepts as basic to the French as "limitation" (*limite*) and "permanence" (*constance*). Along with the dense and massive concept of "mission," these two other concepts form the next "Unity" with the character of each Frenchman. All of French literature, thus a good part of French thought, is the best example of this.

Clarity, accuracy, avoidance of extremes, rhythm, equilibrium, a model for others, high quality together with quantity, plus what de Maistre talks about and what the Abbé Trublet best defined in speaking of Voltaire, which is to say, "the perfection of mediocrity."[41] Summing up all these qualities, plus add-ing a sense of limitation and permanence, we arrive at a great sum—*un grand total*—EQUILIBRIUM. France is a country, perhaps the only one in the world today, which has achieved equilibrium and maintained it despite all the attacks coming from outside. Damn! even at this moment, under total occupation, France maintains her equilibrium. All her literature and thought, her entire concept of man as such, her entire culture, in short, flows directly from this equilibrium. Others, still searching for it, have necessarily taken this equilib-rium as a model. As long as each nation searched for it in the French manner, discord was avoided. But when they began to search each in their own fashion, which is more understandable and natural, conflicts arose.

All French literature is an expression of equilibrium (including the Marquis de Sade)—an equilibrium already achieved, though achieved increasingly at the expense of ideas, but nevertheless an equilibrium that is simply astound-ing. The language itself is a major factor in this equilibrium, since language has an enormous influence on the formation of the character and mind of every nation. Having long ago been "perfected" and set in place, like the Latin from which it emerged, the French language reached its zenith in the eighteenth century and—came to a halt. Having stopped, it set the limits beyond which thought was unable to extend except at the expense of concessions detrimental to the language itself. It is the language that fixed the concepts of "limitation" and "permanence" intrinsic to French nature. In this also France was the first. As the earliest among the languages of the modern world to crystalize and become homogeneous, French became what Latin was for the Middle Ages. But what was once perfect is not perfect forever. Yet, that's what France believes it is.

France was the first to have discovered man, the first best to have defined him in time and in space. This is exactly what de Maistre says at the end of his fragment, speaking of the Revolution and its success. And it was on this conception of man that France came to a halt, considering that the summit had been attained and that man would always remain the same. In a letter to Friedrich Sieburg, responding to his book about France, Bernard Grasset cites a fragment from Charles Péguy, which can serve as the best example of French "limitation" and "permanence" in relation to man.[42] "Humanity will surpass the first dirigibles, as it has surpassed the first locomotives. After telephotography, it will continue to invent 'graphies' and 'scopies' and 'phonies,' all equally 'tele,' and people will circle the earth in no time at all. But this will never be anything but the transient earth. People will enter inside and pierce it through and through, as I do with this ball of clay. But this will never be more than the material earth. And no man or any kind of humanity—this in a certain positive sense—has ever claimed reasonably to have surpassed Plato. I will go further. I will add that a truly cultured man does not understand, cannot even imagine, what it would mean to claim to have surpassed Plato."

Here is the best proof of "permanence." Every Frenchman, without even realizing it, thinks that a certain level of man's knowledge and welfare cannot be exceeded and that this level was attained at the very moment when man began to think. Man does not change—only methods and forms change. Here is the source of French equilibrium, sustained by language and thought; here, the source of tolerance, a condescending smile for everything that rises or tries to rise above the equilibrium, or drops below it. *L'homme ne peut se dépasser.*[43] With this assertion the case is closed.

All this was true at a certain time and place, it was all perfect, but it does not remain perfect. But France believes it. France believes in "permanence," believes in "limitation"—her own limits, which were limits for others, since France was the first to have set them. As long as the whole world was neither here nor there, the French language, France itself constituted the truth, because—and this is indisputable—she managed for a certain time to produce the best synthesis of equilibrium in all domains. At the time de Maistre wrote his *Fragments sur la France*, all this was correct, because France was truly at the forefront—and, furthermore, in all domains. It's important to stress this "in everything," because in talking of France today people tend to distinguish between material and nonmaterial factors, forgetting certain things and quarreling blindly.

One of the fundamental reproaches leveled at France today is that she did not join others in harnessing herself to the wagon of progress, that she kept herself apart. Today we know, however, what was considered "progress" ten years ago has changed its meaning. Every cultured man should have by now understood that the machine in itself does not constitute progress. France understood this instinctively long ago, but has not understood that even this "progress" causes and must cause man to change, that man does not stay the same forever and for all eternity. France defended herself against progress in quotation marks and against progress without quotation marks—and hence her charm. But protecting herself against progress that is purely external, she also protected herself against the progress of thought. This may seem paradoxical unless one understands that this "free thought," this ideal of man, all that the thought of the eighteenth and nineteenth centuries have given us and that France so splendidly materialized (in words) and made digestible—all that yesterday still constituted the truth is today barely a small part of it.

When were France and her culture at the peak of their development? When she was ahead of all others in terms of progress that was not only spiritual but also MATERIAL. Her success and magnificence belong to the era in which, while setting the standard in the advance of ideas, she contributed to external, even technical progress, creating between them a culture, which is to say, an equilibrium. Her own success, one of the most splendid in history (besides Greece), left her with the conviction that HER equilibrium was the greatest man can achieve here on earth and that, come what may, the ideal man will remain the same, his happiness as well. France has managed to be happy—let others do likewise and they will be happy too. As long as France acted *as a totality*—both spiritually and materially—others managed to be happy. Today other nations have surpassed her in material terms, without matching their own progress in spiritual terms. France has partly modernized, without moving forward in the realm of ideas. Misapprehension has grown.

The sense of mission, blind faith in man's unchanging nature, limitation, and permanence—these are the essential elements of France. Meanwhile, the world is moving forward, becoming more complicated. The simple and clear, but superficial philosophy of the seventeenth century is no longer sufficient to solve the problems facing man today. Péguy says that televisions, scopes, and graphs do not change the essence of man and that "a cultured man cannot imagine what it would mean to want to surpass Plato," but he is wrong. It may soon be necessary to surpass Jesus Christ, not Plato, in order simply to live in some kind of equilibrium. Perhaps today, in a certain sense, the hundreds of thousands of people in each of the countless camps in Europe and Asia are already outdoing Jesus Christ every day, simply in order to live. Not all has yet been said, whatever La Bruyère[44] may think.

The comparison of these two fragments—de Maistre and Keyserling—shows this very well. There was a time when the clear and simple philosophy of the eighteenth century was sufficient, when the French concept of man corresponded fully with the concepts held by others, when France created modern man in her image and likeness, and when it suited him well. But today the conflict has turned into a discussion between parents and the young generation, in which the parents are intransigent.

Keyserling's entire introduction to the analysis of France throws into relief what strikes one immediately when observing the French. The Frenchman does not understand the spirit. If he did, he would not debase it today at every turn. Reason cannot be debased, because in man reason is innately a wh——, who always offers everything to everyone, above all to the best client, that is, to me. Reason gives France today all she desires. In the entire process of the Renaissance, in the discovery of nature and man, France took from man the part easiest to grasp—reason. She equated man's development with the development of reason. The French *esprit*, or spirit, has a much greater element of reason than spirit has anywhere else. And this is the line her development took, the line taken by her equilibrium. The French equilibrium, which is less an equilibrium of the spirit than an equilibrium of reason, created a type of man in which reason has killed the spirit, or in less brutal terms—a type of man in whom reason has restrained what the rest of the world, even the Anglo-Saxons, think of as spirit.

Thus, France and the French possess the greatest equilibrium of any country or people. This rationalization, the intellectualization of everything, was carried so far that it became irrational, dogmatic. France got stuck in irrational rationalism, in the *credo quia absurdum*, in the limitless fidgeting within the very limited space of her intellectual horizons. Having fallen into the automatism of reason, into an intellectual Fordism, she is threatened with blindness. And indeed, France increasingly stops seeing, increasingly loses sight of the whole, and understands ever less about the problem of contemporary humanity. Disoriented, she flees into the past, *elle refuse le présent.*[45]

Can the world live without her? I don't think so. Her sense of measure, of limitation, of permanence, and of connection (coherence) will always be needed. But she has dug in her heels, planted herself four-square in her reason, and takes umbrage or smiles condescendingly. "Look at me," she says, "look at my Paris, at my small towns, and at my villages sunk in the well-tended landscape. Where will you find that peace, that 'yesterday' you can so often mistake for 'today'? Where else has happiness—a man's happiness, as small and everyday as bread—been better realized? Where has man ever been as much in harmony with his surroundings and with himself as here, in my home? Where has man been able in general to be more of a man than here, in this land of silence and imposing storms?" It's the truth. But this equilibrium is ever harder to maintain. Rationalized (like collaboration), in harmony with man and the world of a bygone age, it has today become unreasonable, now perhaps even quite lethal. The external "yesterday" of France, still alive and so captivating, cannot last for long in the domain of thought. It is likely to end in a terrible "screw-up."

In his memoirs of childhood, as meandering as the fog, Anatole France perhaps best describes what it is that captivates everyone who has succeeded in dissolving into this atmosphere and giving themselves over to it: ". . . I have known practically all the same sounds and cares of Paris that Boileau described around 1660, in his attic in the Palais. Like him, I heard the cock's crow rending the dawn in the very heart of the city. In the Faubourg Saint-Germain I sniffed the odor of the stables, I saw districts that had preserved their country look and the charms of the past . . . Love of the past is natural to man. The past plucks the most sensitive strings of the small child and the old man . . . And if one wants to know why all human imagination, fresh or faded, sad or gay, turns with curiosity toward the past, one will certainly discover that the past is our only promenade and the only place where we can escape our worries, our daily cares, where we can escape ourselves. The present is sterile and muddled, the future is hidden. All the richness, all the luxury, all the world's charm reside in the past . . ."

France loves the past and anyone who looks into that quiet pond along with her learns to love it, too. But the past cannot be a goal in and of itself, it cannot constitute a limit. Even today the cocks crow in the quiet dawn of Montmartre, and in the small courtyards in the center of town chickens cackle and rabbits hop. Even today a fat, shiny tomcat will doze in the shopwindow or stroll majestically in the police station or Préfecture, fed on portions left over by the prisoners and detainees, spreading peace and quiet all around. But such charms do not extend to everything. France's outward charm provides respite and repose, but her thinking becomes ever more annoying. How welcome it would be if France could also manage to reconcile past and present, to create that enchanting *continuité*, that coherence, in her thinking as well.

However, France does not want to do this—or else no longer can. Ernest Renan wrote in *L'Avenir de la science:* "France is an outstanding example of humanity's analytic, revolutionary, profane, and irreligious age . . . It is possible that one day, having played her part, France may become an obstacle to humanity's further progress and will disappear, for the tasks are essentially distinct. He who analyzes, does not synthesize."[46] The intellectual gulf between the world and France is growing wider at an ever-increasing speed. French intellectuals today willingly leave the job of synthesis—to Russia and her Communism. France is going blind and closing her eyes. The less she understands others, the less they understand her. They turn to her for physical respite, as in a spa, but find no respite for thought. Because her thinking, her concepts, and her notion of man no longer suffice. Increasingly, thought, spirit, and soul shatter against a blind resistance, against the once-famed clarity that today leads to closed-mindedness. Reason cannot be spirit, because reason is a wh——, and spirit cannot be reason, without wh——ing around. France is going blind, is becoming a wh——, still full of charm and subtlety. Like an old lady, smelling of patchouli, dressed up and witty, in the Voltairean mode, she displays her charms, while observing the follies of youth with an indulgent eye. Can she be right? Personally, I don't agree with her. I know only that the desire for instant rejuvenation can lead to serious misunderstandings. These misunderstandings already began under Pétain's "rejuvenating" government and under the label of the *Empire français.* If after the war France continues to conceive of the *empire* in the same terms as before, not only the empire but France herself may well come to an end. One cannot rejuvenate oneself without at the same time *understanding youth.* But France does not want this, she does not want to *understand.*

The echoes resound loudly to this day, deceptive and enticing. Thought tends to jump from one extreme to the other. Quite a while ago, I once wrote that France is above all a land of optical illusions. I may have been right. The image, the outward form, adroitly conceals what's inside. Whence the difficulty of judging calmly. France still *stands up well as an object of the gaze,* but increasingly less well as the object of *thought.* Whoever is satisfied with images, content to "put up with" external appearances, which are the easiest in this case "to put up with," and happy to skim the surface of these calm waters, will have trouble understanding the changes taking place under the surface. Freedom? France has progressed from the freedom to do as one pleases to the freedom NOT TO DO what is not immediately gratifying and in the absence of internal discipline must be a constraint. It's an apathetic, opportunistic freedom, becoming ever less creative and more torpid. The freedom of the eighteenth century, adapted to an entirely distinct type of man, freedom of the spirit above all, has been transformed now into a kind of spiritual slavery, shackled by the endlessly repeated, unchanging ideal. France is deluded. She mechanically recites a rosary of some kind of liberty and moth-eaten slogans, restores antiquities, and goes blind.

March 9, 1943

Yesterday a representative of Gnome et Rhône bicycles called to say they have finally obtained two bicycles for me. I've been waiting for them since last September. They were my idée fixe. I don't know whether I care so much about them because they are really such splendid bikes or because they are so hard to get. The difficulty of obtaining various objects creates a ghastly snobbism. A Dunhill lighter, a Gnome et Rhône bicycle, a suit of "English" wool, cigarettes with a goût américain,[47] and so forth, nowadays destroy any sense of social equality or "classlessness." One dreams of having something or other, in order to have something other people don't have and to feel superior to them in some way. America is probably the only place on earth that manages actually to equalize people, because it gives them what we only dream of and what only very few possess. Scarcity generates the sharpest class consciousness. Russia has probably managed already to create greater class consciousness than anywhere else. And now with your pogony and denshchiki—ho, ho—"off you go to die, tovarishch."[48] And these ordinary tovarishchi are dying. In any case, I have my two bicycles, a pretty sight—and I've calmed down for a bit. This morning I at once took my tires and inner tubes to the agreed-upon bistro, where the good-natured Mr. Sepot was already waiting for me. I started buying these tires and inner tubes already last year, which was not at all easy. I got hold of them by means of negotiations with bicycle-taxi drivers, innumerable encounters in shady bistros in Belleville, and other black-market maneuvers. I love all this! It will be boring as hell when it's again possible to buy things the normal way. The only thing left will be cocaine and morphine, Communism and other stupéfiants.[49] I have a certain affinity with the character of Albertin in an otherwise silly novel by Tristan Bernard.[50] "The release of tension I experienced almost daily after managing to extricate myself from difficult situations produced an altogether considerable amount of satisfaction," says Bernard. At present, the amount of satisfaction I experience at the end of every day is more than considerable.

In the evening I arrived at the bistro, where I found our bicycles waiting.

Marvelous. Entirely of aluminum, light as froth, shiny as a dentist's office, with fantastic gears for riding uphill—in short, a dream. I was as happy as an adult. "As a child" is a silly comparison, because children are too dumb to be truly happy. I had to wait until it grew dark, to avoid taking the two bikes back to the hotel in the daytime, which might have aroused comments with unpleasant consequences from the residents. They would rush to send an anonymous letter to the police, claiming I was involved in the black market. Already, when I pass the concierge in the entryway, I try to maneuver so that she doesn't notice that I have new shoes from Bodnar selling for three thousand francs. One must be very careful, because *la jalousie*, a national emotion, sees everything. The concierge, like a Sphinx, spends the day lying near the entryway. She has no riddle to offer because she herself tries to solve the riddles posed by the new shoes, a new fur coat, hat, or outfit worn by the residents as they come and go. And so as not to make too great an effort, she solves every riddle the same way: *Il fait du marché noir.*[51]

Fortunately, our *patrons* are less inquisitive and—they don't like the concierge. Which is why there is an atmosphere of trust and honesty in our hotel. Our neighbor across the way has an entire grocery shop in his room, everyone listens to bulletins from London "out loud" on unregistered sets. Occasionally someone who would rather not have their papers checked spends the night, and finally the two policemen who live here *sont des chic types*,[52] which is to say, when presented with forged papers, they wink and say, as they return them with a flourish: "Good imitation."

I have bought these bicycles now, not in order to ride them, but in order to have them. They are destined for a trip around France after the war. I arranged with the *patron* to have them stored in the basement. In the evening I took them into the hotel "from the back," from avenue Daumesnil. Then, quickly, one by one, I took them up to the room. The sight of those gems made me want to dance. I spread out a map of France on the table and began to trace our future route. In the cramped room crowded by the two bicycles, I lay under the table and called out various magical names: "Brittany—then turning east, because the Atlantic coast as far as Bordeaux is uninteresting. Skirting the Massif Central and then straight on to Biarritz. Then the Pyrenees . . ." Basia reminds me that I have forgotten about the castles on the Loire, but in the meantime it's impossible to walk across the room. I reluctantly removed the wheels and put everything in a corner. I was totally wound up. Basia looked at me with a smile full of the tenderness with which she might have regarded her ten-year-old son. She asked whether I intended to sleep with these bicycles. Albertin from Bernard's novel whispered that I might very well want to do just that.

March 13, 1943

The bicycles, carefully wrapped like precious mummies, were put to rest in the sarcophagus of the basement. The *patron* took the occasion to hide his new automobile tires. This happens now all the time: something is purchased on the sly, something is silently hidden away. Each person has a million secrets and everything has unheard-of value. The value of absolutely everything has its charm, on condition that the charm does not last too long. From time to time, I sit in my armchair, open a book, and take inventory, gazing around the room, which looks as if nothing special was going on. Meanwhile, there, up on top, are three pairs of soles. I got them for 100 francs a pair, now they're certainly worth 150. Under the bed are ten kilos of sugar. I paid 150 a kilo, now they go for 220—at the very least. English preserves are still in the suitcase under the bed. They're the ones from Dunkirk, already historic. The farmers were burying and then selling them. I paid 40 a jar, now you won't find them even for 200. Ah—those fish in olive oil . . . In another suitcase is Basia's fur coat. We bought it last summer at André Brun. The three new suitcases covered in parchment are destined for our journey to some "freedom reserve." They were expensive, but today for any old thing covered in marbled paper you have to pay 500 or 600 francs. I peek playfully behind the wardrobe. Two new bicycle tires—in reserve. And above them, in the mysterious obscurity, hangs a fat ham wreathed in a dry sausage. I imagine looking through the wall into the kitchen and stick my finger in the pot of butter and schmaltz. Total delight. Thus, I sink deeper into my armchair, I open Hegel, which I cannot finish and surely never will, and keep reading. It's a rare case of intellectual masturbation. I break off and think how pleasant it is to POSSESS, to have something, damn it! And when you need it to have something more. And therefore I increasingly think about leaving Europe. Because people here are so preoccupied with providing for future generations that present generations are left with nothing. André Siegfried, in his splendid *Qu'est-ce l'Amérique*, writes: "In Europe, where opportunities have narrowed, it is certainly more difficult to produce new riches than to distribute those that exist. At least, that's how the public imagines the problem. This is the source of the two European temptations that characterize our old countries: on the one hand, nationalism, which is to say, the conquest and division of territories; on the other hand, revolution, which is to say, the division of wealth or the temptation at least to divide it. Is this not the spectacle that confronts us?"[53] And what a little spectacle! And now, on top of that, the "one and only ideologies." So many vaccines are invented, but no anti-ideological or antinationalist vaccine can be invented. And we're supposed to be living in the age of progress. The League of Nations of the future should concentrate all its efforts on inventing an anti-ideological gas. As soon as a country begins to emit dangerous nationalist or ideological miasmas, boom! down come a few bombs of pleasantly smelling gas. For the aroma, I propose Chanel No. 5. All men would instantly go out in search of someone to take to bed, the young would begin to dream of love, and peace would descend.

Instead of being taught morality or ethics, we are taught idealism. All this idealism, or rather "ideologism"—people are no longer brought up, they are trained in ideologies—has lately aroused in me a storm of protest. Someday I'll burst. For the moment I'm trying to fill the gaps. It's unbelievable the ignorance in which we were raised. And those truths, capital "T," fitting material for antiquarian bookshops, have been and still are presented to us unfailingly as living and "scientific" novelties. And all that addressed to empty bellies. Hungry people will swallow anything, even ideologies.

The psychosis of "the landing" has taken hold of Paris. Already, from hour to hour, the *Débarquement* is expected. Clandestine flyers urge everyone to flee who might be sent to work in Germany. "Take cover in the villages, hide out, don't be afraid of the risks of underground life, because the hour of liberation is near." Paris is buzzing with *on dit*. Meanwhile, it's again time for the seasonal offensive of English propaganda. Somehow I fail to picture this landing, especially in France. It's still too soon. Every night there's an infernal barrage, because the English are flying over Paris on the way to Italy. The Americans have quarreled with the Russians, because the Russians absolutely refuse to publicize the help America is providing and this angers the Americans. They would like Stalin to give them the kind of good coverage they are giving him. The innocents!

March 20, 1943

I'm in bed with the flu. I'm resting. I feel extremely good and I'm very glad the flu was kind enough to pay me a visit. C. arrived from Cracow on leave and we'll give him letters to take back. This Frenchman, who in the fall lacked confidence and knowledge of the world, has now become civilized, has picked up some manners and polish, even learned to speak well, which he was unable to do before. Travel is instructive, so is sleeping with an attractive girl from Cracow (he showed us her photo—*connais pas*).[54] In addition, he took quite a trip. As far as Rostov and back from Rostov with the *Kriegswerkstätte*[55] where he works. The trip left him with sober views on the "proletarian paradise," where, according to him, the German occupation was in many cases more of a paradise than the Soviet regime. He says that the French don't want to believe him and all suspect him of spreading pro-German propaganda. In a tone almost of despair and with the authentic logic of a simple, uneducated fellow, he asked me: "Monsieur André, why is speaking of what I saw in Russia considered German propaganda? One has nothing to do with the other. I am not at all saying that the Germans are good." Ha! *pauvre Candide*. He observed an interesting thing: "When we crossed the former Soviet-Polish border, I felt that Europe had ended." An ordinary workman, not especially intelligent, noticed this, whereas so many people do not want to recognize this obvious truth, that Russia is not Europe, that we are separated by a cultural-spiritual gulf which cannot be bridged, that Russia, despite its progress in material terms—and that very one-sided—means barbarism, brutishness, and the East. The Anglo-Saxons insist that everything must be done to allow Russia to emerge from behind the barbed wire and become "Europeanized." I fear, however, it's more likely that Europe and even England may run the risk of becoming "Bolshevized," since all Europe, England, and America have suddenly "discovered" Russia and stand with their jaws agape. And there's something indeed to gape at. If I feel hatred for this system, it's not because of any class prejudice, but simply because I hate everything that tries to kill the person, that tries to kill me, a unique individual, and that reeks from far away of termites and collectives, of the ignorance and brutishness of the "one and only true ideology." Keyserling may not be a great philosopher, but he sometimes has an excellent sense of the essence of things. In his *Spectrum of Europe*, he wrote only one sentence about the Poles, but that's enough: "Poland is much more emphatically Catholic and Western than any other country precisely because her Slavism makes her especially aware of the difference that exists between her and the Russian spirit." That's enough. I personally feel, most emphatically, the difference that exists between myself and the Russian spirit.

March 25, 1943

I'm lying down and reading Prus's *Novellas*. Excellent. One of the few Polish writers I can't find fault with. He dazzles me with the breadth of his vision, his feeling, and his understanding of the devilish problem of the "Polish character." He views everything, benevolently (though often only apparently, because sometimes bitterness seeps through), and at the same time—as encouragement—provides a glimpse of the treasure troves of virtues slumbering somewhere deep down and buried in the avalanche of misfortunes contained in the words: the history of Poland.

Only now, after getting to know the West, do I for the first time see what

I already felt so strongly back home, that I was simply suffocating. I see how much we have lost and how far we have fallen out of line, losing our anchor. All Poland is such a *bouillabaisse*, such a Polish stew, that one can sometimes hate it. Racially Slavic, culturally Latin, with a Byzantine temperament (Polish Byzantinism, or rebellious servility, deserves a special study), an intellectual German-French mixture with breezes coming from Russia—an infernal concoction, in which we ourselves very often lose our way.

I often really want to shoot myself. Especially after conversations with my countrymen. If it weren't for K., with whom I work, and visits from P., who is the midwife of my thoughts (hard to believe, but that man was a colonel and an engineer to boot and nothing managed to dull his mind), I would probably shoot myself three times a day.

After nine centuries of this extraordinary mess, the Poles are recovering their independence for a brief moment, a great historical pause of fifteen minutes, and after tremendous efforts to turn this tribe into a homogeneous nation, history rings again, and the next lesson begins. Who knows if it's not the worst, the long years of mathematics, with integrals and differentials. If Prus enchants me, it's because, with an indulgent and ironic smile, he puts aside the cavalryman and the young girl, the larks, the meadows, the violets and cornflowers, the rabbits and hares, and teaches us to be a nation not only in the spiritual sense, but above all in the material sense. He teaches us to build from the foundations, not from the roof. A nation is not a roof, that Polish roof in the Byzantine-Gothic-Vistulian-Baroque-Rococo-Insurrectional-Piłsudskian and damn what else style, this roof composed of legends and songs, of recitals, and rah-rah patriotic masochism, full of a tragic sense of greatness, of no interest to anyone else, and complaints about everyone and everything, God included, who for us is not God but a czar (this is not over yet, but only beginning). A nation has foundations as well, foundations we don't like to talk about, because they are as unattractive as all foundations on earth. Because they are not colorful or artistic, do not contain the sound of spurs and the burbling of water in one's head, the neighing of horses or conspiratorial battles. I am "earthy" and "cool-headed" and I don't understand this concert at all. Nothing has ever filled me with greater fear and righteous indignation than speechifying to empty bellies and the happiness of so-called future generations. And telling lies in the name of the fatherland, covered in the thick sauce of tin-soldier nationalism.

Someone told me that for every flight over Germany American pilots get a special bonus and every member of the bomber crew who returns safe and sound after twenty-five flights gets a certain number of dollars and can return to the United States. For him the war is over and that's it! I would like to see a Pole, who after hearing this would not at first cover his face in shame and feel "deeply" indignant (we do everything "deeply"—nothing less). It seemed even to me at first that something was not quite right. For the duty of every good Pole is supposedly to fly until he is shot down for the glory of the fatherland. How can one connect the concept of "dough" with sacrifice for the fatherland? The Americans are right. Each of us admits as much in secret, but God forbid out loud. Hypocrisy on the subject of Poland and the Patria (capital "P"— nothing less) is our national perversion. Patriotic hypocrisy pushes us into the parochialism of our entire culture, which no one in fact understands. We're carried away by foreign writers, but when one of our writers does not include Poland, the Poles, hollyhocks and poppies, thatched roofs, meadows, a servant girl, pregnancy, and abortion (one of our national problems), he is a bad Pole. Like Conrad, who finally settled on the excellent idea of writing in English. And not about thatched roofs or hollyhocks. And although he did more to make Poland better known than even Henryk Sienkiewicz, Eliza Orzeszkowa found it appropriate to chew him out.[56] And even those who admired Conrad nevertheless reproached him deeply for "not having returned." He did not return because he preferred to live in England and every man should have the right to live where it suits him best. Some consider their hometowns the be-all and end-all, and I respect that, but others prefer to roam the world and find more in this world than in any small town. And they are then accused, with sanctimonious indignation, of being "cosmopolitans," which is to say, almost—Jews. And what can be worse—between you and me—than a Jew?

March 26, 1943

If Communism succeeded in fulfilling all its promises, it would stop being Communism and therefore it never will succeed. The humor in this "scientific" ideology consists in the promise of impossible things, which until the end of one's days one can keep "striving for," "giving one's all to," "marching toward," with the mirage ever on the horizon. And because it is unattainable, distant, "for the future generations," one can therefore "believe." That's the key. It's based on faith, the trick is in this faith. That's the detonator of the Communist cartridge. The trick is in the detonator. It's based on abstraction and without abstraction, nothing doing. All religions and metaphysics, all the vials of opium, are chucked out the door, replaced by a "casserole" of hashish, also for the common folk. And the faithful have faith. A sausage is dangled high up and the order is to jump.

And the faithful jump. Higher and higher. And when they jump dangerously high, the sausage is hitched even higher. Because it's a question, not of the faithful reaching the sausage, but of their jumping better and higher, of their jumping "dialectically." And so we jump and will keep jumping until the end of our days and we will all finally turn into grasshoppers. And once humanity has been ennobled and dialectically "insectified" to perfection, we'll be truly happy. And we'll mate and marry with the cicadas (the female of the grasshopper) and it'll be super! I'm already excited, but I don't yet believe it.

March 28, 1943

I have recovered from the flu and went out for a walk. I bought the *Pariser Zeitung* and read as I slowly crossed avenue Daumesnil into the Bois de Vincennes. It's still unpleasantly chilly and spring is not yet in the air. An article summarizing the results of the winter campaign in Russia was a bit sour. Everything begins with *Wir haben verloren, ABER,*[57] and after this *aber* it seems that in fact the Russians have lost this campaign and that the Russian offensive came to nothing. It reminded me of the joke about the gigolo who propositioned every girl on the dance floor. Once when asked whether he wasn't often slapped on the kisser, he answered, yes, but on balance, *per saldo,* he got more of what he wanted than slaps. The Germans insist that *per saldo* they have the upper hand. In addition, the Germans insist that England has sold herself to Russia and that America intends to do the same, in short, quite to the point. Apart from the military communiqués, the German press is beginning to make sense. But this amounts to nothing, because — the press is German.

April 1, 1943

Rommel Africanus has apparently left Africa "for health reasons." An Egyptian eye infection, or in other words, they threw sand in his eyes. He has evacuated in time. Unless they had him evacuated because he had begun to be too popular.

April 3, 1943

Spring. Suddenly it's warm, suddenly the sparrows have begun chirping loudly before going to sleep, suddenly the smell of greenery and apple blossoms is in the air. Like Faust at the sound of the bells, moved by the sounds and smells I declared time-out to thinking and, whispering softly, *"Ich habe schon alles durchstudiert*,"[58] I got rid of Albert-Émile Sorel's *Louise de Prusse*, I dug myself out from under Henri Bergson, Hegel, Spinoza, Huxley, Gustave Le Bon,[59] and other wise treatises, and took up *La Dame aux camélias*.

Returning from the town hall, I dropped into a bistro for a glass of white wine. The bistro doors were wide open, and the sun streaming in warmed up the interior after the long winter nap. The furniture, the shiny coffee machine, and even the stone floor stretched out lazily and breathed a warm air. A black cat was walking slowly along the walls, sitting down from time to time and blinking his eyes. Little rainbow sparks lit up the tips of his whiskers, his fur shone. I stroked him and thought that when the war ended I would have many cats. He arched his spine, bumped his head against my hand, and went off to sit a few feet farther away. The cat's stroll displayed all the pleasures of sunshine. The wine has acquired a different taste, because the sun is splashing inside the glass. The chatterboxes are already at the counter and are talking with the *patron* about the spring. They'll be landing for sure. Notices have already been prepared in the city halls, which will be posted right after the landing. It's already "stated" there, that all men of fighting age must present themselves at the concentration camps. *Si, si, mais oui—j't'assure—on les a vue, ces affiches . . .*[60] What's it to me, the sun is shining and at the moment I'm feeling good.

A fly is stepping around a drop of beer. I want to embrace it and I'm sorry that flies don't let themselves be embraced. There have been so many months without flies. It tasted the beer, moved away, and rubbed its front legs with satisfaction. With its hind legs it stroked its wings, finished grooming itself, and wandered off to another puddle of beer.

Bicycles whiz through the streets. Women in wide skirts display the tops of their attractively painted legs. They are all shapely and one can fall in love with each one for a couple of hours. The "pretty" *patronne* of the radio-electronics shop, whom we call the electric cow (?), has already put on a colorful dress and gazes stupidly ahead. She displays herself to the public together with her irons and camp stoves. The baker's wife and her dun tomcat have fattened up over the winter and now it shows. The bakery was often closed for violations, thus clearly "black market deals" were thriving. I'd like to know whether the baker's wife already has a box at the Comédie-Française. These days all such ladies have subscriptions to the theaters and go around wearing their newly acquired jewels. Money goes from the hands of those who think they deserve it into the hands of those said not to deserve it. But—one has to eat. The women behind the counters in the bakeries, groceries, delicatessens, and dairies are making fortunes, selling under the counter. The fly performed its trial flight and landed on a lightbulb, where it celebrated with a black dot. The policeman from our hotel now dresses in civvies and briskly scoots over to the proprietress of the laundry across the way. She truly has elephantiasis of the legs, but her top parts are still good, as is the cash register. And he's a penniless peasant from the Basses-Pyrénées. What's he got there? A couple of vines and some stones. But lots of sunshine. When the war ends, I'll go south. Now I have to polish up the bicycles and tomorrow we'll go somewhere to see the apple trees in bloom. An apple tree in bloom is one enormous flower. The spires of Notre-Dame now rise up from among the blossoms. I drink a second glass of wine. The chatter-boxes have moved to the table, spread out a small rug, and begun a game of belote. The hard-of-hearing *patronne* has appeared and begun slowly wiping the counter. Deeply deaf. She always confuses "Cognac" with "Armagnac" and "*bière*" with "Byrrh." It's surprising they haven't yet confiscated the zinc of the metal counter. It's been requisitioned everywhere and now there's linoleum, fastened with two slats. The bistros have become dark and dreary, without the shine. Ah—now the belote players are already beginning to shout. I seem to be dreaming that the world has ceased to exist. The lilacs are certainly in bud, and tomorrow the children will be taking donkey rides in the Vincennes zoo. The caged parrots, carried into the open air, will screech and rotate their beaks. They'll be heard as far as the pond. And there will instantly be a lot of litter on the lawns. If the ice cream carts are already out, Basia will buy herself something cold and granular for five francs. She says it's "delicious" . . . I finished my wine. I'm already too hot in my wool socks. It's still chilly in the courtyard in front of our hotel and the artificial grotto emits a cold, humid draft. But the ivy is already completely green and has lost its winter gray.

I sit in my armchair at the open window and read. I'm greedily reading that story of great love. Armand and Marguerite have the smell of spring. A vista opens into the clouds of flowering apple trees. Their story is calm and hopelessly sentimental, like every love. I take some scores out of the suitcase and open the *Invitation à la valse* by Carl Maria von Weber.[61] I look with emotion at the rapid passage that Marguerite was unable to execute smoothly. It's indeed hard to play. I would like to talk with her and tell her she must practice beat by beat and without the pedal. It should sound like the touch of a stick against the wooden pickets when one runs along a fence. I turn the pages and softly whistle the melody that is forever tied to Marguerite. The whole book is nevertheless noble. Like every true love. It seems to me that a person who has never really been in love cannot comprehend this novel. Deep love is always touched with sentimentality and "house on fire," things seemingly banal and inviting parody. I feel a shameless lightness when I read this "soap opera" and my chest trembles slightly. Somewhere deep down I smile through my tears. Marguerite's pale smile is everywhere. The open window admits warm breezes and a ball of dust lying in the middle of the floor has rolled under the bed. The sounds of a piano fill my ears. The gliding tones of the waltz, a white dress in the candlelight, and the rapid notes of the passage, like a spring rain.

April 4, 1943

Sunshine and springtime. It's Sunday. The sparrows have gone mad. The concierge's rabbit has escaped from its cage and cautiously visits the courtyard. With one ear hanging to the side, he is hilarious. A white ball of fluff on his paws. I laugh, because his movements are quite roguish. He creeps slowly into the bushes and suddenly rushes out headlong, as fast as he can. I lean out over the railing and throw crumbs of bread. The sparrows dive down from the tree, snatch their loot, and fly off. The rabbit doesn't really get it. He watches the sparrows with an appealingly helpless expression on his face. You can almost see that something is getting tangled and confused in his head. The concierge has emerged from her "loge," walking like a fattened duck; she quacked something and went into the toilet, naturally not closing the door. She flushed and came out again. In the quiet, sunny morning, the water sounds like a waterfall. Again she quacks to herself and tries to catch the rabbit. The sun is already lighting up the roofs of the houses and will soon be streaming into our room. I'm hungry and look forward to breakfast and my first cigarette. We're going to the park on our bikes. I am absolutely not thinking about anything. I'm living. Hot tea, bread and cheese, then bread and jam. A cigarette. Afterward I'd like to dive into the washbasin. I wander around the room in the buff. A shame it's still too soon to go riding in shorts. Music from the radio floats over from the neighboring houses. Suspended in a cage on some balcony, a rooster being fattened up for Easter suddenly crowed. If only it hasn't brought on the rain. Old Mrs. Horwat, my grandmother's maid, always said that when the rooster crows during the day, it means there'll be a "splash." About one of my cousins, she said, "he's so clean, you can drink coffee out of him." Grandma called her "my dear old Horwatka" and insisted that everything was more expensive in Cracow. Basia and I have decided to eat breakfast earlier and then set off. I go down for the bicycles and suddenly there's an infernal roar. A salvo of all the antiaircraft cannons all over Paris. Then a distant boom, lasting a minute, or maybe two, and the muffled drone of motors. I rushed into the courtyard, but there was nothing to see. They had been flying very high overhead, lost in the blueness of the springtime sky. I prepared the bicycles and we had our meal. We set out. On avenue Daumesnil an uninterrupted line of people trails in the direction of the Bois de Vincennes. Children's carriages are squeaking, there's the shuffle of thousands of feet. Everyone is walking slowly, relaxed and lazy. Latest news—they have bombed Renault. Many people were killed on the Longchamps racecourse when a few bombs fell into the crowd of spectators. The Americans have really blown it—can't they tell where Longchamps is and where Renault? Mass production. Over there it's death, people torn to pieces and houses in ruins, hundreds killed and thousands mourning their dear ones; here it's a sunny day, a crowd of people amusing themselves, a carefree mood bubbling in the glasses of sparkling wine they're drinking on the terraces. *"Garçon, un verre de mousseux!"*[62] Laughter, a fellow kisses his girl, a mother plays with her child, I ride and enjoy the sun. The moment of tension has already passed, the roar and rumbling of the four-engine monsters have sunk into the distance and ceased to exist. Life . . . Flickers of fresh green are already bursting from the trees, trembling in the sun and showing off. Far outside Paris, near Joinville, we sit on the grass. The ground is still damp and chilly. We eat chocolate and biscuits, I roll a cigarette and exhale into the sky. Basia is writing a poem. One of her little poems, simple and childish. She's seeking a rhyme for "grand piano." What an idea! I say: "soprano." "Jędrek, don't be a silly," I hear the poetess answer. I look up into the sky and think of words that can express the feeling of absolute happiness, as juicy as a huge pear. The sunshine is white and fluid; it spreads around and warms. Late in the afternoon we ride to Fontenay to visit Robert and his wife. Both are in the garden digging in the earth. Their gang of children are playing and Filip, the youngest, stands in the doorway. Whatever you say to him, he answers in perfect imitation of what he's heard from the adults, *"Hein? Hein?"* He doesn't know how to talk, but this he's already learned. Basia looks through Jacques's Greek textbooks and observes that she's forgotten everything. I tell her not to worry, because what's most important is what's been forgotten, as someone once said. We eat supper with the family and return at nightfall. It's chilly except for waves of warm air here and there. The apple trees give off their aroma, their whiteness and pale pink glowing in the dusk. The black spines of the Château de Vincennes melt into the darkening sky. Life—ordinary, daily life, can be splendid.

April 6, 1943

I finished *La Dame aux camélias*, which has left me with a sense of longing. I'm not sure for what. Spring has hurried and is bursting forth in all directions. The streets are full of women's painted legs in their sandals, wide floral skirts flutter in the wind, the scent of perfume catches in your nostrils. I always distinguish Rumeur by Lanvin, because I like it best. At the same time funerals are under way for the victims of the bombing the day before yesterday. Among the dead at Longchamps was one of my acquaintances from the Ministry of Labor. Already elderly, he had two passions in his life: the races and the English. He died at the races from an English bomb. A subject for one of Artur Swinarski's epigrams.[63] He was torn to shreds and the remains were identified by a tie pin: a gold riding crop studded with small rubies. All this was recounted today when I went to the ministry to get some papers and forms. Today his place at the table was empty and no one greeted me cheerfully with: "*Monsieur André, comment va la Pologne?*"[64] He's the one who for the last few months would always ask me, with a wink, what Warsaw would be called after the war: "Varsoviebourg or Varsoviegrad?" Despite his Anglophilia, he was afraid that England would sell us out to Russia. He wasn't the only one afraid of that. I have always feared the "Holy Alliance" between America, England, and Russia, which will be concluded first of all at the cost of our independence, if after the war it will be possible to speak of anything like independence at all. According to eyewitnesses, there was a nest of German flak at the racecourse and one of the sportier American bomber pilots flew low and aimed a few bombs at it.

After leaving the ministry, I ended up once again in the sunny stream. Lots of people on rue de Vaugirard. Again, painted legs and painted thighs peeking out from the folds of a skirt on a bicycle. I dropped into the Dupont at Porte de Versailles. Someone had put a franc into the jukebox and the beat of American "swing" filled the place. Finally some human music, not that perpetual Beethoven, Mozart, Schumann, and Schubert. I returned home in the evening. An open window, evening sounds from the house next door, dusk falling. The sparrows wish each other good-night at the top of their lungs. Life, life at any cost. I'm not thinking, because thinking is impossible.

April 9, 1943

They're attacking Tunis *au ralenti*.[65] The war is growing, acquiring fantastic proportions. After this war who would ever want to engage in war again? It began as a war of nations and has ended as a war of continents. This war is more of a world war than the first one, as a contemporary Mr. Prudhomme might say. After this war, who will be able *seriously* to consider arming themselves? Only the great national blocs. If Poland, Czechoslovakia, Yugoslavia, and others recover their independence, will they have the means to acquire arms? They will only be able to arm in the framework of some kind of continental bloc. The next war (I am clairvoyant) can only be "pot luck," just like the current picnic. It's becoming ever more obvious that the structure of the world will consist of spheres dominated by the Anglo-Saxons and the Russians. As long as these blocs don't go to war against each other, war will in fact be impossible, because no one else will be able to afford to conduct a war under contemporary conditions. Who knows if the present war is not already the peak of airpower and if the next war will not dispense with that in favor of a cheaper and also more effective means of destruction. Rocket-fired torpedoes will replace airpower and artillery. Paris will be bombarded from Moscow, New York from London. It makes my head spin. I feel almost physically the speed with which we are rushing along on the unbridled horse of "progress." People look like drunkards. We are drunk, completely intoxicated, and it gets harder and harder for us to "realize" what's really going on. And I doubt whether the end of this war will sober us up. I'm afraid that the resolution of the final issues will be the work of drunkards and that the results will be drunken, as well. Drunkards think everything is possible.

April 12, 1943

The meeting between Mussolini and Hitler lasted from the seventh to the tenth. The communiqué has little to say. The decision was taken to pursue the fight until the final victory. If pigs had wings, as old Rzecki would say. There's a mood of spring thaw on the Asian front. Mussolini seems to have asked Hitler for permission to withdraw the Italian divisions from the Eastern Front. He feels threatened. Indeed, from Tunis to Italy is not very far. But the crux of the matter is that these two clowns have had a meeting, that the clownish newspapers can clown around on this subject and once again underscore that the first commandment of propaganda is to treat everyone like a herd of morons, to whom everything must be explained. They indeed manage to explain everything. When the Russians reach Berlin, they will also be able to explain. And my most urgent desire is to be able to reach the moment when I get to see just HOW.

I would like to re-read — this time not as an assignment and not in abridged form — Zygmunt Krasiński's *Undivine Comedy*. It always seemed to me that of the three Polish "bards" he had the best head. I remember my final exam for the Gymnasium diploma, where I was asked about Pankracy, Krasiński's revolutionary hero.[66] I characterized him as "the incarnation of the devil of history." The professors looked astonished, but I could not provide an explanation of my "thesis." Now it seems to me it wasn't all that stupid after all.

April 13, 1943

Basia is laid up with the flu. So I was the one who went to the market. A sunny April morning, chilly and fresh. The shrill voices of the tradeswomen penetrate the courtyard. The less they have to sell, the louder they shout. In this respect politicians and tradeswomen are no different. The door to the toilet in our courtyard bangs constantly. The banging mixes with the clatter of the street vendors' clogs, as they go in and out of our entryway. "Our" outhouse in the courtyard serves the part of the market near our entry. The concierge naturally takes a cut in goods. Someone's always bringing her something—cheaper and no waiting in line. So on market days she hangs around the toilet, chatting with the visitors. The men talk over their shoulders with the door open, the women conduct their conversations through the door. Sometimes an entire group forms and jokes fly on the subject of who's inside. The gurgle of water, laughter, and the clatter of clogs.

The market is bustling. The housewives make their way along the stands. The "better ladies," their makeup in place, but unbuttoned, uncombed, and unwashed, are the wives of the many civil servants who live around here. Besides, who in today's France isn't a civil servant? You hear the sounds of spiteful arguments over a spot in line, revolutionary cries regarding *priorités* or discussions with the vendors, who today exercise a feudal power over the customers. The tradesman is the lord of life and death. He either bestows his favor or not. What he offers, you must not refuse. What he insists you take, you must take. To buy a pound of something you want you must buy a pound of something else, which you absolutely don't need or which is half-rotten. The infuriated *tricoteuses* hiss through their teeth and curse, but when it's their turn they smile sweetly to the tradeswoman. You have to be nice to her. But the tradeswoman is also furious. She's wasting time and money there, selling what she could sell on the side for three times as much.

I, too, am unwashed, I'm also dressed any which way and I also have a basket on my arm. I join the crowd and breathe in the cheeses here, the mussels there, the fish over there. Or I immerse myself in the smell of moist vegetables and greedily inhale the odor of leeks. I stand in line for radishes and buy a bunch of asparagus. Asparagus are expensive, but you have to seize the chance. I buy some lettuce. It's fresh and firm, dripping water, and I would like to bite into it. The market is a sad sight. Some mussels, some fish, a lot of vegetables, and a lot of yelling. I remember, on the first day after I arrived here four years ago, I ran out in front of the house and it seemed like Sesame had opened its doors before me. Laid out on the tables were mountains of dates and dried figs, bunches of bananas, pyramids of chocolate, and cathedrals of cheese. In other stalls were meat and poultry, crayfish and lobsters. Everything cheap, moreover. But despite the war, in France one still sees traces of wealth. Despite the German plunder, despite the continuous requisitions, there's no famine. There's still a choice, still a certain variety, and it's still possible to arrange one's own "small life." There's a certain something in this air, something that so easily makes one happy. The sun is shining, the tradeswomen are shouting, the smells tease the palate. Everything here seems to be centripetal, not centrifugal. I don't know why, but I'm suddenly reminded of that typically French definition of happiness offered by Sacha Guitry: "Happiness is loving old books and young authors, young women and old friends." This definition has something gastronomic about it, the taste of a good dish, and that's probably why I recall it here. Food is also part of culture. A good meal is worth as much as a good poem or a good painting. Food is not at all "inferior," and a diet of cabbage and potatoes certainly has an effect on culture. What can be more horrible than the goal toward which the world is now heading in leaps and bounds—the collectivization of food, preparation en masse, and distribution in canteens or other such barbaric institutions. I return home with the basket, jump on my bicycle, and ride to work. At noon I'll eat in the canteen. And I want to puke.

April 14, 1943

It's the same everywhere. Basia ran into her school friend on the street. A Jewess. Her husband was taken to a camp, carted off, and all trace of him has vanished. She is hiding under false papers with her three-year-old son. She now lives in the countryside near Fontainebleau. She's lost everything, because her three suitcases were "requisitioned" by the *patron* of the hotel in which she was staying and from which she escaped in the night. When she tried to get them back, the *patron* made clear it would be better for her not to try. Now literally out on the street with her son, she turned to the Quakers, who took her in. There she met I., a Spaniard, a Republican fighter, who fell in love with her. They will probably get married someday.

I. is very nice and we meet from time to time. He was a journalist and tells me a lot about Spain. And while listening to his stories, I often wonder which nation is the most European. The Spaniards or the Poles? What we do after drinking a liter of vodka, they do on an empty stomach. Their instinct for self-destruction is quite extraordinary. He describes Saint John's Eve in Barcelona. A great midsummer festival. In the evening the streets are crammed with people. Each street appoints a leader. Surrounded by his staff, he makes the rounds of houses collecting old furniture. The assembled furniture is piled into a heap and when night falls is set on fire. A foretaste of destruction. The young people hang firecrackers on their belts and that's when the real fun starts. Wine is drunk and firecrackers are thrown. The victims of the firecrackers are the girls, who run away—often scorched. After midnight no girl dares show her face on the street;

the street belongs to the men. The firecrackers keep getting bigger. A kind of madness sets in. The guys dash about, blackened and drunk on the wine and the smell of gunpowder. Before dawn everyone runs down to the sea, where the mussel vendors are already bustling. Everyone eats hot mussels and waits for the sunrise. As soon as the sun emerges from the sea, the whole crowd strips down and jumps into the water.

Despite the colorfulness and the heat radiating from such descriptions, I get the impression of an interior coldness. People seem to be trying, by means of all this, to defrost the chunk of ice lodged in their blood. It all comes across as so alien that I don't think there can be anything in common between us.

I. knew the Pasionaria.[67] A simple woman with an amazing ability to influence the crowd. She has a son and a daughter. The daughter does not resemble her mother at all, which leads to hellish scenes at home. Once, after one of these many fights, as I. recounts, the daughter ran out of the house and ran headlong into a beggar child standing in the street. The child wails: "I have no mother." "And you're complaining, you little snotnose?" answers the impetuous daughter.

He describes the sinister role played by the Communists in that dreadful revolution, which turned into a prolonged civil war. "If it hadn't been for the Communists, the republic might have won. But they had started to create Russia in Spain."

April 15, 1943

This whole story about the twenty thousand Polish officers in Russian captivity who were shot near Smolensk is turning out to be horrendous. The Germans have discovered mass graves filled to the brim with the corpses of our officers and continue to discover new ones. Further investigations are in progress and the Germans even promise to identify individual bodies and publish lists of names. The first investigations demonstrated that the gruesome event occurred in spring 1941. The fact that the officers are Polish of course doesn't matter to the Germans, who are interested only in the propaganda damage to Russia and the Communists. Although the Germans who are reporting this are themselves at the moment murdering not merely tens of thousands but hundreds of thousands of people in concentration camps, the discovery of the mass graves has nevertheless made an enormous impression. As a Pole, I'm interrogated at every turn by skeptical Frenchmen, reluctant to believe it. It's not that the French *do not believe it, they don't want to* believe it, considering it a ruse of German propaganda, and they take their "reluctance to believe" so far as to insist it's the Germans themselves who murdered these men. I answer questions briefly: "I have no objective grounds not to believe the Russians did it." I was convinced from the start that this was essentially the work of the GPU.[68] Upon reflection, I realize I've been waiting these last few months for some such *coup de théâtre*. I feel no surprise—quite the contrary—a sense, rather, of its being quite normal, the consequence of what has slowly been unfolding—in a continuous chain—over many months. Russia's relationship to Poland, despite all the diplomatic posturing, is hostile. To this day the Polish government has not been able to settle the question of the people who were deported to Russia and is not able to locate them. The murder of thousands of Polish officers would be nothing exceptional. Quite the opposite. Not to have murdered them would have been remarkable. This is the extermination of part of the Polish intelligentsia, which Russia knows will never come to terms with the Communist program. Katyń is simply the execution of one of the points in the program Russia has in store for Poland.

But it's not only the French: even many Poles *do not want* to believe it. It's a classic example of faith in illusions, an example of the overwhelming impulse toward hypocrisy and self-deception. Because Russia is fighting the Germans, because Russia is an "ally," because Poland will awake one fine day—obviously, Great, Powerful, and Independent (capital letters even for adjectives). This and thousands of other examples demonstrate the fatal influence of being drunk in the fog of ideology. In talking with people, I always hear: "What a pessimist you are." I'm no pessimist—I simply have the habit of saying "the theater is half empty" when others say "the theater is half full." I try to see things as they are and not through an ideological fog or smoke screen, a morbid optimism. People don't want to think—they *are afraid of* sober thinking and time after time experience disappointments proportional to the intensity of their idealistic optimism, or what else to call this rubbish. A philosophy of *happy-endism*. This lying is the sickness of our age and prevents us from adapting ourselves and finding a better direction for the crazy race we have been swept up in. Thus, the gap keeps widening between man, with his false illusions, and real life. The pain and "sickness of the century" keep getting worse. If you start idealizing whatever comes along, then everything gets distorted. Yet people even consider themselves obliged to idealize sh—— because doing so is easy and above all comfortable. But only apparently. And in the short run.

April 17, 1943

Spent the afternoon in an exhibit of silks from Lyon in the Pavillon de Marsan. Antique silks from the Empire, Restoration, and Louis-Philippe. Amazing drapes woven on both sides, splendid wall coverings and upholstery. These old, thick silks are as meaty and juicy as thick leaves. I snuck up close and touched them with my hand, savoring the contact with the vestiges of former splendor. In the first hall there was Napoleon's throne. Simple, well-proportioned, upholstered in green silk with a golden "N" and bees. In the second hall, the bed of Louis XVIII, wide, comfortable, covered in silk. Further along, more examples of fabrics, doors, and furniture. Such great harmony, peace, and good taste. Finally, already modern things. Interesting that French Art Nouveau should have such charm. It has a lightness and a very special flavor. It's not the heavy and indigestible German or Austrian Jugendstil. French Art Nouveau has a bit of the Parisian woman. The postwar period is weaker. The perpetual search, merely for the sake of searching, with the goal of finding nothing at all, a feature inherent in all the "-isms" (if one knew one would find something, the search would lose its charm, a Cracow artist once told me), extended even to silk. Cold-bloodedness is the key to all art between the wars. It's an art that expresses instincts, not feelings.

The *imprimés* from 1942 are attractive and tasteful in the French manner. After the exhibit we went to Rebattet for ice cream and petits fours. The day was sunny and warm. The trees in the Tuileries are covered in green fuzz, as light as mist. You can see their skeletons clearly, each branch against the blue of the sky, but at the same time already green. An X-ray in color. People are strolling at a summer pace.

April 18, 1943

We got up early and after a solid breakfast I worked on the bicycles. It was a sunny day and already hot. We stuffed our backpack and bags and set off for the forest near Boissy-Saint-Léger. It's less crowded in the afternoon and we usually leave around noon. Charenton dozed impressionistically in the sun. The waters of the Marne glistened with the green of all the new leaves around it. Beyond Alfortville we entered a road lined with apple trees. The apple trees are already past bloom and scatter billions of rose petals. I said to Basia: "Spring snow is falling." Our bicycles kicked up clouds of fallen petals, blown into the air as we sped by. A car drove through in a rose-colored blizzard and vanished in a cloud of flowers. One could gather them off the road by the handful and they were like a carpet under our wheels. Approaching Boissy, we stopped to get something to drink. The sleepy *patron* of a somnolent bistro brought us two glasses of lemonade and then mysteriously disappeared. We sat at a table in front of the building. Lemonade, a piece of chocolate, a cigarette, and a sunny moment of peace. These are the moments I store away forever, that I gather and amass for later on, that I deposit in the current account of my emotions. Then, in an instant, I can sit down, close my eyes, and quickly write out a check, reliving them with the same intensity. I have all of southern France deposited this way. Whenever I want to, I can experience the warm evenings, hear the sounds, breathe the sea and sand. And now I'm lying at the foot of a giant oak, buried up to my neck in the thickets and young saplings. The leaves have already burst from the branches, the shrubs are covered in a frosting of green. I'm afraid they would fall if I touched them. Last year's dry leaves crunch under me and the ground exudes the smell of winter. I don't know why, but the smell of dry leaves and moist earth affects me like a fog: it arouses memories of childhood, memories of the forests near Lida and Nowogródek, the outlines of the castle of Gedymin,[69] the image of a wolf encountered during a horseback ride with my father.

April 21, 1943

Katyń is the "highlight" of the spring season, if it's not unseemly to use this expression. But it's difficult to describe it otherwise. Photographs, broadcasts, interviews, reporting. The entire German propaganda apparatus, as one voice, has "katynized" itself. Forensic medical experts have traveled to the site, so far only from countries friendly to the Germans. The case has been clear from the beginning—at least to me. There's only one grotesque aspect (grim grotesque) in all this and it blunts the edge, namely the fact that the wholesaler is denouncing the retailer and that both belong to the same butchers' guild. What the Russians did in Katyń piecemeal—extraordinary that they murdered them one by one, led them to the ditch one by one, shot each one in the back of the head, and piled the corpses like sardines in a tin can—this the Germans do wholesale, industrial scale. It's amazing that the collectivist ideology in this case employed an extremely individualistic method of execution. How many "hairdressers" they must have needed, because, good God, pistol shooting is exhausting. I used to do a lot of shooting and I know how tired your hand gets, particularly with a pistol. And there, each one, personally, one at a time, one bullet each. They must have dumped some who were not yet dead. Words fail. The cruelty exceeds all bounds and is numbing. There, several tens of thousands have been shot (since it seems that Katyń is only one of their stock of "preserves")—here, hundreds of thousands are dying "their own deaths" in camps and prisons (in addition to Katyń, it's the same there as well). The difference is only apparent—a matter of form. Which is why the reaction to Katyń is not at all what the Germans expected. People don't *want* to believe this. A pity. But it's often the case, when the jackal accuses the hyena, that people tend to take one side or the other, unable to see that both feed on carrion. All this propaganda misses the mark. The Germans have already lied so much that when, as an exception, they tell the truth, no one wants to believe them. A pity. Because if this were believed, many misunderstandings could be avoided after the war. You'd know who you were dealing with. As it is, people have by now given up on Hitlerism, but they haven't given up on Communism. A pity someone else didn't uncover this Katyń, someone who could legitimately say: "not I." Rumors are circulating that the Polish government in London has turned to the International Red Cross in Geneva with a request for expertise. Clearly America and England will not agree to this. The Russians were at first silent, but are now starting to lie through their teeth. They insist it's the work of those "fascist bandits" (pronounced with the same telltale accent as that of the so-called Pole on Radio Moscow). I'm curious to know what's being said about Katyń by the remaining Polish officers and soldiers who miraculously and thanks to the dexterity of General Anders managed to extricate themselves from Russia and are now taking a rest cure in Iran.[70] I imagine those in Iran have no doubts in the matter.

April 25, 1943

Easter. The weather is horrid and we're staying home. Basia is painting, I'm reading to her aloud from a collection by Ferdynand Hoesick about various "acquaintances" from days gone by.[71] Among other things, a letter from George Sand to Franciszek Grzymała concerning her decision to fall in love with Chopin and give herself to him.[72] The letter is very witty and brilliant, but at the same time so frigid and calculating, so businesslike, that reading it makes one realize for the first time the reasons for the breakup in Nohant. Sand does not restrain herself in the least. Her memories of the rendezvous in the darkened room, during which she feels she has "had an effect" on "the young one," her reflections on his pain and homesickness, the claim that she would like to be for him what Venice is for the traveler and that she is ready to do so, if . . . and so on, all this in the end is distasteful and cheap, despite the letter's formal perfection. On his side, feeling, heart, and nobility, though certainly lots of egoism; on hers, the French intellectual tart, in general, a tart, with a talent for writing about what she doesn't really feel. This comes through in all her works. "Writing for Mme Sand is a function," Gautier once said, when telling the Goncourts about his visit to Nohant. I prefer Balzac. He had style. Apparently, at one of Gavarni's[73] receptions, he said: "One day I would like to be as well known, to have a name as popular, as famous, altogether as illustrious, as to allow me to fart in public and for the public to take it entirely in stride." That I can understand.

April 27, 1943

We spent all yesterday at home. Basia was in bed painting, I was organizing the books and reading. I'm trying quickly to catch up, because there's so much I don't know. Great sensation today. The Russians have broken diplomatic relations with the Polish government in London. Is this the beginning of the end? So soon? Moscow asserts that the Polish government in London is fascist (the telltale pseudo-Polish accent again) and that Sikorski has no choice but to move to Berlin. It's another matter, that in Sikorski's place, I would immediately withdraw all Polish forces from action in the west. Let the Americans and English intern us, but not another Polish life.

Now once again everyone is shedding tears over Poland, everyone is talking about "unfortunate Poland." We are terribly in fashion. *"Pologne,"* *"les Polonais,"* *"Polen"* — in all the newspapers and on the radio on both sides of the Rhine. The Germans are outright bawling. I want to go to the N.S. *Volkshilfe* on the Champs-Élysées and say: *"Geben Sie mir eine Fahrkarte nach Katyń hin und zurück."*[74] I'm curious to see whether we will take our patriotism so far as to refuse an invitation to visit Katyń, should the Germans extend one. With us Poles, anything is possible. If the Germans offered me this journey, I would go in a split second. Every eyewitness may prove to be invaluable at some point. Meanwhile, the Germans are transporting English and American officers from among the prisoners of war to visit Katyń. I wonder what these officers think of it and if they will dare talk about it once they are free after the war, under the "Holy Alliance." Taken all together, it's infernally sad. The rupture of relations with the Poles in London determines everything for the future. Russia thus avoids any possible explanations and gains a free hand in dealings with Poland. For let's not fool ourselves—neither England nor America will tie this free hand. When the Soviet army soon enough crosses our border, the real dance will begin. This is certainly not the end of our suffering and our problems. I'm beginning to be less surprised by Mickiewicz and Słowacki, their mysticism, and soporifics such as *The Pilgrims' Book* and Towiański, into the bargain. The end of this war may see a repetition of the "Holy Alliance," the Congress of Vienna, and the Duchy of Warsaw with a Russian governor or a Soviet Konstantin.[75] Poland sticks in everyone's throats. In this entire war, there's been "too much" of one thing—and that's Poland. Very embarrassing. Without Poland it would be much easier to settle the fate of Europe.

There's a macabre but telling cartoon in today's *Le Petit Parisien*. A giant Stalin bends over a tiny Churchill and says, confidentially, shielding his mouth with his hand and looking at the figure of a Polish officer whose back is turned: "The place for a certain Polish general is not in London . . . but in Katyń."

If Sikorski becomes "too much," they'll at least get rid of him, since they can't get rid of all of Poland. An obstacle. In Sikorski's place, I'd be on my guard.

May 1, 1943

The holiday of lilies of the valley. Gray and chilly. The thousands of bouquets of lilies of the valley for sale on every corner seem to be freezing and shaking in the cold, the pale, fragrant flowers huddling in their leaves, as though wrapped in warm shawls. A decree issued this year allows anyone to sell lilies of the valley without a special permit. So the streets are swarming with ragged children and the poor, thrusting bouquets at passersby. Near Gare de Lyon there were more people selling than buying. On the way home I bought a few bouquets. It began to rain and I arrived drenched. I love to return home soaking wet.

In regard to the Soviet-Polish conflict, today's *Le Petit Parisien* says: "To take the Soviets' side is to incur America's displeasure, because the Poles have a lot of influence there." Perhaps, in all the political dirty business that is coming increasingly to the surface in this war, America, as the least "politically sophisticated," will retain a certain purity of intentions and sincerity of action. But this lack of political sophistication harbors another danger, closely tied to the Americans' lack of intellectual sophistication. This danger is Russia's impressive power of attraction, which is perhaps especially impressive to the Americans, who are used to considering *the facts but not the essence* of any issue.

May 5, 1943

Tadzio has arrived with fresh news from Warsaw. Even in Poland people don't want to accept the truth about Katyń. Not surprising, since in Poland Katyń is inescapable, at every turn, at every minute. He reported on the fighting in the Jewish ghetto. Extraordinary and impressive. After an hour's conversation with Tadzio, who made it to Crimea and back, who has seen many things and recounts them briefly but intelligently, I came to the conclusion that instead of resolving a host of problems, this war will produce a whole raft of new ones. At present all the facts suggest that the end of the war will solve NOTHING and only increase the tension between polar opposites. Genuine chaos will set in after the war.

May 8, 1943

Tunis and Bizerte have been taken. It's puzzling how sudden this victory is. Nevertheless, I still don't believe the war will end this year. Optimism is again raging and it constantly makes me sick.

This evening we saw Tchaikovsky's *The Queen of Spades* at Salle Pleyel, presented by a Russian opera company. There were seven scenes of an unbearable perfection. A perfection leading at times to ecstasy, to a catch in the throat. The opera was so well done it's hard to imagine anything better. A gem, a masterpiece of staging, direction, acting, and taste. To make theater out of opera, while not losing the music, the opera itself, is not easy. To maintain the rhythm and balance demands a director of the highest class. And here Yuri Annenkov demonstrated what he can do.[76] There was not the slightest trace of artifice, of showiness. Here theater and opera were so well intermingled and presented as to create a sense of absolute truthfulness. Plus absolute consistency of performance. Hermann sang and acted among others who sang and acted as well as he. I kept thinking about the Reduta, which I grew up around. First in Warsaw in the "Reduta halls" and in the Orangerie (*The Dandy* in the Orangerie, with "O mother fortune, wag your tail—but slowly,"[77] which I recited to myself throughout my Gymnasium years, when I was being examined in mathematics), then in Wilno on Pohulanka Street, then in Warsaw, in the cellars of ZUPU, or whatever it was called.[78] I would sit for hours and listen, watching Poręba, Chmielewski, Kunina, Jaracz, Perzanowska, Drabik, that whole crew literally sacrificing themselves for art.[79] I remember how I cried when Józef Poręba, Stefan Jaracz's younger brother and a very promising actor, committed suicide. As a seven-year-old boy I used to hang around the stage with my cousin Elżunia.[80] I would sit in on rehearsals, on those endless rehearsals, listening to the voice of Uncle Julek (Juliusz Osterwa was married to my mother's sister) and to Mieczysław Limanowski's tirades. Hearing this *Queen of Spades* called up memories and I kept thinking that Osterwa and his Reduta constituted an entire era in our theater. His wife, my aunt, was a charming phenomenon, whom I fell in love with as a child.[81] Jerzy Szaniawski's *The Bird* and *The Paper Lover*, Stefan Żeromski's *Whiter than Snow* and *The Quail*.[82] The image of that amazingly charming woman, who treated me from my earliest years as a grown-up "Man" and who faded slowly with a smile. Her burial in winter 1929. We returned from the funeral on foot, the three of us—Osterwa, Elżunia, and me. Stalls on the street were selling Turkish delight. We stopped and Uncle Julek, smiling through his tears, bought us each a piece. I ate mine, swallowing my tears. In the evening he played in some "cash-cow" farce and all Warsaw went to see him. The sanctimonious held it against him, but he was saving himself from drowning in despair.

How many memories came to mind during the seven scenes of *The Queen of Spades*. For the first time since the beginning of the war. I never reminisce, I'm entirely turned to the future. And suddenly everything came back to me.

The sets were terrific. A few objects cleverly placed against a background of drapes and infused with carefully designed lighting created an atmosphere it is difficult to attain in a theater. It formed a WHOLE, a whole rarely encountered on stage. And this whole affected all my senses, "captivating" me completely. From the first moment I had to "surrender" and could not resist, like an obedient medium.

The second scene, representing the reception at Liza's, combined with the music and costumes, the lighting and the decor, which was superbly suggestive thanks to its restraint, was a treasure. Overall, the scenes were linked together, one after another, and despite their diversity, they struck a single note, creating a coherent whole. Tchaikovsky's music, which I don't actually like, is here genuinely "demonic." Only a Russian could create music like this. We left the theater stunned, with a feeling of "plenitude" one rarely has in such cases. This will remain with me forever. On May 29 they're giving *Eugene Onegin*. Obviously, we're going.

Today is my mother's name day. It reminds me of all the name day celebrations I remember from my childhood. My mother . . . "The state can raise the children." "The family is not a necessary element in the raising of children," and so forth. How outrageous, how idiotic. The withering of warmth, love, and tenderness results in a coldness, a chill, a hardening, more and more evident in people today. People without mothers or fathers, like cut flowers.

May 9, 1943

An exhibit at the Galerie Charpentier called *"Scènes et figures parisiennes."* One of the best exhibits I've recently seen. Ten by Degas, two Manets, three Renoirs, thirteen Toulouse-Lautrecs, a few Berthe Morisots, and a whole bunch of less well-known artists pulled along on the tails of these comets. *La Belle Époque*, the essence of Paris, spicy, exciting, tasteful. Renoir's *Le Café-Concert* (I know it by heart and am always entranced, there's always something new), Degas's ballerinas, the boulevards, theater loges, parks, shopgirls—all the riches of Parisian life in over three hundred canvases, sketches, posters.

What strikes me about modern painting is a certain type of cowardice. The artists paint as though they were afraid of something, although each tries to give the appearance of daring. There's a rather unpleasant hypocrisy in all this. They're afraid of everything—light, drawing, color. Many pieces reflect the terror of being charged with "lack of originality," every painter's nightmare. As a result, this general anxiety often leads to greater uniformity, in contrast to which the less fearful, such as André Dignimont, appear original, though they are probably not.[83] This fear of lacking originality is perhaps most noticeable in painting and poetry. Also certainly in music. Three genres in which form, pure form, plays a very important role. And this competition becomes dangerous, because it may cause us some day to start admiring kitsch once again. Or old junk. Jazz, for example, is the only kind of modern music I can bear and that I genuinely like. Basia at one point said: "It seems to me that these were painted, not with brushes, but with brains and nerves." For sure—we are living in an age of thought, above all thought. And therefore music, poetry, and painting all attempt, above all, to express thought. Whether they succeed, if indeed success is possible, that's the question. In every branch of art in which form and shape are basic elements, the expression of ideas is fiendishly difficult without jeopardizing form itself (or whatever we persist in considering form to be). Hence the impression of willful eccentricity. Only prose still manages to emerge undefeated. Who knows if one day art will not become a treatise of pure logic. And then suddenly someone will notice that bodies are flesh-colored—and it will be a great discovery.

After the exhibit we went to Rebattet for ice cream and petits fours. I find the sight of the old biddies and old fogies, creaking in all their joints, devoted to gluttony, strangely calming. People are stuffing themselves and are content. Here at least you see people who know what they want and what they don't want. Without hang-ups.

May 12, 1943

The Afrika Korps is being quickly liquidated. Today the capture of General von Arnim, Rommel's successor, was announced. The African front has ceased to exist. Gone are the dreams of Egypt, of a rendezvous in the Caucasus via Asia Minor, and of the march on India. It's rumored that the swift capture of Tunis and Bizerte resulted from the collapse in morale of the German divisions, which simply surrendered. In any case, this is no indication of what will come next. I no longer believe the war will end this year. This is just the start of the aerial offensive against Germany. The Germans have already gone on the defensive, all along the line, but they are still strong.

May 22, 1943

A symphony concert at Salle Gaveau. Three symphonies—naturally, Romantic. In the cinema, in theaters, in fashion—the return to Romanticism is everywhere. I'm tempted to order a velvet tailcoat and sleep in a nightcap. Romanticism hovers over the streets, appears in clothing, in window displays. Combined with spring, this creates a very special atmosphere, in which one can forget completely about the war. In the streets, in parks — it's comforting. Peaceful, no cars. It's unlikely Paris has ever been as beautiful as it is now. People ride around on their bicycles and visit the city. A Frenchwoman said to me yesterday: "*Mon Dieu*, how charming our Paris is. I see it for the first time now. Every Sunday I ride around the city on my bike . . ."

Schubert's *First Symphony*, which he wrote at the age of sixteen, still echoing Mozart and Haydn. Colorful ribbons in the air. The Schumann symphony was undistinguished. A good *Larghetto*. The Brahms left me cold.

The concert was a matinee. When we emerged, it was still light. A Saturday evening. I so love these summer evenings, when we walk home together, arm in arm, through the deserted streets. We stop in front of display windows, I spout nonsense and suddenly start walking with a very strange step. Basia pulls away. "What are you up to?" "It's the step of a drawing-room idiot, which Flaubert imitated so well," I answer. "And this is the 'step of the creditor' — Gautier's specialty. You have no understanding of French literature." Basia crosses the street. I catch up with her. "You ought to buy yourself some of those earrings that are in fashion these days, then I will certainly divorce you." Paris is sagging with the weight of costume jewelry, which is actually quite nice. We hop into the metro and return home. Basia will make supper, and then will be unable to extract me from my armchair, to which I am glued, along with whatever book I'm reading.

May 24, 1943

In the course of last night, the English bombed the dams on the Möhne and Eder rivers. They destroyed the dams and water flooded the entire area. There were apparently enormous losses and many victims. As one can easily imagine. It's very sad, although from the military perspective it's a great accomplishment. Technically, it must have been terribly difficult. But all in all, it's beginning to be pointless. The universal bestialization, the enormous destruction, the hundreds of thousands and millions of human lives and the grave that Europe is digging for herself.

May 29, 1943

This evening we heard *Eugene Onegin*. Less successful. It lacked precisely the compact unity of the *The Queen of Spades*. At times it dragged. Some scenes were excellent, but they were disconnected. The performance lasted so long they had to break off before the end, because of the metro. Overall, it missed. At Étoile we could not push our way into the last train on our line. The crush and heat were indescribable. People were behaving like wild animals. In the end we managed to catch the last train to Vincennes and got out at Reuilly-Diderot, going the rest of the way on foot. A warm, dark night.

May 30, 1943

Over the last week, Germany has endured three heavy bombardments. Essen, Dortmund, and Zeiss in Jena. It's the beginning of the systematic destruction of German industry and cities. After the war, when Germany and many industrial enterprises in other countries have been demolished (this is only the beginning), all Europe will be ravaged and hungry. There will be shortages of everything. And help will come, and everything will be so noble, everything will bear a touching and high-minded name. Help for the population of the suffering countries and a lot of other aid. Everything will be good. While on the sly, Germany will be rebuilt. And the press, the radio, and the cinema will once again burst with ideals and lull the population with new slogans. Nothing but the TRUTH will be uttered . . . Paradise.

And then they'll be pulling the strings and new puppets will be at each other's throats. I've completely lost my reason. Whenever I turn on the radio and listen to the drivel from the other side of the Channel, instead of the ordinary, vulgar lies I hear from this side, all I hear are fairy tales. And what noble and beautiful tales they are, and how full of the TRUTH . . . It's enough to make you puke. Both sides are doing the same thing. Both aim to destroy all thinking, to discourage man completely from any kind of mental effort. Because it's only with a herd of sheep that you can do whatever you want. It's sheep, not men, they are raising. And most horrible of all, even the real sheep are not protesting, though as animals they should be wiser. They are certainly bellowing, only we don't want to hear it. Give man ready-made, easily digestible answers to everything, remove all obstacles in his way, lest he trip and in falling begin to think and reason. Why should he read?—give him pictures. Anticipate any question with an answer. Formulate the answer so clearly that it doesn't occur to him to doubt it. Because doubt arouses thinking. No—statistics, the voices of the learned, the "most accomplished" (the pharaohs' high priests?)—everything simple, clear, defined, like "the class struggle," "the laws of history," furniture made of steel, and skyscrapers. Confuse him, delude him, allow him to forget he's a man. Do not touch his interior—stay on the surface, on the surface, comrades! A world—a brave new world!

If not for the law of reaction, which exists in everything, no matter what, one might succumb to doubt completely. And the deeper we fall, the stronger will be the reaction. In thirty or forty years a new man may arise. Europe may become more civilized and freer than in the period of its greatest development to date. I may even live to see that day.

But in the meantime one must have the patience of an angel and keep listening to this amazing rubbish, immense and apocalyptic. Whatever Walter Lippmann says is sacred throughout America, whatever Goebbels writes and Hitler bellows galvanizes the entire nation. And what Stalin does not say, and what Radio Moscow interprets in the style of an elementary schoolboy exercise, enthralls the masses, who yearn for "paradise." They yearn and they believe. What mental poverty all this shows, what obtuseness and dogmatism. Banal, cloying, intellectually worn-out.

May 31, 1943

The decree on mobilization of young men. The cohorts of 1920, 1921, and 1922 must present themselves for registration and transport to Germany. It's practically a military draft. Panic.

They now need Poland. Yesterday's *Pariser Zeitung* cites an article from the Italian Agenzia Stefani: "Refusing to play her designated role in Europe, a role that no one denied her, pulling the chestnuts out of the fire for the enemies of European civilization, who had waited a long time for the opportunity of the war to have the European continent at their mercy, Poland betrayed not only her own interests, but also the interests of all the peoples of the continent, among whom, thanks to the virtues of her people, to her history and her traditions, she had the right to demand an honorable place, which no one had any intention of denying her."

Wonderful! On May 30, 1943, the world discovers that nevertheless something like Poland exists. Because now they're having regrets. A few million excellent soldiers . . . Which they could have had. Not only us—all of Europe. But it should have been done differently. Not in the Prussian manner and not like drill sergeants. The idea itself was not stupid, as is becoming ever clearer now.

June 4, 1943

The French in Algiers have created a Committee of National Liberation. Something like a parliament. Now they'll be in their element. Now they'll be able to stuff themselves, indulge in intrigues, and gab, gab, gab. They will liberate the country by flapping their lips. General Giraud will be at loggerheads

with General de Gaulle, underlings with underlings, commotion, emissaries—
nothing but gab, gab, gab.

June 6, 1943

Meanwhile, in America they're holding a conference called "Hot Springs"
in a town of that name. They're discussing the division of global production
after the war. Virginia is witnessing Homeric battles over pigs, bacon, sugar,
fruit, grain, and so on. The Anglo-Saxon delegation proposed that France, Belgium, Italy, Spain, and the Scandinavian countries concentrate on cultivation
of fruits and vegetables, while Canada, the United States, Russia, Argentina,
and Australia would grow grain. But the Chinese sided with the Americans and
refuse to agree with the others. All such accords are useless unless there's mutual
understanding.

June 13, 1943

Pentecost. Splendid weather. We're going for a swim. Basia is packing the
food, I'm collecting our things. I would like to write, like Mikołaj Rej—with a
feeling of blissful happiness: "When summer comes, remind yourself: savor it,
dear soul. You are blessed with goodness, but only in fearing God and thanking
Him with all your heart."[84] I'm savoring it, imagining the aroma of "succulent
little morsels, mulled wine in a cup of delightful beer . . ." These summer days
are full of flavor, well seasoned, aromatic. Life becomes one long, sensual experience.

A scorcher. We biked to a large pond near Valenton. One of the few natural beaches near Paris and not well known. It was deserted. I pitched the tent,
to have some shade, and then there was nothing but sun and the water. I don't
remember anything else. I recalled the long hours of lying on the sand at the
beach in Gruissan without a thought in my head. Possible to stop thinking and
impossible to think. My throat is parched and I don't even want to talk. Then,
back into the water and after getting out, an amazing appetite. Bread, butter,
cheese, sausage, fresh eggs, wine. Sun, resting, the water, and eating again. Until
the end of the day. We returned when it was already getting dark. At Porte de
Charenton we ate ice cream from a stand and refreshed our palates.

June 14, 1943

A gray day, windy and cold. In the evening we went to visit Robert and his wife. Pleasant, as usual. They invited us once again to spend this year's vacation at their aunt's place in Chambellay. We were very touched by the offer, but we don't yet know what we'll decide to do. Because this year we want to take a bit of "our own" vacation—to hunker down somewhere in a country inn, eat well, and do whatever we fancy. We've been dreaming of such an inn for a long time. I'm tired.

June 20, 1943

The day before yesterday Basia went to Thoméry to see R. I arrived there today. The mood is somber. When I got off the train, Basia and R. told me that yesterday the Spaniard, I., was arrested. He's in prison in Fresnes.

July 1, 1943

I'm not writing, not reading, not thinking—instead I'm making a model of an old French light aircraft. Fascinating. When I get home I glue my wooden sticks in silence, absorbed completely in problems of assembly. Basia looks at me as though I were a lunatic and patiently puts up with the mess in the room, the trash and disorder. A great way to unwind.

I must now help R., because I.'s arrest has left her entirely helpless. I'm making the rounds trying to find some way, but I don't know if anything will come of it.

July 2, 1943

Evening at the Odéon Theater. I like this old house. And the audience is easier to bear than in other theaters. Thanks to the cheap tickets (it's a state theater) there are many young people, some "decent" and thrifty families in the loges, elderly gentlemen, lycée professors, often with the faded ribbons of their decorations in their shabby jacket lapels. The mood is warm and intimate—especially on a calm July evening, when you step out for a smoke on the broad steps in front of the theater and catch the nocturnal scent of greenery and water from the Luxembourg Gardens. Your eye gets lost in the narrow streets full of secondhand bookshops. I know each one by heart and I know what each has to offer. Eskimo ice cream pops are sold during the long intermission. We eat Eskimos in the half-light, leaning against a cool column.

Henry Murger's one-act play, *Le Bonhomme Jadis*, filled with garret romanticism and sympathy for shopgirls.[85] An old, warm-hearted pensioner, naturally
living in an attic room on the sixth floor, helps arrange a meeting between the
boy and girl in the neighboring rooms, penniless and clearly in love. And when
they meet, when they recognize their long-concealed love, the old man offers
them his savings. Here, children, take this purse of gold. There's enough for an
old man with what remains. All this, naive and teary-eyed, in costumes of a bygone age.

Followed by three acts of laughter, qui pro quo, over the top by Victorien
Sardou.[86] *La Papillonne*—the female butterfly—is a sickness that befalls the
majority of married men after several years of marriage. It's the need to change
where they live, their preferences, their habits, the need for adventure and adventures in love. In short, the condition that precedes and encourages their departure from the so-called straight path of faithful marriage. And here we have
Monsieur Champignac, all too happily married, who has come down with the
"*papillonne.*" He falls for the seductions of a flirtatious woman who arranges to
meet him out in the fields under a pear tree, after which he is whisked away by
a charming *soubrette* who takes him to see a certain Italian woman with a fiendishly jealous husband.

All this, however, is the work of the charming, young, and worldly aunt of
Monsieur Champignac's wife. The aunt plays the role of the mysterious Italian woman. A series of qui pro quos, classic and inevitable, one after the other,
makes you laugh and feel good. Once again, costumes from a bygone age, men
comical in brown hats and checkered coats, women charming in dresses with
bustles. Sardou pulls out all the stops, old-fashioned and elegant, despite his
somewhat dicey language—he sparkles and charms.

Noisy, crowded, restless Paris has gone underground, into the metro. Above
ground all is quiet, with the whir of bicycles and old-time Paris. At dawn the
cocks crow, rabbits hop in the courtyards. Paris has become as intimate as an
old and comfortable apartment.

July 5, 1943

They've finished him off. The evening communiqué reported that on the
way back from an inspection in the Near East, Sikorski was killed in a plane
crash in Gibraltar. Tragic.

He was not perhaps a great statesman, but he certainly still had some credit
in England and America. He may have derived his power merely from being
inconvenient, but in our current situation that was a form of power in itself. In

addition, he had the power of a symbol, a symbol of Poland, which in him (of course, from the perspective of foreigners) had survived in exile. For foreigners, he and Poland were virtually one. He had access everywhere, everyone knew him. And in these times, growing ever darker for us, in the land of the blind, the one-eyed was king. We're dogged by misfortune. Who is left? No one. We now have no one. After Darlan, it was Sikorski's turn. I thought the sequence would be different. Two months ago I began to "sense" something and even pasted into my notebook the little cartoon from *Le Petit Parisien*. Who remains in London? Kazimierz Sosnkowski.[87] A great general but no politician. How well this death suits everyone.

July 6, 1943

An inquest and an investigation will have to be conducted in Gibraltar. They ought really to take place in London or Moscow.

The Germans are having a great time. German propaganda has made Sikorski into a virtual saint. Resourceful, brave, capable, anti-Bolshevik, and so on. They shed tears over him and insist, as usual, that "this did not surprise them." It's their latest invention. Since they have begun getting kicked in the behind, nothing surprises them. They know everything in advance. Only somehow they aren't able to profit from their clairvoyance. For "reliable and well-informed Berlin circles," Tunis "was no surprise," and more of the same. That they could at least have managed to understand. Because we understand nothing. For us everything always comes as a surprise. When they trick us and sell us out, it will be a surprise. In any case, an unpleasant one. Because we count only on pleasant surprises. For pleasant surprises we are inclined to sacrifice I don't know how many lives and heroics. We are always expecting a miracle. If I were a king (as the *pontifex economicus maximus* Edward Lipiński used to say), I would issue a decree, that from now on the life of every Pole is a treasure and to sacrifice it under any pretext is a crime.[88] We always believe that in politics loyalty pays. Nonsense. I now see that if we had taken the German side from the beginning, we would be in a much stronger position today than as loyal allies. Even with regard to Russia. If someone came to me today inviting me to join a clandestine organization, I would send him packing. Because, what's the point? For Poland? For the Poland that will not be determined by us? We tend to measure everything by standards of "decency," loyalty, and so on, not ordinary business standards. Thinking about this often drives me to outright blasphemous conclusions. Poland has taken over our minds and paralyzes our thinking. Instead of being *Homo sapiens*, we belong to the race of *Homo polacus*, to a race stupe-

fied by the fatherland, to the company of idiots in thrall to morbid patriotism
and nationalism.

July 7, 1943

This evening we saw Louis Verneuil's *Ma Cousine de Varsovie* with Elvire
Popesco at the Bouffes-Parisiennes.[89] Three acts of absolute idiocy. If at least it
had been more determined in its idiocy. But no — the ending aspires to represent
the so-called "struggle between feeling and responsibility," trying to be "psychological." It's difficult even to describe the plot. In brief, it seems more or less that
Lucienne is the wife of Burel, a former banker exhausted by years of work. The
doctor prescribes a treatment — by means of "literature." And so he sits at home,
this buffoon, and writes — "a novel." That's what's supposed to relax him. But her
husband's presence at home interferes with Lucienne's relations with Hubert,
a friend of the family. Burel, moreover, is beginning to "notice" something. At
this point, the couple receive a visit from their beautiful, eccentric cousin from
Warsaw — by the name of Sonia. Warsaw is obviously "over there," far away — in
Russia. So Lucienne decides to push Sonia in her husband's direction and thus
gain the freedom to indulge in hanky-panky with Hubert. But Burel is also no
fool. On his side he wants to make use of Sonia as well — and how! He therefore
pushes her toward Hubert, so as not to have to share his wife with this friend.
And Sonia "struggles" to decide which side to take in this "conflict," and so on.

The terrific Elvira Popesco, a stunning Romanian coquette, getting on in
age, who speaks French with an affectedly bad accent, delighting the so-called
ultrarefined local public, is a complete professional and certainly a good actress.
That's hard to deny. Her spirited temperament is engaging. But that's the extent
of it. Sonia — the cousin from Warsaw . . . If this war teaches the French anything else (though it won't), it will teach them a bit of geography. But in this case
as well, my optimism may be carrying me away.

Lola has received a letter from the *patronne* of the inn where she spent last
year's vacation saying they will have a place for us. It's a small village in the *département* of the Sarthe, near Chambellay. I'll probably take a longer holiday
and we'll spend part of the vacation with Robert and his family, part in Joué-
en-Charnie.

July 10, 1943

Between Oryol and Belgorod — massacres. The Americans and the English
have landed in Sicily. How long will they keep playing with this Sicily and when

will it be Italy's turn, time for the first steps in "Festung Europa,"[90] as it's called these days? We are a fortress besieged by Barbarians. How splendid, this mutual accusation of "Barbarism"—capital "B." There's a terrible *"circulus viciosus"* here, as one of my aunts from Wilno used to say on every occasion. On the one hand, people are increasingly losing the desire to be free, demanding ever more insistently to be put in chains, more than ever intent on avoiding any risks (freedom is the riskiest of operations, in personal as well as public life). On the other hand, from morning to night they bellow about freedom. What a madhouse. A man must have a drink, as I'm doing right now (already on the fourth glass of Negrita rum), in order to begin to see more clearly. Man does not want to be free; we all basically don't give a fig for freedom—indeed, from our earliest years. Barely do we grow up a bit than we start dreaming of chains. That's why the vast majority of freedom-lovers get married. Don't look far—that's me. Then the bullshitting about freedom sets in. And in the name of freedom one runs oneself ragged, urgently seeking some idea of liberty. But since there's a complete deficit in this domain and an urgent desire for chains, made of roses, as an example, then boom! one chooses an ideology, usually the most fashionable (*la mode avant tout*[91]) and devotes oneself to it mind, body, and soul. And one takes an oath. Nowadays everyone tends to swear on the old scrap of paper called Communism. Because they must—damn them—believe in something. And if one believes in nothing, one says "Things will get better" and "Every cloud has a silver lining." And what if things don't get better? And if it turns out, to the contrary, that there is no silver lining, but the clouds only get darker? And what about my rum, for example? What then? Then would I have to shoot myself or poison myself with gas *à volonté?* And is the sun worth nothing? Does a green tree also amount to nothing? Isn't the cat purring on my lap enough to live for? Belief is everything, right? I believe in cats and rum and sunshine and green trees and freedom. I want the right to drop dead of starvation, if I don't make it on my own. And to live—for goodness' sake, to live a bit as I please, and not according to some sh—— ideology. Amen. I'm thirsty. "Darby M'Graw—fetch aft the rum," as Captain Flint in Savannah demanded.[92] After which he kicked the bucket. But he'd made the most of life, the utmost.

General Sosnkowski has been appointed commander in chief. Fine. A response was needed, so this is it. Besides, it's the only way out, since one doesn't want to appoint traitors. The Russians right now do not need "statesmen"—they need, as they have always needed, run-of-the-mill traitors. This, in great quantity, the London government cannot provide. So better this way. Since there's nothing else left to be saved, there's at least honor. A certain Mikołajczyk as prime minister, a certain Kwapiński deputy prime minister.[93] My grandmother would have asked, "Whose people are they?" And I would have answered, like Madzia Samozwaniec: "Theirs, grandma, not ours."[94] These will certainly not be from the four and forty.[95] Not even from the one and twenty. Long live rum and olives!

July 20, 1943

Everything's arranged. We're leaving on August 2 for Chambellay. We'll stay a week. From there we'll bicycle to Joué-en-Charnie (about sixty km) and settle into the inn for two weeks. Now I can't think about anything else. At home I'm rushing to finish the model airplane (maddeningly difficult to assemble, but I managed) and awaiting our departure. There'll be a comedy with the tickets. At Gare Montparnasse there are lines more monstrous than even Dante could have imagined in his *Inferno*. There are many things he could not have imagined. Well, I don't know — *connais pas*. How dull life will be, when it will be possible to buy tickets the normal way. What will I "grouch" about then?

July 26, 1943

Holiday . . . I already have the ticket and two window seats reserved. It was an entire undertaking. I note this for the sake of future generations, who will leave on vacation from the terrace of their own homes in their own helicopters or spend their holidays home in bed, sucking "geographical candies" labeled "Miami," "Biarritz" or "Cannes"; sleeping for three weeks, dreaming they are on a beach or on the seaside — according to their doctor's prescription, if they're being pedantic. That's for those of modest means. Only the truly rich will travel for real. Crowding will thus be avoided. But we've not yet reached this point, and the very act of purchasing tickets is so complex that the journey itself seems like a needless appendage. One might in fact complain that after all this trouble one must still board the train, make the trip, change trains, not open the door when the train is in motion, not spit on the floor, and so on.

Tickets must be purchased a week in advance. Thus, the day before yesterday I went to Gare Montparnasse and first took a good look around. The lines in front of the ticket windows were so long that if Paris were not so spread out, the last in line would probably be standing in the suburbs. All Paris is leaving. In a friendly chat with the policeman monitoring the herd — which was in fact peaceful — I determined precisely where the line to the cashier starts to form, in which direction, etc. Next I selected a hotel that would put me closest to the finish line. Now came the battle for the room. This is not a simple business. No

hotel keeper today gives a room to anyone he doesn't know or who was not recommended by one of his acquaintances. Without such a personal reference,
it's better just to find a place under a bridge. This system protects the hotel
keeper against the theft of bed linen, one of the most precious items in the
"New Europe." Someone requests a room, pays fifty francs, and vanishes with
all the linen. Professionals do not neglect the curtains, the tablecloths, and the
rugs. A mere fifty francs easily becomes five thousand. Which is why the unknown customer arouses every *patron's* suspicion.

I entered, and before even saying *bonjour* I smiled — oh, so easily and naively,
a bit shyly, with that "Slavic charm" to which they are so susceptible. Then I
made a long speech, as timid as can be, in exquisite French, replete with the
currently fashionable complaints. After two minutes I felt I had him. A discreetly proffered pack of cigarettes, which I urged him to accept, produced a
warm atmosphere and — a room. We continued to chat of course about the war,
about the sacred question of food, and about which *départements* were best to
visit. Butter, eggs, and meat are the deciding factor today in choosing a summer
holiday destination. Paris goes on holiday in order to eat. We parted as old acquaintances.

Yesterday evening I packed my bag: pajamas, soap, a thermos with coffee,
breakfast, an extra sandwich just in case, a sweater, and a book. No tent, though.
At nine in the evening I went "to check in." If Saint Anthony heroically resisted
all the enticements to which he was subjected during his famous temptation, it
was only because he was not sleeping in a Parisian hotel — and near Gare Montparnasse, moreover. In the desert — no big deal! God, or perhaps Satan, spared
him the test of a night in a hotel near Gare Montparnasse and he became a
saint. Since early morning, I've felt like I'm *"in odore sanctitatis."*

I got a splendid room, furnished with a crimson carpet. A bed as huge as a
Midway aircraft carrier. A bathroom, with a bidet like the pond in the Alham-
bra. Alone in such a room, you feel totally abandoned, unneeded, forgotten . . .
Add to this the meager light of the night lamp, suggestively illuminating the
whole room through a lampshade as diaphanous as a woman's negligée, and
the glimmers in the large mirror (oh, what that mirror must have seen . . .), and
the emptiness becomes hopeless. But no matter.

I got undressed, rolled a fat cigarette and lit up, turned off the light and
opened the window, because the evening was very hot. Heavy, humid Paris heat.
Silence. The lights still shone in several apartment windows, the regular muffled
breathing of the locomotives rose up from the train yard. And suddenly, from
one of the buildings across the way, from one of the darkened windows, a muffled woman's cry resounded in the stuffy courtyard. That special cry. I suddenly
felt like a wolf and pricked up my ears. Silence — then, even more subdued, the

same moan. A signal. In the next room, quiet until now, the furniture began to knock about. Followed by some flailing and a prolonged woman's laugh, a laugh squelched by a kiss. The laugh, through clenched teeth, of the female of the species. Again the knocking of furniture. Silence. Then from the other side of the wall next to my bed, a different sound reached me. The monotonous, regular, almost mechanical squeaking of a bed. One minute, two, three— I glanced at my watch hand shining in the darkness—and on it goes. It's getting tiresome, boring, and hopeless. "He's some kind of Stakhanovite," I think, keeping time. Well—finally, brother! I'd worked up a sweat. A deadly silence has fallen, they're bound to bring a stretcher any minute. Meanwhile, on the opposite side, they're stomping around. The rustle and patter of bare feet. The delicate steps of a nymph and the long bounds of a satyr. Laughter, pearly and resonant. The sound of glass and the pop of an opening champagne bottle. Pulled from an ice bucket, the bottle rubs sensuously against the ice cubes. I feel a monstrous thirst and would give anything for a tall *flûte* of champagne, cold and *sec*. Something is biting me. I turn on the light and am hit almost smack in the face by—a swarm of fleas. The champagne of Parisian beds. They burst out on all sides, deft and nimble. I catch one. I turn out the light and silence falls. Suddenly, shrill, piercing, and sharp—"Ow!" . . . "Obviously," I think, "an old trick—he must have stuck an ice cube in the bed under her active parts." He laughs hoarsely and crudely. Now she laughs, too. The customer is always right. I light another cigarette.

The quiet of the sleeping courtyard is suddenly rent by the sound of the radio: "With this we end the sixth news edition of British radio in the Polish language—you will hear us again at one fifteen a.m. Central European Time." For a moment I don't know where I am. A few muted knocks, repeated four times, resound in the courtyard. London. The Polish journal ended at eleven fifteen. A stentorian voice says: *"Ici Londres . . . voici notre . . ."* The French bulletin comes on the tail of the Polish, and begins before it's done. I hear again: *". . . Russie. Les troupes russes, après avoir brisé la résistance allemande dans le secteur nord de Bielogrod, avancent sur . . ."*[96] They are always advancing.

I slept badly. Until late at night I kept hearing all possible Allied bulletins from London. Someone across the courtyard had the volume turned up. Clearly, a case of occupation melancholy. Toward morning I was wrenched from my troubled half-sleep by the cock's crow. Suspended in a cage near a window, the symbol of France was announcing the dawn. I expected to hear the mooing of a cow somewhere, but no. In the Paris of the fourth year of the New Era everything is possible. In the center of the city people are raising rabbits, ducks, turkeys, chickens, and geese, and the chase after fleeing poultry is not an unusual sight, even on the grand boulevards. Goats are transported on the metro; potatoes are weighed on the automatic scales of the underground commuter stations. The smaller hotels post notices: "Raising poultry in the rooms is forbidden." As in the days of Boileau and the Roi-Soleil.

I doze. The alarm rings. I'm nervous. Will I make it to the ticket window before five? I drink my coffee, roll a cigarette, and at twenty to five slip out of the hotel. I scooted across the street and kept close to the wall. Two policemen arrived on bicycles but didn't notice me. There's no joking with the curfew. Quietly and slowly I reached the place where the line began to form — and I was not the first one. I was already merely the twelfth. Those ahead of me were professionals. Sleeping somewhere inside the station, in spots known only to themselves, among the baggage carts, in some nook. They make a living this way, getting 150 to 200 francs for a ticket. If one calculates three tickets a day, they earn 20,000 francs a month, or as much as the director of a large factory, plus the whole day free. Because the ticket windows open at seven in the morning and whoever is first can already go home by eight. It's one of the most demoralizing consequences of the war. How will the hundreds of thousands of people who today earn large sums of money like this manage after the war to work and earn a living the normal way? How to cure this generation of the habit of wheeling and dealing and of relying on under-the-counter profits, on the considerable sums of money that "fall from the sky"?

These people are talking business. Which branches have the most traffic, that the nights are chilly. One of them begins a discussion about how much he should take in exchange for his hideout, "since I also intend to buy myself a vacation. Then I'll play the fat bourgeois and you, François, can stand in line to buy my ticket." Laughter. Suddenly we were surrounded by several policemen. I glanced at my watch. Five to five. They have the right to a nasty prank. Exactly. The order sounds tough: "Each of you should prepare to pay a fifteen-franc fine and off you go to the police station." *Adieu les vacances*, I thought. The assembled company protests. The policemen laugh and nudge us toward the cashiers. Just a joke. Bursts of laughter and lively conversations with the "authorities." The French complain about their police — fine — but only because they don't know ours. Most policemen here sabotage all official orders designed for the persecution of citizens. Before the "roundups" of Jews, many are warned in advance of the danger, and often when someone is asked for documents on the street and shows a counterfeit ID, the policeman will whisper: "Good fake, *allez-y*" — smiles and tells him to get going. Marcel Déat, a pillar of the collaboration, wrote wittily in *L'Oeuvre* that "one is not sure the majority of police are sure, but one is sure a majority are not."[97] There's no greater tribute.

We stand in orderly fashion at the door. Two hours to wait until the ticket windows open. The instant five o'clock sounded, the deep morning silence was broken by knocking and the stamping of feet. The entryways of all the houses around the station banged open all at once, and the contestants took off. One hears the stamping of feet and the clatter of wooden soles—the first already come running in, panting, out of breath. Five minutes later, there are two hundred people standing behind me. Calm will now last until the first metro. In the meantime, the cyclists pull up. The bicycles whirr. It's a race to the finish, from the spot where the bicycles are abandoned. They are thrown to the ground or propped against a wall and the riders hustle to get in line. I'm sure that records in bicycle sprinting are being broken daily.

Then comes the stamping of hundreds of feet. The metro, like an enormous geyser, disgorges a stream of people. The first train. A thick mass, emerging from underground, floods the long ramp. In a few minutes I have a long line of two thousand people behind me. They will wait here until evening. The policemen make the rounds, defusing quarrels and arguing with people who curse them out because they're unable to vent their anger on anyone else. There's obviously no question of reading them the riot act for disrespecting authority. The crowd's anger is well founded: each one was sure he would be "the first" and now cannot understand by what miracle so many can already be ahead of him. The policemen understand this. Better a few curses thrown their way than to have to break up fights . . .

The ticket windows open. The policeman counts off fifteen people and ushers us into the sanctuary. I go to the window for my Paris-Brest line, ask for two good seats (slipping twenty francs into *mademoiselle*'s tiny hand), and immediately receive two window seats along with a pleasant smile, for good measure. It's the same everywhere now. Everyone gives and everyone takes. These aren't bribes. They are *cadeaux*—gifts. They create an intimacy. The relationship between the official and the customer changes instantly into a pleasant familiarity and on the next occasion one is already dealing with a friendly acquaintance.

I leave the cashier and see that the crowd is humming and laughing. The policemen are conversing animatedly with the people. I ask what's going on. I don't believe what I hear. The police on the morning shift have brought the great news, completely unbelievable: Mussolini has resigned!!! And suddenly, amid the laughter and the racket, someone struck up a little song, composed on the spot to the melody of the tarantella: "*le Duce, le Duce a démissionné, Duce, Duce, on aura la paix . . .*"[98] The crowd picked up the words and the melody and seemed to be bursting with joy. All the contempt of a people that has always been free, a people for whom freedom is the essence of life—whatever it may be—infused this scornful little song, mocking the "Caesar of Fascism." There was no hatred in it—only the impression of a completely indescribable contempt. This contempt, which a crowd can have only for a clown who just yesterday they were compelled under threat to consider a God. All the same, clearly no one ever took Mussolini seriously. I'm sure the same news about Hitler would arouse a different reaction. Because Hitler is a clown, but unfortunately a tragic clown, a sinister clown. The crowd was humming and the Germans passing by pretended not to understand. Each one was followed by a thousand jeering glances. I went out in front of the station. I like the square in front of Gare Montparnasse. A sunny morning. I stopped for a glass of white wine. I wanted to sit on the threshold next to the large cat and warm myself in the sun. To sit and observe, just looking around and not thinking. At Dupont's across the way the jukebox was playing and Danielle Darrieux was singing "Premier Rendez-Vous,"[99] colorful girls were flitting along the boulevard on their bicycles, pumping with their slender legs. I took the cat on my lap and bending over whispered in his ear: I have my tickets and Mussolini is gone.

July 29, 1943

At first they wrote that the Duce had stepped down for reasons of health. But in the end it was impossible to conceal that he had been deposed by the Great Fascist Council. The king has taken power, Marshal Badoglio has created a government, and as of today the Fascist Party has been dissolved.[100] People have not really grasped the exceptional significance of this fact. They consider it only from the point of view of strategy. They don't observe the most important thing—one of the greatest ideological bankruptcies the world has ever seen. This is not the collapse of a government like any other *régime*, it's the collapse of the idea that for twenty years dominated Italy and on which practically all the nations of postwar Europe more or less relied, the idea that inspired Germany, Franco's Spain, Turkey, and us—Poland. Its rapid collapse seemed impossible, yet it crumbled in the space of several hours. This day will force all fascists and all believers in whatever "one and only ideology" the world over to examine their consciences. This is simply the collapse of a religion—almost as if the pope had dissolved the Church. The bankruptcy of the idea for which hundreds of thousands of people have perished over the last four years.

How prophetic the words of the great twentieth-century humanist Guglielmo Ferrero sound today. When exiled by fascism, he wrote in his excellent study of 1926, *Entre le passé et l'avenir*, that while all the proper monarchies had fallen after the last war, "fascism alone, instead of overthrowing the monarchy, took it prisoner, forcing it to assume absolute power in the hope of being able to make use of it: one day we'll see if they calculated correctly."[101]

Today we see that they calculated badly.

August 2, 1943, L'Etre Clément

I'm lying in bed, a lamp is burning on the night table. The rest of the large room sinks into semidarkness. Against the wall is a black prie-dieu, and over it a crucifix. An enormous Breton armoire with iron fittings. On a small stool in the corner is a Hussar's uniform from the 1890s. The uniform of Madame Bazin's husband. The window is ajar, the night is misty, saturated by the daylong rain. Drops of mist, slowly falling from the trees and from the branches rubbing against the windowpanes, drum on the metal window frames. In the garden and in the forest behind the river owls are laughing. Somewhere a ripe pear has fallen and plopped on the ground.

In this house, in this room, amid the quiet and monotonous tapping of the drops, all of today seems like a distant memory. Early this morning we set out from Paris. A couple of hours on bicycle, supper in the dining room, the drawing room, the vestibule with ancient weapons, Madame Bazin—everything has become a dream, in which reality is hard to recall. I'm overcome with lethargy. I listen to the drops of mist, I gaze around the room, at the photographs of women in crinolines and men in the uniforms of those bygone days.

The train left at nine o'clock. Naturally, the station was crammed, but we fortunately made our way through all the obstacles. Inside the train, it was bearable. I go out to buy some of those magazines which are in fact German, though published in French, with the difference that they lie even more than those that are actually German. Returning from the newsstand, I notice that platforms carrying antiaircraft weapons are attached to the rear of all trains heading for the coast. We are traveling under armed guard. Small huts have been constructed on the platforms *für die Mannschaft.*[102] The soldiers are cooking, drying their linens. A Frenchman passes me and asks how I like this traveling circus. I answer that I'd prefer a real circus with real monkeys. We start up. The weather gets worse. After Chartres there's a downpour. In Le Mans it's still pouring. In Sablé the rain has stopped. The day is overcast and warm. I like this kind of weather. We doze. After one o'clock we reach Angers. Basia and I emerge from the station.

A quiet square, deserted streets, the sky covered in gray clouds. *Peace.* The world doesn't seem to exist beyond this town. Paris, the newspapers, the war, the *Wehrmachtsberichte*—all have disappeared. There are streets and alleys, an old bus coughing and wheezing, an empty café with a garden, a small bistro and several inhabitants drinking wine. No sanatorium can calm the most strung-out nerves in less time than the French provinces. Here the remains of that balanced life still persist, here one lives in the hour as it is rung by the old clock, and not a dozen hours or days in advance. In this sameness, this apparently monotonous existence, Time has nevertheless not been driven out and variety has not been extinguished. Nothing here is identical, although everything seems to be the same. Everything is mysteriously intense.

It makes me sad to think that entire continents, such as Russia, the United States, and South America, have all become identical, that a house built on the Atlantic is the same as a house built on the Pacific, that a city on the Dnieper is the same as a city on the Volga. If Americans take their vacations in Europe, it's precisely because it offers them variety, because after a few hours of travel they are indeed *somewhere else*. I'm now, for example, in the square in front of the station in Angers, I'll go through several little towns and arrive at Mme Bazin's. With every passing hour, I'll be in a different place, although French towns, with their gray houses and rows of shutters, all look the same. I'll drink wine made only here, and two weeks later I'll eat butter that tastes different from butter in Brittany or Normandy. Sinclair Lewis's *Main Street*, which I read long ago, begins to echo in my head: "Always, west of Pittsburg, and often, east of it, there is the same lumber yard, the same railroad station, the same Ford garage, the same creamery, the same box-like houses and two-story shops" . . . the same, the same . . . and so on until infinity.[103]

Here I begin to lavish my affection on the narrow alleys with their gutters, the small, uncomfortable houses, and the old furniture. It's foolish to renounce progress, but it's a crime to drool with enthusiasm over a large factory or a four-motor bomber, considering them the height of human ingenuity. One must accept as quite ordinary the fact that man achieves many things, and while assimilating progress, one must at the same time keep it under control . . . Here, on quiet afternoons, one feels the value of Peace and Harmony, which are perhaps outmoded, but also enriching, a value that is underestimated, neglected, and disdained. Drinking my white wine, I plunge into the glass and dissolve. I am Peace.

We fetch our bicycles from the baggage compartment. By some miracle they have arrived whole and undamaged. But that's only because I took half of them with me, dismantling whatever I could in Paris. This is what everyone does these days. Only a very naive person puts his bicycle in with the baggage including its leather saddle, light, chain, and pump. Sitting on the curb, I saddle our steeds.

We cross the city on foot. The streets are cobbled and hilly. Angers is asleep, the inhabitants drift through the streets like gossamer. We keep to the walls and towers of the ruined castle. It rises, black and moss-covered, above the bouquets of chestnut trees. We cross the bridge over the Maine. The sky is gray, there are a few barges and a laundry boat on the leaden river. Women hunched over or kneeling are washing their laundry in the river. The whiteness of the white linen is dazzling against all the shades of lead-gray. A sleepy rain is falling. We put on our rain capes. They are made of stiff oilcloth. We both look like dark-green beetles. We ride along. We pass tiny Avrillé—deserted and ashen. The road is quiet. The wet asphalt shines and it's like riding on a mirror. Occasionally a bicycle whizzes past us, occasionally we pass someone walking along the edge of the road. Going downhill, we feel like we're flying through space. All we hear is the purr of the wheels and the rustle of our capes. The whimpering of birds comes at us from the roadside trees, here and there a fat crow caws raucously, in lazy flight. A frightened rabbit scampers across the road. The sun has emerged from behind the clouds and spreads rusty colors, filtering light through the banks of fog and humidity. The rain has let up. We stop—*we have the time*. We sit by the road and eat our afternoon snack. The smell of wet vegetation. Pear juice runs down our chins. Pears are plentiful this year. A bus passes, weaving strangely. I light my pipe and simply feel good. Infinitely good. Then onward . . . A row of chestnut trees follows the road, bunches of fruit dangle casually from the tangled blackberry bushes. Now there's a large pond and on its banks the château belonging to the Marquis de Charnassé. Sheep and cows are grazing. The water in the pond is smooth and placid. Soon, between two walls of blackberries, we come upon Chambellay and find ourselves in front of Madame Bazin's house. I open the white gate.

The two ladies emerged from the house and greet us. Madame Bazin kisses us on the forehead. We collect our things and enter the dark vestibule. And there, Madame Bazin, with a combination of sophisticated elegance and simple refinement, says: "I was thinking that you and your wife have become accustomed to the view from the windows and to the furniture, so it would give me great pleasure if you again stayed in my room upstairs."

This affected me strangely. A tactfulness completely unheard of today, that "view from the windows"—an insignificant thing, but so subtle, the entire sentence, as though read aloud from Balzac—dislodged me from the present and I recovered a lost time. I gave her a long kiss on the hand and whispered *"merci."* I almost had tears in my eyes. I slowly climbed the stairs and entered the yellow room, to the same view from the windows, to the same furniture. I looked out at the lawn, the garden, the river, and the meadows beyond the river, surrounded by wooded hills. The same view—a year later. I felt at home. In this very view, in this very furniture I had left a piece of myself. I recover it now and converse with the self of last year. Basia has fallen asleep, tired from the journey. In the distance owls are laughing. A large drop of water knocked on the metal window frame and a rustle ran through the black trees. The clock on the church tower has now struck one.

August 4, 1943

This year it's more relaxed here. Perhaps because there are fewer people. They bring us breakfast in bed, then we go downstairs. I don't know what's happening with me, but I have no desire even to speak. I sit somewhere in a corner and silently assemble a small model airplane for the boys. Then I move to another corner, sit and gaze straight ahead. I wander around the house, along the walls hung with old weapons. I enter our room and sit in an armchair, letting images just flow through my head. It feels good. I don't want to and I can't read, I don't want to think or speak. I gaze out the window onto the lawn in front of the house. Basia is sitting on the ground, with her skirt spread out around her, and paints. A group of children sit in silence, heads bent over her drawing. They can sit this way for hours and watch as the pencil runs over the paper, as the colors fill in the drawing. They are quiet and polite—practically spellbound. And in the distance little Philippe is taking a walk, tottering along on his first ramble. From time to time he sits down, looks around, as if continually searching for something he cannot find.

The chill in the room is that of an old house that has not been heated for years. A warm breeze comes in through the windows. The church clock strikes the hour twice, so the people out in the fields can hear it clearly. Toward evening the sky clouds over and long, ash-gray hours set in. Everything here is whiter than in Poland and the word "gray" never occurs to me. I wander around the house and listen to Balzac. He speaks to me in images. When at the ash-gray hour I lean against the old chest of drawers and observe the room with the toilet concealed in the wall, with the crucifix over the prie-dieu, I see a different house—the one on the Loire—La Grande Bretèche.[104] I listen to Doctor Bianchon's short account of the Comtesse de Merret. Am I listening? No. Seeing, rather. The small *cabinet de toilette* in Mme de Merret's bedroom was four foot deep. Through my half-closed eyes, I see her leaning against the fireplace. She has heard him enter. The other one was hidden there inside. The Comte de Merret removes the crucifix from the wall. "I swear," murmur the bloodless lips. "Louder . . . and repeat: I swear before God that there is no one there." And then a wall rising slowly, brick by brick. The door of the little *cabinet* vanishes behind it.

All of this seems real, still living, as though it were only yesterday. I never really know whether the scent of the rooms, people's words, and the views remind me of Balzac or whether he reminds me of them. If all this is him—or else, if he is all of this. It's only at such moments that one feels the existence of a great, limitless One. It's only then that I understand Keyserling's fine observation that what Dante's *Divine Comedy* was for the Middle Ages, Balzac's *Human Comedy* was for the nineteenth century. It is without compare.

I've already seen the mayor. He was so pleasant, placid, and encyclopedic . . . I also saw the priest walking in front of the church reading his breviary with an eye that let nothing around escape him. I said, *"Bonjour, Monsieur le curé,"* and he mumbled back: *"Bonjour, bonjour."* He already knows us, because all Chambellay knows us. "They are all blabbermouths with sharp tongues," as Rosalie said about Vendôme, when speaking with Bianchon. And we also know that the old Comtesse de C., who lives in the little palace, has had it up to here with the housemaid who has worked for her for forty-five years. They will have to separate . . . That will be a subject for conversation. The day after tomorrow the new prefect is supposed to arrive and address the farmers. Yet another new prefect. They're always changing. The government has begun to cooperate so closely with the Germans that no decent man wants to cooperate with the government. In the administration it's a constant merry-go-round.

I enter the drawing room. There are many interesting books there. *Bernadotte, Les Amants de Venise* — the story of George Sand and Alfred de Musset's visit to Venice, and some others as well.[105] I don't have the strength to pick up a single one of them. I prefer to lean out the window and listen to the wind stirring in the black spruce surrounding the house. The quacking of ducks, the squeak of the pump, and the murmur of running water reach me from the nearby farm. Sometimes Robert sits in the drawing room and writes letters. I hide behind the piano and listen to the scratching of the pen on paper. In the absolute quiet around us, the sound is strangely soothing. Listening to someone write — it's funny . . .

August 5, 1943

How long the days are here. Every day here is as long as a week in Paris. Life seems so short that people feel they must cram in as much as possible. For me, the most happens when nothing happens. Every day here is indeed a good piece of life. What is the value of a day in which there's no moment to reflect or to be able not to reflect at all? Life changes us little by little into beings who think only by halves, dealing in scraps like rag collectors of thought. The average intellect of modern man, including my own, rather resembles a shattered mosaic, a strange *puzzle*, impossible to assemble as a whole. The fragments can be dazzling, but the center is missing, the piece from which one can start building the whole. When one doesn't know what to build with one's thoughts, where to begin assembling the puzzle, one tries to escape them.

The thinking of people around here is nothing special, it remains within the modest bounds of the material world, most often focused on money, food, and possessions, but it *does constitute* a whole, which is based on something. And this constancy, this order, "despite everything," can be felt at every turn. The whole atmosphere is permeated above all with individualism. And perhaps this is exactly what has such a soothing effect. Here everyone is a *type*, everyone is someone, represents something. Simply because he's connected to the land, to his house, to his livestock. Here I am beginning to understand the meaning of property and its influence on man's internal formation. A man who has something of his own cannot become a termite, cannot become a wheel in the soulless machine of the collective. If Communism began by abolishing private property, if it turned the peasants into some kind of bureaucrats or state employees, it did so precisely because it sensed the danger and the impossibility of making termites out of people connected in any way to property. If France, despite the industrialization of the nineteenth and twentieth centuries, retained its individualism, it's because everyone *had something*, everyone tried *to have* something, or dreamed of *having* something. Property of any kind, no matter what, strengthens the backbone of individualism. A man who has something does not feel like one of many, but will always be more himself, a unique specimen. Land and its possession are the feeling of *unicité* to the nth degree. All the slogans of the worker-peasant movement therefore strike me as idiotic lies. The worker has nothing in common with the peasants—they are two opposite poles.

If the world today is moving in the direction of ever greater dehumanization, insectification, collectivization—it's because the number of people who possess nothing, who become workers having nothing of their own to sell, besides labor power and their brains, keeps growing. A man without property ceases to be an individual and, although it seems like a paradox, becomes a greater egotist. He turns into what has been dubbed the "average man," the "man on the street," the "unknown soldier" (I would abolish the cult of the *unknown* corpse, so humiliating for mankind), turns into a leaf floating without resistance on every breeze of the latest ideology. His logic becomes the logic of the crowd, which is to say, none at all. Thus, the *type* is dying out, extinction threatens the unique human specimen—inconvenient, sometimes scandalous, but "impermeable" to catchwords, slogans, and idiotic formulas.

The prefect who will speak here tomorrow will encounter, not a crowd, but an assembly of people, each of whom will be thinking in his own individual way and will not be taken in by empty phrases. Three-quarters of the words, formulas, and unproven "absolute" truths (the special quality of absolute ideological truths—and their strength)—will come to grief against the house, the livestock, the revenue, the *property*. The extremism of the so-called progressive social and political ideologies really appeals only to those who have nothing. Every revo-

lution therefore begins with the revolution of the masses who have no attach-
ments, who own nothing, who are anonymous. But their devotion always conceals the desire to possess. Communism will one day go to hell, if only because
it has given nothing, even taken away what people still had, even the illusion
of possession. It will someday fall apart under the pressure of the masses, who
will want *to have something*, it will be devoured by its own children. And the
greater the number of people deprived of property, of something they can call
their own, the more likely massacres will be to succeed, the easier it will be
to die for any old slogan, for any old ideology touted by some "prophet." The
socialized world will give rise to many more conflicts, much greater mayhem,
than any other. Ideological colonialism will be much bloodier than the old-style
economic type, which had at least the advantage of being wrapped in very thin
ideological tissue paper. Russia will soon obtain colonies in Central Europe. But
this will not be colonialism, this will be "the triumphal march of progressive ideology." The first bars of this march can already be heard in every bulletin from
Moscow. There's also a nightmarish nationalism, the seductive casing in which
the bitter pill will be administered. There's plenty of territory—you have only to
look at the map of the world. Entire continents are open, continents that have
not yet gone through the scarlet fever of puerile nationalism. I do not rejoice, I
do not applaud. The end of this war, as it is beginning to appear, will not solve
anything and will only increase existing tensions. But everything will unfold
smoothly, because Russia has in its possession the best sedative—a "great ideology." And this war, instead of being the death knell of all ideologies, is already
at this moment providing ammunition for another one, just as totalitarian, just
as ruthless, and even more "exotic" (from the perspective of Christian civilization) than Nazism or fascism.

A heavy, two-wheeled cart, drawn by three horses, harnessed single file,
passed along the road. Everyone who encounters it says "good day," exchanges a
few words with the farmer trudging along next to it in his heavy wooden shoes.
Everyone knows him and he knows everyone. He is someone, represents something. He is not lost in the mass and there is no one else here exactly like him.
When tomorrow the prefect displays before him the colorful array of propaganda formulas now in fashion (there is the same fashion for ideologies as for
women's hats, only alas the fashion in ideology is always more costly than the
fashion in hats), his thinking will be *his own* thinking, shaped by the style of
thinking established by ancestors who have lived here for ages. His thinking
will be the further extension of thinking begun already long ago. It will be aus-
tere and knotty, but will have something to rest on. Except that the number of
people deprived of any points of reference is continually growing. The average

man has nothing, possesses nothing. He has lost any feeling for his past or memory of it. His thinking cannot be the "further extension" of anything because he doesn't consider himself a "continuation." He is anonymous, conceived out of nothing, rootless, subject to every ideological gust, every breeze and gale let loose ever more skillfully and perfidiously. The average man has lost his *autonomy* in every aspect of life. Having lost his physical freedom and continuing to lose it even further, he is losing his internal freedom, the last bastion of humanity. And in fact he doesn't want it. Today the average man *does not want* freedom. That's why it's so easy for him to stick his neck under every new yoke. Having nothing, he feels threatened at every turn. With no past, he fears both the present and the future. This fear grows with every passing decade. For the mirage of a safe future, for the illusion of the ideological present, he enthusiastically exchanges his freedom—a thing without value, when in fact you don't really own anything. The masses today yearn to be in chains, they are blind, ready at any moment to give up the worthless remnants of their property—in exchange for promises and the noose. And they will get them. In the near and distant future, neither will be wanting.

I am lying in a deckchair and setting off fireworks. But these fireworks can often set me on fire. I'm torturing myself. The sparrows dive from the high pines into the fruit trees and peck at the pears. Truths are farther away than we're led to believe. I don't know why, but it occurred to me just now that if I were asked to name the female character I love most in all the books I've ever read, I would answer without hesitation: "Lena from Conrad's *Victory*."[106] Thinking about it all, I increasingly ask myself the insoluble question, whether I am not indeed Heyst.

August 6, 1943

Michel calls us to lunch. He makes the rounds of the house, ringing the cow's bell. We come downstairs and stand behind our chairs. The children sing a short prayer horribly out of tune. Madame Bazin sits down—all follow her. Conversation begins, always somewhat disjointed. Yesterday the Russians took Oryol, the English finally managed to take Catania, the Americans have Munda. Clearly, no one believes the war will end this year. Now that Robert is director of a large factory in N., he has come in contact with the Germans for the first time and tells me about them. It sounds like a blind person describing colors. I don't think any Frenchman is capable of grasping the psychology of another people. They're like poor radio receivers—that pick up only a single station: the National Radio. Thus, after lunch, as we sit in the corner of the drawing room over coffee and a cigar, I usually give him short lectures. He listens carefully and, like every Frenchman, is moved by a certain admiration, or perhaps rather, respect, for intellect. And—like every Frenchman—he picks up only the strictly rational components. It's curious that a nation with such talent for analysis understands nothing about psychology or psychoanalysis. It seems to me a big mistake to claim that the French invented the "psychological novel." These are analytical novels—a kind of inorganic chemistry in literature. Only Balzac has gone farther, beyond the limits of cold, precise dissection—and to this day he is misunderstood. The world admires him for qualities that France does not understand at all. A foreign admirer of Balzac and a French devotee of this nineteenth-century Freud have little chance of understanding each other, no matter how long they try. The French admire him for everything he *said*—we are inclined to stress everything he did not say, but which is so wonderfully conveyed. A dialogue about Balzac resembles train tracks that run parallel toward the same goal but never meet. In general, conversations with the French remind me of train tracks: I have the impression they understand me, but it turns out that they are only running *parallel*. When it comes to people, they are masters of inorganic chemistry, but organic chemistry eludes them. This irrational rationalism dazes them with its clarity.

Between one sip of coffee and the next, while inhaling a strong cigar, I try to adapt to this mode in our conversations. I turn up the flame, in order to break through the darkness of clarity and reach the remotest corner of the soul, which is true understanding. This is an excellent exercise for me, all the more so because French *esprit* is not a mysterious jewelry box: it is usually opened, not with spells or black magic, but with one push on a hidden button. The button is always concealed in the choice of words that arouse a Frenchman's high spirits or emotionality. It's easiest to get through to a Frenchman via his spiritedness—with sparks of wit. When I discuss the Germans with reference to Keyserling's excellent analysis of the embryonic state of the German character; when I discuss their cult of power, emerging from the deep conviction of their own internal weakness and pliability; when I mention the nationalism of a people that values nationalism so highly because it so easily loses its national identity and submits to foreign influence; when I mention overcompensation—we do not understand each other. But when I mentioned the title of an article about the Germans by Emil Ludwig, when I said "bandits and musicians," the jewelry box opened.[107] The title was the spark. I had no difficulty explaining Ludwig's thesis, that someone who listens intently to Beethoven's *Ninth Symphony* in the evening, the next morning will retain little of what is called "the noble feelings." In the morning he remains a bandit—a free, unconstrained hoodlum. "*Vous comprenez, la* Neuvième Symphonie *constitue un dérivatif pour tous les instincts nobles et généreux. Restent le bandit et l'assassin.*"[108]

We get up to go. As we part, I hear Robert muttering to himself with a laugh: "*Bandits et musiciens.*" I had found the hidden button. Three words—and personal contact. When I told him about the Germans three years ago, he didn't want to believe me.

In the afternoon we go to the river to bathe. I'm teaching little Michel to swim. The elder one, Jacques, has begun to show symptoms of "pure intellect"—he's afraid of the water and of physical exertion. He's in danger of becoming one of the many intellectual orchids. I'm sorry for the boy. How grateful I am to my father, though sometimes brutal in his methods, for developing my body in the image and likeness of a man. Now I swim as well and easily as I think. I think with my entire self. I cannot, by contrast, bear pure intellectuals, whom I loathe. They are so often inhuman. They are either hard as rock or slimy as reptiles. I jump off the bridge and swim alongside Basia. We have fun—conversing in glances and smiles.

August 7, 1943

The day after tomorrow, we're moving on. A grand ramble along quiet roads, through quiet little towns. No watch, no time . . .

Evening. Overcast and warm. The dusk fell slowly. The trees, the hedgerows, the castle were flattened. Silhouettes. The harvest has long since been gathered and the stubble has already turned gray. Every field, large and small, is surrounded by a square hedgerow, out of which rise strangely bent and twisted wild pear and apple trees, amputated yearly for firewood. In the oxidized dusk they looked like figures. We sat down by the road. It was so quiet that a beetle in flight whirred like an airplane motor. A falling leaf knocked against a branch. The air was still and not even the fine grass shook. We spoke in a whisper. The darker it got, the more the beetles whirred.

From time to time a bat plunged silently and dropped in its velvety flight below the dark crowns of the trees. And in the small field opposite, a rabbit rolled around. It rolled like an egg, higher, lower . . . Stopped and listened. Two others ran out of the hedgerow to join it. They ate the grains of wheat left on the ground. After a while more showed up. Others kept arriving and the field turned into a great dining hall. They jumped about, rolled around, and froze in place.

I was sure they were talking, laughing, and dancing. We became children, watching them. We kept looking for something else among the rabbits . . . Perhaps the fairy who had cast a silent spell on this corner of the world, perhaps little elves or dwarfs in red bonnets . . .

August 8, 1943

Sunday. Morning Mass in the church. Excellent sermon. The parish priest, from an aristocratic Spanish family, has the culture I always envy when I encounter French clergy. A courageous and powerful sermon, distinctly antitotalitarian. His superb style, precision, and ability to mention so many things without calling them by their names transfixed not only me but the entire audience. First he touched on the visions of a certain young woman and what the Virgin Mary said to her. This was still before the war. It must be admitted that these visions not infrequently came to pass. But much could have been foreseen without the Virgin Mary, and today all the more so. The world's intoxication with Communism facilitates prophecies greatly. Ideologies are the very latest intoxicants, for which there are no antidotes.

Afterward, I listen to the radio—Strauss waltzes. I wondered whether all the discoveries in the realm of telecommunication in fact enrich our lives. They seem to do so, but all they add in fact is variety. This strikes me now, in particular, after the deep shock of this morning's sermon. I see most clearly the paradox of our time: the more technology facilitates human contact, bringing continents and individual people closer together, continually improving the means of long-distance communication, the weaker this communication becomes, the more alien people seem to each other. Personal contact—the only enriching and fertile kind—disappears from life. Today, it's the Thing, the object, that inserts itself at every turn between man and man. Whole continents are connected, but the sense of estrangement grows, man himself becomes an object. The *person*, the subject, disappears.

Contemporary literature is beginning to suffer chronically from the absence of Types and resorts to action in which the same people are always involved. The psychological conflicts of contemporary man increasingly boil down to sexual conflicts, which are unmanageable for him because he has nowhere to look for answers to questions about the instincts, about blind forces. The contemporary novel, with few exceptions, is exhaustingly monotonous, soon forgotten, leaving no trace. This phenomenon appears in all fields of art, which tends increasingly to employ "mechanical" devices to achieve its effects on man. Literature, music, painting all operate today by means of shocks. It's a kind of electrotherapy or injection of curare. Instead of addressing the noblest layers of the human soul, they try above all to play on the nerves. When I visit an exhibit of contemporary painting, when I listen to contemporary music, I always feel as if I've received an electric shock. Whereas here, the walls of this house, the words spoken by people who still retain their individuality, emanate an amazing warmth. In the afternoon, I went to see the mayor to have our identity cards stamped with "*Départ.*" Monsieur C. was again incomparable in his dullness. He belongs to the category of people who pretend to be on a first-name basis with everything—all of science, politics, cosmology, geography—and who solemnly intone such great ideas as, for example, the important fact that great rivers flow by great cities or expound the enlightened view, from the perspective of urban planning, that if cities were built in the countryside, they would have healthier air. Ten minutes of conversation and the smell emanating from the combination of biped and halfwit in one person affected me like the smell of lukewarm sugar water. I feel sick. The Goncourts observed, brilliantly, that this type of man wants to have his portrait hung in the drawing room—in his National Guard uniform, aloft in a hot-air balloon.

We discussed the war. How long would it last? Monsieur C. asserted playfully that although everything suggested that the war was eternal, there was nothing to fear—"even eternity has an end." I said he was *très spirituel.* Overcome with satisfaction, he seemed to be rubbing his short legs hidden under the table. Through the half-open door appeared the *infanta* of the C. family, an overdressed redheaded girl. I naturally addressed a few compliments to this red heifer. Monsieur C. confessed "in confidence," that she was *très intelligente* and was already reading *nos classiques.* Remarkable, no? And that he will soon be arranging for Latin lessons. Clear? Not to speak of music. But, naturally. I remembered that I already knew someone like this—the daughter of the scheming Monsieur Roque in Flaubert's *L'Éducation sentimentale.* Such people marvelously improve themselves by means of their children.

Our last evening. After supper we gathered in Madame Bazin's room. She put out the fortune-telling cards. Everyone laughs and—lets themselves believe just a bit. Robert will be facing many difficulties. In his new position, very high placed but challenging, he will have all too many. Pauline, in the last months of pregnancy, looks terrific. She is one of those women who do not feel like a woman when not expecting a child. This will be their third during the war.

I go up to our room, take a last look at the old weapons and the old engravings on the walls, listen to the creak of the stairs.

August 10, 1943

We're at the inn Under the White Horse. But everyone says the Hôtel du Cheval Blanc. It sounds better and gives the owners more status.

Yesterday morning we packed our bags and were accompanied by Robert and the boys to the nearest village, where we set out on our own. A deserted road, morning fog, and complete quiet. Larks danced in the delicate mists above the fields, suspended in the air as though on the thinnest string. The sound of wings flapping as the crows fly low overhead, and far ahead of us a rabbit has run across the road. These are the moments I always try to capture, in which I often seem actually to experience the ineffable *now*. Time. I'm reminded of Saint Augustine's *Confessions*. Time is the past, the present, and the future. There is no more past, it is gone—the future has not yet arrived, and the present, dissolving in both the past and the present, is intangible. In fact there are three tenses: the present of things past, of things present, of things future. Riding along the quiet road, immersed in a strange plenitude, I'm especially aware of the great fiction of time, the intangibility of the present. Everything in man is either in the past or in the future. The present is experienced *through* those two times. There are, however, moments in which there exists only what is—moments too fleeting to be measured, but nevertheless splendid, because replete. Only the feeling of complete plentitude makes it possible to capture this *now*. But in such moments time itself disappears, ceases to be. And perhaps this absence of time, this complete detachment from the mathematical nature of time, is what is filling us both with something entirely indescribable, something very, very rich.

Hundreds of meters disappear behind us, the watch hands move forward, but I'm still in one place. I run my eyes over the stubble, the meadows, the clumps of trees, and follow the vanishing road. I'm filled with a great silence. Can one say one has "traveled," when one covers hundreds of kilometers in only a few hours, stopping—or not stopping—here and there? I am convinced that having ridden my bicycle from Angers to Le Mans, I will have a greater right and better reasons to claim to have taken a real journey than a person who has gone from Paris to Saigon in three days. Which of us has experienced more? My journey offers me experience, as I slowly reach my destination. The goal fades, no longer a thing in itself, the distance is no longer an enemy but a friend with whom one engages in an enriching and fulfilling conversation. It's like those puzzles on the first page, with answers on the last. To hop from Paris to Saigon is to glance at the puzzle, and without even giving it a try, go directly to the ready answer. This system is not enriching, does not expand, does not demand reflection. Man then becomes a creature most resembling a flea, as Keyserling says. No flea would hop gaily, without misjudging its landing point, if while hopping it had also to devote itself to cultivating its interior life. What makes man unique is his openness to the world (Max Scheler's *Das weltoffene Tier*[109]). But how to maintain one's openness to the world, without being able to observe anything except what can be noticed when speeding at five hundred km an hour? Man shuts himself in and becomes a flea.

This world here, the farms, with their roadside dung heaps, that we pass slowly by, the great, two-wheeled carts—everything is full of warmth. Sablé is swarming with vacationers. Paris has taken up residence for two months. Elegant, casual attire, as though on the Riviera. All the people hang around, bored, but stay for the food. Food is the only entertainment in this provincial town, which has—O horror!—only one cinema. There are many nouveaux riches. They immediately stand out. They are not dressed—they are *overdressed*. We eat lunch. At noon it's sultry and stifling. We continue on our way. After a while, we enter Joué.[110] A church, a square, a road lined by two rows of houses. We stop at the inn. A single day of rambling has "demoralized" us completely. Inside the inn, we feel uncomfortable. The room is tiny and cramped, with a view onto the square in front of the church.

Before supper we washed in the deep basin known here as a *cuvette* and went downstairs. At our table, besides Lola and Janka, were the innkeepers, a young man, and a married couple, dentists from Paris, with a hysterical five-year-old daughter. After the dining room in Chambellay, after the pure and beautiful French language, as beautiful as only true French can be, when spoken by people who know how to use it, here we felt the difference. It's awful, how badly most of the French speak French. In any case, in Poland dentists did not speak *like this*. By contrast, the food was fantastic. Pâté, tomatoes with sour cream, salad, cake, and black coffee. I can scarcely breathe.

August 11, 1943

We are slowly getting used to things. I visited the mayor to get the stamp of "Arrival." This mayor runs a general store. Something like the Galeries Lafayette in a town with seven hundred inhabitants. All important administrative questions are resolved in the store. The mayor is old and amiable. Usually he gives the impression of being good-natured and a bit simple-minded. But on special occasions, he assumes quite a different expression, which reveals the profound intelligence of an ordinary man, ennobled by time.

After entering the date under the rubric "Arrival," he pulled from his pocket a carefully wrapped stamp and pressed it over his signature. I was touched to observe that it was still the old stamp of the Republic, with a seated Marianne, her arm resting on something and something wrapped around her head. I observed that it was nice to see the traditional symbol, nowadays replaced by Pétain's "*Francisque*," which is to say, a two-edged ax in a bundle of sticks, obviously those carried by lictors in Roman times (young, strong, vital, like concentration camps, hit squads, militias). At this, the old mayor smiled slyly and admitted under his breath: "That's why I always keep it on me, so it can't be taken away. I will never change the stamp—*je suis républicain, monsieur.*"[111] Such people will be unaffected by *Bekanntmachungen*,[112] orders, statutes, and new, totalitarian slogans. The Republic, with its freedom of the individual and respect for human rights, runs in the blood of old citizens such as these. The Declaration of the Rights of Man and Citizen, freedom, and the Republic are tangible, material, like banknotes, wine, and bread. But today, when the German renaissance of the Third Reich, as propagated by Vichy, penetrates ever deeper into the organism of France and rejuvenates it by means of denunciations, prisons, punishments, and concentration camps, the number of such people in official positions keeps shrinking. They are replaced by petty traitors with new stamps. Two-edged, like that ax . . .

But it's not only the mayor—practically the entire population around here is "anti-." The *only* citizen who ever refused to accept his ration cards, since become famous throughout France, hailed from this region. He said that neither his grandfather nor his father had used "anything like this" (*de ça*) and therefore he, too, would say no thank you to "that" (*pour ça*). The land he owned and worked would support him without "that" (*sans ça*). This is also where a certain solitary old peasant, who said he would not work his land for the Germans, left home, and hires himself out to others, repairing shoes, stoves, and harnesses. His land is being run by the state, but the old man is perfectly happy. These people exude something different, something invigorating, because they have managed to remain themselves. They have resisted all those regulations that are supposed to better organizzze us, immunizzze us, strengggthen us, unify and rejuvenate us, introduce a new order and make us happy now and in the hour of our death—Amen. Damn!

There are moments when I'm seized by extreme anarchism—an anarchism not even dreamt of by those who wave banners demanding, "Death to Everyone!"

This is anarchism to the point of hysteria, almost to insanity. I would be capable of refined murder. Today I understand why the unemployed cook's helper decapitated the commandant of the Bastille, de Launay, with his penknife, in cold blood.[113] He decapitated, not a person, but the Bastille, the *system*. The atrocities of the Revolution were atrocities committed against the system and the people who incarnated it. Murder and brutality were directed at the system *through* people. The people in themselves did not count, they aroused no pity, because they were murdered *en passant*—while the murderer looked past them, listening not to the victims' groans but only to the creaking of the system's joints. When it is not people who are being murdered but the *thing* they represent, there can be no question of pity. Man becomes blind, deaf, insensitive— he becomes as objective and dry as the *system and organization* he's toppling at a given moment. And so this first savage reflex, monstrous in its consequences, is basically innocent. It is not a crime. Crime begins when murder and violence turn into *systems* and *organizations*, when they are planned. Revolutions are not cruel when driven by instincts that are uncoordinated and basically healthy, the instincts of the masses who "have had enough." The unemployed cook's helper beheading de Launay with a dull penknife was not a criminal—he had had enough and the others had had enough. The Russian peasant disemboweling the Volga River magnate had simply had enough. They were not criminals. These the Lord will not set on the left on Judgment Day and they will find a place among the righteous, though the blood of innocents will still be dripping from their hands. But Marat, Robespierre, Dzierżyński, Stalin, Himmler, and Hitler, though none may have killed a man with his own hands, are the most horrible of criminals. Because they transformed blind murder into a system, because they reduced a great and invigorating flame to a "low heat," because they routinized the outburst, because they besmirched the sanctity of crime. The greatest crime is to besmirch crime. There are certain grand and noble exceptions that cannot be made into rules. Crime is among them.

Today, only *today* do I understand the bloodthirstiness of people "who have had enough," do I *truly* understand the cook's helper at the Bastille—and I envy him. I envy him and I understand him, at those moments when I have to write a letter and cannot find white paper in the mayor's shop, but only lined paper— so I rip a few sheets from this notebook and write my letters on them. Because my hysterical anarchism, which may be stupid, but has gotten the better of me, considers writing on lined paper a limitation on my individuality—on my person. I understand it, when I make the rounds of the Parisian town halls and see how, with each passing week and month, the mountain of card files, annotations, information, and questionnaires, both secret and public, keeps growing. When each of us figures not as an individual but as a number, and when we are treated like file cards, as more important than the person, than I am, than the great *exception*, that, being a *man*, I am in nature. When I accompany workers destined for deportation to be examined by the medical commissions that, with a quick glance, dispatch them like cattle to the slaughter. When I think of the millions of people behind barbed wire and in prison cells, and when I'm afraid to *imagine* what's going on there—I understand the cook's helper at the Bastille and I understand the point at which a man can be tempted to reach into his pocket—for a matchbox or a dull penknife.

Here I relax. Breakfast in the room, dress is casual. A shirt, linen trousers, and espadrilles. We go out into the fields, taking a book, not intending to read it. The area is hilly. Among the hills there are small country roads. Large meadows surrounded by hedgerows. Cows and sheep graze.

August 12, 1943

Our table has been enriched by another person, who constitutes its ornament. The Comte de R., who until yesterday had been suffering from the *maladie de vacances*, which is to say, indigestion, appeared today for the first time since our arrival. We had learned of him from stories told by the other guests. I took to him right away, and by dessert we were talking freely. Nothing may be more agreeable than establishing a relationship in the course of conversation that moves quickly upward in short spirals. The Count is tall and handsome, in his forties, a typical specimen of the French aristocracy, perhaps not profound, but nevertheless interesting and charming. Characters of this kind display superb technique, sophistication, and freedom. Absolute ease moving in any situation, in every role. An excellent talent for what could be called "sketching," an absolutely inimitable talent. A subtle wit and ease. An appealing lack of "seriousness"—the "seriousness" of people who live their lives from A to Z, and even when they get to the end of the alphabet are unable to forget its beginning.

The Comte de R. began life at the letter "P"—which explains the purity of his vision, his unrealistic view of the lower orders and childishly naive opinion of his social inferiors. The Count is a democrat and a devotee of the peasants. Such absolute democratism and idealization of the peasantry, such exorbitant belief in the perfection and advantages of the common folk, can be found only among aristocrats, twenty-year-old young men (and not in our day), and idealists prone to intellectual abstraction. Except that this idealism, which usually appears in the form of the dry, pitiless idealism of Robespierre, in his case is sunny, heartfelt, and sentimental. His ideas about the ennobling influence of nature are drawn directly from the ideology of Jean-Jacques Rousseau, and he considers the only acceptable sociologist to be Charles Fourier and his phalansteries. He is heir to that branch of the French aristocracy that instigated the Revolution and even when standing before the guillotine smiled and continued to believe in the *bonté innée du peuple*.[114] Therefore, although his opinions are extreme, they are not provocative. It's the equivalent of stamp collecting—a harmless obsession. One senses right away that if he had the chance to put his ideas into practice on a grand scale, he would not, thank God, be able to do so. His great innate culture would be a natural restraint. People like these make clear why fascism draws its gun at the word "culture," why they and the Communists wipe out anyone who betrays authentic traces of culture. Because these ideologies know that people like this are not useful to them. Incapable of extremism, of decisive action taken to the edge, they elude all totalitarianisms, black, brown, or red, and *infect* other people.

Culture, according to the Frenchman, is an equilibrium. The Comte de R., despite his Fourierism and belief in the goodness of the people, is well balanced. His philo-peasantism and his democratism are nevertheless a mania, which is condemned and used by his family, to its own advantage. It considers him out of his mind and tries, by means of this ploy, to deprive him of the inheritance. The inheritance is the local château—*cum woodis et forestis*. The Count now lives in Joué near this castle, close enough to impede the plans of his brother, who wants to inherit the castle entirely for himself. The château is under seal, the income from the tenant farmers goes to a notary, no one benefits, and the legal proceedings continue. As former military attaché to the French embassies in Vienna and London, the Count now lives on a modest pension. His brother, a wealthy industrialist, has the time to prolong the contest over the inheritance, in order to compel the democrat to renounce his rights. Such people remind me instantly of the perfectly apt comment by Antoine de Rivarol: "Some people gain nothing from their fortunes but the fear of losing them."[115] The Count and his brother at present indeed have nothing else. What's worse, others get nothing out of it, either . . . These stories of inheritance in France can be entirely medieval.

Over a delicious cake with whipped cream, we discuss current affairs, jumping from topic to topic. Man? If today man seems to have little value, it's first of all because he has forgotten his own real worth, because he thinks he amounts to nothing in spiritual terms and has lost the sense of his uniqueness, whoever he may be. The consequence has been the internal devaluation and depreciation of man in man. Only this could have led to what fifty years ago seemed to us impossible.

Rapidly exchanging thoughts, often in shorthand, we outline the situation, defining the position in which we have found ourselves. We've been taught to take everything literally, discouraged from thinking "with tolerance." We've been taught to attach importance to words, not to *meaning*. We've forgotten how to search for meaning, using words to obscure the traces of reasonable inquiry. The entire twentieth century did nothing but teach people to attach importance to the words uttered by important minds with a greater or lesser sense of responsibility. We foundered in obscure scholasticism, which has led to perhaps the greatest paradox of our time: a generation, raised in the cult of reality, that has entirely lost the sense of reality. Today's man is in most cases a barograph. Like the barograph, which registers changes in pressure, without knowing or understanding the significance of what it reports, man registers reality without really grasping what's going on. He registers reality in the form of fear, suffering, hopelessness, passing relief, and surges of hope. But the arc of these changes is only the result, not the reality, not its essence or meaning.

Vous savez, Sainte-Beuve somewhere said: "*Il faut subir son temps pour agir sur lui.*"[116] One must bear (like pain, like suffering) one's era in order to act upon it. But not in one's sleep, not under narcosis. Some operations cannot be performed with anesthesia, even local. One cannot perform surgery on our era, using the anesthesia of optimism and idealism—of *uniqueness.* Because the issue increasingly concerns not so much the rights of man but man himself.

We are alone. On the wall the clock is ticking, the clatter of dishes being washed comes from the kitchen. There are conversations that, despite their somber conclusions, are invigorating. There are people nowadays, and there will be others in times to come, who may succeed in salvaging what remains of what until very recently was indisputably the greatest achievement of mankind: freedom of thought, independence of mind.

On the wall the clock is ticking. "Minds are waking up—how good it is to be alive," wrote Ulrich von Hutten four centuries ago.[117] Do you catch the scent of these words? They contain everything.

August 13, 1943

An interesting book on the influence of the Chinese language and literature on Chinese thought. It turns out, in effect, that the Chinese language and its grammar are much more logical than the grammar of Western civilizations. The addition of endings for the plural and the feminine gender is illogical. For example, *trois femmes fardées.* If the number "three" is indicated, the ending "s" is superfluous, because we know there are three women, and not one. And since the subject is women, the addition of the feminine ending "e"—the second "e"—is unnecessary, because we know that it's not about men. When we say "three wo*man* with makeup" we know everything and basically do not distort the meaning. The word and its concept, what it conveys, become more stable. Further consequences follow. Most basically, Western languages, by virtue of their plasticity and the ability to twist certain words and—what's worse—attach them to ideas they don't perfectly match, are more abstract and less apt for the expression of *exact* ideas. In expressing ideas, all Western languages run the danger quite simply of *missing the target*, especially when it comes to abstractions, because each one of our words has a large margin on both sides. That's why it's not surprising that when it comes to abstract thinking and abstract ideas, the same written text can be interpreted in endless ways. It's well known that the Bible or the Gospels, not to speak of the Apocalypse, Marx, Engels, Hegel, and Lenin, can be interpreted in a thousand and one ways, that certain great ideas already lend themselves to complete distortion on the level of interpretation, all the more so when put into practice. Such distortions can lead to bloody misunderstandings. The second greatest cause of death on earth results from the misinterpretation of great ideas. The Western languages turn out to be too impoverished to express concepts related to the highest reaches of spirit and reason. That's why all Western thought, including the Western religions, is characterized essentially by a terrible vagueness, especially beyond a certain level. This vagueness leads to multiple interpretations, each of course the "one and only," in the name of which the followers of the same great idea attack each other, as at present in the case of Germany and Russia, both children of the same early nineteenth-century German philosophy. It contains no doctrine of the individual, because Fichte's entire doctrine of the "Self" says nothing about the individual, and becomes completely deadly in Hegel's doctrine of the State. Two impersonal doctrines, two doctrines of the State, developing from the same roots, joined in most ferocious battle. It's remarkable that in the West most bloody conflicts are the result, not of the clash of one idea with another, but of the battle between two interpretations of the same Idea, which was supposed to unite us. I therefore begin to wonder whether our vaunted materialism is not in fact an erroneous interpretation of certain ideas but rather the most convenient and easiest one. Could this materialism in fact be the cause of bloody abstraction? Because we want imperatively to render tangible what by its very nature must remain as it is. By interpreting the Gospels, we feel we are making them more accessible, we feel we are coming closer to Christ. I am nevertheless not sure if we are not then in fact the farthest away from God. The interpretation of Nietzsche's "Superman" has led to the creation of the "Subman," while the interpretation of Marx's thoroughly materialistic doctrine has caused its adherents to bog down in a complete abstraction, surrounded by dogmas that prevent them from seeing reality. This sounds like an outright diabolic joke invented by matter itself. I wonder increasingly whether it's not actually this abstraction, which is to say the absolute desire to materialize concepts and ideas that cannot in fact be materialized, that is the main cause of our terrible misunderstandings and whether in that case we are not the acolytes of an insane religion, a hundred times more abstract and esoteric than anything of the sort the East has created. The East never dared attempt to materialize spirit. In this, it may perhaps demonstrate greater realism than we do.

The Chinese ideograms, which is to say words that express exactly what we lack words to express, diminish the possibility of ideological misunderstandings—and fist fights. Things we interpret in different ways and on which we are unable to agree, thus leading us to "impose an understanding" on each other in a purely external and painful manner, the Chinese materialize in words that enable them to move more freely in certain areas of thought and thereby avoid conflicts or limit them to struggles within clearly defined spheres. Obviously, this strict, exclusive, and unique meaning of words places the "limitations" on thought that we are accustomed to calling "typically Chinese." This exact and precise language has generated the equilibrium of Chinese thought and its "ossification"—a relative concept and appropriate only in contrast to our Western activeness and our apotheosis of action. One thing is certain, namely, that it's easier in Chinese to express MEANING, and that's already significant and spares many misunderstandings. The lack of such precision in words is particularly apparent today, when certain words and concepts linked to them have become so fluid that the same sentences can be uttered on two separate occasions, regardless moreover of the speaker's intellectual standpoint. The West today perhaps best illustrates the parable of the Tower of Babel. In fact, the West has gone farther—marvels occur within the confines of a single language. The same communiqué or commentary, expressed in practically the same words in London and in Moscow, means something completely different. The use of certain words, such as "Freedom," "Justice," "Democracy," and the "Person," has become impossible without miles of commentary, without defining the speaker's intellectual position, his doctrinal adherence, religion, origins, grandfather, father, mom, personal preferences, brand of toothpaste, most frequent dreams, and shoe size. Without such commentary, each of these concepts can represent thousands of different things, millions of freedoms, and billions of laws.

I'm looking for a place to swim. These small rivers that wind among the hills are not for swimming. The innkeeper showed me a small pond on the map, five kilometers from here. In the late afternoon I set out in that direction. After a half-hour's search, I ended up suddenly in another world. The forest road widened into a small hollow, and the large beeches growing around it covered the sky. The days are already getting shorter—here it was almost night. After a while, I came upon a dilapidated mill, asleep at the foot of a high embankment that cut across the hollow. A narrow stream of water dropped from the embankment, vanishing into the ruins of the mill, reemerging calmly and quietly from under the crumbling walls. I mounted the embankment. Enclosed on both sides by wooded hills and nestled against the embankment slept a quiet pond. The sky was ashen, dusk was falling. It was hot and humid, the temperature and smell of a hothouse. In this complete, absolute silence, in this godforsaken place, amid the exuberant and luscious vegetation, I felt as if I had traveled back suddenly several million years to the era of dinosaurs and other Mesozoic monsters. The impression was so strong that for a moment I was convinced that some strange fish *must* exist here that exist nowhere else.

A small, stony beach stretched out on the right side. The stones were reddish, among them many little dry, black cushions with long spikes. A strange aquatic plant cast onto the shore. The water was pinkish. In the middle of the lake something splashed, and from the other end, completely concealed by water lily leaves, came mysterious slurping sounds. Again, in the middle of the pond a fish broke the surface of the water and sliced it silently, like a knife. Bubbles of gas rose from the bottom and burst on the surface. I stood on the bank, absorbed in watching and listening. Everything here was otherworldly. For the first time in France I did not feel like I was in a garden. Despite my strange fear and shivers of repulsion, something drew me toward the water. I stripped off my shorts and shirt. Naked and shivering, I fought with my disgust. The touch of a floating stem shocked me as though I'd touched a snake. I felt a wave of shivers running down my spine. The water had been warmed by the summer sun. I splashed myself and groped to see whether anything was protruding from the bottom and, like a torpedo, swam the crawl to the very middle.

A few seconds, and I was in my element. I swam around the edge of the pond. Only when my foot occasionally reached the ice-cold lower layer of water did I recoil uneasily, feeling again that I was not on this earth. The water, the night, a mysterious charm, the silent trees, the dark clouds, and the heavy air penetrated me so deeply that I felt myself to be a creature, a part of this murky nature. Like the time at Gruissan when I was pulled out to sea by a fishing boat and then detached myself a few kilometers from shore and swam back, alone, for two hours, on that moonlit night, so here I once again felt the primal force of life: the bubbling and pulsing of my blood, the amazing work of my muscles, and every beat of my heart. Each part of my body stopped being just a part and became the whole of me. I lay flat on the water and saw only the dark clouds, flowing slowly and smoothly across the sky. I drank to the dregs the extraordinary pleasure of life. Can one love God any more than in such moments, when one feels oneself "thus" to be His work? The most successful of nature's creations, with the limitless capacity to develop, with so much still to achieve in order to become a Man. In such brief moments, I pray, not in thoughts or in words, but with my whole being. I feel life.

Regaining the shore, I shook off the water like a dog and got dressed. Following the paths through the forests and fields, I returned home. All evening Basia and I discussed Jan Parandowski's *The Olympic Discus*.[118] I have absorbed his humanism practically since childhood. Maybe that's why I feel a bit unhappy in times such as these . . .

August 15, 1943

After lunch we get on our bikes and ride over to the pond and stay there until evening. It's marvelous. Every day we discover something new: a strange aquatic plant, giant ferns, or clusters of blackberries, which we gobble up after a swim. Most often we are alone, but occasionally an old man comes and cuts the sharp grasses near the shore as bedding for his livestock. When the sun drops in the west, half the pond is swallowed in shadow. Silvery green frogs sit on the lily pads and croak or click in the dead silence of the hot afternoon. The sky is pale blue, the water calm and as smooth as a blue mirror on which someone has left the traces of a breath. A delicate mist mutes the colors. We swim together, making the circuit of the pond, and dry ourselves sitting on a large, rose-colored rock. Basia sits under an umbrella. We bought it for fourteen francs in a small shop in a nearby town. Surprised at the low price, we were told by the elderly madame that she's had them on hand since 1912. She even showed us the bill. Then they cost three francs.

The hours are long and calmly follow the movement of the sun—all as it should be. Today is Sunday, but we did not go to church. The parish priest here is Irish by origin. He's called Cunningham. He has preserved an Irishman's hatred for England along with some last drops of blood remaining from those born rebels. The English say the first word an Irishman utters when he enters the world is "no." This priest thinks the Germans deserve support simply because the entire opposite camp is discredited by England being in it. He therefore gives implicitly pro-German sermons, or if not pro-German then certainly anti-Anglo-American. The mayor refuses to greet him and confided to me that *il pourrait être plutôt sultan que prêtre . . .*[119] Moreover, the way the sacristan rings the bells gives one goose bumps and makes one want to gnash one's teeth. Church bells are also an instrument.

We were joined in our excursion to the pond today by Comte de R. He borrowed a bicycle and we rode over together. A splendid fellow. His wit enlivened the entire afternoon. While we swam, he walked along the shore, telling us about this area, which he has known since childhood. We inspected the strange cushionlike plant. In certain regions, apparently, they are often eaten. The Count sliced one open with his penknife and gave us a "scientific" lecture. It was one great, magnificent spoof of the professorial mode—stupid and puffed up, alas often found among academic types. He perfectly captured the tone, the dry, irrefutable objectivity, of men in whom science has killed all wisdom, heart, and sense of humor. I sat on the ground, writhing with laughter. He reminded me of the puppetlike figures of some of my professors, who in this very same tone injected us young spirits with the cult of fact, of the man of abstraction, and of the subordination of everything to science. The Count went wild. He drew upon an entire reserve of extraordinary platitudes, ending with a patriotic disquisition, invoking Marshal Pétain, on the importance of raising oily plants in the state interest. I howled and laughed through my tears.

After we emerged from the water, the Count stood on a rock and began to read an excerpt from Keyserling's *South American Meditations*.[120] He had a hint of the pastor about him. Saggy clothing and a straw hat lent him authority. In a strong voice, with a marvelous, musical accent, the kind retained only by the last of the truly cultured French, he read: "Even if politicians are the most honest people on earth, politics is nevertheless *by its very nature* rape, seduction, plunder, exploitation, theft, and, at best, the assertion and coldly egotistic defense of personal interests. Machiavelli's *The Prince* has not only been surpassed, but left well behind by the modern statesman, who speaks on every occasion, without flinching, of ideals and the law. Espionage, counter-espionage, provocation, exploitation of the weakness of others, a stubborn insistence—worthy of Shylock—on observing treaties, or the hypocritical attempt to circumvent them, all this is routine for any foreign policy crowned with success. In this sense, I find no profession more ignoble. The worst part of this profession is not its notoriously criminal character, which appears only now and then, but its claim to represent or to defend 'the law.' Politics is *always* unjust, morally speaking, *always* bad. This is why so many criminal characters have been such great statesmen ... There is in this regard only *a single* solution that is neither cowardly, nor suspicious, nor dishonest: to recognize that politics belongs to the lowest reaches" (*les bas-fonds*), "in the sense that the intestinal functions belong to the lowest reaches. *And therefore* to put these base elements at the service of what is superior—to the greatest possible extent. Not in the Machiavellian sense, which considers evil to be good insofar as it is useful, nor in the spirit of the Jesuitical maxim, that 'the end justifies the means.' But in the sense that one accepts the tragic fate that the lowest reaches must necessarily form part of man; that they can never become moral or spiritual. But that nevertheless one cannot achieve the Good on earth except by means of this Evil that remains *forever* Evil."

We sat a while in silence. These intense words, resounding clearly in the sultry silence, this declamation, this text as it was "acted out" and extracted from the letters on the page, like music from a score, made a great impression on us. Especially on me. I felt an affinity with the intensity and unpredictability of the ideas. Basia, after reading something I wrote, once told me: "Try to restrain yourself, tone yourself down! You have the temperament of the first man of the Renaissance." I burst into laughter. I would have such a temperament if there was any Renaissance on the horizon. Rather, what I see before me is darkness, the depths of ideological stupidity pervading the earth, like a black cloud, an abyss of dogmas and scholasticism, of fanatical and obtuse religion. Where did it start? In Asia. What degeneration!

Together, we discuss everything in this passage. How much truth it contains . . . Today, we see where we have been led, and will continue to be led, by this perpetual talk of ideals and rights and by the attempts to present as spiritual and moral things that fundamentally are neither spiritual nor moral. When I commit an evil deed, I never cover it up, I don't pretend it's justified, or moral, or spiritual. Evil, when acknowledged, is easier to bear than evil cloaked in hypocrisy. What leads us today to these nightmarish ideas? What is the cause of the *greatest* suffering of all? Neither physical torments nor murders nor persecutions, but lies, monstrous lies and hypocrisy, the justification of everything as spiritual and moral. The Germany and Russia might be forgiven everything if, doing what they do, they did not *speak. That's* what is unforgivable.

August 17, 1943

We occupy our spare moments in amassing food. We were "introduced" to certain farms, presented to the farmers' wives, and we now ride over to purchase our supplies. I've already mailed home two kilos of butter and four dozen eggs. The *patron*'s wife will keep them for us in cold storage until we return. The prices are so low as not to be believed. I feel as if I'm stealing, not buying. A dozen eggs for 45 francs, a kilo of butter for 120 francs. Four years of war have passed and here it seems as though the war never happened. When we stop by the farms in the evening and chat with the farmers (a long conversation before concluding a sale is required, or they'll say we have bad manners and give us nothing), we feel like we're dreaming. The silence of dusk descends on the dirty yard in front of the house, with its eternal manure pile practically on the doorstep. Black trees and bushes are outlined sharply against the darkening sky, lit at the bottom by the last rays of the sun, which has already long sunk below the horizon. It's only at this time of day that they come alive. Each one is different, each takes the form of a figure. Every type can be found among them, and their age can be determined from their outlines. Old pear trees, wild, disheveled, and bent, unkempt apple trees. The bushes and hedgerows are like the crowds: turbulent, wild, clamorous. And how many different characters there are! Riding along the road or waiting for the farmer's wife to bring us eggs or butter from her storeroom, we discuss the trees as though they were people. It's hard not to smile at the sight of the old willow kneeling at the roadside, with the sham humility of a pious devotee filled with passive spite. Some trees are good, some malicious, ironic, peaceful, or full of inner anxiety. All this comes into view only at dusk.

We so love these hours, when the moon keeps stealing more and more light from the sun and coats the remains of the day with a metallic wash. From the henhouses we hear the interrupted flutter of wings as the hens settle into their perches. One or the other gives a cackle or clucks before going to sleep. Planted in rows in their cramped henhouse, they remind me of a railway compartment. They look like travelers. In this position it's probably impossible to really sleep. From the rabbit cages come the sounds of silent quarrels. These are wordless arguments, in which irritation is expressed in abrupt stamping. The rabbits are masters of pantomime, and their silent fury is more furious than the fury of any other creature. The modesty of means amplifies the effect. Hearing these hard, choppy, brutal noises, it's hard to believe they are produced by animals in whom everything is so soft. The ducks love to wander about at night. They stick their feet enthusiastically into the mud and with a low whisper, ending as a whimper, pull them out in order to stick them in again somewhere else. They slurp with their beaks in the thick soup of the manure pile, emitting loud quacks from time to time, sounding rather vulgar.

The farmer's wife sometimes puts out chairs in front of the house and we sit and talk. In the darkness, our faces become bright spots and only our words remain. They question us about the war, about Paris. They listen to us as though we were people from distant continents. They like it when we tell them about the hunger and scarcity in the cities, about the difficulties and awful conditions in the heavily populated areas. About the bombings. Sparks of irony then light up their eyes and I sense that their smiles compress hundreds of wrinkles, each revealing a hidden joy, a *Schadenfreude* concealed in expressions of sympathy. The city folk, always arrogant and supercilious, conceited and disdainful, repulsed by the farmers' dirty hands and the manure piles in front of their houses, are these days at their mercy. They keep arriving, abase themselves, whine, and pay through the nose. They flatter, send presents, and plead. The locals see this and laugh. As they sell their goods and take the money, they make it clear above all that they're offering a gift, "because it pleases them to do so." Let the city folk not get the impression that only money counts.

Us they like. They sense instinctively that everything that surrounds them, which has become foreign and exotic to citified Frenchmen, is intelligible to us. We tell them about Poland, about the poverty of the villages, about the hard struggle with the capricious Polish climate. Here, half the work takes care of itself. And when we admire the beautiful old furniture, passed down from generation to generation, the heavy cupboards and great chests with iron fittings, they feel that our excitement is not affected, not meant as flattery.

We return in the dark. The bicycle dynamos purr quietly and our lamps spread a muted light on the paving before us. Somewhere in the distance owls are laughing, and against the dark granite of the sky bats are tracing complicated lines.

August 19, 1943

I have spent the entire afternoon writing letters. I don't like writing letters, because I never manage to make them short. They usually concern matters I haven't been able to discuss in person. The task makes me realize how far we've today lost the art of letter writing. Nowadays, it's not really letter writing, but a cheaper way, on paper, to send a wire or use the telephone. Anyone who can't afford a telegram or a phone call writes "a letter." Correspondence, and in its wake, or perhaps along with it, also the art of conversation, has disappeared from modern life. People have stopped being sensitive to the style and form of communication, written as well as spoken. The industrial-commercial style predominates in both arenas. A pity. A pity above all that the correspondence of many good writers and great thinkers of our day will not exist, only because they were in many cases able to communicate with others in other ways, beside letters. We'll miss those notes, however brief, that convey so much. Like Balzac's note: "My dear Posper" (in his haste, he omitted the "r" in Prosper), "come to Laurent-Jan's this evening. There'll be some well-dressed wh—— there. — Balzac." After all, the most valuable of all Flaubert's work is his correspondence. Perhaps in fact because he considered letter writing less important and did not torture his style.

I've taken another two days off and we're not leaving until the twenty-fourth. We're sending some of our things by bus to Le Mans, and we ourselves will go by bike. This may be our last vacation during the war. It's unlikely we'll be able to get away next year. The war has lasted four years already, but for France it has not yet begun. For France, and to a considerable degree for other countries, the war will begin only — after the war. The Germans have created an equilibrium, which is in fact a disequilibrium, terrible in its long-term consequences. When it bursts, the chaos will be indescribable. The French laugh when I advise them to save up for later. When I tell the farmers they should invest whatever they are keeping under the mattress in inventory and buildings, because what today costs one hundred francs will cost five hundred after the war, they regard me with suspicion.

We're gathering these peaceful moments and storing them for the future. Not much more will happen this year. They can take Italy, in Russia the Germans can retreat, as usual, and the game will continue. Nevertheless, I don't believe there'll be a landing this year. The second front will have to be postponed for much later. For the time being, clouds of heavy bombers fly over us at night, headed for Germany or Italy. For half an hour, sometimes an hour, the monotonous roar of hundreds of thousands of horses — deep and ominous. Halifaxes, Stirlings, and long Lancasters are in the air. They can be identified by the photographs they scatter, and people are moved by their wailing. Obviously, only when they listen in places where it's still calm . . . In Paris we are moved, but in a different way.

The quiet, sunny days pass by. Splendid weather and August heat. The scent of sunbaked trees, stones, and earth. The afternoons seem somehow smoky and the roadside blackberry bushes are covered in dust. The muffled din of the electric threshing machines reaches us from afar. The machine quietly swallows up the fluffy sheaves, slows down and exhausts itself, then, having spit out the hay, starts thumping again, louder and more freely. The penetrating whistle of a small, narrow-track locomotive that rumbles and hisses threateningly, wanting absolutely to seem grown-up, resounds in the distance. The miniature red and green carriages flit among the trees, twisting and turning, like a train on a carousel.

Having rested briefly after lunch, we go to the garage for our bicycles. We squint our eyes, blinded by the sun, and the sudden transition from our chilly room to the scorching-hot garden makes us shiver. At such moments one would rather float through the air than walk on the ground. One's arms and legs become lazy, one's thoughts get tangled up. I feel like a fly sitting on old-fashioned fly paper, unsticking itself in one place, only to get stuck again in another. We get on our bikes and set off. We come awake only in the shade of the trees, near the water, or in the refreshing chill of the giant ferns. We hunt for mushrooms and dry them in the sun. We eat the huge blackberries, sunbaked and sweet. The scents awake memories and fill us with waves of longing. We talk. Alone together, we feel everything most intensely. Love and friendship . . . One must simply understand, always try to understand. Love?—Like everything, it also demands work—ordinary, everyday work. Even love cannot be left to sail in the wind, without a rudder. Nothing is as fallible as the so-called infallible instincts.

August 21, 1943

Today I went to Sainte-Suzanne with a young man who grew up here. It's a small town, thirty km from Joué, recognized (*classé*) as an architectural monument. The young fellow is twenty-two and graduated from Arts et Métiers with a diploma in engineering. An only child, a typical *fils à papa*, of the local type. Relatively sure of himself, relatively narrow in his views, but still ready to learn despite the sixteen years of intellectual torture to which he has been relentlessly subjected. I study him like a typical product of the system of abstract education that treats people like algebraic equations, and the entire world and all humanity as guinea pigs.

Engaging my companion in conversation is difficult. All my efforts to broaden his perspective come up against his impulse to narrow it down. I would have to pass through a bottleneck containing an ideological shrine, a system. It is the product of prolonged, strenuous labor that originated in the eighteenth century, when a certain Helvetius claimed that the humblest of Alpine shepherds could be transformed at will into a Lycurgus or a Newton. This labor persisted throughout the nineteenth century and today has finally borne fruit. Today, in fact, we have a housepainter and corporal in the image of Lycurgus and a failed Georgian priest as a modern Pericles, a demigod.[121] The efforts in this direction have indeed been effective. When Paul Painlevé became prime minister, he said in one of his speeches that he based all his policies on the precision of geometric theorems.[122] Is anything different happening in the world today? This young fellow, like millions of other young people in Germany, the Soviet Union, the United States, and Asia, believes that "anything can be done," when inspired by one or another theory, ideology, or system. As Guglielmo Ferrero wrote after the last war: "If ancient civilization collapsed, it was because at a certain point it lost any hope of improving the State. Modern civilization is threatened by very great difficulties for the opposite reason: it believes too much in the possibility of all kinds of progress, including political progress." What is meant by "political progress" and faith in its possibilities, a blind faith, we understand today. Developing his idea, Ferrero continues: "In short, we are so sure of being able to create the perfect State that we do not hesitate to sacrifice everything we yesterday still considered of incalculable value: liberty, for example. The ancients wanted to perfect the State, but they knew they could only do so within certain limits. We have lost the awareness of these limits. We regard political institutions as if they were made of wax and as if each generation can shape them according to its own idea, as if we can introduce all the changes and results that our concept of the public good demands, as though we had the freedom to choose among all the political doctrines that the human mind is capable of creating."

And in fact these millions of "well-bred" young people have lost all sense of limits. They reject everything on the basis of some theory or fleeting half-truth. The young were always idealistic, rebellious, simplistic in their understanding, and apodictic. This is completely understandable. But when I observe today's youth, I notice something particularly monstrous: an even-tempered cold-bloodedness. This is not a hot and stormy idealism that blinds your eyes, an idealism of flared nostrils and flushed cheeks, of thunderbolts hurled to left and right, of a heightened pulse. My generation in Poland still above all retained a hot-blooded negation, a healthy anarchism that at the same time desired what was good and noble, tender and young. Today this young fellow, together with millions of others, reasoning coldly and "scientifically," know to a frightening degree exactly what they want. Mankind and the most difficult of life's problems are in their hands no more than a fly whose wings, legs, and head can be torn off. Because that's what some theory, system, or ideology demands. And they *believe* it. That's perhaps the most horrible part. They *want to believe*. In my encounters with this new mentality, I increasingly have the impression of seeing an artfully chiseled shrine enclosed in a bottle. These days, the entire educational process in Germany, America, and especially the Soviet Union involves the precise chiseling of the mind and the arranging of shrines in bottles. The current war already shows the result of this direction in intellectual development, because all the regimes that followed the last war, without exception, were "improvements" that rejected all limits. Communism took this endeavor to the point of aberration. Life exacts a cruel revenge, all the crueler the more one hides behind theories, utopias, and blind FAITH in a system. During the Revolution, when France fabricated one constitution after another, Arthur Young smiled in pity and wrote from the other side of the English Channel: "How imprudent to throw oneself into the arms of theory in order to create a constitution."[123] He would probably be sickened at the sight of what's happening in the world today. Throwing himself into the arms of theory, the new man wants not merely to form constitutions but indeed to create entire systems! And what theories! Theories interpreted by corporals and by boors from Georgia, from the Tatars, and from the steppes.

The Renaissance? The Renaissance began with the loss of faith. The man of the Renaissance began to reflect, to think, to criticize, TO STOP BELIEVING. What about us? Having uncoupled ourselves from religion, "the opium of the people," we at all costs want to believe, we want to attach ourselves to a different raft. And so? We therefore drug ourselves with vulgar substitutes. Communism is today the same "opium of the people" as religion once was. But Communism has the drawback that it can be verified by experience. And that's where it stumbles. For I continue to believe that people are not complete fools, that generation after generation cannot be duped. Here's what I would like to repeat every thirty seconds to the young man riding next to me on this peaceful road: "Stop believing, you little squirt! And if you want absolutely to believe in something, then believe only in something that cannot be empirically proven. One can believe truly only in God, paradise, and hell because no one will ever prove them to you. So go ahead and believe and at least we know today that this belief of yours will harm no one." But it's hard to talk with him. He keeps chiseling away, making small pieces to insert with pincers into the neck of the bottle in which he's assembling his small shrine. If at least he were building a model boat, or a grandfather clock, or a miniature Château de Chambord, but no—A SHRINE. A shrine in the style of the great nonsense of the nineteenth century.

Sainte-Suzanne is lovely. An old town on a hill, still partly surrounded by the walls of a medieval fort. Inside the walls are small houses, small gardens, and narrow streets. To climb the walls we had to ask for the key to one of the garden gates. The gardens are charming. Tucked under the ramparts, smelling of greenery and vegetables, filled with tobacco bushes planted on the sly. All of France is planting tobacco, drying and cutting it, supplementing the meager cigarette ration. Each of these small gardens is France. France cannot be understood without "understanding" these gardens.

The walls offer a panoramic view of the fog-covered fields and forests. In the center is a castle. It now belongs to some bankrupt Italian count and has been taken over as the site of a summer camp for the *Jeunesse française*, or some other *Pétainjugend*.[124] A splendid and overgrown courtyard, on which a sweaty Führer surrounded by boys has put up tents and booths for tomorrow's fair. A mass of paper, rags, strings, planks, and tarps.

The castle is falling to pieces. The magnificent Renaissance building, lightly restored in eighteenth-century Rococo, is crumbling. Unhindered and unquestioned, we went inside. It's hard to imagine anything more beautiful and at the same time sadder. The rooms still contain some of the old furniture. Marvelous old Renaissance cabinets, carved chests, chairs, and armchairs. And amid all this, the campers' mattresses, straw thrown around, empty food tins, the stubs of candles that had dripped onto the furniture, dirt, and *Kraft durch Freude*.[125] We were entirely alone. I opened one of the cupboards and was struck dumb. There was a leather toiletry case on one of the shelves. I opened it. Tarnished silver fittings on crystal bottles, a heavy mirror, brushes—gems from the late Louis-Philippe period. There they remain, forgotten, out of fashion. I had the urge to "save" them from this site of destruction.

In another place I came upon a pile of newspapers from the 1880s tossed into a corner by the dynamic youth. I sat in an armchair and began to read a long article aimed at General Boulanger.[126] France was threatened by a dictator. The title—"Caveant Consules"—Beware, consuls! Fascinating. Advertisements by fashion houses with their prices. Splendid. I lost the sense of present time. Correspondence from Moscow. The author cites Napoleon's opinion of Russia, uttered on Saint Helena: "I intended to go to India. The English greatly feared my enterprise. That's why they recently settled in Alexandria. But one day they'll see what will happen to them with the Russians, who are not far from India and are already in Persia. Russia is a power that is advancing surely and rapidly toward world domination." Naturally, together with France, as this correspondent desires. The Entente Cordiale[127] was not on the agenda. I gathered up several newspapers, and with the fervor of an archaeologist, ferreted around in all the corners.

In one small room on the third floor I found a chest filled with albums of musical scores, among them many in handwritten copies by a certain Comtesse de B. Who could that have been? I stood with an album of Strauss waltzes, dating from 1848, and fell to dreaming. The wind whistled through the fantastic framework of the roof, which resembled lace made of rafters. In some of the rooms the ceilings have already fallen in and it's only the sooty fireplaces that hang one above the other, still attached to the walls. I was filled with sadness and anger. Such disdain for this deserted and unneeded castle, now reduced to ashes, the jewel of an architecture that did not consider a house a machine to live in. It's bad to look only back, but also bad to look only forward, perhaps not to look at all? The entire cultural heritage of Mama-Europe is today prey to the mentality of people without a past or of European boors. Standing in this castle I felt the menace—perhaps for the first time so directly—of this deluge. From the east, brutes and barbarians are pushing forward, from the west, healthy and ruddy creatures are flying in their four-engine flying fortresses. And inside, the European boor, pretending to defend culture, wants to destroy what's left of it. A truly moving spectacle. I began to laugh and listened to my laugh echo in the empty rooms.

My young companion came running up to me every now and then, calling: "*Venez donc et regardez*—I'm sure it's an authentic antique—*ça vaut au moins 100,000 francs.*"[128] The French sense of thrift and love of the past in terms of the value it represents rebelled forcefully within him.

We both returned excited and indignant. He suddenly became more appealing. He was pretty good at estimating the value of this old stuff, and that's already something. Maybe he's not so hopeless . . .

After lunch I lay down and read the old newspapers. I felt, in reading them, as though I were stealing. In fact, I had indeed stolen something—I had stolen time, as I once used to steal sweets or jam from the old cupboard.

August 22, 1943

Today we were with Comte de R. in his château. That is, not so much "in" it as "near" it. Because it's sealed and even he has no right to enter. It's about three km from Joué. The afternoon was scorching, but in the deep pathways lined with hedgerows and ferns, there was a damp chill. The Count told us how the Chouans had ventured into the region when they were fighting the "blues" of the Republic. The old, hollowed-out trees and the endless little fields, surrounded by hedgerows and banked earth, looked like hundreds of little fortresses. Indeed, not much has changed here since then. The only roads are those once laid out by Napoleon. He used the roads to pacify the royalists, but our path runs across the fields. We keep lifting the heavy wooden barriers enclosing the pastures. They creak and squeak, smelling of old, sunbaked wood. Cows stand motionless in the shade of the bushes or trees. Like statues. Above them thousands of flies and gnats dance in crazy zigzags.

The château is a big old house on a hill. As usual, the rear of the house, opening into a large park, is the most beautiful part. The shutters are closed. The place is deserted. A long allée cuts through the park. Two rows of giant old trees create a misty, bluish shade below. Between the house and the shady park is a garden. Fruit trees, vegetable patches, and climbing rosebushes along the pathways.

Among the tools in the shed we find a sickle on a long handle and we go to the pond to cut the giant pinkish-white flowers. Neither lilies nor water lilies. Melancholy permeates everything. I observe the Count's slender profile. He was born here and knows every nook and cranny. He is at home but the home is not his. He has come here, just as we have, to look around. I bend over the pond and snip some large, wet flowers and feel a sense of regret. Will this house and park ever acquire inhabitants who, having moved in, will not trample on the period and spirit it represents? As yesterday in Sainte-Suzanne, so today I had the sense of something ending. Ending all the more tragically, since it's the *spirit* that's coming to an end—something indefinable, which dies slowly but irrevocably.

We follow the allée. Like the main nave of a cathedral. Along the sides are the remains of the park. Artificial grottos, rocks and miniature bridges, strange dwarf trees and bushes—the entire stock of Romantic decoration. The sense of a time lost forever is depressing. We circle the adjacent forest. The Count regales us with the complications of the family inheritance, of sales, investments, payments, annuities. It's just as complicated as any financial intrigue in Balzac. And as in reading Balzac, so here I understand nothing of it. I understand the words "notary," "signature," "deadline," and so on. I say *oui*, I get the general idea but miss the details. I note only that the French *noblesse* has long ago forgotten the formulas of *noblesse oblige*, that the sense of dignity and aristocracy of the spirit are no stronger among them than among the rest of the French population. The authentic type of *Grand seigneur* may have existed here once upon a time, but it disappeared centuries ago. The average Pole, Spaniard, Hungarian, or Turk has a far greater sense of honor and dignity, certainly indicating a greater "nobility" (in the positive sense of the term), than the French *noblesse* of today. Alongside his often great qualities, every Frenchman also harbors a bit of Figaro, the rascal. If I never have trouble making myself understood to a Spaniard, but almost always to a Frenchman, that is why. I have still not managed to explain to any Frenchman why we Poles are not collaborating. I've managed to convince a few of them, but then only partly. I'm referring obviously to the older generation. The young have begun to mobilize on a grand scale. One could be nasty and say it's because the Germans have only now begun to step on toes . . .

In conversation today with Comte de R., hearing his arguments, I felt unpleasantly embarrassed. There are things one simply cannot discuss with a Frenchman, no matter how cultured. The memoirs of the Duchesse d'Abrantès, in which ambition and a sense of dignity play a large role, whether in relation to individual figures or to entire nations, can serve as a clinical example of what France and a representative of one of the oldest families of the French *noblesse* understand by the concept of *amour propre*. The nature of the welcome accorded foreign armies in Paris in 1815 and the way the French conducted themselves prompted General Blücher to refuse to attend official receptions, writing "various things" about the *Franzosen* in letters to his wife.[129] When Flaubert arrives in Paris in 1871, he writes to Ernest Feydeau:[130] ". . . for good Parisians, Prussia does not exist. They make excuses for the Prussian gentlemen, they admire the Prussians, they want to become Prussians. Never, *mon vieux*, have I felt such enormous disgust with men. I would like to drown humanity in my vomit." That's what I too wanted to do in June 1940 and often want to now. But, as this same Flaubert writes in another letter, one could just as well say today: "This poor France is not at all pleasant at the moment: truly—neither noble nor spiritual. But in the end—it's France."

And that's what everyone will say one day. Just as one forgives a pretty woman more readily than anyone else, so one more readily forgives France . . .

August 23, 1943

This morning in the shadow of the church I ran into the mayor. Playfully winking an eye, he said: "*C'est fini en Sicile . . .*" Well, finally! Now they'll be landing in southern Italy. Yet again, everyone thinks the end is near. Not me.

Tomorrow is the end of this summer dream. I don't know who thought up the saying that "work ennobles." I only know that I was always ennobling myself the most when I had nothing to do. Instead of pitying people who have to spend the best years of their lives earning a crust of bread, it's made out to be heroic. I'm returning to Paris with aversion. I would much rather settle down in the countryside and do nothing. My boundless reserves of exuberance and energy are slowly dwindling. Awaiting me are a few shady and risky business affairs, demanding action and speed—after which I frankly intend to come to a standstill. Autumn has to be calm—war and peacefulness: books, theater, walks. Besides, it's the last chance. It's time, damn it, for this French idyll and these Parisian pastorals to end. Next year may be worse. France is still being coddled . . .

Work, work . . . The myth of work in our day is murderous. Work, work, we work, I work . . . People are stupefied by work, a religion of work has been created, work has become an end in itself—the one and only true one. At no other time have so many things been the "one" and "true." Furthermore, all the most horrible forms of work are glorified. The entire approach to work in our day is distorted. Nowadays, I don't laugh at all or ridicule the fact that in 1936 France created a Ministry of Leisure (*Ministère des Loisirs*). The myth of work and the distortion of the question of work have gotten to the point where a majority of people do not know what to do in their free time. Everyone knows how to work, but how to relax and do nothing—hardly anyone. Culture is nevertheless *also* the art of "doing nothing." The first task of the new people of the coming new age will have to be the regulation of concepts. We standardize screws and threads, why not do the same for words and their meanings. But at the moment nothing is being done except scientifically (this is real science!), stuffing people's heads with old nonsense. The whole problem of Work is posed today in an entirely abnormal fashion. What is considered work today is certainly not ennobling. Work in offices and in automated factories, put on a pedestal, worshiped, surrounded by a halo, gussied up, elevated to a place of special dignity, among other kinds of work (for example, twiddling thumbs and catching flies) does not ennoble. This kind of work so stupefies, coarsens, and befuddles that it destroys all reason, as well as the benefits of relaxation. The art of doing nothing is also dying out. A person who is unable to do nothing turns into an insect. Only a perverse mind can admire bees or ants. I pity them. As long as work becomes an end in itself, art for art's sake, the "bee-ification" and "ant-ification" of man has no chance of ending. Fewer and fewer people today create anything, even at home, after work; more and more only re-create what has already been created. We have fallen into the crazed and crazy dance of Work. The Stakhanovite is a symbol, an idol. No—it's an aberration, an error. Three-quarters of what we today call work, salivating with affection and hypocrisy, and surround in myth, three-quarters of it could be executed by clever chimpanzees (constantly threatening to strike because of the stupidity of the work) and intelligent squirrel monkeys. It is unacceptable for man to be debased to this degree and moreover to consider the result to be excellent, unique, heroic, and robust. Work is a sad necessity. But as in every other area, on this point too the lies are terrible and the euphemisms in which we slosh around, wet up to our ears, are monstrous. In this regard, France was always candid and only now, influenced by the "New Renaissance," have the ax, the hoe, the saw, and the pliers moved to front stage. In general, it becomes increasingly clear that if a man does not break stones or is not a sewer cleaner or a dirty *travailleur*, he doesn't have the right to live. We live in a time in which things and people are deliberately debased. A monstrous demagogy is everywhere, it's even in fashion. Yes, there's a fashion even for that. A fashion for Work, a fashion for primitive man, for the *bête humaine.* The more boorish a nation becomes, the more splendid a future it has. This may very well also be a means of rejuvenation. Rémy de Gourmont said somewhere that the ignorant masses provide the nation with a splendid reserve of life force.[131] Unfortunately completely ignorant masses no longer exist, because everything has been done to turn them into semi-ignorant masses. And that's the worst of it.

An ocean of hypocrisy. A Pacific of cretinism and blindness has breached its shores and inundates everything. But perhaps this must be, perhaps it's for the better. Apprentice confectioners are allowed to eat their fill of cake. We too may one day sicken ourselves with all of that. It's the last day of vacation and I drown my despair in rum. Happily, my type of work is bearable to the extent that it allows me great freedom in the area of "doing nothing." In the notebooks I've filled with writing I see most clearly the enormous role played in a man's life by "doing nothing" and the opportunity of "doing nothing." In addition, there is dear K., who often grabs some of my papers and says: "I'll do this for you, you should write in peace." Who knows if what is called French culture does not in fact emerge to a large measure from this kind of opportunity. Until now, France has resisted the cult of work. Salaried work is in many cases

here a secondary occupation. It's very rare for a Frenchman to identify completely with what he does for a living. The Frenchman puts his heart into what
he does after work, at home. Hence the leisurely pace in offices, the great latitude in factories, and the disregard for regulations, decrees, and so on. This is
occasionally very annoying, but it allows the worker to remain a person and not
a machine. In this regard, France may in future serve as an excellent counter-
weight. The French will never agree to being totally absorbed in work; they will
not allow themselves to be made into termites. They are saved by their gardens,
their *passions*, which often are more profitable than their actual professions.
Three-quarters of French literature has been created "after hours" or even "during hours." People who are not sucked dry by salaried work can try their hand
at something besides the lathe or the adding machine. And most important of
all, no employer here would dare demand extra work without extra compensation—on behalf of the state or for the general good, and so on. When sacrifice is
demanded, the rates are set first. Then they all sing the "Marseillaise" and everyone is happy, while the minister has the chance to deliver a *sublime discours* and
emphasize the *magnifique geste du peuple.*[132] When it's a question of the state,
the French understand a lot, but they always end with: *Sommes quand même
pas des esclaves . . .*[133] And they look with disdain on the Germans next to them.

   If today the possibilities keep diminishing for people to live fully and make
a living by doing something they really like, they should have that possibility, if
only in psychological terms. But this is impossible when mass production, and
indeed work in general, is treated as a religion. But work, as it has become today,
cannot be idealized. But when we are ordered to find happiness in our work,
we are being compelled to do just that. Happiness cannot be found in reproduction; repeating a prototype has nothing human about it. The cult of work
in today's form is nothing but a distraction, a dumbing down, a bureaucratiza-
tion of the human soul and of the modest remains of reason. Meanwhile, the
problem becomes more acute, because reality proves to be something different.
The cult of work cannot be maintained in the face of today's technological development. True—but liberating people from the yoke of the cult of work runs
the risk of freeing the individual, allowing him to escape the collective, if only
in spiritual terms. And this cannot be allowed . . . Anything can be done with a
man stupefied by work.

August 25, 1943

   The charm is gone. Back in Paris, but I've had it. My thoughts return constantly to a little house, in a small town, somewhere in France. I envy Comte
de R. He has remained there in the little dimly lit room he rents from his old

nanny. Sounds of the world reach him there like sounds from beyond the walls. Day and night last twenty-four hours. Despite my three weeks of rest, I feel tired. I'm tired in advance, merely at the thought that I *will be* tired. Living constantly in the future tense, the complete absence of the present (whatever one is doing at a given moment becomes automatically unimportant), is the most exhausting. I'm forcing myself along, dragging myself from day to day, like a heavy sack of potatoes.

We left yesterday afternoon. Heartfelt good-byes. Bicycles weighted down. Eggs, a chicken, butter . . . Joué disappeared behind a turn in the road, leaving the ribbon of asphalt shining in the sun. The train was to depart Le Mans at six in the evening. We had lots of time. We rode slowly, avidly absorbing the remaining hours. The road was splendid. Tall, slender poplars on either side, like columns. Elsewhere, a long arbor of low, spreading plane trees. Winding roads along the edge of the hills and sleepy little towns. In one of the villages we hear the bulletin from London. *Ici Londres* . . . The familiar voice reaches us through the open window. We stop and listen. On the entire road there's no one but us, the houses seem deserted. The sun is burning and it's so quiet you can hear the rustle of a lone hen bathing in the sand. The Russians have taken Kharkov. The great offensive that began on July 5 is expanding. They are pushing the Germans back to the Dnieper.

We take the inclines slowly. At the top, the road flattens out, like a see-saw. We descend silently, smoothly. A row of trees, closing in before us, opens up and recedes quickly to the sides. Le Mans can be sensed from afar. The wind carries the smell of dust. When we enter the city, I look around with hatred. Comte de R. has infected me with his Fourierism and rural idealism. We bump along the cobblestones of Le Mans, avoiding the tram rails. Charcoal-fueled cars smoke like laundry irons and leave long trains of trash and dust in their wake. The narrow-track railway station radiates the heat of scrap iron baked by the sun and the dull odor of grease. An oven. People trail along the streets, sweaty and dusty.

I have to force myself to complete the formalities, deliver the bicycles, purchase the tickets. The train is already waiting at the platform. We find two seats. The cider in the thermos has not withstood the trip and has exploded. Cider is dripping from the baggage rack onto my head. I sip off a bit, close the thermos again, but nothing helps. It keeps fermenting in the thermos. The compartment is stifling. The plush seats are sticky. Finally, we're moving. We watch the houses and fields speeding by. I'm reminded of the times, in childhood, when vacation ended and I watched the fields and forests disappearing behind us, shedding tears of regret deep in my heart.

The travelers begin to eat. It's a display of excess, debauchery. No one eats ordinary bread. All pull out white *pain brioché,* butter, hard-boiled eggs, sausage, ham, cold meats, roast chicken, fruit. Aromatic, amber-colored calvados flows from little flasks with metal caps. Authentic Camembert, melted by the heat, has turned into a thick cream with the sharp odor of hydrogen sulfide and ammonia. There's a smacking of lips glistening with grease, a blissful licking of greasy fingers, as paper wrappers and nutshells fly out the window. Scraps are thrown on the floor. It's at once an orgy and a holy rite, which the French alone invest with a quite special tone and mood. One not only senses the relish with which they eat; one sees it. Eating is not merely the satisfaction of hunger. It's a sensual delight. No bite here passes the lips unnoticed, no atom of food evades the critique of the palate. A little girl carefully opens the box of Camembert, taps it delicately with her little finger, and passes it to her mother, saying reassuringly: "*Maman, it est bien fait.*"[134] The French, from childhood, are connoisseurs of food and its quality. Their gluttony is repellent, but at the same time a sign of culture. Eating indiscriminately from tins and kettles, simply to relieve one's hunger, is good for lovers of *Eintopfgerichten*[135] and other barbarians. Cuisine is an art and demands artistry. The ability to distinguish among varieties of oysters, fruit, meat, cheese, and wine, the art of composing a "menu" demand the same degree of culture as the art of distinguishing good paintings from bad or of selecting one's reading. A certain French worker employed by the Germans once said to me: "*Monsieur,* people who eat *like that* cannot be masters of the world."

The sun is setting, the small train stations make a racket as we rush through them. Beyond Versailles are the first of the far-flung Parisian suburbs. Small houses with little gardens, built any old how, without rhyme or reason. Paris is surrounded by one of the most beautiful natural regions of any great city, but built up in the ugliest fashion. From afar the area looks like a heap of rubble, sprouting weeds. At Vaugirard, we pass the gloomy cube of the municipal refrigeration plant. A cold crematorium. The train slows down—the bridges over the inner boulevards rumble.

Gare Montparnasse.

A thick human stream trickles toward the exit. Heavy suitcases stuffed with food. On the broad square in front of the station the crowd disappears into the crevices of the metro. The trains clatter. The hens suffocating in baskets are cackling, the geese extend their long necks from backpacks, opening their thirsty beaks, a goat in a sack squirms and kicks. Armfuls of withered wildflowers. Spots of color, flat and muted in the dull electric light. Drops of sweat, dribbling slowly from brows to cheeks. *Dis donc, y a une place!*[136] Stepping on toes, pushing. Fat, greasy, sweaty laughter. The dirty, wet floor of the train car, stinking of rotten fish.

In our room it's hot and it smells of dust. On the table are cups with the remains of moldy tea, a piece of dried-up bread, pear cores swarming with disgusting little flies. In the room it's still the second of August.

We open the windows and undress. I wash my sticky, dirty hands.

The long, sunny, peaceful days are gone. Days that were full and whole, permeated with . . . What? I don't know. Perhaps with what sounds so modest, but is so expressive: *Douce France*.

September 1, 1943

The fifth year of the war has begun. How lucky our parents were. They had only three months until the end. Merely three months. And for us? Perhaps another year, perhaps more . . . The war is only now just beginning. In fact, it hasn't yet begun. Instead of being resolved, all the problems are becoming more complicated. It was a lot easier two years ago than today for me to imagine the end of the war. Today I don't see it, or if I do see it, it's in a much more distant future. When the waters are truly muddied, it takes a long time for the dirt to settle again on the bottom. Today the muddying is complete, total. In everything. The world has changed, people have changed, so have thoughts, tendencies, ideas. Return to "what was before" is impossible. So, then what? Man's capacity to affect what is usually referred to by the general term "evolution" is essentially rather limited. The end result will truly be the victory of forces that clash under the surface, unseen, and gain the upper hand. It's difficult to impart direction to these forces. They can be ignited, but it's difficult to control them, just as it's difficult to control fire or flood. And in this war, to this very day, nothing is done but continually ignite new forces. It's hard for me to comment, because I'm sitting in a fortress, having no contact with the besiegers. I don't know what direction thinking has taken THERE, on the other side. But what emerges from over there is incoherent and unsteady. England and America still think of us as they used to. Meanwhile, Europe has changed, much more than they realize. The four horrible, long years of the "New Europe" have instructed us in cold realism, they have taught us to take a hard look at the truth. It's not easy to lull us to sleep any old how, not easy to dazzle us with words. In the general confusion, amid the allusions and half-truths, one thing is clear: Russia. Russia knows what she wants—and has taken action. She hides nothing. Russia knows that every year of this life makes us more than ever "ready for anything." And she will take advantage of it.

September 3, 1943

I had some business in town this morning, but near Saint-Germain I was caught by an alarm. I sat down in the garden by the church and began to read. Soon shelling began. Everyone was herded into the doorways. I entered a doorway on place Saint-Germain and struck up a conversation with an elderly gentleman. A lycée teacher from Bordeaux. We talked about books. He spoke about Bernanos, whom he knows personally.[137] We wound up discussing the present. The artillery was firing. Two formations flew overhead, high up. From time to time they shone in the deep sapphire of the sky, like fish in the depths, their white underbellies glistening. Four-engine flying fortresses. The shelling has grown even stronger. Thousands of shells were bursting in the sky and the planes were floating among the rotund clouds. Suddenly a whistle. I nipped into the doorway. Cries on the street. People were running from the direction of Gare Montparnasse. Rue de Rennes disappeared in clouds of dust. Panic. A bomb fell nearby. The police again drive people into the buildings. We look at each other. My professor is blissful. Something doesn't add up. Why these bombs in the center of the city? Meanwhile, someone rushes into the doorway and cries: "The English have landed in Calabria." These are strange moments. I seem to be dreaming. My heart beats rapidly and at the same time I'm overcome by a terrible fatigue. I would like to stop existing for a moment. A large cloud of smoke and dust is drifting down the street and coming toward us. Only the silver crests of police helmets shine through the cloud, as the officers hustle the curious into the buildings. Silence descends. Gone is the charm of my pleasant conversation with the bearded gentleman, scattered to the winds are the names of Bernanos, Balzac, Flaubert, and Maupassant. I hear only the final question, to which I did not manage to respond: "Have you read anything by Roger Martin du Gard?"[138] No—I haven't. There's so much more I want to read. But when? Where to begin? And what for? To be smashed into dust and disappear in the smoke? The fire engines wail, the sirens continue to blast. The alarm is over. The sun is shining, the sky is sapphire, the bistros open their doors with a clank, and people take their seats under the colorful umbrellas on the terraces. I sit down, too. *Garçon, un verre de rhum.*[139] I'd like to get drunk.

Then I get on my bike and ride off. I have to take a detour because the streets are blocked. Bombs had fallen on rue de Rennes and rue du Cherche-Midi. Near Gare de Montparnasse a six-story building was destroyed. Clouds of dust, police, fire brigades. Ambulance sirens are blaring. A few bombs had also fallen near Porte de Versailles and on rue de la Croix-Nivert. Perhaps one of those American bombardiers was in a good mood, got angry at the "flak" positioned all over Paris, and let loose a couple of little bombs. In his place I would have lobbed a few too. What's up? Is it war or party-time in this Paris? Up here we're flying, they're shooting at us, as if we were ducks, and there down below they're discussing Balzac, Maupassant, Bernanos. You're right, young fellow, from Illinois or Texas.

Our factory is in a frenzy. Everyone is rushing to the telephone. All of Paris is phoning right now—their families, acquaintances, relatives, friends. Paris has been bombed . . . O my goodness! All of three bombs in five rows and what a fuss! I've the urge to declaim Virgil's *Bucolics.*

September 8, 1943

Madness, joy, delirium. The Italians have capitulated. In fact, they capitulated long ago, the capitulation itself was signed a few days ago, but only announced today—"at a convenient moment for the concerned parties." Mussolini has been imprisoned by Badoglio's government. This evening, the war seemed to have ended. Excuse me!—for whom?

September 13, 1943

Marvelous! Detachments of German parachutists have liberated Mussolini. Reading today's description of this historic event, I felt like I was reading something by Dumas, *père.*

An impregnable castle in the mountains (impregnable, really!), the imprisoned dictator, probably along with his concubine—a mixture, right out of Dumas—*The Count of Monte Cristo, The Three Musketeers,* and Cagliostro himself.[140] Too bad he was in fact abducted and the Germans, who were entirely surprised by the Italians' treachery (*Vous êtes vulgaire, mon cher. Ça s'appelle une volte-face*[141]), managed to extricate themselves from a situation, which on September 8 seemed hopeless. I don't share the general enthusiasm. The English and the Americans were apparently also taken aback. The American Fifth Army landed with difficulty in the Gulf of Salerno and is trying desperately to withstand the shelling of the German divisions, which have withdrawn skillfully from southern Italy. The English Eighth Army under the renowned Montgomery is trying desperately to join up with the Americans. Five days after the Italians' total capitulation, instead of landing immediately at several points and taking control of Italy as far as Lombardy, thus blocking the German retreat, the English and Americans have allowed the Germans to form a line of defense on territory suitable for defense. They've messed up big-time. They will later have to sacrifice many men to make up for what they could have accomplished in one blow with minimal losses. Lots of noise but little military advantage. Near

Naples, General Clark is barely holding on to a scrap of a beachhead, the Germans are attacking methodically, the English want to link up with Clark—total bedlam and a nuisance.[142] But the point is, a lot can be said. I appear to be stupid because I notice things, while others seem wise because they don't. For a while now, no one has wanted to see anything. And no one does.

September 15, 1943

If this keeps up the Germans will push the Americans into the water. They are already crowing about victory, but it's too early. Crowing is meant to obscure the details of the Italian treachery, which is piquant.

This evening I visited Antek and his wife, who had arrived from the countryside to spend a few days in Paris. Suddenly the alarm. We went onto the balcony. The "flak" began to rage. From the western suburbs was heard the dull thunder of bombs. After a while, large bomber squadrons appear in the early evening sky. They are heavy and move slowly among the hundreds of clouds of bursting shells. They fly relatively low, in V-shaped groups of twenty-six. The booming of the antiaircraft guns becomes incessant and Paris trembles. Suddenly, there's a burst of fire in one of the squadrons. Seconds. Like a flare of magnesium. The machine disintegrates in the air. The wings fall, twisting like dry leaves. Will they jump? No—nothing. We stare as though watching a film. I feel my legs shaking slightly under me. Only one single parachute opens. One of eight or ten has jumped. A gap opens in the squadron, the machines calmly reassemble. Another plane replaces the one that was lost—the others follow. And again, a flame in the next squadron. Antek's wife has a fit of hysterical weeping. We take her down to the basement. She slowly regains her calm. People stand in groups in the empty streets and talk with each other. Basia observed the whole corrida from the little window in our kitchen. We both feel a heartbreaking sense of injury, but it is mixed with disgust. To stand calmly and watch as people are being murdered.

September 18, 1943

Well—the stitch dropped in Salerno has been recovered and the situation amended. The Russians are monotonously advancing. I'm curious to see whether the Germans manage to hold the line for a while at the Dnieper. Unable to escape the enemy, they are obliged to keep fighting as they retreat. Horribly exhausting, but they do it very well. In any case, the twilight of the gods is approaching. I'm waiting now for "the 44."[143]

We are slowly preparing for winter. Potatoes, fruit preserves—it's not hard to get food if you have money. I'm always tired. I understand people who have a vocation for the cloistered life. I would now be capable of shutting myself off in a retreat for months at a time. To sink into the silence, melt into the monotony of a monk's gray existence. To stroll along the overgrown pathways, touched by autumn gold, of a neglected garden and read Saint Thomas Aquinas and Saint Augustine . . . To sit on a stone bench, write, and flick away the little spiders, stubborn little ants, and green garden fleas landing on my paper. Then to gaze through the bars of a Gothic window at the huge, red sun crossed by a few streaks of bluish clouds. Someone would bring me a meal and a candle. And at midnight I would rise to say my prayers . . .

Meanwhile, racing my bicycle through streets roasted by the hot summer. Despite the preautumnal chill, the stones still radiate heat, the dust is still summery. My business affairs have done well. I bought some pretty things for Basia. For myself, I'm buying books.

September 25, 1943

The Russians have taken back Smolensk, and Mussolini has established a republican-fascist government.[144] Everything is now possible. How far have we still to go? Stalin may perhaps invite the Romanov dynasty to resume the throne, while he plays the role of Rasputin. He is well qualified. This "republican-fascist" government affects me like "achoo" powder. I want to sneeze, wipe my tears, and sneeze myself to death over this boundless ocean—of what? Stupidity? Cretinism? Charlatanism? These words don't begin to convey what it's about. It's an ocean of filth, sprayed with perfume, in which the great madhouse of so-called humanity is bathing. Mussolini is creating a "republican-fascist" government, Stalin is defending democracy (democratic Communism—that's coming next. Good joke!), Hitler is defending Western culture—in general, everyone is defending something. And the individual man, with what's left of the brain in his head, must defend himself against sneezing himself to death and going mad. Everyone's greatest concern at the moment should be to emerge, not just more or less intact from this whirlwind, but with a remnant of sanity. This will be hardest of all. One thing is certain: even with the greatest reserve of common sense, a person compelled to spend a week listening to everything on the radio and reading everything appearing in print could be committed to a mental hospital without a doctor's prescription. One look at him would be enough. Overall, it's not what's happening but what's being said and written that has all the marks of the coming of the Antichrist. There's only so much that can possibly happen and what actually does happen—will pass. But once the night of the soul and the darkness of thought are unleashed, the dawn will be long in coming.

I feel all this in my bones. As though I were placed between the two plates of a printing press and being squeezed ever more tightly. But at the same time I cannot scream out. Some things leave me mute. All that remains is my soul wailing in hellish silence. The last two nights have been filled with explosions and flares bursting in the sky. The English are off to bomb Italy. Last night a wounded bomber, burning like a torch, flew low over half of Paris, then crashed into the roof of the Grands Magasins du Louvre. The charred remains of the crew were found on the streets around it. Quite an attraction . . .

September 26, 1943

I've become a mechanical reading machine. It's no longer the Dnieper line. The Russians have crossed the Dnieper in six places; the fighting is now at Kiev. Getting warm, warm—getting warmer. Soon they will begin to "liberate" us. And will liberate us for the next fifty years.

Armory's "50 ans de vie parisienne." The Dreyfus Affair, a picture gallery of bygone personalities and faded names. Willy and Colette, Rachilde, Paris 1900.[145] Poorly written, topical. It's the fashion, hence the splash.

September 28, 1943

Persistent rumors of a Soviet-German armistice. It's already in the air; already the first steps have been taken through Turkish intermediaries. It looks like Russian blackmail, by means of which they hope to impose certain things on their "dear allies." Rumors launched by the Communists on orders from Moscow.

October 1, 1943

The rumors of a Soviet-German agreement have become so persistent that today the Germans officially denied them.

In France organized resistance is beginning to make itself felt. Young men slated for deportation to Germany are organizing brigades, which the English supply with weapons from the air. The brigades are causing trouble. Beginning by setting fire to the harvests and destroying agricultural machines. The peasants do not want to surrender anything voluntarily, so ordinary robberies are now becoming more frequent, as are murders of collaborators. Innocent people and political opponents fall victim as well. Until now France has been calm, but that calm may be coming to an end.

The English and the Americans have gotten bogged down in southern Italy and will spend the winter there. Things could have gone better . . . The Russians are advancing, the Germans are slowly losing the fruits of all their victories.

October 5, 1943

M. and his wife wrote me from Monceaux to say they had slaughtered a pig and inviting me to come. Monceaux is eighty km from Paris, in the *département* of the Oise. I like them very much. He used to drive a mail truck, she's a charming, subtle woman typical of the middle classes as encountered only in Pomerania. Two years ago, they settled in the countryside, where he works as an agricultural laborer. Finding two bare rooms and living conditions as primitive as only an agricultural worker in France can bear (beyond belief), they have earned practically everything by their own hard work and intelligence. He himself has made their simple furniture, built cages for the chickens and rabbits, a pigpen, and after work hours planted a sizable kitchen garden. Having arrived here from Paris with three suitcases, they today have what almost amounts to a small farm—naturally the envy of all their French neighbors. Because, when it comes to foreigners, the French do not want to recognize the enormous labor they put in, but see only the results. They think everything is easier for the Poles, everything does better. Why this should be, the envious Frenchman doesn't wonder. He considers it an injustice, bad-mouths the *sale étranger*,[146] observes that the Pole keeps eating better and better and lacks for nothing, but the Frenchman won't lift a finger to improve his own caveman existence. Because he's lazy. He doesn't see that the stupidest Pole is more intelligent than he is, is not afraid to work, shows initiative and ingenuity, and "is good at everything" because he wants to be. And because he has to be. The Frenchman only envies him, whines, and understands nothing. For the Frenchman, everything is always "unfair." *C'est pas juste*—is heard from dawn to dusk. Especially when it comes to foreigners.

Polishness is puzzling. Some devil has gotten into the Polish people. They are all managing, all have cash, buy and sell, earn money, spend money and eat, take vacations, go for cures. The Poles are good at everything: the factory hand or mechanic knows how to fatten a pig, raise chickens, repair anything, make his own soap, candles, sausages, cupboard or chicken coop, plant tobacco, grow the best tomatoes, and so on. We are a people made for life in emigration, because only as immigrants do we accomplish miracles. At home we lose momentum and everyone dreams only of becoming—a civil servant. If only Poland and that holy fatherland of ours would stop messing with our heads, we would develop into some of the most remarkable human material, on the move, blossoming, earning our living. We might even start thinking, which is usually not in our nature.

I set out early, around eight in the morning. A gray, chilly, misty day. A long road through the sooty suburbs. Only at Saint-Denis did I hit a good highway. Autumn. The yellowed grass, the rust-colored trees, the disheveled gardens with the remains of cabbage, lettuce, and carrots. I feel good. I'm on my own and merge with the rain around me. I munch on chocolate and keep going. The kilometers disappear slowly. I pass a château sunk in a neglected park. On the crumbling walls a black inscription says *"Vive le Roi!"* One should smile, but I don't smile. This arrogance imbued in us by the nineteenth century is comical. All because humanity began, with difficulty, to understand a thing or two and call things by their names. Every imbecile began to consider himself "learned" and regard everything as "ridiculous." Because it's not "progressive," superficial, idiotic, "available to everyone," shallow and easy. Education has begun to rely on picture books, and the Communist books win all the prizes in this respect. Stupidity and rotten arrogance don't stop growing.

In Chantilly I enter the twilight of the forests. At the very entrance to the city, there's a splendid allée, leading to the Menier castle. *Chocolat Menier.* Racehorses, ridden by jockeys the size of pygmies, trot along the roadside paths. The jockey and the sacristan may be the two most repulsive specimens of the white race. Their colorful jackets flit through the forest shadows. In the center of Chantilly German telephone operators walk around with bags of grapes *und sie lachen und essen.*[147] The sight of these women arouses the sexual murderer in me. I buy a kilo of large black grapes. When I pass Creil I'll rest and eat them. The road from Chantilly to Creil is straight and monotonous. The fog thickens and little drops settle on my jacket and mustache. The smell of northern France, the climate that's found in the novels of Maxence van der Meersch.[148] Creil is crawling with workers of various nationalities. The Germans are building air-fields in the area. The guttural sounds of Algerians and Moroccans talking in the streets, Negroes flashing the whites of their eyes, energetic Polish curses, m-f——s, in the sing-song accent of the southeastern region. I pass the station. I wonder when the English will bomb it. They'll certainly have plenty to hit. Dozens of locomotives, hundreds of freight cars. In a little town beyond Creil, I take refuge in a roadside bistro. I have a coffee and eat my bread and cheese. The *patron* has been fastidiously wiping the clean counter for the last hour. A fat guy entered and the two began to whisper in the corner. I overheard the words "car" and "two tons." Some underhanded deal involving rationed goods, no doubt. They sealed the transaction with a dose of cider. I went on my way.

An hour later I enter Clermont. The lunch hour silence. Around two I reach

Monceaux. M. and his wife welcome me joyfully. I consume an enormous pork cutlet and after lunch lie down for a nap. The indescribable feeling of blissful calm and silence. I sense the fatigue in my extended legs. The last of the summer flies buzz against the windowpanes, the sounds of chickens and ducks rise from the courtyard. I peer at the sooty ceiling and listen to M. washing the dishes in the adjoining kitchen. The splash of water running and water draining, the clatter of forks and knives. I am nothing but peaceful rest.

October 6, 1943

After a breakfast enlivened by all the various products of the pig slaughter (liverwurst, headcheese, sausages), I went outside with a book to take a walk. A barely sunny day, but warm. I followed the allée between overgrown ponds. Everything was golden yellow. Small poplar leaves rained from the trees, sparkling in the sun like sequins. Sweet flag and reeds, yellowing and withering at the tips, rustled in the light breezes. Through the breaches in the dying vegetation appeared scraps of pale blue sky, covered in a silver mist. The silence of an autumn morning. I love to read while walking. I read and my thoughts slide forward in short spurts, like the pond skaters. I watch them from the edge of the pond. The water buckles under their delicate legs, as though it were made of thick plastic. They skim across the water, chasing after something invisible. Fine, golden leaves keep raining from the trees into the water.

I don't know why, but on silver-and-gold autumn days like this, the past, those bygone times, seems much more vivid. One after another, memories of those past years come to life, with their insignificant events. I don't recall important things, but minor everyday details: when my mother gave us plums. Covered in gray fuzz, they recalled the mossy bottles of old wine. On Sundays, after Mass, we went to the promenade in the Błonia park in Cracow and bought "Sphinxes." On one broiling summer night I helped the Franks finish the display windows in Janek Grosse's shop. A steamy summer night in Cracow . . . Longing and regret, that this won't return, that the little things, in particular, are gone forever. Tears come to my eyes, uncontrollably, the leaves fall faster and faster from the trees. The pond skaters skim across the water, a fish splashes. And when I close my eyes, a tear catches, then breaks away and flows slowly down my cheek. Lick it away, as you used to . . . It tickles as it settles into the corner of my mouth. Longing trembles in my breast, a grieving for those times past, as for someone who has died. The wind has swept upward and showered the wrinkled water with another handful of golden confetti. Life hurries on, ever more traces are left behind. I return for lunch and stuff myself for old time's sake, because even the pork cutlets evoke memories. Toward evening I visit the farms belonging to M. and his wife and to S. and his wife. Chicken coops, pigpens, rabbit hutches — all built with their own hands from old bricks, scavenged boards, scraps of old metal. They have made use of every last piece of refuse, putting everything together after work until late in the night. What the Frenchman discards the Pole repairs, renovates, and makes use of. S.'s two children wear thick leather sandals that S., a metal turner by trade, made from old shoes found in the trash. Their French neighbors visit them and say enviously: *Mais vous êtes capitalistes!*[149] They're right. Every Pole is a born capitalist. And would be one, if conditions were favorable. And if he didn't have Poland continually squeezing his brains. Poland is becoming a State, the State is becoming an official, and in the end the State, the minister, the official, and everyone else — that's Poland, a big mess and everyone acting the idiot. As a result, instead of people like M. or S. producing fruit juice, you have the State Fruit Juice Factory, and S. and M. are driving mail trucks.

October 7, 1943

A mild, sunny day. I set out early and pedaled slowly, stopping from time to time. After forty kilometers I sat down by the road to eat. A truck filled with apples drove past. The fellows tossed me three large apples. *"Pour votre dessert,"*[150] cried the Frenchman seated on a mountain of baskets. I waved and smiled back at them. Excellent apples. Continuing on, I simply dawdled. It was a shame to rush past the forests and the remaining vegetation. Again a city. In Chantilly I managed cleverly to avoid a gendarme patrol checking the contents of bicycle packs. My lard, meat, eggs, and flour were in danger — not to speak of myself. The attempt to suppress the black market is idiotic. By one in the afternoon I was home. The three days had refreshed me.

October 9, 1943

This evening we saw Pagnol's *Fanny* with Raimu at the Théâtre des Variétés.[151] Raimu may be the best French actor. In films as well as the theater, he is head and shoulders above the entire French acting crew. Every word and gesture are imbued with naturalness, intelligence, culture, subtle charm, and goodness. These are his last appearances before joining the Comédie-Française, where he will make his debut in Molière's *Le Bourgeois gentilhomme*. This inspires many intrigues and much jealousy. Because the mummies in the Comédie-Française cannot accept the fact that a "boulevard actor" (the equivalent of a tightrope walker) should soil the boards of the premier stage of France. Now, in farewell, Raimu is playing on the boulevards, as the unforgettable César in *Fanny*.

Pagnol is all charm. All his plays, his film scripts, though resembling each other, are always full of something that's never boring—heart. They radiate the warmth of the south, the carefree spirit, chattiness, good nature, and kindheartedness of people whose joys and sorrows, laughter and tears are always bathed in the rays of the sun. They convey the atmosphere of the still, hot afternoon hours, of quiet evenings and conversations over the inevitable glass of yellowish-green pastis. And everything punctuated by powerful gusts of emotion, like the blasts of the mistral. One has to know the south, that other France, to experience and understand it, in order truly to appreciate the small details, the words and movements, with which Pagnol constructs his plays and creates Art. There's usually a combination of monologues and gestures with simple, straightforward action, as often encountered in real life. His characters are human and what they do they do for real. A pure heart beats in their breasts and their simplicity is not a pose. Life in the south intermingles with the sun, the wine, the olive oil, creating a wonderful mixture, in which the greatest sorrow is bound to find solace. Tear-filled eyes find rest on the sapphire surface of the sea, the wind rustles in the canopies of the pines, the nostrils fill with the odor of fried olive oil and fish, and the cool, dim interior of a small bistro beckons with its calm. Because it's so good to live there, life in itself counts most of all. If it doesn't turn out one way, it will turn out another—and likely just as good, peaceful, and gentle.

Marius has gone away and left Fanny. He has been lured by the desire to encounter different worlds; the breath of the seas and foreign continents has swept him off and left the woman stranded. He has abandoned two hearts, torn by longing—the hearts of both Fanny and César. Months pass without any news. Fanny can no longer disguise the fact that she will become a mother. Conversations, confidences, outbursts of anger, and tender words. Panisse declares himself to Fanny. The scene in Panisse's shop is magnificent, a smiling mélange of southern *vantardise*, the panache of words and gestures with the nobility of true and genuine emotions. On the ruins of one happiness another happiness blooms. And when Marius reappears, he has to leave, because that's what life demands, because it will be better that way.

If this play will never age, the actors who have now been appearing in it for over ten years have nevertheless themselves managed to age. *Fanny* is still running in Paris with the original cast. This is undoubtedly possible only in Paris and it has a touching charm. But if it is not bothersome in the older characters, like César, Panisse, and Fanny's mother, time has left its mark on Marius and

Fanny. Orane Demazis and Berval, both in their middle years, are the young couple.[152] Marius's protruding belly and Fanny's no longer young face and figure somewhat spoil the image and atmosphere.

But above it all presides Raimu. His performance is a masterpiece. He never seems to be repeating himself, but each time creates his role from scratch. This may explain the bewitching freshness and charm in each glance, gesture, and word.

I half-closed my eyes and felt the smells, the warmth, and the breath of air. Evenings in Carcassonne and Narbonne. The tough, dust-covered greenery of the trees and vines. The sea, the sun. There, in that sun, in the dim chill of a bistro, in a glass of rum, in the long hours of complete solitude at the seashore, a part of me was born. And a part of me has remained down there forever . . .

We emerged from the theater onto the dark boulevard. People were leaving the cinemas and theaters and vanishing underground. In the stuffy passageways of the metro little bouquets of roses were being sold. From down there in the south.

October 13, 1943

Great! Today in conversation with a Frenchman on the subject of the current moment, I expressed the timid concern that this whole era might be seen as a stain on the history of France. To which he answered in all seriousness: "This period will never be part of the history of France. It will be included in the history of the occupation." This, this, exactly THIS, and nothing else, is what dooms them. Blind as bats. They are duped even more by nationalism and *la France éternelle* than we are duped by Poland.

October 16, 1943

This evening we saw *Duo* in the Théâtre des Ambassadeurs. It's Paul Géraldy's adaptation of the Colette novel.[153] I didn't understand much of it, because I feel that in relation to women of this type and to this kind of "problem" I would react differently. But it's possible I find it hard to understand because I belong to a different breed. For the same reason, just as I find it hard to understand des Grieux in *Manon Lescaut*, so Michel, despite the sympathy I felt for him up to the very end, failed to move me.

Alice is a fashion designer, Michel the administrative director of a large fashion house. They have arrived for a weekend at their small farm somewhere in France. Inadvertently, stupidly and needlessly, Michel discovers that once long ago, while he was in London, Alice had cheated on him with a fabric supplier and financier named Bordier. It's a cruel blow, because Michel loves Alice and he immediately decides that Alice's betrayal was merely a "lapse" of the senses and that the accident had no bearing on her feelings for him. He grits his teeth and gets control of himself. One must be up-to-date, *à la page*. He even makes jokes and kids around—and life goes on.

He feels nevertheless that there is no way to avoid an explanation. He doesn't have the strength to entirely dismiss the event. Suddenly an interrogation. One question after another. Was Alice acting on emotion, or was it merely an "accidental" impulse of the senses? Just a small flicker of emotion, without consequences, Alice assures him. Michel calms down and puts it out of mind. After the storm, the sky is once again blue. But for the second time, he overestimates his own strength. It so happens that Bordier drops in to see them on his way to Paris to discuss some financial matters, a question of possible loans and credits for the fashion house. Michel cannot control himself. He grabs Bordier by the scruff of the neck and kicks him out the door. Not even smashing his face in. I kept thinking: "Michel—go to it!—on the jaw! grab him by the tie and bash him one!"—but with this guy, nothing of the kind. My blood boiled. The drama heats up again.

Michel is ashamed of his "weakness." He apologizes to Alice for having been carried away. As for me—I just don't get it. Instead of giving Alice, in turn, a good whack, he apologizes. If it had been merely an ordinary burst of sexual desire, he tells her, he could more easily have accepted the fact. But Alice had given Bordier not only her body but also a part of her feelings. That he could not accept. "I lied!" Alice cries, "it was only an ordinary *coup de sens*." She swears it's true, and proves it by reading him a trivial passage from a letter Bordier had sent her the morning after. Michel is crushed. He feigns calm, but as soon as Alice has fallen asleep, exhausted by their squabbling, he leaves the house and—drowns himself.

Three acts of dialogue, in progression—*piano, forte, con fuoco*. Géraldy has done a great job building up to the finale and has tailored it all to the stage. He has made the most of the misunderstandings. But all the same I understood nothing. The ending in particular made me laugh. How could he drown himself? Couldn't he swim? For a man in such circumstances there is only one way to drown himself: in alcohol. And why take it out on himself? Why not on Alice and Bordier, if he wants to take it out on someone? The play seems to me to touch on the problem of the contemporary male. If so, then it's an interesting case.

There's no doubt that in our age of machines and boredom, real men are disappearing. Men now react to the thousands of events and situations in life more like hysterical women. While women are gaining strength in the face of adversity, parrying the blows of life with ever greater resistance and fortitude, men are becoming more hesitant and unsure. Women are much better at enduring the war. Men are fighting, because they have to. Many are heroic. But if one were to look more deeply, I'm not sure it wouldn't turn out that even on the front lines hysteria affects many things. It's a war of hysterical men and for that reason is so cruel. Who knows if the male is not already disappearing, even in war. Not to mention everyday life. Men are becoming more vulnerable. Physically and especially morally, men are ever more prone to falling apart. It's not the masculine modern woman who resembles a hermaphrodite, but it's the man who has become fluid, elusive, vague. How much harder it is today to form the image of a man. "Weak" women have become rare, but weak men are increasingly common. The number of confident women grows, the number of resolute men diminishes. The civilization that is emerging threatens men much more than women. Women withstand monotony more easily and are prepared to sacrifice a lot for the sake of order, security, and concord. Monotony is more destructive to men. We become as fussy as women, sensitive in the negative sense, vindictive, lacking in flair. We're overtaken by moods in which we try to fight off the sense of responsibility: hysteria, a tendency to slackness, fickleness.

Michel is an excellent example of modern man, that miserable man forced into routines, regimented, numbered, hemmed in by hours and minutes, pressured by automatism—all this external discipline in which inner discipline is lost. He has no desire to give Bordier a normal "drubbing." Bah—he justifies himself by saying he just gently shoved him out the door. He doesn't dare to give his wife a spanking. That would be too crude, but it might have given both of them some relief. He doesn't dare to leave her, because life without her would be even more barren and gray, reduced to his hours in the office and his paperwork. He doesn't want to start life over again, because he lacks the imagination—the flame has died out. This typical specimen of the derivative man of our age doesn't have the strength to find a resolution in some kind of creativity or adventure. He tries to solve the problem intellectually, by thinking it through, trying to master something in himself by means of reason with which reason in fact cannot cope. And therefore he drowns himself. Well, go ahead, drown yourself. Serves him right!

The performance is excellent, although Valentine Tessier overdoes the insolence.[154] She speaks and behaves so provocatively that in Michel's place I would have slapped her around from the first to last act. This kind of performance fundamentally alters the intensity of the play and distorts its meaning.

For its part, the audience was stunning. The "Dames" and "Messieurs," the hoi polloi enriched by the black market, who come to the theater, not for the three acts, but for the two intermissions. The sight of them made me think I was in a theater in the Wild West among the gold diggers.

October 17, 1943

A conference of the so-called Allies has opened in Moscow.[155] Eden, Hall, Molotov, various military men, and so on. A poker game among horse thieves. Moscow wants a second front, insists, demands, and apparently threatens. The English are playing politics with their innate stupidity, which gives the impression of a "great and skillful diplomacy." The Americans, for their part, invoke their deliveries to Russia and let it be understood that without them the Soviets would be having a hard time, but the Soviets do not want to reach an agreement. Since they all need each other, there is nevertheless hope they'll come to some kind of understanding. If in a year "all this" begins to end, that will be a good thing. Better, nevertheless, not to think about "how."

Two powerful and unassailable convictions prevail everywhere these days. The most sensible people reduce everything first of all to defeating the Germans: "As soon as the Germans are defeated, we will enter a new era." In a word, Liberty, Equality, Fraternity, Prosperity, Independence—*wsio, tout, everything, alles.* "As soon as the Germans are defeated, I'll get married, butter will be cheaper, paradise on earth." Simple, clear, certain. The basket is ready with raisins, dried fruit, and nuts without coupons. The second dogma is that Russia is changing. No, that the Russians have already changed. They are perfect angels, lambs, a truly great people. Of course, it's agreed, "certain" things are unavoidable at the beginning (rather long this beginning, for a beginning), but there's no doubt, that . . . In any case, all these accusations are false, just reactionary propaganda, lies. Katyń—my God—the facts are unclear, it's a controversial matter. All this reveals a subconscious clinging to whatever comes along, the absolute desire *to believe.* The Soviets and Communism have become substitutes for religion. Belief in them has taken the place of the lost faith in everything. Pulled by the centrifugal movement of the world and of humanity, man grows ever more centrifugal and does not want to "spin off" at a sharp curve. And therefore he blunders from one idiocy into even greater idiocies.

October 21, 1943

Autumn. Mornings, when I leave for the office, workers dressed in faded work blues are sweeping the withered leaves on avenue Daumesnil. They gather them into great piles along the sidewalk and set them afire. A meaty, greasy smoke wafts through the streets. The type of smoke changes with the time of year. Summer smoke is different from autumn smoke. Now it's chilly and gray. Another wartime winter is approaching.

I have discovered a small bookshop on rue Saint-Sulpice where they have agreed to try to find me "difficult" books. A diminutive bookbinder is in charge. Books, particularly good ones, have become no less objects of the black market than butter, sugar, and counterfeit bread coupons—in general everything. A slew of translations from English, many publications from before the war and now banned, have their own exchange rates, just like the dollar and the louis d'or. My bookbinder (he's called Bardache—a very Balzacian name) has initiated me into the labyrinth of the current market. I sit in his cubbyhole behind the shop, glassed-in at the top, rolling cigarettes for him and for myself (his fingers are sticky from glue and he can't roll them, but it doesn't bother him in the least that I lick the paper) and I watch as he glues the leather binding to the sewn books. He has found me Max Scheler, Jung, and Spengler, whom I wanted to revisit after a number of years. He speaks about Pierre Louÿs,[156] about many of his books, of which it's unclear whether they were written by him or imitated for use in brothel waiting rooms. He quotes me dizzying prices for certain éditions de luxe.

I inhale with pleasure the smell of glue and old paper. Then I wander around the shop, skimming through the books on the shelves. I'm assembling a small library. But many things are impossible to obtain. I therefore order them. Bardache unleashes a whole pack of hunting dogs into the chase for any given title, while I wait. I pay more dearly, but I can afford it. One cannot be fully human without a certain amount of extra cash in one's pocket. Without a piece of sausage and the means, however minimal, to satisfy one's cultural needs, the spirit becomes entirely inhuman, which means eminently inclined to create ideologies, according to which half of humanity must be slaughtered in order for the author of the ideology and those of his kind to be able to eat and have the means to satisfy their elementary cultural needs. In fact, all "the one and only true" ideologies are the products of starvelings—if not physical, then certainly moral or spiritual.

Below a certain threshold, one cannot be a human being. One may possess all the features of humanity, one may keep oneself going, but at an enormous cost that is certain to distort the soul. The possession of a certain culture without at the same time having the possibility of satisfying, if only partly, the needs to which that culture gives rise, leads people to perversions more or less harmful to those around them. Moral or spiritual starvelings are far more dangerous than physical starvelings. It is easier to satisfy physical hunger. Spiritual hunger persists and even grows when the other kind is sated. A man with a certain culture is not and cannot be complete, if he must repeat all day long: "If only I had . . . I would buy . . ." Some day the myth of Communism will crumble to dust, and the cause will be, on the one hand, that Communism will multiply the needs it calls "elementary" without, on the other hand, providing the means to satisfy them. At the heart of today's entire conflict is the quarrel between two methods of "feeding." Some want to move forward, they want to realize their dreams (America). Others want to destroy dreams altogether, reducing everyone to the lowest level; they want to teach people not "to want," they want them to get unaccustomed to moral hunger, they want perhaps to destroy hunger simply by means of hunger (Russia).

I'm performing an experiment on myself. Once I had resolved the problem of sausage, I stood up straighter. Once my imagination stopped dancing a wild saraband around some book title or other, my muscles flexed. Because in many cases I CAN BUT I CHOOSE NOT TO. "I can but why should I?" gives me dignity. Even with regard to myself.

October 23, 1943

This evening in the Théâtre Saint-Georges for Balzac's *L'École des ménages*. I went to the theater worried and fearful. It was the kind of anxiety you feel for someone you dearly love and you know has taken the wrong turn. I feared a disgrace, in short, a flop—and I was right.

Concerning Balzac's theatrical talents opinions are divided. Some insist there was no chance he would be successful in the theater—others maintain he didn't have enough time to master the technique and, had he lived longer, would certainly have found his own style in this as well. Hard to say. One thing is certain, which is that Balzac himself had no great confidence in his own abilities in this domain and always sought a partner when writing a play. Things usually ended with the partner letting him down and Balzac himself—amid the torments and pangs of childbirth—putting his first attempt in the drawer. When he was threatened by increasing debts, when his normal earnings were not enough to cover his bills, Balzac's theatrical nerve came to life. The theater! An end to debts and a fortune awaiting. For the theater interested him only from the monetary point of view. "A hundred fifty performances"—he would cry to his friends—"at 50,000 francs a night, which means 750,000. And now, do the math: 12 percent author's rights, which means over 80,000 francs pure profit. Not to speak of the brochure in 80,000 copies at 3 francs apiece—30,000 . . ."

And the play he had put aside, unfinished and covered in the dried sweat of his all-night efforts, of the titanic struggle of his vast imagination with the narrow demands of the theater, emerged from the drawer onto the table. That's what happened with *L'École des ménages*.[157]

After his great journey to Corsica and Sardinia, where a silver mine he had wanted to buy and which—amazingly!—was indeed a solid and valuable investment (for that reason the deal had failed) was snatched from under his nose, after his visit to Italy and in Guérande (his romance with Hélène de la Valette), the year 1838 was relatively unprofitable. *The Cabinet of Antiquities, The Splendors and Miseries of a Courtesan's Life,* completion of *The Rise and Fall of Cesar Birotteau, The House of Nucingen,* and *A Daughter of Eve.* Only modest cash revenues. Meanwhile overdue bills are threatening. In February 1839 he needed 6,000 francs to cover his debts. What to do? The theater! His friend, Armand Pérémé, used his influence and Balzac signed a contract with Anténor Joly, director of the Théâtre de la Renaissance, which provided 6,000 francs for the immediate delivery of *The School of Matrimony,* another play due in five months, the next in eight months . . .[158] Saved!

He instantly extracts from the drawer *The First Shopgirl* (*La Première Demoiselle*), which in 1838 had already displeased Mme Hańska but which delighted Mme Sand.[159] Balzac changed the title. *The Shopgirl* became *The School of Matrimony.* "I'll launch a drama based on ordinary petit-bourgeois life, as a trial balloon," he apparently wrote to Mme Hańska, "without fuss, something inconsequential, to see what people will say about something that presents them with the absolute truth." Naturally, he engaged a partner. That was Charles Lassailly.[160] Together they set to work. For sixteen days and sixteen nights they wrestled with the insurmountable difficulties of the stage. Exhausted, crushed, squeezed like a lemon, he appears in Joly's office with *School of Matrimony* in hand. Joly does not accept the play. The "absolute truth," the "drama based on ordinary petit-bourgeois life"—these were not then in fashion. The theater wanted theater in the worst sense of the word. It wanted plays à la *Antony* of Papa Dumas or *Hamlet* with a *happy-end,* which Papa Dumas had so well tailored to the Parisian public.[161] *Happy-end* is not at all an American invention. The mass culture that had just begun to sprout in France demanded then, as it does today, a *happy-end* and optimism. Balzac's *School of Matrimony* sank into oblivion until—1943. Between the moment when the pitiless Joly rejected the miserable author's play and the present autumn there is a void, which nevertheless connects those moments and makes them both seem contemporary. Heading for the theater, I felt that Balzac was still alive. I was moved, a bit lost in time, and terribly anxious. Unfamiliar with *The School of Matrimony,* not even having read it, I trembled at the idea that Honoré might "overdo it," as Tadeusz Boy-Żeleński once wrote concerning Mme Hańska, that he might get carried away.[162] And Honoré did "overdo it." Even with respect to the demands of theater today, so much more progressive than back then.

Profiting from the absence of her husband and assisted by her two daughters, Anne and Caroline, after Anne, aided by Monsieur Duval, Mme Gérard's brother, and Roblot, the cashier of the firm, has conceived a cunning plot, Mme Gérard fires Mlle Adrienne, the first of Monsieur Gérard's shopgirls and the only one he trusts. But before Mlle Adrienne has actually moved out, Gérard, hastening his return, unexpectedly appears at home. He is unpleasantly surprised not to find his confidante and only friend in this family nest of vipers. The drama explodes, full of tension, violent and headlong. Love (for Gérard has understood that he loves Mlle Adrienne with the final love of an aging man), as well as cunning, jealousy, and hatred, lead all the characters in the course of three acts to some kind of epilogue. But what kind? In the course of three powerful acts, in some scenes achieving the somber grandeur of a disturbing, almost Ibsenesque realism, the situation becomes so complicated that no solution seems possible. Gérard wants to leave his family and go away with Adrienne, but he cannot resolve on this step. To live from now on without Adrienne is impossible. To leave Adrienne in the household and return to the status quo will be hell. To renounce happiness? Not possible. To experience it from a distance, after burning all his bridges behind him? Also, no. Compromise? Excluded.

I confess that the first three acts struck me by their modernity. The issue raised was considered unsuitable to the theater by the theatrical standards of 1839. The "absolute truth" here takes the form of shocking scenes, acceptable to us today but certainly in Balzac's day belonging to the "unmentionable." The reason no doubt for Mme Hańska turning up her nose and for George Sand's delight. Because Balzac says out loud what Sand only thought (and did) and which, despite everything, she—the great Aurore—did not dare express in *this* fashion. Joly rejected the play because the public of that day would not have swallowed such an obvious scandal. Even Balzac had to take this into account and he therefore introduced the astounding epilogue. It was supposed to be a communion wafer, the spiritual coating intended to make the bitter pill easier for the public to swallow, but at the same time also that "unheard-of" something that so delighted the *enfant terrible* of French literature and of all of France. He indeed overdid it. The epilogue, it seems, is based on an actual event (?), which Balzac "got wind of" somewhere in 1838. He attached it, with his usual passion and apparently at the instigation of the Duchess de Metternich, to the rest of the play.

The fourth act represents the Gérards' drawing room. The candles on the chandelier have been lit. We see the black coats of a notary and some officials. They have been summoned for the signing of a document, or rather as official witnesses to the fact that Gérard and Mlle Adrienne, there present, are not in command of their faculties. At the moment Gérard was entering the carriage in which he and Adrienne were to run away, both had lost their memories and all contact with reality. They had stopped being able to see or recognize each other. They continue to live side by side, talking with each other, yearning for each other, recounting their love, and waiting for death to unite them forever. A mystical, sky-blue and silver ending. The communion wafer.

After three acts of a brutal terre à terre, after the explosion of feelings and instincts of flesh and blood, the epilogue is like a glass of tepid water. It ruins everything, deflates all the tension. The three powerful acts crumble into sugary mysticism, the whole thing shatters completely.

For me, nevertheless, Balzac has returned to life. Basia and I felt his presence and in discussing certain scenes we both smiled. That's him exactly, "such" as he was, at this moment, at that moment, in this sentence, in that scene, in this character. How proud he must have been of the epilogue . . . of the epilogue, in particular.

Despite the fashion for Balzac, the theater was empty. *The School of Matrimony* will not make it and will fail, despite the brilliant state of theater at the moment. I feared this from the first and was not mistaken.

The refined Constant Rémy (Gérard) is very good, Mary Morgan (Adrienne) is splendid.[163]

1944

January 26, 1944

I have not been writing. When the future becomes entirely predictable, when it's clear that night is descending, what reason is there to write? I've now been in the hospital for five days. At first it was an illness, a swelling on the left side of my neck that kept growing, a fever, until finally the doctor pronounced it to be a *ganglion*, or some such name, and an emergency operation was needed. Apparently, at the last moment the situation was even dangerous. K. as usual proved so thoughtful, so resourceful, that thanks to him I have my own separate compartment in the common ward. Life in the ward "runs its course," but I am not part of it.

This morning an old duffer died. He moaned softly. When the doctor arrived, he was no longer moaning. He had breathed his last. Involuntarily, I blew into the air, as though blowing out a candle, and thought, "That's life." Screens were placed around the old man's bed and life continued "on its course." A young fellow lay next to him. He was brought in yesterday after a serious operation to remove the open safety pin he had swallowed (where these days had he found a safety pin?) from his throat. Yesterday, the fellow was barely alive, today he's already up and laughing. Now he's gone to the hospital concert. I didn't go to the concert because I didn't want to get dressed. The hours drag by, one after another, hours without periods or commas, time with no punctuation. I go to the bathroom for a cigarette — it's forbidden to smoke in the ward — and am reminded of my Gymnasium days. I read and reflect. Actually, I now have what I've been dreaming of for weeks. Peace, enough time, and the feeling of being "cut off." I'm a bit cut off from the world. Meanwhile, events in the world are speeding ahead — speeding toward an end that is paradoxical and tragic. Like a menacing shadow, with every passing day the specter of Russia stretches farther and farther into the future, moving firmly toward victory, toward *the only* victory, and subordinating everything to itself. And so? And so, must Eastern Europe fall under the domination of that mechanized barbarism, of that brute, of the ideology that kills everything in man that makes him a man? After so many years of lying, of that repulsive lying that stifles and shackles thought, after so many years of empty and inhuman *dogmas,* must we plunge yet again into lies, dogmas, and state-run hypocrisy? It could well be . . . What am I afraid of? I'm afraid, for heaven's sake, that I'll once again *be ordered* to believe in something. *Ordered* to believe that some democracy or Communist system is perfect and "the one and only." That once again any piece of sh—— will be turned into *ideals and ideologies,* that once again lies and propaganda will be put on a pedestal and made into a new God. I have enough troubles with the old one . . .

So, what's the point of this war? And who does it serve? People sense the end is approaching, but they don't rejoice. Everyone feels a certain anxiety, however, as though before being plunged into even greater darkness. How greatly have people's moods changed in the past half year . . .

I sit alone and I don't want to think, I'm afraid of thinking and of thinking things through. How simple everything would be if one could believe, for example, in the simplicity of Radio Moscow.

January 27, 1944

I gaze at the grayness outside the window. My dressing has been changed. The doctor rummaged in my wound and it hurt. Man is obliged to agree with everything that falls to his lot. It's the only way of finding peace. Protest against the bad sides of life leads to nothing, all the more so when the "bad sides" are in the past. Protest should aim for the future. That's the only constructive form of protest. The horror of Communism is its continual protest aimed at the past, the past of an early capitalism that no longer has anything to do with reality. Protest aimed at the present and the future are heresies there. And their *happy end* does me in.

January 28, 1944

Still in the hospital. The incision is healing slowly. Bed no. 3 is occupied by an elderly Frenchman, an old-fashioned, mustachioed Breton. I go over to chat, or rather to listen to his endless stories. He works coloring flowers, a profession peculiar to Paris. He colors heather lilac, as well as various grasses and other everlasting flowers. He talks about the previous war. He was in the Balkans. He returned from Constantinople to Salonica on a ship where typhus was raging. People were dying all around and in the silence of the steamy weather there was the continual sound of water splashing, as the corpses were dropped into the sea.

He's pious, a touchingly pious believer, without a drop of sanctimony. He belongs to the congregation of the Sacré-Coeur and has his own banner, which he carries in all the processions. He's very proud of this banner. He paid three thousand francs for it before the war—"and that's without the pole, the fittings, or the case," he adds, with a wink. He lies in bed reading the New Testament—in Latin. Clearly, he understands nothing, it's just to keep his spirits up. He lent me the little book and I read all morning. I swallowed the New Testament in one gulp. In Latin it had a special charm. Truly beautiful descriptions of the life of Christ. So direct that at times it seemed to me it was only yesterday when he went around preaching, when he revealed to the world of his time a great and unknown thing: Mercy and love of thy neighbor, human dignity even among those most abased, although *"Beati qui persecutionem patiuntur propter justitiam: quoniam ipsorum est regnum caelorum"* seems to me somewhat demagogic.[1] It seems a bit discriminatory, as, for example, when only the sons of workers and peasants have the right to higher education.

The scene in the Temple with the Pharisees is splendid. In every conversation with Communists I would also like to call out: *"Quid me tentatis, hypocritae? Ostendite mihi numisma census . . . Cujus est imago haec, et superscriptio? Dicunt ei: Caesaris. Tunc ait illis: Reddite ergo, quae sunt Caesaris, Caesari: et, quae sunt Dei, Deo."*[2] It's quite cinematic.

Evening. The air is heavy. The central heating sucks all the refreshing moisture from the air. Only a stench remains—the stench of sweaty bodies, urine, and illness. Happily, I can open the window and in my compartment I am separate from the rest of the ward. The collective—the ideal of the future world. Damn it! I have decided to be subjective, radically subjective. In this era of groveling "objectivity," there's no other way to behave.

Around eight, a patient who was operated on this afternoon had a hemorrhage. I hear the burbling in his throat, as in an old sink, and the splash of blood spurting out in streams. Moaning, burbling, and sloshing. Silence. The nurses run back and forth. The on-duty physician arrived. The man was dying. He belched long and deeply. Then it was over. Already they are surrounding his bed with screens. My God—is this anything special? I blew into the air and again extinguished an imaginary candle. How many people are perishing at this moment, at this very second, out there on the fronts, in German and Russian concentration camps, everywhere. I am also unimportant. It's a lottery.

It's stuffy in the ward and I'm sweating. I hold a handkerchief sprinkled with eau de cologne under my nose and think about Petronius. I probably won't be able to fall asleep. It's quiet again in the ward. Soon they turn out the lights. We sleep with the carrion. They did not even open the windows. No doubt so the corpses do not catch a *congéstion*. I can't stand it. I light a cigarette in bed, although it's forbidden. But no one notices. I sit on the bed and gaze at the lilac dusk. Sleeping is out of the question. I get dressed and sit with a book in the armchair next to the night lamp. Soon a nurse comes and orders me back to bed. This is not allowed. I didn't even look up and pretend to continue reading. I must already be healthy, because I'm simply itching for a fight. The nurse keeps chattering. The rules, order, the on-duty doctor. I close the book with a smack (Pascal's *Pensées*), bang it on the table, and yell: "*Je m'en fous, vous comprenez*[3]—I can't sleep and I want to read."

Another flood of words. The doctor-in-chief will come, etc. "Let him come and I'll talk with him. *Foutez-moi la paix.* I can't sleep. It's hygiene, *nom de Dieu*, sleeping with carrion in the same room in this foul air."[4] The male nurse appeared and tries to take me by the hand. I was waiting for that. "*Attention, mon vieux, ne me touche pas,*[5] or you'll be carried out of here on a stretcher." He took fright. Lets go of me and leaves me in peace. Chatter in the corridor. I'm in heaven. I keep reading. At eleven two fellows appear with a stretcher to take out the venerable corpses. They rummaged a bit there in the dim light and after a while passed right by me. The stretcher was covered in a black tarp. The nose and toes were visible. And thus did a man take his leave. I waved and said under my breath, "*Salut.*" The nurse again approached and asked if I intended to go to bed. *Non, merde!* She left. I slit open the pages of my book and went to bed at midnight. The ward was stifling. When one of them starts to cough, all start coughing. The one across the way with cancer of the trachea snorts and wheezes, like an old locomobile. Stench. I opened the window and in flew a mosquito. In January, a mosquito! I curse out loud, because it's buzzing around my face. It bit my hand and I finally killed it on my forehead. Now I can sleep.

January 29, 1944

The incision is not healing. It keeps oozing. I'm horribly anxious. This is a prison. I'm completely unfit for collective living. It depresses me. I want to break and smash everything. If only Jędrek Przybylski were with me, we'd start a classic fracas, imported direct from Dębniki and Podzamcze, the tough quarters of Cracow. I remember how his father once had pneumonia. His papa loved the bottle but the doctor had laid down the law. Mama went out and Jędrek suddenly hears his father's basso voice: "Andrzej, my one and only son, your father will soon be dead . . ." Jędrek had begun to cry, thinking his father was already kicking the bucket, when his father continued: "and in this my final hour I ask you to nip out and bring me a pint of lager from Ritterman's." Jędrek handed papa his beer and papa didn't kick the bucket at all. There was one feat I always envied him: that rascal spent all his time preparing for final exams—in the

Phoenix.[6] He drank coffee, danced with all the hostesses and taxi dancers, and in the breaks between tangos and English waltzes, he crammed. And passed. And I didn't. To this day I'm convinced it's because I didn't study in the Phoenix. I must be in a really bad way, if I'm beginning to reminisce. Elegant dance lessons. The two Wyrwicz girls, Magda Grosse, Szarska—the cream of Cracow. And for drinks there was lemonade. I would run right afterward for a vodka, to forget the taste of the lemonade. I'm in a really bad way. I would love some rum, but there's no way to get it. Basia doesn't want to bring any. Perhaps I should repeat the scene with Przybylski's papa: "O wife, my only, my beloved . . ." Damn! I'll trade some tobacco for wine with one of these stiffs.

In the afternoon there was a "concert." I went. One of the rooms, apparently a lecture hall (such filth, such filth), is arranged like an amphitheater. The public entered. Goya, by contrast, is nothing but a pipsqueak. His battlefields are ordinary still lifes. Here the still life was living. These patients are miserable, filthy, and stinking. Painted girls from the dermatology ward (*c'est notre siphilisation*, as one of my French acquaintances likes to say when we discuss our present times), sickly faces, bare legs, and hospital gowns. The whole amphitheater resembled a woman's Spanish comb, filled with dandruff from top to bottom. It had the atmosphere and palette of an engraving of a fifteenth-century hospital. Human rags and dregs. The "artists' performance" began.

An old, skinny granny with a beaky nose provided the piano accompaniment. A young man rattled out a few lethargic songs. It's interesting that this nation with no musical ear and no sense of rhythm should have such a passion for singing. Then a *jeune fille* from the collection of overused maidens squeaked out a few off-key songs. A threadbare prima donna, retired from service, next cranked out something from the repertoire of 1925 and blew the audience playful kisses, inviting them to join in the refrain. And the dandruff hummed along.

The director of the troupe then gave a performance. He recited a poem from which it appeared that all those wearing rosettes of the Legion of Honor were perfect scoundrels who did not deserve them, while those who had actually shed blood "*pour la Frrrance*" had nothing. The dandruff applauded like mad. I did, too, just to convince myself that I still can. I can, which means I still belong to the human race. Because the main thing is to applaud, to know how to applaud. Next, he recited a long poem by François Coppée (worse even than coughing or Victor Hugo), titled "The Strike of the Blacksmiths."[7] Finally a kind of *chanteuse fantaisiste* resembling an old Komsomol girl, party cell member, or *Chekistka* (one of my aunts from Wilno always used to say: "Women are always crueler than men—just look at those Cheka women"[8]) sang songs for the audience in *argot*. Something like "I'm Afraid to Sleep Alone"[9] and proposed to the men in the audience that they sleep with her. As she sang, she went down into the amphitheater and selected one particular young stinker, whom she kissed on both sweaty cheeks at the end of the song. I felt sick to my stomach and left. I was revived only by the sight of sparrows bathing in a puddle. The sun was setting and the sparrows, puffed up like grayish-brown feather dusters, splashed around in the water. I envied them. While inside, the dandruff continued to enjoy themselves. My eyes retained the image of the packed hall and the ghastly head of a woman missing her chin and lips. And the rows and rows of heads, bizarre and horrible. The navy-blue gowns, the dirty bandages, the women's bare legs, bluish with veins. Torn shoes and slippers, the overpainted faces, the greasy hairdos and earrings. Amid all that, the skeletal rattle of the piano and the lady "singers" from the graveyard of broken-down artists, hopping about and blowing kisses to living corpses.

I'm thinking about Jasiek.[10] I've been here nine days and I'm already at the end of my rope. For him it's been four years. Day after day. It must be horrendous—a camp.

I'm reading Édouard Dujardin's memoirs of Houston Stewart Chamberlain, the Germanicized Englishman who wrote the once famous, racist, and anti-Semitic *Grundlagen des neunzehnten Jahrhunderts*.[11] The Nazis consider him their prophet. The English, after all, are versatile. In one of his letters to Dujardin, Chamberlain writes: "I recently sent my maid to hear *Tannhäuser* and she returned in raptures: 'How beautiful,' she said, 'but how much more beautiful it would be without the music.'" That's the voice of common sense. The maid must have been exceptionally intelligent. She said more or less the same thing as Frobenius in his *History of Civilizations*, which asserts about the nineteenth century that in music Weber began the work of destruction, which Wagner then continued.[12] Frobenius defines it as "pointless virtuosity," as "organized, or rather, mechanized sounds." Indeed, it cannot be said of Wagner that he is a master of the art of restraint. Chamberlain's scullery maid sensed this.

January 30, 1944

For two days now the nurses have been changing my dressing and I can't find out anything. I've asked for the doctor to change it today. The doctors here are strange. They have none of the "divine spark" that characterizes German, Austrian, or Polish doctors. No sense of a calling or artistry. They are functionaries who consider this job no better than any other. No interest in their patients at all. Today's intern behaves like a demigod, like an indifferent Parisian tomcat. Aren't they taught about patient psychology? He busied himself with me, examined me, poked around, and repeated their eternal *ça va, ça va très bien*. "But why doesn't it heal?" I ask. "Because we only lanced the tumor without removing it and it's now slowly draining—*ça suit son cours.*"[13] That comforted me a little. I returned to my compartment, sat down in the chair, and fainted. I came to when they were undressing me. I'm obviously weak. It infuriates me. It's the first time in my life that my body, of which until now I could demand anything I wanted, has failed me. But obviously this, too, one must accept.

January 31, 1944

But, it seems that indeed *ça va.* The nurses are beginning to drop hints that I may be sent home and come back for the dressings. We'll see. The only thing that "cools" me off is the chill in our hotel room. But it's a mild winter. Amazing—this year is the first time I've missed the snow and the dry cold. It's spring outside. I'm weak.

Hitler gave a speech on the eleventh anniversary of Nazism. When pressed, he squeals. If Germany loses the war, it will be the end not only of the German people but of half of Europe and all of European culture. Perhaps. Except, what would happen if Germany won?

February 1, 1944

I intend to stay in this cursed hospital because it makes sense. They're giving me injections to build up my strength and I'm eating sugar. Since January 14, I haven't eaten any sugar and as a result my organism has been thrown off-balance. I've always needed sugar more than anything else. Today's *L'Écho de la France* (all France will soon be called "L'Écho de la France") has an interesting article called "Russian-Polish Conflict Enters a Critical Phase." It's the title of an article in the English *Economist,* which is quoted in the French paper, followed by a summary. It's rather amazing, moreover, that it should have appeared both in England and here.

"The Polish-Russian disagreement is considerably more extensive and complicated than the discussion of the border in itself. On both sides, it's a question of trust and mutual antipathy . . . The Russian declaration contains a certain number of entirely unsupported statements of a polemical nature concerning the Polish government, which is far from being 'isolated from its people' and which, in any case, represents the nation more completely than any other Polish government ever has, despite the political mistakes and *faux pas* it may have committed. The Russian declaration contains the threat to form a new government in Poland, originating in the Union of Polish Patriots[14] in Moscow. It is important to make clear that this kind of government will be regarded by all the Allied powers as a 'phantom-government,' and that it should not expect to be recognized. It is apparent that the most sensible step for Moscow now to take in order to facilitate a Polish-Russian rapprochement would be to dissolve the Union of Polish Patriots and initiate actual negotiations with the neighboring countries."

Quite interesting. On the other hand, today's *Matin* reports that Stalin has granted autonomy to the Soviet republics on the English model, a move intended also to serve as the resolution of the Polish problem. *Znachit*, as the Russians say—meaning Poland as an autonomous Soviet republic. This suits me just fine, at least it's clear, because I've expected essentially nothing else for a long time. But please leave me out of it, because I don't want to be "autonomous."

The wound doesn't stop oozing. It's already the second week. They say that *ça se vide* and that *c'est long*.[15] The devil take them. So I'm stuck in the hospital. I'll have to consider it a rest cure.

Jean Giraudoux died yesterday of an attack of uremia. An entirely unexpected death. One of the literary celebrities of contemporary Paris has expired. At the moment, in fact, his *Sodome et Gomorrhe* is playing at the Théâtre Hébertot with Edwige Feuillère.[16]

February 2, 1944

A new law about labor conscription for men aged sixteen to sixty and women from eighteen to forty-eight. New transports to Germany are in preparation.

I'm finishing Louis Bromfield's *La Mousson. Hintertreppenlitteratur.*[17] Some pretty good descriptions next to passages, often a dozen pages long, of complete barbarism. Unclear what the whole thing is about.

I read in today's paper that a new radio station has opened in Paris. It's called *"radio-diffusion permanente."* It broadcasts information from seven in the morning to ten at night. Nonstop.

Great! There's a kind of madness in this. We've reached the point at which the entire city may be reduced to a state of complete stupefaction. It would be enough to install speakers every fifty meters in all the streets, broadcasting the same thing over and over around the clock. We're already being trained for the future world.

Once again, night is coming. The nights are the worst. At eight they shut the lights. I don't fall asleep until eleven, sometimes not until midnight, and then I fall into paroxysms of sleep, waking around one, then three, then five in the morning. Most often I lie and reminisce. I reminisce calmly, with no regret that something has ended.

February 3, 1944

The Germans assert that in recent days they have dropped over a thousand tons of bombs on London. Churchill announces the coming of important battles that will inflict great suffering on all Englishmen. The *Daily Herald* speaks of final preparations for the boldest invasion in history. They will be fighting in the service of Russia.

In France the battle against gangs of "terrorists" has begun. The doctor, when pinned down, told me that everything is going well, but the process cannot be hurried. Too bad. I'm reading and taking notes.

February 4, 1944

Well, at last—they have removed the full dressing, the oozing has stopped, they've applied some gauze, and now it should heal. In a few days it may all be over. These hospitals are truly medieval. Yesterday morning they discovered that one of the patients in our ward has scarlet fever. He remained here with us until today and only toward evening did they take him to the isolation ward.

Today it snowed. It melted at once, but looking out the window at the dance of flakes cheered me up somehow. A thick snow with wind is like music for me. It plays. An entire symphony. Each flake strikes a particular note. On its own it means nothing, but along with the others, it creates a melody.

February 5, 1944

Now it's really healing. They brought the X-ray of my lungs and the doctor said everything was fine. I lie in bed surrounded by books. The doctor who came today stopped and began to inspect them. He looked at me and—was at once transformed. In this country, known as so cultured, the sight of a dozen books acts like a secret password. The doctor sat on the bed, began to leaf through Bergson, then Pascal, and deigned to start a conversation. When finally he left, I concluded that the degradation of France has reached the point where a member of the so-called intellectual elite feels more in common and greater affinity with another of his kind than anywhere else. Who knows if we are not approaching a time when two people meeting even in the absence of witnesses will begin by patiently "sniffing each other out," like two dachshunds (all humanity will by then have come to resemble nothing but dachshunds), after which one will casually, as if just to himself, drop the name of a forbidden philosopher or writer. "Pascal," he will whisper. The other will then embrace him and say, "my brother." They will then shed some tears and arrange to meet at night in some ruins, so they can spend an hour discussing Pascal. But even that will be difficult, because their words will be drowned out by the loudspeakers of some *"radio-diffusion permanente,"* placed every twenty-five meters, and because the dream and goal of every city official will be to install street lighting so pervasive and powerful that people will not be able to gaze upward and see the starry sky. The starry skies conceal the most treacherous traps for the thinking of the new man. A few of them might *begin* to think. I'm starting to believe that Alexander the Great became great simply because he preferred to journey to India, rather than implement the "Utopia" Aristotle had written for him.

Yesterday the Russians took Równe and Łuck. It's beginning.

They have just told me that I can leave the hospital if I want to. I instantly phoned Basia and asked her to bring my coat and hat. I have a three-week-old beard and look like Fridtjof Nansen.[18]

February 6, 1944

Home again. What a joy! It's really cold here, but I feel completely different. As though released from prison. Right away, I shaved. People have brought me various things. Everyone whom I've always been ready to assist with various problems, whom I've managed to help, in simple human terms, expecting nothing in exchange—all have made me feel how fond of me they are. One brought groats from his own reserves and *a single apple* (his only one, which he received as a gift from somebody—which really moved me). Another person arranged to get me a chicken. I., the Spaniard, brought me prunes and jam from the Quakers. M. and his wife sent a chicken and two dozen eggs from their farm. W. and S. brought butter, bacon, flour, a jar of jam, groats, some apples, and some heads of cauliflower—and no one would take any money. Dr. K., my nominal boss, has been occupied exclusively, it seems, with obtaining jam, apples, and other edibles for me. He is truly tireless in helping others. There are few people in my life for whom I have had such respect.

I knew that many people liked me, but I didn't know how much.

. . . .

June 2, 1944

Once again, I've stopped writing for several months. What's the use? Now I'm writing only from a chronicler's sense of duty, as one would keep one's diary until the last moment on a sinking ship.

I left home at six in the morning and rode through Porte de la Chapelle. Remains of the bombardment. Buildings ripped open, streets large and small broken up. The morning was chilly and overcast. Beyond Saint-Denis I was on a main highway. All around, empty and parched. For the past two months there hasn't been a drop of rain and the suburban house gardens are as bare as at the approach of autumn. The flower beds have become piles of dust. Farther on, in the fields, the wheat has dried out at the root. Half an hour later I entered Chantilly. A chill everywhere and the green smell of the leafy forests. Then Creil, already bombed several times. Train carriages like accordions. These harmoniums invite you to play a lively and joyful melody of perfect destruction. The swollen bellies of the locomotives, slashed and punctured with holes, the coils of their entrails twisted, flaming pipes hanging out. Rails and switch points crushed into the ground churned up by the bombs. Enormous craters all around. Solid American mass production. I have by now pedaled sixty km. I dismount, settle down in a small wood, and have something to eat. My mouth is dry and the wine tastes twice as good. I lie down and cover up because it's chilly. I doze. Little birds are chirping in the bushes, the beetles promenading through the grass make a penetrating sound. Total silence. I fall into a heavy half-sleep and wake at noon. Cloudy. Somewhere airplanes buzz. The daily, monotonous music, interspersed with drumming. I hurry on. The road goes through the parched fields. If only for a bit of rain. I wish for rain as though I were myself a plant. I pity each tuft, each blade of grass. In the midst of all this, the crimson poppies burn insolently, increasing the feeling of drought and thirst. After one I arrive at M.'s house. They are pleased with my visit. His wife smiles with her exquisite eyes and says: "You will get some rest with us." Indeed, I'll get some rest. Finally. I'll eat a large plate of potato dumplings and drink rhubarb compote. After lunch I lie down and fall asleep. I wake toward evening. The sun is setting behind the forests, the weather has cleared up. Overhead two formations of heavy bombers fly past, surrounded by fighter planes speeding from all sides. They shimmer and howl. Like a herd of sheep driven by barking sheepdogs.

In the evening on the radio: the march on Rome, the Germans are beaten, Velletria and Valmontone have fallen. Before I fell asleep, another two-hour concert of engines, monotonous and relentless. It's totally incredible how many of them the Americans have manufactured. Only in order to lose the war.

June 3, 1944

At five in the morning the butcher arrived. A tall, thin Frenchman. I got up with M. and decided to be present at the execution. The pig did not want to leave the pigpen. It sensed the butcher—that was totally clear. They tied it to a peg by the hind leg. M. sat astride it and held it down. It squealed. Considering that the slaughter was illegal, its behavior was beneath criticism. An ax blow to the forehead. It fell over with a moan (a scene from Zola). A long knife thrust into the heart and a fountain of blood. The wife used a large saucepan to catch the blood, which she stirred to prevent it from congealing. For headcheese and blood sausage. Poor old "Mikuś" was gone. The couple say it's their last pig. They won't raise another one because, after all, the English are landing. About everything people now say: "It's not worth it, because they're landing." Mikuś's corpse is covered in straw, which is burned to singe the bristle and dirt. The same operation is repeated after the fatty hulk is turned on the other side. In the morning chill, it's pleasant to warm myself at the smokeless fire. I feel good and peaceful. The singed pig is scrubbed with a stiff brush and painstakingly scraped with a sharp knife. The hind legs are sliced open and the tendons are extracted from under the skin. They are strong enough to hold 140 kilos of dead weight; they are used to attach it to a special ladder. The ladder with the hanging pig is propped against a wall. A long caesarean incision. The bladder. The warm innards fall into the saucepan. Stench. The coils of fat go directly onto the table, where M. cuts them and throws them into the kettle on the stove. We have breakfast. Scrambled eggs, bread, "coffee" with milk. The butcher cleans the intestines. Eighteen meters of thin entrails and thick, blue-gray bowels for headcheese. Dirty work. He squeezes the excrement as if from tubes and rinses the entrails with hot water. What an excellent pig. Lard four fingers thick. The head, the liver, the kidneys, the lungs and heart—all make their way into a great kettle in the courtyard, under which a fire is lit. The butcher quarters the meat. We immediately get to work. We cut the front of the hams for dry sausages. Many sausages, because when they land, it may be necessary to flee . . . Not from THEM. From the Germans, who will be rounding up the men. In the afternoon the production of sausages, liverwurst, headcheese, and blood sausage. Up to our elbows in the heaps of meat, we have no appetite. We drink only "coffee" and eat bread and butter. We put the meat for salting into barrels and hunt the large flies that attempt to endow us with their offspring. It's a cool day, so everything will keep. We finish at midnight.

Tomorrow or the day after, they'll be in Rome. We listen to a station called "*Soldatensender Calais.*"[19] An English diversionary station, superb of its kind. It must have been created by fantastic specialists, in cahoots with English intelligence. The Germans are said to listen to it passionately. Disaster in Italy.

June 4, 1944

Sunday. Exhausted, we slept late. For breakfast, "coffee," bread with headcheese, liverwurst, and then again "coffee." I stuffed myself. I took a blanket and went to the forest for some sun. It's warm. I dozed off until lunch. For lunch, fried liver. Stuffed myself again. In the evening, supper and the radio. Rome has been taken. English fighter planes have been flying all day today, monitoring the highways and shelling trucks. They fly at an altitude of ten to fifteen meters. They feel right at home. Not a single German plane. Not bad.

June 5, 1944

The English have been out hunting since early morning. Sleek machines pop out from behind the forests, take the obstacles like thoroughbreds, howl, and are gone. Now louder, now softer, the roar of engines sounds like barking. At ten in the morning I was lying in the woods near the station. A locomotive arrived to pick up freight cars loaded with some sort of cargo, I don't know what. But they had spotted it already. They circled around for a bit, to let people get away, and then they stitched it up artistically. Two straight seams and the steam hissed magnificently — it was over. The engineer went into raptures. The destruction filled him with joy. Even I catch myself thinking of locomotives or other "functioning" objects as scandalous, if not blasphemous. I envy those pilots. Expressions such as "into dust," "into powder," "into pablum," "to smithereens" keep running through my head. Sparks are flying.

After yesterday's sunny weather, today it's raining. I lie in bed and listen with pleasure to the monotonous splashing and drumming in the gutters. I greedily drink in the water along with the plants.

June 6, 1944

I set out on my bike around ten a.m., loaded up with lard, eggs, butter, and sausage. Mixed weather. Sun, wind, clouds, passing downpours, and cold. And then, a moment of sun. I have changed my route. Mouy, Beaumont, Paris. The main roads might be "too hot." They've been flying again, entire packs of them, since early morning.

The road is hilly, splendid. Great forests of giant ironwood trees. The shallow valleys are like gardens. I want to start swatting off the airplanes, like mosquitoes. It seems that any moment they will swarm down on me. At Baumont I cross the Oise by boat because yesterday all the bridges were bombed. Dead fish are floating near the shores. My boatman tells me that after yesterday's bombardment of the railroad bridge over five hundred kilos of fish were caught. Today all of Beaumont had fish for lunch. The mood is strange. When I ask people in the small towns which direction to take, they answer rather secretively and suspiciously, inspecting me from head to toe. Groups of Germans —

in threes and fours — stand at the crossroads, waiting for cars. After Presles I'm caught by a downpour and duck into a roadside bistro. An old woman gives me an "apéritif" super-sweetened with saccharine and informs me that "under the circumstances one must be careful whom one talks to . . ." I don't understand, but I say "*ah, oui, oui.*" I offer her some bread with headcheese. She thanks me with a glass of cognac. I continue on my way. I reach Paris at four. At Porte de la Chapelle — the sound of an alert. A passerby says: "It's already the eighth today." A record. Soon the end is signaled. On boulevard Magenta people are crowding around. A German bus has hit a civilian truck and knocked it over. It looks like a beetle turned on its back. Another alert. The sirens are choking and hiccupping. I sit on a bench and have a smoke. Around five I'm home. "I was worried about you." — Why? — "What? Don't you know? THEY'VE LANDED."

I wait for the current before I can turn on the radio. Finally, around eight: "Eleven thousand airplanes, transport gliders, paratroopers, four thousand vessels, not counting barges." They are here, they are here . . . fighting in Normandy, all the way from Cherbourg as far as Deauville. And the Word became flesh.

June 8, 1944

The English have taken Bayeux and the separate bridgeheads have come together, creating a uniform front eighty km long and ten km deep. Additional forces keep landing.

Paris is calm, life continues as usual. They are bombing the outskirts of Paris and in the provinces. I bore myself reading Paul Hazard's *La Crise de la conscience européenne.*[20]

June 10, 1944

As a reward to the population for its calm behavior, the Oberbefehlshaber, commander of Paris, has extended the curfew until one a.m. to allow people to go to the movies. The cinemas open late because the current doesn't switch on until late. The situation with food is becoming difficult. People are lining up for bread in front of the bakeries. The Allies have already built two airfields in Normandy. They're coming.

June 11, 1944

All is calm. Only today, around eight in the morning, were the English, American, and Soviet flags finally removed from the column on place de la Bastille. Yesterday the police confiscated a whole supply of English and American flags from a merchant on the boulevards. Enough to fill an entire truck. Must be a collaborator.

We stayed home all day. I try to read, but it doesn't work. Such attempts at reading are like beating nails into gnarled wood. Recently I've had terrible gnarls in my thoughts. This evening Robert dropped in, very anxious, because he's lost contact with his family in Niort.

Lots of articles about Poland in the American press in connection with Stanisław Mikołajczyk's visit with Roosevelt.[21] Mrs. Roosevelt even wrote an article on Poland, which was published in several hundred newspapers. Poor old Poland. Mrs. Roosevelt did not, apparently, appear in Cracow folk costume. A stroke of luck! Otherwise everyone would have said the deal was done and all for the best.

June 12, 1944

Four years ago, on June 12, hidden among tires piled in a truck, I escaped from Paris. It was the same warm weather, and the dull drumming of artillery sounded from afar. The Germans were crossing the Seine. Crowds of people were heading south, along roads too narrow to hold them. Today there have already been four alerts, a string of bombs rumble in the distance, planes buzz in the clear blue sky. And not a single German machine. I have the sense, indeed I'm convinced, that these are the most beautiful moments of the war.

Around four in the afternoon, I was at the Ministry of Labor to see the director of the section on "foreigners." I like him a lot. Tall, slender, subtle. He loves Proust and is himself a bit Proustian. In the cold room, shaded by curtains, peonies in full bloom stood on his desk, enormous and fragrant. This bouquet of flowers threw me back suddenly to another era, perhaps to À *la recherche du temps perdu*. I told him: "These flowers and you yourself seem to me to form a whole." He smiled and understood what I meant to say. We discussed the latest events, then moved on to Maurice Maeterlinck.[22] I told him about Flaubert's correspondence, which led us to consider Maupassant, whom we find so particularly appealing these days. Is it his style? His lack of pity? I don't know. I continue to see the bunch of peonies and their perfume keeps coming in waves.

We emerge together into rue de Vaugirard, which is drenched in sunshine. He tells me that Jean Anouilh's *Antigone* is terrific and recommends the performance.[23] Then suddenly he stops: "*Monsieur*—two hundred kilometers from here a terrible struggle is taking place . . ." Yes, indeed—life is strange. We part. I get on my bike and ride home. From time to time a German car, "decked" in foliage, speeds through the sunny street. Harder thus to spot them on the roads over which ONLY Allied planes are stubbornly growling. A taste of their own medicine . . .

I sit on a café terrace on boulevard Saint-Germain. Bicycles and the colorful patches of pretty women flash by in the sun. On warm days all the women seem to be "open," like flowers. Perhaps it's only the ghost of an impression, because the bouquet of peonies remains before my eyes. The Americans have taken Carentan.[24]

June 13, 1944

At night the alerts don't let up. All Paris is sleep-deprived and a bit drowsy. People doze off in the metro. They are starting to feel the pinch of hunger — even vegetables are scarce. Next month, it's said, bread coupons will no longer be distributed and one will have to register in the bakeries. I can't stand bakers. They're already starting to behave as though THEY were the ones who had been supplying the bread. They act as if they are the government. A government of bakers, that would be horrible indeed.

After yesterday's sunny weather, today it's again overcast. People are worried this will hinder the operations of the air force. And yet the French are starting to mutter and grouse. When the English arrive they will ruin the economy. They've already landed with "fake" francs, and afterward they'll only exploit us, and la-di-da, tra-la-la, hiss-boom-ba . . . everything in a tone of embittered irony. I like the French very much, but at the moment I'm fed up and during lunch in the canteen I let my colleagues have it. When the Germans arrived with occupation marks, that was fine. People quickly adapted. When the English arrive with occupation francs, which certainly will be worth more and have better backing (if only the backing of greater power), it's not fine. Sensible, because otherwise the peasants would immediately demand a dollar for an egg and a pound for a pound of butter. "Well, if you're so tired and weak, then simply admit that the Latin race, to which you belong, is in full decline and stop bullshitting. And if there's something you don't like, do something about it. Bad-mouthing and irony, and *esprit*, even of the best sort, achieve nothing. For a hundred years everyone has been 'exploiting' you, the English at the head of the line, and you only manage to grumble, pity yourselves, and shed tears over *la pauvre France*." I got a bit carried away and K. nudged me under the table. I was sure they would jump on me. But, no. And that's what really got me worried . . .

Now that the Allies have landed and it's obvious they have every chance of holding on, people say with disdain: "Well, they had four years to prepare," or "They wage war with matériel, not people — no big deal." Such complaints often remind me, rather cruelly, of the behavior of an accomplished but aging actress who cannot admit that certain roles are no longer for her and is unable to switch to a more suitable repertoire.

The English have imprisoned a sizable division of those gray-clad German telephone operators. I detest these German women — even more than the German men.

June 14, 1944

I'm having breakfast and suddenly the alert. In a moment, the roar of motors low over the rooftops and a long barrage of machine gun fire. A German has been sighted and is being pursued across the roofs. A few minutes later bombs thunder somewhere nearby. I'm always worried about the local train station. (O you train station . . .) Just in case, we go down into the metro. It's already crowded there. A boy with a puppy in his arms stands against the wall. I ask him if his puppy is also afraid. He answers me seriously: "*Mais si, Monsieur,* look how he trembles." The children are playing tag along the tracks and shouting. A group of young men and women, workers from the nearby factory, have found places and settled down. Laughter, kisses, the girls sit on the boys' laps. One fellow lights a cigarette and passes "the smoke" around. The girls gasp and clear their throats.

I brought along Pierre-Maxime Schuhl's *Machinisme et philosophie.*[25] To counteract the misuse of inventions, Francis Bacon in his *Novum Organum* appeals to "common sense and holy religion." Go ahead, O you poor man of the twentieth century, and appeal to "common sense and holy religion," when both reason and religion have already in part become prehistoric concepts. In any case, reason, for sure. The fat, Goliathlike shopkeeper keeps returning to the shelling above our neighborhood: "When I heard them up there firing away, I thought *ça va mal* and told my customers to leave." And a little while later, repeating: "When I heard . . ." Too bad they didn't shoot *him.* Maybe he's a baker? Horrible. People like him are convinced that victory in the war is intended for their own benefit, in particular.

The alert ended at ten, and fifteen minutes later I rode over to the factory. On the Pont d'Austerlitz two women had set up their easels and with complete calm were painting the eternal view of the Seine and Notre-Dame. After the long alert, after the thunder of the bombs and the flutter of the air battle overhead, there was something infinitely reassuring about those easels. An elegant black van belonging to the champagne firm of Pommery-Greno drove past me, full of thick bottles. I was overcome with such a thirst that I dropped into the nearest bistro and drank a glass of sparkling wine with ice.

In the evening I listened to the radio and caught a German broadcast, which reported that in response to a shortage of soap, a campaign has been launched there under the slogan, *"Dreck ist nicht gefährlich."*[26] Some professor has written in a medical weekly that whether a mother puts her child to bed unwashed or washed has absolutely no effect on the child's health. What a shame that this campaign had not been launched when I was a child. Those evening baths were pure torture. I have decided to make up for it and go to bed tonight without washing. *"Dreck ist nicht gefährlich."* O God—what a nation!

June 15, 1944

Alert. I therefore left our "Salle des Fêtes" and rode to Bagneux, to the park. German fighter planes from the nearby airfield of Villacoublay were scattering in all directions, escaping low over the rooftops.

I lie on the grass, as dry and hard as wood chips. Again, splendid weather, not a drop of rain. The air is so transparent that from here I clearly see the Sacré-Coeur, fifteen km away as the crow flies. I lie on my back, reading a short book about Mme Hańska, called *L'Étrangère*, by the Polish writer Sophie de Korwin-Piotrowska.[27] I don't like her approach to the subject. Mme Hańska is depicted as an ethereal being, which doesn't work at all, since it's well known she was the owner not only of far-flung estates but also of a rather rotund body. The 209 pages contain everything: sleigh rides, the harvest festival, Józef Hoene-Wroński, the emir Wacław Rzewuski, the confederations, the Philomaths and the Philarets, Polish stew, Romanticism, etc.[28] Naturally, in Neuchâtel there was the one kiss (nothing happened on the island, God forbid!—they spent their time singing hymns) and "Balzac had a presentiment that his liaison with Mme Hańska would bring them no joy, nothing except spiritual exaltation." They loved each other in the "mystical heavens." Why write such things? Their meeting in Saint Petersburg in 1843 was certainly not, however, so "mystical." On the way back from Saint Petersburg to Paris, Balzac stopped in Dresden. He's somewhat disappointed when Dresden fails to move him as expected. He then writes: "I will therefore have to return to Dresden with you, in order for the paintings there to speak to me. Aside from the women by Rubens, nothing else moved me, except that the Rubens women reminded me of a certain Eve . . ." I can't swear the quotation is exact, but I remember this was certainly the gist of it. How much more eloquent this is. It immediately conjures up Mme Ewelina. And how natural and intelligible, how agreeably not "mystical." I don't know the Rubens paintings in Dresden, but I assume they're no different from the ones in Vienna or here. As it happens, I don't like Rubens. A painter of round, flesh-colored hams. Too bad that monographs or biographies written in Poland, about any subject or person, are never actually about them: the person or ruin described is only a pretext for raising the "Polish Question." Poland muddles everything for us. And the result is the ethereal Mme Hańska, who in reality must have weighed some two hundred pounds.

The alert is over. A shame. The Germans return to the airfield, skimming the rooftops. Meanwhile, I'm thinking about Balzac, about the gossip that surrounded his journey. It was said the czar had paid him to write a book to answer and correct the Marquis de Custine's "caricature" of Russia.[29] Sometimes it all sounds quite absurd . . . And with an element of reproach . . .

Since all the bridges crossing the Seine have been bombed, the entire German *Nachschub*—their reinforcements—are going through Paris. I get pleasure watching them heading for the front, sweaty and exhausted. I'd like to sidle up to those stopped cars and say with an innocent air: "What do you think? Did Balzac understand painting?" before turning on my heel, like a little boy, boasting that he has a watch, ha, ha, and you don't have one . . .

Once again, there are lines in front of all the shops. We are drying our bread.

June 16, 1944

The vocational school attached to our factory recently held competitive entrance exams. The candidates are fourteen years old. Today I looked over the compositions on the theme, "Why do you want to enter this school?" Among the many hackneyed, rote, and prefabricated answers, quite a few were spontaneous. For example, these: "In three years I will be hired by a state factory and then, after thirty years of work, a peaceful life will begin, retirement." Another expanded the idea: "And when I have retired" (*la retraite*), "I'll build myself a little house with the money I've saved and I'll be able to be happy." I cite word for word. *Vivat*—life begins after sixty. Happiness, too. Not bad for fourteen-year-old boys. Farsighted. One wrote frankly that he "would be happy to enter this school, because they feed you well." This I appreciate, it's a lot better.

I don't know what to think of this, without being unfair or allowing our Slavic toughness, often affected, to get the upper hand. One thing I'm sure of: it's not a good thing when a fourteen-year-old boy already knows what retirement is and considers it the height of his ambitions, his chance at happiness. It's perhaps a sign of the fundamental exhaustion of the race. An apt illustration of Gustave Le Bon's characterization of the Latin races.[30] In their confessions the boys demonstrate an absolute readiness to submit to the authorities, to put themselves at the mercy of the state. So where is the famed French individualism? Le Bon asserts that statism is what every Frenchman in his heart truly yearns for. I'm ready to agree. I told Robert that the boys' exercises had shocked me. He smiled sadly. He is one of those valiant Frenchmen, those who are today perishing by the thousands in battle. But there are few of them and judging by these exercises I'm beginning to fear their numbers will continue to decline. I would be hard-pressed if someone today asked me: "What do you think? Is France 'done for'?" But I fear for its future in the times that are upon us.

The Germans announced today that they have deployed a secret retaliatory weapon, with which they intend to demolish London. London says that yesterday and last night England was attacked by pilotless planes. A type of flying bomb.[31] How quickly does humanity adapt to each new age. At the same time, London reported that Japanese steelworks have been bombed by Superfortresses, one and a half times larger than those we now see every day. Their range is six thousand km. These Superfortresses belong to a unit of the World Air Force, based in Washington.[32]

Hearing all this, I involuntarily shifted in my seat, because I suddenly felt short of breath. I loosened my collar. And when I came to write about it, I kept repeating: "You're not writing science fiction—you're recording the facts." The strong sensation of an abyss yawning under my feet. I stand over it, and seeing nothing, I don't know what to think. I shut the radio and, somewhat numb, began to rummage in the bookshelves, like a chicken in its cage. I must have had a chicken's idiotic expression on my face. I took down Bergson's *Les Deux Sources de la morale et de la religion*. Flipping through it and reading the underlined sentences, I came upon this strange thought: "There are, besides, societies that remain at the same level, which is necessarily rather low. Since they nevertheless do change, what occurs is not an intensification of their original traits, which would constitute a qualitative step forward, but their multiplication or exaggeration: inventiveness, if one can still use the word in this case, no longer requires an effort. From a belief that responded to a need one will have moved to a new belief, which externally resembles the preceding, which accentuates one or another superficial trait, but that no longer has a purpose. From then on, while marking time, one continuously adds and enlarges. By the double effect of repetition and exaggeration, the irrational becomes absurd and the peculiar becomes monstrous."[33]

I wonder if we have not been marking time for quite a while now, merely adding and enlarging continuously. Not the intensification, but only the ordinary magnification and exaggeration of the original features.—Ah, *mon cher*, isn't this all for effect . . . My God. The flashy display of ideas, of citations, at a time when the most *ordinary*, everyday words give rise to entire worlds, immense and unbounded. "To drink," whispered somewhere by thousands of scorched lips, "to eat," "to live" — to live at any cost. And that world apart, bluish and calm, like the dawn, which arises today around the small word "silence." *Silence*. Give us this day our daily bread and silence . . .

I am stunned and cannot keep up. My thoughts are collapsing under me, like the legs of a man who's been hit on the head. The approaching age will demand vulgar simplification in all domains, simply for life to go on. And I'm afraid of such simplifications. This is no "aristocratic" fear — no, simply the fear of a mind accustomed, despite everything, to a bit of thinking without simplification.

June 18, 1944

Afternoon in Robert's family garden in Fontenay. A gray, cold day. Robert was digging in the garden, as befits a true Frenchman. I sat under a currant bush and ate my fill. It's only the second time this year that I've tasted fruit. I pounced on the juicy clusters with the voracity of a locust. I ate and ate and ate. And only from time to time, in order to sweeten my lips, puckering with acid, I switched to the sweet gooseberries. Afterward I lay on the grass and gazed at the sky of ash-gray taffeta. The wind tore at the black leaves of the chestnut trees.

The Americans have reached Barneville and cut off the Cotentin Peninsula, including Cherbourg. The Russians continue to advance. Four years ago today Pétain requested a cease-fire. I can still see that day.

June 20, 1944

This morning on the Pont d'Arcole, on the way to the Préfecture of police. Three trucks loaded with wounded Germans stop on the bridge. The less severely wounded are sitting and dangling their legs over the sides. Dirty, pale faces, dusty and torn uniforms, bloodied bandages and rags. Others sit in the middle, away from the sides, with their eyes closed. In this heap of gray-green dirt everything white and purple stands out sharply. A group of Parisians has gathered around the trucks, keeping a certain distance. The two sides regard each other in silence. The trucks start up. This is already an army in total disarray. The Russians have taken Vyborg. Heavy fighting in Normandy.

This evening Robert came for supper. He has had news of his family and has revived. We discuss Maurice Dekobra, pornographic literature, brothels and prostitution, in general, the difference between a brothel and a house of assignation, in particular.[34] And the latest Parisian joke: the war continues and everyone has already died. Alone, two super-fighter planes, one English and one German, are still chasing each other around the globe. Somewhere near the equator they meet. They exchange fire and both planes plummet into the wilderness, burying both pilots in the wreckage. A great male ape, sitting in a tree, observes all this and says to his mate: "Well, old lady, now we have to begin everything all over again."

Afterward, I., the Spaniard, also arrived. He had returned from Runka's place near Fontainebleau and brought us a box of excellent cherries. I pounced on them. When I asked if the Soviets would begin a general offensive, he answered: "Yes, because they need to wipe out the remaining Communists and pave the way for the Stalinists." As a former militant Red Republican, he has fixed views on the subject of the so-called battle for the freedom of the proletariat, and so forth. "I'm no longer going to risk my neck so that those who scream about liberty, the people's rights, and tyranny can sit in comfortable armchairs and trample on freedom and the people's rights, when they themselves are worse tyrants than those against whom the battle was originally directed."

He told me about his good friend from the days when he himself, aged fifteen to twenty-two, was an anarchist. Juan García Oliver was one of the aces of Spanish anarchism. His life was divided between terrorist activity and stays in prison. He appeared before almost all the courts of Spain. After the Republic was overthrown, he became—minister of justice in Francisco Caballero's cabinet in 1937.[35] I. went to see him, accompanied by the lawyer who had defended the present minister in a series of trials for terrorism. The two men entered the minister's magnificent office—"in Spain ordinary janitors have magnificent offices, not to speak of ministers!" adds I. He was in the uniform of a republican officer and therefore saluted, while the lawyer went up to his former client and familiarly took his hand: "*Que tal Juan*—how happy I am . . ." or something of the kind. Juan García Oliver regarded him coldly, spurned the lawyer's hand, and drawled: "Not Juan, but *minister of justice*." The lawyer took it as a joke. The minister pressed a button. "Please see these two gentlemen to the door." "He was nevertheless a good minister of justice," adds I. "He knew all the police commissars and all the prisons. He had the chance to make their acquaintance when he was escorted from place to place with chains around his wrists." I. concludes from this, in addition: Whoever has once held high position is loath to descend from his throne. And in today's Russia more and more people are occupying thrones. When I ask him what he therefore thought about popular movements and so on, he answers me wittily: "I believe in God, but I don't believe in priests."

June 21, 1944

Yesterday the Germans shut down the "*Service social d'aide aux émigrants.*" Many Poles received subsidies there, which have now been halted, leaving them in the lurch. Naturally, Dr. K. began right away to imagine how we might, if only partly, replace that *service*. He is inexhaustible. We began to calculate roughly how much the two of us had managed (more him than me) to extract from the French during the war for assistance to the Poles. We came up with about two million francs. "And we've ended up with nothing," he said with a laugh. "Because we two honest idiots make a perfect match," I replied.

General Anders, Józef Gawlina, and Kazimierz Papée were received by the pope.[36] Thus, Poland is saved. I nevertheless contemplate the splendid future with unease, as D. wrote humorously when sending us butter from La Ferté-Bernard. His letter took as long to reach us as the latest note from my mother in Cracow. This is because, as D. writes, "since there was so little traffic on the rails, the stationmaster closed the station and took off with his family to the countryside." France is nevertheless charming. I dream of becoming a stationmaster.

Before supper I had to ride over to place de la Bastille yet again. A young, wet-behind-the-ears policeman, signaled me to stop on avenue Daumesnil because I was riding in the middle of the street. On the right side the paving is uneven. He began to inspect my papers and demanded a fine of fifteen francs. That so infuriated me — I was in a rush, to boot — that I tore my papers from his hands and gave him the fifteen francs with the words "here's your tip — *merde*" and went on my way. He didn't make a peep. When I turned around, he was still standing in the same place. I felt ashamed and rode up to apologize and this time to chew him out "logically." In the end he was abashed and excused himself by saying "he had to do his duty." I said I agreed with him, but on condition he do it intelligently. "*Intelligemment, vous comprenez, intelligemment.*" When I left, we were in full agreement. A bit more and I could have gotten him to apologize for being a policeman in the first place.

June 22, 1944

Early this evening, around seven, there was a big air raid. They were bombing something in the northwest outskirts of Paris. Probably storage tanks for gasoline or oil, because a thick cloud of smoke rose in the west above Paris, obscuring the whole sky. The bombers flew over the center of the city — about a hundred of them. They could be seen clearly. I stood in a doorway at Châtelet and though the flak was intense I poked my nose out to get a good look. People stood and observed the parade, hopping back into the doorways only when the shells exploded directly over us. Black crosses in V-formation slowly moved against the whitish sky. Suddenly there was a cry in the street, a long moan. In the last formation a flame flared up, then died out. *Touché!* The heavy machine breaks away, spirals, jerks up for a moment, and, spinning in ever tighter circles, drops to the ground. People simply moan. The unfeigned, genuine sympathy of the crowd.

June 23, 1944

Several bombs from yesterday's air raid fell in the very center of Paris. Today I was ordered to turn around on rue Censier. At the intersection of Censier and rue Geoffroy Saint-Hilaire the street was piled with debris, the buildings were in ruins, the windowpanes shattered.

I received my biweekly salary today once again in a new thousand-franc bill. Currently, three different thousand-franc bills are in circulation. The printing of new banknotes has for quite a long time been the only type of French manufacture that is truly flourishing.

A shortage of salt in the countryside means that the peasants have stopped slaughtering pigs. We haven't had a bite of meat since the beginning of the month. Hitler ordered the crew at Cherbourg to fight to the finish. Meanwhile, a virtuoso Japanese violinist has arrived in Germany, where Goebbels gave her an authentic Stradivarius. She will be presented to the Führer in order to play him a few *Lieblingsstücke*, his favorite pieces. Perhaps, "Maciek has died, has died . . ."[37]

June 24, 1944

At Janka's name day party. Discussion of France, Balzac, Mme Hańska, and Hoene-Wroński. I couldn't talk about Hoene-Wroński, because I haven't read him and in general am not drawn to him. But I took a sideways shot at him, to the indignation of the gathered company. With Hoene-Wroński it's once again about POLAND, and not about Hoene-Wroński. It's quite possible that the sale of the "absolute," or rather its selling off piece by piece, and moreover for a hefty sum, was not in itself fraudulent enough to qualify him as a fraud, so he is not so different from Cagliostro or Zbigniew Dunikowski (the one of gold).[38] (How can you say this . . .) Cyprian Norwid likewise had no means of publishing, not only his ideas, but, what's worse, his poems.[39] Why didn't he do the same thing? Instead of selling one of Raphael's drawings to the French for a fat sum (he was penniless), he *gave* it to Poland, while earning his living as a simple workman.

Otherwise, the subject was the war—with four interruptions for "parlor alerts." A Frenchwoman among the guests said she had seen Sacha Guitry two days ago at a painting exhibit in the Galeries Charpentier. Accompanied by an extremely young girl. If he continues like that he will begin finding his girl-friends in kindergartens. On that occasion, he apparently read from a section of his new book, called *From Jeanne d'Arc to Philippe Pétain.*[40] This is what's called "perfect whoredom," something like perfect pitch. Not to mention the combination of those two names. Frenchmen of that sort make one want to write a book called *From Napoleon to Tino Rossi.*[41]

In the metro, as we were returning home in the evening, a drunken street-walker gave proof of her patriotism by cursing out a lonely German soldier. "*J'suis Frrrrançaise,* I'm not afraid of him, I'm not afraid of prison, *merde . . .*" Her friend, a bit less drunk, tried to calm her. But the result was quite the reverse. In broken German, fragments of filthy insults and words learned in bed, when patriotism did not prevent her from sleeping with the Germans, she kept on be-rating the Kraut. This is also "perfect whoredom" and I'd like to know if Sacha Guitry will do the same thing. The soldier stood still, like a rigid statue by Arno Breker.[42] He didn't flinch. He understood everything and only smiled imper-ceptibly. People also smiled. She got off at place d'Italie, still cursing from the platform. No doubt tonight she will give herself gratis — to some Frenchmen.

The Americans are hammering their way through the fortifications at Cher-bourg. The Russians have smashed through the German lines on both sides of Vitebsk. In London it's "unpleasant," in Paris there are minor alerts.

June 25, 1944

A marvelous day. Blue sky without a wisp of cloud. Around one o'clock we set out on bicycle for the Bois de Vincennes, taking lunch with us. Avenue de Tremblay, running through the forest toward the racecourse, has been trans-formed into a "corso." I've never seen so many people. Thousands of bicycles, packed horse-drawn buses from the last century, coaches, cabriolets, and car-riages. A happy crowd strolling in the sun. The floral skirts of girls on bikes flap as they pedal, revealing their legs. Someone is singing, someone whistling. Along the sides, under the trees, people are taking their walks. The war? Not a trace. It's a cheerful Sunday from the good old days of peace. Looking around, I think of yesterday's bombardment of Versailles, in which 225 persons were killed and over 500 injured. But all that seems like a bad dream. We spread out our blan-ket, have our lunch, then I read and fall asleep.

We return around seven. The same crowd is streaming from all sides toward Paris. Flower bouquets on bicycle handlebars. As we near home we're caught in an alert. Shelling. Three bomber formations cut across on a diagonal. Three planes are shot down, as might have been expected. The evening raids are deadly. They are clearly visible.

Cherbourg is already practically taken. During the raid on Berlin the cathedral crypt was destroyed and the tomb with Frederick II's remains was demolished.[43]

June 27, 1944

Basia found nothing today at the market. She stood in line for two hours for a smidgen of white cheese resembling plaster. With the addition of powdered milk from our reserves, we'll be able to eat it. Lunches in the factory canteen have one less course. Dr. K. and I go around hungry and furious.

Guglielmo Ferrero's *Aventure — Bonaparte en Italie, 1796–1797.*[44] Excellent. Long ago, reading Napoleon's correspondence, I got the impression that the entire glorified and celebrated Italian campaign has been cloaked from head to toe in legend. Ferrero dispassionately reveals the truth and disperses the halo that for 150 years has surrounded Bonaparte's head.

Most important, the plan for the campaign was worked out by the Directory, being the collective effort of the young officers of the Revolution and bellicose civilians. Bonaparte followed it to the letter. The march on Ceva and its conquest, the peace with Piedmont in Cherasco. The continuation of the campaign, or rather the adventure, is just as surprising for Bonaparte as for the Directory. Italy not only shows no resistance, but simply capitulates. The young general's small army, forty thousand strong, poorly armed and famished, would have succumbed to its own audacity had it not been for Italy's lethargy. The old world, locked in the forms of the *ancien régime*, was shocked by the sight of these audacious ragamuffins, trampling and crushing everything: order, harmony, laws, time-tested principles and beliefs. Bonaparte's victory? The application of General Guibert's advanced military methods, violating all the principles and codes of eighteenth-century warfare, which managed to limit the mutual slaughter by certain laws and as much as possible moderate its effects.[45] Bonaparte crosses the Po River, not where General Beaulieu is entrenched, but in his rear.[46] Brilliant. Yes, but in so doing Bonaparte violates the neutrality of the Kingdom of Parma, an action no eighteenth-century commander would have taken. He is agile, moves quickly. Yes, but he marches without supplies, feeding the army off the countryside. A method unknown in the military customs of the eighteenth century. He is victorious because he tramples and devastates. He liberates force and unleashes violence, later becoming its prisoner. Bonaparte's conquests in Italy, his march on Vienna, Austria defeated and suing for peace, the establishment of republics, and the emergence for the first time of the future emperor's lion's claws. His victories are the result of new methods, of brutality introduced into the intricate gentleman's game that war had become in the *siècle galant*. March on Vienna? The risky undertaking of a young daredevil who only by a miracle emerged whole. Generals Hoche and Moreau[47] failed to cross the Rhine at the same time and Bonaparte found himself in Austria alone, with revolution and chaos in his rear, the full force of Austria and the threat of famine before him. Vienna's momentary terror quickly passes and then Bonaparte, not Austria, is in need of peace. His preliminary conditions are therefore mild. He realizes he has to retreat and would like to do so with honor. Peace negotiations would have lasted for months, while Bonaparte senses that even in Paris his legend is already on the wane. Campo Formio is the fruit of the threats and pleas, the arguments and virtual insults thrown by the young commander at the icy diplomats of the monarchy. Not everything happened the way it has since been represented. And once unleashed on the plains of Lombardy, chaos, the trampling of rights and of the "rules of the game," has persisted until this day. The cult of power and hatred blinds us. Hence the legend of Bonaparte. Violence begets violence, when one party tramples on rights, everyone else tramples on them, too. Violence swells, like an avalanche, under which the first to disturb the delicate equilibrium of snow particles perishes. But along with him others also perish, and often the entire culture and civilization that had prevailed until then. Russia will one day have to raise a monument to Hitler . . . She will get rid of the cursed Jews, the "*prokliatye evrei*," and introduce them into Europe. That, even Peter the Great didn't manage to do. And next to the Bronze Horseman another horseman will arise.[48] This one would have to be on a donkey.

Robert is so worried about his family that he intends to go to Niort by bicycle. A difficult journey of over four hundred km. But I'm not surprised at him. It's another thing altogether, when it comes to having six children, which nowadays is simply a throwback. We, thank God, don't have a single one, and yet it always seems to me that too much weight is given to this whole business.

June 28, 1944

This morning an unconfirmed report that Philippe Henriot, minister of propaganda and archtraitor, was assassinated last night.[49] At midday, one twenty p.m. exactly, Laval addresses the country and confirms the morning rumor. "He died a hero's death," says Laval. I listen to this along with all my office mates, men and women, standing under the open window of the janitor's apartment, from which the radio blares. In the general silence, one woman snarled: "Shut your trap—*sale Auvergnat*." Approving laughter. After Laval's speech—the "Marseillaise." Screams of protest, and the janitor is obliged to turn off the radio. The poor old "Marseillaise" . . . But this will not be considered part of the history of France—it will belong to the history of the occupation. Main result: Henriot will have stopped screeching every evening on the radio. He was dangerous. His powerful and convincing dialectic, clever, very Cartesian, and seemingly modeled on the best Moscow examples, presented many things very much *à la française.*

Early in the evening I met Mr. Zygmuś. It's been a long time since I've seen him, because he ran into some "trouble" concerning dollars and decided that it was best to lie low. As usual, a bit drunk. When I ask how things are going, he mumbles: "Ah, very well. We have meat every day, we drink Bordeaux, and we wait for things to improve." He invites me into his shop: "You should come by. There's always a drop of gin or cognac stashed away."

The Russians have taken Mogilev, there's fighting in Bobruysk. They're approaching Minsk from two sides. Finland is not capitulating and has signed a treaty with the Germans, who are supposed to send reinforcements. The Finns have an *esprit de suite*[50] that I admire. Who knows whether such an *esprit de suite* would not have served Poland better . . . But talking with Hitler was out of the question, and that's all there is to it. The commanders at Cherbourg, General von Schlieben and Admiral Hennecke, have apparently surrendered in a most scandalous way.[51] They abandoned their excellent bunkers and surrendered before the rest of the army. Their behavior was so shocking that the American officers chewed them out roundly. A Frenchman said to me today, as calmly as can be: "You know, the Americans have proved to be excellent soldiers. The capture of Cherbourg was flawless. Even the French could not have done it better . . ." This is what's called "perfect chauvinism," rather embarrassing. For me, very embarrassing, even. And for the French, destructive—it will do them in.

June 29, 1944

On the avenue at Porte de Châtillon an enormous herd of cows. Traffic came to a standstill. The cows were being herded by a dozen or so German soldiers with rifles slung over their shoulders, helmets on their belts, and sticks in their hands. The sight was so unusual and comical that people burst into raucous laughter. Someone cried out: "They are the POWs from Normandy"— and a salvo of laughter. But soon the practical side got the upper hand: "They're taking our meat ration; maybe this was supposed to be for us." The cult of the beefsteak, I want to say the "sacred" beefsteak, shows up in everything. Meanwhile, the soldiers are running around and chasing the stupefied beasts off the sidewalks. An image from the Goncourt journals appeared vaguely before my eyes: a herd of livestock was dispatched to Paris in 1870. Are the Germans planning to defend themselves here?

Life in the city proceeds as usual. Most people expect that in a month the Allies will be here. They have already gotten used to the landing in Normandy and are now waiting for the "real landing." This means that Normandy is not the most important operation. Thus, it's said: "As soon as they really land, then . . . and so on." People have caught the sickness of gigantism. Not surprising. A daily supply of numbers such as a thousand bombers under the protection of fifteen hundred warplanes, the litany of bombed cities, and various other computations, can easily turn heads. Blind intoxication on power—power, furthermore, that belongs to someone else.

On the Eastern Front the German retreat is beginning to look like an enormous disaster. Eight days from the onset of the attack. The salvos of 224 (?) cannons are thundering in Moscow, the words of Stalin's long and pompous orders of the day keep pouring out, strangely familiar, reeking of 150-year-old mustiness. But in Russia they're the latest hit. And this musty philosophy, this musty vocabulary, will now be ruling over Poland, over half of Europe? It's *the very same style*, to the letter, in which the Directory's orders of the day were written 150 years ago. The similarity is striking and disheartening: "Eternal glory to the conqueror of Lodi! Glory and honor to the supreme commander, the general who prepared the audacious attack on the bridge at this city, overtaking the host of French warriors, withstanding the enemy's murderous fire and doing what it took to defeat him! Honor to courageous General Berthier, who thrust himself to the head of the dangerous and terrible republican column, which trampled and struck down the foe! Honor to generals Masséna, Cervoni, Dellemagne, to the brigade commanders Saluces, Dupas and Sugni, to Captain Toiret of the third grenadier battalion! Glory to the brave second riflemen's battalion, which decided the fate of that day! Glory to the brave division led by General Augereau and to its commanders! Glory to the government commissar Saliceti!" Oof—I've exhausted myself. The power of the French revolutionary style is astounding. This style is still alive and Stalin knows how to arouse his brutal hordes, who die for the cause that keeps them in chains. In the Russian orders of the day, the style continues to resonate to this very day.

Everything has happened so quickly that people are only now beginning to realize what's going on. Vitebsk, Orsha, Mogilev, Bobruysk. Russia, O Russia! It seems the whole world is looking in that direction, as toward the magnificent rising sun. There is no cure for blindness. No one wants *to see, to understand*. The power of mass suggestion, universal and absolute. "The Russians will change, they have changed already." Perhaps they will change, but have they changed? I was talking the day before yesterday with R., who lived in the Wilno region from 1939 to 1941. I have different views on this question, however. My so-called idées fixes . . .

The Germans have changed their minds. Three weeks ago the Eastern Front was the most important, but now there's been a total change of sets. In Italy and in Russia they're applying a "flexible defense" until they defeat the Anglo-Americans in the west. Then the attack on Russia. *Opiat'*—once again—on to Stalingrad, as Wiech would have said.[52] Simple, as simple as can be. Piece of cake.

The latest weapon is officially called the V-1, short for *Vergeltung*, or Reprisal No. 1. Others are in the works. Pretty pathetic.

I'm very curious to see whether we Poles ever manage to create any other style beside the "noble" style. In any case, after the war we will be seriously tempted by the "martyrdom" style coupled with typically Polish buffoonery. And then I'm also curious to discover whether after the destruction to which Poland has already been subjected, more of which is surely to come when the Russian front slowly moves across, whether after this destruction we will make the effort to organize and build everything absolutely "the way it used to be," or whether we will muster the courage to create something new. At any rate, I'm sure that a certain snobbish-noble affectation will resurface very quickly, regardless of the regime that awaits us. And if the regime is Communist, then farewell, we're done for—that utopia will devastate us more effectively than the entire century of partitions and both world wars. One cannot mention this, because Russia has cast a MAGIC SPELL over the sanest of minds. It's positively medieval how people are afraid to speak up. A psychosis, compared to which Nazism seems at the moment but an inept imitation.

But let's not forget one thing: The world, dear sir, is always watching us. They don't say anything, dear sir, but they always take us as an example. Because the Poles, dear sir, as you know . . . ha . . . damn! . . . you know. The Poles, you understand . . . how to put it, dear sir . . . Exactly: HOW TO PUT IT?

June 30, 1944

I finally got hold of a kilo of butter. A mere seven hundred francs. Besides that, a bunch of radishes in the market, bought *under the counter* from a tradeswoman selling yarn and thread. We eat peas, our remaining potatoes, and pasta. Two hours after a meal, I'm hungry again.

Henriot's remains were displayed in front of the Hôtel de Ville and Parisians paraded past the coffin, leaving bouquets of flowers. Some people are even capable of that . . . Seven hours before his death, Henriot had assisted at the send-off of French SS volunteers. *Paris-Soir* ran a photo of that ceremony. The train cars carried banners reading: "*Vive la France, Heil Hitler, Vive Henriot!*" This is not the history of France, but the history of the occupation . . .

I'm again flipping through Stefan Żeromski's *Conversion of Judas* and it bothers me.[53] No—not bothers—that's an understatement. Why "the toiling people," "need," "the stench"? Why, beyond the hero Ryszard Nienaski's idealism, does one sense above all the dirty laundry, the filthy handkerchiefs, and the dirty room with a samovar, and why does all this seem to lack "purpose"? Żeromski so detested Russia, yet was so deeply affected by her. It's ridiculous, how much my personal memories prevent me from reacting calmly to this great writer.

I remember how as a little boy I was invited by Żeromski and his wife to attend a kind of *Kinderbal*. At one point it was decided to show me the moon. I entered a dark room, Żeromski threw a coat, apparently his own, over my head and ordered me to look carefully through the extended sleeve, as if through a telescope. And suddenly he dumped a glass of water, from the front, through the sleeve. The water ran down my face and into my nose, I began to choke and cough terribly, almost vomiting my party snacks. But this was not the most important part. At this very moment the door was thrown open and light fell into the room. The light revealed the other children, laughing at me. I know I somehow understood that, too, but I clenched my fists at the sight of Żeromski. He stood to the side, watching as I choked, and laughed quietly, with malice and satisfaction. This laughter, somehow yellowish green, I now see in everything of his I read. I know it's not fair, but I can't do anything about it. It's amazing that this memory is one of the clearest I have retained from early childhood. The yellowish-green laugh. Still in Gymnasium, I got a failing grade for using this description. I was very proud of that grade.

July 2, 1944

Sunday. We're at home. Afternoon tea at Lola's. Eight guests in a minuscule room, but it's pleasant. After the others had left, Basia and I went out with Lola to explore the cinema programs in our neighborhood. The same old, antediluvian films. How comical, ugly, and unaesthetic the women's outfits look, now out of fashion. When they were fashionable this was not the view. Only ideologies are timeless. For the past hundred years the fashion has been the same and now the mustiest ones have become the last word.

Endless streams of bicycles are returning from the Bois de Vincennes. In the evening Robert drops by, bringing a large piece of meat and *real* Camembert. Someone traveling to Paris had delivered a package from his family in Niort. Naturally, he stayed until midnight, but I can talk with him forever.

In Russia it's criminal what's going on. They have crossed the Berezina River where it's 120 km wide, they have taken Wilejka and Stołpce, they're cutting off the German retreat from Minsk. It's reported that in the past ten days the Germans have lost 230,000 men and another 200,000 are threatened with encirclement in the Minsk region. What's happening? Have the Germans completely faltered in this sector? It looks that way. The English are repulsing the German counterattacks on the Tilly-Caen line.

July 3, 1944

Gray and stifling. As of tomorrow several metro lines will be entirely shut, whole sectors on other lines. The metro in an abridged edition. The buses linking Paris with the distant suburbs are also no longer running. Life is gradually slowing down and the bicycle is becoming the only means of locomotion.

These days we're living on green peas. Every day I get two kilos of peas in the factory, sometimes a bit of lettuce. I'd rather drink vinegar and munch cornichons. The Russians are doing as they please. It seems that over there the German army has practically ceased to exist.

In the afternoon I dropped into my bookstore to see if they had found me any of the books I ordered. I really like to slip into the bindery and finger the newly bound books. The smell of glue and leather, conversations with Bardache. Today he lent me the first volume of van der Meersch's *Corps et âmes*.[54]

The price of counterfeit bread coupons has jumped from 150 to 250 francs. After work I dropped in on Mme R. We discussed the Soviets. Like everyone else, she too "believes." In answer to my remarks about Russia, which she qualified as "narrow-minded" and "not progressive," she trotted out the great argument: "But nevertheless what great musicians Russia has produced. Tchaikovsky, Glazunov, Rimsky-Korsakov, Rachmaninov, Scriabin, Prokofiev . . ." "I have always feared and been extremely wary of countries that have produced many musicians, and great musicians at that," I answered her. But she no doubt did not get it.

July 4, 1944

Air raid alerts all morning. Incredible stories are making the rounds in Paris about butter being sold by German drivers transporting gasoline and ammunition to Normandy. Everyone says that here or there the Germans are selling butter for one hundred francs a kilo. Except that no one knows exactly where and when. At any rate, imagination is creating tons of butter and Paris has a butter fixation.

Otherwise, the Germans' next secret weapon is also supposed to be a flying bomb, or rather a rocket with considerably longer range. As far as Washington. That would be useful, but alas it's probably not true. The Russians have taken Polotsk, heavy fighting in Normandy.

July 5, 1944

For three days now the electric power has come on only at ten p.m. They say that in a few days there won't be any lights at all. All transports of workers to Germany have been suspended.

July 6, 1944

On the way to work I crashed into a German car. An enormous tractor was blocking the entrance to a garage and when I passed it, I didn't notice a car coming out of the driveway. Fortunately, I instinctively lifted my leg and only the pedal hit the bumper. The pedal was bent inward, practically into a hook. But somehow I managed not to fall over. The Germans stood and watched. I couldn't restrain myself and mouthed off, rudely: *"Ihr habt ja keine Hupe drinnen, was? Zu viel Arbeit auf das Ding zu drücken wenn ihr rauskommt . . ."*[55] I was terrified and couldn't even escape. But they just looked at me with their bovine eyes, after which they tried to prove to me that it was my fault. Well, well. I snapped out: *"Erzählen Sie mir keine G'schichten."*[56] But this time using polite address. I took the bike by the frame and went into a French garage across the street to ask for tools. But the young mechanic, who had seen the whole collision, snatched the bicycle from my hands and set about fixing it himself. Half an hour later, I was able to go on my way. The mechanic kept talking all the time about Russia. He didn't even mention Normandy.

Hitler has dismissed Marshal von Rundstedt as commander in chief in the west and replaced him with Marshal von Kluge.[57] Clearly he's afraid of Rommel, although Rommel is close at hand. In addition, yesterday the Führer gave a turbid speech to the *Reichsindustrieleiter*, who, led by Albert Speer, paid him a visit.[58] Afterward, Speer decorated them all with medals. The recent epidemic of medals being awarded to all and sundry reminds me a bit of extreme unction. This evening in the cinema we saw *Goupi Mains Rouges*.[59] A terrific film concerning a peasant family, an entire peasant clan. The newsreels showed Caen reduced to nothing. For lunch peas, for supper peas and bread—and lines for bread.

July 7, 1944

The offices of the civilian German administration in Paris, or the notorious Hôtel Majestic, and the Gestapo archives have been transferred to Nancy. Could this be the beginning of the evacuation of Paris?

July 8, 1944

This evening a small and very pleasant gathering at P.'s place . . . One of the hostess's students, a young Frenchwoman, spoke excellent Polish. It took her only a few years to learn Polish and she now reads Żeromski without a dictionary. Discussion of Żeromski. My opinions shocked absolutely everyone. Many people seem immediately to doubt whether I am at heart really a "good Pole." At the very least, certainly not 100 percent . . . Tadzik P. timidly criticizes Żeromski's language. I acknowledge all the virtues of his extremely rich language, the floods of unexpected adjectives, and the "*swing*" (shocked looks) of adverbs, but I sharply attack the "spirit" of his work. Why does he make dirty things even dirtier than they are in fact, while what's repulsive becomes cloying and indecent? What's the point of the nocturnal scene in which a lady examines Nienaski's "nuts" (chair legs were buckling . . .) while they're riding in a carriage?[60] Bolesław Prus, by contrast, will always be of his time while also timely. Prus conveys the spirit of eternal harmony, the indestructible quality found in every fragment of Greek sculpture. In Żeromski the disharmony and disorder, the "*polnische Schweinerei*,"[61] and the incompleteness are overwhelming—they are structural.

Naturally, a revolt breaks out against me. The same old story: I haven't just criticized Żeromski—I've *insulted* Poland. Because he's "so Polish a writer" (*tant pis pour lui*[62]). What's the meaning of "so Polish"? I don't consider him to be "so Polish" at all. Then out come the heaviest guns, which are supposed to reduce you to ashes: "He loved Poland so much." Well, what of it? A devilishly useful argument, this Poland, when all others fail. The "Jerusalem Balsam" we use for every ailment. Results guaranteed. When you don't have the courage or desire to think things through, bring out the red-and-white Polish stop sign . . .

We return before ten o'clock, taking the metro to Châtelet, but miss the connection. We go the rest of the way home on foot. Over an hour's walk through dark, empty streets. A melancholy rain is falling and the night is stifling.

The Americans have taken La Haye-du-Puits. Their air force is pulling out all the stops. What a lot of them they've made. The Russians have taken Baranowicze and are fighting in the outskirts of Wilno.

July 9, 1944

No electricity all day and one can't listen to the radio. People say that soon there won't be any gas or electricity at all, and the newspapers delicately hint that people should start leaving Paris. I do some reading, then I resole Basia's sandals. Shortly before four o'clock we set out to visit Szymon K. and his wife for afternoon tea. A number of metro lines have been closed, so we have to change twice to reach Opéra.

K. is an expert on painting and snaps up Polish canvases at auction, often for a song. Recently he landed a Gierymski.[63] A view of the Panthéon from a bridge over the Seine. I don't know of any French painter quite as "Parisian" as Aleksander Gierymski. His Paris captures the heart of Paris, with all the essentials.

I love their place. It has the feeling of a "real apartment," the likes of which are already beginning slowly to recede into the past.

July 10, 1944

Paris has become a city of bicycles. Everyone wants to buy a bicycle. The shoddiest piece, thrown together from worthless, cracked, and dented parts, costs seven, eight, or nine thousand francs. A bicycle tire costs up to two thousand francs. Around six in the afternoon, the streets are jammed. You have to watch out, because among the thousands of riders many are just beginners, and you never know until the last minute what they're going to do. Right after lunch I returned home, because I didn't have the strength to spend the afternoon brooding over tiresome paperwork. I lay down and slept for three hours. Outside, the sky was gray, rain was splashing against the windows. By seven Basia had returned from school. We looked over her sketches. She was worn out by the metro. These days it's wild in the metro. A. then stopped in briefly and filled the room with the babble of a twenty-two-year-old child. "The Russians have already taken Wilno, and I've got this swelling, because I scratched a pimple with a dirty penknife and the doctor prescribed herbal tea to cleanse the blood and when I'm reading I like to pick my nose . . ." "Which you then enjoy eating," I finished for him, soon kicking him out the door. I feel sorry for the fellow. The "baby of the litter," spoiled by his mother and his aunt. Well, the Russians have begun "liberating." Lida is already "liberated." Baranowicze, too. The collaborationist Parisian weekly, *La Gerbe*, recently published a questionnaire asking leading French lights their opinions on the bombing of cathedrals.[64] Many writers, scholars, physicians, and others refused to answer. By contrast, Céline, the celebrated Louis-Ferdinand Céline, the fascist, pro-German Céline, answered splendidly. If that's what it took to end the slaughter (*cette tuerie*), he would sacrifice all the French cathedrals and gladly add all the German ones, too.[65] Literally. They had counted on his voice and his foul mouth and crude style. But Céline played them a sneaky trick. Universal indignation among the occupation hounds, howling and barking.

I agree with him. What are all the cathedrals worth, why even mention cathedrals, those dead stones, while rivers of innocent blood are flowing? We don't deserve cathedrals. What's the good of cathedrals for humanity SUCH AS IT IS? I'm told I'm a "pessimist." But I'm simply afraid of all the great splendors promised for after the war. They are decidedly too beautiful—this democracy, these reforms, this parrrrradise.

After lunching in the canteen, I stopped in to chat for a bit with Świątek. A fount of Cracow gossip. We came to the conclusion that Camus's *Le Malentendu* now running at the Théâtre des Mathurins was an obvious plagiarism of Karol Rostworowski's *The Surprise*.[66] Świątek told me that *The Surprise* had been submitted to a competition announced by a Cracow theater, and that he was the one who convinced Rostworowski to submit it by promising in advance he would win first prize. The promise was justified by the fact that none of the plays already submitted had any value and the jury was in an awkward position. Zygmunt Nowakowski was also part of this cabal.[67] Świątek described the various reactions of the members of the jury. *The Surprise* undeniably beat all the other submissions by a long shot. However, it was not favored by the majority of the jury. Leon Chwistek said his wife had read it and found it weak, undeveloped.[68] By contrast, Emil Haecker in *Naprzód* expressed his appreciation and exclaimed: "This must be the son of a peasant, a man of the people, who has never held a pen in his hand but has talent. Real, red-blooded, healthy proletarian talent."[69] Haecker must later have had egg on his face, when the peasant son turned out to be—Count Rostworowski. Rostworowski said he based *The Surprise* on an actual event. A very similar story apparently occurred in some Belorussian village and Franciszek Pusłowski seems to have known the details.[70] *Le Malentendu* is a strict copy, to the point even that the plot unfolds not in France but somewhere in Moldavia.

The armies are advancing on all fronts. The Russians are expected to take Wilno any time now. The Polish Underground Army is openly joining the action there.[71] The Poles are fighting the Germans at Wilno on behalf of Soviet Lithuania.

This evening Tadzik P. came to see us, then Lola, too, arrived. We talked all evening. We Poles have a very weak grasp of reality. We imagine that the English, the Americans, and the Russians are arranging everything for our benefit, for us in particular, and in general that they have no other concern except Poland. How could it be otherwise? Because of the 303rd Division, because of Monte Cassino, because the Home Army is helping the Russians take Wilno, because of General Maczek's division, and so on.[72] One can imagine that the Allies will be so indebted to us that until the resurrection of Poland (after the years of Soviet occupation) we will be able to lounge around and do nothing but sign "received" for the sums we will have been repaid. But what if we are expected to keep on paying? That's entirely likely. How many Poles have the Russians already deported and how many more will be deported in the future?

July 12, 1944

The food situation has become tenuous. Lunch in the canteen was inadequate and insubstantial. An hour later I was hungry. And then, B., an extremely nice young Frenchman, gave me a long lecture about a new philosophy, or rather philosophical system, whose name can be translated as "existentialism." He called it the philosophy of the future. I listened and listened and although I'm not entirely dense, I understood nothing. I observed one of the women workers, who pulled a white breast from under her blouse and began to nurse her infant. A car at a gas station. Finally, B. asked: "*Avez-vous compris?*" I was so hungry that I would willingly have replaced that child at the breast. "*Oui,*" I answered, "from this it follows that if not for the hope that one will eventually die, one should shoot oneself at once." I love Thought, I'm very fond of Thought, but of Thought in which there is the smell of foliage at dawn, in which there are veins full of hot blood, like the bluish veins on that mother's breast. I would really like something new, but not the kind of "progress" that makes every effort suddenly to glorify what should already have been consigned to the archives for good.

I arrived home famished. There are lines all over the city, lines for everything. Naturally, people are always quarreling, because they're irritated. Unkempt and stinking harpies look around to find someone at whom to discharge their foul tongues. Greed and envy, jealousy and hatred distort every face.

Around ten in the evening, terrible cries in our courtyard. Gray-haired Gorgons rush in from all sides. What's going on? PEACHES. A carload of peaches is being sold here, right in front of our building. I grab a basket and rush out. There's already a long line. A Fury, whose bun of dull, greasy hair, unwashed since birth, tickles my chin, stands right in front of me. The women jabber, quarrel, jump out of line to "take a look." Is there enough or not? The biddy ahead of me turns and says: "There will certainly not be enough." "That doesn't matter," I answer calmly. "Then why are you standing here?" "Just for the fun of it, because I like to stand in line." She increases her distance a bit, suspicious, and finally stops stroking me with her bun. From time to time she looks at me out of the corner of her eye and says nothing more. It's getting dark and I can't read. Finally, it's completely dark and the tradeswomen yell that they can't give change, because it's impossible to see. In any case, the good peaches have run out and selling *au plateau* begins. For ten francs, directly into the basket, without being weighed. They dump about three kg of rotten peaches into my basket and I hurry home, because it's leaking. We go through them, cut away the rotten pieces, and save the rest. Better this than nothing. Before the war mountains of such peaches were left over in Les Halles. Today they're selling them at ten francs, after an hour and a half of waiting in line, and we're still very happy. It's a Communist method of making people optimistic and content. Long ago I tamed two pigeons. They fly up to the windows every day and fear nothing. Today I was ashamed to catch myself thinking, what if . . . hm . . . pigeon tastes pretty good.

July 13, 1944

Today there was a revolution in the factory. Some cabbages had appeared in the food cooperative. About three hundred grams each, or three cabbages for every ten persons. What to do? Cut them up? Renounce one's share? People discussed and argued for an hour. Finally, I proposed we draw lots. They agreed. The losers looked like they were ready to eat the winners together with their cabbages. Me included. C. said, with a crooked smile, that I'd done very well with my "good" idea, meaning I'd proposed the lottery because I knew in advance that I would win. I made a face at her and said: "*J'suis pas bête, moi, hein? . . .*"[73] We're not yet at the point of famine, things have only gotten a bit more difficult, but people are already prepared to eat each other up. I suddenly feel a terrible revulsion, looking at these faces. I seem to see their exposed guts, with the stinking coils of their intestines. People barely mention the war. The talk is all about food, everything is seen from the perspective of grub.

On the Eastern Front—a deluge. The Russians have taken Wilno, they're at Pinsk, heading for Grodno and Białystok, encircling, breaking through. In Normandy things are going well.

July 14, 1944

Le quatorze juillet. The "Marseillaise" is blaring on Radio Paris, in Vichy, in Algiers, from London. Broadcasts of celebrations in liberated France.

July 15, 1944

This evening a long bicycle ride. Along the Seine, boulevard Saint-Germain, to the Odéon. We looked at the program. Perhaps we'll go next week. Then we sat in the Luxembourg Gardens. A warm, overcast evening. A child insisted on poking a long stick into our spokes. He then went over to the pond and thoroughly drenched the back of his stroller. Some boys launched a motorized boat. Silence, the rattle of the mechanical toy, the early evening calm of the sky, the bouquet of trees and flowers. Vegetables are now growing where lawns used to be. Beans and roses. At nine thirty they began to signal the closing. We continued on our way. Boulevard Montparnasse. Empty streets. Just a few sleepy customers on the terraces of Le Dôme and La Coupole. Men are carrying women on their bicycles. Sidesaddle, behind. A charming sight. Boulevard des Invalides. Old private mansions, the gold dome of the Invalides. We ride past the Polish Embassy. The German Institute is now located there. Soon it will be "*rraus*"—out on its ear. The palaces on quai d'Orsay, the Chamber of Deputies. We enter boulevard Saint-Germain and finally take a seat on the terrace of the Deux Magots. The clock on the church steeple strikes ten and it's getting dark. We take the cavelike rue Bonaparte down to the Seine. The silhouette of Notre-Dame and the clasplike arcs of the bridges blur in the darkness. The water is black and oily. Then place de la Bastille and repulsive rue du Faubourg Saint-Antoine. At ten thirty we reach home, imbued with the silence and peace of this strange city. Paris is magnificent now. This is the Paris that will remain forever in my memory. London talks a lot about the Polish character of the Wilno region. A waste of breath . . .

July 16, 1944

It took almost two hours to boil the water for tea. The gas is so weak that cooking anything has become almost impossible. It's horrible, it's monstrous, unbearable, blah, blah, blah. Suddenly a horrible scream in the staircase. My neighbor, the fat one, runs out of her room, the asthmatic old man next door emerges with his gorillalike tread, I hear a commotion, a sentence here and there: "*C'est fini, rien à faire, c'est perdu.*"[74] Thinking of the Normandy front and trembling slightly, I also fly out of my room. It turns out to be something much worse: our neighbor had gone to the WC with his ration cards in the unbuttoned back pocket of his trousers. And all the cards had fallen down the "chute." He realized what had happened only after he'd covered the cards with the remains of what he'd obtained in exchange for them. What a ruckus! "Over there, you can see them, but it's too deep." The *patron* came upstairs—for a big conference. To call the fire department or not? Are the firemen needed or can we do without them? Maybe a poker will suffice? I returned to my room. After a while, cries of joy. "*Ça y est. Quelle chance.*"[75] They have been washed and are drying on the windowsill. Jubilation and with good reason, because it's a big deal to get them replaced. A person without ration cards is in general a nobody. Under suspicion, an operator, not a citizen. In short, null. Oof.

Leafing through the Goncourt diaries, I come upon this scene: "Crossing the reading room in the National Library, I noticed a man absorbed in reading. He was holding the hand of the young woman seated next to him. When I passed by again two hours later, the man was still reading and still holding the young woman's hand. It was a German couple. NO . . . IT WAS GERMANY!" In my delight, I want to smash everything in the room. I spend the entire day re-playing this scene. Fantastic. Like a bolt of lightning. Lightning-sentences writ-ten by Jules Goncourt. His brother Edmond would never have managed such subtlety. Written with a toothpick dipped in red wine.

After lunch, the Bois de Vincennes. We lie on the grass after eating part of our rabbit, radishes (today the vegetable allowance was a mere five hundred grams a person), bread and butter, and gooseberries. I don't understand why they don't sell food by the dose in the pharmacies. Poor organization. On the path next to us a skinny fellow, a Titi or Coco, is teaching his large, fat darling to ride a bicycle. He sends her off on her own steam into the road, having patted her broad behind. The sound echoed through the trees. The saddle disappeared into her crevices and she seemed to be sitting directly on the bar. An alert.

We hear the buzz of airplanes. Soon shells start bursting above us. A terrible din. We enter a nearby arbor, to avoid being hit on the head by shrapnel. People are running out of the clearings and out of the woods. After a while all quiets down and people spread out again. Children resume their ball games (and Titi teaches his hippopotamus to ride a bike). Later we're in Robert's garden. He misses his family and is out of sorts. We lie on the grass and talk about the pro-cess of deep metal rolling, both hot and cold. Then about technology in general. It seems to me there are times at which a single move of profound reflection is more valuable than a thousand moves forward in one's own automobile or air-plane. Even if it is one's own.

July 17, 1944

An old article in the "socialist" (or rather, national socialist) weekly, *Germinal*, which has since stopped publishing, fell into my hands today. The title is "Plato's Socialism" and the author is a certain Félicien Challaye.[76] To cite a passage: "The first clearly articulated socialist theory in the history of European thought is the theory developed by Plato (428–348) from the fifth century before the Christian era." (ah, the Christian era . . .) "An encouraging start: the first, in chronological order, of our great comrades is a mighty genius, a profound philosopher, and a magnificent artist."

No big deal, I can swallow that, but this "comrade Plato" gave me indigestion all afternoon. This evening, again quite by accident (I don't read these rags), I glanced at *Signal*, dedicated to "The Spirit of Europe."[77] A photograph of a sculpture of Plato and a short biography, including the phrase: "He is the first Western nationalist."

I crumpled it up thoroughly, crushed it into the ground, and wanted to pray to Flaubert. O you saintly Flaubert, you who once wrote to Louis Bouilhet: "But we who derive no profits, we are alone, *alone*, like the Bedouin in the desert. We must cover our faces, wrap ourselves in our coats, and lower our heads into the storm— and always—unremittingly—until the last drop of water, until the final beat of our hearts." No—if after the war everything is not done to ensure that Plato is above all Plato, ordinary Plato, simply Plato, all will be lost. If nothing is done, then one will have to move somewhere Plato has never been heard of. There are still such places on earth. That would decidedly be better and easier to bear. I no longer remember who used the phrase "tetragon of stupidity," but it's great. Except, how much power will be needed to smash all the tetragons that are lining up these days one after the other. Tetragons of lying, hypocrisy, mistaken ideas, mystifications, one-and-only true IDEOLOGIES. Our civilization—appearances to the contrary notwithstanding—does not sin so much in deed. It sins horribly in thought and speech. "I am suffocated by the floods of hatred I feel for the stupidity of my age. The shit rises in my gorge, as in a strangulated hernia," writes Saint Flaubert in a different letter. Tragically, it's not the proletariat or the plebs who are stupid but the so-called enlightened classes who are becoming stupider by the minute. "The enlightened classes need to be enlightened," writes Flaubert in yet another letter. "Begin with the head. It's the sickest; the rest will follow on its own."

Will it be possible to express outrage in the society of the comrades of "comrade Plato"? Basia phoned to say she was riding to school on the bike. Into town on her own, for the first time. She will demolish half of Paris . . . We've arranged to meet at half past five at the intersection of Raspail and Saint-Germain and return home together.

Membership card, French camping association, 1946. (Polish Institute of Arts and Sciences of America [PIASA], New York)

(right) Jan Birtus, Basia and Andrzej Bobkowski, Gruissan, August 1946. (Instytut Badań Literackich, Polish Academy of Sciences, Warsaw)

(below) Andrzej Bobkowski taking notes, Guatemala, 1950s. (Fondation Jan Michalski, Montricher, Switzerland)

20.5.1940

Cisza i upał.Paryż opustoszał i pustoszeje z dnia na dzień.
Odbywa się to jednak jakby pokryjomu.Ludzie wyjeżdżają chyłkiem,zapewniając
znajomych do ostatniej chwili,że "my się nie ruszamy".I tylko coraz częściej
dostrzega się na ulicach samochody,prześlizgujące się z ciężkim bagażem umoco-
wanym na dachu i mknące na południe.Nie należy ich dostrzegać.Ale niepewność
i tajemnica opadły na miasto.Idąc ulicą ciągle łapałem się na tym,że najnor-
malniejsze zjawiska codziennego życia wydawały mi się tajemnicze.Samochody
jeździły tak jakoś dziwnie,jakby ciszej i prędzej,a na dworcach "métro" cze-
kało się nie tylko na pociąg,lecz na coś więcej.W powietrzu wisiały kłamstwo
i niedomówienie.

Dopiero dziś rano ta próżnia w dołku,z którą każdy chodził,zniknęła.Weygand
mianowany wodzem naczelnym na miejsce Gamelin'a,Pétain w rządzie.Weygand od-
razu objął dowództwo i pojechał na front.Oczywiście zaczęły chodzić słuchy
o zdradzie:podobno Gamelin popełnił samobójstwo,są dowody,że...itd.Wierzy się
w Weygand'a,wierzy się,że naprawi i załata.Tymczasem pierwszą fazę tej bitwy
Francuzi przegrali na całej linii.

Niemcy są już w Arras i w Amiens,starają się otoczyć Armię belgijską.

21.5.1940.

Reynaud powiedział dziś w Senacie prawdę,a raczej część prawdy.
Okazało się,że Armia Gen.Corap,broniąca linii Ardenów na odcinku Mézières -
Sédan była źle skompletowana,obsadzona dywizjami źle uzbrojonymi - w listo-
padzie zeszłego roku widziałem ich chodzących po mieście w nocnych pantoflach,
a ponadto mosty na Meuse nie zostały wysadzone.Poprostu skandal.Najsilniejsze
uderzenie Niemców poszło oczywiście w tym kierunku,bo napewno wiedzieli oni
o tym,zanim Mr.Reynaud został poinformowany.Ale za to tradycji stało się za-
dość:wszyscy są podniesieni na duchu tym skandalem.Francuzi klną,złorzeczą
i wkońcu dochodzą do ostatecznej konkluzji,że "teraz my im pokażemy" i "Wey-

First page of the typed copy of the manuscript. (Instytut Literacki–Kultura, Le Mesnil-le-Roi, France)

Andrzej Bobkowski at his Remington typewriter, Guatemala, 1950s.
(Fondation Jan Michalski, Montricher, Switzerland)

(above) Andrzej Bobkowski in front of his house in Guatemala
City, 1950s. (Instytut Literacki–Kultura, Le Mesnil-le-Roi,
France)
(below) Basia and Andrzej Bobkowski in the courtyard of the
University of San Carlos of Guatemala, Guatemala City, 1950s.
(Instytut Badań Literackich, Polish Academy of Sciences,
Warsaw)

Andrzej Bobkowski in the Adirondack mountains, April 1961.
(Muzeum Literatury im. Adama Mickiewicza, Warsaw)

I met up with Basia. She had traversed all of Paris without incident. I was re-luctant to believe it, but there it was. What has this war not made of people . . .

"You really didn't knock anyone down?"

"No. Everyone avoided me. But my head hurts from the sun."

An answer in the style of *das Ewig-Weibliche*.[78] Everyone avoided her . . . I tell her I have a kilo of mushrooms and two kilos of peaches and sixteen hun-dred grams of young potatoes. She smiles and forgets for a moment about her headache.

"For once we won't have green peas and pasta," she says in the voice of a shrinking violet.

Off we go. On place Saint-Germain we sit on the terrace of Café Bonaparte and drink ice-cold sparkling "cider." It's a stifling afternoon with a fresh wind. Streams of bicycles flow around us. Work lets out at this hour. The number of bicycles is simply dizzying, everyone gets around on bicycles.[79] The sun, a deep blue sky without a single cloud. Bicycles, short gingham skirts and silk dresses, sandals, the display of legs up to the waist, as the wind lifts the light fabrics. I can hardly breathe for feeling the wonder of life.

We go down rue Bonaparte on foot. Basia takes a look at "her" second-hand shop, I inspect the books. Then we ride home, continuing along the Seine. After supper a gathering at Lola's. We discuss the Russians. Someone at some point had said that, overall, things weren't so bad. And clearly Lola was glad of it. Be-cause, like millions, she too *doesn't want to* see. When I speak about *the truth of the matter*, she presents me with little factlets. Such facts are created in order to conceal the essence of things.

July 18, 1944

A giant parade was apparently held in Moscow. Fifty-seven thousand Ger-man prisoners of war, led by captured German generals, marched through the Moscow streets. One can well imagine what this march must have meant for the dozen German generals. They walked like the barbarians behind the chariot of a victorious Roman. They, the generals of Great Germany, of *Großdeutsch-land* . . .

But when one recovers from the first impulse of satisfaction and when one recalls that this is the twentieth century, that THIS and many more terrible things have been happening, even after all that has been written and repeatedly underscored by the spilling of blood, one is overcome by darkness. Besides the crashing of the bombs, I increasingly seem to hear the crash of culture crum-bling into ruins, the culture of the Declaration of the Rights of Man and other such nonsense.

July 19, 1944

Paris talks of nothing else but sugar. Because in other *départements*, five kilos of sugar per person are being distributed in advance for the "O ticket." Expeditions from Paris to the provinces in search of sugar are therefore being organized. Our factory has sent a car with the "tickets" of all the personnel. For the second day, there's talk of nothing but sugar. What does anyone care if Livorno and Ancona have fallen, if the Americans have taken Saint-Lô, if the Russians are fourteen kilometers from Lwów and are fighting on the outskirts of Brest-Litovsk? Sugar. Will there be any sugar or not?

July 20, 1944

After leaving the office I took a tumble at the first turn. Dumb and avoidable—I myself don't know how it happened. The skin of my entire left arm and hand is as shredded as a bloody steak. I was so furious that I got back on the bike and was at Porte d'Orléans before I stopped at a pharmacy to get it bandaged.

Sweltering. The air is stifling, overheated, and inert. Heat radiates from the asphalt, like a furnace. Cars, bicycles, the drone of motors fueled by wood gas, their sickening exhaust. At Alésia I became dizzy and as a precaution dismounted. Pain was shooting through my left arm. Finally, I reached the side streets. The streets near the Prison de la Santé were still barricaded behind trestles with barbed wire. For July 14, the prisoners staged a revolt and are said to have killed several guards. The newspapers didn't report it. Now the rebels are being "pacified."

Basia tells me our *épicier* asked her today: "What do you think of the latest developments? Shouldn't Poland have to restore Russia's ethnic boundaries?" Basia retorted calmly: "Don't you think France should give Indochina back to the Indochinese, Madagascar back to the Malagasy, and Algeria to the Algerians?" That stopped the grocer cold. It's beyond belief the degree to which everything "catches on," when it comes to Russia. There's nothing but Russia. It's not so bad when the masses are stupid, because the masses are always stupid, but real hell begins when the masses start to use terms such as "ethnic boundaries." Nevertheless, France, with its veneer of sophistication, is connected to the Soviets by a secret and very powerful thread, the spiritual thread of boorishness, of those who speak of "ethnic boundaries," while ill at ease with a knife and fork. There's something else as well: only Russia today extends the kind of promises its own system makes impossible to attain. And therefore people all believe in it. Communism has replaced religion these days and has become what it accuses other religions of being: the opium of the people. The French have always had a strong inclination for practically unattainable things and a deep belief in things actually unattainable. Hence the pervasive sympathy for the Soviets.

Another serving of news this evening. An attempt to assassinate Hitler. Alas, Hitler was only singed, though a number of his associates were wounded. A clock-bomb exploded in the *Führers Hauptquartier*. It seems significant and suggests an organized conspiracy. But there's little precise information.

The Russians are spreading like a flood. They have taken Augustów and are a dozen kilometers from East Prussia.

July 21, 1944

Unfortunately, the attempt on Hitler's life did not succeed. Rumors abound. I don't listen, because what's the point? Graf von Stauffenberg, one of the *"blaublütige Schweinhünde und Reaktionäre,"* messed up badly and that's what counts.[80] The death throes continue.

B. came to see me today, pulled a slide rule from his pocket, and calculated, to the third decimal point, that if the Russians keep going at their recent pace, and if the Allies do not step it up in Normandy, then in two months they will meet in Montmartre. I'm very fond of him, but although today he was merely joking, I nevertheless include him in the category of intellects I call "Cartesian wells." These are people who approach every phenomenon in life with slide rule in hand. How frightening it would be—a world of people with slide rules.

Afternoon tea at N.'s. He's a young chemical engineer who in his student days befriended the writer Maxence van der Meersch. Apparently, many people from the medical world of Lille appear in van der Meersch's *Corps et âmes*, which is why that splendid novel was attacked so harshly.[81] The N. family are practicing Catholics and active members of the Family Association. The goal of the association is to defend the family. For example, when the owner of a building does not want to rent an apartment to a family with many children, it intervenes. When someone—naturally wealthy, eminent, universally respected, and so on—seduces an underage girl, by enticing her with sweets, then the association uses its connection with a great lawyer (only a great lawyer—one of less stature would not succeed) to get him tried and sentenced. Otherwise, such a gentleman—wealthy, eminent, universally respected, a chevalier of the Legion of Honor—might well have extricated himself from the consequences, as has usually been the case (and certainly still is). The current parish priest, an active and enterprising man, has organized the sale of vegetables for the poor, a day camp for poor children, with lunch for five francs. The work continues to pile up, because thanks to all this, the number of "Catholics" has been growing enormously and everyone suddenly remembers that once upon a time they were baptized and took first communion. When asked what he thought of all the misfortunes of the present war, the priest told N.: "Without these misfortunes, everyone would have forgotten about God." Madame N. adds: "In fact — from the moment of the landing, more and more people have been coming to church."

Tomorrow I must ask B. to calculate for me on his slide rule the number of people who might be re-converted by the dropping of a single bomb. I want to draw up a table beginning with fifty-kilogram bombs. Very simple. Then I'll send it to the Americans and to Rome. I'll include a slide rule, so that other human issues might also be resolved with its help. Then we'll build a shrine containing slide rules and establish a new religion — sliderulism. And everything will be just fine.

July 22, 1944

It's being said that Hitler has engaged in peace talks with the Soviets and that they have arrived at a preliminary understanding. That for this reason the English wanted to get rid of him by means of this Stauffenberg. That in any case the Germans have already signed an armistice agreement, and stopping the Russians at one place or another is a matter of days or even hours. Just rumors, perhaps, but perhaps not. Where do they come from?

That somebody Mikołajczyk has announced that he's ready to go to Moscow for talks with Stalin. Yet another one who "believes." The Soviets adore people like this.

A street scene. A cool, refreshing July morning. The streets are still empty and quiet. In front of one of the houses on rue Broca a tall woman in mourning stands in the middle of the street, behind her a boy with a giant wreath that hides him entirely. A man still in his nightshirt, his hair uncombed, leans out of the second-story window. They engage in a lively conversation. I stop. In the empty street every word can be heard.

"I came to show you the wreath . . . it's for the funeral of poor Pierre . . . it's expensive, but just look, made of real flowers. It won't last, but it's so pretty . . ."

Like a great rising sun, the man's wife appeared at the window. She intruded herself slowly — SHE ROSE — until she completely obscured what in common parlance is known by the word "husband." Her large bust splashed noiselessly over the windowsill, restrained loosely by her ragged nightgown (exactly like the skin of milk when poured into a cup — plop), and hung over the street. Captive balloons. She poked out her head, bristling with the barbed wire of curlers, and a stream of exclamations descended from above:

"So beautiful. These flowers are just as good as artificial ones. Poor Pierre. And just think, it's all because of food." The woman below pushes the boy holding the wreath toward the window. "So that's how it is, they have to use real flowers, because tin can't be had. You realize" (the curlers are now talking back into the room) "it's the food. The stomach. No meat, no wine. And today it's the funeral."

The woman in mourning maneuvers the wreath, pushing the boy this way and that.

"You see—I watered it just this morning, to keep it fresh."

I continued on my way. Damn, what times these are. Not even any tin to make wreaths. What have we come to? Scandalous! I would not agree to die now for all the money in the world.

July 24, 1944

Our factory food cooperative is showing unexpected resourcefulness. Today I received five kilos of sugar for 15 francs. (On the black market sugar costs 165 francs.) In addition, vegetables almost every day. We are again eating very well, all the more so since Świątek is always on the lookout for fruit. Plums, peaches, gooseberries, sour cherries. Świątek is great. A mine of Cracow anecdotes. What jokes he tells about Leon Chwistek. Świątek is always elegant, dressed to the nines, and perfumed. Poor man, consumed by FEAR. For fear of the Germans he got himself locked in a madhouse by pretending to be insane. It was only Dr. K. who somehow found him out and managed to get him released. K. is the only one who could have done it. And now he helps support this ruin of a man out of his own pocket.

This afternoon I met Basia on boulevard Raspail. She rides daringly around Paris and insists it's not very hard, "because you have to ride as though no one else was on the street." I understand—that's no doubt why everyone avoids her. When she gets on her bike, I close my eyes and block my ears, because the first ten meters defy all the laws of equilibrium. But she has such force of character that even these laws bend to her will. We drink cold beer in La Européen opposite Gare de Lyon. The Parisian metro has been reduced to a few main lines and apparently what goes on there is hard to believe. I prefer not to see it.

This evening I have a bitter taste in my mouth, from thoughts that have been preying on me for the past half hour. The day before yesterday, after the occupation ("liberation") of Chełm, the Russians played "Jeszcze Polska"—"Poland has not yet died." Today they announced the conquest—excuse me, the "liberation"—of Lublin, and again, "Jeszcze Polska."[82] Well, and the Union of Polish

Patriots in Moscow has declared the government in London to be illegal and has created a Committee of National Liberation and some kind of National Council, which has supposedly already gone into operation.[83] From the moment I heard about this, the aria "Ridi Pagliaccio!" from *Pagliacci* automatically began sounding in my ears. Laugh, you Polish soldier-clown, you Polish pilot-clown and sailor-clown, and you gentlemen-clowns. Let's all of us laugh. In return for five years of suffering, for five years of "firm resolve," for refusing to collaborate with the Germans, for not having our own Pétain or Quisling, for concentration camps, roundups, and executions. For all of that, you have a Poland that begins in Chełm, you have a National Council with Wanda Wasilewska.[84] They're liberating us, freeing us, giving us a great and independent Poland. We've been waiting five long years and finally it's the "dawn of freedom," the red star. Well, let's rejoice, let's laugh, let's clap our hands, O clowns! Laugh, damn it—let's go, heartily, all together! Offer flowers to the termites of the New World, to the ambassadors of Paradise, to Generalissimo Stalin's free citizens. Write some odes. "Poland will not yet have died as long as THEY still live."

I'm ridiculous, pathetic, and stubborn. Because I can see only one thing: that in fighting against totalitarianism, we become mired in something even worse. I writhe in pain. Not a Polish pain—no—a cosmic pain.

July 25, 1944

The Goncourts describe their reaction to reading documents from the Revolution, which they are studying for one of their plays: "Yes, deprive the Revolution of its blood, and the exclamation 'what stupidity!' will come to your lips when confronted with this chaos of cannibalistic idiocies and flesh-eating rhetoric. You have to read it to believe, to believe that this occurred in France not quite a hundred years ago . . . And what hypocrisy, what lies, this Revolution. The slogans, the formulas, the speeches, the history, everything in that era is a lie. Ah, what a book one could write, under the title, FRAUDS OF THE REVOLUTION!"

Yes—deprive the Russian Revolution of blood and what is left? Stupidity and lying and hypocrisy raised to the nth degree in comparison with the French Revolution. And today this stupidity, this hypocrisy, and the greatest ideological mendacity in history, are touted as the ONE-AND-ONLY TRUTH. The intellectual level of humanity has never sunk so low.

For example: Molotov issued a proclamation saying that the Soviet government has concluded an agreement with the Polish Committee of National Liberation in Chełm, according to which the goal of the Soviet Army is the liberation of Poland, the creation of a strong and independent Poland, without interference in the administration of the country and without the imposition of any form of government not in accordance with the desires of the people. Accept this and you can get yourself drunk on water. But people believe. Millions believe. Delightful.

In response, London has declared that the Polish Telegraph Agency *has been authorized* to issue a communiqué saying that the members of the so-called Committee of National Liberation are little-known figures and cannot represent the Polish nation. The committee consists of representatives of the very small Communist Party in Poland and does not reflect the desires and aspirations of the people of Poland. Who can have authorized the Telegraph Agency to publish such nonsense? These figures are known, indeed well known, I myself know half of them personally. Wanda Wasilewska, living with that bricklayer from Cracow, Maniek Bogatko—was there anyone who didn't know them?[85] Everybody knew them, they spent days on end at the workers' university.[86] Bolesław Drobner—an unknown?[87] The same goes for General Rola-Żymierski?[88] Andrzej Witos and General Berling are perhaps less well known.[89] But if you add the entire Socialist Youth and the Pacifist Club, headed by Józef Cyrankiewicz, will they also be considered unknown?[90] The point is, they are so well known that one can already predict who will be forming the Polish Vichy. Though the situation is not quite the same . . . Unknown?—everything at once so familiar. Julek and Frydek will no doubt soon emerge as "deputy ministers," Józef will certainly become a big fish, because he always had a knack for power, and Kryśka will regret she stopped going out with him. Unknowns—it makes me weep . . . I had no nose, a fatally weak sense of smell. Or rather, it was too acute: even before the war they all smelled too much to me of Cuir de Russie.[91] And therefore I was considered a "muddlehead."

For ten days the Russians have been standing at the East Prussian border. At first this caused a great stir. But then it all died down. Why are the Russians advancing so quickly on Polish territory, faster than on any other sector of the front? Why haven't they taken even one step across the East Prussian border? A single occupied acre of East Prussia would be much more effective as propaganda than the occupation of Poland. Is it possible the Russians may still be expecting SOMETHING and that's why they haven't entered Prussia? I'm suspicious and I tremble with fear for Poland.

July 27, 1944

Yesterday Goebbels gave a big speech and explained how the plot had unfolded. He then talked about the total mobilization of which he is in charge.

He insisted that the assassination attempt and the revolt could only redound to the country's benefit. I'm sure that three-quarters of the German population believed him. I myself couldn't, somehow. He promised a new weapon, new inventions, and in general the start of a new war.

As of today, the Paris post office refuses to take letters for Warsaw. In Paris, the stubborn rumor is making the rounds that Hitler and Stalin have signed an armistice, which is supposed to begin on August 1.

After leaving the office I had a long conversation with B. (without the slide rule this time). We discussed the future of the world. I reminded him, finally, of a certain scene from the Goncourts, whom I'm reading now in the evenings to calm myself down. During a long discussion of the scientific far-sightedness of Marcellin Berthelot and Claude Bernard,[92] someone said: "If things continue like this, one day there will be no other solution but for the Honorable Old Man with the beard to descend to earth and in the deep voice of a museum guard to say: *Messieurs, on ferme.*"[93] We both laughed. And German transports were rolling through the streets.

July 28, 1944

D. writes from La Ferté-Bernard: "I will certainly soon end up in prison or in a hospital, since I have the irresistible desire to bash in the kisser anyone who says with sincere goodwill, 'Well? Poland will soon be liberated. The Russians are at this place or that.' I hear this sentence a dozen times a day from people I had always considered normal and intelligent. I'm beginning to fear for my own sanity, since madmen always think everyone around them is mentally ill, and I myself have come to that conclusion."

Here in Paris I also want to bash people in the kisser, but I would have to mechanize the process, because it's Paris and it's not a dozen people a day, but tens and hundreds who daily display their good manners by congratulating me right and left (literally everyone). They already take me for a nut case, because they're trying to make me feel good and I'm ready to scream *merrrde* and tell them they're crazy. No one, absolutely no one, wants to believe me. Sometimes I have the sensation of a nightmare, of suffocating, of a fly caught in a spider's web. With each "liberated" city, these morons congratulate me. I've stopped responding.

July 29, 1944

Basia went off, on her own, by bicycle all the way to Neuilly to the wedding of one of her friends. I was tempted to say the rosary. I had lunch at a restaurant in Fontenay. For a few beans with two sausages no longer than a finger each, for a tiny triangle of "Camembert" with a small carafe of "cider" (the bread was my own), I paid 113 francs. I returned home at two and lay down for a nap. Later in the afternoon, Basia biked back from Neuilly, on her own, and when she entered the room she was as elegant and animated as though she'd emerged from a Rolls-Royce, not dismounted from a bicycle. She inspected my hand and had the nerve to say: "I worry now about you when you're on your bicycle." Hell. Of course, because not everyone "avoids *me*."

Take a small group of friends, all of whom you like very much, one at a time. But when together, it's like this: discussion of new systems of gas burners producing strong flames when the pressure is low, of little stoves that run on paper (you crumple the paper into balls, you keep throwing them in, and that's how you cook), of the Russians (the usual nonsense), of butter from Normandy (like talk of ghosts—everyone speaks about them, but few have seen them)—in short, meh meh, meow meow, and haw haw.

Yesterday I managed to lay my hands on an entire leg of lamb and on Sunday we'll have a lot of meat. But suddenly the gas has died. In Paris—a tragedy. There's no electricity in the daytime, at night it starts only at quarter after ten. And only for the lights. Women cannot get their perms. But a solution even for that has already been found: One of the grand hair salons—Antoine, I believe—has constructed an apparatus run by a tandem bicycle. They have hired four racing champions who take turns pedaling for eight hours. A music hall in Montmartre intends to illuminate the stage with the aid of similar tandems. The cinemas and theaters have been closed for two weeks now. All the concierges are saying that *ça ne peut pas durer comme ça*,[94] because today some dying woman in the hospital said the war would end on a Sunday, the thirteenth. The closest falls on August 13. In general, what is paradise compared with the UNRRA?[95] Poor J. complained to me today that her husband is probably cheating on her. I think it's true, but I told her not to worry, because the UNRRA *vous arrangera tout ça.*[96]

That Mikołajczyk has already reached Tehran and tomorrow should be in Moscow.[97] The Russians are on the outskirts of Warsaw.

July 30, 1944

Late afternoon in the Bois de Vincennes. We were sitting near the pond and I was telling Basia about our future. If we have our own little house with a garden, in summertime Basia will make lots of fruit preserves and I will make fruit wine and liqueurs. But if we live in a housing block and wear Model No. 1 clothing and eat according to the weekly menu and read some *Proletarian*

Poland, edited by a former member of the National Union of Socialist Youth, then Basia will not be making fruit preserves, nor I fruit wine and liqueurs. We will be going to meetings to discuss Marx, Lenin, and Stalin, and will convince ourselves that life has only now become beautiful and it's all "for the good of Poland." So, no—I don't see why the subject is always Poland and why every-thing must be for the sake of Poland. That I was born Polish is just as acciden-tal as my belonging to one particular social class and not another, as my being white and not black. Social class and skin color are prejudices you can thumb your nose at, but the fatherland, that's absolutely sacred. Why? Nationalism has also become a religion, and the more primitive it is and the more fanatical, the more it demands respect. Now people are already saying: "Our duty is to return to Poland, no matter what the future holds." Why? Man alone is not a fiction—all else is fiction. The whole world can be a fatherland and every man a brother. What counts on earth is man, above all man. But in Poland excuses are already being found for "not returning." I myself won't return for the sake of Poland. Why? I won't return, because I simply don't want to and if I have the chance to explore the world, because it beckons me, because the world and other people interest me, because life in the corked bottle of the fatherland doesn't suit me one bit. But one doesn't have the right to do this. Why? Mikołaj-czyk has not yet reached Moscow. Anxiety. As though anything depended on that. French radio from London said that Konstantin Rokossovsky comes from a noble Polish family.[98] Important, indeed. As our bard Mickiewicz has said: "A great scoundrel, as is usually the case with Poles that turn Muscovites in the czar's service."[99] Rokossovsky is at the outskirts of Warsaw. And now we will certainly throw ourselves into a "heroic battle" in order to deliver Warsaw—to Rokossovsky. From a Polish, and most important, a noble family. To be Polish is indeed often infernally complicated. The myth of nationality is one of the great myths that refuses to crumble. The Lord God has been dispensed with, religions have been dispensed with, but nationality and nationalism have not. Quite the opposite. This myth still has a great future before it. And so long as it persists, a HUMANE world will remain a dream. There will still be a world of myths, not people.

This war will resolve nothing. Bitterness, disgust—disgust with everything, and I'm unable to get it out of my mind and unable to let anyone convince me to do so.

July 31, 1944

No news about Mikołajczyk, Romer, or Grabski.[100] They should already be in Moscow. "Maybe Stalin has had them arrested?" people ask. He's too clever for that—he needs dupes like these, because without their help he will convince no one that Poland is still Poland. And when it comes to Poland, the Poles want nothing so much as to be convinced.

August 1, 1944

Mikołajczyk is in Moscow. The Russians have apparently concentrated a million men outside Warsaw. Inside Warsaw all that remains are the German army and the Gestapo.

August 2, 1944

Yesterday, the Polish Underground Army launched an open battle to liberate Warsaw. Warsaw is apparently burning and there are battles in the streets. What's it all for? Thoughts, thoughts, I'm full of thoughts and afraid of words, any of which can be misleading.

One of my French colleagues told me today, "in confidence," winking mysteriously, that if the Americans have conducted such a successful offensive in recent days, it's because they've had French advisers. *"Vous savez, les Américains se laissent conseiller.*[101] The English never listened to us. And that's why they never advanced." This attitude may be fatal to them. This Frenchman reminded me of Sieburg's *Dieu est-il Français?* Another Frenchman, a teacher in our vocational school, sat down at my table during lunch and, also "in confidence," practically in a whisper, insisted the V-1 was just the beginning, the Germans have prepared other surprises. "You'll see," he says, "the V-5. It's a French invention, which the Germans have only perfected." (The fatal attitude: Germans never discover anything themselves, they only perfect French inventions.) He didn't want to tell me what it was, but finally whispered: "These are bombs, which in a range of three hundred meters lower the air temperature to minus 300 degrees Celsius, and in a range of thirty kilometers to minus 30."

I looked at him and said I pitied his students. I observed that I thought this complete nonsense, because, in the first place, a temperature of absolute zero amounts to minus 273 degrees Celsius, but in practice one can approach it (minus 272 degrees) only by the liquification of helium, which the Germans do not have—perhaps you know better, I don't teach in a vocational school—and, in the second place, because the explosion of a bomb using liquid air would be able to lower the temperature only over a very limited area. To which my "special informant" objected: "The revolt of the generals was motivated by their desire to use these terrible inventions right away, but Hitler objected. He didn't want to resort to such savage methods of war."

Whispering softly, I asked him who was paying him to say things LIKE THIS and asked for the address of the office that was paying. I'd also like to earn something on the side.

He belongs to a type of moral sadist one frequently encounters these days. People like this devote themselves to creating anxiety, spreading fear and despair. They feel strong in their cruel stupidity when they see people growing weaker around them. I have learned not to exclude anything and I don't exclude the existence of things even worse than these refrigerator bombs. The technical possibilities for destruction are limitless. But I'd have no compunction deep-freezing people like this "special informant."

The Americans are securing Brittany. They've taken Rennes and broken through the front. In Warsaw, terrible fighting. The Underground Army has taken control of the Mokotów district, Filtry and the Lubecki complex in Ochota, and the Avenue of the Polish Army in Żoliborz.[102]

August 4, 1944

I'm a passionate reader of graffiti in Parisian *pissoirs*. The exchange of thoughts among anonymous people unknown to each other, this nameless correspondence on the tin-covered walls, a bit above the spot that gets sprinkled, is often terrific. French chattiness and *émotivité* do not miss an opportunity for expression.

Today I saw an entire discussion. First note: "Bravo Soviets—the USSR will win." Underneath, a remark in red pencil: "Moron—soon you'll have to be fighting against them." Even lower, a short conclusion, impressively calm. Some "college student." "Not necessarily" (*C'est pas sûr*).

On rue de Vaugirard someone wrote: "*Stalingrad—sic transit gloria mundi Germanorum.*" Some distinguished scholar with a classical education. But he annoyed the common folk, because a series of graffiti followed, along the lines of: "*Merde*—write in French if you want to be understood." "*T'es Chinois, toi?—On est chocolat avec ton latin*"[103] (must be some southerner), etc. I therefore added my bit at the end: "*Vox populi—vox Dei.*"

In Warsaw—barricades, the main post office, a skyscraper, the gasworks, the electric station, and a number of districts are in the hands of the Poles. They say the Germans are driving the population to the barricades, while themselves hiding behind them. I would like to stop thinking. Mikołajczyk spoke for two and a half hours with Stalin. It looks as if the Polish government in London may have ordered the uprising in order to have a so-called ace in hand. A lovely ace . . . I'm afraid to pronounce the word "absurd," but it tempts me at every turn, when I think about this. All the more so, since the Russians have not advanced an inch in the last four days. Another word that I fear and that constantly buzzes in my head is "provocation."

August 5, 1944

Early evening, beside the pond in the Bois de Vincennes. Deserted. I'm reading aloud from Antoine de Saint-Exupéry's wonderful *Terre des hommes*.[104]

Horrors are occurring in Warsaw. This suits the Russians very well and it's why they're in no hurry to take the city . . . The Americans are on the verge of securing Brittany as they approach the Loire. From the other side they are already approaching Brest and Lorient. The Russians have taken Stryj and are fifty kilometers from Cracow.

August 6, 1944

The Goncourts write that humbug is killing France. They're right. We're all being killed by humbug and myths.

Around eight we're going to visit W. and his wife. Ordinary people, but nice. A few months ago I found him work, or rather I recommended him to the Polish cobbler-officers (ah, those officer-cobblers). He began to work there making fashionable ladies' shoes and today earns a good living, making the same kind of shoes at home. The couple welcome us with a magnificent supper. It's quite astounding how much money ordinary people are willing to spend (when they have it) on food. Meat, potatoes, everything swimming in fat, very expensive fat (butter at 700–800 francs a kilo, lard at 400–450). W. confesses he spends almost everything he makes on food.

It occurred to me after we left that the hatred felt by the proletariat focuses less on what the "intelligentsia" possesses than on what *sets it apart*. They know, or rather sense, that they would not be able straightaway, in a single generation, to attain what they *truly* covet, even if they had money enough. It's not the money they envy but above all the *knack* of knowing how to spend it. Those uneducated women, now suddenly enriched, have more money than we do and spend enormous amounts on clothing. But they are still envious, still on the other side of the barricades, because they don't know how to *make the right choices* and can't achieve the *look* of the modest and inexpensively dressed women of the "intelligentsia." They want to capture something intangible— and are therefore filled with hate.

The Russian pressure on Warsaw has let up and the communiqué from General Bór in Warsaw is bitter, although most of the city is in our hands.[105] In Moscow, Mikołajczyk, Romer, and Grabski have met with representatives of the "Polish" Committee of National Liberation. That's great diplomacy for you.

August 7, 1944

Warsaw has become an inferno. Literally the entire population is fighting. While the Russians look on. Once the Germans have slaughtered the Poles, the Russians will take Warsaw. That will mean some tens of thousands fewer of the best citizens, which is to say tens of thousands fewer opponents of Communism and of Soviet Poland. This is crystal clear. Who knows whether earlier Polish generations weren't right when they sang the refrain, "Whoever says the Muscovites, / Are brothers to the Polish tribe, / I will shoot between the eyes, / Before the church of the Carmelites."[106] I cannot keep repeating "it will somehow work out" and I can never consider the Muscovites our brothers. What do we expect? The radio communiqués are all mum about Warsaw, which is always a sore point. And there in Warsaw those poor boys and girls surely believe the whole world is watching; they think they are dying before the eyes of the world. Poland is not only a problem for the Poles, it's a problem for the world, a problem that troubles everyone's sleep.

Let's be really and truly honest: emigration is not an escape ON BEHALF OF Poland, it's an escape FROM Poland, from graves, from misfortune, from continual, hopeless efforts. It's an escape from endless troubles, from endless work without compensation, from enthusiastic death. One can justify oneself in many ways, but what remains at bottom is the ordinary and very human sense of the right to happiness. If one can't find it in one place, one looks somewhere else. That is, unless one is inclined to torment oneself and find lofty pretexts for doing so. It's understandable—pure, unadorned unhappiness is unbearable and a little bouquet of flowers of one kind or another will always be welcome. That's *à propos* K.'s remark yesterday, delivered with a bitter smile: "One does not return from emigration." And I surely will not return.

August 8, 1944

This morning at the Ministry of Labor. Conversation with C. We recalled the old film based on a novel by H. G. Wells, in which after the end of a massive war, war still continues.[107] Chieftains, gang leaders, and the commanders of private armies fight among themselves. We're headed in that direction. A gloomy conversation, but refreshing. It seems to me that "enlightened pessimism" is a bracing elixir in a time of "enlightened illiteracy." In every conversation with this man, I sense a melody winding among the words. We talked about loneliness, about Leonardo da Vinci. All the while I had before my eyes an image I'd seen long ago.

Once, as I was riding along the Sarthe River, I stopped at Solesmes Abbey.[108] It was a sunny September morning. I entered the church and stood before the partly open door leading to the sacristy. Bright shafts of sunshine fell through the even brighter stained glass of the windows and cut through the obscurity of the vast, vaulted room in gentle bands. Outlined against the walls were great mahogany closets that displayed the total darkness of their gaping interiors. In the middle of the room, on a long table covered with a dark green cloth, glittered gold goblets encrusted with stones, along with crystal cruets and a few unfolded chasubles. Two monks, walking slowly and calmly, appeared for a moment, then vanished, dispersing the streaks of sunlight, cutting across them, bending them in different directions. The light jumped about, died down, then reignited, playing an exquisite étude on the objects laid out on the table. It seemed to me that I was listening to the light. I stood, watching and listening. And at the same time overflowing with a longing too immense to express. Today, talking with C., I felt it had then above all been the longing for a sense of harmony. It's at moments such as these that people often convert, that they find their way to faith. Perhaps it was the longing for longing. These days, do we truly long for anything? The human heart has become an engine, an ordinary engine, geared to operate for so and so many hours of work for a world without a heart, for a world of steel engines, a world in which man is the slave of production and consumption. "Clearly," says C., "the comparison is exaggerated, but if we keep following this road, won't you, I, and others like us begin to feel the way Leonardo felt in his day? We are not stuck in the past, as some would like us to think we are—as SOMEONE in particular would like us to think. Not true. We are already advancing beyond our time, suited not to the atmosphere of this era, but rather to the era that must arrive if man is not to become an insect. Stupidity is always the most stubborn thing, but it is not eternal." As we were parting, he added another couple of sentences, with a smile: "Odd, it's only now that I've begun to grasp the meaning of the medieval monasteries. That's where people met in order to escape the night that surrounded them, to isolate themselves from ignorance, and talk with each other, as we are doing now, without the risk of burning at the stake."

I torment myself, because I'm unable to posture, even in relation to myself. While writing, I urge myself: "Go buy a little bunch of violets, why don't you; pour your soul into some beautiful words and propel yourself out of time, the Werther of the refrigerator age."[109] But I can't.

Aside from that, "the ordinary days pass by, like barnyard animals" (Maria

Kuncewiczowa).[110] Paris, like the animals in the zoo, is waiting for the advent of extraordinary days. The Americans have taken Le Mans and are fighting at Angers. Meanwhile in Warsaw, the Germans are murdering the Poles. The Polish Underground Army is doing the best it can, the Russians are looking on and — rubbing their hands.

August 9, 1944

It is not so difficult to describe things you've noticed. It's much more difficult to notice in the first place. A true writer is not someone who writes well but someone who notices the most.

August 10, 1944

Exceptional weather. The Côte d'Azur, not Paris. A cloudless, deep blue sky over the entire city. Dark sapphire in the center, brighter at the horizon, and evolving from clear blue to opalescent white. At noon an alert. The heavy machines rumble and only a few shots are heard. If at this moment Paris is being defended by a single battery at each corner of the city, that's already a lot.

In the afternoon we heard that the railway workers have gone on strike. The metro will stop on Saturday at one thirty p.m. and remain closed until one thirty p.m. on Monday. Clearly, no one will go to work. In Paris anticipation has set in. They are already at Chartres. The city buzzes with rumors. The Americans have indeed pulled off a terrific tank maneuver. He's got talent, that Patton. The Germans continue to counterattack in Normandy. It's truly hard to understand what kind of plan they have.

The situation in Warsaw is critical. Jan Kwapiński in London declared that help is on the way (????) and will be effective (????).[111] He urges the Poles to keep calm and lets it be known that Polish circles in England are indignant and bitter. Easy to understand. Russia's bad faith is obvious. But how could they have expected anything else? Mikołajczyk, after a second round of talks with Stalin, left Moscow today. He declared that he is optimistic (O God . . .), although on a whole series of points he and Stalin failed to reach agreement. In short, zero. Meanwhile, in Warsaw . . . Władysław Raczkiewicz has named Tomasz Arciszewski as his successor.[112]

Tadzik and Lola came for supper. Naturally, the subject was Warsaw. Bitterness, nothing but bitterness. This overshadows the fact that here in a few days the occupation may end and takes away the desire to rejoice. In the evening we go for a stroll along the Seine. The sun has set and night is falling. The black spires of Notre-Dame are outlined against a rose-colored sky, turning dove gray. In the distance, the Eiffel Tower floats like a mist in the sky. A pleasant chill comes off the water. A steel mammoth, swaddled in branches, rattles its way down the street. The lone German Tiger crawls forward and vanishes in the dark. Its powerful exhaust still belches blue flames and scatters sparks in its wake.

August 11, 1944

Anticipation is in the air and growing. In the afternoon, people were saying that American patrols were reaching Trappes. Trucks are parked in front of the German hotels, loaded with suitcases, boxes, and old furniture. The weather is stifling. In the Falaise pocket a Polish tank division has gone into action under the command of General Maczek. What are we Poles now fighting for? It's a waste of every soldier's life. The Germans report that in the Wilno region the Russians have disarmed our Home Army and arrested its officers. That would be logical and I see no reason not to believe it. Stalin has apparently demanded from Mikołajczyk that Poland renounce its mutual aid treaty with England. This doesn't seem likely to me. Why would Stalin care about our treaty with England? What drives me crazy is when people talk about Russia as if it were a completely normal country, the partner of England and America, and so on. Real ignorance, truly medieval. This is the same totalitarianism as any other, but one's not allowed to admit it. Reversing Ulrich von Hutten's famous remark, I constantly want to say: "Minds have gone to sleep, how terrible it is to be alive."[113] Overall, Soviet totalitarianism is worse than Hitler's, because it consumes the soul as well, gnawing away more deeply, attacking the whole man. But no one wants to SEE this.

The Germans have begun rounding up bicycles. The gendarmes are "officiating" today at Porte d'Orléans and in Nanterre. Old or new, everything ended up on trucks, headed for the "bicyclized" divisions of Great Germany.

August 12, 1944

An alert. I'm sitting in "my" garden in Bagneux. Ribbons of smoke wind across the deep blue sky. Two silvery formations of pterodactyls have laid their eggs far away and one can now hear the groans of the artillery chasing after them. Children from a nearby school sit in the shelters in the garden and have a singing lesson. The teacher stands near the exit and teaches the boys to sing "Tipperary." The childish voices squeal: "It's a long, long way to Tipperary—it's a long, long way to go . . ." Just so—you have a long road ahead of you, my children. Then they sang the "Marseillaise." In the Fontenay market today little flags—for the time being French—were on sale for eighty-two francs. Starting at dawn, you could hear the cannons. A distant sound, barely noticeable. Coming from the direction of Versailles.

In the afternoon we stayed home. Silence. In the courtyard a painter, hired by our *patron* especially for the job, is repainting the sculpture that stands in front of the hotel. It will be good as new—*couleur de bronze*. When I asked the wife what had induced them to spend so much money, she smiled mysteriously.

Not much news this evening. The Red Army has suddenly lost all its momentum. After the Warsaw massacre it will surely get it back. Fighting is still going on in Warsaw—impressive and tragic. The Riviera, both Italian and French, is being bombed. There will certainly be a landing in the south. The Americans have announced that they will release no news of troop movements for the next two days so as not to benefit the Germans.

August 13, 1944

Good weather, sunny, very hot with gusts of gentle wind. A sweltering silence and only from afar do you hear dull explosions, mixed with the distant buzz of airplanes. From time to time the Germans fly overhead, skimming the rooftops. It seems the Germans have begun to arrest the Parisian police and early today they were seizing bicycles on place de la Bastille. In the afternoon we're invited to tea by Szymon K. and his wife and we'll go on our bikes. If they take them, fine—I have nicer ones in the cellar. Around four we set out. The city is a strange sight. Empty. A few people drag themselves through the streets, a few bicycles pass by. German trucks are rushing about everywhere, in every direction. Occasionally, a magnificent Tiger rolls by, churning up the asphalt with its steel caterpillar treads. Handsome tanks.

In the deserted, overheated city one hears the constant roar of motors. The mood is a bit strange. During the visit, Basia and I were seized by a terrible attack of vomiting. Something must have disagreed with us and it happened again on the way home. Near the Seine, Basia feels so weak that I carry her in my arms across the street and put her on a bench. A stifling, August night, as in the south. At home we both go to bed, completely drained by the attacks. The room is suffocating. An oven.

Warsaw is fighting. The radio provides excerpts from Arciszewski's speech to the nation. A lot of good it will do them. Why are these young people doomed to such heroism, which no one will want to hear about? Russia, as usual, wants neither the Poland as she is nor the Poland she would like to become. The Germans and the Russians are both annihilating THE SAME THING; they are united in annihilating THE SAME THING. The Germans in farewell, the Russians as a welcome. From the beginning I have been using the words "Russia" and "Russians" as much as possible, because the issue here has nothing to do with Communism or a change of regime. These are but appendages—the heart of the matter is Russia, perennial Russia, which does not know or understand the concept of "freedom," to the extent of not needing it at all. Only Russia has been capable of taking Marxism, the theory elaborated by Marx and his acolytes that was partially correct in its time, and creating such a caricature, such a "tetragon of stupidity," before which man is entirely powerless. And it's perhaps exactly that impotence that today is wrecking the most enlightened minds and plunging them into darkness. With respect to this night that is falling, the Middle Ages seem like a Renaissance. The Russians are planted there, on the other side of the Vistula and watching, as thousands of young people, in an outpouring of utmost nobility, are fighting with stones against the most modern of armies. There is such cynicism in the Russian gesture that it defies one's capacity to react and becomes abstract in its perfection. To the many things we cannot pardon them, they have added things that are simply unpardonable. Since childhood, I have always hated them. Today I hate them as "purely" as their cynicism is "pure." One should not hate, but there may be times when certain hatreds are so justified that to deny them would be to deny one's own self.

August 14, 1944

Morning in the city. More activity in the streets than yesterday. Sunshine and the azure of the sky. In the gardens and on the benches along the boulevards, the Bouvards and Pécuchets engage in mysterious conjectures. Where are the Americans? The Germans and the women of Paris run around in skimpy clothing. An exhibit of masculine torsos and feminine thighs, painstakingly painted to look as though they were tanned. The street resembles the finale at the Folies-Bergères. The side streets are quiet, except for the distant wailing of motors and the clanking of speeding tanks.

Indeed, in this sunshine, in the sudden bursts of chill wind announcing good weather, everything seems entirely absurd. How can one die in such sunshine? I think about the boys and girls in Warsaw, of these magnificent boys, who want to die in the sun, or simply must. Why has fate always doomed the Poles to such heroism? All the radio reports about Warsaw contain a note of embarrassment. Too much heroism. Once again we are alone in confronting something only we can grasp and understand. No matter who or what demands the sacrifice of our lives—gets it. Just provide a pipeline into which our blood can flow—and we'll deliver it, in streams, anywhere and for anyone; just say "death" and, crying "life," we are as one.

I've eaten nothing since morning and am once again retching. Pure bile. I only regret that I don't have enough of it to cover the entire Louvre, the entire world. Perhaps it's these thoughts. I'm sitting on the steps of the Louvre and trying to think, in order not to think at all. I'm tossed between the pathos and the cynicism of my generation, wishing the future generation more cynicism and less pathos. In this world of cynics, the cynics outrun us. Our road has come to an end. Remember, then, children: cultivate cynical hatred, silent, devious, cold, and without pathos. In the world of Volpones, be Super-Volpones.[114] When reality exceeds all limits and enters the domain of the absurd, the choice is between cynicism and pathos. A line of thought—what is it? This line breaks under the impact of a single contraction of the heart. One can know oneself the way one knows the multiplication tables—and suddenly forget everything. Again I feel sick, in a moment I'll shake with convulsions and vomit behind a column, but I'll be laughing and hoping that maybe I'll succeed in vomiting up myself. Or in vomiting whatever it is that causes me to sob loudly in the sunshine, as I write these stupid, useless sentences. The Great Improvisation, the childish confession of a shithole century.[115] Children—believe in NOTHING, in absolutely NOTHING. It's very difficult, but healthier. Reserve your passion, if you must have it, for women and for God.

A woman approached with a small dog and sat down next to me. Raise little dogs instead of ideologies—it's healthier. A cloud of sparrows descended from the Tuileries. The roar of motors.

Evening. General Bór-Komorowski is sending desperate cries for help from Warsaw. Thinking is impossible. Poland is too much to bear in this war. We are not heard. Mme Sikorski's appeal to the women of the world is a voice crying in the wilderness. Mikołajczyk met with Anthony Eden, and the *Times* maintains that the chances of an agreement are good, because "the Polish Committee in Moscow has SHOWN IT IS NOT COMPLETELY INFLEXIBLE." On whose orders and for what purpose did Warsaw throw itself into the fight? The greatest heroism, when it has no clear purpose, arouses only pity, nothing more. It's regarded as the heroism of a madman who throws himself under the train in order to stop it. When it comes to Russia, an explanation has already been found. One hears a lot about the adaptation of Russian carriage axles to fit the narrower European tracks. Next, they'll be widening the tracks to allow the Asiatic rabble to enter deeply and smoothly into Europe.

Eisenhower's order to all the invading powers is full of mysterious gravity.

The stink of death. The Americans are keeping radio silence and so their where-abouts are unknown. There's one thing I don't understand: when I checked the map on August 9, I could figure out what the Americans were up to, but I couldn't understand why the Germans remained in Normandy, all the way from Domfort through Mortain, Vire, and Thury-Harcourt, as far as Caen. Why do they keep exerting themselves to counterattack, instead of retreating to the Seine, while there's still time? They may yet escape, because they're masters at it, but the feathers will fly. The American maneuver is classic, first-rate.

August 15, 1944

The police are on strike, the metro is not running. I go over to Lola's. The *patronne* of her hotel is married to a policeman and it seems the police have indeed disappeared from the streets of Paris. The husband also did not show up for duty and plans to spend the night away from home. They have lent me today's *Petit Parisien* carrying Commandant von Choltitz's notice to the people of Paris.[116] He warns against demonstrations: "I will not hesitate to employ the most brutal methods of repression . . ." And so polite. I listen to the communi-qué: the Allied forces have landed in the south, between Nice and Marseille. This is now truly an invasion in the grand manner. I don't understand the Ger-mans. They commit one blunder after another. Defending the line of the Seine has become impossible, it seems. It's quite likely Paris will remain in one piece thanks to this. The Germans have only now begun to retreat and the Americans seem to have prevented them from moving in the direction of Paris, pushing them toward the west. De Gaulle has called on the French to launch a general strike and resume work only when the Allies enter. Groups congregate at Porte d'Orléans until eleven p.m. (curfew), waiting for the Americans. *Douce France.* No change in Warsaw. There, they are dying in the sunshine.

August 16, 1944

A strike's a strike—I'm staying home. I call the office only at eleven. It turns out that K. has arrived on foot. From Passy to Châtillon. It's therefore unseemly for me to stay at home, so I get on my bike and ride over. Lots of activity in town, once again there are lines in front of the bakeries. Right after work I bring Szy-mon K. the sugar I managed to get at our factory cooperative. It's an inferno in town. Overcast, with suffocating heat. At Alésia the Germans are directing traf-fic. A swollen river of trucks, bicycles, and pedestrians flows through the streets. Under the circumstances, riding a bicycle becomes a circus act. On boulevard

Raspail German trucks are stationed in front of all the hotels. They are packing up in a hurry, feverishly, collecting hotel bedding, mattresses, and furniture. I stood next to a truck full of night tables (??) and watched. I couldn't tear myself away. They were running around in their shirts, sweaty and out of breath, and loading—night tables. Why the devil night tables? And I kept whispering quietly to myself: "They're fleeing." My heart was in my mouth. Not a single policeman in the city and incredible traffic. Crowds of people walking miles on foot. Complete mayhem at place de l'Opéra. More traffic than I can remember even before the war. On boulevard des Italiens I dismount and run across on foot. At K.'s I get some rest. The stress of crossing eight kilometers of the city has exhausted me. The drone of motors can be heard from rue Lafayette. Truck after truck, filled with suitcases, parcels, bundles. They're leaving. But at the same time, K. tells me, they are hoping to return. Wherever they have rented apartments and paid up until January 1, 1945, they ask the landlords to extend their leases. They're not beaten yet. But despite everything, I don't have the feeling that this is the END. K. and I talk things over. Moscow's position on Poland is crystal clear. Warsaw is the best dress rehearsal—this Warsaw in arms, getting help—from England. Because it's closer . . .

Starting tomorrow, so-called Plan D goes into effect in Paris. Truly "D"—as in "*Dreck.*" Gas completely shut off, electricity only from eleven thirty p.m. to midnight, total halt to the metro, and registration for rations of cooked or raw meals. The Germans are detonating military installations around Paris.

August 17, 1944

This morning, I take some sugar to Tadzik P. Then I ride over to the Ministry of Labor to get an extension on Lola's work permit. Tadzik has given me coupons for two liters of spirits for the stove and in addition we also have some wood coal. All I need is to find a stove. The day before yesterday there were stoves all over Paris, but suddenly they have all vanished. I'm at a loss. And suddenly right in front of me on rue de Vaugirard, I notice a cyclist with a large sack on his baggage rack, in which metal objects are clinking. I approach and strike up a conversation. I ask if he isn't carrying wood-coal-burning stoves in his sack. Yes, he says. I start to laugh and he's puzzled. I'm laughing because the way we're living these days gives you a sixth sense. In the clamor of the street, in the midst of this crazy traffic, to hear the jangle of metal objects, to connect it with the very stoves I've been looking for, to go after them and not be mistaken—this is really an animal instinct. Because, from the very first moment I was certain that he *must* have stoves in his sack. He's taking the stoves to a shop in Issy-les-

Moulineaux. I ride alongside him. At Porte de Versailles several private cars pass by, marked with a red cross and carrying wounded officers. Faces covered in blood, eyes closed, gray-green dolls thrown into a corner of the back seat.

In Issy-les-Moulineaux I follow the cyclist into the shop through the BACK DOOR, and although fifty people have already signed up for stoves, I negotiate one for myself. In an adjoining bookshop I find General Gourgaud's diary of Saint Helena, one of the most interesting documents of Napoleon's final years.[117] And apparently one of the most reliable.

In the afternoon it's rumored that Chartres, Dreux, and Orléans have already been taken by the Americans, that the Americans are already fifty kilometers from Paris, and that Paris will be declared an open city. The Germans have thirty-six hours to leave Paris. After work, I went to see Dr. K. in Passy. The Germans are decamping pell-mell. On avenue Mozart they're loading up the equipment of entire garages. Motorcycles are rushing about. Din and bedlam. I cross Paris from one end to the other. At Trocadéro small groups of people stand and watch the distant fires. German cars hurry in all directions. Tanks and cars wait under the trees of the cours Albert I. The soldiers are dirty, unshaven, ragged. An officer runs around in a shirt and cap, yelling and cursing. No one pays any attention. Men are lying in the dust of the allée and sleeping. Others sit against the trees, staring blankly ahead. At moments I have trouble believing my eyes. Light tanks are positioned along the Seine. The soldiers have crawled out of them, covered in soot from head to toe, and sit or doze, leaning against the machines. Crowds of people watch them in silence. And down below, at the water's edge, a veritable Côte d'Azur. The Parisians are bathing in the Seine in the middle of the city, profiting from the absence of police. Girls are shrieking, people are calling out, laughing. And there's the usual forest of fishing poles and crowds of fishermen. A matchless sight, simply idyllic. Private cars now appear among the military vehicles. People throw them hateful glances and say: *"Les collaborateurs s'en vont."*[118]

Groups stand at the intersections waiting for civilian trucks to take them closer to home. *Auto-stop* on all the streets. Cyclists stand on the corners of place de la Bastille and warn people not to ride across the square, because *les Boches* are grabbing bicycles. The wave of bicycles breaks and flows around the edges.

The *patronne* of my hotel confides that she has a big problem. She has ordered various flags and banners from Galeries Lafayette, but the metro is not running and she can't get there. The statue in front of the hotel, already painted the *couleur de bronze*, is waiting to be attired in the Allied colors. I entreated the *patron* and his wife not to include the Soviet colors, and they agreed. The naked goddess Pomona will wear a tricolor sash and hold three small flags in her hand. Like a *girl* in the final tableau at the Folies-Bergères. All the dry cleaners in the neighborhood are working overtime coloring fabric to make flags. People even bring their bed linen to be dyed. The men sit in the bistros and discuss the events. The Germans are expected to blow up some warehouses in Vincennes and people look at each other with sparks of courage and audacity in their eyes: "No reason to be afraid . . ." It has all the appearance of a well-produced farce with a *happy end*. It doesn't occur to them for a second that things might have been different. My God—how unabashed they are at the good hand they've drawn in this game. From the very beginning.

August 18, 1944

I'm not going to the office but staying home. Explosions have been heard since early morning. The Germans are blowing up everything around. Then the drone of airplanes and three series of bombs not far from us, because the door shakes on its hinges. Around noon we go to the market. More good weather. The mood in the market is sunny. Basia asks for lining material. It's 150 francs a meter and no textile "points." The stall is selling everything without points. We prepare lunch on the wood-coal stove. Today's curfew begins at nine in the evening. A young man living in our hotel who belongs to the Organization of the Resistance (*la Résistance*) brings Basia tricolor armbands and asks her to paint them with the Cross of Lorraine (the Gaullist sign) and the inscription "12e Arr."[119] These are armbands for the commissars of the Republic in our district. Around seven we go for a walk. All the bistros are crammed. The people are drinking beer and watching the Germans leave. And the Germans keep leaving. The dream of Europe has come to an end.

The evening bulletins are full of news. The Germans have lost the Battle of Normandy and they are retreating to the lower Seine without any apparent desire to fight. The Americans are on the outskirts of Paris. The RAF and the South Africans are trying to supply Warsaw with arms and ammunition. All the way from England . . . because the Russians consider Warsaw too far away . . . Twenty bombers have already been lost in the skirmishes over Warsaw.[120] I don't have the strength to think about it.

August 19, 1944

Great agitation since early this morning. Disjointed conversations heard in the entryway and finally Lola drops in. It's over, flags are waving, crowds fill the streets. Lola hugs us, we are moved. In the courtyard the *patron* affixes a tricolor sash to our statue. Energetic debate on how to affix it. Someone says: "*Elle aura un beau soutien-gorge.*"[121] Our hotel is bustling and the phone rings off the hook, because it's the general headquarters of the "Résistance." I get dressed and go downstairs. It seems, however, that it's not over yet. These are only the automatic reflexes of the French. The Germans have not quitted Paris completely.

This afternoon gunshots echoed in the streets. German cars drive through and shoot from time to time, just in case. No one goes into the streets anymore. It seems the Préfecture of police is burning and there are "battles" on boulevard Saint-Michel. Paris is trying to imitate Warsaw. In our town hall, the "Résistance" has already deposed the mayor and provisional elections have been held. The young man from our hotel has been elected *conseiller municipal* and we therefore drink to his health. All this is at least as uplifting as a vaudeville by Eugène Labiche.[122] I have the constant urge to laugh. Other young men arrive—every fourth one has a tiny lady's pistol, no bigger than a powder compact. But, no problem—let's make the Rrrrevolution, let's depose the mayor, let's arrest the collaborators. Naturally, the neighborhood small fry. The greatest motive for such arrests is usually that "she sold such and such at such and such a price." Because we are mainly arresting the local tradeswomen and grocers. Our *patronne* insists on being shown the list of names of the candidates for arrest and at each name exclaims: "Oh, I know that one, she deserves it—she's made a fortune on the black market . . . Oh, there, there—that one—he was always threatening us . . . yes, yes . . . that other one, be tough on her, *c'est juste . . .*" Revolution, like hell it is.

The residents of two buildings stand in the entry chattering away. When the sound of shelling is heard, the concierge latches the gates and the chatter redoubles. The shelling dies down, the gates cautiously reopen, and the braver types sit on a bench on the boulevard. The street is deserted and people go from one entry to the next, gabbing. Toward evening a squadron of "our" fighter planes flies low overhead—handsome Mustangs. O joy—everyone at the windows. I think of Warsaw . . . The evening communiqués say that the Americans have reached the Seine between Mantes and Vernon and are trying to circle Paris from the east. Very wise, because then Paris will fall automatically. The encirclement of Paris appears to be a plan to surprise Marshal von Kluge once again from behind.[123] In the city, a comic-opera bombardment.

August 20, 1944

A powerful storm last night. Bombardment of the city all morning. In the afternoon everything calms down and notices appear on the walls. Thanks to the German promise not to attack public buildings occupied by the provisional authorities and their promise to withdraw from Paris, an armistice has been concluded between them and the "Résistance." Great. They did a bit of shooting, showed off a bit, and one day later—agreement. Both sides stop taking potshots, people are going out for walks—and all's well. People wait calmly for the munificent intervention of the Americans. Like a fairy tale for polite children. One day, one fine day, all this will be known as "the heroic throwing off of the occupier's yoke by French patriots and the common folk of Paris," and so on. It seems, however, that the performance has begun a bit prematurely, that they have miscalculated the moment, thinking the Americans would be arriving today. Which explains why they quickly signed the armistice. This suits the few remaining Germans just fine, since they would rather surrender to a regular army and to the Americans than to the "heroic" rabble.

Toward evening we strolled with Lola along the Seine. The flashy cars of the "Résistance" dash through the streets carrying a few pipsqueaks armed with popguns. Young doctors on motorcycles, wearing shorts and Red Cross armbands, with elegant nurses like *sex baggage* riding behind. Shake gently before using . . . The helmets painted white with red crosses suit the nurses very well. Photogenic. Fit for a picture. And on the Pont de Bercy, the Germans calmly withdraw their remaining trains, locomotives, and railway cars. They stand on the bridge with their machine guns pointed at the street, grim and threatening, but in the end no one does anyone any harm. I walk by under their gun barrels much more calmly than if these were the pipsqueaks of the FFI (Fifi).[124] I think of Warsaw . . . And of Tadzio. "Mr. B.—here everything is much gentler. The climate is gentler, cows don't butt with their horns, dogs don't chase cats, instead of bedbugs there are only shy fleas, the Germans are behaving humanely, and now France is liberating herself, bouquets in hand, with negotiations, with notices, under anesthesia," as my Tadzio would have said. Like that time on the "Romain" bridge in 1940. Everything is proceeding painlessly and swiftly. I have Basia and Lola on my arms and I consider the difference. And despite myself, I think of Grottger's drawings and of Manet or Renoir.[125] (The difference in mood is the same.) Emigration is the flight from Grottger's drawings. In a nutshell, plain and simple.

It's quiet along the Seine. On the anchored barges and flatboats, underwear is drying, chickens walk along the banks, and rabbits, who "have the day off," hop from the barges and flatboats, while motionless fishermen sit alongside. The French flag flies cautiously from a few houses. People sit in the doorways and listen to the stories of the "heroes."

The evening bulletins say the Americans are in Melun, in Fontainebleau, that they're headed for Montargis. In Warsaw it's hell. No negotiations there and no talks.

August 21, 1944

The Americans are playing hide-and-seek near Paris. They have crossed the Seine both west and east of the city and are said to be in Corbeil.

We stay home and wait. The initial joy has already passed and we feel as though we were already liberated. In Paris, no one's in charge. Some remaining Germans are still wandering about, the "Résistance," which is to say the Fifi, are making the rounds.

This evening we can't catch any bulletins, because the electricity shuts down after twenty minutes. We went for a walk. Peace and quiet. "War and Peacefulness."

August 22, 1944

We've been hearing the sound of cannons since this morning. Shelling in the city has resumed. People are now certain the Americans will arrive any moment, which is why gunfire has started up again. Paris "is fighting." In the afternoon I pay a visit to G. The inhabitants are sitting outside their buildings in all the streets. A revolutionary mood. No one is working and it's only now that the entire *peuple de Paris* can be seen. They are now all PRESENT. On our boulevard it's still tolerable, but in the side streets the crowd reigns. Naturally, the mood is belligerent and bossy. New notices are constantly being posted on the walls. People stand and read them, carefully, with an air full of dignity and self-assurance. They follow up with amazingly logical and intelligent comments. The words *"c'est logique, c'est très intelligent, c'est juste"*[126] are uttered in an unctuous tone of solemn approval. Anything at all can now be published, the most astounding idiocies can be written—and everything is received with ritual gravity, the sage furrowing of one's brow, and the ceremonial scratching of one's behind. Newspaper vendors whizz through the streets on their bicycles. In a second they are surrounded and the whole stack of liberated newspapers is bought up. Of course, the first to appear was the Communist *L'Humanité*.[127] Demanding the return of the deserter Maurice Thorez.[128] *C'est logique.* In addition, promising to raise wages by 40 percent and introduce the forty-hour week. The assembled company nods in approbation. *C'est logique.* Promise them paradise now and they'll believe. Communism's power of attraction lies in this promise and in THE FAILURE TO KEEP IT. It's the clever dangling of a sausage on a string and, when the masses actually try to grab it, raising it higher and higher still. The point is not for them to reach it but to jump ever higher and better, as the almighty State and Party desire. From time to time permission is given to take a little taste of the sausage and hope is extended: "See how good it is—a bit more jumping and you can have some more." And so, generation after generation dies in the faith, transmitting it to their offspring. Faith is what counts.

The citizens read the scribbles of the social prestidigitators, after which they deliberate in the bistros over a glass of wine. The newspapers feature big head-lines: "*Paris conquiert sa liberté par les armes*," "*Paris se libère lui-même*,"[129] and in general France is liberating herself on her own, with the barest help from the Allies. A week from now there'll be no more talk of the Americans or the English. The cock—it would be hard to find a better symbol for this nation. The entire company, gabbing away in the doorways and in the bistros, beat their wings and crow, flap their combs—and wait for American chocolate and tinned food. But when a German motorcycle appears in the distance, it takes but three seconds for the street to empty, the gates to lock, and hand-to-hand combat to break out at the keyholes, so that people can "see." Paris "is fighting."

Ce Soir[130] writes that, at three in the afternoon, the Germans used tanks to attack the Hôtel de Ville and the Préfecture of police, but were repulsed, that Paris is "bristling with barricades," that at place de la République and on boule-vard de Bonne-Nouvelle the fighting involves "light artillery." Cock-a-doodle-doo! Because at four p.m. I am at place Voltaire, which is to say, a kilometer from République, and I watch the crowds duck suddenly into the doorways. The Germans pass by, hurling two grenades just in case, which are so loud that three minutes after the explosion, no one dares poke their nose outside.

Toward evening we go for a walk. In the doorways, people are selling lettuce and radishes, who knows from where. We buy some extra just in case. We take shelter for a moment in a bakery, as a German motorcycle passes by, shooting in all directions. The Germans are afraid, and people are afraid—everyone is afraid.

The evening bulletins report heavy fighting in Warsaw. The insurgents have captured telephone headquarters with the help of flame-throwers taken from the Germans. They've also begun to produce their own mine-throwers and shells and have started making their own armored vehicles. One has already been put into operation and the armor held. All of Poland should be transported to America and after fifty years America will be—Polish. And it will be great. By contrast, here "Paris is fighting." And you, O world, piss yourself in admiration for *la France éternellement héroïque et insoumise*.[131]

The Germans have shifted troops from Italy to the south of France. No doubt another of the corporal's intuitive plans . . . A stifling night. Two (literally: two) shots were fired in the street. It's Paris fighting. *Paris conquiert sa liberté par les armes.*[132] General Koenig has been appointed military governor of Paris.[133] Cock-a-doodle-doo!

August 23, 1944

No idea what's happening. We stock up on water, just in case. Chlorine at 0.05 gram per liter of water. Distant cannon fire continues to resound. Another stifling day, but overcast. A few shots in the streets from time to time. At four thirty I turn on the radio and suddenly we hear that "Paris is free." Reporting from the streets of New York, people shouting and singing at the news that Paris has been liberated. Followed by a speech larded with a unique oceanic grandiloquence: "After four days of bloody battles Paris has been liberated. The date of August 23 will forever remain a date . . . The Paris that bowed, but has never broken . . ." Something is off-target in this story concocted on credit, because just as the radio is bellowing about the liberation of Paris, planes are flying overhead and German artillery is shelling them, as it hasn't managed to do for a long time. And when we emerge in front of the house, we learn that barricades are being erected on place Daumesnil. We drop in on Lola. Lola is fit to be tied. She had gone to the hairdresser, where she found a twelve-year-old boy whose mother had sent him to get a permanent. "Here they're building barricades, cannons are roaring all day long, and a mother sends her twelve-year-old boy for a permanent. What a country . . ." We go visit the barricades. Some cobblestones dug up from the road, a few old beds and kitchen stoves dragged from the attics, public benches, a few sacks filled with sand and lopped-off tree branches. Makes a good picture. If a butterfly made a heavy landing, the thing would disintegrate in a flash. Notices on the walls: "General mobilization," "Men, women, children—come build barricades. May the good people of Paris demonstrate they have not forgotten the traditions of 1830 and 1848 . . ." Cars drive by and throw leaflets. One great farce, with an expertly orchestrated "mood." And everyone gives an excellent performance.

The evening newspapers are crowing. They offer recipes for the manufacture of antitank bottle-bombs. "The German tanks will no longer be invincible. This form of resistance (bottles) perfectly suits the popular and spontaneous character of the Parisian uprising and recalls the improvisations of 1830, 1848, and the Paris Commune." One can have a good time and bring joy to the world. Alas, the world will take this very seriously. The date of August 23 may well go down in history as the date of the liberation of Paris, although no one has yet set eye on an Allied soldier. But that's convenient. Paris can therefore be said to have "liberated herself." I only fear the Germans may tire of this game of insurrection and commit a real massacre somewhere as a lesson. Until now, most of the dead and wounded have been recruited among the bystanders.

This evening, it's *opiat'* — once again, as the Russians would say — about liberated Paris.

August 24, 1944

Another day of waiting. It's pouring. There's no more shooting, because the powder is wet. But Paris is fighting. By afternoon everything is literally covered in flags. It's said they're already at Porte d'Orléans.

August 25, 1944

Silence in the city. I therefore decide to take a ride around. It's a splendid day. By now both French and Allied flags are flying from all the windows. It looks wonderful. The gray, sooty walls of the buildings have turned into flower beds. Everything is happening the way it could only have been imagined. The Germans have not blown up anything, they've destroyed nothing. Near Gare de Lyon I have to take a detour to avoid some shooting. Germans and collaborators still at large are shooting from the rooftops. At place de la Bastille a few shots are fired. Not a soul. But from the direction of the Pont d'Austerlitz I hear an ever-increasing din. I approach. A crowd. I see the first tanks and trucks. The soldiers are waving, people are shouting. Before my eyes are great pyramids of tanks, American helmets, and small *jeeps*. The roar of motors, the clanking of tank treads, and the delirious crowd. I stand under a tree and watch and I feel as if I'm dreaming. But no. More keep coming. Green shirts, trousers, and gaiters. Here at last are the others. The ones who have been expected for so many long years, now it's really THEM. Barely three months after the landing, they are in Paris. They look magnificent. A different world is entering Paris, freedom is entering. Perhaps not perfect, perhaps . . . perhaps . . . , but what is that handful of reproaches compared to the darkness that has reigned until now and that is descending upon the eastern half of Europe at this very moment. For how long? I suddenly realize that tonight I'm no longer threatened by a search, by an unexpected knock on the door, by any . . . My God. As if in a fog, I see more trucks with soldiers in green shirts and helmets covered in netting. I realize that tears are streaming down my face, that I'm shouting along with the others, waving. At the sight of these smiling faces under their heavy helmets, faces moving in rhythm, I find I'm exclaiming to myself in Polish, with wild enthusiasm: "They're chewing gum!" And I laugh at myself. So, fine, OK—but in the world we have known until now no one has been chewing gum. This gum melted my heart.

Then the great, boundless joy gives way to sadness. A column of ambulances stops near me. The vehicles are driven by pretty young girls with impeccable *maquillage*. I lean against one of the ambulances and watch as trucks and tanks keep coming across the bridge. I suddenly begin to cry, almost sobbing under my breath. A young woman driving an ambulance looks at me and asks suddenly, in English, why I'm crying.

"I'm Polish and I'm thinking about Warsaw," I answer softly. "Here they can be happy, but we still cannot."

A moment of awkward silence. The girl reaches into her pocket, offers me a Chesterfield, and mumbles a brief word. I took the cigarette and fled. I couldn't not accept it. But, no—there are things that cannot be resolved even with millions of cigarettes, tinned food, and other gifts. No, no, and no. I held that first cigarette of my favorite kind, and finally lit it. It smelled a bit of eau de cologne, a bit like soap, but finally like a Chesterfield. I smoked it, thinking it contained a world incapable of understanding certain things. Perhaps because that world was never forced to smoke anything worse than a Chesterfield. Tanks and vehicles were driving through the streets, and above this happy city floated a great cry of joy.

THE END

AFTERWORD: OUT OF THIS NETTLE

Grażyna Drabik

Andrzej Bobkowski found himself in a unique position in 1940. A young, adventurous Pole, he was on his way, together with his wife, Basia, from Poland to Argentina, exploring the world, celebrating his recent marriage, and looking forward to a new job, which was awaiting him in Buenos Aires. The German invasion of Poland in September 1939 cut him off from his family and friends. The German invasion of France, a few months later, stranded him in Paris, without any resources besides his wits. He found work in a French munitions factory, which in June 1940 had to be evacuated to the south of France. After a few weeks in limbo in Carcassonne, Bobkowski was desperate to return to Paris, to rejoin his wife and search for new ways of dealing with his displacement. But trains were not running. France was divided into two zones: free and occupied. Travel was rigidly controlled. The whole world was in the process of a dramatic and still not fully comprehensible re-making—of frontiers, alliances, and worldviews.

Bobkowski and a young worker from the factory named Tadzio purchased bicycles and, on September 6, 1940, began the ride toward Paris. On the way, Bobkowski took daily notes and made a record of the ride—along the coast of France from Narbonne to Nice, climbing through the Maritime Alps, crossing the demarcation line in Chalon-sur-Saône, and finally approaching Paris—that reads like a fascinating fusion of reportage, astute political commentary, personal reflection, and lyrical musings.

The Paris to which these two wanderers return at the end of September 1940 is a very different city, transformed by the presence of German soldiers and the rules of an occupied country. Back in his temporary home, Bobkowski continues to take notes, finding grounding in this task of keeping the record. He talks about hardships and moments of joys, big news from the frontlines and small local incidents. He observes the evolution of Parisian life in its struggle for survival—seemingly innocuous compromises that profoundly affect all social relationships. He evokes the feeling of uncertainty and a strange mood marked by a mixture of the new and the familiar. Together with him, we observe how what was until recently considered "abnormal" and impossible slowly becomes acceptable and "normal."

He writes almost daily, with only a few interruptions in the steady flow, until August 25, 1944, composing a kind of symphony of the occupied city: a record of the war geographically happening "somewhere else," yet changing every aspect of daily life "here." The literary quality of the notes is of the highest order as they speak to us in a distinct individual voice: youthful, sharply critical of politics, attentive to signs of hypocrisy, yet also capable of tenderness and sensitivity to human vulnerabilities. The commentary is provided from the dual perspective of insider and outsider: a Pole observing the French; a devout anti-Communist noting the growing influence of Communist ideology; an educated European becoming aware of the destruction and decadence of Western civilization.

The range of themes tackled in the course of this "note taking" is impressive. The developments of the war, of course, command an enormous amount of Bobkowski's energy. His attention is at first primarily focused on the impact of Germany's attack on France: the swiftness of the Nazi victory; the new Vichy government's conciliatory eagerness to accommodate the German occupiers; the French army's evident unpreparedness and unwillingness to fight; the civilian population's chaotic reactions; England's puzzling restraint . . .

These observations inform a larger discussion of German authoritarian tendencies. With Soviet Russia a rapidly growing presence on the eastern fringes of Europe, they broaden into a consistent critique of totalitarianism in general. Bobkowski identifies the totalitarian ideology and political system as manifested in his times by two matching forms: German Nazism and Russian Communism. Their destructive power results from the simplistic premise, which they share, that by imposing a rigid order, they can resolve all human problems and change human nature. The recourse to violence that both systems perpetuate negates the value of the lives of the present generations in the name of false promises of a bright future: for the victorious Germans in one case and for the liberated "downtrodden masses" in the other.

His critique is not only political but also ethical. The tyranny of such ideologies is deadly for the human spirit, as it deprives humanity of the freedom essential for human dignity and of a chance to shape one's life in accordance with one's needs, aspirations, efforts, and abilities. Like a stern moral tale, the *Notebooks* become a warning against treating human beings as political instruments and disregarding the "here and now." Bobkowski's is a passionate protest against outright pillage and violence, as well as against various forms of manipulation in the name of lofty future ends.

But the book cannot be reduced to a gloomy diagnosis of military, political, and ethical disasters. On the contrary, the *Notebooks* pulsate with positive energy. We follow a rich thread of reflection on the importance of balance between spiritual and material needs, evident in the praxis of living, yet often undervalued by excessive theorizing or intellectual detachment. There is a steady vein of cultural commentary, extolling the pleasures of reading a good book, attending theatrical performances, or listening to music. The joy of being alive is rooted in a specific time and place: in awareness of the weather, attention to the landscape, and the whole gamut of sensual experiences of the physical being.

Divagations on civilization and culture range from attempts to identify general traits of "European civilization" to the peculiarities of the Polish or French "character." On this point, Bobkowski's critique takes broad aim, attentive especially to various forms of social pretense and hypocrisy. Perhaps the harshest words of criticism are reserved for the Polish intelligentsia, his own social milieu, which he ridicules for being snobbish, undeservedly self-important, contentious, and what Bobkowski considers as perhaps its greatest sins: being petty and selfish.

We even find a love story hidden amid the reports of political developments and philosophical arguments, between the news from the front and from the neighborhood. Only a couple of times Basia steps out from the shadows. We are told little of her activities (she studies painting) or of her opinions (she laughs quite a lot at Bobkowski), but we do know enough to have a sense of her independent spirit and of the bond between the two. She is present from the very first page to the last, though her importance is explicitly declared only in a couple of moving passages that convey the strength of their attachment and mutual reliance: "We are alone, we two, and each of us clings to the other as if to a ship's mast in a storm."

It's the story of a "real life" love, too, which takes us back to Cracow, when Bobkowski was barely nineteen years old. He met Barbara Birtus in 1932 at his aunt's house, when she was tutoring his young nephews. In short: "Jędrek," as he was called by his family, and "Basia," the diminutive form of her name, met, they talked, and they remained together for life. Their marriage on Christmas Day 1938 was quick and quiet, and most of their relations, besides a few of their closest family and friends, were informed after the fact. Three months after the wedding, the young couple left Cracow, never to return, traveling to Paris with the intention of obtaining Argentinian visas.

In its thematic diversity and in the seemingly "natural" way in which Bobkowski weaves the numerous threads, the *Notebooks* recall another unusual and hard to classify creation. Cervantes embarked on writing a simple story of adventures, and yet within the messy, open-ended format, through a series of simple episodes "on the road" and long conversations "at the inn," he managed to render his entire real world and the world of his dreams. In telling the story of Don Quixote, he presents a vivid picture of his Spain: its friars and its Moors, the snobbish and cruel aristocrats and the foolish common men capable of equal cruelty, the prisoners in shackles condemned to absurdly harsh sentences, the brave damsels opposing the dictums of their fathers, the young noblemen dressed up as shepherds, and the shepherds talking like poets . . .

The *Notebooks* display a similarly broad outlook and generosity of spirit. Its form is open, its content suggestive of the old-fashioned ideals of love, honor, and freedom. Tragic elements are tempered by humor—sometimes picaresque and carefree, at other points sharply satirical. Like Cervantes, Bobkowski proclaims the right to make individual choices and speak in one's own name, even if judged foolish by others, and insists on the necessity of individual responsibility for one's deeds, which can be practiced only under conditions of freedom. And as in *Don Quixote de la Mancha*, the greatest "adventure" witnessed by the reader is the main character's transformation.

The process of remaking oneself starts with an unexpected feeling of detachment—the sudden, almost physical sensation of "breaking away" that Bobkowski signals for the first time, with a note of astonishment, at the very beginning of the *Notebooks*. The moment occurs during the dramatic exodus from Paris, in the aftermath of his impulsive decision to leave the city, while witnessing the chaos of crowded roads and confronting the fear of the unknown. Bobkowski relishes the newly discovered sense of liberation and sketches an apt analogy a couple of weeks later, when he finds on the street a single colorful bead loosened from a string of other beads. He carries this bead in his pocket as a symbol and reminder of the separation from his past and the possibilities of the present.

His growing self-awareness is inexorably linked with the act of writing, and Bobkowski describes various moments of this active creation of his new identity: being open to the world. Listening. Being like the instrument to be played by the surrounding colors, sounds, and silences. Observing attentively. Searching for words to describe anew the world and one's place in it. Trying to re-create on a page the experience, the sensations, the fleeting impressions, the thoughts pressing inside the skull. That is, attempting to complete the impossible task. Impossible, states Bobkowski, yet undertaken day after day. With the reminder that "it is not so difficult to describe things you've noticed. It's much more difficult to notice in the first place. A true writer is not someone who writes well but someone who notices the most."

We gain a better understanding of this process of self-creation as the writer by noting Bobkowski's admiration of other writers and artists. He values Balzac's capacity to identify the power of money and vividly show in his novels how the possession of money, or the lack of financial resources, shapes the fate of individuals. He praises Flaubert for his ambition to chisel the sentence to a point of perfection in precision and clarity. He is enchanted by the elemental humor that runs like a powerful undercurrent through the historical novels of Henryk Sienkiewicz. He admires Katherine Mansfield for her attention to small things and her understatement that leaves space for the reader's own discoveries in her stories "in which nothing happens, and yet so much has occurred."

The fact that he loves Chopin, and every year goes on a pilgrimage to his grave in Père Lachaise, is not surprising, as the great composer is his compatriot and another displaced soul trying to mark his place in a "foreign land" by wits and talent. It's especially illuminating, however, to see what Bobkowski finds so special in Chopin as the model artist. He admires his capacity to devote hours and hours to playing basic exercises, the patience and endurance involved in such practice. He praises Chopin's sound "business sense"—the expectation of just payment for the completed compositions. Yes, inspired art, yet depending on work, and work again, and a "sober view of things."

Later in the *Notebooks*, a transformed narrator emerges: feeling liberated from his social milieu, its strictures and expectations, and aware of a new, freely chosen path. Bobkowski is at peace with himself, in spite of the tragic circumstances that confront him. He is aware of his hard-won victory, grateful for a chance to "find himself," and full of exuberant energy: *Everything pleases me, everything around is like music.* "The moods of individual streets and the vistas, caught on the fly, revolve inside me like a parade of dancing couples, each in a different costume. I take great gulps of something I cannot define. Youth? I feel good because I'm young and strong; because I'm myself and I think more freely than ever before. And because I have Basia. What more do I need?"

The *Notebooks*, although presented in a linear manner, aim to transform this daily record of events, observations, and reflections into a story and to tell it in a convincing manner. It's a story with two main characters: the individual and the collective. The individual protagonist, as noted above, undergoes a positive transformation, finding a sense of the fullness of life, with an echo of the Kantian "moral law within" and "the starry heavens above."

The collective character, France, fares much worse, and its dramatic arc ends on a tragic note. At the crossings of the two fates, we witness various ups and downs and emotional oscillations: Bobkowski's love for *"douce France"*; his admiration for French culture as the pinnacle of European civilization; his pleasure in the French joie de vivre, nourished by a taste for sensual experience and instinctive resistance to the rigidity of strict order; his appreciation of France as the only place where he could have experienced the revelatory illumination of self-discovery; his terrible disappointment with France's petulance and prompt submission in confrontation with the enemy; the consolation he finds at any sign of the impulse for "insubordination."

The tears that Bobkowski sheds in the final moments recorded in the *Notebooks* are explicitly prompted by what was happening in his home city of Warsaw. By the end of August 1944 it was engulfed in flames, its last tragi-heroic gesture of resistance, the Warsaw Uprising, doomed by the overwhelming force of the dual enemy: the occupying German army and the "liberating" Soviet soldiers, already standing on the eastern bank of the Vistula River. But the tears were also flowing for his cultural home, France, which was rightfully rejoicing at the arrival of the Anglo-American liberators yet willfully blind to the dangers of Soviet power and its allied Communists acting from within.

A couple of years later, in the short essay "From the Back," Bobkowski adds an epilogue to this story of love and heartbreak: "Europe—first and foremost is defined by the European man, but unfortunately, this is now a dying and decaying breed. Europeans have become 'pacotille,' mutton, and have lost the distinct characteristics that guaranteed their former glory: entrepreneurship and resourcefulness, prompt readiness to undertake reasonable risk, independent judgment, reasonable insubordination. To the contrary—today's Europeans have become obedient, and submissive to the State, their own and foreign."

He transforms this mournful dirge into a mandate for action. With $150 in their pockets, not a word of Spanish, minimal knowledge of the region, and a touch of Conradian readiness for the unknown, in June 1948 Andrzej and Basia Bobkowski embark on the ship *Jagiełło* and cross the ocean in the direction of Guatemala, which will become their new home and final resting place.

The openness of form permits Bobkowski to include various styles in the telling of his story. Indeed, one of the striking characteristics of the *Notebooks* is the ease and seeming naturalness with which they accommodate multiple genres. We can enjoy lively descriptions of the rural countryside or urban scenes. The reportage invites us to share in adventures "on the road" and conversations "at the tent" when the modern-day Don Quixote and Sancho Panza ride across southern France and the Alps, with bicycles serving as their steeds. We are offered character sketches drawn with barely a few lines, like the drawings of Paul Gavarni, which Bobkowski appreciates. We read extensive theater and film reviews. We may laugh at the satire ridiculing social pretenses. Sometimes, we have to plow through long philosophical ruminations or summaries of the arguments of other authors.

This diversity of genres, the multiple styles invoked at different occasions, the quotations reproducing on the page the fragments of conversations of individuals of different classes and regions, the continuous changes in tone—all posed special challenges in the task of translating the *Notebooks*. The title itself presented an interesting puzzle. *Szkice piórkiem* refers to quickly drawn sketches, created with a few brushes of the quill. Chosen by Bobkowski for the title, the phrase seems to clash with the size of the book and gravitas of its content. It suggests the author's distance from his creation, perhaps a touch of self-irony, and invites also a certain light-heartedness in various possible responses.

Polish is agile and fluid, and it comfortably accommodates quite a degree of disorder, especially in the spoken form. Its vocabulary, often enamored with the distant rural past and attached to remote points of reference (ah, *"kontusz"*—how the word reverberates! and how sadly devoid of such echoes is "robe," which the dictionary provides as its correct translation), is nevertheless open to borrowings from other languages and marked with a touch of the Polish anarchic spirit. The attention to specific shifts in diction and to nuances of individual words was essential to do justice to a prose as controlled as Bobkowski's, sympathetic in composition to nouns and verbs, unadorned by metaphors, aiming for the precision of expression, and only occasionally permitting itself a dance with adjectives.

I find this quality of Bobkowski's writing, his restraint and control of the seductive power of words, particularly attractive. Interestingly, in his linguistic discipline and attention to ethical questions, I recognize the characteristic qualities of Polish poetry, in particular an affinity with the humanistic spirit of Wisława Szymborska's and Zbigniew Herbert's poems.

Bobkowski's place in Polish literature is marked by dramatic reevaluations and readjustments. Before the *Notebooks* could be published in his native country, they appeared in Paris (published by Kultura, in 1957), London (Kontra, 1985), and in French translation in Switzerland (Noir sur Blanc, 1991). As noted earlier, from 1948 on he lived in Guatemala and kept his distance from the émigré political and social turmoil. He remained almost completely unknown in Poland; his name was forbidden, assiduously guarded by censors. At the time of the first publication of *Szkice piórkiem* in Poland in 1995, more than three decades after his death, the stars were aligned favorably. The date was right, after the fall of the Communist system, the critics were hungry, and the audience ready.

The appearance of a new kid on the block had quite a spectacular effect. His somber "wartime diary" gained the endorsement of Roman Zimand, a serious and perceptive literary critic. Its bright blue cover shone like a beacon announcing something new and exciting. Propelled by the revisionist impulse of post-

Communist momentum, the *Notebooks* were recognized as a vital "document of the epoch," and he was enshrined among other great names of the twentieth-century "memoir canon," next to three writers who lived, worked, and published in Poland: Zofia Nałkowska, Maria Dąbrowska, and Stefan Żeromski, and two famous émigré authors: Witold Gombrowicz and Gustaw Herling-Grudziński.

Bobkowski seemed to fit the role well, adding a new perspective to the larger story of World War II. And yet he stood apart, uncomfortable in the pantheon and regarded by many a bit suspiciously. Before their diaries were published, all five authors were already firmly established as professional writers, each with a recognized body of work: collections of short stories, novels, literary essays, and in Gombrowicz's case, controversial but widely known plays. Only Bobkowski had nothing to his name besides a few short stories, a handful of equally short essays, and occasional commentaries dispersed in the émigré press.

The *Notebooks* or Bobkowski's life couldn't be securely enclosed in any familiar cultural paradigm. The "outsider" status added to the mystique already surrounding the author. His biography was known only in its basic outlines, and the facts of his life traced an unusual path, tempting colorful speculation. Indeed, the joy ride of enthusiastic "followers" spiraled at the beginning of the twenty-first century into a whole field of "Bobcology." Bobkowski was widely quoted, often out of context, even more widely praised, with some of his phrases used as slogans of cultural rebellion. He gained a dubious "celebrity" status, known more for what he did in life (or didn't do) than for his creative work.

Two more recent developments have added another layer to this story. The original manuscript of the *Notebooks* was "discovered" in New York: nine copybooks, densely filled with Bobkowski's elegant and unusually legible handwriting. I use quotation marks, because these modest school-like notepads had been lying quietly for years in the archives of the Polish Institute of Arts and Sciences of America (PIASA), stored in plain cardboard boxes, donated by Basia Bobkowska at the end of her life in 1982. Access to the manuscript revealed substantial editorial changes Bobkowski introduced in preparation for the publication of the book, opening new channels of interesting and productive discussion.

Perhaps of even more wide-ranging consequence was the dedicated researchers' and editors' work that resulted in the publication of fascinating correspondence with the most important figures of postwar Polish cultural life, both in Poland and in emigration. Bobkowski's epistolary exchanges with Jerzy Giedroyc, Tymon Terlecki, Jerzy Turowicz, Jarosław Iwaszkiewicz, Józef Wittlin, Mieczysław Grydzewski, et al. are complemented by letters to his relatives, among them a particularly significant trove sent to his mother, Stanisława, and uncle Aleksander Bobkowski.

With ten volumes of diversified correspondence and a couple of book collections that present his short stories and essays, Bobkowski can no longer be regarded as an "author of one book"; he is more than a "diarist" to be appreciated for providing a documentary record. The letters are extraordinarily rich in content and attentive to form. Their style is controlled and conscious of the intended audience. In short, they are propelled by a creative impulse and they highlight the unusual quality of Bobkowski as a writer: his capacity to present a grand vision and address major existential questions in the humble form of a letter or notebook.

In his correspondences, as in the *Notebooks*, Bobkowski is distrustful of big words and declarations but does not shy from expressions of emotion. The letters redefine the image of Bobkowski as a dispassionate and removed "lone wolf." They reveal the depth of his personal connections, cultivated with attention and full engagement. They also testify to his powers of effective communication. Perhaps the best example of this gift is provided by his correspondence with Aniela Mieczysławska that traces the full arc of their relationship: from casual contact between total strangers, addressing each other formally, to a close friendship founded in mutual trust and appreciation. The transformation is achieved through an exchange of mere "words on paper," which essentially is the meaning of literature.

The *Notebooks* themselves can be regarded as a kind of correspondence addressed to the individual reader. As in a letter, the voice speaking to us from these pages is direct and seeks to establish emotional connection. It is forceful, self-disciplined, and enormously appreciative of the rich texture of living. It offers warnings and admonishments and encouragements. It prompts us to reflect; challenges to recognize the ease with which we might slide into submissiveness; criticizes a tendency toward excessive rationalization; denounces false promises of ideologies and the traps of self-deception; shows the seductiveness of too much ease and comfort. And like a steady refrain, over and over it repeats the urgent appeal to see—to see the beauty of the shimmering light, of a small French town on the slopes of the mountains, of plain decency, of an honorable gesture.

Let the last word belong to another writer who in the face of tyranny, on a large and small scale, managed to convey the tragic and comedic elements of the human lot and never grew tired of denouncing the corrosive effects of the ethics of the "means justify the ends." I quote a line from Shakespeare, following Bobkowski, who in turn took it from Katherine Mansfield. These are words spoken by Hotspur, a young nobleman with a modest role in the big drama of Henry IV, which Bobkowski might have noticed while reading Mansfield's short story "Bliss," where they serve as epigraph. Or perhaps Bobkowski copied them when he visited the New Zealand writer, one journeyman and wanderer paying homage to another, at the cemetery in Avon-Fontainebleau, where they are engraved on Mansfield's plain tombstone. And so the words travel from page to page, across centuries and continents, still resonant: have no fear, go forth.

"'Tis dangerous to take a cold, to sleep, to drink; but I tell you, my lord fool, out of this nettle, danger, we pluck this flower, safety."

ACKNOWLEDGMENTS AND TRANSLATORS' NOTE

This translation is based on the text of the first edition: Andrzej Bobkowski, *Szkice piórkiem (Francja 1940–1944)*, 2 vols. (Paris: Instytut Literacki, 1957). A recent edition reproduces this text exactly, with only minor typographical corrections.[1] The original notebooks on which the published text is based can be found in the archives of the Polish Institute of Arts and Sciences of America (PIASA) in New York City.[2] The published version diverges from the notebooks in various ways, some of which have been identified by the Polish scholar Łukasz Mikołajewski.[3] We do not mark the divergences in our notes, but follow the text as Bobkowski himself wanted it to appear.

On many occasions we have consulted the French translation by Laurence Dyèvre, which we gratefully acknowledge.[4] All translations from the French and German are our own, with the exception of the verse by André Maurois and a line from Adam Mickiewicz, *Pan Tadeusz*.[5]

Many individuals helped us locate and identify pertinent photographs and documents. In particular, we would like to express our appreciation for the generous advice offered by Maciej Nowak, author of a study of Bobkowski's work[6] and of an upcoming biography. Andrzej Bernhardt, Małgosia Czerwińska, Jarosław Klejnocki, Bożena Leven, Vera Michalski-Hoffmann, Weronika Orkisz, Wojciech Sikora, Mikołaj Sokołowski, and Ewa Zając provided extraordinary access to the archives under their care, permitting us to select the visual materials that enrich this volume.

Grażyna Drabik owes particular thanks to Małgosia Balasińska, Basia and Boguś Barański, Jacek and Lidia Drabik, Aili Flint, Krystyna Iłłakowicz, Jola and Wojtek Marczyk, Basia Nikonorow, Chris Rzonca, Antoine Vivas, and Maryla Wodzyńska for their friendship and understanding during this long journey. She would also like to thank Paul and Bell Chevigny, whose civic courage and dedication to social justice have taught her the true strength of the American spirit and the value of persistence against the odds. She greatly regrets that Austin Flint, who introduced her to the toughness and joy of the English language, cannot participate with us in celebrating this completed work.

She would like to acknowledge the grants received from the City College of New York, the Professional Staff Congress of the City University of New York

(PSC-CUNY), and the Kościuszko Foundation, which allowed her to focus on the *Notebooks* during the summers of 2015 and 2017, as well as to thank Carla Cappetti, Yana Joseph, András Kiséry, Geraldine Murphy, and Michelle Valladares, her colleagues at City College, for their support and advice.

Finally, Grażyna would like to dedicate this English version to Nicolas and Luka, with hope that it will offer them special insights into the complexities of history and the power of imagination.

For her part, Laura Engelstein would like to thank Alison MacKeen for proposing this project and John Donatich, the director of Yale University Press, for including us in this remarkable series of literary translations. She would also like to thank Laura Jones Dooley for her sensitive editing, good humor, and moral support, and Margaret Otzel for her editorial wisdom and responsiveness. On the home front, she thanks Michael Geyer for his unflagging patience and encouragement and for the benefit of his wide-ranging knowledge and expertise. Isabella contributed by interrupting.

NOTES

Introduction

1. Andrzej Bobkowski (hereafter AB) to Tymon Terlecki, February 20, 1958, in AB, *Listy do Tymona Terleckiego, 1956–1961*, ed. Nina Taylor-Terlecka (Warsaw: Biblioteka "Więzi," 2006), 95.

2. Józef Piłsudski (1867–1935), founding head of state (1918–1922) of the Second Polish Republic, returning to power in 1926, after a coup d'état.

3. Barbara Bobkowska, née Birtus (1913–1982): http://andrzej-bobkowski.pl/zycie /Basia.

4. Katarzyna Plucińska-Smorawska, *Między historią a literaturą: O Szkicach piórkiem Andrzeja Bobkowskiego* (Warsaw: Neriton, 2005), 10, 12–14.

5. AB and Zbigniew Koziański, "Sprawozdanie z działalności Biura Polskiego przy Atelier de construction de Châtillon w czasie okupacji niemieckiej," in Jerzy Giedroyc and AB, *Listy, 1946–1961*, ed. Jan Zieliński (Warsaw: Czytelnik, 1997), 696–702.

6. Włodzimierz Bolecki, "Kultura (1946–2000)," in *The Exile and Return of Writers from East Central Europe: A Compendium*, ed. John Neubauer and Borbála Zsuzsanna Török (Berlin: Walter de Gruyter, 2009), 154.

7. http://www.kulturaparyska.com/en/historia/.

8. AB to Giedroyc, July 25, 1957, in Giedroyc and AB, *Listy*, 468.

9. AB to Giedroyc, August 6, 1957, in ibid., 472.

10. AB to Giedroyc, September 5, 1957, in ibid., 478.

11. AB, *Szkice piórkiem (Francja 1940–1944)*, 2 vols. (Paris: Instytut Literacki, 1957). For a complete list of his publications, see Maciej Nowak, *Na łuku elektrycznym: O pisaniu Andrzeja Bobkowskiego* (Warsaw: Biblioteka "Więzi," 2014), 459–460.

12. Roman Zimand, "Posłowie: Wojna i spokój" (1983), in AB, *Szkice piórkiem* (Warsaw: CiS, 2007), 542.

13. London: Kontra, 1985; Warsaw: Towarzystwo Opieki nad Archiwum Instytutu Literackiego w Paryżu, Wydawnictwo CiS, 1995. AB, *En guerre et en paix: Journal, 1940–1944*, trans. Laurence Dyèvre (Montricher: Les Éditions Noir sur Blanc, 1991); AB, *Wehmut? Wonach zum Teufel? Tagebücher aus Frankreich, 1940–1941*, vol. 1, trans. Martin Pollack (Hamburg: ROSPO, 2000).

14. Ołeś Herasym, "O recepcji *Szkiców piórkiem* Andrzeja Bobkowskiego na Ukrainie," in *Andrzej Bobkowski wielokrotnie*, ed. Krzysztof Ćwikliński, Andrzej Stanisław Kowalczyk, and Maciej Urbanowski (Warsaw: Biblioteka "Więzi," 2013), 251, 253.

15. AB, *Vijna ì spokij: Francuz'kij šodennik, 1940–1944*, trans. O. Gerasim (Kiev: Kritika, 2007).

16. Original entry for August 4, 1942, quoted from the archival manuscript in Łu-kasz Mikołajewski, *Disenchanted Europeans: Polish Émigré Writers from* Kultura *and Postwar Reformulations of the West* (Bern: Peter Lang, 2018), 371.

17. Hermann Alexander Graf von Keyserling (1880–1946), a Baltic German born in Livonia (then part of the Russian empire, now divided between Latvia and Estonia), was a popular travel writer and armchair philosopher. He was known for his *Reise-tagebuch eines Philosophen: Der kürzeste Weg zu sich selbst führt um die Welt* (1919), *Das Spektrum Europas* (1928), and *Südamerikanische Meditationen* (1932). AB, "Key-serling," *Horyzonty*, no. 7 (1946): 1–7; no. 8, 8–13; rpt. in AB, *Ikkos i Sotion oraz inne szkice*, ed. Paweł Kądziela (Warsaw: Biblioteka "Więzi," 2009); Jan Tomkowski, "Tes-tament Keyserlinga (O Andrzeju Bobkowskim)," in *Sporne postaci Polskiej literatury współczesnej: Następne pokolenie*, ed. Alina Brodzka and Lidia Burska (Warsaw: IBL, 1995). See mention of Keyserling in Léon Werth, *33 Days*, intro. Antoine de Saint-Exupéry, trans. Austin Denis Johnson (1996; Brooklyn, NY: Melville House, 2015), 58, citing Lucien Febvre's description of Keyserling as one of "philosophy's journalists."

18. Andrzej Bobkowski Papers, PIASA Archives, Fonds No. 45: http://www.piasa .org/archives/fonds-045.html.

19. Łukasz Mikołajewski, "Pamięć fabularyzowana. Powojenne poprawki w *Szkicach piórkiem* Andrzeja Bobkowskiego," in *Buntownik, Cyklista, Kosmopolak: O Andrzeju Bobkowskim i jego twórczości*, ed. Jarosław Klejnocki and Andrzej St. Ko-walczyk (Warsaw: Biblioteka "Więzi," 2011); Mikołajewski, *Disenchanted Europeans*.

20. Zimand, "Posłowie," 544–545.

21. Maciej Nowak, "Patrzę inaczej," in Klejnocki and Kowalczyk, *Buntownik*, 174–187; Łukasz Mikołajewski, "Odpowiedź Maciejowi Nowakowi," in ibid., 188–196; Maciej Urbanowski, "*Szkice piórkiem*—autentyk czy powieść?," *Dekada Literacka*, no. 15 (75) (1993), rpt. in Maciej Urbanowski, *Szczęście pod wulkanem: O Andrzeju Bobkowskim* (Warsaw: LTW, 2013), 21–22.

22. Andrzej Chciuk, "O Andrzeju Bobkowskim i jego listach," *Wiadomości*, year 17, no. 32/33 (854/855) (August 12/19, 1962), 3; Zimand, "Posłowie," 546.

23. AB, "Biografia wielkiego Kosmopolaka," *Kultura*, no. 9 (1960): 19–20.

1940

1. General Maxime Weygand (1867–1965) went to Poland in 1920 to advise Piłsud-ski in the Polish-Soviet War (1919–1921), which established the borders of the indepen-dent Polish state. He retired in 1935 but was recalled as commander in May 1940; he advocated capitulation. Briefly Pétain's minister of defense, he energetically applied the anti-Jewish laws. Although he openly criticized Germany, he was a willing col-laborator until his dismissal under German pressure in November 1941. The Germans arrested him in November 1942. He was imprisoned as a collaborator in 1946 but was cleared in 1948. General Maurice Gamelin (1872–1958), unsuccessful commander of the French military in 1940 during the Battle of France. Marshal Philippe Pétain (1856–1951), head of state of Vichy France, 1940–1944.

2. Paul Reynaud (1878–1966) resigned as prime minister on June 16, 1940, and was replaced by Pétain. Reynaud had insisted that France keep fighting.

3. General André-Georges Corap (1878–1953) commanded the Ninth Army in the Battle of France and was relieved of his post on May 19, 1940. Paris was occupied on June 14. On June 17, Pétain announced that France would ask for an armistice, and on June 22, France and Germany signed an armistice that took effect on June 25.

4. Decisive Polish victory over the Red Army in August 1920, during the Polish-Soviet War.

5. Identity cards for foreign workers.

6. Flowers, Susanne, cute.

7. We're closing.

8. The Parc de Bagatelle is part of the Bois de Boulogne.

9. Come on, now, don't cry.

10. Adolf Dymsza, stage name of Adolf Bagiński (1900–1975), a popular Polish film and theater actor known before the war for his comic cabaret performances.

11. François Chappel was chief engineer of the Châtillon factory.

12. To get some air.

13. Long live madmen.

14. Tadeusz Wylot, see Introduction.

15. Words of the "Marseillaise": "form your battalions—let's march, let's march!" For "march" he substitutes "flee."

16. Polish September refers to the German invasion of Poland, beginning September 1, 1939. The weather was unseasonably hot and sunny.

17. A play on *Kaiserwetter*, meaning very sunny weather.

18. Włodzimierz Terlikowski (1873–1951), Polish painter.

19. *Gallia est omnis divisa in partes tres* . . . "All Gaul is divided into three parts." Julius Caesar, *Commentarii de Bello Gallico*, trans. W. A. McDevitee and W. S. Bohn (1869), 1:1 (available at http://www.sacred-texts.com/cla/jcsr/dbg1.htm; hereafter cited as Caesar, *Bello Gallico*).

20. Next time don't forget him.

21. Prewar café and restaurant in Warsaw known for late-night dancing.

22. It's signed, it's signed.

23. Finished—we are too intelligent to break our necks . . .

24. *Ogniem i mieczem* (1884), a popular historical novel by Henryk Sienkiewicz (1846–1916) set in seventeenth-century Poland during the Cossack uprising led by Boghan Khmelnytsky against Polish rule in Ukraine. It is part of the enormously popular trilogy *With Fire and Sword* (*Ogniem i mieczem*), *The Deluge* (*Potop*), and *Fire in the Steppe* (*Pan Wołodyjowski*), first published in installments in 1884–1888.

25. Since the victory, the spirit of pleasure has triumphed over the spirit of sacrifice. People have made demands but were unwilling to serve. They have not wanted to make the effort; today unhappiness greets them.

26. Jean Prouvost (1885–1978), newspaper publisher, became minister of informa-

tion in Reynaud's government on June 6, 1940, then was high commissioner for information in Pétain's government, resigning on July 10, 1940.

27. Chestnut cream.

28. As much as you want.

29. The Battle of Dakar in September 1940 was an unsuccessful attempt by the Allies to capture the strategic port in French West Africa (modern-day Senegal) in order to overthrow the colonial administration and install a Free French government under General Charles de Gaulle (1890–1970).

30. *Marseille Trilogy*, consisting of three plays, *Marius* (1929), *Fanny* (1931), and *César* (1936, as a film), by Marcel Pagnol (1895–1974), celebrated French writer and filmmaker.

31. Belote was a popular two-hand card game.

32. Naughty Toto, the meat is not for you—oh, no!

33. Coffee for the gentleman!

34. Your case has been examined and the commissioner will sign this at five o'clock.

35. Tomorrow afternoon.

36. Ann Bridge (1889–1974), British novelist. Her first novel, *Peking Picnic* (1932), was based on her experience as the wife of a diplomat in China.

37. But one must not confuse these two things.

38. What would you like, poor dear?

39. Does Monsieur know that café?

40. Monsieur knows that for sure.

41. Captain Flint is said to have died in Savannah, Georgia, shouting, "Darby M'Graw—fetch aft the rum." From Robert Louis Stevenson, *Treasure Island* (1883).

42. High mountain range in southern Poland.

43. Staś Tarkowski and Nel Rawlison, principal characters in Sienkiewicz, *In Desert and Wilderness* (*W pustyni i w puszczy*, 1911), a popular young adult novel of adventure, set in nineteenth-century Egypt and Sudan during the Madhi revolt in Sudan, in which the two young friends, fourteen-year-old Staś and eight-year-old Nel, are kidnapped by rebels.

44. Julian Tuwim (1894–1953), author of popular satirical verses, cabaret sketches, librettos, and songs, was one of the most important poets of the interwar period.

45. *Wspólny pokój* (*The Common Room*, 1932), novel by Zbigniew Uniłowski (1909–1937), a critical representation of the 1920s–1930s Warsaw artistic milieu.

46. Italian: Dangerous to lean out.

47. Madame, again, please.

48. Gustave Flaubert (1821–1880), known for his purity of style.

49. André Maurois (Émile Salomon Wilhelm Herzog, 1885–1967), *Climats* (1928), the story of two unhappy marriages. Abbé Prévost (1697–1763), *Manon Lescaut: L'Histoire du Chevalier des Grieux et de Manon Lescaut* (1731).

50. I understand.

51. Here on the left, my dear!

52. An excursion, what? Ouyi, we're out for a jaunt.

53. Two operas are based on the novel by Prévost: *Manon Lescaut* (1893) by Giacomo Puccini (1858–1924) and *Manon* (1884) by Jules Massenet (1842–1912).

54. Michał Konstanty Bogucki (1860–1935), translator of Greek literature, taught Greek and Latin at Saint Ann's Gymnasium in Cracow, also known as Nowodworski Collegium, one of the best secondary-level educational institutions in interwar Poland.

55. "*Postea quam in vulgus militum elatum est qua arrogantia in conloquio Ariovistus usus omni Gallia Romanis interdixisset, impetumque in nostros eius equites fecissent, eaque res conloquium ut diremisset, multo maior alacritas studiumque pugnandi maius exercitui iniectum est*" (When it was spread abroad among the common soldiery with what haughtiness Ariovistus had behaved at the conference, and how he had ordered the Romans to quit Gaul, and how his cavalry had made an attack upon our men, and how this had broken off the conference, a much greater alacrity and eagerness for battle was infused into our army; Caesar, *Bello Gallico*, 1.46).

56. An allusion to registered or "controlled" prostitution, a system instituted in the 1830s in which prostitutes were given medical inspections and yellow identity cards. La Roquette was a prison. In the novel the lovers try to escape their troubles by moving to New Orleans. They do not escape them. Des Grieux is called "*un homme de qualité.*"

57. The quotation combines two separate phrases: (1) "*Germani multum ab nostra consuetudine differunt*" (The Germans differ much from these usages; Caesar, *Bello Gallico*, 6:21); and (2) part of the sentence "*Latrocinia nullam habent infamiam, quae extra fines cuiusque civitatis fiunt, atque ea iuventutis exercendae ac desidiae minuendae causa fieri praedicant*" (Robberies which are committed beyond the boundaries of each state bear no infamy, and they avow that these are committed for the purpose of disciplining their youth and of preventing sloth; ibid., 6:23).

58. "*Ac fuit antea tempus, cum Germanos Galli virtute superarent, ultro bella inferrent, propter hominum multitudinem agrique inopiam trans Rhenum colonias mitterent*" (And there was formerly a time when the Gauls excelled the Germans in prowess, and waged war on them offensively, and, on account of the great number of their people and the insufficiency of their land, sent colonies over the Rhine; ibid., 6:24).

59. How hot it is.

60. Amantine-Lucile-Aurore Dupin (George Sand, 1804–1876), French novelist and lover of Frédéric Chopin (1810–1849), among others.

61. Juliusz Słowacki (1809–1849), Polish Romantic poet.

62. Do we like him? . . . I meant an intellectual crane. ("La grue" means "crane" but also "whore.")

63. Gaius Plinius Caecilius Secundus (61–113 CE), Roman magistrate.

64. Denis Diderot (1713–1784), *Jacques le fataliste et son maître* (1796).

65. Interwar Warsaw cafés frequented by artists and writers.

66. "Mountain morons": there is no such compound word in German; AB's invention.

67. Związek Niezależnej Młodzieży Socjalistycznej (ZNMS), socialist youth organization, 1917–1948, continued in emigration, 1946–1952.

68. A short sword or dagger used in Roman times.

69. It's not good to eat.

70. Phrase used by Kosma and Damian, twin sons of Old Kiemlicz, secondary characters in Sienkiewicz, *The Deluge*.

71. How ticklish they are, now.

72. Lowest rank in the German, Swiss, and Austrian armies.

73. See note 24, above.

74. Światopełk Karpiński (1909–1940), Polish poet and satirist.

75. Nickname for Andrzej.

76. Albert Einstein (1879–1955) stayed abroad after 1933. Thomas Mann (1875–1955) fled in 1933. Franz Werfel (1890–1945), Austrian Jewish writer, fled in 1938.

77. The Route Napoléon, opened in 1932, follows the route from Elba to Grenoble, crossing the Alps, taken by Napoleon Bonaparte in 1815.

78. The Château de Malmaison, west of Paris, was the residence of Empress Joséphine and, after her death in 1814, Napoleon's last residence in France in 1815 before his exile to Saint Helena.

79. In Margaret Mitchell's *Gone with the Wind* (1936), Scarlett O'Hara says, "I'll think about that tomorrow." The film premiered in December 1939.

80. Monsieur Bonbonski, a telegram for you. (Bonbonski, literally, Mr. Candyman, is a distortion of Bobkowski.)

81. "Reduta Ordona" (1832), a poem by Adam Mickiewicz (1798–1855), the bard of Polish Romanticism, recounts an episode in the uprising of 1830–1831 (known in Polish as the November Uprising), an unsuccessful attempt to liberate the part of Poland under Russian rule since the late eighteenth-century partitions. Facing the overwhelming Russian forces, Ordon, defender of a redoubt on the outskirts of Warsaw, decides to blow up the last reserves of ammunition and weapons.

82. On the Polish-Soviet War, see note 1, above.

83. Well, you know, I don't like Jews.

84. Mother, why do you always talk about your Jews? The gentleman is not interested in knowing your opinions on that subject.

85. But it's very complicated.

86. Yes, it's a beautiful city.

87. The Polish priest Franciszek Antoni Cegiełka (1908–2003) was attached to the French Catholic mission in France in the 1930s. In October 1940 he was arrested by the Gestapo and spent time in Sachsenhausen and Dachau. In 1948 he emigrated to the United States, where he remained until his death.

88. Stanisław Przybyszewski (1868–1927), Polish dramatist and poet whose naturalistic writings were famous for their decadent and provocative character.

89. Jerzy Edward Schnayder (1891–1974), Polish specialist in classical languages and philosophy who taught from 1926 to 1939 at Saint Ann's Gymnasium in Cracow.

90. "The Poles cannot feel joy without shouting and uproar." Quoted in Latin by the character Zagloba, in Sienkiewicz, *Fire in the Steppe.*

91. Kazimierz Przerwa-Tetmajer (1865–1940), poet in the Young Poland movement.

92. Budrys: from the popular ballad "Trzech Budrysów" (1828) by Mickiewicz.

93. "My, Pierwsza Brygada" (We are the First Brigade), also known as "Marsz Pierwszej Brygady" (March of the First Brigade) and "Legiony to żołnierska nuta" (The legions are a soldier's song), associated with the Polish Legions organized by Józef Piłsudski during World War I.

94. The Totenkopfhusaren (Totenkopf-Husaren), elite Prussian cavalry divisions.

95. Reference to "Ballada o pannie Franciszce." "Mazurek Dąbrowskiego," the Polish national anthem, was written in 1797 by Józef Wybicki (1747–1822), one of the organizers of General Jan Henryk Dąbrowski's Polish army in Italy. The opening line is: "Jeszcze Polska nie zginęła" (Poland will not have perished . . . as long as we live). Kamil Norden (Jadwiga Maria Migowa, 1891–1942), Polish journalist, writer, and feminist who died in Ravensbrück.

96. "Moscow, ravaged by fire, delivered to the French?"—a line from Mikhail Lermontov (1814–1841), "Borodino" (1837), not Alexander Pushkin (1799–1837), author of *Eugene Onegin.*

97. Ernest Renan (1823–1892), French philosopher and historian, famous for his natural history of religion: *Vie de Jésus* (1863), and *Essai psychologique sur Jésus-Christ* (1921). Oswald Spengler, *Decline of the West,* 2 vols. (1918, 1922).

98. Antoni Słonimski (1895–1976), *Rodzina* (1933).

99. Słonimski, *Lekarz bezdomny* (1930). Otwock, a suburb of Warsaw.

100. Constantin Güys (1802–1892), Dutch-born Crimean War correspondent and illustrator. Edmond de Goncourt (1822–1896), *La Fille Élisa* (1877).

101. Egon Schiele (1890–1918), Austrian Expressionist painter.

102. Hermann Hesse (1877–1962), *Narziß und Goldmund* (1930).

103. Please have some.

104. Why soap? They wash so little.

105. Warsaw suburb.

106. Sir James Jeans (1877–1946), popular English astronomer.

107. Adam Styka (1890–1959), Polish-born artist who painted North African and North American scenes.

108. Busy main street in the prewar Warsaw Jewish quarter.

109. Arnold Böcklin (1827–1901), German Symbolist painter.

110. A slight misquotation of Shakespeare, *Henry IV, Part 1,* act 2, scene 3: "'Tis dangerous to take a cold, to sleep, to drink; but I tell you, my lord fool, out of this nettle, danger, we pluck this flower, safety." Correctly quoted as the epigraph to Katherine Mansfield's story collection *Bliss* (1920). Mansfield (née Beauchamp, 1888–1923), New Zealand writer known for her short stories.

111. Jeanne Pacquin (1869–1936) and Edward Molyneux (1891–1974), fashion designers.

112. Luxury single-car railway train in 1930s Poland.

113. But not much, you know; now . . . *Oh là là*, it's really hard.

114. Fort near Gdańsk that repulsed the German attack in September 1939, as did Warsaw.

115. Camping forbidden.

116. From the oldest Polish hymn, "Bogurodzica," from the fifteenth century, in which Adam is referred to as "God's creature" (Adamie, ty boży kmieciu).

117. Town in central Poland, a major railroad junction yet without other distinguishing characteristics, standing here both for a relatively important place and for provincialism.

118. Mickiewicz, *Pan Tadeusz* (1834), epic poem and central work of Polish Romantic literature.

119. Gotthold Ephraim Lessing (1729–1781), *Nathan der Weise* (*Nathan the Wise*, 1779), a play advocating religious tolerance.

120. AB creates a pun, combining Polish and German: "*Fräulein V. hat grosse Zaleten, aber auch grosse Waden.*" Literal English: "Miss V. has great virtues (*zaleta*, Polish), but also great faults/calves" (*wada*, fault, Polish; *Wade*, calf, German). English/German pun equivalent: "*Fräulein V. hat grosse Plusen, aber auch grosse Schuld-ers*" (Miss V. has great pluses, but also great shoulders; *Schuld*, fault, German).

121. Lessing's comedy *Minna von Barnhelm oder das Soldatenglück* (1767).

122. Oscar Wilde (1854–1900), *Lady Windermere's Fan* (1892). "Dzień Esika w Ostendzie" (1907), satirical poem by Tadeusz Boy-Żeleński (1874–1941).

123. You sure have a huge appetite.

124. Are you German?

125. Warsaw didn't want to surrender . . . But France . . . it's shameful!

126. Our men? . . . They eat, they show up, they sleep.

127. René Descartes (1596–1650), French philosopher, mathematician, and scientist. François Marie Arouet Voltaire (1694–1778), French Enlightenment philosopher. Ferdinand Foch (1851–1929), French general and supreme Allied commander during World War I. Louis Hubert Lyautey (1854–1934), French general and colonial administrator who served in Indochina, Madagascar, and Morocco and was briefly minister of war.

128. We will win because we are stronger.

129. Characters in Sienkiewicz, *In Desert and Wilderness*. Kali, an African boy of princely origins, is held as a slave by the Sudanese Bedouins. Freed by Staś, Kali becomes his loyal servant and close friend, a companion in a series of adventures.

130. Sienkiewicz, *Listy z podróży do Ameryki*, 2 vols. (1876–1878).

131. Helena Mniszek (Helena Mniszkówna, 1878–1943), *Trędowata* (*The Leper*, 1909), a melodramatic novel in which a young aristocrat marries a poor governess.

132. Don't be afraid, dear sir . . . as you say . . .

133. You know a bit about our history?

134. It's the tune that makes the song.

135. You are unfortunate.

136. *Wiadomości Literackie*, a Warsaw literary weekly with a liberal sociopolitical outlook, covered a broad range of issues and presented both well-known and new writers. After 1939, it was published in London, from 1940 to 1944 as *Wiadomości Polskie, Polityczne i Literackie*, and after the war as *Wiadomości*, which became a major outlet for Polish émigré writers.

137. Gdynia, a Baltic seaport that enjoyed government-sponsored urban development in the 1920s and 1930s. Centralny Okręg Przemysłowy (Central Industrial District), an industrial center in Silesia built between the wars. Bank Gospodarstwa Krajowego (Bank of the National Economy).

138. *Strzępy meldunków*, 1936 memoirs of General Felicjan Sławoj-Składkowski (1885–1962), minister of internal affairs, 1926–29 and 1930–31, and chief of army administration, 1931–35. The Castle (Zamek), President Piłsudski's residence. Klonowa Street, residence of General Edward Rydz Śmigły (1886–1941), marshal of Poland from 1936.

139. Aldous Huxley (1894–1963), *Ends and Means: An Enquiry into the Nature of Ideals and into the Methods Employed for Their Realization* (1937).

140. We're not that dumb.

141. The front door will be closed.

142. Of my irresistible Slavic charm.

143. Essex, a small, affordable car produced in Detroit, 1918–1922. Reduta (The Redoubt), an experimental theater-lab founded in 1919 by AB's uncle Juliusz Osterwa (1885–1947), actor, theater director and theoretician, and Mieczysław Limanowski (1876–1948), geologist, university professor, theater theoretician, and director, inspired by the teachings of Konstantin Stanislavsky. In 1925 Reduta relocated to Wilno, on Pohulanka Street; in 1931 Osterwa brought the group back to Warsaw. Though its activities were ended by World War II, Reduta remains a point of reference and inspiration for many artists.

144. Jules Verne (1828–1905), *Les Enfants du capitaine Grant* (1867–1868).

145. Józef Weyssenhoff (1860–1932), author of works satirizing the traditional Polish aristocracy.

146. Commonly used all-purpose remedy.

147. Stendhal (Marie Henri Beyle, 1783–1842), *The Charterhouse of Parma* (1839), the story of an Italian nobleman caught up in the Napoleonic wars.

148. On Saturday and Sunday one does not work.

149. Too difficult.

150. "Ballada Alpuhara," from Mickiewicz, *Konrad Wallenrod* (1828).

151. Moorish king who resists the Spanish attack in Mickiewicz, *Konrad Wallenrod*.

152. Cigarette for the mountaintops.

153. Jan Parandowski (1895–1978), *Dysk Olimpijski* (1933), which earned a bronze

medal at the 1936 Olympics in Berlin and the Polish Literary Academy's prize for literary achievement in 1937.

154. Small town.

155. The highest peak, at 1,310 meters, of the Gorce Range in Małopolska.

156. I don't care.

157. Léon Blum (1872–1950), moderate socialist, premier of France, 1936–1937, 1938, 1946–1947, and opponent of Vichy during the war.

158. Seat of the Polish government in Paris.

159. Come on, wait.

160. Ivan Bunin (1870–1953) left Soviet Russia in 1920, was awarded the 1933 Nobel Prize in literature, and died in France.

161. Lines from Mickiewicz's poetic drama *Dziady* (*Forefathers' Eve*, 1860): "*Na głowie ma kraśny wianek, / W ręku zielony badylek, / A przed nią bieży baranek, / A nad nią leci motylek.*"

162. Polish resort in the Tatra Mountains.

163. Cliff overlooking the ancient Roman Forum from which miscreants of various kinds, including traitors, were thrown to their deaths.

164. Mariette Lydis (1887–1970), Austrian painter, known in Paris in the 1930s.

165. Chalon-sur-Saône, situated on the demarcation line that from June 17, 1940 until 1944 marked the boundary between the *zone occupée* in northwestern France and the *zone libre* in the south.

166. Napoleon met with Czar Alexander I on July 7, 1807, on a raft in the middle of the Neman River, where they signed the Treaty of Tilsit ending the War of the Fourth Coalition, in which the Prussians were defeated.

167. Perhaps now that will also change; one never knows.

168. Who's there? — It's us. — Oh, good, good. We'll have rain tonight.

169. Do you have a pass?

170. Tomorrow, come back early tomorrow morning. Today it's too late.

171. You never know what it depends on, probably the officers' mood.

172. Gentlemen, I present your new lodgers!

173. I have to take a look and see if there are any clients.

174. Go ahead, go ahead, it's good for your personal hygiene! — You know her? — What do you say! . . .

175. Well, well, you know, that's Paris . . .

176. Leo Viktor Frobenius (1873–1938), German ethnologist who worked in the Congo and proposed a theory of culture as a living organism.

177. Miss Dora, what did he mean? . . . The Germans today consider the State to be mankind's highest form of order. According to Hegel's philosophy, the State is the highest value on earth and as such demands the sacrifice of everything, including human life . . . Miss Dora, this judgment is false. It is faaaaalse, it is insane!! . . .

178. Are you refugees?

179. Where were you born?

180. Wiener-Neustadt, sixty-five kilometers south of Vienna, is the site of a military academy established in the eighteenth century. AB was in fact born there; his father was a staff officer in the Austrian army. The joke: In Vienna, near Vienna-Neustadt. The correction: In Vienna-Neustadt, near Vienna . . . Anton, he is actually your countryman.

181. What a nice guy.

182. No, no, you can keep going.

183. Heinrich Heine (1797–1856), *Deutschland: Ein Wintermärchen* (1844): *"Ihr Thoren, die Ihr im Koffer sucht! / Hier werdet Ihr nichts entdecken! / Die Contrebande, die mit mir reist, / Die hab' ich im Kopfe stecken"* (You fools that search inside my trunk! / There's nothing there for you to find: / The contraband I bring along, / Is hidden in my mind).

184. Wait a moment.

185. G'd morning. "Gut-Mugging" is the distortion.

186. Order above all.

187. Here you are, you can continue. Why are you returning to Paris?

188. Do you understand?

189. Why not just admit you don't have the money for the train ticket . . .

190. Don't make a fuss.

191. Especially since we're neither sick nor tired.

192. Rudyard Kipling (1865–1936), "Boots" (1903): "Seven—six—eleven—five—nine-an'-twenty mile to-day— / Four—eleven—seventeen—thirty-two the day before— / (Boots—boots—boots—boots—movin' up an' down again!) / There's no discharge in the war!" From Ecclesiastes 8:8 (KJV): "There is no man that hath power over the spirit to retain the spirit; neither hath he power in the day of death: and there is no discharge in that war."

193. On Dakar, see note 29, above.

194. Field gray, the color of German army uniforms.

195. Decent fellows—and so well brought up.

196. The miser Père Grandet, a character in Honoré de Balzac (1799–1850), *Eugénie Grandet* (1833).

197. Nicholaas Gerard Pierson (1839–1909), Dutch liberal economist and statesman. Ludwig von Mises (1881–1973), Austrian liberal economist and sociologist. Enrico Barone (1859–1924), Italian socialist economist. AB's reference may derive from N. G. Pierson, Ludwig von Mises, Georg Halm, and Enrico Barone, *Collectivist Economic Planning: Critical Studies on the Possibilities of Socialism*, ed. F. A. von Hayek (1935).

198. Edward Lipiński (1888–1986), socialist economist, member of the Polish Socialist Party, and founder of the Institute of Prices and Business Cycles, was professor at Szkoła Główna Handlowa (Warsaw School of Economics), 1923–1940, where AB studied.

199. Gentlemen in musty gray.

200. "Bo to się zwykle tak zaczyna" (1934), a slow foxtrot, popular in the 1930s, which dramatizes the falling in and out of love.

201. They're nice, you can't complain . . .

202. Admiral Joachim Murat (1767–1815), Napoleon Bonaparte's brother-in-law and a fancy dresser, had no connection to the circus but was executed by firing squad after Napoleon's fall.

203. Charlie Chaplin's film *Police* (1916).

204. A blond whore.

205. Rudi—you just have to take my photo!

206. You see, . . . the director and the beautiful girls from Paris.

207. Anatole France (1844–1924), French novelist who won the 1921 Nobel Prize in literature. Alphonse Daudet (1840–1897), popular French writer.

208. He smokes his nasty cigarettes and whistles his Paris songs.

209. It's for your wife—don't lose it.

210. Large, propeller-driven airplanes designed by the British Bristol Aeroplane Company.

211. F——— off, you old rattle, we're not thieves . . . Shit!

212. Every evening THEY count my coupons.

213. Take it, eat, . . . you are young . . .

214. Too bad . . . I'm not afraid . . . THEY . . . THEY have forbidden us to sell . . .

215. Guy de Maupassant (1850–1893), French writer known for his short stories.

216. There's a difference, all the same.

217. Your lights, gentlemen!

218. But here is my light . . .

219. I'm asking for your lamps. This is my only lamp.

220. It's not like before—times have changed . . .

221. Back home.

222. General Pierre Jacques Étienne Cambronne (1770–1842) fought with Napoleon at Waterloo. When called upon to surrender to the British, he is supposed to have said, "*La garde meurt et ne se rend pas!*" (The guard dies and does not surrender!) In another version, he is supposed to have said simply: "*Merde!*" (Shit!—figuratively, "Go to hell!") This version became known as *le mot de Cambronne* (Cambronne's witticism).

223. Go ahead, go ahead, dig in, help yourselves . . . go ahead.

224. Only for the German army.

225. Nurse.

226. Right turn!

227. Ancient city in Campania, in the south of Italy.

228. "Father," a Russian term of respect and affection used for Orthodox priests and formerly also for the czar.

229. Ignacy Rzecki, character in *The Doll* (1890), a novel by Bolesław Prus (Alek-

sander Głowacki, 1847–1912). On the one hand, Rzecki is an old-fashioned type, private and humble, loyal in his personal relationships, and dedicated to his modest work. On the other hand, he has an adventurous past (he fought for Hungarian independence in 1848), cultivates the myth of Napoleon as the harbinger of liberty and democracy, and carries in his heart the Romantic ideals of freedom and love.

230. Léon Gambetta (1838–1882), French statesman, briefly headed the Third Republic at its inception in 1871.

231. Louis-Philippe (1773–1850), king of France (1830–1848); his name was attached to a certain style, particularly of furniture.

232. Georgina Elisabeth Ward, Countess of Dudley (1846–1929), a noted beauty. *La Duchesse de Langeais*, 1834 Balzac novel.

233. As a safety precaution.

234. You have to be clever.

235. Dom Plastyków, seat of the Union of Polish Artists in Cracow.

236. Go on, my friend, time to get off . . .

237. Ah, would you believe it! . . . What a bastard . . .

238. Nasty weather.

239. How are you? Fine, thanks, OK. You interested? No, my sweet, no thanks.

240. One must earn one's modest living, and that's all.

241. Steady customers.

242. "Boże coś Polskę" (God save Poland), Catholic hymn dating from 1816 that competed with "Jeszcze Polska" (Dabrowski's Mazurka) for the national anthem after 1918. "Rota" (The Oath), text 1908 by Maria Konopnicka (1842–1910), music 1910 by Feliks Nowowiejski (1877–1946).

243. Women who supposedly sat beside the guillotine, knitting, as the executions took place.

244. Someone who cuts ahead in line.

245. We know all about these pregnant women . . .

246. Olida was a brand of inexpensive pâté, used in French army rations during World War I.

247. No point waiting.

248. Jersey is a British crown dependency off the coast of Normandy. Its residents were evacuated under German occupation, July 1, 1940–May 9, 1945, and the island was supplied from France until the D-Day landing in 1944 interfered with shipments.

1941

1. Radio Londres, the Free French radio transmitted in French via the BBC.

2. You see, madam is Polish. We'll get them, isn't that right, madam?

3. Adam Asnyk (1838–1897), Polish Positivist poet. *"Trzeba z żywymi naprzód iść, / Po życie sięgać nowe, / A nie w uwiędłych laurów liść / Z uporem stroić głowę."* "Daremne żale" (Vain regrets, 1877).

4. Piłsudski: see Introduction, note 2, above. Roman Dmowski (1864–1939), Polish

national leader. Ignacy Daszyński (1866–1936), prime minister of the Second Polish Republic.

5. Maurois: see 1940, note 49, above. His successful first novel, *Les Silences du colonel Bramble* (1918), concerned World War I.

6. Axel Munthe (1857–1949), Swedish physician and psychiatrist who served in the British ambulance corps during World War I. He published *Red Cross, Iron Cross* anonymously in 1916 and in his own name in 1930.

7. Popular term for the red wine issued to French soldiers in World War I.

8. No, sir, besides it's already rationed: one wife for a lifetime.

9. Heinrich Schliemann (1822–1890), German archaeologist, pioneer in excavations of the classical world.

10. Sacha Guitry (Alexandre-Pierre Georges Guitry, 1885–1957), born in Saint Petersburg of French actor parents, was a leading "boulevard" actor and playwright who also made and appeared in films. During the German occupation, he continued to work in the theater and in film, leading to charges of collaboration after the war, of which he was ultimately cleared. *Vive l'Empereur! ou le Soir d'Austerlitz* was first performed at the Théâtre de la Madeleine in 1941.

11. The weather is nevertheless good.

12. A certain type of fencing, particularly popular in Germany, used the saber (*Schlager*).

13. Słowacki: see 1940, note 61, above.

14. Andrzej Tomasz Towiański (1799–1878), messianic metaphysical Polish philosopher; he stands for a mixture of sound political aspirations (including Polish independence) and some beautiful but vague ideals (liberty, democracy, tolerance, including recognition of the Jews as the Christians' "older brothers"), all saturated with mystical obsessions. The "Wild Steppes" refers to the Zaporozhian Cossacks, who rebelled against the Polish kings in 1648 and are mentioned in Sienkiewicz. In Russian and Ukrainian, "Wild Field" (*Dikoe pole*) refers to the sparsely populated steppe between the Black and Azov Seas.

15. Madam, I eat only lobster with mayonnaise.

16. Sébastien-Roch Nicolas, known as Chamfort (1741–1794), French writer known for witty epigrams and aphorisms. Critical of the Jacobins, he committed suicide to avoid prison.

17. Emile Hácha (1872–1945), president of Czechoslovakia in March 1939 and under Nazi occupation. He agreed to cooperate with the Germans when threatened that the country would otherwise be destroyed, but he may also have aided the resistance; in the end he is described as having become a Nazi puppet.

18. "Kupą Mości Panowie" — "Kupą tu, waszmościowie, kupą!": from Sienkiewicz, *The Deluge*. A popular phrase used in reference to attacks and defense.

19. At the same time . . . They are even.

20. *Indiana* (1832), George Sand's first novel.

21. Alexandre Dumas, *fils* (1824–1895), *La Dame aux camélias* (1848). Balzac, *La*

Cousine Bette (1846). Alexandre Dumas, *père* (1802–1870), *Les Trois Mousquetaires* (1844). Théophile Gautier (1811–1872), *Mademoiselle de Maupin* (1835). Madame de Sévigné (1626–1696). Mademoiselle de Lespinasse (1732–1776), *salonnière* who published her *Letters* in 1809.

22. Octave Aubry (1881–1946), French author of a series of historical novels featuring Napoleon I and Napoleon III.

23. The oil painting *L'Indifférent* (1717) by French painter Antoine Watteau (1684–1721).

24. The Syria-Lebanon campaign was the Allied invasion of Vichy French–controlled Syria and Lebanon in June–July 1941.

25. Karl Czerny (1791–1857), Austrian composer who wrote sonatas used as exercises by piano students.

26. An armchair *whose* armrests ended in bronze sphinx heads *whose* paint was flaking off . . .

27. Joseph Conrad (1857–1924), *The Shadow Line* (1917).

28. Wood was used for shoe soles during the occupation, when leather was scarce.

29. Tanagra figurines, dating from fourth century BCE, known as Tanagras from the site in Boeotia (Greece) where great numbers were found.

30. Lost.

31. The Sikorski-Maisky Treaty, which annulled the Soviet-Nazi partition of Poland of September 1939, was signed in London on July 30, 1941, by Polish prime minister General Władysław Sikorski (1881–1943) and Soviet ambassador to Britain Ivan Maisky (1884–1975). Under its provisions, the Soviets agreed to the formation of a Polish army on Soviet territory under supreme Soviet command. All Polish citizens imprisoned in the Soviet Union, including POWs, were granted "amnesty." Sikorski was killed on July 4, 1943, when his plane crashed into the sea near Gibraltar.

32. What were they guilty of?

33. Paul Gavarni (Sulpice Guillaume Chevalier, 1804–1866), French caricaturist and illustrator. Honoré Daumier (1808–1879), French artist known for political satire.

34. One mustn't try to understand.

35. Władysław Anders (1892–1970), general in the Polish army who fought in the Polish-Soviet War (see 1940, note 1, above). He took part in the Battle of Mława after the German invasion of Poland in 1939 but was captured by Soviet forces near Lwów on September 29, 1939, and imprisoned in Moscow. Released after the Sikorski-Maisky Treaty, Anders was charged with forming a Polish army to be composed of Polish refugees and deportees in the Soviet Union, to fight alongside the Red Army. The contingent that became known as the "Anders Army" managed in March 1942 to secure its transfer from Soviet territory to Iran, Iraq, and finally Palestine. As the Polish Second Corps it distinguished itself during the Italian campaign at Monte Cassino in May 1944. After the war Anders became inspector general of the Polish forces in exile. He is buried at Monte Cassino.

36. Crusade against Bolshevism . . . Crusade against the Boche (slang for Germans).

37. Marshal Semyon Budenny (1883–1973) led the famous Red Cavalry during the Russian Civil War. The Battle of Kiev (July–September 1941), in which he played a role, was a major defeat for the Red Army.

38. Mineral water labels from Vichy say (or said): *"autorisation de l'état."* Some labels were marked *"Vichy-État."*

39. La Légion des volontaires français contre le Bolchevisme was created after the Nazi invasion of the Soviet Union on the initiative of Jacques Doriot (1898–1945) and other collaborators. France had not declared war on the Soviet Union and the legion did not have official Vichy government endorsement, though Pétain wished it good luck. The volunteers ended up serving in the German army.

40. "I will redouble the activity of the police." Pétain's address to the French people delivered at Vichy, on August 12, 1941: *"un vent mauvais. L'inquiétude gagne les esprits, le doute s'empare des âmes."* Admiral François Darlan (1881–1942), commander of the French navy at the start of the war, continued as minister of the navy under Pétain and in February 1941 became prime minister. In April 1942 he was forced to resign by Pierre Laval (1883–1945), who became head of government. He traveled to Algeria the day before the Allied invasion on November 8, 1942, and made a deal with the Allies to fight on their side, which outraged de Gaulle. Darlan helped save the remaining French fleet from being captured by the Germans. On December 2, 1942, he was assassinated by an anti-Vichy monarchist who was then executed.

41. It's not at all interesting, war.

42. Members of Sikorski's cabinet: August Zaleski (1883–1972), minister of foreign affairs; Marian Seyda (1879–1967), minister preparing the peace conference; and Kazimierz Sosnkowski (1885–1969), minister without portfolio and liaison with Polish resistance. The three ministers resigned in protest over the Sikorski-Maisky Treaty.

43. Szymon Konarski, also Szymon Jaxa-Konarski (1894–1981), director of the Polish bank in Paris, ran a Polish bookstore and published his memoirs: *Cztery lata w okupowanym Paryżu* (1963). Roman Mirosław Rosinkiewicz (1895–1943), Polish aeronautical engineer who in September 1939 helped evacuate technical personnel to Romania; he then himself made it to France, where he remained until his death.

44. Cécile Sorel (1873–1966), French stage actress in *Madame Capet (Marie-Antoinette, reine de France)*, by Marcelle Maurette (1903–1972), Théâtre du Gymnase, June 1941.

45. Richard Strauss (1864–1949), *Salome*, a modernist opera based on the Oscar Wilde play, was first performed in 1905. The opera contains the Dance of the Seven Veils, by means of which Salome gets King Herod to agree to have John the Baptist beheaded.

46. Drunk as a Pole.

47. Maria Karolina Zofia Felicja Leszczyńska, or Marie Leszczyńska (1703–1768), queen consort of France. Called Queen Marie of France, she was the daughter of King Stanisław I of Poland, was married to Louis XV, and was the grandmother of Louis XVI.

48. General Carl-Heinrich von Stülpnagel (1886–1944) commanded the Seventeenth Army in the invasion of the Soviet Union and participated in the murders of Jews and partisans. In February 1942 he became commander of German-occupied France. At the same time, he conspired with other officers involved in the plot to assassinate Hitler. After the failed attempt of July 20, 1944, Stülpnagel tried unsuccessfully to kill himself; he was executed on August 30, 1944.

49. Rzecki: see 1940, note 229, above.

50. Sienkiewicz, *Trilogy*: see 1940, note 24, above.

51. German expression for factotum, a servant who does everything needed, a "Girl Friday."

52. Stanisław Wokulski, the main character in Bolesław Prus's novel *The Doll* (see 1940, note 229, above), begins as a revolutionary, fighting for Polish independence from Russia in 1863, but ends as a wealthy businessman. His love for a vain, aristocratic woman does him in, though not before he visits Paris, where he contemplates investing his fortune for the good of humanity.

53. *Trois Valses* (1938), the French musical film adaptation by German director Ludwig Berger (Ludwig Bamberger, 1892–1969) of the operetta by Oscar Straus (1870–1954), is a love story spanning three generations, with a happy ending. Yvonne Printemps (1894–1977), French singer and actress. Pierre Fresnay (1897–1975), French stage and film actor.

54. "Pieśń strzelców," from *Pieśni zbudzonych* (1863), by Władysław Ludwik Anczyc (1823–1883), composed in connection with the 1863 Polish insurrection against Russian rule.

55. The inscription reads: "*À la voix du vainqueur d'Austerlitz / L'empire d'Allemagne tombe*" (At the voice of the victor of Austerlitz / The German empire falls).

56. *Mireille* (1864), opera by French composer Charles Gounod (1818–1893).

57. "The Needle," mentioned in entry for January 3, 1941.

58. Józef Beck (1894–1944), Polish statesman, diplomat, and Piłsudski supporter who evacuated with the Polish government in 1939 to Romania (where he died of tuberculosis). In 1941 his whereabouts were unknown, and it was rumored that he had reached the United States.

59. Saint Philip, whom one fools.

60. Colonel Wojciech Fyda (1894–1944), fought in the Polish-Soviet War; was military attaché at the Polish embassy in Paris from April 1936 to November 1939. Arrested eventually by the Germans, in April 1944 he was deported to Mauthausen, where he died on May 7, 1944.

61. Balzac, *César Birotteau* (1837), novel about a successful Parisian cosmetics entrepreneur who goes bankrupt as a result of property speculation. In the end he pays off his debts, then dies suddenly, his honor restored.

62. "*Blut und Boden*" (blood and soil), the Nazi slogan; the *Winterhilfswerke* (winter relief work) was an annual Nazi fund drive to support the indigent. The French version was *Secours d'hiver*.

63. But you know I will give you everything you want. Give me bread and that will do. You are all the same a bit of a skunk.

64. You can take that as yet another sign of French decadence.

65. Hôtel Astoria, a Belle Époque luxury hotel used as German headquarters during the occupation.

66. *Rassenschande*, race defilement, sexual relations between so-called Aryan and non-Aryan persons, a Nazi crime. Maupassant, *Bel Ami* (1885), novel about a young man sleeping his way to a career. The Austrian Willi Forst (1903–1980) starred in and directed this film, which appeared in Germany in 1938–1939.

67. The field commander of Nantes, Lieutenant Colonel Karl Hotz (1877–1941), was assassinated by the Resistance on October 20, 1941. On October 22, 1941, forty-eight hostages were shot in reprisal, five in Paris.

68. They have no style, don't have the touch . . .

69. It's a game!

70. Jacques Pierre Bainville (1879–1936), French historian and journalist, Action française supporter. *Napoléon* (1931) was a popular history best seller.

71. Book 11 of *Pan Tadeusz* is called "The Year 1812." The first line is: "*O roku ów! kto ciebie widział w naszym kraju!*" (O memorable year! Happy is he who saw you in our land!)

72. *Good Soldier Schweik* (Švejk, 1921–1923), antiwar novel by Czech writer Jaroslav Hašek (1883–1923) about a soldier in World War I, naive and honest, who bumbles his way through the war.

73. A veritable battle of annihilation.

74. German-language daily published from January 1941 to August 1944.

75. If it pleases the English gentlemen to launch an offensive, whether in Norway or on our German coast, in Holland, in Belgium, or in France, we can only tell them: Go ahead, you will retreat more quickly than you have come!

76. If I were to summarize the overall success of this campaign to date, then the number of prisoners of war has now reached about 3.6 million, that is, 3,600,000 prisoners, and I will not allow any English blockhead to come along and say that this is unproven. If a German military office has counted something, then it's correct! (thunderous applause).

77. I hope that we will soon be able to implement a few more measures by which we will bit by bit slowly but surely strangle them.

78. I hope, be able, slowly but surely.

79. So I can only say to Mr. Roosevelt: I do not need experts for expertise. My head alone is enough for me. I need no brain trust to support me. If any change should happen, it develops first in my brain and not in anyone else's, certainly not in the brains of experts. Neither am I a Gymnasium student [. . .] who draws maps in a school atlas.

80. If now the American president Roosevelt, who was already responsible for Poland's entry into the war, which we can today definitively prove to him . . .

81. Georges Scapini (1895–1976), French lawyer and politician who headed the

Vichy diplomatic service in charge of French prisoners of war in Germany. He was tried and acquitted of collaboration in 1952.

82. Have you tried to get London on 1,500? Yes. It works great . . .

83. Pierre Blanchar (1892–1963), French actor. The film in question is *Le Jouer d'échecs* (*The Chess Player*, 1927). It contains a scene in which the Polish anthem of independence, "Boże coś Polskę," is sung. The title of Fyodor Dostoyevsky's 1866 novel *Igrok* (in English, *The Gambler*) is closer to the Polish title: *Gracz* (*The Player*), but the film is based not on Dostoyevsky but on the novel *Le Jouer d'échecs* (1926) by Henry Dupuy-Mazuel (1885–1962).

84. Small town in central Poland, in 1941 under German occupation.

85. Piasecki was a famous Cracow chocolate manufacturer.

86. Abbé Nicolas Charles Joseph Trublet (1697–1770) wrote on moral questions and in particular criticized Voltaire.

87. Joseph Conrad, *Lord Jim* (1900), concerns a man guilty of having committed an act of cowardice.

88. Joseph (1740–1799) and Étienne (1745–1790) Montgolfier, French industrialists and inventors.

89. DKW ("Dampfkraftwagen"), German motorcycle and automobile concern. During the war it produced military equipment. Also referred to as DKW-Grün, Kriegswerkstätte (War Production).

90. Marshal Semyon Timoshenko (1895–1970), Soviet commissar of defense (May 7, 1940–July 19, 1941), replaced by Stalin; in November–December 1941, he was in charge of the Rostov area.

91. Cakes, chocolate, candy, champagne (in German).

92. They've had it!

93. *Les États-Unis d'aujourd'hui* (1927) by André Siegfried (1875–1959), French geographer and political writer.

94. District.

95. The French birthrate will rise.

96. The Battle of Mers-el-Kébir (July 3, 1940) involved a British naval attack on the French navy on the coast of French Algeria.

97. Dmitry Merezhkovsky (1865–1941) in fact died on December 9, 1941. He was a literary critic, novelist, and leading figure in the Symbolist movement and in the early twentieth-century Russian Orthodox lay revival. Merezhkovsky left Soviet Russia in December 1919, headed first for Poland, continuing on to France in March 1921. Merezhkovsky denounced the Soviet regime as the "Kingdom of the Antichrist." The title AB refers to was in fact a historical novel: *Voskresshie bogi* (*Resurrection of the Gods: Leonardo da Vinci*, 1901). While in Warsaw, Merezhkovsky had connections to Piłsudski, with whom AB's family was also linked.

98. Towiański: see note 14, above.

99. Sienkiewicz's novel *Bez dogmatu* (1891) presented a "portrait of a generation," privileged and talented but lacking commitment and clear direction.

100. He thinks, he thinks, he gets a beating, and he keeps thinking.

101. Announcement.

102. Don't you find that just a little bit—strange?

103. The German worker invites you. Go work in Germany.

104. Idiot, imbecile, nitwit . . .

105. Sienkiewicz's novel *Rodzina Połanieckich* (1894), like *Bez dogmatu* a moral-psychological portrait, was criticized by the literary critics but loved by readers.

106. *Marie Stuart* by Marcelle Maurette.

107. Kazimierz Krukowski (b. Zawisza, stage name Lopek, 1901–1984), wildly popular Jewish Polish cabaret performer, film actor, and writer.

108. Field Marshal Walther von Brauchitsch (1881–1948), commander in chief of the German army, 1938–1941, was dismissed on December 19, 1941, after the failed Moscow campaign. He was arrested after the war but died of a heart attack before his trial.

109. You would like, Sir? I would like an azalea.

110. Only temporarily, you understand, the events.

111. The case is examined in the archives.

112. Orchestra seat.

113. Not bad, your story.

114. Saint Joseph, the patron saint of cuckolds.

115. Excerpt from Balzac, *Le Curé de village* (*The Village Priest*, 1839).

116. Excerpt from Balzac, *Mémoires de deux jeunes mariées* (*Letters of Two Brides*, 1842).

1942

1. Sienkiewicz, *In Desert and Wilderness:* see 1940, note 43, above.

2. Jan Ksawery Koźmiński (1892–1940), Polish painter and illustrator. He was arrested by the Nazis in October 1939 and shot in 1940.

3. Wanda, a beautiful young princess from Cracow, refused a marriage proposal from the German knight Rydygier, who threatened to destroy Cracow if she did not agree. To avoid the destruction of her city, she threw herself into the Vistula River.

4. They are bigger Huns than Pétain.

5. Sienkiewicz, *Krzyżacy* (1900), translated in English as *Knights of the Cross*.

6. You know, this is very good, it's anti-Hun . . . *oh là là*, take it.

7. It's hard for them.

8. Good day, Madam Duval, how are things? / Good day, Madam Lepont, fine, thanks, and you? / Yes, thanks, just fine. Ah! What nasty weather . . . / Yes, it's cold today . . . the fog . . . / And your husband, is he feeling better? / Yes, his leg is still a bit swollen, but what can you do . . . With this kind of weather . . .

9. Good day, Mr. Paul, how are things? / Thank you, Madam, and yourself? / Yes, things are calming down. Tough work all the same, with those boxes . . .

10. World famous.

11. To do everything humanly possible . . . with people who are, after all, nobodies.

12. Cato the Elder (234–149 BCE), Roman statesman and historian. "I consider that Carthage must be destroyed."

13. Lucien de Rubempré is the hero of Balzac's *Illusions perdues* (*Lost Illusions*, 1837–1843). He also appears in *Splendeurs et misères des courtisanes* (*Splendors and Miseries of a Courtesan's Life*, 1838–1847).

14. Where you can get a decent inexpensive meal.

15. Don't be shy, Sir, play, play.

16. Former prison in Paris, from which victims were taken to the guillotine.

17. Say, pal, move a bit to the right, we can't get through.

18. Poor girl.

19. She went up to the kitchen for, for . . .

20. Yes, she went up to the first floor to recover from the emotions of the ground floor—spiritually. Play on words: *monter* / *se remonter*.

21. And instead of getting some cold water, she got a coat, two dresses, sheets, and a few silver spoons as souvenirs . . .

22. No, no, nevertheless, it's shameful—shit—a gang of scoundrels.

23. Camille Desmoulins (1760–1794), revolutionary executed by the guillotine. A bronze statue in his honor in the garden of the Palais-Royal was destroyed in 1942.

24. Fresh, peaceful landscapes, tender green prairies, melancholy streams, clumps of alder and ash, a gentle, pastoral natural scene. George Sand, *Valentine* (1832).

25. Local army command.

26. "Be what you will, but above all know what you want to be." Albert Leo Schlageter (1894–1923), Freikorps member arrested and executed after the war for sabotaging French forces occupying the Ruhr.

27. On schedule.

28. They're clearing out, we'll be free.

29. Pétain's speech of January 1, 1942, published on January 4, 1942.

30. A European power, France recognizes her responsibilities towards Europe. A civilizing power, she has retained, despite her defeat, a privileged spiritual position in the world.

31. [The unusual situation] will suggest to Germany, we hope, an attenuation of the conditions she has imposed on us after her victory. The sincere rapprochement between the two nations, desired by the Governments and by the peoples, will follow from this. Our dignity will be restored; our economy will be relieved.

32. But the conduct of a French policy inspired by French interests alone demands the tightening of French unity. For our spiritual unity is in danger.

33. In the partial exile forced upon me, in the partial liberty I am allowed, I try to fulfill my duties.

34. Wise guy, con man.

35. He's not a woman and when women do this they're not satisfied with one year.

36. This fellow is one of yours.

37. Characters in Balzac's *Comédie humaine*: Vautrin, a disguised criminal, takes

Lucien under his wing, tries to save him when he is imprisoned, but Lucien commits suicide in his cell. Vautrin escapes all attempts to trap or stop him.

38. Would not have corrected the truth.

39. The guard.

40. You don't need to . . . !

41. Ramrod straight and self-important.

42. And I thank the Préfecture for it.

43. Yes, yes, because . . . you understand.

44. Fine.

45. Why isn't he working?

46. The poor young man has TB.

47. And what are you? Why have you come with him?

48. I work in Paris. He is my friend. He's young, he's stupid—he needs help. He speaks no German . . .

49. Oh, well, OK.

50. Well, let's get out of here . . . / You never know, you know . . . / The citizen's dignity.

51. Come at two o'clock.

52. G. Lenotre, *Paris révolutionnaire: Vieux papiers, vieilles maisons* (*Revolutionary Paris: Old Papers, Old Houses*, 6 vols., 1900–1929), reprinted many times. G. Lenotre was the penname of Louis Léon Théodore Gosselin (1855–1935), French historian and playwright.

53. Wheelchair. Georges Couthon (1755–1794), close to Robespierre in the Jacobin faction, along with whom he was guillotined on July 27, 1794.

54. Louis Antoine Léon de Saint-Just (1767–1794), fervent advocate of the Terror, guillotined on July 28, 1794. Jean Charles Pichegru (1761–1804), general of the French revolutionary wars who later turned against Bonaparte and sided with the royalist opposition. He attempted to overthrow Bonaparte's regime but was arrested. Found strangled in prison, he was rumored to have been murdered.

55. Oh, that . . . and what country are you from? English or Italian? / Half one, half the other.

56. Marie-Joseph Paul Yves Roch Gilbert du Motier, Marquis de Lafayette (1757–1834). The first in line of the ruling House of Capet was Hugh Capet (941–966).

57. Literally "hall of lost footsteps," a large hall or vestibule leading into offices and rooms in an administrative building.

58. As a result of the partitions, Warsaw had come under Russian imperial rule, unlike Cracow, which had been Austrian.

59. At the general information bureau.

60. Then I cannot.

61. Anthony Eden (1897–1977), British foreign secretary at the time.

62. Florence L. Barclay (1862–1921), English romance novelist. *The Rosary* (1909) was her most famous novel.

63. Robert Taylor (1911–1969), Hollywood leading man.

64. I'm listening.

65. Excellent worker, always perfect, meticulous, careful.

66. I don't know. On this January 30 I can say only one thing for certain: how this year will turn out, I do not know. Whether the war will end, I do not know.

67. Lord, give us the power to preserve our freedom, for our German people, our children and grandchildren, and not only for our German people, but also for the other peoples of Europe. For this is a war for all of Europe and therefore for all mankind.

68. A small nest egg, a small fortune.

69. A bill is still something.

70. Where does so much money come from? Ernst Wagemann (1884–1956), prominent German economist.

71. The Phoney War, name given to the period September 1939–April 1940.

72. Social security.

73. Richard Lewinsohn (1894–1968), *Histoire de la crise, 1929–1934* (1934). Lewinsohn was the economic writer for the left-leaning German newspaper *Die Weltbühne*.

74. Józef Papkin is a character in the comedy *Zemsta* (*Revenge*, 1834) by Polish writer Aleksander Fredro (1793–1876). He boasts about his courage but is in fact a coward.

75. Ah, so, the Americans. You'll see.

76. The Battle of Eylau (1807) pitted France against Prussia and Russia during the Napoleonic Wars. It was a great massacre in which the French seemed victorious but had no clear victory. Cambronne: see 1940, note 222, above.

77. It's for my wife. / Since when are seats in the metro reserved?

78. Let him be, he's a boor. / Boor . . . look at this boor!

79. Adolphe Borchard (1882–1967), French pianist and composer who wrote for films in the 1930s.

80. The tragedies *Phèdre* (1677) and *Iphigénie* (1674) by Jean Racine (1639–1699).

81. Very annoying. A pain in the ass.

82. Boors get out.

83. Władysław Reymont (1867–1925), Polish novelist, winner of the 1925 Nobel Prize in literature, whose best-known work was the four-volume *Chłopi* (*The Peasants*, 1904–1909).

84. For God's sake.

85. The French brothers Edmond (see 1940, note 100, above) and Jules de Goncourt (1830–1870) published the *Journal des Goncourt: Mémoires de la vie littéraire* (Paris, 1887–1898). Here they describe Voltaire's *Candide, ou l'optimisme* (1759) as "*du La Fontaine prosé et du Rabelais écouillé.*" Jean de La Fontaine (1621–1695), author of fables in verse. François Rabelais (c. 1483/94?–1553), French Renaissance author of the bawdy work *La Vie de Gargantua et de Pantagruel* (1532–1564).

86. "The Golden Liberty of the Polish Nobility" refers to the political system of the Polish-Lithuanian Commonwealth, in which the nobility controlled the parliament.

87. From the late seventeenth century to the mid-eighteenth century the Saxon kings Augustus II and Augustus III ruled Poland.

88. Kraft durch Freude, Nazi leisure organization and slogan.

89. Character in Rabelais, *La Vie de Gargantua et de Pantagruel.*

90. German battleships.

91. Quasimodo is the main character in Victor Hugo (1802–1885), *Notre-Dame de Paris (The Hunchback of Notre-Dame*, 1831), set in medieval Paris. Hermann Hesse, *Narziß und Goldmund.*

92. French actress Annabella (Suzanne Georgette Charpentier, 1907–1996) was involved romantically with Hollywood actor Tyrone Power (1914–1958) while she was still married to another man; their subsequent marriage in 1939 caused trouble for her movie career.

93. In the Riom Trial (February 19, 1942–May 21, 1943), Pétain's government tried to blame the 1940 defeat on leaders of the Third Republic. Among those tried were former prime ministers Léon Blum (see 1940, note 157, above), Édouard Daladier (1884–1970), and Paul Reynaud (see 1940, note 2, above), as well as Maurice Gamelin (see 1940, note 1, above). Riom is a city in central France.

94. As much gas as you like.

95. Nazi propaganda portrayed Communism as a conspiracy of Jews and Freemasons, hence the joke about England, the Soviet Union's ally.

96. Bristol Blenheim, British light bomber.

97. Louis de Broglie (1892–1987), French physicist and mathematician who won the Nobel Prize in physics in 1929 for his research on neutrons and the development of a new field of "wave mechanics."

98. To allow everyone to demonstrate their solidarity and express their disdain.

99. France is wounded. Anglo-Saxon barbarism. The French people and the French worker in mourning.

100. Residential neighborhoods.

101. And they should leave us the hell alone.

102. Now it's real love.

103. Shit . . . That makes 90 francs altogether with the room.

104. Lucie, change the room, give him number 43.

105. Love is made here.

106. If they let them get away with it at Riom.

107. Podfilipski, character from a novel by Józef Weyssenhoff (see 1940, note 145, above).

108. "People were asking me why they were fighting. Well, I had trouble answering them." General Antoine-Marie-Benoît Besson (1876–1969) surrendered to the Germans in June 1940.

109. Józef Maria Hoene-Wroński (1776–1853), Polish messianic philosopher, mathematician, and physicist.

110. Zofia Nałkowska (1884–1954), Polish writer and member of the Polish Academy of Literature between the wars, known for controversial topics and feminism.

111. Balzac, *Le Cousin Pons* (1847), novel in which the musician Sylvain Pons has a passion for collecting art but is cheated out of his collection by avaricious people who take advantage of him.

112. François Pinet (1817–1897) launched a fashion shoe wear company in 1855.

113. Tsarskoye Selo was the czar's country seat, outside of Saint Petersburg.

114. No, no thanks, it's really too much, oh well, I'll take one, to make you happy.

115. Gavarni: see 1941, note 33, above.

116. Basically I owe you a dinner . . . I missed by a year.

117. It doesn't really tempt me.

118. So I'll go to Poland.

119. Balzac, *Le Lys de la vallée* (*Lily of the Valley*, 1835), novel in *La Comédie humaine*.

120. Stakhanovites were Soviet workers rewarded for exceeding their norms. *Der schaffende Mensch* (*Homo faber*, man the creator), concept employed by Max Scheler (1874–1928), influential German philosopher, Catholic convert, practitioner of philosophical anthropology.

121. Jean Baptiste Antoine Marcellin de Marbot (1782–1854), First Empire general. His *Mémoires du Général Baron de Marbot* (1891) describe the Napoleonic era.

122. François-René, Vicomte de Chateaubriand (1768–1848), French writer, politician, diplomat, and historian known for his autobiography, *Mémoires d'outre-tombe* (1849).

123. Józef Wittlin (1896–1976), Polish novelist, poet, and translator, best known for the novel *Sól ziemi* (*Salt of the Earth*, 1935). François Mauriac (1885–1970), novelist, journalist, and winner of the 1952 Nobel Prize in literature.

124. "The courage, devotion, self-denial, patriotism of Paris have been much acclaimed . . . One single word suffices: Paris does without butter." Gautier (see 1941, note 21, above), *Tableaux de siège: Paris, 1870–71* (1871).

125. You're used to it.

126. The Yellow Peril. Kaiser Wilhelm II (1859–1941), reigned 1888–November 9, 1918, when the monarchy was abolished.

127. Emperor Franz Joseph I of Austria (1830–1916), reigned 1848–1916.

128. *Mam'zelle Bonaparte*, a film by Maurice Tourneur (1876–1961) released January 1942, is a historical drama set during the reign of Louis-Napoleon Bonaparte.

129. *La Fille du puisatier* (*The Well-Digger's Daughter*, 1940). Raimu, stage name for French actor Jules Auguste Muraire (1883–1946), best known for playing César in Pagnol's *Marseille Trilogy* (see 1940, note 30, above).

130. *L'Assassinat du père Noël* (*Who Killed Santa Claus?*, 1941), French drama directed by Christian-Jaque (1904–1994).

131. *Le Jouer d'échecs*: see 1941, note 83, above.

132. *Nuit de décembre* (*Night in December*, 1940), directed by Kurt Bernhardt (1899–1981), in which the main character is a pianist. Forced to flee Germany in 1933

because he was Jewish, Bernhardt later worked in Hollywood under the name Curtis Bernhardt.

133. Edwige Feuillère (Edwige Caroline Cunati, 1907–1998), leading French actress of film and stage. *La Dame aux camélias*, adapted in 1852 by Alexandre Dumas, *fils*, from his novel. The film *La Duchesse de Langeais* (1942), directed by Jacques de Baroncelli (1881–1951), based on Balzac's novel.

134. Is France on trial or is it a French trial?

135. Literally "a herd not an army"—in French there's a pun. In English, perhaps: a farce and not a force.

136. The famous Saint-Nazaire Raid or Operation Chariot. On March 28, 1942, the British made a daring amphibious attack on the dry dock at Saint-Nazaire, a port in Normandy. Although there were many German casualties, many British were captured and killed, and military historians now consider it a mistake. In the Zeebrugge Raid of April 23, 1918, the Royal Navy attacked the German inland naval base at Bruges; the assault was only a partial success.

137. Impregnable.

138. Automobile and truck manufacturing plant, planned by Ford France in 1937, that opened in 1940 shortly before the German invasion. The cars were called Matfords. The plant was requisitioned by the Germans.

139. You're hurting me.

140. Gnome et Rhône, major French aircraft engine manufacturer. They also made bicycles; see entry for March 9, 1943. Goodrich made tires and other rubber products.

141. Jacqueline Delubac (1907–1997), third wife of Sacha Guitry.

142. *Bouvard et Pécuchet*, unfinished satire by Flaubert, published posthumously in 1881, which concerns the adventures of two Parisian copy clerks.

143. Frobenius (see 1940, note 176, above), known for the concept of culture as a living organism (*die Kulturen als lebendige Organismen*).

144. Jacques Doriot: see 1941, note 39, above. Marcel Déat (1894–1955), journalist, former socialist, and collaborator during the occupation. Laval (see 1941, note 40, above) became prime minister on April 18, 1942. He was executed in 1945 as a traitor.

145. Jacques Benoist-Méchin (1901–1983), *L'Histoire de l'armée allemande* (*History of the German Army*, 1936–1938). Benoist-Méchin was a right-wing politician and Vichy collaborator.

146. Alfred Falter (1881–1954), Silesian industrialist, engineer, and economist.

147. We'll be like Poland.

148. And everything's all very well arranged.

149. Luckily, because, imagine . . . we're suffering enough already and moreover . . . only imagine what that would have been . . .

150. Local tax on goods brought into the city.

151. Allusion to a line from Julian Tuwim's satirical ballad *"Piotr Płaksin"*: *"gdzieś w mordobijskim powiecie."* For Tuwim, see 1940, note 44, above.

152. Keep up the conversation.

153. Chouans, peasant rebels in western France who rose against the republican government in 1793.

154. We were too happy.

155. A small but nice society.

156. Field Marshal Gerd von Rundstedt (1875–1953) participated in the invasion of France and the Russian campaign, was dismissed in December 1941, and was recalled in 1942 as commander in chief in the west.

157. For German cars only.

158. Field Marshal Wilhelm Keitel (1882–1946), Hitler's senior military adviser, was tried and sentenced to death at Nuremberg.

159. Everything's for the best in this best of worlds—Voltaire, *Candide*.

160. General de Marbot: see note 121, above.

161. André Masséna (1758–1817), one of Napoleon's marshals.

162. You are my countryman, then. I'm also from Wiener-Neustadt and the young fellow is from Baden.

163. Well, well—you should be happy . . .

164. Yes—it's simply shameful.

165. Look at this . . .

166. And to think how much it costs, this crazy game-playing . . . and what's the purpose, why . . . because the so-called Führer was an idiot from the get-go . . .

167. Dance halls.

168. Timoshenko: see 1941, note 90, above.

169. Probably *Der Ring des Polykrates*, a ballad by Friedrich Schiller (1759–1805), about the tyrant of Samos, who boasts about his victories, thus causing his luck to fail.

170. What do you want?—that's life. When it's going well, enjoy it—and that's all there is.

171. Jacques Bainville (see 1941, note 70, above), *Histoire de deux peuples: La France et l'Empire allemand* (*The History of Two Peoples: France and the German Empire*, 1915).

172. Richard Walther Darré (1895–1953), Reichsminister of food and agriculture, 1933–1942.

173. Genuine 4711 eau de cologne.

174. "Soviet Aims in Europe" . . . the Soviets would like to occupy Trondheim, Bergen, and Norwich with their hinterland.

175. Leader, army, air force, permit, headquarters, military commander.

176. The decree, dated June 1, 1942, went into effect on June 7, 1942.

177. Reinhard Heydrich (1904–June 4, 1942), Reichsprotektor of Bohemia and Moravia, murdered by Czech partisans.

178. Precisely, on the coast.

179. Those English—they should leave us the hell alone—at least in vacation season.

180. General Erwin Rommel (1891–1944), gifted commander and national hero, later opposed Hitler, who forced him to commit suicide.

632   Notes to Pages 322–332

181. Workshop for the unemployed.

182. Foreign workforce.

183. And above all do not send your men to work in Germany.

184. Yes, yes—you're doing a great job, my friend.

185. But there are many of us like that—have courage—we'll get them.

186. On June 21, 1942, Rommel took Tobruk (a Libyan port near the Egyptian border) from the English, who had captured it in January 1941. The Allies regained Tobruk in November 1942.

187. Military commander.

188. Mikhail Zoshchenko (1895–1968), inspired Soviet-era comic writer who mocked the foibles of Communist society and got into trouble for it, but survived.

189. Mr. and Mrs. are not at home.

190. Hurry up, miss.

191. Zero percent butterfat.

192. That dirty guy from the Auvergne.

193. Inferiority complex.

194. About France.

195. German culture is naturally the greatest.

196. Daddy's boys.

197. After the vacation.

198. What heat.

199. *Le Lit à colonnes* (*The Four-Poster Bed*, 1942), directed by Roland Tual (1902–1956).

200. AB refers to the roundup of July 16–17, 1942, in which 13,500 Jews were first confined to the Vélodrome d'hiver, a skating rink in the 15th arrondissement, and then sent to concentration camps.

201. Keyserling: see Introduction, note 17, above. "One must submit to one's era in order to affect it." AB here cites a variation of a phrase actually coined by Charles Augustin Sainte-Beuve (1804–1869), in "Le Comte Joseph de Maistre," *Revue des Deux Mondes* 3 (1843). AB cites Sainte-Beuve's original formulation ("*Il faut subir son temps pour agir sur lui*") in the entry for August 12, 1943. See 1943, note 116, below.

202. Rommel: see note 180, above; here he is compared to Scipio Africanus, Roman hero of the Second Punic War.

203. Round-trip.

204. Von Brauchitsch: see 1941, note 108, above.

205. General Fedor von Bock (1880–1945) served as commander during the 1939 invasion of Poland, as well as during the invasion of France and the 1941 invasion of the Soviet Union, including the unsuccessful assault on Moscow.

206. Private museum founded in 1927 by Ernest Cognacq (1839–1928), proprietor of the Samaritaine department store.

207. Jean-Baptiste-Camille Corot (1796–1875), French landscape and portrait painter.

208. Jules Michelet (1798–1874), known for his *Histoire de France* (1833–1867), was ferociously anticlerical, an attitude reflected in his celebratory *Histoire de la révolution française* (1847–1853).

209. In 1941, Hitler's deputy Rudolf Hess (1894–1987) flew to England to try to turn the British against the Soviet Union but was taken prisoner.

210. Nazi concept of the "people's community."

211. Well, how do you do, what do you know! Those people from Dieppe have all the luck.

212. German artist Arno Breker (1900–1991), whose highly stylized Neoclassical work was admired by Hitler.

213. The German grenadiers. Possible reference to the poem by Heinrich Heine, "Die Beiden Grenadiere" (The Two Grenadiers, 1822): *"Nach Frankreich zogen zwei Grenadier', / Die waren in Rußland gefangen."* (Two grenadiers were returning to France, / They had been captured in Russia.) Heine's grenadiers are French, returning to find Napoleon captured. The poem was set to music by Robert Schumann.

214. Hit of white wine.

215. Compression of lines from "Przepowiednia z Tęgoborza" (Prophecies from Togoborz, 1893), concerning the defeat of the "black eagle" when it ventures to the east. The "spiritualist" verses, of uncertain authorship, published in 1939, were popular during the war.

216. Careful what you say. The enemy is listening in.

217. Sablé-sur-Sarthe and Chambellay, towns in the Loire region in west-central France.

218. The Battle of Salamis (480 BCE) was fought between the Greek city-states and the Persian Empire and ended in Greek victory.

219. Historically unique.

220. The Battle of Schleiz (October 9, 1806) resulted in French victory against the Prussians and Saxons. The French general Nicolas Joseph Maison (1771–1840) was not involved in this battle.

221. Murat: see 1940, note 202, above.

222. General Jean Lannes (1769–1809). General Louis Nicolas Davout (1770–1823).

223. Battle of Prenzlau (October 28, 1806). General Bogislav Friedrich Emanuel von Tauentzien (1760–1824). Frederick Louis, Prince of Hohenlohe-Ingelfingen (1746–1818). Prince Augustus of Prussia (1779–1843).

224. General Antoine Charles Louis de Lasalle (1775–1809).

225. Bolesław Wieniawa-Długoszowski (1881–1942), Polish general, Piłsudski's military adjutant; from 1938 to June 13, 1940, he was Polish ambassador in Rome.

226. William I, Elector of Hesse (1743–1821), was expelled from his domain in 1806 and replaced by Napoleon's brother; he returned in 1813. General Édouard Mortier (1768–1835).

227. Venus's punch.

228. From the station? Yes, yes, from the station, going home.

229. A few kind words.

230. Balzac, *Le Médecin de campagne* (*The Country Doctor*, 1833).

231. Maurois: see 1940, note 49, above. "In your salon, style 'Directory' / (Lavender-blue and lemon-yellow) / Ancient armchairs sit, hail-fellow, / In a fashion contradictory, / With a sofa lacking history / (Lavender-blue and lemon-yellow)." André Maurois, *The Silence of Colonel Bramble*, trans. Thurfrida Wake, verses trans. Wilfrid Jackson (New York: John Lane, 1920), 40.

232. Frédéric Moreau is the hero of Flaubert's *L'Éducation sentimentale* (1869).

233. Rabble.

234. It's high time you got here.

235. The Comités de salut public, created in 1793, were the arm of Robespierre's Jacobin dictatorship. Militärbefehlshaber, military commander. Antoine Quentin Fouquier-Tinville (1746–1795), French prosecutor during the Revolutionary Terror, was known for his zeal.

236. Balzac, *Modeste Mignon* (1844).

237. The bugs that have appeared this year.

238. To have a personal talk.

239. Actions against speeches (. . . speeches because of actions), dilettantish opponents, goals attained.

240. Gigantic construction, the European crusade, the Folk Community we fought hard for, and so on. AB's interjection plays on the echo: *Kreuzzug* (crusade) and *Kreuzworträtzel* (crossword puzzle).

241. Gaius Petronius Arbiter (27–66 CE), Roman noble and reputed author of the comic novel *Satyricon* in the reign of the emperor Nero.

242. If, for example, in the next few months we advance to the Don, following the Don finally reach the Volga, storm Stalingrad, and also take it—you can rely on that (prolonged stormy applause)—in their eyes . . . this is nothing.

243. Now in particular it's the occupation of Stalingrad itself that will be completed, as a result of which this blocking position will be deepened and strengthened. You can be sure that no one will dislodge us from that place again. (Thunderous applause.)

244. Until proven otherwise.

245. Mr. Churchill, you have never yet scared me. But you are right that we need to wonder, for if I had an enemy of stature, then I could calculate approximately where he would attack. But when confronted with military idiots, one naturally cannot know where they will attack—it might well be a totally crazy undertaking. And that's really the only unpleasantness, that you never know with this mental case (Roosevelt) or with this chronic drunk what they will do next.

246. *The Fabulous Destiny of Désirée Clary* (1942).

247. What wine have Mr. and Mrs. chosen?

248. Jean-Baptiste Bernadotte (1763–1844), marshal of France under Napoleon I,

fought in 1812 with Czar Alexander I against Napoleon and in 1818 became king of Sweden and Norway.

249. Marie Leszczyńska: see 1941, note 47, above.

250. That's the crux of it.

251. Jean Victor Marie Moreau (1763–1813), French general who helped Napoleon to power, was subsequently involved in various plots, changed sides, and, after a time in the United States, returned to Europe and participated in the 1812 campaign against Napoleon. He is buried in Saint Petersburg and was considered a traitor by Napoleon's side.

252. Pierre Lecomte du Noüy (1883–1947), well-known French biophysicist and philosopher. *L'Avenir de l'esprit* (1941).

253. The Couvent d'Études des Dominicains was established in Étiolles only in 1938. It housed teaching priests, brothers, and Dominican students from different nations.

254. It's big, but it's not beautiful.

255. You're not allowing me to be polite.

256. But you know, they swam in the absolute.

257. They are fanatics from the time of the Holy Inquisition.

258. Laure Junot, Duchess of Abrantès (1784–1838) and wife of General Jean-Andoche Junot (1771–1813), became Balzac's lover in 1828. Her memoirs appeared in eighteen volumes from 1831 to 1834.

259. The oak leaf, symbol used as a mark of distinction in military medals and decorations.

260. What do you know, they said that . . . they explained that . . . I can't repeat it . . .

261. Paul Raynal (1885–1971), French playwright; *Napoléon unique* (1937).

262. Joseph Fouché (1759–1820), minister of police under Napoleon I. Charles Maurice de Talleyrand-Périgord (1754–1838), French bishop and long-serving diplomat, played an important role during the years of Napoleon's conquests.

263. Louis Marie Prudhomme (1752–1830), French writer, satirist, and author of *L'Europe tourmentée par la Révolution de France, ébranlée par dix-huit années de promenades meurtrières de Napoléon Bonaparte* (*Europe Tormented by the French Revolution, Shaken by Eighteen Years of Murderous Excursions by Napoleon Bonaparte*, 1815), as well as a dictionary of famous women (1830).

264. Tradeswomen selling baubles.

265. Edmund Karol Feliks Krzymuski (1852–1928) belonged to the classic school of legal jurisprudence in Poland.

266. Letizia Ramolino (1750–1836), a native of Corsica, was the mother of Napoleon I.

267. Spat.

268. Henri Giraud (1879–1949), French general, chosen by Dwight Eisenhower to lead French troops in North Africa, a position he assumed after Admiral Darlan (see 1941, note 40, above) was assassinated.

269. I really don't know whether these were all only mistakes.

270. One shouldn't waste words responding to the lies of this old gangster.

271. We will defend Africa against anyone.

272. Konrad Wallenrod, hero of the narrative poem *Konrad Wallenrod*, by Adam Mickiewicz. The concept of "Wallenrodism" implies changing sides, treachery, and regard for one's own safety.

273. Propaganda office.

274. Axel Heyst is the main character of Joseph Conrad's novel *Victory* (1915).

275. Artur Grottger (1837–1867), Polish artist known for his grand paintings of historical scenes, but especially for stylized portraits of the patriotic insurrectionists and their families.

276. Kees van Dongen (1877–1968), Dutch-French painter of the Fauves school.

277. Aldous Huxley (1894–1963), *Point Counter Point* (1928).

278. A public assistance hospital.

279. The small but nice society from Vichy.

280. Reference to Piłsudski's coup d'état of May 1926.

281. Most obediently, as in the epistolary formula, "your most obedient servant."

282. Lys Gauty (1900–1994), French cabaret and music hall singer popular in the 1930s. After the Liberation she was reproached for having sung on Radio Paris, used by the German propaganda office, and for having toured Germany with Strength through Joy.

283. After losing the Battle of Maciejowice in 1794, Tadeusz Kościuszko (1746–1817) was supposed to have said: *"Finis Poloniae"* (This is the end of Poland). He denied having said it, and it may have come from Prussian propaganda designed to weaken Polish morale in fighting for independence.

284. Henry Becque (1837–1899), French dramatist. *La Parisienne* premiered in 1885. *Don't Walk around in the Altogether!* by Georges Feydeau (1862–1921) premiered in 1911. Alice Cocéa (1899–1970), Romanian-born French actress and singer.

285. Gabrielle Réjane (1856–1920), French stage and early silent film actress.

286. André Antoine (1858–1943), French actor, director, author, and theater manager. The Théâtre Libre, which he founded in Paris in 1887, was distinguished by innovative staging of French, German, Scandinavian, and Russian naturalist writers, as well as numerous new plays rejected by other theaters.

287. André Dignimont (1891–1965), French illustrator, painter, and engraver.

288. Maison Boucheron, a luxury jewelry house founded in 1858.

289. Bicycle-taxis.

290. "I consider that Laval and Pétain should dangle on the gallows after the war." Echoing the famous Latin quotation: *"Ceterum censeo Carthaginem esse delendam"* (I consider that Carthage must be destroyed), calling for the destruction of the enemies of the Roman Republic. AB mixes some Polish into the adapted Latin.

291. Charles Dullin (1885–1949), major French actor, teacher, and sponsor of contemporary drama.

292. Madame Vauquer is a character in Balzac's *Père Goriot* (1835).

293. No, it's impossible, it's crazy.

294. I only do those who are leaving.

295. References to family addresses in Cracow.

296. Aleksandra Billewicz (Oleńka), the young Polish noblewoman who is the main female protagonist in Sienkiewicz's *The Deluge*.

297. Character in Bolesław Prus, *The Doll* (see 1940, note 229, above).

1943

1. André Gide (1869–1951), French winner of the 1947 Nobel Prize in literature, was originally sympathetic to the Soviet Union; he was invited to visit and expressed his disillusionment in *Retour de l'U.R.S.S.* (1936). Étienne Bonnot de Condillac (1714–1780), French Enlightenment philosopher. Jean-Jacques Rousseau (1712–1778), referring perhaps to *Considérations sur le gouvernement de Pologne* (1770–1771). For Michelet (see 1942, note 208, above), perhaps the exchange with Alexander Herzen. Marquis de Custine (1790–1857), *La Russie en 1839* (1843), a highly critical travel journal that had an enormous impact on how foreigners saw Russia. Jacques Bainville (see 1941, note 70, above), *La Russie et la barrière de l'Est* (1937).

2. Alfred Nicholas Rambaud (1842–1905), French historian; *L'Histoire de la Russie depuis les origines jusqu'à l'année 1877* (1878).

3. Reference to the separate peace concluded at Brest-Litovsk in March 1918 between Soviet Russia and the Central Powers in World War I, in which Russia abandoned its allies, France and Britain. The Red Army originally abolished insignia of rank but subsequently restored them.

4. Abdül-Hamid II (1842–1918), the last autocratic sultan of the Ottoman Empire.

5. The Battle of Velikiye Luki (November 19, 1942–January 16, 1943) took place at this strategically located town on the east-west line between Moscow and Riga.

6. Nikolay Berdyaev (1874–1948), neo-Orthodox idealist philosopher who was expelled along with other non- and anti-Marxist Russian thinkers from Soviet Russia in 1922. His philosophy has been characterized as Christian Existentialism. *Novoe srednevekov'e: Razmyshlenie o sud'be Rossii* (*The New Middle Ages: Reflection on the Destiny of Russia*, 1924) discusses Russia's relationship to Europe.

7. Mickiewicz, *Księgi narodu polskiego i pielgrzymstwa polskiego* (1832), a political pamphlet written after the defeat of the 1830 uprising against Russian rule. Słowacki (see 1940, note 61, above), *Król-Duch* (1845–1849), a historico-philosophical Slavonic epic.

8. Cyprian Norwid (1821–1883), Polish poet, dramatist, and artist.

9. Slowly but surely.

10. The Siege of Leningrad lasted from September 8, 1941, to January 27, 1944, when the Red Army finally liberated the city. More than 600,000 people died in the siege, mostly from starvation. In January 1943 Soviet forces managed to secure a link to the city, over which some supplies could be transported, somewhat alleviating the blockade.

11. Hannibal is before our gates—Cicero. Danger in delay—Livy.

12. What have you done with your army?

13. Battle of Eylau: see 1942, note 76, above. Balzac, *Le Colonel Chabert* (1832).

14. General Hans-Jürgen von Arnim (1882–1962), World War I veteran who commanded various Wehrmacht divisions—in the battles for Poland, in the invasion of the Soviet Union, and in North Africa.

15. At the point of death. General Friedrich Paulus (1890–1957) was promoted to field marshal by Hitler during the Battle of Stalingrad, as a way to pressure him not to surrender his remaining army, on the grounds that officers of that rank did not surrender. Paulus surrendered anyway on January 31, 1943.

16. Propaganda Office in France.

17. Sudden outbursts.

18. *Pontcarral, colonel d'empire*, film by Jean Delannoy (1908–2008), which opened in December 1942 and was considered an appeal for resistance.

19. The human beast rampant. In heraldry, "rampant" indicates an animal standing erect with paws raised, as in a "lion rampant."

20. Hermann Esser (1900–1981), German journalist and early Nazi adherent.

21. Robert de Beauplan (1882–1951), early supporter of Pétain who denounced Nazi anti-Semitism in 1939 but soon became an ardent collaborationist and anti-Semite. From 1942 he was political editor of the pro-German *Le Matin* and spoke on Radio Paris. Although he was arrested and condemned to death in 1946, his sentence was later commuted to life imprisonment.

22. François de Curel (1854–1928), French novelist and playwright.

23. Negotiations subsequent to the Sikorski-Maisky Treaty of July 1941 were intended to define Poland's eastern border. After World War I Lwów was part of the Second Polish Republic. In 1939 the city was incorporated into the Ukrainian Soviet republic. Lviv is today located in the nation of Ukraine.

24. Meaning unclear.

25. Arise Germany! And Germany is arising. Every night. "Arise Germany!" was Goebbels's slogan for mobilizing for total war.

26. Joseph de Maistre (1753–1821), *Considérations sur la France* (1797).

27. "Considérations sur la France," in *Oeuvres complètes de J. de Maistre*, vol. 1 (Lyon: Librairie générale catholique et classique, 1884), 76–78.

28. France obtains the most prying, meticulous, scribbling, paper-pushing, inventorying, monitoring, verifying, neatest, in short an administration more like a cleaning lady than any administration ever known. Balzac, *Les Employés* (1837).

29. Guglielmo Ferrero (1871–1942), Italian historian, journalist, and novelist; *Entre le passé et l'avenir* (*Between the Past and the Future*, 1926).

30. Balzac, *Le Député d'Arcis* (1854).

31. Zoshchenko: see 1942, note 188, above. Arkady Averchenko (1881–1925), Russian playwright and satirist who left Soviet Russia in 1920.

32. Paul Valéry (1871–1945), "Rhumbs" (1926) and "Autres Rhumbs" (1927), *Tel Quel* 2 (1943).

33. Sébastien Le Prestre de Vauban (1633–1707), celebrated French military engineer.

34. Victor de Riqueti, Marquis de Mirabeau (1715–1789), French economist of the Physiocratic school; *L'Ami des hommes, ou Traité de la population* (1759).

35. The Pharoah Sesostris, mentioned by Herodotus in his *Histories* as having led an army to Asia Minor, then west into Europe, defeating the Scythians and Thracians. *La Chanson de Roland*, twelfth-century epic poem. *Amadis de Gaula*, chivalric romance popular in sixteenth-century Spain.

36. "Fragments sur la France," in *Oeuvres complètes de J. de Maistre*, 188–196.

37. Keyserling, *De la souffrance à la plénitude* (*From Suffering to Abundance*, 1938). AB's version seems to deviate in small details from the French text.

38. Jacques Bénigne Bossuet (1627–1704), French bishop and theologian. Nicolas Boileau-Despréaux (1636–1711), French poet and critic.

39. Siegfried: see 1941, note 93, above. Albert Thibaudet (1874–1936), French essayist and literary critic. Daniel Halévy (1872–1962), French historian.

40. Friedrich Sieburg (1893–1964), German journalist, writer; *Gott in Frankreich?*, in the 1930 French translation *Dieu est-il français?* (*Is God French?*).

41. Trublet: see 1941, note 86, above.

42. Bernard Grasset (1881–1955), influential French publisher. Charles Péguy (1873–1914), poet, essayist. Letter from Péguy to Sieburg, "Sur la France," in *Dieu est-il Francais?*

43. Man cannot surpass himself.

44. Jean de la Bruyère (1645–1696), philosopher, moralist.

45. She rejects the present.

46. Renan (see 1940, note 97, above), *L'Avenir de la science* (*The Future of Science*, 1890).

47. American taste.

48. In Russian: "epaulettes," "orderlies," "comrade." See note 3, above.

49. Narcotics.

50. Tristan Bernard (Paul Bernard, 1866–1947), French playwright, novelist, and journalist.

51. He's involved in the black market.

52. Are classy guys.

53. André Siegfried (see 1941, note 93, above), *Qu'est-ce que l'Amérique?* (*What Is America?*, 1937).

54. I don't know her.

55. "War production" factory, apparently in Cracow. Could be part of DKW-Grün (see 1941, note 89, above).

56. Eliza Orzeszkowa (1841–1910), popular Polish writer and representative of the Positivist movement whose many novels addressed social conditions in partitioned Poland.

57. We have lost, BUT.

58. I've already studied everything thoroughly.

59. Albert-Émile Sorel (Jeanne Marguerite Renouard, 1876–1938), *Louise de Prusse* (1937). Henri Bergson (1859–1941), influential French philosopher. Gustave Le Bon (1841–1931), French sociologist best known for *Psychologie des foules* (*Psychology of the Crowd*, 1895).

60. Yes, I assure you, they've seen the notices.

61. Carl Maria von Weber (1786–1826), *Aufforderung zum Tanz* (*Invitation to the Waltz*, 1819), the first Romantic concert waltz.

62. Waiter, a glass of champagne!

63. Artur Maria Swinarski (1900–1965), Polish poet, playwright, and satirist, active in 1930s Polish cabarets.

64. Mr. André, how's Poland doing?

65. At a slow pace.

66. Zygmunt Krasiński (1812–1859), Polish Romantic poet. *Nieboska komedia* (*Undivine Comedy*, 1833) is a drama in which revolutionary and reactionary forces confront each other. Pankracy was a leader of the revolutionary camp, ready to justify anything in the name of the revolution. The "three bards" are the Romantic poets Słowacki, Mickiewicz, and Krasiński.

67. Dolores Ibárruri (1895–1989), Basque Communist activist and heroine of the Spanish Civil War.

68. State Political Administration, Soviet security department, predecessor of the KGB.

69. Gedymin (Gediminas), grand duke of Lithuania (1315–1341).

70. Anders Army: see 1941, note 35, above.

71. Ferdynand Hoesick (1867–1941), Polish publisher and bookseller, author of the first monograph on Chopin.

72. Franciszek Grzymała (1790–1871), Polish author who emigrated to Paris after the 1830 uprising and collaborated with Mickiewicz.

73. Gavarni: see 1941, note 33, above.

74. Give me a round-trip ticket to Katyń.

75. Grand Duke Konstantin Pavlovich (1779–1831), governor of Russian-ruled Poland during the 1830 Uprising.

76. Yuri Annenkov (1889–1974), who was active in pre-1914 modernist theater in Russia, emigrated in 1924 to Paris, where he worked as a theater and film scenic designer.

77. *Fircyk w zalotach* (*The Dandy's Courtship*, 1781), a lighthearted comedy of manners by Franciszek Zabłocki (1752–1821). Zabłocki used colloquial language, folk sayings, and proverbs, such as the one quoted here.

78. Reduta: see 1940, note 143, above.

79. Józef Poręba (1895–1923), actor and comanager of the Reduta. Zygmunt Chmielewski (1894–1978), theater and film actor. Ewa Kunina (1889–1963), actor.

Stefan Jaracz (1883–1945), actor, cofounder of the Union of Polish Theatrical Artists. Stanislawa Perzanowska (1898–1982), actor and director. Wincenty Drabik (1881–1933), stage and costume designer.

80. Elżunia is the diminutive form of Elizabeth, here referring to the daughter of Wanda and Juliusz Osterwa (see 1940, note 143, above).

81. Wanda Osterwina, *née* Malinowska (1887–1929), theater and film actress, wife of Juliusz Osterwa, and member of the Reduta from its beginning in 1919 until her death. Limanowski: see 1940, note 143, above.

82. Jerzy Szaniawski (1886–1970), essayist and author of many plays, including *Papierowy Kochanek* (*The Paper Lover*, 1920) and *Ptak* (*The Bird*, 1923). Stefan Żeromski (1864–1925), prominent writer, playwright, cultural commentator, and social activist who was president of the Union of Polish Writers and wrote novels of "engagement" highlighting social and psychological conflicts and positivist ideals. The premiere of Żeromski's play *Ponad śniegiem bielszym się stanę* (*Whiter than Snow Shall I Be*) on November 29, 1919, initiated the activities of Reduta. *Uciekła mi przepióreczka* (*The Quail*, 1924) was first performed at Reduta in 1925.

83. Dignimont: see 1942, note 287, above.

84. Mikołaj Rej (1505–1569), Renaissance writer and father of Polish literature; a reference to the fragment from Rej's *Żywot człowieka poczciwego* (*The Life of an Honest Man*, 1558), a treatise in verse on the ideals of the good life.

85. Henry Murger (1822–1861), French novelist and poet whose semiautobiographical stories about the life of a poor writer and his artist friends, *Scènes de la vie de bohème* (*The Bohemians of the Latin Quarter*, 1847–49), became the basis for Puccini's opera *La Bohème*.

86. Victorien Sardou (1831–1908), *La Papillonne* (1862). George Bernard Shaw dismissed Sardou's formulaic plays as "Sardoodledom."

87. Sosnkowski: see 1941, note 42, above.

88. Lipiński: see 1940, note 198, above.

89. Louis Verneuil (Louis Collin Du Bocage, 1893–1952), *Ma Cousine de Varsovie: Comédie en trois actes* (1923). Elvire Popesco (1894–1993), French actress of Romanian origin.

90. Fortress Europe.

91. Fashion above all.

92. From Robert Louis Stevenson, *Treasure Island*: see 1940, note 41, above.

93. Stanisław Mikołajczyk (1902–1966). Born in the German province of Posen (Polish Poznań), a member of the Polish Socialist Party, he fought in the Polish-Soviet War, was prime minister of the Polish London government from July 14, 1943, to November 24, 1944, joined the Soviet-backed government in Poland after the war, resigned in 1947 over falsified elections, and died in the United States. Jan Kwapiński (Piotr Chałupka, 1885–1964) did not return to Poland after the war and died in London.

94. Magdalena Samozwaniec (1894–1972), Polish writer.

95. Reference to Mickiewicz, *Dziady* (*Forefathers' Eve*). "His name forty and four" are the words heard by Father Piotr, a central character, while praying in his prison cell. Father Piotr envisions Poland as a new Christ betrayed by the world (with France in the role of Pilate). The tragic vision is tempered by the prophecy of a new messiah (named mystically by the number 44) and the triumphant resurrection—spiritual and political—of Poland.

96. London speaking . . . here is our . . . / . . . Russia. Russian troops, after having broken the German resistance in the sector north of Belgorod, are advancing toward . . .

97. Déat: see 1942, note 144, above.

98. The Duce, the Duce has stepped down, Duce, Duce, we'll have peace now . . .

99. Danielle Darrieux (1917–2017), French singer and film star. The film *Premier rendez-vous* opened in 1941.

100. Marshal Pietro Badoglio (1871–1956). On July 25, 1943, Mussolini was arrested by King Victor Emmanuel III and Badoglio became prime minister. Italy signed an armistice with the Allies on September 3, 1943, and Badoglio remained the nominal head of government until June 9, 1944.

101. Ferrero: see note 29, above.

102. For the men—the crew.

103. Sinclair Lewis, *Main Street* (1920), chapter 22.

104. "La Grande Bretèche" (1831), short story by Balzac.

105. *Bernadotte* could be a book about the historical figure. Charles Maurras (1868–1952), French writer and founder of the right-wing Action française; *Les Amants de Venise: George Sand et Musset* (1916). Alfred de Musset (1810–1857), French dramatist, poet, and novelist who described his love affair with Sand in *La Confession d'un enfant du siècle* (1836).

106. Conrad, *Victory*: see 1942, note 274, above. Lena and Heyst are lovers. When Lena dies, Heyst commits suicide.

107. Emil Ludwig (Emil Cohn, 1881–1948), German-Swiss writer born in Breslau (now Wracław), known for popular biographies.

108. You understand, the *Ninth Symphony* provides a diversion for all the noble and generous instincts. What remains is the bandit and the murderer.

109. Animal open to the world. Max Scheler: see 1942, note 120, above.

110. Joué-en-Charnie is a town in the Loire Valley.

111. I am a Republican, sir.

112. Notices.

113. Bernard René de Launay (1740–1789) was in charge of the Bastille on July 14, 1789, when it was stormed by the mob. He was lynched, stabbed, and beheaded by a butcher.

114. Innate goodness of the people.

115. Antoine de Rivarol (1753–1801), royalist writer during the Revolution.

116. For Sainte-Beuve's line, as cited by Keyserling, see 1942, note 201, above.

117. Ulrich von Hutten (1488–1523), German humanist, reformer, and critic of Roman Catholicism.

118. Parandowski: see 1940, note 153, above.

119. He's more like a sultan than a priest.

120. Keyserling, *Südamerikanische Meditationen* (1932). They were clearly using the French translation.

121. Claude Adrien Helvétius (1715–1771), French Enlightenment philosopher. Lycurgus of Sparta (800–730 BCE), lawgiver who established basic institutions. Pericles (494–429 BCE), Athenian statesman, orator, and general.

122. Paul Painlevé (1863–1933), French mathematician and statesman who served as prime minister in 1917 and in 1925.

123. Arthur Young (1741–1820), English writer on agriculture and economics, known for *Travels in France* (1792), his impressions of the Revolution. The source of this alleged quotation may be: "It will now be seen, whether they [the French] will copy the constitution of England, freed from its faults, or attempt, from theory, to frame something absolutely speculative: in the former case, they will prove a blessing to their country; in the latter they will probably involve it in inextricable confusions and civil wars, perhaps not in the present period, but certainly at some future one."

124. Les Chantiers de la Jeunesse (1940–1944) was a youth organization that inculcated Pétainist ideology, formed after the defeat to replace the military draft. *Pétainjugend* is a play on Hitlerjugend, the Nazi youth organization.

125. Strength through Joy: see 1942, note 88, above.

126. General Georges Ernest Boulanger (1837–1891), political figure who became the center of an authoritarian movement in France in the 1880s.

127. Anglo-French agreement signed in 1904.

128. Come take a look. This is worth at least 100,000 francs.

129. Gebhard Leberecht von Blücher (1742–1819), Prussian general who fought against Napoleon at Leipzig and Waterloo.

130. Feydeau: see 1942, note 284, above.

131. Rémy de Gourmont (1858–1915), French Symbolist poet, novelist, critic.

132. A moving speech. A magnificent gesture of the people.

133. All the same, we're not slaves.

134. Mama, it's ripe.

135. Stews.

136. What do you know? a seat!

137. Georges Bernanos (1888–1948), conservative, Catholic French writer.

138. Roger Martin du Gard (1881–1958), French novelist, 1937 Nobel Prize in literature. His major work depicts life on the eve of World War I, in which he himself had fought.

139. Waiter, a glass of rum.

140. Alexandre Dumas, *père*: see 1941, note 21, above; *Joseph Balsamo* (1846–1848) features the character Joseph Balsamo, also known as Cagliostro.

141. You are vulgar, old man. That's called a volte-face.

142. General Mark W. Clark (1896–1984), commander of the U.S. Fifth Army.

143. "The 44" or "four and forty," shorthand for a messiah; see note 95, above.

144. The so-called Italian Social Republic, or Republic of Salò (September 23, 1943–April 25, 1945).

145. Armory (Carle Lionel Dauriac, 1877–19 —), *50 ans de vie parisienne (souvenirs et figures)* (*Fifty Years of Parisian Life: Memories and Personalities*, 1943). Rachilde, pen name of Marguerite Vallette-Eymery (1860–1953), French novelist and playwright.

146. Dirty foreigner.

147. And they are laughing and eating.

148. Maxence van der Meersch (1907–1951), French writer whose father was Belgian. His novels are set in northern France, where he was born.

149. But you are capitalists!

150. For your dessert.

151. Raimu: see 1942, note 129, above.

152. Orane Demaise (Henriette Louise Burgart, 1904–1991), French actress for whom Pagnol created the role of Fanny in *Marius*. Berval, stage name of Antonin Pasteur (1891–1966), French theater and film actor.

153. Paul Géraldy (1885–1983), French playwright and poet; *Duo* is based on the Colette novel (1934) of the same name.

154. Valentine Tessier (1892–1981), French theater and film actress best known for her performance in Jean Renoir's adaptation of *Madame Bovary* (1932).

155. The Moscow Conference (October 18–November 11, 1943) involved foreign ministers Anthony Eden (Britain), Cordell Hull (United States), and Vyacheslav Molotov (Soviet Union). China joined in signing the Declaration of the Four Nations that emerged.

156. Pierre Louÿs (1870–1925), French Symbolist writer known for his eroticism.

157. Balzac's *L'École des ménages* (*The School of Matrimony*) was a flop when it opened in 1839.

158. Armand Pérémé (1804–1874). Anténor Joly (d. 1852), French journalist and theater director.

159. Evelina Hańska (Ewelina, *née* Rzewuska, 1805–1882), a young, rich, well-educated Polish aristocrat living on her husband's estate in Volhynia, initiated a correspondence with Balzac in 1832. The two first met in person in Switzerland in 1834 and continued a love affair in letters for many years, meeting occasionally in Saint Petersburg, Holland, and Italy. They married only in 1850, nine years after her husband's death, and came to Paris five months before Balzac's own death.

160. Charles Lassailly (1806–1843), French writer.

161. Alexandre Dumas, *père*, *Antony: Drame en cinq actes et en prose* (1831), enjoyed a contrasting success.

162. Tadeusz Boy-Żeleński: see 1940, note 122, above.

163. Constant Rémy (1882–1957), French actor. Michèle Morgan, stage name of Simone Renée Rousel (1920–2016), French actress, famous after the war for roles in French and Hollywood films.

1944

1. Matthew 5:10 (KJV): "Blessed are they which are persecuted for righteousness' sake: for theirs is the kingdom of heaven."

2. Matthew 22:18–21 (KJV): "Why tempt ye me, ye hypocrites? Shew me the tribute money. Whose is this image and superscription? They say unto him, Caesar's. Then saith he unto them, Render therefore unto Caesar the things which are Caesar's; and unto God the things that are God's."

3. I don't give a damn, understand?

4. Back off! . . . for God's sake.

5. Watch it, fellow, don't touch me.

6. Feniks, a café and fashionable dancing club, opened in 1933 in an Art Deco building in central Cracow.

7. François Coppée (1842–1908), French poet and novelist; "La Grève des forgerons" (1869). Known as a poet of the common people, Coppée later espoused right-wing views and was among the enemies of Dreyfus.

8. Komsomol, Soviet youth organization. Cheka (Extraordinary Commission), the Soviet political police.

9. "Ja się boję sama spać," popular song performed by Zula Pogorzelska (1898–1936), Polish actress and cabaret singer.

10. Jan Birtus, Basia Bobkowska's brother.

11. Édouard Dujardin (1861–1949), *Rencontres avec Houston Stewart Chamberlain: Souvenirs et correspondance* (1943). Houston Stewart Chamberlain (1855–1927), *Grundlagen des neunzehnten Jahrhunderts* (*Foundations of the Nineteenth Century*, 1903).

12. Frobenius: see 1940, note 176, above. The closest title to the one AB cites is *Kulturgeschichte Afrikas* (*The Cultural History of Africa*, 1933).

13. It's taking its course.

14. Związek Patriotów Polskich, created in the Soviet Union in June 1943 as the core of what was to be the postwar Communist government in Poland.

15. It's draining; it takes a long time.

16. Jean Giraudoux (1882–January 31, 1943). *Sodom and Gomorrah* opened in 1943. Feuillère: see 1942, note 133, above.

17. The novel *The Rains Came* (1937), by American author Louis Bromfield (1896–1956), was published in French as *La Mousson* (*The Monsoon*, 1939). *Hintertreppenlitteratur*, "backstairs-literature," suggesting literature of popular appeal that reached ordinary households.

18. Fridtjof Nansen (1861–1930), Norwegian explorer of the North Pole.

19. Soldiers' Station, Calais.

20. Paul Hazard (1878–April 13, 1944), French historian; *La Crise de la conscience européenne* (*The European Mind*, 1935).

21. Mikołajczyk: see 1943, note 93, above.

22. Maurice Maeterlinck (1862–1949), francophone Belgian writer, winner of the 1911 Nobel Prize in literature.

23. Jean Anouilh (1910–1987), French dramatist; *Antigone*, his most famous play, premiered in February 1944.

24. Battle of Carentan (June 8–13, 1944), during the Battle of Normandy, between U.S. airborne forces and the German Wehrmacht. Allied victory closed the gap between the two Allied landing zones.

25. French philosopher Pierre-Maxime Schuhl (1902–1984), *Machinisme et philosophie* (1938). Schuhl, who was Jewish, spent the war in a concentration camp for officers at Colditz, near Leipzig.

26. Dirt is not dangerous.

27. Sophie de Korwin-Piotrowska, *L'Étrangère, Éveline Hańska de Balzac* (*The Foreign Woman*, 1938).

28. Hoene-Wroński: see 1942, note 109, above. Orientalist Wacław Rzewuski (1786–1831) was a leading figure in Polish Romanticism. The confederations were groups of nobles during the period of the Polish partitions. The Philomaths and Philarets were student secret societies at the University of Wilno, suppressed in 1823, whose members included Mickiewicz.

29. Marquis de Custine, *La Russie en 1839*: see 1943, note 1, above.

30. Le Bon: see 1943, note 59, above.

31. The new V-1 rockets, launched on June 13, 1944, were not true rockets but indeed pilotless planes. The "V" came from the German *Vergeltungswaffen*, or weapons of reprisal.

32. Boeing B-29 Superfortress fighter planes, or heavy bombers, were used by the U.S. Army Air Force from 1942 and later were deployed to drop the atomic bombs on Japan. There was no "World Air Force."

33. Henri Bergson, *Les Deux Sources de la morale et de la religion* (*The Two Sources of Morality and Religion*, 1932).

34. Maurice Dekobra (Maurice Tessier, 1885–1973), French writer popular between the wars; he spent the war years in the United States before returning to France.

35. Juan García Oliver (1901–1980). Francisco Largo Caballero (1869–1946), leader of the Spanish Socialist Workers' Party and prime minister of the Second Spanish Republic, 1936–1937.

36. Anders: see 1941, note 35, above. Józef Gawlina (1892–1964), bishop-chaplain to the Polish army. Kazimierz Papée (1889–1979), ambassador for the Polish London government to the Vatican.

37. "Umarł Maciek, umarł . . ." Nineteenth-century Polish folk song.

38. Count Alessandro di Cagliostro (Giuseppe Balsamo Cagliostro, 1743–1795), Italian occultist and magician. For the Dumas novel about this character, see 1943, note 140, above. Zbigniew Jan Dunikowski (1889–1964), Polish engineer who claimed to make gold from sand and ran into various legal difficulties.

39. Norwid: see 1943, note 8, above.

40. Sacha Guitry, *De Jeanne d'Arc à Philippe Pétain* (1942).

41. Tino Rossi (1907–1983), popular French singer and film actor.

42. Breker: see 1942, note 212, above.

43. On May 24, 1944, an incendiary bomb destroyed much of the structure of the Berlin Cathedral, including the crypt. Frederick II of Hohenzollern (1712–1786), who had participated in the partitions of Poland, was at the time buried, not there, but in Potsdam. Hitler had had his tomb transferred for protection to a salt mine, from which it was removed by the U.S. Army after Germany's defeat.

44. Ferrero, *Aventure: Bonaparte en Italie, 1796–1797* (1936).

45. Jacques Antoine Hippolyte, Comte de Guibert (1743–1790), French general and military theorist.

46. General Johann Peter, Baron Beaulieu (1725–1819), Austrian general defeated by Napoleon in 1796 during the Italian campaign.

47. General Lazare Hoche (1768–1797). General Jean Victor Marie Moreau (1763–1813) later became the emperor's rival.

48. From Alexander Pushkin's *Bronze Horseman* (1837), a narrative poem about Peter the Great (1672–1725), to whom Catherine the Great (1729–1796) erected a monument in the form of a horseman. In fact, Peter the Great could not have expelled the Jews from Russia because the Jewish population entered the Russian empire only with the partitions of Poland under Catherine the Great.

49. Philippe Henriot (1889–June 28, 1944), anti-Communist, anti-Semitic member of the Catholic nationalist right who supported the Nazis after the invasion of the Soviet Union. From January 1944 he gave regular radio speeches as Vichy minister of information and propaganda. Assassinated by a member of the Resistance, he received an elaborate state funeral.

50. Tenacity, perseverance.

51. General Karl Wilhelm von Schlieben (1894–1964). Admiral Walter Henneke (1898–1984).

52. Wiech (Stefan Wiechewski, 1896–1979), Polish humorist who often used popular speech, particularly Warsaw dialects, to comic effect. Here the word *opiat'* is simply Russian for "again."

53. Żeromski (see 1943, note 82, above), *Nawracanie Judasza* (*The Conversion of Judas*, 1916).

54. Van der Meersch (see 1943, note 148, above), *Corps et âmes* (*Bodies and Souls*, 1943).

55. What's the problem, you guys — don't you have a horn in there? Too much effort to press the thing when you're coming out . . .

56. Don't tell me any stories.

57. Rundstedt: see 1942, note 156, above. Field Marshal Günther von Kluge (1882–August 19, 1944) committed suicide after the failed coup against Hitler, though he was not actively involved in the conspiracy.

58. German industrialists. Albert Speer (1905–1981), Reich minister of armaments and war production.

59. *Goupi Mains rouges* (*It Happened at the Inn*, 1943), French mystery film di-

rected by Jacques Becker (1906–1960) about an old woman whose family is suspected of murdering her.

60. Reference to Żeromski's trilogy, *Zamieć* (*The Blizzard*, 1916–1919), in which the character Ryszard Nienaski is a young architect full of ideas and projects for social reform.

61. Polish mess.

62. Too bad for him.

63. Aleksander Gierymski (1850–1901), modernist Polish painter.

64. *La Gerbe* (*The Sheaf*), a German-subsidized weekly published 1940–1944 by pro-Nazi French intellectuals.

65. Louis-Ferdinand Céline (1894–1961), modernist French writer, Nazi sympathizer, and anti-Semite.

66. *Le Malentendu* (*The Misunderstanding*, 1943) by Albert Camus (1913–1960) premiered on June 24, 1944, in the Théâtre des Mathurins. Karol Hubert Rostworowski (1877–1938), Polish playwright and musician, came from a gentry family and was an arch-Catholic and anti-Communist. The tragedy *Niespodzianka* (*The Surprise*, 1928–1929), about a couple who kill a wealthy young man who has come to visit, hoping to get his money and not knowing that they are murdering their own son, won the national book prize in 1932.

67. Zygmunt Nowakowski (Zygmunt Tempka, 1891–1963), Polish writer, journalist, and director.

68. Leon Chwistek (1884–1944), Polish painter, philosopher, and mathematician.

69. Emil (Samuel) Haecker (Haker) (1875–1934) was editor of the Cracow socialist newspaper *Naprzód* (Forward).

70. Franciszek Xawery Pusłowski (1875–1968), Polish art collector, poet, translator, officer of the Polish army, and government figure.

71. Armia Krajowa (AK), or Polska Armia Podziemna (1944–1945), of the Polskie Państwo Podziemne (Polish Underground Government), loyal to the Polish London government.

72. General Stanisław Maczek (1892–1994), Polish tank commander. No. 303 ("Kościuszko") Polish Fighter Squadron in the Royal Air Force. The Battle of Monte Cassino (January 17–May 19, 1944) acquired a special meaning for the Poles as a symbol of heroic courage and military savvy, but also of terrible loss of life.

73. I'm no dope, what?

74. It's all over, nothing can be done, it's lost.

75. We've done it! What luck!

76. Félicien Challaye (1875–1967), French philosopher and journalist, author of *La Formation du socialisme: De Platon à Lénine* (1937). A former Dreyfusard and pacifist, he supported Vichy during the war. *Germinal*, collaborationist weekly associated with Marcel Déat that appeared April 28–August 11, 1944.

77. *Signal*: Nazi propaganda magazine.

78. "The eternal feminine"—the phrase used notably by Goethe (1749–1832).

79. Except for Jews, who were forbidden to have bicycles. See Jacques Biélinky,

Journal, 1940–1942: Un Journaliste juif à Paris sous l'Occupation, ed. Renée Poznanski (Paris: Cerf, 1992), 208 (entry for May 14, 1942). The cost of this prohibition is obvious.

80. Count Claus von Stauffenberg (1907–July 21, 1944), whom AB calls a "blue-blooded swine and reactionary," though it's unclear whose phrase he is ironically invoking, was among the group of German officers who attempted to kill Hitler on July 20, 1944, for which he was executed.

81. Van der Meersch, *Corps et âmes:* see note 54, above.

82. "Jeszcze Polska," Polish national anthem: see 1940, note 95, above.

83. The Polish Committee of National Liberation, known as the Lublin Committee, was proclaimed on July 22, 1944, as an alternative to the London-based Polish government in exile. It grew out of the Union of Polish Patriots, another Moscow-created organization (see note 14, above).

84. Wanda Wasilewska (1905–1964), Polish-Soviet Communist figure.

85. Marian Bogatko (1906–1940).

86. Towarzystwo Uniwersytetu Robotniczego (TUR).

87. Bolesław Drobner (1883–1968), member of the Polish Socialist Party and of the Lublin Committee, loyal to the Soviet-backed regime.

88. Michał Rola-Żymierski (Łyżwiński, 1890–1989), ranking Communist Party member, marshal of Poland in 1945, and Polish minister of defense, 1945–1949.

89. Andrzej Witos (1878–1973), member of the Union of Polish Patriots and the Lublin Committee. General Zygmunt Berling (1896–1980), whose political choices are too complicated to be summarized here.

90. Związek Niezależnej Młodzieży Socjalistycznej (1917–1948). Józef Cyrankiewicz (1911–1989), Polish socialist and, after 1948, Communist; premier of the Republic of Poland, 1947–1952, and premier of the People's Republic of Poland, 1954–1970.

91. A Chanel perfume created in 1924 to commemorate Coco Chanel's affair with a Russian aristocrat.

92. Marcellin Berthelot (1827–1907), French chemist. Claude Bernard (1813–1878), French physiologist.

93. Gentlemen, we're closing.

94. Things can't go on like this.

95. The United Nations Relief and Rehabilitation Administration, founded in November 1943, was mainly occupied with care of refugees and displaced persons after the war.

96. The UNRRA will take care of all that.

97. The Anders Army exited the Soviet Union for Tehran en route to Palestine, where it served under British command.

98. Konstantin Rokossovsky (1896–1968) was born in Velikiye Luki, Russia, to a family of Polish ancestry, but his father was a railroad engineer. He fought in the Russian imperial army in World War I, joined the Red Army in 1917, was purged in the 1930s, but returned to his command in World War II. He fought at Stalingrad and became marshal of the Soviet Union and later minister of defense in the postwar Polish Communist government. While the Warsaw Uprising was under way, Rokossovsky

commanded the Soviet forces that had reached the Vistula River but withheld support for the insurgents, waiting for the uprising to be suppressed.

99. "*Łotr wielki, jak się zwykle dzieje / Z Polakiem, który w carskiej służbie zmoskwicieje.*" Mickiewicz, *Pan Tadeusz*, bk. 9. Adam Mickiewicz, *Pan Tadeusz, or the Last Foray in Lithuania*, trans. George Rapall Noyes (London: J. M. Dent, 1917), 226.

100. Tadeusz Romer (1894–1978), diplomat, foreign minister of the Polish government in London. Stanisław Grabski (1871–1949), president of the National Council in London, 1942–1945, favored cooperation with the Soviet Union.

101. You know, the Americans accept advice.

102. Key districts in central Warsaw.

103. Are you Chinese, or what?—We're chocolate with your Latin.

104. Antoine de Saint-Exupéry (1900–July 31, 1944), *Terre des hommes* (*The Land of Men*, 1939), autobiographical essays, translated in English as *Wind, Sand, and Stars*.

105. General Tadeusz Bór-Komorowski (1895–1966) gave orders to begin the Warsaw Uprising on August 1, 1944, and surrendered to the Germans on October 2, 1944. Prime minister of the Polish government in London, 1947–1949, he died in London.

106. The ditty: "*Kto powiedział, że Moskale / Są to bracia dla Lechitów, / Temu pierwszy w łeb wypalę / Przed kościołem Karmelitów,*" a short, popular version by Rajnold Suchodolski (1804–1831) of the lofty patriotic song "Kościuszko's Polonaise" (1792).

107. The British film *Things to Come* (1936), about a war that lasts thirty years, was based on various works by H. G. Wells (1866–1946).

108. Abbaye Saint-Pierre de Solesmes, Benedictine monastery about 250 km southwest of Paris, between Paris and Rennes, founded in the eleventh century.

109. Johann Wolfgang von Goethe, *Die Leiden des jungen Werthers* (*The Sorrows of Young Werther*, 1774).

110. Maria Kuncewiczowa (1899–1989), Polish novelist.

111. Kwapiński: see 1943, note 93, above.

112. Władysław Raczkiewicz (1885–1947), president of the Republic of Poland, 1939–1947. Tomasz Arciszewski (1877–1955), socialist politician and prime minister of the London government, 1944–1945.

113. Von Hutten: see 1943, note 117, above. The original saying is: "Minds are waking up—how good it is to be alive!"

114. *Volpone; or, The Fox*, comedy by Ben Jonson (1572–1637), a satire of greed and lust. The title character is a scheming Venetian gentleman.

115. "The Great Improvisation": a lengthy monologue in Mickiewicz's *Forefathers' Eve* (see 1943, note 95, above), recited in prison by Konrad, an idealized Romantic poet. Beginning as his confession and a prayer, the poem turns into a confrontation and desperate rebellion in the face of the silence of God.

116. *Le Petit Parisien* was the official voice of the Vichy regime during the war. General Dietrich von Choltitz (1894–1966) became known for defying Hitler's order to destroy Paris in 1944, instead surrendering to the Free French.

117. Gaspart Gourgaud (1783–1852), *Journal de Sainte-Hélène, 1815–1818* (1899, reissued 1944).

118. The collaborators are leaving.

119. Twelfth arrondissement.

120. The Warsaw Airlift was an Allied operation undertaken in August and September 1944 to deliver supplies to the Polish Home Army fighting in Warsaw. Flights originated in Italy; the Soviets did not grant flyover rights or provide access to their air bases.

121. She'll have a pretty brassiere.

122. Eugène Labiche (1815–1888), French playwright known for vaudeville.

123. Field Marshal von Kluge: see note 57, above.

124. Forces françaises de l'intérieur (French Forces of the Interior), name given by de Gaulle to the Resistance fighters.

125. Grottger: see 1942, note 275, above.

126. It's logical, it's very intelligent, it's fair.

127. The newspaper *L'Humanité* was established in 1904 by Jean Jaurès and the French Socialist Party; after 1920, it was the organ of the French Communist Party, clandestine during the war until the Liberation.

128. Maurice Thorez (1900–1964), leader of the French Communist Party, 1930–1964, spent the war years in Moscow.

129. Paris is winning her freedom by force of arms, Paris is liberating herself on her own.

130. *Ce Soir* was an evening newspaper established in 1937 by the French Communist Party to compete with *Paris-Soir*. Banned in August 1939, along with *L'Humanité*, it reappeared in August 1944 and was discontinued in 1953.

131. Eternally heroic and rebellious France.

132. Paris is winning her freedom by force of arms.

133. Marie-Pierre Koenig (1898–1970), French general, leading commander in de Gaulle's Free French forces, named commander of the French Forces of the Interior in 1944.

Acknowledgments and Translators' Note

1. AB, *Szkice piórkiem* (Warsaw: CiS, 2007).

2. PIASA Archives: Fond No. 45: Andrzej Bobkowski Papers: http://www.piasa.org /archives/fonds-045.html.

3. Łukasz Mikołajewski, "Pamięć fabularyzowana: Powojenne poprawki w *Szkicach piórkiem* Andrzeja Bobkowskiego," in *Buntownik, Cyklista, Kosmopolak: O Andrzeju Bobkowskim i jego twórczości,* ed. Jarosław Klejnocki and Andrzej St. Kowalczyk (Warsaw: Biblioteka "Więzi," 2011); Łukasz Mikołajewski, *Disenchanted Europeans: Polish Émigré Writers from* Kultura *and the Postwar Reformulations of the West* (Bern: Peter Lang, 2018).

4. AB, *En guerre et en paix: Journal, 1940–1944,* trans. Laurence Dyèvre (Mon-

tricher: Les Éditions Noir sur Blanc, 1991). There is also a German translation of the first volume: *Wehmut? Wonach zum Teufel? Tagebücher aus Frankreich, 1940–1941,* vol. 1, trans. Martin Pollack (Hamburg: ROSPO, 2000), which we have not consulted.

5. André Maurois, *The Silence of Colonel Bramble,* trans. Thurfrida Wake; verses trans. Wilfrid Jackson (New York: John Lane, 1920), 40. Adam Mickiewicz, *Pan Tadeusz, or the Last Foray in Lithuania,* trans. George Rapall Noyes (London: J. M. Dent, 1917), 226.

6. Maciej Nowak, *Na łuku elektrycznym: O pisaniu Andrzeja Bobkowskiego* (Warsaw: Biblioteka "Więzi," 2014).

INDEX OF NAMES

Names starting with "de," "le/la" and "von/van" may be alphabetized by the subsequent part of the name based on common usage.

Abbeville, 4

Abdül-Hamid II, 380, 389, 637n4

Action française, 642n105

Adria, 338

Afrika Korps, 445

Agenzia Stefani, 448

Aisne, 9

Alexander I (Czar), 137–138, 614n166, 634n248

Alexander the Great, 529

Algeria, 562, 620n40, 623n96

Amiens, 3

Anczyc, Władysław Ludwik, 621n54

Anders, Władysław, 197–198, 440, 542, 619n35

Angers, 461–463

Angoulême, 24, 25, 26

Anjou, 329, 330, 347

Annabella (Suzanne Georgette Charpentier), 286, 628n92

Annenkov, Yuri, 443, 640n76

Anouilh, Jean, 534, 646n23

Antibes, 99–100

Anti-Bolshevik Legion, 198, 226

anti-Semitism, 63, 186, 187, 231, 525, 638n21, 647n49, 648n65. *See also* Jews

Antoine, André, 370, 636n286

Arciszewski, Tomasz, 576, 578, 650n112

Ardennes, 3

Ariovistus, 48, 609n55

Aristotle, 529

Arles, 78

Armia Krajowa, 648n71. *See also* Polish Underground Army

Armory (Carle Lionel Dauriac), 505, 644n145

Arnim, Hans-Jürgen von, 388, 445, 638n14

Arras, 3, 4

Asnyk, Adam, 177–178, 189, 617n2

Association Cinématographique Européenne, 188

Atelier de Construction, viii

Aubry, Octave, 189, 619n22

Augereau, Pierre, 548

Augustine, Saint, 473, 504

Augustów, 563

Augustus (Prince of Prussia), 338, 633n223

Augustus II (Saxon king), 628n87

Augustus III (Saxon king), 628n87

Auschwitz, 283

Auxerre, 154–156

Avallon, 152–153

Averchenko, Arkady, 402, 638n31

Bach, J. S., 93, 215

Bacon, Francis, 536

Badoglio, Pietro, 460, 502, 642n100

Bagiński, Adolf (Adolf Dymsza), 10, 607n10

Bainville, Jacques Pierre, 216, 317, 379–380, 622n70, 631n170, 637n1

Balzac, Honoré de, xi, 50, 71, 138, 150, 161, 165, 187, 189, 190–191, 212, 235, 240–242, 270, 287, 299, 303, 331, 332, 341, 346–347, 348, 359, 375, 387, 401, 402, 440, 463, 464, 469, 487, 494, 516–519, 537, 538, 543, 596, 615n196,

Balzac, Honoré de (continued)
  621n61, 629n111, 630n133, 633n230,
  634n236, 635n258, 636n292, 638n28,
  644n157, 644n159
Bandol, 60, 84–87
Banque de France, 242, 276, 278
Baranowicze, 554
Barcelona, 435
Barcelonnette, 121–122
Barclay, Florence, 274, 626n62
Baroncelli, Jacques de, 630n133
Barone, Enrico, 150, 615n197
Bayard pass, 124
Bayeux, 533
Beaulieu, Johann Peter, 545, 647n46
Beaumont, 532
Beauplan, Robert de, 391–393, 638n21
Beauvallon, 93
Beck, Józef, 210, 621n58
Becker, Jacques, 648n59
Becque, Henry, 370, 636n284
Beethoven, Ludwig van, 204, 432, 469
Belgian Red Cross, 62, 73
Belgorod, 453
Belvès, 31
Benoist-Méchin, Jacques, 307, 630n145
Berdyaev, Nikolay, 381, 382, 393, 637n6
Berger, Ludwig, 621n53
Bergson, Henri, xi, 428, 528, 539,
  640n59
Berlin, 338, 352, 369, 383, 385, 396, 441,
  545
Berling, Zygmunt, 567, 649n89
Berlioz, Hector, 303
Bernadotte, Jean-Baptiste, 354, 634n248
Bernanos, Georges, 501, 643n137
Bernard, Claude, 568, 649n92
Bernard, Tristan (Paul Bernard), 420,
  421, 639n50
Bernhardt, Kurt (Curtis), 629n132
Berthelot, Marcellin, 568, 649n92
Berval (Antonin Pasteur), 511, 644n152
Besson, Antoine-Marie-Benoît, 293,
  628n108
Béziers, 70
Biélinky, Jacques, 648n79

Birtus, Barbara (Basia). *See* Bobkowski,
  Barbara Birtus (Basia)
Bizerte, 443, 445
Bizet, Georges, 156
Blanchar, Pierre, 221, 303, 623n83
Blenheim, Bristol, 628n96
Blücher, Gebhard Leberecht von, 494,
  643n129
Blum, Léon, 128, 286, 292, 343, 408,
  614n157, 628n93
Bobkowski, Aleksander, 599
Bobkowski, Barbara Birtus (Basia), vii,
  viii, ix
Bobkowski, Stanisława, 599
Bobruysk, 547, 548
Bocage, Louis Collin du (Louis Ver-
  neuil), 453, 641n89
Bock, Fedor von, 331, 632n205
Böcklin, Arnold, 83, 611n109
Bogatko, Marian (Maniek), 567, 649n85
Bogucki, Michał Konstanty, 609n54
Boileau-Despréaux, Nicolas, 408, 418,
  458, 639n38
Bois de Boulogne, 372, 607n8
Bolsheviks, 232, 235, 267, 353, 379, 380,
  387, 397
Bonnard, Pierre, 84
Borchard, Adolphe, 281–282, 627n79
Bordeaux, 19, 23, 232
Bór-Komorowski, Tadeusz, 573–574,
  580, 650n105
Bossuet, Jacques Bénigne, 408, 639n38
Bouilhet, Louis, 560
Boulanger, Georges Ernest, 492,
  643n126
Boulogne, 4
Boulogne-Billancourt, 343
Bourg, 137–141
Bourges, 16–18
Boy-Żeleński, Tadeusz, 93, 518, 644n162
Brahms, Johannes, 446
Brauchitsch, Walther von, 235, 331,
  624n108
Breker, Arno, 334, 633n212
Brest, 263, 264, 284, 573
Brest-Litovsk, 562, 637n3

Bridge, Ann, 39, 608n36
Brittany, 310–311, 319, 327, 329, 572, 573
Broglie, Louis de, 289, 628n97
Bromfield, Louis, 527, 645n17
Budenny, Semyon, 198, 620n37
Bunin, Ivan, 130, 614n160
Burgart, Henriette Louise (Orane Demaise), 511, 644n152
Burke, Edmund, 397
Byron, George Gordon, 40

Caballero, Francisco Largo, 541, 646n35
Cabet, Étienne, 393
Caen, 552
Cagliostro, Alessandro di (Giuseppe Balsamo Cagliostro), 502, 543, 646n38
Cahors, 32
Calais, 4, 5
Camargue, 78–79
Cambronne, Pierre Jacques Étienne, 160, 280, 616n222
Camus, Albert, 555, 648n66
Cannes, 97–99
Capet, Hugh, 626n56
Carcassonne, 34, 35–39, 44–45, 65–68, 592
Carentan, 535, 646n24
Casablanca, 384
Catherine de Medici, 404
Catherine the Great, 647n48
Catholicism, 163, 343, 356–358, 382, 407, 424, 563, 610n87, 617n242, 648n66
Cato the Elder, 250, 625n12
Caussade, 33
Cegiełka, Franciszek Antoni, 65, 163, 172–173, 201, 610n87
Céline, Louis-Ferdinand, 555, 648n65
Cervantes, 594–595
Cervoni, Jean-Baptiste, 548
Ce Soir (French Communist Party newspaper), 588, 651n130
Cézanne, 189
Challaye, Félicien, 560, 648n76
Chalon-sur-Saône, 137, 141, 147–148, 592, 614n165

Chałupka, Piotr (Jan Kwapiński), 454, 576, 641n93
Chambellay, 330, 335, 341–350, 455, 463–472
Chamberlain, Houston Stewart, 525, 645n11
Chamfort, Sébastien-Roch Nicolas de, 187, 357, 618n16
Chanel, Coco, 649n91
Les Chantiers de la Jeunesse (Pétainist youth organization), 643n124
Chantilly, 256–257, 507
Chaplin, Charlie, 152
Chappel, François, 12, 159, 213, 607n11
Charlemagne, 56, 404
Charles I (English king), 406
Charpentier, Suzanne Georgette (Annabella), 628n92
Chateaubriand, François-René, vicomte de, 301, 629n122
Châtillon, viii, 5, 8, 161–162, 202, 209, 213, 220, 233, 242, 357
Cheka (Soviet Extraordinary Commission), 645n8
Cherbourg, 533, 540, 543, 544, 545, 547
Chmielewski, Zygmunt, 443, 640n79
Choltitz, Dietrich von, 581, 650n116
Chopin, Frédéric, 160–161, 204, 216, 220–221, 281, 324, 440, 596, 609n60
Chouans, 311, 631n153
Christian-Jaque, 629n130
Churchill, Winston, 216, 218, 219, 284, 315, 326–327, 333, 353, 384, 442, 528, 634n245
Chwistek, Leon, 555, 565, 648n68
Cicero, 637n11
Clark, Mark W., 503, 643n142
Clary, Désirée, 353–354
Clermont-Ferrand, 36, 88
Cocéa, Alice, 370, 371–372
Cognacq, Ernest, 632n206
Cohn, Emil (Emil Ludwig), 469, 642n107
Col de Cayolle, 120
Colette, 511, 644n153
Cologne, 317, 319

Committee of National Liberation, 448, 566

Condillac, Étienne Bonnot de, 379, 637n1

Conrad, Joseph, xiv, xv, 191, 306, 365, 426, 468, 623n87, 636n274

Coppée, François, 524, 645n7

Corap, André-Georges, 3, 607n3

Corot, Jean-Baptiste-Camille, 327, 332, 632n207

Côte d'Azur, 97, 101

Courbet, Gustave, 315, 327

Couthon, Georges, 268, 626n53

Cracow, viii, 221, 287, 423, 508, 523, 573, 594, 626n58

Cranach, 356

Creil, 507

Creusot, 358

Crimea, 242

Cunati, Edwige Caroline (Edwige Feuil-lère), 303, 527, 630n133

Curel, François de, 396, 638n22

Curie, Marie, 204

Curtis (Kurt Bernhardt), 629n132

Custine, Marquis de, 379, 538, 637n1

Cyrankiewicz, Józef, 567, 649n90

Czerny, Karl, 190, 619n25

Czytelnik (publisher), ix

Dąbrowska, Maria, 599

Dąbrowski, Jan Henryk, 611n95

Daily Herald (British newspaper), 528

Dakar, 36, 148, 198

Daladier, Édouard, 286, 292, 304, 628n93

Dante Alighieri, 455, 464

Darlan, François, 199, 311, 363, 364, 365, 366, 367–368, 452, 635n268

Darré, Richard Walther, 317, 631n172

Darrieux, Danielle, 460, 642n99

Das Reich (Goebbels), 384, 386, 389

Daszyński, Ignacy, 178, 618n4

Daudet, Alphonse, 153, 616n207

Daumier, Honoré, 170, 197, 619n33

Dauriac, Carle Lionel (Armory), 505, 644n145

Davout, Louis Nicolas, 338, 633n222

Déat, Marcel, 307, 458, 630n144, 648n76

Deauville, 533

Debussy, Claude, 281, 282

Declaration of the Rights of Man, 318, 320, 475, 561

Dégas, Edgar, 207, 444

De Gaulle, Charles, 50, 138, 194, 195, 215, 365, 366, 367, 449, 581, 608n29, 620n40

Dekobra, Maurice (Maurice Tessier), 540, 646n34

Delannoy, Jean, 638n18

Dellemagne, Claude, 548

Delubac, Jacqueline, 305, 630n141

Demaise, Orane (Henriette Louise Bur-gart), 511, 644n152

Descartes, René, 56, 94, 300, 408, 612n127

Desmoulins, Camille, 255, 268, 625n23

Dickens, Charles, 365

Diderot, Denis, xii, 282, 609n64

Diego Suarez (Madagascar), 314–315

Dieppe, 332–334

Dignimont, André, 372, 445, 636n287

DKW-Grün, 224, 225, 639n55

Dmowski, Roman, 178, 617n4

Dongen, Kees van, 366, 636n276

Doriot, Jacques, 307, 620n39, 630n144

Dostoyevsky, Fyodor, 221, 303, 381, 623n83

Drabik, Wincenty, 443, 641n79

Drobner, Bolesław, 567, 649n87

Duchesse d'Abrantès (Laure Junot), 359–360, 387, 494, 635n258

Dujardin, Édouard, 525, 645n11

Dullin, Charles, 374, 636n291

Dumas, Alexandre, *fils*, 189, 630n133

Dumas, Alexandre, *père*, 189, 332, 502, 517, 643n140, 644n161

Dunikowski, Zbigniew Jan, 543, 646n38

Dunkirk, 5, 8, 357

Dupin, Amantine-Lucile-Aurore. See Sand, George

Dupuy-Mazuel, Henry, 623n83

Dürer, Albrecht, 356
Dymsza, Adolf (Adolf Bagiński), 10, 607n10
Dzierżyński, Feliks, 476

L'Echo de la France (French newspaper), 526
Economist, 526
Eden, Anthony, 514, 580, 626n61, 644n155
Einstein, Albert, 60, 610n76
Eisenhower, Dwight, 580
El Agheila, 370, 375
El-Alamein, 330–331, 359
Engels, Friedrich, 67, 294, 299, 480
English Red Cross, 173
Erfurt, 338
Essen, 402
Esser, Hermann, 391, 392, 638n20
Étiolles, 355–358
Eugénie, Empress, 331
Eylau, Battle of, 338, 638n13

Falter, Alfred, 309, 630n146
Ferrero, Guglielmo, 401, 460, 489–490, 545, 638n29
Feuillère, Edwige (Edwige Caroline Cunati), 303, 527, 630n133
Feydeau, Georges, 370–371, 494
FFI (Forces françaises de l'intérieure), 586, 587, 651n124
Fichte, Johann Gottlieb, 480
Flaubert, Gustave, 45, 165, 187, 189, 332, 342, 351, 446, 472, 487, 494, 534, 560, 596, 608n48, 630n142, 633n232
Foch, Ferdinand, 94, 612n127
Forst, Willi, 214, 303, 622n66
Fos, 79
Fouché, Joseph, 360–363, 635n262
Fouquier-Tinville, Antoine Quentin, 345, 634n235
Fourier, Charles, 477
France, Anatole, 153, 418, 616n207
Franz Joseph I, 302, 318, 629n127
Frederick II of Hohenzollern, 545, 647n43

Frederick Louis (Prince of Hohenlohe-Ingelfingen), 338, 633n223
Freemasons, 51, 288, 305, 628n95
French Red Cross, 10, 76
Fresnay, Pierre, 207, 621n53
Friedland, 338
Frobenius, Leo Viktor, 145, 306, 525, 614n176, 630n143, 645n12
Fyda, Wojciech, 621n60

Gable, Clark, 366
Gambetta, Léon, 165, 617n230
Gamelin, Maurice, 3, 286, 292, 304, 606n1, 628n93
Gap, 124
García Oliver, Juan, 541, 646n35
Gauguin, Paul, 327
Gautier, Théophile, 189, 301, 331, 332, 440, 446, 629n124
Gauty, Lys, 369, 636n282
Gavarni, Paul, 196–197, 298, 440, 597, 619n33, 629n115
Gawlina, Józef, 542, 646n36
Gedymin, castle of, 439, 640n69
Géraldy, Paul, 511–512, 644n153
La Gerbe (The Sheaf), 554–555, 648n64
German National Socialism, 242, 297, 311
Germinal (collaborationist weekly), 560, 648n76
Gestapo, 66, 147, 163–164, 177, 189, 201, 208, 264–265, 267, 553, 571
Gibralter, 232, 451, 452
Gide, André, 294, 379, 410, 637n1
Giedroyc, Jerzy, ix, xiv, 599
Gierymski, Aleksander, 554, 648n63
Giraud, Henri, 363, 367–368, 448, 635n268
Giraudoux, Jean, 527, 645n16
Glazunov, Alexander, 551
Gniesenau (German battleship/cruiser), 284
Gnome et Rhône, 305, 420, 630n140
Goebbels, Joseph, 195, 383–384, 386, 448, 543, 567–568, 638n25

Goethe, Johann Wolfgang von, 352,
648n78, 650n109
Gombrowicz, Witold, ix, 599
Goncourt, Edmond de, 74, 282, 331, 332,
440, 472, 548, 559, 566, 568, 573
Goncourt, Jules de, 282, 331, 332, 440,
472, 548, 559, 566, 568, 573
Goodrich manufacturing plant, 305,
630n140
Göring, Hermann, 152, 166, 184, 222,
226, 312, 354–355, 385
Gosselin, Louis Léon Théodore
(G. Lenotre), 626n52
Gounod, Charles, 145, 209–210,
621n56
Gourgaud, Gaspart, 583, 651n117
Gourmont, Rémy de, 496, 643n131
Grabski, Stanisław, 570–571, 574,
650n100
Grasset, Bernard, 415, 639n42
Gregory of Tours, 294
Grenoble, 126, 131, 134–135
Grottger, Artur, 365, 586, 636n275
Gruissan, 40–44, 46–62
Grydzewski, Mieczysław, 599
Grzymała, Franciszek, 440, 640n72
Guatemala, ix, 597, 598
Guéret, 21–22
Guibert, Jacques Antoine Hippolyte,
comte de, 545, 647n45
Guillaumes, 118
Guitry, Sacha (Alexandre-Pierre Geor-
ges Guitry), 183–185, 353–354, 435,
543–544, 618n10, 630n141
Güys, Constantin, 74, 611n100
Gdynia, 102, 613n137

Hácha, Emile, 187, 618n17
Haecker (Haker), Emil (Samuel), 555,
648n69
Halévy, Daniel, 409, 639n39
Halle, Battle of, 338
Hańska, Ewelina, 517, 518, 537–538, 543,
644n159
Hašek, Jaroslav, 622n72
Hazard, Paul, 533, 645n20

Hegel, Georg Wilhelm Friedrich, 92, 93,
299, 337, 422, 428, 480, 614n177
Heine, Heinrich, 146, 615n183, 633n213
Helvétius, Claude Adrien, 489, 643n121
Hennecke, Walter, 547, 647n51
Henri IV (French king), 408
Henriot, Philippe, 546–547, 549–550,
647n49
Herbert, Zbigniew, 598
Herling-Grudziński, Gustaw, 599
Herodotus, 639n35
Herzen, Alexander, ix, 637n1
Hess, Rudolf, 332, 633n209
Heydrich, Reinhard, 318, 631n177
Himmler, Heinrich, 476
Hitler, Adolf, 19, 30, 48, 58, 60, 92,
95, 137, 164, 182, 193, 211, 214–219,
228–229, 235, 276, 292, 302, 306, 312,
314, 331–334, 338, 352, 353, 363–364,
369–370, 377, 383, 385, 388, 391–
392, 398, 433, 448, 460, 476, 504,
526, 543, 546, 547, 552, 563, 564, 568,
571, 577, 621n48, 633n212, 638n15,
647n43, 649n80, 650n116
Hitlerjugend, 643n124
Hoche, Lazare, 546, 647n47
Hoene-Wroński, Józef Maria, 294, 537,
543, 628n109, 646n28
Hoesick, Ferdynand, 440, 640n71
Home Army, 577
Horace, 72, 138
Hot Springs, conference of, 449
Hotz, Karl, 622n67
Hugo, Victor, 223, 628n91
Hull, Cordell, 644n155
L'Humanité (Communist newspaper),
587, 651n127, 651n130
Hutten, Ulrich von, 479, 577, 642n117,
650n113
Huxley, Aldous, 105, 366, 428, 636n277
Hyères, 89–90

Ibárruri, Dolores (Pasionaria), 436,
640n67
International Red Cross, 440
Iwaszkiewicz, Jarosław, 599

Jacobins, 407, 618n16, 626n53, 634n235
Jagiełło (ship to Guatemala), 597
Jaracz, Stefan, 443, 641n79
Jaurès, Jean, 651n127
Jeans, James, 78, 611n106
Jersey, 617n248
Jews, 17, 63, 92, 186–188, 224, 225, 231,
    234, 288, 294, 305, 318, 319, 329–330,
    412, 426, 435, 442, 458, 546, 606n1,
    610nn83–84, 611n108, 618n14,
    621n48, 628n95, 630n132, 632n200,
    638n21, 646n25, 647n48, 648–
    649n79
Joan of Arc (Maid of Orléans), 56, 411
Jonson, Ben, 650n114
Joly, Anténor, 517, 518, 644n158
Joséphine (Empress), 360–363, 610n78
Joué-en-Charnie, 453, 455, 474, 478,
    489, 493, 498, 642n110
Juan les Pins, 99–100
Julius Caesar, 45–46, 48–49, 55,
    607n19, 609n55
Jung, Carl, 515
Junot, Jean-Andoche, 359, 635n258
Junot, Laure (Duchesse d'Abrantès),
    359–360, 387, 494, 635n258

Karpiński, Światopełk, 57, 58, 610n74
Katyń, xi, 437, 439–440, 441, 442, 514
Keitel, Wilhelm, 312, 631n158
Keyserling, Hermann Alexander Graf
    von, xi, xii, 330, 403, 407–410, 411,
    417, 424, 464, 469, 473, 484, 606n17,
    632n201, 639n37, 642n116, 643n120
Kharkov, 316, 317, 318, 320, 338, 377,
    388, 498
Khmelnytsky, Boghan, 607n24
Kiev, 198, 206, 505, 620n37
Kipling, Rudyard, 148, 615n192
Kluge, Günther von, 552, 585, 647n57,
    651n123
Koenig, Marie-Pierre, 589, 652n133
Kołakowski, Leszek, ix
Komsomol, 524, 645n8
Konarski, Szymon, 201, 620n43
Konopnicka, Maria, 617n242

Konstantin Pavlovich, Grand Duke,
    640n75
Kontra (publisher), 598
Korwin-Piotrowska, Sophie de, 537,
    646n27
Kościuszko, Tadeusz, 370, 636n283
Koźmiński, Jan, 244, 624n2
Kraft durch Freude (Strength through
    Joy), 284, 492, 628n88
Krasiński, Zygmunt, 433, 640n66
Kreiskommando, 257, 625n25
Krukowski, Kazimierz (Lopek), 31–32,
    234, 624n107
Krzymuski, Edmund Karol Feliks, 361,
    635n265
Kultura (journal), ix
Kultura (publishing house), ix, xiv, xv,
    598
Kuncewiczowa, Maria, 575–576,
    650n110
Kunina, Ewa, 443, 624n79
Kupiansk, 387
Kwapiński, Jan (Piotr Chałupka), 454,
    576, 641n93

Labiche, Eugène, 585, 651n122
La Bruyère, Jean de, 417, 639n44
Lafayette, Marquis de, 269–270,
    626n56
La Fontaine, Jean, 282, 627n85
La Haye-du-Puits, 554
La Mure, 126–129
La Napoule, 97
Lannes, Jean, 338, 359, 633n222
La Rouchefoucauld, François de, 357
La Salette, 118
Lasalle, Antoine Charles Louis de, 338,
    633n224
La Seyne, 87–88
Lassailly, Charles, 517, 644n160
Launay, Bernard René de, 475, 642n113
Laurel, Stan, 79
Laval, Pierre, 307, 309, 311, 318, 322, 323,
    325, 327, 336, 350, 359, 374, 389, 392,
    398, 546, 620n40, 630n144,
    636n290

League of Nations, 422
Le Bon, Gustave, 428, 538, 640n59
Lecomte du Noüy, Pierre, 355, 635n252
Leipzig, 338
Le Lavandou, 90–91
Le Mans, 350, 498, 576
Lenin, Vladimir, 380, 480, 570
Leningrad, 383, 386, 388, 637n10
Lenotre, G. (Louis Léon Théodore Gosselin), 626n52
Leonardo da Vinci, 284, 575
Leopold (King of Belgium), 5, 62
Lermontov, Mikhail, 611n96
Lespinasse, Mademoiselle de, 189, 618n21
Lessing, Gotthold Ephraim, 612n119, 612n121
Leszczyńska, Maria, 204, 354, 620n47, 635n249
Lewinsohn, Richard, 279, 627n73
Lewis, Sinclair, 462
Lida (Polish town), 554
Limanowski, Mieczysław, 443, 613n143
Limoges, 24
Lipiński, Edward, 150, 452, 615n198
Lippmann, Walter, 448
Liszt, Franz, 165, 281, 324
Livy, 138, 637n11
London, Jack, 42
Lorient, 573
Louis XIV (French king), 56, 94, 407–408
Louis XV (French king), 620n47
Louis XVI (French king), 7, 620n47
Louis XVIII (French king), 438
Louise (Queen of Prussia), 338
Louis-Philippe (French king), 165, 183, 295, 437, 492, 617n231
Louÿs, Pierre, 515, 644n156
Lübeck, 338
Lublin, 565
Lublin Committee, 649n83, 649n87, 649n89
Ludwig, Emil (Emil Cohn), 469, 642n107

Luther, Martin, 92–93
Lwów (Lviv), 396–397, 638n23
Lyautey, Louis Hubert, 94, 612n127
Lycurgus, 489, 643n121
Lydis, Mariette, 136, 611n164

Machiavelli, 484
Maczek, Stanisław, 577, 648n72
Madagascar, 96–97, 311, 314–315, 562
Maeterlinck, Maurice, 534, 645n22
Magdeburg, 338
Maisky, Ivan, 619n31
Maison, Nicolas Joseph, 338, 633n220
Maison-Laffitte, ix
Maistre, Joseph de, xi, 397, 403–407, 411–416
Malmaison, 61
Manet, Édouard, 207, 347, 444, 586
Mann, Thomas, 60, 610n76
Mansfield, Katherine, 60–61, 85, 130, 596, 600–601, 611n110
Marat, Jean-Paul, 476
Marbot, Jean Baptiste Antoine Marcellin de, 300, 313, 629n121, 631n160
Mareuil, 26
Marie Antoinette, 252–253, 255
Marie-Louise (Duchess of Parma), 361
Maritime Alps, 99, 106, 113, 118, 592
Marseille, 78, 80–81
Martigues, 79
Martin du Gard, Roger, 501, 643n124
Marx, Karl, 92, 187, 299, 480, 570, 579
Mary Magdalene, 254
Masséna, André, 313, 548, 631n161
Matford manufacturing plant, 304, 630n138
Le Matin (pro-German newspaper), 293, 318, 391–393, 527, 638n21
Maugham, Somerset, 42
Maupassant, Guy de, 155, 214, 534, 616n215, 622n66
Mauriac, François, 301, 629n123
Maurois, André, 46, 51, 178, 342, 618n5, 633n231
Maurras, Charles, 642n105

Mecklenburg-Schwerin, von (Prince), 338

Meersch, Maxence van der, 507, 551, 563, 644n148

Melun, 157

Merezhkovsky, Dmitry, 228, 623n97

Mers-el-Kébir, Battle of, 228, 623n96

Michelet, Jules, 332, 379, 380, 633n208, 637n1

Mickiewicz, Adam, 91, 204, 220, 373, 381, 382, 441, 570, 610n81, 611n92, 612n118, 614n161, 636n272, 637n7, 640n66, 642n95, 646n28, 650n99, 650n115

Mieczysławska, Aniela, 600

Mikołajczyk, Stanisław, 454, 534, 564, 569, 570–571, 572, 574, 576, 577, 580, 625n93

Mikołajewski, Łukasz, xiii

Miłosz, Czesław, ix

Ministry of Labor, 7, 321–322, 432, 534, 574, 582

Ministry of Leisure (Ministère des Loisirs), 495

Ministry of Production (Secrétariat d'État à la Production Industrielle), 213

Minsk, 547, 551

Mińsk Mazowiecki, 221, 224

Mirabeau, Victor de Riqueti, Marquis de, 404, 639n34

Miramar, 97

Mises, Ludwig von, 150, 615n197

Mitchell, Margaret, 610n79

Mniszkówna, Helena, 98, 612n131

Mogilev, 547, 548

Molière, 71, 94, 165, 374, 408, 509

Molotov, Vyacheslav, 514, 566, 644n155

Molyneux, Edward, 612n111

Monceaux, 506, 508

Montaigne, 187

Montauban, 33

Monte Carlo, x, 106–109, 110–112

Monte Cassino, 648n72

Montereau, 157

Montgolfier, Étienne, 223, 623n88

Montgolfier, Joseph, 223, 623n88

Montgomery, Bernard, 360, 370, 374, 384, 502

Montluçon, 18–20

Montpellier, 73–78

More, Thomas, 393

Moreau, Jean Victor Marie, 354, 546, 635n251, 647n47

Morgan, Michèle (Simone Renée Rousel), 519, 644n163

Morisot, Berthe, 444

Mortier, Édouard, 338, 633n226

Mounet, Lily, 362

Mozart, Wolfgang Amadeus, 204, 432

Munthe, Axel, 179, 618n6

Muraire, Jules Auguste (Raimu), 302, 509–510, 511, 629n129, 644n151

Murat, Joachim, 152, 166, 338, 616n202, 633n221

Murger, Henry, 451, 641n85

Musset, Alfred de, 465, 642n105

Mussolini, Benito, 331, 369, 433, 459–460, 502, 504, 642n100

Nałkowska, Zofia, 294, 599, 629n110

Nansen, Fridtjof, 529, 645n18

Napoleon Bonaparte, 56, 61, 94, 134, 137–138, 144, 152, 164, 204, 214, 306, 331, 338, 354, 359, 387, 388, 438, 493, 545–546, 583, 610n77, 614n166, 616n202, 626n54, 634n248, 635n251, 635n262, 635n266

Napoleon III (Louis-Napoleon Bonaparte), 303, 629n128

Narbonne, 46, 51, 52, 56, 69–70, 592

National Socialism. *See* German National Socialism

National Socialist Party, 391, 392

Nemours, 12, 14–16

Nero, 352, 634n241

Nice, 100–105, 109–112, 592

Nietzsche, Friedrich, 92, 480

Norden, Kamil, 66, 611n95

Normandy, 533, 548, 551–552, 557, 563, 576, 581, 584, 617n248, 646n24

Norwid, Cyprian, 543, 637n8

November Uprising (Poland), 610n81
Nowakowski, Zygmunt (Zygmunt Tempka), 555, 648n67
Nowowiejski, Feliks, 617n242

Oklahoma (U.S. ship at Pearl Harbor), 227
Opel (plane manufacturer), 312
Oryol, 453
Organization of the Resistance (*la Résistance*). *See* Résistance
Orsha, 548
Orzeszkowa, Eliza, 426, 639n56
Osterwa, Elżunia, 641n80
Osterwa, Juliusz, 443, 613n143, 641n80, 641n81
Osterwina, Wanda (Wanda Malinowska), 641n80, 641n81
Ovid, 138

Pacifist Club, 567
Pacquin, Jeanne, 612n111
Pagnol, Marcel, 37, 81, 302–303, 509–510, 608n30, 629n129, 644n152
Painlevé, Paul, 489, 643n122
Papée, Kazimierz, 542, 646n36
Papkin, Józef, 280, 627n74
Parandowski, Jan, 121, 483, 613n153
Parc de Bagatelle, 9, 372, 607n8
Pariser Zeitung (German-occupied Parisian newspaper), 229, 276, 397, 427, 448
Paris Opéra, 10, 185, 198, 209, 329, 331, 366, 554, 582
Paris-Soir (daily newspaper), 550, 651n130
Pascal, Blaise, 523, 528–529
Pasionaria (Dolores Ibárruri), 436, 640n66
Pasteur, Antonin (Berval), 511, 644n152
Patton, George S., 576
Paulus, Friedrich, 388, 638n15
Pearl Harbor attack, 227
Péguy, Charles, 415, 417, 639n42
Pérémé, Armand, 517, 644n158
Pericles, 489, 643n121

Périgueux, 26, 29
Perzanowska, Stanislawa, 443, 641n79
Pétain, Philippe, viii, 3, 19, 28–29, 40, 85, 94, 105, 138, 160, 163, 167, 181–182, 195, 199, 212, 219–220, 222–223, 226, 242, 244, 257–259, 278, 286, 292, 297, 307, 309, 311, 325, 345, 350, 354, 363, 364, 365, 367, 369, 370, 389, 392, 398, 419, 475, 484, 540, 566, 606n1, 607nn2–3, 620nn39–40, 628n93, 636n290, 638n21
Peter the Great, 379, 546, 647n48
Le Petit Parisien (Vichy regime newspaper), 442, 452, 581, 650n116
Petronius Arbiter, Gaius, 352, 522, 634n241
Philarets, 537, 646n28
Philomaths, 537, 646n28
Pichegru, Jean Charles, 268, 626n54
Pierson, Nicholaas Gerard, 150, 615n197
Piłsudski, Józef, viii, 178, 605n2, 606n1, 611n93, 613n138, 621n58, 623n97, 633n225, 636n280
Pinet, François, 629n112
Pinsk, 557
Plato, 415, 417, 560
Plinius Caecilius Secundus, Gaius, 51, 609n63
Plucińska-Smorawska, Katarzyna, 605n4
Pogorzelska, Zula, 645n9
Polenreferat, 264–265
Polish Academy of Literature, 629n110
Polish Bureau, viii
Polish Committee in Moscow, 580
Polish Committee of National Liberation, 566–567, 574, 649n83
Polish Finance Ministry, viii
Polish House (Paris), 172–173, 175, 179
Polish House (Toulouse), 34
Polish Institute of Arts and Sciences of America (PIASA), xiii, 599
Polish Ministry of Commerce and Trade, viii
Polish Red Cross, 99, 103, 126, 131–134
Polish Socialist Party, 641n93, 649n87

Polish Telegraph Agency, 567
Polish Underground Army, 571–572, 576
Polish Underground Government (Polskie Państwo Podziemne), 648n71
Polotsk, 552
Popesco, Elvire, 453, 641n89
Poręba, Józef, 443, 640n79
Porte de Versailles, 8
Power, Tyrone, 628n92
Prenzlau, 338
Prévost, Abbé, 608n49, 609n53
Prince of Wales (British warship), 228
Printemps, Yvonne, 207, 621n53
Prinz Eugen (German cruiser), 284
Prokofiev, Sergei, 551
Proust, Marcel, 347, 534
Prouvost, Jean, 29, 607n26
Prudhomme, Louis Marie, 432, 635n263
Prus, Bolesław, 207, 377, 424, 425, 553, 616n229, 621n52, 637n297
Przerwa-Tetmajer, Kazimierz, 66, 611n91
Przybyszewski, Stanislaw, 65, 610n88
Puccini, Giacomo, 641n85
Puget-Théniers, 113–114
Pushkin, Alexander, 66, 611n96, 647n48
Pusłowski, Franciszek Xawery, 555, 648n70

Quimperlé, 16
Quisling, Vidkun, 566

Rabelais, François, 407, 627n85
Rachilde (Marguerite Vallette-Eymery), 505, 644n145
Rachmaninov, Sergei, 122, 551
Racine, Jean, 94, 627n80
Raczkiewicz, Władysław, 576, 650n112
Radio London, 197, 215, 220, 226, 235, 319, 332, 364, 457, 498, 617n1
Radio Moscow, 440, 448, 521
Radio Paris, 220, 307, 332, 558, 636n282, 638n21
Radio Vichy, 231
Raimu (Jules Auguste Muraire), 302, 509–510, 511, 629n129, 644n151
Rambaud, Alfred, 379, 637n2

Ramolino, Letizia (Madame Mère), 360–362, 635n266
Ravel, Maurice, 42, 324
Raynal, Paul, 360–363, 635n261
Red Cross: Belgian, 62, 73; English, 173; French, 10, 76; International, 440; Polish, 99, 103, 126, 131–134
Reduta, 443, 613n143, 640n79, 641n81, 641n82
Rej, Mikołaj, 449, 641n84
Réjane, Gabrielle, 370, 636n285
Rémy, Constant, 519, 644n163
Renan, Ernest, 67, 332, 419, 611n97
Renault (manufacturer), 290, 305, 431
Rennes, 572
Renoir, Jean, 644n154
Renoir, Pierre-Auguste, 327, 444, 586
Renouard, Jeanne Marguerite (Albert-Émile Sorel), 428, 640n59
Repulse (British warship), 228
Résistance (Organization of the Resistance), 366, 584–587, 622n67, 647n49, 651n124
Reymont, Władysław, 282, 627n83
Reynaud, Paul, 3–4, 15, 19, 607n2, 628n93
Rimsky-Korsakov, Nikolay, 551
Riom, 286, 292, 293, 303, 318, 398, 628n93
Rivarol, Antoine de, 478, 642n113
Riviera, 65, 83, 93, 111, 364, 578
Robespierre, Maximilien, 268, 476, 477, 626n53, 634n235
Rodin, Auguste, 193
Rokossovsky, Konstantin, 570, 649n98
Rola-Żymierski, Michał (Łyżwiński), 567, 649n88
Rollan, Henri, 362
Romer, Tadeusz, 570–571, 574, 650n100
Rommel, Erwin, 320, 330–331, 359, 360, 370, 375, 384, 388, 427, 552, 631n180, 632n186, 632n202
Roosevelt, Eleanor, 229, 338, 364, 534
Roosevelt, Franklin D., 15, 205, 216, 219, 227, 229, 326, 353, 364, 384, 534, 622nn79–80, 634n245

Rosenberg, Alfred, 92
Rosinkiewicz, Roman, 201, 222, 620n43
Rossi, Tino, 544, 646n41
Rossini, Gioachino, 44
Rostov, 224, 377, 385, 388
Rostworowski, Karol, 555, 648n66
Rousel, Simone Renée (Michèle Morgan), 519, 644n163
Rousseau, Jean-Jacques, 379, 477, 637n1
Rubens, Peter Paul, 537
Rundstedt, Gerd von, 311, 552, 631n156
Russian Free Press, viii, ix
Rzewuski, Wacław, 537, 646n28

Sable-sur-Sarthe, 335, 338–340, 474
Sade, Marquis de, 414
Sainte-Beuve, Charles Augustin, 479, 632n201, 642n116
Sainte-Suzanne, 489, 491–493
Saint-Exupéry, Antoine de, 573, 650n104
Saint-Gilles, 78
Saint-Just, Louis Antoine Léon de, 268, 626n54
Saint-Maxime, 93
Saint-Nazaire, 304, 630n136
Saint-Raphaël, 94–95, 123
Saint-Sulpice, 22, 23
Saint-Tropez, 93
Salamis, Battle of, 337
Salerno, Gulf of, 502, 503
Salvation Army, 210
Samozwaniec, Magdalena (Madzia), 455, 641n94
Sand, George (Amantine-Lucile-Aurore Dupin), 50, 165, 188, 189, 190, 221, 256, 332, 440, 465, 517, 609n60, 642n105
Saragossa, 359
Sardou, Victorien, 451, 625n86
Scapini, Georges, 220, 622n81
Scharnhorst (German battleship/cruiser), 284
Scheler, Max, 474, 515, 629n120
Schiele, Egon, 75, 611n101
Schiller, Friedrich, 631n169
Schlageter, Albert, 257, 625n26

Schlieben, Karl Wilhelm von, 547, 647n51
Schliemann, Heinrich, 182, 618n9
Schnayder, Jerzy Edward, 65, 611n89
Schneider-Creusot plants, 358
Schubert, Franz, 204, 432, 446
Schuhl, Pierre-Maxime, 536, 646n25
Schumann, Robert, 432, 446, 633n213
Schwerbel, Counselor, 163–164, 172–173, 177–178, 201, 208, 228
Scipio Africanus, 632n202
Scriabin, Alexander, 44, 551
Senlis, 247–249, 251–256
Sens, 156
Sesostris, 404, 639n35
Sevastopol, 320, 322, 326, 388
Sévigné, Mme de, 189, 618–619n21
Seyda, Marian, 200, 620n42
Shakespeare, William, 187, 374, 600, 611n110
Shaw, George Bernard, 641n86
Sicily, 453–454
Sieburg, Friedrich, 411, 415, 571, 639n40
Siegfried, André, 226, 409, 422, 623n93
Sienkiewicz, Henryk, 27, 57, 97, 160, 204, 207, 228–229, 230, 341, 426, 596, 607n24, 608n43, 610n70, 611n90, 612n129, 618n14, 618n18, 623n99, 624n105, 637n296
Signal (French newspaper), 560
Sikorski, Władysław, 196, 219, 227, 396–397, 402, 441, 442, 451–452, 619n31, 620n42
Sikorski-Maisky Treaty, 196, 619n31
Sławoj-Składkowski, Felicjan, 613n138
Słonimski, Antoni, 71, 73, 92, 611n98, 611n99
Słowacki, Juliusz, 50, 186, 188, 381, 441, 609n61, 637n7, 640n66
Śmigły, Edward Rydz, 613n138
Socialist Youth (*see* Związek Niezależnej Młodzieży Socjalistycznej), 53, 567, 570, 610n67
Soldatensender Calais (radio station), 531
Somme, 4, 9

Sorel, Albert-Émile (Jeanne Marguerite Renouard), 428, 640n59
Sorel, Cécile, 202, 620n44
Sosnkowski, Kazimierz, 452, 620n42
Sosnkowski, Marian, 200, 454, 620n42
Spandau, 338
Speer, Albert, 552, 647n58
Spengler, Oswald, xi, 67, 515, 611n97
Spinoza, 428
Stalin, Josef, 152, 164, 217, 227, 229, 353, 379, 380, 384, 390, 423, 442, 448, 476, 504, 527, 548, 564, 568, 570–571, 572, 576, 577, 623n90
Stalingrad, 331, 333, 335, 337, 346, 352, 360, 370, 376, 377, 383, 386–388, 390, 549, 634nn242–243, 638n15, 649n98
Stanislavsky, Konstantin, 613n143
Stanisław I (King of Poland), 620n47
Stauffenberg, Claus von, 563, 564, 649n80
Stendhal (Marie-Henri Beyle), 113, 613n148
Stettin, 338
Stevenson, Robert Louis, 641n92
Stołpce, 551
Strauss, Richard, 471
Stryj, 573
Stülpnagel, Carl-Heinrich von, 206, 214, 215, 621n48
Styka, Adam, 80, 611n107
Suchodolski, Rajnold, 650n106
Sully-sur-Loire, 16
Świątek, Leon, 555, 565, 648n68
Swinarski, Artur Maria, 432, 640n63
Szaniawski, Jerzy, 443, 641n82
Szymborska, Wisława, 598

Tacitus, 138
Tadzio (Tadeusz Wylot), x, xii
Talleyrand-Périgord, Charles Maurice de, 360–363, 635n262
Tamerlane, 410
Tauentzien, Bogislav Friedrich Emanuel von, 338, 633n223
Taylor, Robert, 627n63

Tchaikovsky, Pyotr Ilyich, 443, 444, 551
Tempka, Zygmunt (Zygmunt Nowakowski), 555, 648n67
Terlecki, Tymon, 599, 605n1
Terlikowski, Włodzimierz, 21, 607n18
Tertullian, 410
Tessier, Maurice (Maurice Dekobra), 540, 646n34
Tessier, Valentine, 513, 644n154
Tetmajer, Kazimierz (*see* Przerwa-Tetmajer), 66
Thibaudet, Albert, 409, 639n39
Thomas Aquinas, 504
Thorez, Maurice, 587, 651n128
Timoshenko, Semyon, 224, 316, 623n90, 631n168
Tobruk, 188, 322, 330, 632n186
Tolstoy, Leo, 187, 304, 306, 381
Toruń, viii
Toulon, 87–89, 95, 148, 368, 369–370
Toulouse, 34, 96
Toulouse-Lautrec, Henri de, 444
Tourneur, Maurice, 629n128
Towiański, Andrzej Tomasz, 229, 382, 441, 618n14
Trappes, 577
Tripoli, 384
Trublet, Nicolas Charles Joseph, 223, 414, 623n86
Tsarskoye Selo, 296, 629n113
Tual, Roland, 632n199
Tunis, 388, 432, 443, 445
Turowicz, Jerzy, 599
Tuwim, Julian, 44, 608n44, 630n151
Twain, Mark, 352

Underground. *See* Polish Underground; Résistance
Uniłowski, Zbigniew, 608n45
Union of Polish Artists, 617n235
Union of Polish Patriots (Związek Polskich Patriotów), 526–527, 565–566, 645n14, 649n83, 649n89
Union of Polish Theatrical Artists, 641n79
Union of Polish Writers, 641n82

University of Wilno, 646n28
UNRRA (United Nations Relief and Rehabilitation Administration), 569, 649nn95–96
Uriage, 126, 131

Valéry, Paul, 135, 403
Valette, Hélène de la, 517
Vallette-Eymery, Marguerite (Rachilde), 505, 644n145
Valmontone, 530
Van der Meersch, Maxence, 507, 551, 563, 644n148
Van Gogh, Vincent, 327
Var valley, 99, 104, 120
Vatican, 357, 358. *See also* Catholicism
Vauban, Sébastien le Prestre de, 403, 639n33
Velikiye Luki, Battle of, 383, 637n5
Velletria, 530
Verneuil, Louis (Louis Collin du Bocage), 453, 641n89
Victor Emmanuel III (Italian king), 642n100
Virgil, 502
Vitebsk, 548
Vizille, 130
Voltaire, François Marie Arouet, 94, 223, 282–283, 284, 399, 414, 612n127, 623n86, 627n85, 631n159
Voronezh, 376
Voroshilovgrad, 388

Wagemann, Ernst, 627n70
Wagner, Richard, 92, 93, 204, 334, 525
Ward, Georgina Elisabeth, 617n232
Warsaw, viii, xi, 89, 571–574, 576–582, 584–588, 591, 597, 626n58, 650n102, 651n120
Wasilewska, Wanda, 57, 566, 649n84
Watteau, Antoine, 189, 619n23
Weber, Carl Maria von, 429, 525, 640n61
Wellington, Viscount (Arthur Wellesley), 313
Wells, H. G., 574, 650n107

Werfel, Franz, 60, 610n76
Westerplatte, 89, 117, 612n114
West Virginia (U.S. ship at Pearl Harbor), 227
Weygand, Maxime, 3, 19, 219, 222, 606n1
Weyssenhoff, Józef, 111, 613n145, 628n107
Wiech (Stefan Wiechewski), 549, 647n52
Wiener Neustadt, Austria, viii, 146, 314, 615n180
Wieniawa-Długoszowski, Bolesław, 338, 633n225
Wilde, Oscar, 71, 74, 86, 161, 216, 365
Wilejka, 551
Wilhelm II (German kaiser), 302, 629n126
William I (Elector of Hesse), 633n226
Wilno (Vilnius), 80, 110, 443, 549, 554–557, 558, 577
Witos, Andrzej, 567, 649n89
Wittlin, Józef, 301, 599, 629n123
"World Air Force," 539, 646n32
Wybicki, Józef, 611n95
Wylot, Tadeusz (Tadzio), x, xii

Young, Arthur, 490, 643n123

Zabłocki, Franciszek, 640n77
Zaleski, August, 200, 620n42
Żeromski, Stefan, 443, 550, 553, 599, 641n82, 648n60
Zimand, Roman, 598
ZNMS (Związek Niezależnej Młodzieży Socjalistycznej; *see* Socialist Youth), 610n67
Zola, Émile, 221
Zoshchenko, Mikhail, 324, 402, 632n188, 638n31
Związek Niezależnej Młodzieży Socjalistycznej (ZNMS), 53, 567, 570, 610n67
Związek Polskich Patriotów (*see* Union of Polish Patriots), 526–527, 565–566, 645n14, 649n83, 649n89

ANDRZEJ BOBKOWSKI (1913–1961) was the author of short stories and essays, as well as the journal of his years in wartime France, which has established his reputation as a master of modern Polish prose.

GRAŻYNA DRABIK teaches contemporary literature at City College and Macaulay Honors College at the City University of New York. She translates Polish poetry into English and Portuguese, including, with David Curzon, the collection of poems by Anna Kamieńska, *Astonishments*. She is currently working on a translation into Polish of the great Brazilian poet Adélia Prado.

LAURA ENGELSTEIN is the Henry S. McNeil Professor of Russian History Emerita at Yale University and Professor of History Emerita at Princeton University. A member of the American Academy of Arts and Sciences and a Corresponding Fellow of the British Academy, she has published widely on the history of late imperial Russia and lives in Chicago and New York.

WITHDRAWN

8-19